NCERT SOLUTIONS

with Chapterwise **Study Notes**

MATHEMATICS 10th

Author
Astha Singhal
Sudarshan Prakash

ARIHANT PRAKASHAN (Series), MEERUT

卐 **Administrative & Production Offices**

Regd. Office

'Ramchhaya' 4577/15, Agarwal Road, Darya Ganj, New Delhi -110002
Tele: 011- 47630600, 43518550

卐 **Head Office**

Kalindi, TP Nagar, Meerut (UP) - 250002
Tel: 0121-7156203, 7156204

卐 **Sales & Support Offices**

Agra, Ahmedabad, Bengaluru, Bareilly, Chennai, Delhi, Guwahati, Hyderabad, Jaipur, Jhansi, Kolkata, Lucknow, Nagpur & Pune.

卐 **PRICE** ₹375.00

卐 **PO No :** TXT-59-T065443-06-25

Published by Arihant Publications (India) Ltd.

For further information about the books published by Arihant, log on to www.arihantbooks.com or e-mail at info@arihantbooks.com

Follow us on   

Preface

Feeling the immense importance and value of NCERT books, we are presenting this book, having the **NCERT Exercises Solutions**. For the overall benefit of the students we have made this book unique in such a way that it presents not only solutions but also detailed explanations. Through these detailed and through explanations, students can learn the concepts which will enhance their thinking and learning abilities.

We have introduced some Additional Features with the solutions which are given below:

- **Explanatory Solutions** Along with the solutions to questions we have given all the points that tell how to approach to solve a problem. Here we have tried to cover all those loopholes which may lead to confusion. All formulae and hints are discussed in full detail.
- Also included **Thinking Process** and **Mistake Alert** to understanding 'How to solve question' and points of mistakes.
- **Note** We have provided notes also to solutions in which special points are mentioned which are of great value for the students.

Apart from all those who helped in the compilation of this book a special note of thanks to all. With the hope that this book will be of great help to the students, we wish great success to our readers.

Astha Singhal
Sudarshan Prakash

Contents

Real Numbers

CHAPTER 01

Important Points

01 The Fundamental Theorem of Arithmetic Every composite number can be written (factorised) as the product of powers of primes and this factorisation is unique, apart from the order in which the prime factors occur.

Fundamental theorem of arithmetic is also called as Unique Factorisation theorem.

Composite number = Product of primes

or

Any integer greater than 1 is either a prime number, or can be written as a unique product of prime numbers.

e.g., (i) $2 \times 11 = 22$ is the same as $11 \times 2 = 22$. (Ignoring the order)

(ii) 6 can be written as 2×3, where 2 and 3 are prime numbers.

(iii) 15 can be written as 3×5, where 3 and 5 are prime numbers.

Note The prime factorisation of a natural number is unique, except for the order of its factors. *e.g.*, $210 = 2 \times 3 \times 5 \times 7 = 5 \times 2 \times 3 \times 7$

(iv) 12 is formed by multiplying the prime numbers 2, 2 and 3 together, $12 = 2 \times 2 \times 3$

$\Rightarrow$ $12 = 2^2 \times 3$

Note 4×3 does not work, as 4 is not a prime number.

02 HCF and LCM by Prime Factorisation Method

(i) HCF of two or more numbers = Product of the smallest power of each common prime factor involved in the numbers.

(ii) LCM of two or more numbers = Product of the greatest power of each prime factor involved in the numbers.

(iii) For any two positive integers a and b, we have

$\text{HCF}(a, b) \times \text{LCM}(a, b) = a \times b$

$$\Rightarrow \quad \text{HCF}(a, b) = \frac{a \times b}{\text{LCM}(a, b)}$$

and $$\text{LCM}(a, b) = \frac{a \times b}{\text{HCF}(a, b)}$$

03 Irrational Numbers A number is called irrational if it cannot be expressed in the form $\frac{p}{q}$, where p and q are integers and $q \neq 0$. *e.g.*, irrational numbers are $\sqrt{2}, \sqrt{3}, \sqrt{15}, \pi, -\frac{\sqrt{2}}{\sqrt{3}}$, 0.1011011101111......, etc.

The sum or difference of a rational and an irrational number is irrational. The product and quotient of a non-zero rational and irrational number is irrational.

A number whose decimal expansion is non-terminating and non-repeating is an irrational number.

Note Let P be a prime number. If P divides a^2, then P divides a, where a is a positive integer.

Exercise 1.1

Question 1 Express each number as a product of its prime factors.

(i) 140 (ii) 156 (iii) 3825 (iv) 5005 (v) 7429

Sol.

(i) We use division method as shown below

2	140
2	70
5	35
7	7
	1

$\therefore \quad 140 = 2 \times 2 \times 5 \times 7 = 2^2 \times 5 \times 7$

(ii) We use the division method as shown below

2	156
2	78
3	39
13	13
	1

$\therefore \quad 156 = 2 \times 2 \times 3 \times 13$

$= 2^2 \times 3 \times 13$

(iii) We use the division method as shown below

3	3825
3	1275
5	425
5	85
17	17
	1

$\therefore \quad 3825 = 3 \times 3 \times 5 \times 5 \times 17$

$= 3^2 \times 5^2 \times 17$

(iv) We use the division method as shown below

5	5005
7	1001
11	143
13	13
	1

$\therefore \quad 5005 = 5 \times 7 \times 11 \times 13$

(v) We use the division method as shown below

17	7429
19	437
23	23
	1

$\therefore \quad 7429 = 17 \times 19 \times 23$

Question 2 Find the LCM and HCF of the following pairs of integers and verify that LCM × HCF = product of the two numbers.

(i) 26 and 91 (ii) 510 and 92 (iii) 336 and 54

Sol.

(i) 26 and 91

2	26
13	13
	1

7	91
13	13
	1

$26 = 2 \times 13$ and $91 = 7 \times 13$

∴ LCM of 26 and 91 = $2 \times 7 \times 13 = 182$

and HCF of 26 and 91 = 13

Now, $182 \times 13 = 2366$ and $26 \times 91 = 2366$

Hence, LCM × HCF = product of two numbers

(ii) 510 and 92

2	510
3	255
5	85
17	17
	1

2	92
2	46
23	23
	1

$510 = 2 \times 3 \times 5 \times 17$

and $92 = 2 \times 2 \times 23$

∴ LCM of 510 and 92

$= 2 \times 2 \times 3 \times 5 \times 17 \times 23 = 23460$

and HCF of 510 and 92 = 2

Now, $23460 \times 2 = 46920$

and $510 \times 92 = 46920$

Hence, LCM × HCF = product of two numbers

(iii) 336 and 54

2	336
2	168
2	84
2	42
3	21
7	7
	1

2	54
3	27
3	9
3	3
	1

$336 = 2 \times 2 \times 2 \times 2 \times 3 \times 7$

and $54 = 2 \times 3 \times 3 \times 3$

∴ LCM of 336 and 54 = $2 \times 2 \times 2 \times 2 \times 3 \times 3 \times 3 \times 7 = 3024$

and HCF of 336 and 54 = $2 \times 3 = 6$

Now, $3024 \times 6 = 18144$ and $336 \times 54 = 18144$

Hence, LCM × HCF = product of two numbers

Question 3 Find the LCM and HCF of the following integers by applying the prime factorisation method.

(i) 12,15 and 21 (ii) 17, 23 and 29

(iii) 8, 9 and 25

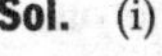

Sol. (i)

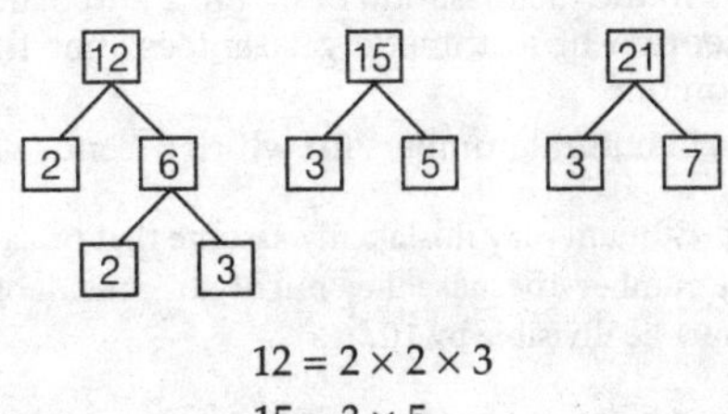

$$12 = 2 \times 2 \times 3$$
$$15 = 3 \times 5$$
$$21 = 3 \times 7$$

Here, 3 is common prime factor of the given numbers.

$\therefore$ HCF (12, 15, 21) = 3

LCM is product of the greatest power of each prime factor of 12, 15 and 21.

$\therefore$ LCM (12, 15, 21) = $2^2 \times 3 \times 5 \times 7 = 420$

(ii) 17 23 29

There is no common factor as 17, 23, 29 are primes. Therefore, HCF is 1.

LCM is the product of the greatest power of each prime factor of 17, 23 and 29.

$\therefore$ LCM (17, 23, 29) = $17 \times 23 \times 29 = 11339$

(iii) First we write the prime factor of each of the given numbers.

$8 = 2 \times 2 \times 2 = 2^3, 9 = 3 \times 3 = 3^2, 25 = 5 \times 5 = 5^2$

$\therefore$ LCM = $2^3 \times 3^2 \times 5^2 = 8 \times 9 \times 25 = 1800$

and HCF = 1

Hence, HCF (8,9,25) = 1 and LCM (8, 9, 25) = 1800

Question 4 Given that HCF (306,657) = 9, find LCM (306, 657).

Sol. We have, HCF (306, 657) = 9

We know that,

Product of LCM and HCF = Product of two numbers

$\Rightarrow$ LCM $\times 9 = 306 \times 657$

$\Rightarrow$ LCM $= \dfrac{306 \times 657}{9} = 22338$

Hence, LCM (306, 657) = 22338

Question 5 Check whether 6^n can end with the digit 0 for any natural number n.

Sol. If the number 6^n ends with the digits zero. Then, it is divisible by 5. Therefore, the prime factorisation of 6^n contains the prime 5. This is not possible because the only primes in the factorisation of 6^n are 2 and 3 and the uniqueness of the fundamental theorem of arithmetic guarantees that there are no other prime in the factorisation of 6^n.

So, there is no value of n in natural numbers for which 6^n ends with the digit zero.

> ***Mistake Alert*** Student may mistakenly assume that 6^n can end with digit 0 for some natural number n because they might not consider that a number ending with 0 must be divisible by 10.

Question 6 Explain why $7 \times 11 \times 13 + 13$ and $7 \times 6 \times 5 \times 4 \times 3 \times 2 \times 1 + 5$ are composite numbers?

Sol. We have, $7 \times 11 \times 13 + 13 = 1001 + 13 = 1014$

The prime factorisation of 1014 is given by

$$1014 = 2 \times 3 \times 13 \times 13$$

So, it is the product of more than two prime numbers.

Hence, it is a composite number.

and $\quad 7 \times 6 \times 5 \times 4 \times 3 \times 2 \times 1 + 5 = 5040 + 5 = 5045$

$\Rightarrow \quad 5045 = 5 \times 1009$

It is the product of prime factor 5 and 1009.

Hence, it is a composite number.

Question 7. There is a circular path around a sports field. Sonia takes 18 minutes to drive one round of the field, while Ravi takes 12 minutes for the same. Suppose they both start at the same point and at the same time, and go in the same direction. After how many minutes will they meet again at the starting point?

> ***Thinking Process*** The total time taken for completing 1 round of circular path will be the LCM of time taken by Sonia and Ravi for completing 1 round of circular path respectively *i. e.*, LCM of 18 minutes and 12 minutes.

Sol. It can be observed that Ravi takes less time than Sonia for completing 1 round. As they are going in the same direction, they will meet again at the same time $18 = 2 \times 3 \times 3$ and $12 = 2 \times 2 \times 3$

LCM of 18 and $12 = 2 \times 2 \times 3 \times 3 = 36$

So, Sonia and Ravi will meet again at the starting point after 36 min.

> ***Mistake Alert*** In such types of problems students may confuse to calculate the LCM or HCF of the numbers.

Exercise 1.2

Question 1 Prove that $\sqrt{5}$ is irrational.

Sol. Suppose, on the contrary, $\sqrt{5}$ represents a rational number. Then, $\sqrt{5}$ can expressed in the form $\frac{p}{q}$, where p, q are integer and have no common factor and $q \neq 0$.

$\therefore \quad \sqrt{5} = \frac{p}{q}$

On squaring both sides, we get

$$5 = \frac{p^2}{q^2} \Rightarrow p^2 = 5q^2 \quad \ldots(i)$$

$\Rightarrow \quad$ 5 divides $p^2 \Rightarrow$ 5 divides p (Note on page 2)...(ii)

Let $\quad p = 5m \Rightarrow p^2 = 25m^2$

On putting the value of p^2 in Eq. (i), we get $25m^2 = 5q^2 \Rightarrow 5m^2 = q^2$

$\Rightarrow \quad$ 5 divides $q^2 \Rightarrow$ 5 divides q ...(iii)

Thus, from Eq. (ii), 5 divides p and from Eq. (iii), 5 also divides q. It means 5 is a common factor of p and q. This contradicts the fact that there is no common factor of p and q.

Hence, $\sqrt{5}$ is an irrational number. **Hence Proved.**

Question 2 Prove that $3 + 2\sqrt{5}$ is irrational.

Sol. Let us assume, to the contrary, that $3 + 2\sqrt{5}$ is a rational number.

Now, let $3 + 2\sqrt{5} = \frac{a}{b}$, where a and b are coprime and $b \neq 0$.

So, $\quad 2\sqrt{5} = \frac{a}{b} - 3$

$\Rightarrow \quad \sqrt{5} = \frac{a}{2b} - \frac{3}{2}$

Since, a and b are integer, therefore $\frac{a}{2b} - \frac{3}{2}$ is a rational number.

$\therefore \sqrt{5}$ is a rational number.

But $\sqrt{5}$ is an irrational number.

This show that our assumption is incorrect.

So, $3 + 2\sqrt{5}$ is an irrational number. **Hence Proved.**

Note Coprime numbers are the numbers that are prime relative to each other. *e.g.*, 5 and 9 do not have a common factor, so they are coprime But 9 is not a prime number.

Question 3 Prove that the following are irrationals.

(i) $\frac{1}{\sqrt{2}}$ (ii) $7\sqrt{5}$ (iii) $6+\sqrt{2}$

Sol.

(i) Let us assume, to the contrary, that $\frac{1}{\sqrt{2}}$ is rational. That is, we can find coprime integers p and q $(q \neq 0)$.

Such that $$\frac{1}{\sqrt{2}} = \frac{p}{q} \Rightarrow \frac{1\times\sqrt{2}}{\sqrt{2}\times\sqrt{2}} = \frac{p}{q}$$

$$\Rightarrow \frac{\sqrt{2}}{2} = \frac{p}{q} \Rightarrow \sqrt{2} = \frac{2p}{q}$$

Since, p and q are integers, therefore $\frac{2p}{q}$ is rational, and so $\sqrt{2}$ is rational.

But this contradicts the fact that $\sqrt{2}$ is irrational.

So, we conclude that $\frac{1}{\sqrt{2}}$ is an irrational. **Hence Proved.**

(ii) Let us assume, to the contrary, that $7\sqrt{5}$ is rational. That is, we can find coprime integers p and q $(q \neq 0)$ such that $7\sqrt{5} = \frac{p}{q}$.

So, $$\sqrt{5} = \frac{p}{7q}$$

Since, p and q are integers, therefore $\frac{p}{7q}$ is rational and so $\sqrt{5}$ is rational.

But this contradicts the fact $\sqrt{5}$ is irrational. So, we conclude that $7\sqrt{5}$ is an irrational. Hence Proved.

(iii) Let us assume, to the contrary, that $6+\sqrt{2}$ is rational. That is, we can find integers p and q $(q \neq 0)$ such that

$$6+\sqrt{2} = \frac{p}{q}$$

$$\Rightarrow \sqrt{2} = \frac{p}{q} - 6 \Rightarrow \sqrt{2} = \frac{p-6q}{q}$$

Since, p and q are integers, $\frac{p-6q}{q}$ is rational and so $\sqrt{2}$ is rational.

But this contradicts the fact that $\sqrt{2}$ is irrational.

So, we conclude that $6+\sqrt{2}$ is an irrational. **Hence Proved.**

DIKSHA APP Questions

☐ Multiple Choice Questions

Q.1 If HCF of two numbers is 1, the numbers, are called relatively ________ or ______.

(a) Prime, Coprime (b) Composite, Prime
(c) Both *a* and *b* (d) None of these

Sol. (c) If HCF of two numbers is 1, then they may be coprime, prime or composite.

Q.2 For what least value of 'n' a natural number, $(24)^n$ is divisible by 8 ?

(a) 0 (b) –1
(c) 1 (d) no value of n is possible.

Sol. (c) Prime factorisation of $24^n = (2^3 \times 2)^n$

Let $n = 1$

$\therefore$ $24^n = (2^3 \times 3)^1 = 8 \times 3$

Which is divisible by 8.

So, the least value of n is 1.

Q.3 $7 \times 11 \times 13 \times 15 + 15$ is a

(a) composite number (b) prime number
(c) whole number (d) both composite and whole number.

Sol. (d) We have, $7 \times 11 \times 13 \times 15 + 15 = 15030$

Prime factorisation of 15030 is given by $15030 = 2 \times 3 \times 3 \times 5 \times 167$

So, it is the product of more than two prime numbers 2, 3, 5 and 167

Hence, It is a composite number and also a whole number.

Q.4 The HCF of 5^{13} and 2^{26} is

(a) 0 (b) 1 (c) 13 (d) 26

Sol. (b) Since, 5^{13} containg multiples of 5

and 2^{26} containg multiples of 2.

So, There are no common factor between 5^{13} and 2^{26} other than 1.

Hence HCF of 5^{13} and 2^{26} is 1.

Q.5 Two positive integer a and b are written as $a = x^3y^2, b = xy^3$, the LCM of (a, b) is

(a) x^3y^3 (b) xy^2 (c) x^2y^2 (d) xy^3

Sol. (a) We have, $a = x^3y^2 = x \times x \times x \times y \times y$

and $b = xy^3 = x \times y \times y \times y$

$\therefore$ $\text{LCM}(a, b) = x \times x \times x \times y \times y \times y = x^3y^3$

Q.6 How many prime factors are there in the prime factorization of 5005 ?

(a) 2 (b) 4 (c) 6 (d) 7

Sol. (b) $5005 = 5 \times 7 \times 11 \times 13$

Hence, total number of prime factors is 4.

Q.7 Which of the following is not an irrational number?

(a) $6 + \sqrt{9}$ (b) $5 - \sqrt{3}$

(c) $\sqrt{2} + \sqrt{3}$ (d) $4 + \sqrt{2}$

Sol. (a) Here, $6 + \sqrt{9} = 6 + 3 = 9$

Since, 9 is rational number.

Hence, $6 + \sqrt{9}$ is not an irrational number.

Q.7 The HCF and LCM of two numbers are 9 and 360 respectively. If one number is 45, then other number is

(a) 180 (b) 720 (c) 36 (d) 72

Sol. (d) Given, HCF and LCM of two number are 9 and 360, respectively and one number is 45.

Let us suppose, another number is x.

Since, HCF $(a, b) \times$ LCM $(a, b) = a \times b$

$$\text{HCF}(45, x) \times \text{LCM}(45, x) = 45 \times x$$

$$\Rightarrow \quad 9 \times 360 = 45 \times x$$

$$\Rightarrow \quad x = \frac{9 \times 360}{45} \Rightarrow x = 72$$

Hence, other number is 72.

☐ Subjective Type Questions

Q.1 What is the HCF of the smallest prime number and smallest composite number ?

Sol. The smallest prince number is 2.

The smallest composite number is 4.

$$2 = 2 \times 1 \text{ and } 4 = 2 \times 2$$

$$\text{HCF}(2, 4) = 2$$

Q.2 Show that 12^n can never end with the digit zero for any natural number n.

Sol. If the number of 12^n for any n, were to end with the digit zero then it would be divisible by 5. This means that prime factorisation of 12^n would contain the prime 5.

This is not possible as, $12^n = (3 \times 2^2)^n = 3^n \times 2^{2n}$

So, the only prime factors of 12^n are 2 and 3.

So, by uniqueness of the fundamental theorem of arithmetic guarantees that there are no other primes in the factorisation of 12^n.

So, 12^n can never end with the digit zero for any natural number n.

Q.3 Can 15^n end with the digit 0, for any natural number n, justify your answer.

Sol. If the number 15^n for any n, were to end with zero then it would be divisible by 2.

This means that prime factorization of 15^n would contain the prime 2. but this is not possible because the only primes in the factorisation of 15^n are 3 and 5.

So, there is no value of n in natural numbers for which 15^n ends with the digit zero.

Q.4 $13 \times 19 \times 29 + 29$ prime or composite ? Justify

Sol. We have, $13 \times 19 \times 29 + 29 = 7192$

The prime factorisation of 7192 is

$$7192 = 2 \times 2 \times 2 \times 899$$

So, it is a product of two prime numbers 2 and 899

Hence, it is a composite number.

Q.5 Two alarm clocks ring at regular intervals of 50 seconds and 48 seconds. If they first beep together at 12 noon, at what time will they beep again for the first time?

Sol. Both the alarm clocks will beep together after the time interval which is multiple of both 50 and 48. Which means that the required time will be the LCM of 50 and 48.

$\therefore$ we have $50 = 2 \times 5 \times 5$

and $48 = 2 \times 2 \times 2 \times 2 \times 3$

$\text{LCM}(50, 48) = 2 \times 2 \times 2 \times 2 \times 3 \times 5 \times 5 = 1200$

$\therefore$ The alarm clocks will beep again after 1200 seconds *i.e.*, $\frac{1200}{60} = 20$ minutes *i.e.*, at 12 : 20 pm.

Mistake Alert This question creates the confusion that what we have to calculate HCF or LCM. So, always remember for collective timing, we always take LCM of quantities.

Q.6 Two triangles have the side of lengths 34 cm and 85 cm respectively. What is the greatest length of tape that can measure the sides of both of them exactly ?

Sol. Side of first triangle = 34 cm

and side of second triangle = 85 cm

The required length of tape is the HCF of 34 and 85.

Now, $34 = 17 \times 2$

and $85 = 17 \times 5$

$\therefore$ HCF (34, 85) = 17

Hence, greatest length of tape will be 17 cm.

Q.7 Two tankers contain 850 litres and 680 litres of pertrol respectively. Find the maximum capacity of a container which can measure the petrol of either tanker in exact number of times.

◎ *Thinking Process* For maximum, always take HCF and for minimum always take LCM.

Sol. To find the maximum capacity of a container which can measure the petrol of either tanker in exact number of times, we require the HCF of 850 and 680.

2	850
5	425
5	85
17	17
	1

2	680
2	340
2	170
5	85
17	17
	1

$850 = 2 \times 5 \times 5 \times 17$

and $680 = 2 \times 2 \times 2 \times 5 \times 17$

HCF (850, 680) = $2 \times 5 \times 17 = 170$ litres

Hence, the maximum capacity of the container is 170 litres.

Q.8 If x is rational and $\sqrt{y}$ is irrational, then prove that $x + \sqrt{y}$ is irrational.

Sol. Let us assume on the contrary that $x + \sqrt{y}$ is rational, so $x + \sqrt{y}$ can be written in the form $\frac{a}{b}$, where a, b are integers and $b \neq 0$.

$\therefore$ $$x + \sqrt{y} = \frac{a}{b}$$

$\Rightarrow$ $$\sqrt{y} = \frac{a}{b} - x$$

Since, $\frac{a}{b}$ and x both are rationals, therefore $\frac{a}{b} - x$ is also rational

So, $\sqrt{y}$ is rational.

This contradicts the fact that $\sqrt{y}$ is irrational.

Hence, $x + \sqrt{y}$ is irrational. **Hence Proved.**

Polynomials

CHAPTER 02

Important Points

01 Degree of a Polynomial The exponent of the highest degree term in a polynomial is known as its degree.
In other words, the highest power of x in a polynomial $f(x)$ is called the degree of a polynomial $f(x)$.

e.g.,

(i) $f(x)=5x+\frac{1}{3}$ is a polynomial in the variable x of degree 1.

(ii) $g(y)=3y^2-\frac{5}{2}y+7$ is a polynomial in the variable y of degree 2.

Note (i) Degree of a polynomial is always a non-negative integer.
(ii) Expressions like $\frac{1}{x-2}$, $2\sqrt{x}$, $\frac{1}{x^3+3x+4}$ etc. are not polynomials.

02 Constant Polynomial A polynomial of degree zero is called a constant polynomial.

e.g., $f(x)=8$, $f(x)=-\frac{5}{2}$

Note The constant polynomial 0 or $f(x)=0$ is called the zero polynomial.

03 Linear Polynomial A polynomial of degree one is called a linear polynomial.

e.g., $f(x)=3x+5$, $g(y)=7y-1$, $p(z)=5z-3$

More generally, any linear polynomial in variable x with real coefficients is of the form $f(x)=ax+b$, where a and b are real numbers and $a\neq 0$.

Note A linear polynomial may be a monomial or a binomial because linear polynomial $f(x) = \frac{7}{5}x - \frac{5}{2}$ is a binomial whereas the linear polynomial $g(x) = \frac{2}{5}x$ is a monomial.

04 Quadratic Polynomial A polynomial of degree two is called a quadratic polynomial.

e.g., $f(x) = 5x^2$, $f(x) = 7x^2 - 5x$, $f(x) = 8x^2 + 6x + 5$

More generally, any quadratic polynomial in variable x with real coefficients is of the form $f(x) = ax^2 + bx + c$, where a, b and c are real numbers and $a \neq 0$.

Note A quadratic polynomial may be a monomial or a binomial or a trinomial, *e.g.*, $f(x) = \frac{1}{5}x^2$ is a monomial, $g(x) = 3x^2 - 5$ is a binomial and $h(x) = 3x^2 - 2x + 5$ is a trinomial.

05 Cubic Polynomial A polynomial of degree three is called a cubic polynomial.

e.g., $f(x) = 8x^3$, $f(x) = 9x^3 + 5x^2$,

$f(y) = 11y^3 - 9y^2 + 7y$, $f(z) = 13z^3 - 12z^2 + 11z + 5$

06 Polynomial of Degree in Standard Form A polynomial in one variable x of degree n is an expression of the form $f(x) = a_n x^n + a_{n-1} x^{n-1} + \dots + a_1 x + a_0$, where $a_0, a_1, a_2, \dots, a_n$ are constants and $a_n \neq 0$.

In particular, if $a_0 = a_1 = a_2 = \dots = a_n = 0$ (all the constants are zero, we get the constants zero), we get the zero polynomial which is denoted by 0. The degree of zero polynomial is not defined.

Note We can express zero polynomial as $f(x) = 0 = 0 + 0x + 0x^2 + 0x^3 + \dots$

Hence, degree for the zero polynomial is not defined.

07 Value of a Polynomial at a Given Point If $p(x)$ is a polynomial in x and α is a real number. Then, the value obtained by putting $x = \alpha$ in $p(x)$ is called the value of $p(x)$ at $x = \alpha$.

e.g., Let $p(x) = 5x^2 - 4x + 2$, then its value at $x = 2$ is given by

$$\begin{aligned} p(2) &= 5(2)^2 - 4(2) + 2 \\ &= 5(4) - 8 + 2 \\ &= 20 - 8 + 2 = 14 \end{aligned}$$

Thus, the value of $p(x)$ at $x = 2$ is 14.

08 Zero of a Polynomial A real numbers k is said to be a zero of a polynomial $f(x)$, if $f(k) = 0$.

e.g. Zero of $p(x) = 5x + 7$ is $p(x) = 0 \Rightarrow 5x + 7 = 0 \Rightarrow x = -\frac{7}{5}$

Hence, $x = \frac{-7}{5}$ is the zero of the polynomial $p(x) = 5x + 7$.

09 Zero of a Polynomial is Precisely the Abscissa of the Point, where the Graph Intersects X-axis

(i) A linear polynomial has at the most one zero.

(ii) A quadratic polynomial has at the most two zeroes.

(iii) In general, a polynomial of degree n has at the most n zeroes.

(iv) In polynomial, $p(x)$ of degree n has atmost n zeroes *i.e.*, it can cross x-axis n times.

10 Graph of a Polynomials In algebraic or in set theory language, the graph of a polynomial $f(x)$ is the collection (or set) of all points (x, y), where $y = f(x)$.

(i) Graph of a linear polynomial $ax + b$ is a straight line.

(ii) The graph of a quadratic polynomial $(ax^2 + bx + c)$ is $\cup$-shaped, called as parabola.

If $a > 0$ in $ax^2 + bx + c$, the shape of parabola is opening upwards '$\cup$'.

If $a < 0$ in $ax^2 + bx + c$, the shape of parabola is opening downwards '$\cap$'.

11 Discriminant of a Quadratic Polynomial

For $f(x) = ax^2 + bx + c$, $b^2 - 4ac$ is known as its discriminant D.

Hence, $D = b^2 - 4ac$, $D \geq 0$.

Case **I** If $D > 0$, graph of $f(x) = ax^2 + bx + c$ will intersect the X-axis at two distinct point, x-coordinates of points of intersection with X-axis is known as 'zeroes' of $f(x)$.

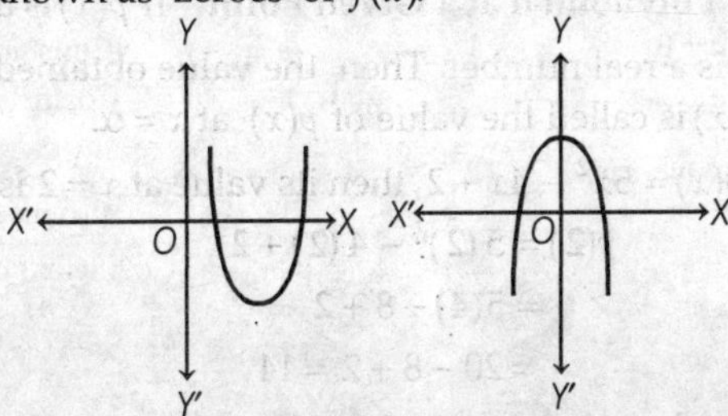

Case **II** If $D = 0$, graph of $f(x) = ax^2 + bx + c$ will touch the X-axis at one point only.

$\therefore$ $f(x)$ will have only one 'zero'.

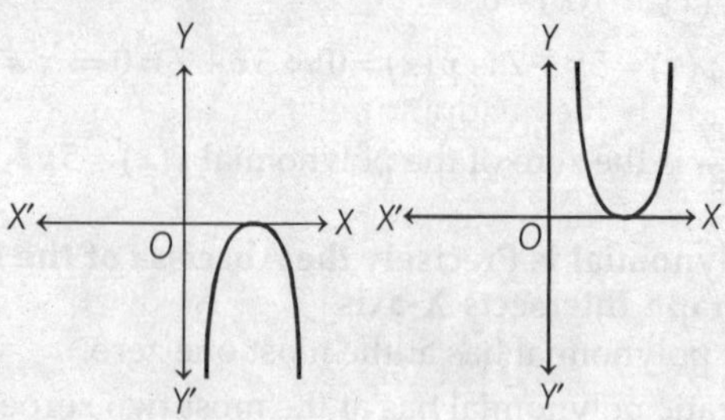

Case **III** If $D < 0$, graph of $f(x) = ax^2 + bx + c$ will neither touch nor intersect the X-axis.

$\therefore$ $f(x)$ will not have any real zeroes.

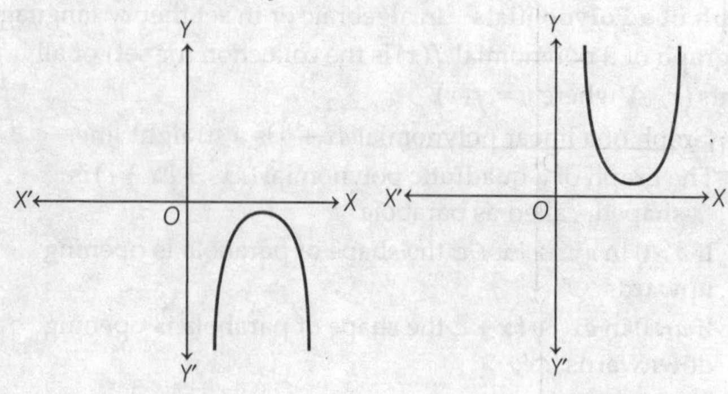

12 Relationship Between the Zeroes and the Coefficient of a Polynomial

Type of polynomial	General form	Almost Number of zeroes	Relationship between zeroes
Linear	$ax + b, a \neq 0$	1	$k = -\frac{b}{a}$, i.e., $k = -\frac{\text{Constant term}}{\text{Coefficient of } x}$
Quadratic	$ax^2 + bx + c, a \neq 0$	2	Sum of zeroes, $(\alpha + \beta) = -\frac{\text{Coefficient of } x}{\text{Coefficient of } x^2} = -\frac{b}{a}$ Product of zeroes, $(\alpha\beta) = \frac{\text{Constant term}}{\text{Coefficient of } x^2} = \frac{c}{a}$

13 How to Make a Quadratic Polynomial with the Given Zeroes

Let the zeroes of a quadratic polynomial be α and β.

$$\therefore \quad x = \alpha, x = \beta$$
$$x - \alpha = 0, x - \beta = 0$$

Then, obviously the quadratic polynomial is

$$(x - \alpha)(x - \beta) \quad i.e. \; x^2 - (\alpha + \beta)x + \alpha\beta$$

i.e., x^2 – (Sum of the zeroes) x + Product of the zeroes

Exercise 2.1

Question 1 The graphs of $y = p(x)$ are given in figures below, for some polynomials $p(x)$. Find the number of zeroes of $p(x)$, in each case.

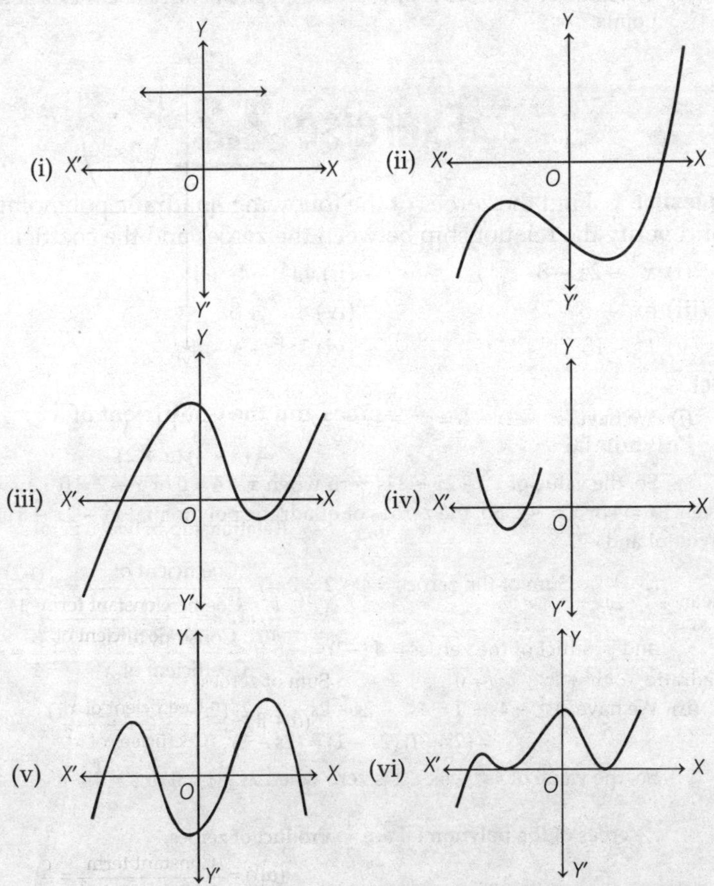

◎ *Thinking Process* To find the zeroes of $p(x)$, count the points, where the graph crosses on intersect the X-axis.

Sol.

(i) There are no zeroes as the graph does not intersect the X-axis.

(ii) The number of zeroes is one as the graph intersects the X-axis at one point only.

(iii) The number of zeroes is three as the graph intersects the X-axis at three points.

(iv) The number of zeroes is two as the graph intersects the X-axis at two points.

(v) The number of zeroes is four as the graph intersects the X-axis at four points.

(vi) The number of zeroes is three as the graph intersects the X-axis at three points.

Exercise 2.2

Question 1 Find the zeroes of the following quadratic polynomials and verify the relationship between the zeroes and the coefficients.

(i) $x^2 - 2x - 8$ (ii) $4s^2 - 4s + 1$

(iii) $6x^2 - 3 - 7x$ (iv) $4u^2 + 8u$

(v) $t^2 - 15$ (vi) $3x^2 - x - 4$

Sol.

(i) We have, $x^2 - 2x - 8 = x^2 - 4x + 2x - 8 = x(x-4) + 2(x-4)$

$= (x-4)(x+2)$

So, the value of $x^2 - 2x - 8$ is zero when $x - 4 = 0$ or $x + 2 = 0$, *i.e.*, when $x = 4$ or $x = -2$. So, the zeroes of quadratic polynomial $x^2 - 2x - 8$ are 4 and –2.

$\therefore$ Sum of the zeroes $= 4 - 2 = 2 = -\dfrac{\text{Coefficient of } x}{\text{Coefficient of } x^2} = -\dfrac{(-2)}{1} = 2$

and product of the zeroes $= 4(-2) = -8 = \dfrac{\text{Constant term}}{\text{Coefficient of } x^2} = -\dfrac{8}{1} = -8$

(ii) We have, $4s^2 - 4s + 1 = 4s^2 - 2s - 2s + 1 = 2s(2s-1) - 1(2s-1)$

$= (2s-1)(2s-1) = (2s-1)^2$

So, the value of $4s^2 - 4s + 1$ is zero when $2s - 1 = 0$ or $s = \dfrac{1}{2}$.

$\therefore$ Zeroes of the polynomial are $\dfrac{1}{2}$ and $\dfrac{1}{2}$.

$\therefore$ Sum of the zeroes $= \frac{1}{2} + \frac{1}{2} = 1 = -\frac{\text{Coefficient of } s}{\text{Coefficient of } s^2} = -\left(\frac{-4}{4}\right) = 1$

and product of the zeroes $= \left(\frac{1}{2}\right)\left(\frac{1}{2}\right) = \frac{1}{4} = \frac{\text{Constant term}}{\text{Coefficient of } s^2} = \frac{1}{4}$

(iii) We have, $6x^2 - 3 - 7x = 6x^2 - 7x - 3 = 6x^2 - 9x + 2x - 3$

$= 3x(2x - 3) + 1(2x - 3)$

$= (3x + 1)(2x - 3)$

The value of $6x^2 - 3 - 7x$ is 0, when the value of $(3x + 1)(2x - 3)$ is 0, *i.e.*, when $3x + 1 = 0$, or $2x - 3 = 0$, *i.e.*, when $x = -\frac{1}{3}$ or $x = \frac{3}{2}$

$\therefore$ The zeroes of $6x^2 - 3 - 7x$ are $-\frac{1}{3}$ and $\frac{3}{2}$.

Therefore, sum of the zeroes $= -\frac{1}{3} + \frac{3}{2} = \frac{7}{6}$

$= -\frac{\text{Coefficient of } x}{\text{Coefficient of } x^2} = -\frac{(-7)}{6} = \frac{7}{6}$

and product of zeroes $= \left(-\frac{1}{3}\right)\left(\frac{3}{2}\right) = -\frac{1}{2} = \frac{\text{Constant term}}{\text{Coefficient of } x^2} = -\frac{3}{6} = -\frac{1}{2}$

(iv) We have, $4u^2 + 8u = 4u(u + 2)$

The value of $4u^2 + 8u$ is 0 when the value of $4u(u + 2) = 0$, *i.e.*, when $u = 0$ or $u + 2 = 0$ *i.e.*, when $u = 0$ or $u = -2$

$\therefore$ The zeroes of $4u^2 + 8u$ are 0 and –2.

Therefore, sum of the zeroes

$= 0 + (-2) = -2 = -\frac{\text{Coefficient of } u}{\text{Coefficient of } u^2} = -\frac{8}{4} = -2$

and product of zeroes $= (0)(-2) = 0 = \frac{\text{Constant term}}{\text{Coefficient of } u^2} = \frac{0}{4} = 0$

(v) We have, $t^2 - 15 = (t - \sqrt{15})(t + \sqrt{15})$

The value of $t^2 - 15$ is 0 when the value of $(t - \sqrt{15})(t + \sqrt{15})$ is 0, i.e. when $t - \sqrt{15} = 0$ or $t + \sqrt{15} = 0$ *i.e.*, when $t = \sqrt{15}$ or $t = -\sqrt{15}$.

$\therefore$ The zeroes of $t^2 - 15$ are $\sqrt{15}$ and $-\sqrt{15}$.

Therefore, sum of the zeroes $= \sqrt{15} + (-\sqrt{15}) = 0$

$= -\frac{\text{Coefficient of } t}{\text{Coefficient of } t^2} = -\frac{0}{1} = 0$

and product of the zeroes $= (\sqrt{15}) \times (-\sqrt{15}) = -15$

$= \frac{\text{Constant term}}{\text{Coefficient of } t^2} = -\frac{15}{1} = -15$

(vi) We have, $3x^2 - x - 4 = 3x^2 + 3x - 4x - 4$

$$= 3x(x + 1) - 4(x + 1) = (x + 1)(3x - 4)$$

The value of $3x^2 - x - 4$ is 0 when the value of $(x + 1)(3x - 4)$ is 0, *i.e.*, when $x + 1 = 0$ or $3x - 4 = 0$, *i.e.*, when $x = -1$ or $x = \frac{4}{3}$

$\therefore$ The zeroes of $3x^2 - x - 4$ are -1 and $\frac{4}{3}$.

Therefore, sum of the zeroes $= -1 + \frac{4}{3} = \frac{-3 + 4}{3} = \frac{1}{3}$

$$= -\frac{\text{Coefficient of } x}{\text{Coefficient of } x^2} = -\frac{(-1)}{3} = \frac{1}{3}$$

and product of the zeroes $= (-1)\left(\frac{4}{3}\right) = -\frac{4}{3} = \frac{\text{Constant term}}{\text{Coefficient of } x^2} = -\frac{4}{3}$

Question 2 Find a quadratic polynomial each with the given numbers as the sum and product of its zeroes respectively.

(i) $\frac{1}{4}, -1$ (ii) $\sqrt{2}, \frac{1}{3}$ (iii) $0, \sqrt{5}$ (iv) 1, 1

(v) $-\frac{1}{4}, \frac{1}{4}$ (vi) 4, 1

◎ ***Thinking Process*** To find the quadratic polynomial use the formula x^2-(sum of zeroes) x + product of zeroes.

Sol. Let the polynomial be $ax^2 + bx + c$ and its zeroes be α and β.

(i) Here, $\alpha + \beta = \frac{1}{4}$ and $\alpha\beta = -1$

Thus, the polynomial formed

$$= x^2 - (\text{Sum of the zeroes})\, x + \text{Product of the zeroes}$$

$$= x^2 - \left(\frac{1}{4}\right)x - 1 = x^2 - \frac{x}{4} - 1$$

The other polynomials are $k\left(x^2 - \frac{x}{4} - 1\right)$

If $k = 4$, then the polynomial is $4x^2 - x - 4$, where k is constant.

(ii) Here, $\alpha + \beta = \sqrt{2}$ and $\alpha\beta = \frac{1}{3}$

Thus, the polynomial formed

$$= x^2 - (\text{Sum of the zeroes})\, x + \text{Product of the zeroes}$$

$$= x^2 - (\sqrt{2})\, x + \frac{1}{3} \text{ or } x^2 - \sqrt{2}x + \frac{1}{3}$$

$\therefore$ Other polynomial are $k\left(x^2 - \sqrt{2}x + \frac{1}{3}\right)$, where k is constant.

If $k = 3$, then the polynomial is $3x^2 - 3\sqrt{2}x + 1$.

(iii) Here, $\alpha + \beta = 0$ and $\alpha\beta = \sqrt{5}$

Thus, the polynomial formed

$$= x^2 - (\text{Sum of the zeroes})\, x + \text{Product of the zeroes}$$
$$= x^2 - (0)x + \sqrt{5}$$
$$= x^2 + \sqrt{5}$$

(iv) Given, sum of zeroes = 1

Product of zeroes = 1

Let the polynomial $P(x)$ be $ax^2 + bx + c$ and its zeroes be α and β as we know

$$\text{sum of zeroes} = \frac{-\text{Coefficient of } x}{\text{Coefficient of } x^2} = \frac{-b}{a}$$

$$\Rightarrow \quad \alpha + \beta = \frac{-b}{a} = 1$$

$$\text{and product of zeroes} = \frac{\text{Constant term}}{\text{Coefficient of } x^2}$$

$$\Rightarrow \quad \alpha \cdot \beta = \frac{c}{a} = 1$$

Thus, the polynomial formed is

$$P(x) = x^2 - (\text{Sum of zeros})x + (\text{Product of zeros})$$
$$= x^2 - (1)x + 1$$
$$= x^2 - x + 1$$

Hence, the polynomial $P(x) = x^2 - x + 1$

(v) Given, sum of zeroes $= \frac{-1}{4}$, Product of zeroes $= \frac{1}{4}$. Let the polynomial be $ax^2 + bx + c$ and its zeroes be α and β as, we know

$$\text{Sum of zeroes} = \frac{-\text{Coefficient of } x}{\text{Coefficient of } x^2}$$

$$\Rightarrow \quad \alpha + \beta = \frac{-b}{a} = \frac{-1}{4}$$

$$\text{and product of zeroes} = \frac{\text{Constant term}}{\text{Coefficient of } x^2}$$

$$\Rightarrow \quad \alpha \cdot \beta = \frac{c}{a} = \frac{1}{4}$$

Thus, the polynomial formed is

$$P(x) = x^2 - (\text{Sum of zeros})x + \text{Product of zeros}$$

$$P(x) = x^2 - \left(\frac{-1}{4}\right)x + \frac{1}{4}$$

The other polynomial are $k\left(x^2 + \frac{1}{4}x + \frac{1}{4}\right)$

If $k = 4$, then polynomial is $4x^2 + x + 1$.

(vi) Given, $\alpha + \beta = 4, \alpha\beta = 1$

$\therefore$ $$\alpha + \beta = -\frac{b}{a} = 4$$

and $$\alpha\beta = \frac{c}{a} = \frac{1}{1} = 1$$

Thus, polynomial formed is

$P(x) = x^2 -$ (Sum of zeroes)x + Product of zeros

$P(x) = x^2 - (4)x + 1$

$\Rightarrow$ $$P(x) = (x^2 - 4x + 1).$$

DIKSHA APP Questions

☐ Multiple Choice Questions

Q.1 The Linear polynomial $p(x) = -9x + 3$ has exactly one zero which is ....

(a) $\frac{-1}{3}$ (b) $\frac{1}{3}$

(c) $\frac{3}{1}$ (d) 3

Sol. (b) We know, a zero of a linear polynomial, $ax + b$ is $\frac{-b}{a}$.

So, the zero of $-9x + 3$ is $\frac{-3}{-9} = \frac{3}{9} = \frac{1}{3}$.

Q.2 A real number α is called a zero of the polynomial $p(x)$, then

(a) $p(\alpha) = -1$ (b) $p(\alpha) = 1$

(c) $p(\alpha) = 0$ (d) $p(\alpha) = -2$

Sol. (c) A real number α is called the zero of the polynomial $p(x)$, if $p(\alpha) = 0$.

Q.3 Which of the following is a polynomial ?

(a) $x^2 + \frac{1}{x}$ (b) $2x^2 - 3\sqrt{x} + 1$

(c) $3x^2 - 3x + 1$ (d) $x^2 + x^{-2} + 7$

Sol. (c) We know that an expression is called a polynomial if the exponent of the variable is a non-negative integer.

Hence, $3x^2 - 3x + 1$ is a polynomial.

Q.4 If one root of $5x^2 + 13x + k = 0$ is the reciprocal of the other root, then find the value of k.

(a) 2 (b) 3 (c) 5 (d) 6

Sol. (c) Let one root be α. Then the other root is $\frac{1}{\alpha}$.

We have the polynomial $5x^2 + 13x + k = 0$

We know, product of zeroes $= \frac{\text{Constant term}}{\text{Coefficient of } x^2} \Rightarrow \alpha \cdot \frac{1}{\alpha} = \frac{k}{5}$

$\Rightarrow \quad 1 = \frac{k}{5} \Rightarrow k = 5$

Q.5 If the sum of the zeros of quadratic polynomial $3x^2 - kx + 6$ is 3, then the value of k is

(a) 3 (b) –3

(c) 6 (d) 9

Sol. (d) We have given quadratic polynomial $3x^2 - kx + 6$, sum of the zeros is 3.

Let us suppose, α and β are the zeroes of polynomial $3x^2 - kx + 6$.

Now, sum of zeroes $= -\frac{\text{Coefficient of } x}{\text{Coefficient of } x^2}$

$\Rightarrow \quad -\frac{(-k)}{3} = 3$

$\Rightarrow \quad \frac{k}{3} = 3$

$\Rightarrow \quad k = 9$

Hence, $\quad k = 9$

Q.6 If one zero of the polynomial $P(x) = (m^2 + 4)x^2 + 13x + 4m$ is reciprocal of the other, then value of m is

(a) 1 (b) –1

(c) 2 (d) –2

Sol. (c) Let one zero be α then other zero is $\frac{1}{\alpha}$

We have the polynomial $P(x) = (m^2 + 4)x^2 + 13x + 4m$

We know, product of zeroes $= \frac{\text{Constant term}}{\text{Coefficient of } x^2}$

$\Rightarrow \quad \alpha \cdot \frac{1}{\alpha} = \frac{4m}{m^2 + 4}$

$\Rightarrow \quad 1 = \frac{4m}{m^2 + 4}$

$\Rightarrow \quad m^2 - 4m + 4 = 0$

$\Rightarrow \quad m^2 - 2m - 2m + 4 = 0$

$\Rightarrow \quad m(m - 2) - 2(m - 2) = 0$

$\Rightarrow \quad (m - 2)(m - 2) = 0$

$$\Rightarrow \quad (m-2)^2 = 0$$
$$\Rightarrow \quad m = 2$$

Hence, value of $m = 2$.

Q.7 The zeroes of a polynomial $x^2 + 5x - 24$ are

(a) one positive and one negative (b) both positive
(c) both negative (d) both equal

Sol. (a) We are gives a polynomial $P(x) = x^2 + 5x - 24$

Let $\quad x^2 + 5x - 24 = 0$

$\Rightarrow \quad x^2 + 8x - 3x - 24 = 0$

$\Rightarrow \quad x(x+8) - 3(x+8) = 0$

$\Rightarrow \quad (x+8)(x-3) = 0$

So, $\quad (x+8) = 0$ or $(x-3) = 0$

If $\quad x + 8 = 0$

$x = -8$

If $\quad x - 3 = 0$

$x = 3$

Hence, zeroes of the polynomial $P(x) = x^2 + 5x - 24$ and -8 and 3.
i.e., One positive and one negative.

Q.8 A quadratic polynomial, whose zeroes are -3 and 4 is

(a) $x^2 - x + 12$ (b) $x^2 + x + 12$
(c) $2x^2 + 2x - 24$ (d) $\frac{x^2}{2} - \frac{x}{2} - 6$

Sol. (d) We are given zeroes of polynomial -3 and 4 the required polynomial $P(x)$ is

$P(x) = x^2 -$ (sum of zeroes)$x +$ (product of zeros)

$\Rightarrow \quad P(x) = x^2 - (-3+4)x + (-3 \times 4)$

$\therefore \quad P(x) = x^2 - x - 12$

We know, multiplying or dividing $P(x)$ by any real number does not affect the zeroes of polynomial.

So, $P(x) = x^2 - x - 12$

$= \frac{x^2}{2} - \frac{x}{2} - 6$ $\quad [\because$ Multiplying $P(x)$ by $\frac{1}{2}]$

Q.9 If one root of the equation $(k-1)x^2 - 10x + 3 + 0$ is the reciprocal of the other, then value of k is

(a) 3 (b) 4
(c) 1 (d) None of these

Sol. (b) We are given the polynomial $(k-1)x^2 - 10x + 3 = 0$

Let one root be α, then other root is $\frac{1}{\alpha}$

Now, product of roots $= \frac{\text{Constant term}}{\text{Coefficient of } x^2}$

$$\Rightarrow \quad \alpha \cdot \frac{1}{\alpha} = \frac{3}{(k-1)}$$

$$\Rightarrow \quad k-1 = 3 \Rightarrow k = 4$$

Hence, the value of k is 4.

Q.10 Polynomial of degree n has

(a) Only 1 zero
(b) Atmost n zeroes
(c) Exactly n zeroes
(d) More than n zeroes

Sol. (c) Degree of polynomial = Number of zeroes of polynomial

Q.11 Graph of a quadratic polynomial is

(a) Straight line
(b) Circle
(c) Parabola
(d) Ellipse

Sol. (c) Graph of a quadratic polynomial is parabola.

Q.12 Quadratic polynomial having zeroes 1 and –2 is

(a) $x^2 - x + 2$
(b) $x^2 - x - 2$
(c) $x^2 + x - 2$
(d) $x^2 + x + 2$

Sol. (c) We are given zeroes of polynomial 1 and –2 required polynomial $P(x)$ is given by $P(x) = x^2 - (\text{Sum of zeroes})x + (\text{Product of zeros})$

$$P(x) = x^2 - [1 + (-2)]x + [1 \times (-2)]$$

$$\Rightarrow \quad P(x) = x^2 + x - 2.$$

Q.13 The quadratic polynomial, the sum of whose zeroes is 0 and one zeroes is 5 is

(a) $x^2 - 5$
(b) $x^2 - 25$
(c) $x^2 + 25$
(d) None of these

Sol. (b) We are given, one zero of polynomial is 5

Let other zero be α.

$\because$ Sum of zeroes is 0.

$$\therefore \quad 5 + \alpha = 0 \Rightarrow \alpha = -5$$

Then, required quadratic polynomial $P(x)$ is

$$P(x) = x^2 - (\text{Sum of zeroes})x + (\text{Product of zeroes})$$
$$= x^2 - (0)x + [5 \times (-5)]$$

$$\Rightarrow \quad P(x) = x^2 - 25.$$

Hence required polynomial is $P(x) = x^2 - 25$.

Q.14 If one of the zero of the quadratic polynomial $x^2 + 3x + k$ is 2, then the value of k is

(a) 10
(b) −10
(c) 5
(d) −5

Sol. (b) Let $P(x) = x^2 + 3x + k$

We know,

$$\text{Sum of zeroes} = -\frac{(\text{Coefficient of } x)}{(\text{Coefficient of } x^2)}$$

We have, one of the zeroes of $P(x)$ is 2.

Let other zero be α.

Therefore, $\alpha + 2 = -3$ ... (i)

$$\text{Product of zeroes} = \frac{(\text{Constant term})}{(\text{Coefficient of } x^2)}$$

$\Rightarrow \quad 2 \times \alpha = k$

$\Rightarrow \quad \alpha = \frac{k}{2}$ ...(ii)

On substituting value of α from Eq. (ii) in Eq. (i), we get

$$\frac{k}{2} + 2 = -3$$

$\Rightarrow \quad \frac{k+4}{2} = -3$

$\Rightarrow \quad k + 4 = -6$

$\Rightarrow \quad k = -10$

Hence, the value of $k = -10$.

☐ Subjective Type Questions

Q.1 Are 1 and 4 the zeroes of the quadratic polynomial $x^2 - 5x + 4$?

Sol. We have, $x^2 - 5x + 4 = x^2 - x - 4x + 4$

$$= x(x-1) - 4(x-1) = (x-4)(x-1)$$

$\because \quad x^2 - 5x + 4$ is zero, when $(x-4)(x-1) = 0$

i.e., either $(x-4) = 0$ or $(x-1) = 0$

$\Rightarrow \quad x = 4$ of $x = 1$

Hence, 1 and 4 are 2 zeroes of the polynomial $x^2 - 5x + 4$.

Q.2 The graph of $y = p(x)$ for the polynomial $p(x)$ is given below. Find the number of zeroes of $p(x)$.

Sol. The number of zeroes is 3 as the graph cuts X-axis at three points.

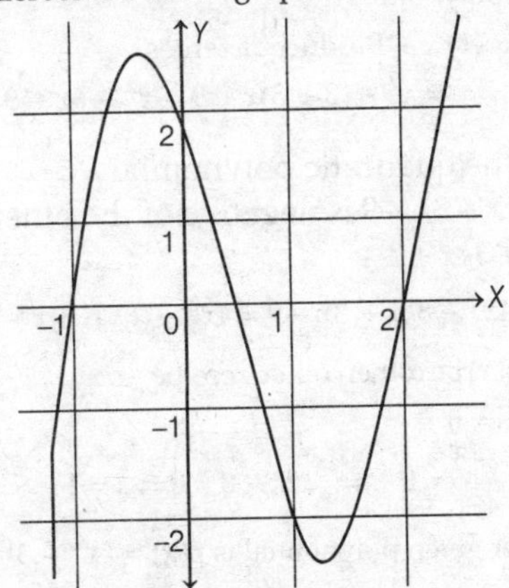

Q.3 Find the value of m if one of the zeroes of the polynomial $3x^2 + mx + 4$ is 1.

Sol. Given polynomial is $3x^2 + mx + 4$.

One of the zeroes of the polynomial is 1. Let other zero be α.

Product of zeroes $= \dfrac{\text{Constant term}}{\text{Coefficient of } x^2} \Rightarrow 1 \cdot \alpha = \dfrac{4}{3} \quad \Rightarrow \alpha = \dfrac{4}{3}$

Now, sum of zeroes $= \dfrac{-\text{Coefficient of } x}{\text{Coefficient of } x^2} \Rightarrow \dfrac{-m}{3} = \left(1 + \dfrac{4}{3}\right) = \dfrac{7}{3}$

$\Rightarrow \qquad \dfrac{-m}{3} = \dfrac{7}{3} \Rightarrow m = -7$

Q.4 If one of the zeroes of the quadratic polynomial $f(x) = 4x^2 - 8kx - 9$ is equal in magnitude but opposite in sign of the other, then find the value of k.

Sol. Let one zero be α. Then the other zero is $-\alpha$.

We have, the polynomial, $f(x) = 4x^2 - 8kx - 9$.

Sum of zeroes $= \alpha + (-\alpha) = 0$

$= \dfrac{-\text{Coefficient of } x}{\text{Coefficient of } x^2} = \dfrac{8k}{4} = 0$

Hence, $\qquad k = 0$

Q.5 If α and β are zeroes of a polynomial $x^2 + 6x + 9$, then form a polynomial whose zeroes are $-\alpha$ and $-\beta$.

Sol. We have, $x^2 + 6x + 9 = x^2 + 3x + 3x + 9$

$= x(x + 3) + 3(x + 3) = (x + 3)(x + 3) = (x + 3)^2$

$x^2 + 6x + 9$ will be zero when $(x + 3)^2 = 0$

i.e., $x = -3$

$\Rightarrow$ $\alpha = -3, \beta = -3 \Rightarrow -\alpha = 3, -\beta = 3$

So, the required polynomial is

x^2 – (sum by zeroes) x + Product of zeroes

$$= x^2 - (3 + 3)x + 9 = x^2 - 6x + 9$$

Q.6 If one zero of the quadratic polynomial $f(x) = 4x^2 - 8kx + 8x - 9$ is negative of the other, then find the zeroes of $kx^2 + 3kx + 2$.

Sol. We have, $f(x) = 4x^2 - 8kx + 8x - 9 = 4x^2 - (8k - 8)x - 9$

Let one zero of $f(x)$ be α then other zero be $-\alpha$.

So, sum of zeroes = 0

$$\Rightarrow \quad \frac{8k - 8}{4} = 0 \quad \Rightarrow \quad 8k - 8 = 0 \Rightarrow k = 1$$

Now, let the other given polynomial is $p(x) = kx^2 + 3kx + 2$

$$= x^2 + 3x + 2 \qquad [\because k = 1]$$

$$= (x + 2)(x + 1)$$

So, zeroes of $p(x)$ are –1 and –2.

Q.7 Find the zeroes of the quadratic polynomial $3x^2 - 2$ and verify the relationship between the zeroes and the coefficients.

Sol. Let $p(x) = 3x^2 - 2 = (\sqrt{3}x)^2 - (\sqrt{2})^2 = (\sqrt{3}x - \sqrt{2})](\sqrt{3}x + \sqrt{2})$

So, zeroes of $p(x)$ are $\frac{\sqrt{2}}{\sqrt{3}}$ and $= \frac{-\sqrt{2}}{\sqrt{3}}$.

Now, Sum of zeroes

$$\frac{\sqrt{2}}{\sqrt{3}} - \frac{\sqrt{2}}{\sqrt{3}} = 0 = -\frac{(\text{Coefficient of } x)}{(\text{Coefficient of } x^2)}$$

and product of zeroes $= \left(\frac{\sqrt{2}}{\sqrt{3}}\right)\left(\frac{-\sqrt{2}}{\sqrt{3}}\right) = \frac{-2}{3} = \frac{(\text{Constant term})}{(\text{Coefficient of } x^2)}$

Hence, verified the relationship between the zeroes and the coefficients.

Q.8 For each of the following, find a quadratic polynomial whose sum and product respectively of the zeroes are as given. Also find the zeroes of these polynomial by factorisation.

(i) $\frac{-8}{3}, \frac{4}{3}$ (ii) $-2\sqrt{3}, -9$

◎ **Thinking Process** If α, β are the zeros of $P(x)$, then required polynomial $P(x) = x^2 - (\alpha + \beta)x + \alpha\beta$ and if α is a zero of $P(x)$ then, $P(\alpha) = 0$.

Sol.

(i) $\because$ $\alpha + \beta = \frac{-8}{3}$ and $\alpha \cdot \beta = \frac{4}{3}$ [Given]

$\therefore$ $f(x) = x^2 - (\alpha + \beta)x + \alpha\beta$

$\Rightarrow$ $x^2 - \left(\frac{-8}{3}\right)x + \frac{4}{3}$ [Formula]

Multiplying or dividing $f(x)$ by any real number does not affect the zeroes of polynomial.

So, $f(x) = 3x^2 + 8x^2 + 4$ [Multiplying by LCM 3]

For zeroes of $f(x)$, $f(x) = 0$

$\Rightarrow$ $3x^2 + 8x + 4 = 0$

$\Rightarrow$ $3x^2 + 6x + 2x + 4 = 0$

$\Rightarrow$ $3x(x + 2) + 2(x + 2) = 0$

$\Rightarrow$ $(x + 2)(3x + 2) = 0$

$\Rightarrow$ $x + 2 = 0$ or $3x + 2 = 0$

$\Rightarrow$ $x = -2$

or $x = \frac{-2}{3}$

$\therefore$ $\alpha = -2$

and $\beta = \frac{-2}{3}$

(ii) $\alpha + \beta = -2\sqrt{3}$ and $\alpha\beta = -9$ [Given]

$\therefore$ $f(x) = x^2 - (\alpha + \beta)x + \alpha\beta$ [Formula]

$= x^2 - (-2\sqrt{3})x + (-9)$

$\Rightarrow$ $= f(x) = x^2 + 2\sqrt{3}x - 9$

For zeroes of polynomial $f(x)$, $f(x) = 0$

$\Rightarrow$ $x^2 + 2\sqrt{3}x - 9 = 0$

$\Rightarrow$ $x^2 + 3\sqrt{3}x - \sqrt{3}x - 9 = 0$

$\Rightarrow$ $x(x + 3\sqrt{3}) - \sqrt{3}(x + 3\sqrt{3}) = 0$

$\Rightarrow$ $(x + 3\sqrt{3})(x - \sqrt{3}) = 0$

$\Rightarrow$ $x + 3\sqrt{3} = 0$ or $(x - \sqrt{3}) = 0$

$\Rightarrow$ $x = -3\sqrt{3}$

or $x = \sqrt{3}$

$\therefore$ $\alpha = -3\sqrt{3}$

and $\beta = \sqrt{3}$

Q.9 Find the zeroes of the polynomial $x^2 + \frac{1}{6}x - 2$

Hence, verify the relationship between the zeroes and the coefficients.

Sol. We have, $x^2 + \frac{1}{6}x - 2$

$$= \frac{6x^2 + x - 12}{6} = \frac{(2x+3)(3x-4)}{6}$$

Zeroes of the polynomial are $\alpha = \frac{-3}{2}$ and $\beta = \frac{4}{3}$

Now, $\alpha + \beta = \frac{-3}{2} + \frac{4}{3} = \frac{-1}{6}$

and $\frac{-b}{a} = \frac{-1}{6}$

$\therefore$ $\alpha + \beta = \frac{-b}{a}$

$\alpha\beta = \frac{-3}{2} \times \frac{4}{3} = -2$ **Hence verified.**

Also, $\frac{c}{a} = \frac{-2}{1} = -2$

$\therefore$ $\alpha\beta = \frac{c}{a}$ **Hence verified.**

Q.10 What value of k, (-4) is a zero of polynomial $x^2 - x - (2k+2)$?

Sol. Let $P(x) = x^2 - x - (2k+2)$

Since, (-4) is zero of $P(x)$, so $P(-4) = 0$

Therefore,

$\Rightarrow$ $(-4)^2 - (-4) - (2k+2) = 0$

$\Rightarrow$ $16 + 4 - (2k+2) = 0$

$\Rightarrow$ $-(2k+2) = -20$

$\Rightarrow$ $2k + 2 = 20$

$\Rightarrow$ $k + 1 = 10$

$\Rightarrow$ $k = 9$

Hence, value of $k = 9$.

Q.11 Write the quadratic polynomial whose sum of zeroes is 2 and product of zeros is –3.

Sol. Let the polynomial be $ax^2 + bc + c$ and it zeroes be α and β.

Here $\alpha + \beta = 2$ and $\alpha\beta = -3$

Thus, the polynomial formed

$$= x^2 - (\text{Sum of zeroes})x + (\text{Product of zeroes})$$
$$= x^2 - 2x - 3$$

Hence, the polynomial is $x^2 - 2x - 3$.

Q.12 What will the value of k if zeroes of $P(x) = 2x^2 - 7x + k$ are reciprocal of each other ?

Sol. Let one zero of polynomial $P(x) = 2x^2 - 7x + k$ be α. Then, other zero is $\frac{1}{\alpha}$

Now, product of zeroes $= \frac{\text{Constant term}}{\text{Coefficient of } x^2}$

$$\therefore \quad \alpha \cdot \frac{1}{\alpha} = \frac{k}{2}$$

$$\Rightarrow \quad k = 2$$

Hence, value of $k = 2$

Q.13 If on division of a non zero polynomial $P(x)$ by a polynomial $g(x)$, the remainder is zero, what is the relation between degree of $P(x)$ and $g(x)$?

Sol. Since, $P(x)$ divides $g(x)$ completely.

Their either degree of $P(x) <$ degree of $g(x)$ or degree of $P(x) =$ degree of $g(x)$.

Q.14 If sum and product of zeroes of $ky^2 + 2y + 3k$ and equal, find k.

Sol. We are given *a* polynomial $ky^2 + 2y + 3k$.

and Sum of zeroes = Product of zeroes

Now, sum of zeroes $= -\frac{\text{Coefficient of } x}{\text{Coefficient of } x^2} = -\frac{2}{k}$

Product of zeroes $= \frac{\text{Constant terms}}{\text{Coefficient of } x^2} = \frac{3k}{k}$

as Sum of zeroes = Product of zeroes

$$\therefore \quad \frac{-2}{k} = \frac{3k}{k}$$

$$\Rightarrow \quad k = -\frac{2}{3}$$

Hence, value of $k = \frac{-2}{3}$

Q.15 If a and b are the zeroes of the polynomial $f(x) = 2x^2 - 7x + 3$, find the value of $a^2 + b^2$.

Sol. We are given the polynomial

$$f(x) = 2x^2 - 7x + 3$$

and zeros of polynomial are a and b

$$\text{Now, Sum of zeroes} = -\frac{\text{Coefficient of } x}{\text{Coefficient of } x^2}$$

$$(a + b) = -\left(\frac{-7}{2}\right) = \frac{7}{2}$$

$$\text{Product of zeroes} = \frac{\text{Constant term}}{\text{Coefficient of } x^2}$$

$$\therefore \quad (a \cdot b) = \frac{3}{2}.$$

As we know that

$$a^2 + b^2 = (a + b)^2 - 2ab$$

$$= \left(\frac{7}{2}\right)^2 - 2 \times \frac{3}{2}$$

$$= \frac{49}{4} - 3$$

$$= \frac{37}{4}$$

Pair of Linear Equations in Two Variables

CHAPTER 03

Important Points

01 Algebraic Expression A combination of constants and variables, connected by four fundamental arithmetical operations of +, –, × and ÷ is called an algebraic expression.

e.g., $6x^2 - 5y^2 + 2xy$ is an algebraic expression.

02 Equation An algebraic expression with equal to sign (=) is called the equation. Without an equal sign, it is an expression only.

e.g., $6x + 12 = 0$ is an equation but only $6x + 12$ is an expression.

03 Linear Equation in One Variable An equation which involves only one variable with highest power 1, is called a linear equation in that variable.

e.g., Each one of the equations given below is a linear equation in one variable

(i) $5x - 18 = 3 - 4x$

(ii) $\frac{y-1}{2} - \frac{y+5}{4} = 6 - y$

04 Solution of a Linear Equation in One Variable A value of the variable which when substituted for the variable in the equation, makes its two sides equal, is called a solution (or root) of the equation.

05 Linear Equations in Two Variables A linear equation in two variables (unknown) x and y are usually represented in the form $ax + by + c = 0$, $a \neq 0$, $b \neq 0$; a, b and c are real constants.

06 Solution of Linear Equation in Two Variables Any pair of values of x and y which satisfied the equation $ax + by + c = 0$, $a \neq 0, b \neq 0$ is called a solution of linear equation.

Geometrically, each solution (x, y) of a linear equation in two variables, $ax + by + c = 0$, corresponds to a point on the line representing the equation and *vice-versa*.

07 Graphical Method of Solution of a Pair of Linear Equations

Step **1.** Read the problem repeatedly to detect the unknown which is to be found.

Step **2.** Represent the unknown by x and y etc.

Step **3.** Use the conditions given in the problem to frame an equation in the unknown x and y.

Step **4.** Prepare the proper tables for both the situations.

Step **5.** Draw the graph of both the equations on the same scale of representation.

Step **6.** Detect the coordinates of the point of intersection of the graphs.

Case I The two lines will intersect in one point. If $\frac{a_1}{a_2} \neq \frac{b_1}{b_2}$, then the graph will represent two intersecting lines. Point of intersection is the only one solution of the system.

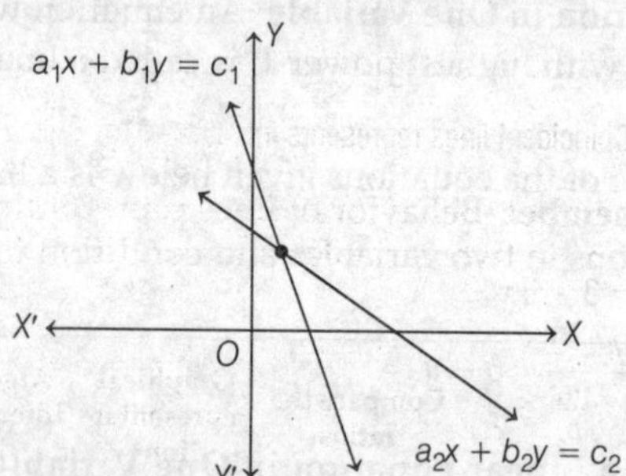

▲ Intersecting lines represent one solution

Case II The two lines will not intersect, *i.e.*, they are parallel. If $\frac{a_1}{a_2} = \frac{b_1}{b_2} \neq \frac{c_1}{c_2}$, then the graph will represent two parallel lines. Therefore, the system has no common solution.

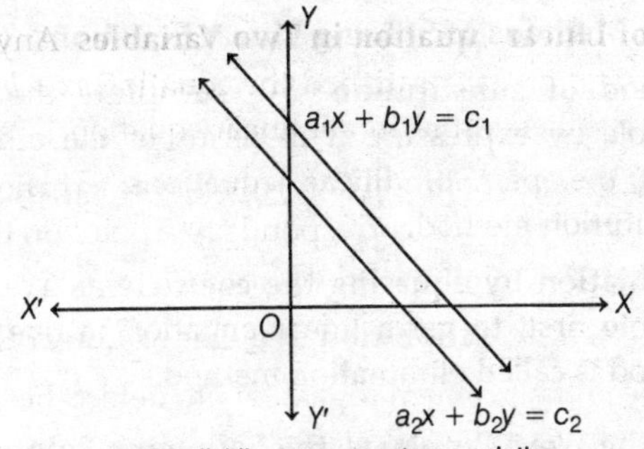

▲ Parallel lines represents no solution

Case **III** The two lines will be coincident. If $\frac{a_1}{a_2} = \frac{b_1}{b_2} = \frac{c_1}{c_2}$, then graph will represent two coinciding lines. Therefore, system has infinitely many solutions.

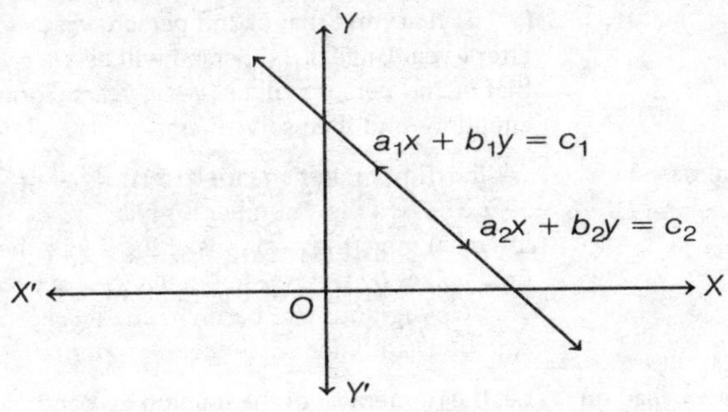

▲ Coincident lines represents infinitely many solutions

08 Point to Remember Behavior of lines representing a pair of linear equations in two variables and condition for solvability as follows.

Pair of lines	$\frac{a_1}{a_2}$	$\frac{b_1}{b_2}$	$\frac{c_1}{c_2}$	Compare the ratios	Graphical representation	Algebraic interpretation	Conditions for solvability
$x - 2y = 0$ $3x + 4y - 20 = 0$	$\frac{1}{3}$	$-\frac{2}{4}$	$\frac{0}{-20}$	$\frac{a_1}{a_2} \neq \frac{b_1}{b_2}$	Intersecting lines	Exactly one solution (unique)	System is consistent
$2x + 3y - 9 = 0$ $4x + 6y - 18 = 0$	$\frac{2}{4}$	$\frac{3}{6}$	$\frac{-9}{-18}$	$\frac{a_1}{a_2} = \frac{b_1}{b_2} = \frac{c_1}{c_2}$	Coincident lines	Infinitely many solutions	System is consistent dependent
$x + 2y - 4 = 0$ $2x + 4y - 12 = 0$	$\frac{1}{2}$	$\frac{2}{4}$	$\frac{-4}{-12}$	$\frac{a_1}{a_2} = \frac{b_1}{b_2} \neq \frac{c_1}{c_2}$	Parallel lines	No solution	System is inconsistent

09 Algebraic Methods of Solving Linear Equations

(i) **Method of substitution** We substitute the value of one variable by expressing it in terms of the other variable to solve the pair of linear equations. This is known as substitution method.

(ii) **Elimination by equating the coefficients** We eliminate one variable first, to get a linear equation in one variable. This method is called elimination method.

10 To Solve the Word Problems, the Following Points should be kept in mind.

Problem type		Steps to be followed
1.	**Age Problem**	If the problem involves finding out the ages of two persons, take the present age of one person as x and of the other as y. Then, a years ago, age of 1st person was $(x-a)$ years and that of 2nd person was $(y-a)$ and after b years, age of 1st person will be $x+b$ years and that of 2nd person will be $(y+b)$ years. Formulate the equations and then solve them.
2.	**Problem based on Numbers and Digits**	Let the digit in unit's place be x and that in ten's place be y. The two digit number is given by $10y+x$. On interchanging, the positions of the digits, the digit in unit's place becomes y and in ten's place become x. The two digit number becomes $10x+y$. Formulate the equations and then solve them.
3.	**Problems based on Fractions**	Let the numerator of the fraction be x and denominator be y. Then, the fraction $= \frac{x}{y}$. Formulate the linear equations on the basis of conditions given and solve for x and y to get the value of the fraction.
4.	**Problems based on Distance, Speed and Time**	We know that speed is defined as Speed = Distance / Time, Distance = Speed × Time and Time = Distance / Speed. To solve problems related to speed of boat going downstream and upstream, let the speed of boat in still water be x kmh^{-1} and speed of stream be y kmh^{-1}, then the speed of boat downstream $= x+y$ and speed of boat upstream $= x-y$.

	Problem type	Steps to be followed
5.	**Problem based on Commercial Mathematics**	For solving specific questions based on commercial mathematics, the fare of 1 Full Ticket may be taken as ₹ x and the reservation charges may be taken as ₹ y. So that, one full fare = $x + y$ and one half fare = $\frac{x}{2} + y$. To solve questions of profit and loss, take the cost price of 1st article as ₹ x and that of 2nd article as ₹ y. To solve questions based on simple interest, take the amount invested as ₹ x at some rate of interest and ₹ y at some other rate of interest.
6.	**Problems based on Geometry and Mensuration**	Make use of the angle sum property of a triangle ($\angle A + \angle B + \angle C = 180°$) in case of a triangle. In case of a parallelogram, opposite angles are equal and in case of a cyclic quadrilateral, opposite angles are supplementary.

Exercise 3.1

Question 1 Form the pair of linear equations in the following problems and find their solutions graphically.

(i) 10 students of class X took part in a Mathematics quiz. If the number of girls is 4 more than the number of boys, find the number of boys and girls who took part in the quiz.

(ii) 5 pencils and 7 pens together cost ₹ 50, whereas 7 pencils and 5 pens together cost ₹ 46. Find the cost of one pencil and that of one pen.

Thinking Process First make the linear equations by the given information and plot the graph of the two equations by the help to table find the intersection point of two lines.

Sol.

(i) Let the number of boys be x and the number of girls be y.
Then, the equations formed are

$$x + y = 10 \quad \ldots(i)$$
$$y = x + 4 \quad \ldots(ii)$$

Let us draw the graphs of Eqs. (i) and (ii) by finding two solutions for each of the equations.

$\therefore$ Table for line, $x + y = 10$

x	0	10	3
$y = 10 - x$	10	0	7
Points	A	B	E

Table for line, $y = x + 4$

x	0	−4	3
$y = x + 4$	4	0	7
Points	C	D	E

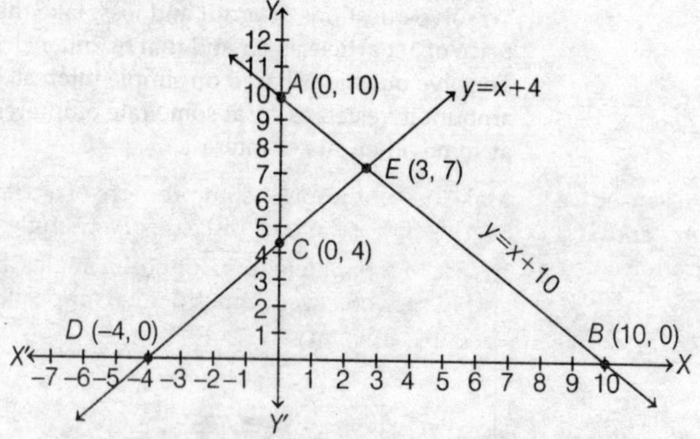

Plotting these points, we draw the lines AB and CE passing through them to represent the equations. The two lines AB and CE intersect at the point $E(3, 7)$. So, $x = 3$ and $y = 7$ is the required solution of the pair of linear equations.

i.e., Number of boys = 3,

Number of girls = 7

Quick Solution

For ease in plotting and tabular representation take one point by taking $x = 0$ and other point by taking $y = 0$.

Table for line $x + y = 10$

x	0	10	3
$y = 10 - x$	10	0	7
Points	A	B	E

Table for line, $y = x + 4$

x	0	−4	3
$y = x - 4$	4	0	7
Points	C	D	E

Here, point $E(3, 7)$ is same in both table. Hence, required solution of pair is $(3, 7)$.

(ii) Let us denote the cost of one pencil be x and one pen be ₹ y.

Then, the equations formed are

$$5x + 7y = 50 \quad \text{...(i)}$$

and

$$7x + 5y = 46 \quad \text{...(ii)}$$

Table for line, $5x + 7y = 50$

x	10	3
y	0	5

Table for line, $7x + 5y = 46$

x	8	3
y	–2	5

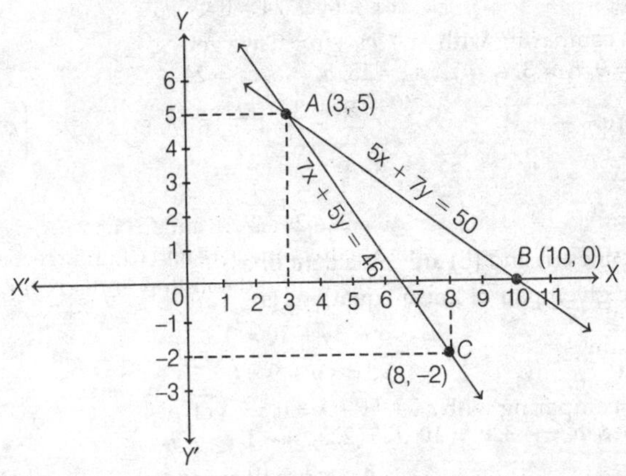

Plotting these points, we draw the lines AB and AC passing through them to represent the equations. The two lines AB and AC intersect at the point $A(3, 5)$. So, $x = 3$ and $y = 5$ is the required solution of the pair of linear equations *i.e.*, cost of one pencil, x = ₹ 3 and cost of one pen, y = ₹ 5.

Mistake Alert Taking one point by taking $x = 0$ and another by taking $y = 0$ is easier only when the point doesn't result in a fractional coordinate. *e.g.*, in Q.1 (ii) if we take $x = 0$ in $5x + 7y = 50$.

Then, $y = \frac{50}{7}$ which is difficult to plot.

Question 2 On comparing the ratios $\frac{a_1}{a_2}$, $\frac{b_1}{b_2}$ and $\frac{c_1}{c_2}$, find out whether the lines representing the following pairs of linear equations intersect at a point, are parallel or coincident.

(i) $5x - 4y + 8 = 0; 7x + 6y - 9 = 0$

(ii) $9x + 3y + 12 = 0; 18x + 6y + 24 = 0$

(iii) $6x - 3y + 10 = 0; 2x - y + 9 = 0$

Sol.

(i) The given pair of linear equations is

$$5x - 4y + 8 = 0 \quad \ldots(i)$$

and $$7x + 6y - 9 = 0 \quad \ldots(ii)$$

On comparing with $ax + by + c = 0$, we get
$a_1 = 5, b_1 = -4, c_1 = 8; a_2 = 7, b_2 = 6, c_2 = -9$

Here, $$\frac{5}{7} \neq \frac{-4}{6} \quad \left(\because \frac{a_1}{a_2} \neq \frac{b_1}{b_2}\right)$$

So, lines (i) and (ii) are intersecting lines.

(ii) The given pair of linear equations is

$$9x + 3y + 12 = 0 \quad \ldots(i)$$

and $$18x + 6y + 24 = 0 \quad \ldots(ii)$$

On comparing with $ax + by + c = 0$, we get
$a_1 = 9, b_1 = 3, c_1 = 12; a_2 = 18, b_2 = 6, c_2 = 24$

Here, $$\frac{9}{18} = \frac{3}{6} = \frac{12}{24} \quad \left(\because \frac{a_1}{a_2} = \frac{b_1}{b_2} = \frac{c_1}{c_2}\right)$$

$\Rightarrow$ $$\frac{1}{2} = \frac{1}{2} = \frac{1}{2}$$

So, lines (i) and (ii) are coincident lines.

(iii) The given pair of linear equations is

$$6x - 3y + 10 = 0 \quad \ldots(i)$$

and $$2x - y + 9 = 0 \quad \ldots(ii)$$

On comparing with $ax + by + c = 0$, we get
$a_1 = 6, b_1 = -3, c_1 = 10; a_2 = 2, b_2 = -1, c_2 = 9$

Here, $$\frac{6}{2} = \frac{-3}{-1} \neq \frac{10}{9} \quad \left(\because \frac{a_1}{a_2} = \frac{b_1}{b_2} \neq \frac{c_1}{c_2}\right)$$

$\Rightarrow$ $$\frac{3}{1} = \frac{3}{1} \neq \frac{10}{9}$$

So, lines (i) and (ii) are parallel lines.

Question 3 On comparing the ratios $\frac{a_1}{a_2}, \frac{b_1}{b_2}$ and $\frac{c_1}{c_2}$, find out whether the following pairs of linear equations are consistent or inconsistent.

(i) $3x + 2y = 5; 2x - 3y = 7$

(ii) $2x - 3y = 8; 4x - 6y = 9$

(iii) $\frac{3}{2}x + \frac{5}{3}y = 7; 9x - 10y = 14$

(iv) $5x - 3y = 11; -10x + 6y = -22$

(v) $\frac{4}{3}x + 2y = 8; 2x + 3y = 12$

Sol.

(i) The given equations can be rewritten as

$$3x + 2y - 5 = 0, \quad 2x - 3y - 7 = 0$$

On comparing with $ax + by + c = 0$, we get

$a_1 = 3,\ b_1 = 2,\ c_1 = -5;\ a_2 = 2,\ b_2 = -3,\ c_2 = -7$

Here, $\dfrac{a_1}{a_2} = \dfrac{3}{2}, \dfrac{b_1}{b_2} = \dfrac{2}{-3}$

Thus, $\dfrac{3}{2} \neq \dfrac{2}{-3}$, *i.e.*, $\dfrac{a_1}{a_2} \neq \dfrac{b_1}{b_2}$

Hence, the pair of linear equations is consistent.

(ii) The given equations can be rewritten as

$$2x - 3y - 8 = 0; \quad 4x - 6y - 9 = 0$$

On comparing with $ax + by + c = 0$, we get

$a_1 = 2, b_1 = -3, c_1 = -8;\ a_2 = 4, b_2 = -6, c_2 = -9$

Here, $\dfrac{a_1}{a_2} = \dfrac{2}{4} = \dfrac{1}{2}, \dfrac{b_1}{b_2} = \dfrac{-3}{-6} = \dfrac{1}{2}, \dfrac{c_1}{c_2} = \dfrac{-8}{-9} = \dfrac{8}{9}$

Thus, $\dfrac{1}{2} = \dfrac{1}{2} \neq \dfrac{8}{9}$, *i.e.*, $\dfrac{a_1}{a_2} = \dfrac{b_1}{b_2} \neq \dfrac{c_1}{c_2}$

Hence, the pair of linear equations is inconsistent.

(iii) The given equations can be rewritten as

$$\frac{3}{2}x + \frac{5}{3}y - 7 = 0; \quad 9x - 10y - 14 = 0$$

On comparing with $ax + by + c = 0$, we get

$a_1 = \dfrac{3}{2}, b_1 = \dfrac{5}{3}, c_1 = -7; a_2 = 9, b_2 = -10, c_2 = -14$

Here, $\dfrac{a_1}{a_2} = \dfrac{\frac{3}{2}}{9} = \dfrac{1}{6}, \dfrac{b_1}{b_2} = \dfrac{\frac{5}{3}}{-10} = -\dfrac{1}{6}$,

Thus, $\dfrac{1}{6} \neq -\dfrac{1}{6}$, *i.e.*, $\dfrac{a_1}{a_2} \neq \dfrac{b_1}{b_2}$

Hence, the pair of linear equations is consistent.

(iv) The given equations can be rewritten as

$$5x - 3y - 11 = 0; \quad -10x + 6y + 22 = 0$$

On comparing with $ax + by + c = 0$, we get

$a_1 = 5, b_1 = -3, c_1 = -11;\ a_2 = -10, b_2 = 6, c_2 = 22$

Here, $\dfrac{a_1}{a_2} = \dfrac{5}{-10} = -\dfrac{1}{2}, \dfrac{b_1}{b_2} = \dfrac{-3}{6} = -\dfrac{1}{2}$,

$\dfrac{c_1}{c_2} = \dfrac{-11}{22} = -\dfrac{1}{2}$

Thus, $-\dfrac{1}{2} = -\dfrac{1}{2} = -\dfrac{1}{2}$

i.e., $\dfrac{a_1}{a_2} = \dfrac{b_1}{b_2} = \dfrac{c_1}{c_2}$

Hence, the pair of linear equations is consistent (or dependent).

(v) The given equations can be rewritten as

$$\frac{4}{3}x + 2y - 8 = 0; \quad 2x + 3y - 12 = 0$$

On comparing with $ax + by + c = 0$, we get

$$a_1 = \frac{4}{3}, b_1 = 2, c_1 = -8; \quad a_2 = 2, b_2 = 3, c_2 = -12$$

$$\Rightarrow \qquad \frac{a_1}{a_2} = \frac{\frac{4}{3}}{2} = \frac{2}{3}, \frac{b_1}{b_2} = \frac{2}{3}, \frac{c_1}{c_2} = \frac{-8}{-12} = \frac{2}{3}$$

Thus, $\frac{2}{3} = \frac{2}{3} = \frac{2}{3}$, *i.e.*, $\frac{a_1}{a_2} = \frac{b_1}{b_2} = \frac{c_1}{c_2}$

Hence, the pair of linear equations is consistent (or dependent).

Question 4 Which of the following pairs of linear equations are consistent or inconsistent? If consistent obtain the solution graphically?

(i) $x + y = 5, 2x + 2y = 10$ (ii) $x - y = 8, 3x - 3y = 16$

(iii) $2x + y - 6 = 0,$ $4x - 2y - 4 = 0$ (iv) $2x - 2y - 2 = 0,$ $4x - 4y - 5 = 0$

Sol.

(i) Given pair of lines is $x + y = 5$ and $2x + 2y = 10$

On comparing with $ax + by + c = 0$, we get

$$a_1 = 1, b_1 = 1, c_1 = -5; a_2 = 2, b_2 = 2, c_2 = -10$$

Here, $\frac{a_1}{a_2} = \frac{1}{2}, \frac{b_1}{b_2} = \frac{1}{2}$ and $\frac{c_1}{c_2} = \frac{-5}{-10} = \frac{1}{2}$ $\therefore \frac{a_1}{a_2} = \frac{b_1}{b_2} = \frac{c_1}{c_2}$

So, the given pair of linear equations are coincident.

Therefore, these lines have infinitely many solutions.

Hence, the given pair of linear equations is consistent.

Now, $$x + y = 5 \qquad \ldots(i)$$

$$\Rightarrow \qquad y = 5 - x$$

Table for $y = 5 - x$

x	0	5
$y = 5 - x$	5	0
Points	*A*	*B*

and $$2x + 2y = 10 \qquad \ldots(ii)$$

$$\Rightarrow \qquad y = \frac{10 - 2x}{2}$$

Table for $y = \dfrac{10-2x}{2}$

x	0	2	5
$y = (10-2x)/2$	5	3	0
Points	C	D	E

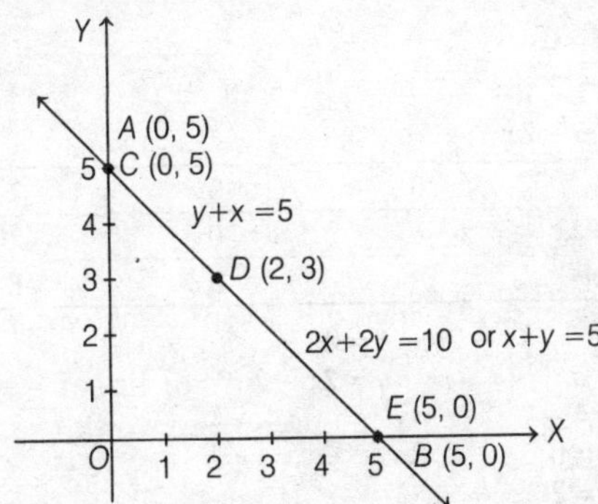

Plotting the points $A(0, 5)$ and $B(5, 0)$, we get the line AB. Again, plotting the points $C(0, 5)$, $D(2, 3)$ and $E(5, 0)$, we get the line CDE. We observe that the lines represented by Eqs. (i) and (ii) are coincident.

(ii) Given pair of lines is $x - y = 8$, $3x - 3y = 16$

On comparing with $ax + by + c = 0$, we get

$$a_1 = 1, b_1 = -1, c_1 = -8; a_2 = 3, b_2 = -3, c_2 = -16$$

Here, $$\frac{a_1}{a_2} = \frac{1}{3}, \frac{b_1}{b_2} = \frac{-1}{-3} = \frac{1}{3}$$

and $$\frac{c_1}{c_2} = \frac{-8}{-16} = \frac{1}{2}$$

∴ $$\frac{a_1}{a_2} = \frac{b_1}{b_2} \neq \frac{c_1}{c_2}$$

Hence, the lines represented by the given equations are parallel. Therefore, it has no solution. Hence, the given pair of lines is inconsistent.

(iii) Given pair of lines are $2x + y - 6 = 0$ and $4x - 2y - 4 = 0$

On comparing with $ax + by + c = 0$, we get

$a_1 = 2, b_1 = 1, c_1 = -6; a_2 = 4, b_2 = -2, c_2 = -4$

Here, $$\frac{a_1}{a_2} = \frac{2}{4} = \frac{1}{2}, \frac{b_1}{b_2} = \frac{1}{-2}$$

and $$\frac{c_1}{c_2} = \frac{-6}{-4} = \frac{3}{2}$$

$$\frac{1}{2} \neq \frac{-1}{2} \neq \frac{3}{2}$$

∴ $$\frac{a_1}{a_2} \neq \frac{b_1}{b_2} \neq \frac{c_1}{c_2}$$

So, the given pair of linear equations is intersecting, therefore these lines have unique solution.

Hence, given pair of linear equations is consistent.

We have, $2x + y - 6 = 0$

$\Rightarrow$ $y = 6 - 2x$

When $x = 0, y = 6$

When $x = 3, y = 0$

When $x = 2, y = 2$

Table for $y = 6 - 2x$

x	0	3	2
$y = 6 - 2x$	6	0	2
Point	A	B	E

and $4x - 2y - 4 = 0$

$\Rightarrow$ $y = 2x - 2$

When $x = 0, y = -2$

When $x = 1, y = 0$

When $x = 2, y = 2$

Table for $y = 2x - 2$

x	0	1	2
$y = 2x - 2$	–2	0	2
Point	C	D	E

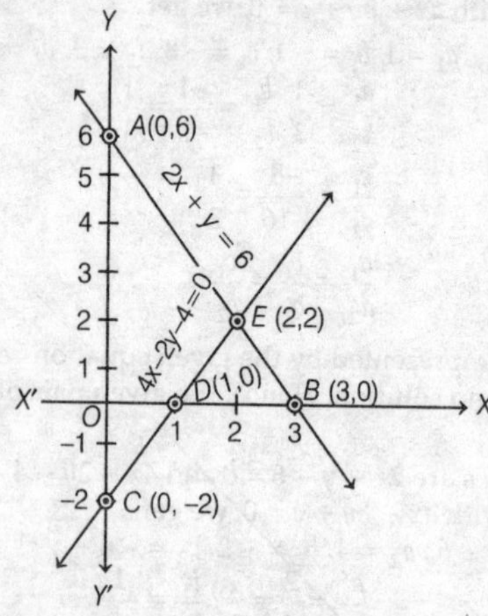

Plotting the points $A(0, 6)$ and $B(3, 0)$, we get the straight line AB. Plotting the points $C(0, -2)$ and $D(1, 0)$, we get the straight line CD. The lines AB and CE intersect at point $E(2, 2)$.

(iv) Given, $2y - 2x - 2 = 0$ and $4x - 4y - 5 = 0$

On comparing with $ax + by + c = 0$

Here, $a_1 = 2, b_1 = -2, c_1 = -2; a_2 = 4, b_2 = -4, c_2 = -5$

Here, $\frac{a_1}{a_2} = \frac{2}{4} = \frac{1}{2}, \frac{b_1}{b_2} = \frac{-2}{-4} = \frac{1}{2}, \frac{c_1}{c_2} = \frac{-2}{-5} = \frac{2}{5} \Rightarrow \frac{1}{2} = \frac{1}{2} \neq \frac{2}{5}$

$\therefore \quad \frac{a_1}{a_2} = \frac{b_1}{b_2} \neq \frac{c_1}{c_2}$

So, the given pairs of linear equations are parallel.

Therefore, these lines have no solution.

Hence, the given pair has inconsistent.

Question 5 Half the perimeter of a rectangular garden, whose length is 4 m more than its width, is 36 m. Find the dimensions of the garden.

Sol. Let the length of the garden be x metre and its width be y metre.

Then, perimeter of rectangular garden = 2 (length + width) = $2(x + y)$

Therefore, half perimeter = $(x + y)$

But it is given as 36 m.

$\therefore \quad (x + y) = 36 \quad \ldots(i)$

Also, $\quad x = y + 4$, i.e., $x - y = 4$ (Given) $\quad \ldots(ii)$

For finding the solution of Eqs. (i) and (ii) graphically, we form the following tables **Table for $x + y = 36$**

x	20	24
y	16	12

Table for $x - y = 4$

x	10	16	20
y	6	12	16

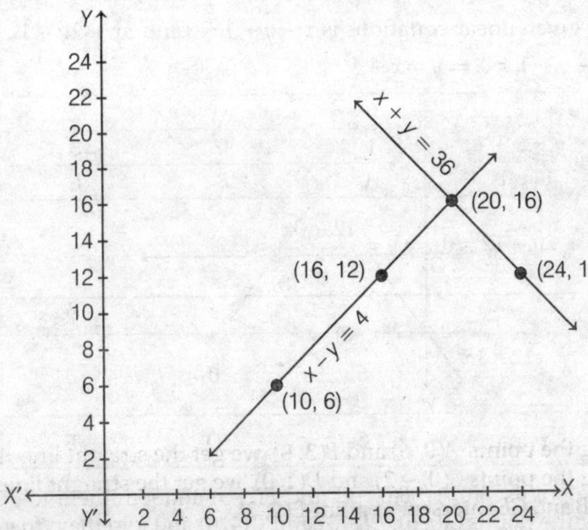

Draw the graphs by joining points (20, 16) and (24, 12) and points (10, 6) and (16, 12). The two lines intersect at point (20, 16) as shown in the graph.

Hence, the required length = 20 m and width = 16 m

Question 6 Given the linear equation $2x+3y-8=0$, write another linear equation in two variables such that the geometrical representation of the pair so formed is

(i) intersecting lines (ii) parallel lines

(iii) coincident lines

Sol. Given linear equation is

$$2x + 3y - 8 = 0 \quad \text{...(i)}$$

(i) For intersecting lines, $\frac{a_1}{a_2} \neq \frac{b_1}{b_2}$

$\therefore$ Any intersecting line may be taken as $5x + 2y - 9 = 0$.

(ii) For parallel lines,

$$\frac{a_1}{a_2} = \frac{b_1}{b_2} \neq \frac{c_1}{c_2}$$

$\therefore$ Any line parallel to Eq. (i) may be taken as $6x + 9y + 7 = 0$.

(iii) For coincident lines,

$$\frac{a_1}{a_2} = \frac{b_1}{b_2} = \frac{c_1}{c_2}$$

$\therefore$ Any line coincident to Eq. (i) may be taken as $4x + 6y - 16 = 0$.

Question 7 Draw the graphs of the equations $x-y+1=0$ and $3x+2y-12=0$. Determine the coordinates of the vertices of the triangle formed by these lines and x-axis and shade the triangular region.

Sol. Pair of given linear equations is $x - y + 1 = 0$ and $3x + 2y - 12 = 0$.

For $x - y + 1 = 0, \Rightarrow y = x + 1$

x	0	–1	2
$y = x + 1$	1	0	3
Points	A	B	E

For $3x + 2y - 12 = 0, \Rightarrow y = \frac{12 - 3x}{2}$

x	0	4	2
$y = \frac{12 - 3x}{2}$	6	0	3
Points	C	D	E

Plot thing the points $A(0, 1)$, $B(0, -1)$ and $E(2, 3)$ and join them to get a line AB. Similarly plot the points $C(0, 6)$, $E(2, 3)$ and $D(4, 0)$ and join them to get a line CD. Clearly, the two lines intersect each other at point $E(2, 3)$. Hence, $x = 2$ and $y = 3$ is the solution of the given pair of equations.

The line CD cuts the X-axis at the point $D(4, 0)$ and BE cuts the X-axis at the point $B(-1, 0)$. Hence, the coordinates of the vertices of the triangle are $E(2, 3)$, $D(4, 0)$ and $B(-1, 0)$.

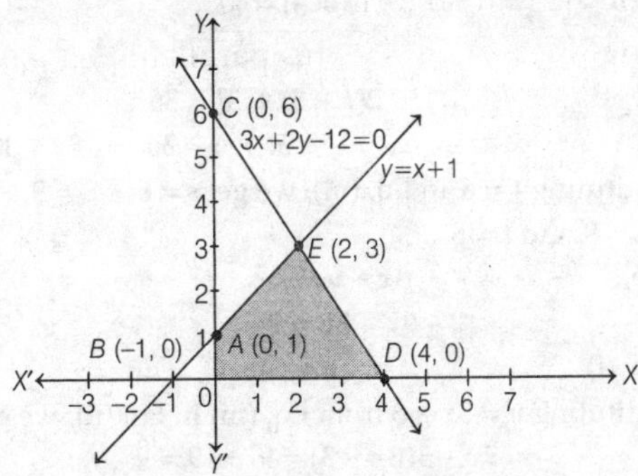

Exercise 3.2

Question 1 Solve the following pair of linear equations by the substitution method.

(i) $x + y = 14$, $x - y = 4$

(ii) $s - t = 3$, $\frac{s}{3} + \frac{t}{2} = 6$

(iii) $3x - y = 3$, $9x - 3y = 9$

(iv) $0.2x + 0.3y = 1.3$, $0.4x + 0.5y = 2.3$

(v) $\sqrt{2}x + \sqrt{3}y = 0$, $\sqrt{3}x - \sqrt{8}y = 0$

(vi) $\frac{3x}{2} - \frac{5y}{3} = -2$, $\frac{x}{3} + \frac{y}{2} = \frac{13}{6}$

Sol.

(i) We have, $x + y = 14$ ...(i)

and $x - y = 4$ ...(ii)

From Eq. (ii), $y = x - 4$ ...(iii)

Substituting $y = x - 4$ from Eq. (iii) in Eq. (i), we get

$$x + x - 4 = 14 \Rightarrow 2x = 18 \Rightarrow x = 9$$

On substituting $x = 9$ in Eq. (iii), we get

$$y = 9 - 4 = 5 \Rightarrow y = 5$$

Hence, $x = 9,\ y = 5$

(ii) We have, $s - t = 3$ ...(i)

and $\frac{s}{3} + \frac{t}{2} = 6$ ...(ii)

From Eq. (i), $s = t + 3$ ...(iii)

On substituting $s = t + 3$ from Eq. (iii) in Eq. (ii), we get

$$\frac{t+3}{3} + \frac{t}{2} = 6$$

$$\frac{2(t+3)+3t}{6} = 6$$

$\Rightarrow$ $$2(t+3) + 3t = 36$$

$\Rightarrow$ $$5t + 6 = 36 \Rightarrow 5t = 30 \Rightarrow t = 6$$

On substituting $t = 6$ in Eq. (iii), we get $s = 6 + 3 = 9$

Hence, $s = 9$ and $t = 6$

(iii) We have, $3x - y = 3$ ...(i)

and $9x - 3y = 9$ ...(ii)

From Eq. (i), $y = 3x - 3$ ...(iii)

On substituting $y = 3x - 3$ from Eq. (iii) in Eq. (ii), we get

$$9x - 3(3x - 3) = 9 \Rightarrow 9 = 9$$

It is a true statement. Hence, every solution of Eq. (i) is also a solution of Eq. (ii) and *vice-versa*.

On putting $x = k$ in Eq. (i), we get

$$3k - y = 3 \quad y = 3k - 3$$

$\therefore x = k$, $y = 3k - 3$ is a solution for every real k.

Hence, infinitely many solutions exist.

(iv) We have, $0.2x + 0.3y = 1.3$ ...(i)

and $0.4x + 0.5y = 2.3$

$\Rightarrow$ $$\frac{4}{10}x + \frac{5}{10}y = \frac{23}{10}$$ ...(ii)

From Eq. (i), $$\frac{2x}{10} + \frac{3y}{10} = \frac{13}{10}$$

$\Rightarrow$ $$2x + 3y = 13 \Rightarrow 3y = 13 - 2x$$

$\Rightarrow$ $$y = \frac{13 - 2x}{3}$$ ...(iii)

On substituting the value of y from Eq. (iii) in Eq. (ii), we get

$$\frac{4}{10}x + \frac{5}{10} \times \frac{(13 - 2x)}{3} = \frac{23}{10}$$

$\Rightarrow$ $$4x + \frac{5}{3}(13 - 2x) = 23$$

$\Rightarrow$ $$12x + 5(13 - 2x) = 3 \times 23$$

$\Rightarrow$ $$12x + 65 - 10x = 69$$

$\Rightarrow$ $$2x = 69 - 65 = 4 \Rightarrow x = 2$$

On substituting $x = 2$ in Eq. (iii), we get

$$y = \frac{13 - 2 \times 2}{3} = \frac{9}{3} \Rightarrow y = 3$$

Hence, $x = 2$ and $y = 3$

Mistake Alert Be careful while transfering the term from LHS to RHS and from RHS to LHS because the sign changes accordingly.

(v) We have, $\sqrt{2}x + \sqrt{3}y = 0$ ...(i)

and $\sqrt{3}x - \sqrt{8}y = 0$ ...(ii)

From Eq. (ii), $\sqrt{8}y = \sqrt{3}x \Rightarrow y = \frac{\sqrt{3}x}{\sqrt{8}}$ ...(iii)

On substituting the value of y from Eq. (iii) in Eq. (i), we get

$$\sqrt{2}x + \sqrt{3} \times \left(\frac{\sqrt{3}x}{\sqrt{8}}\right) = 0$$

$$\Rightarrow \quad \sqrt{2}x + \frac{3x}{\sqrt{8}} = 0$$

$$\Rightarrow \quad \sqrt{2} \times \sqrt{8}x + 3x = 0$$

$$\Rightarrow \quad \sqrt{16}x + 3x = 0 \Rightarrow 4x + 3x = 0$$

$$\Rightarrow \quad 7x = 0 \Rightarrow x = 0$$

On putting $x = 0$ in Eq. (iii), we get $y = 0$

Hence, $x = 0$ and $y = 0$.

(vi) We have, $\frac{3x}{2} - \frac{5y}{3} = -2$ ...(i)

and $\frac{x}{3} + \frac{y}{2} = \frac{13}{6}$ ...(ii)

From Eq. (ii),

$$\frac{y}{2} = \frac{13}{6} - \frac{x}{3} = \frac{13 - 2x}{6},$$

$$\Rightarrow \quad y = 2 \times \frac{(13 - 2x)}{6}$$

$$\Rightarrow \quad y = \frac{(13 - 2x)}{3} \quad \text{...(iii)}$$

On substituting the value of y from Eq. (iii) in Eq. (i), we get

$$\frac{3x}{2} - \frac{5}{3} \times \frac{(13 - 2x)}{3} = -2$$

$$\Rightarrow \quad \frac{3x}{2} - \frac{5}{9}(13 - 2x) = -2$$

$$\Rightarrow \quad 18 \times \frac{3x}{2} - 18 \times \frac{5}{9}(13 - 2x) = -2 \times 18$$

(Multiply by 18 on both sides)

$$\Rightarrow \quad 27x - 10(13 - 2x) = -36$$

$$\Rightarrow \quad 27x - 130 + 20x = -36$$

$$\Rightarrow \quad 27x + 20x = 130 - 36 \Rightarrow 47x = 94$$

$$\Rightarrow \quad x = \frac{94}{47} \quad x = 2$$

On substituting $x = 2$ in Eq. (iii), we get

$$y = \frac{13 - 2 \times 2}{3} = \frac{9}{3} = 3$$

$$\Rightarrow \quad y = 3$$

Hence, $x = 2$, and $y = 3$

Question 2 Solve $2x+3y=11$ and $2x-4y=-24$ and hence find the value of m for which $y=mx+3$.

Sol. We have, $2x + 3y = 11$ ...(i)

and $2x - 4y = -24$ ...(ii)

From Eq. (ii), $4y = 2x + 24$

or $y = \frac{x+12}{2}$ ...(iii)

On substituting the value of y from Eq. (iii) in Eq. (i), we get

$$2x + 3\left(\frac{x+12}{2}\right) = 11$$

$\Rightarrow$ $4x + 3(x + 12) = 11 \times 2$

$\Rightarrow$ $4x + 3x + 36 = 22$

$\Rightarrow$ $7x = 22 - 36$

$\Rightarrow$ $7x = -14 \Rightarrow x = -2$

On substituting $x = -2$ in Eq. (iii), $y = \frac{-2+12}{2}$

$\Rightarrow$ $y = \frac{10}{2} = 5$

On substituting $x = -2$ and $y = 5$ in the equation $y = mx + 3$, we get

$$5 = m \times (-2) + 3 \Rightarrow 5 = -2m + 3$$

$\Rightarrow$ $2m = 3 - 5 = -2 \Rightarrow m = -1$

Hence, $m = -1$

Question 3 Form the pair of linear equations for the following problems and find their solution by substitution method.

(i) The difference between two numbers is 26 and one number is three times the other. Find them.

(ii) The larger of two supplementary angles exceeds the smaller by 18 degrees. Find them.

(iii) The coach of a cricket team buys 7 bats and 6 balls for ₹ 3800. Later, she buys 3 bats and 5 balls for ₹ 1750. Find the cost of each bat and each ball.

(iv) The taxi charges in a city consist of a fixed charge together with the charge for the distance covered. For a distance of 10 km, the charge paid is ₹ 105 and for a journey of 15 km, the charge paid is ₹ 155. What are the fixed charges and the charge per km? How much does a person have to pay for travelling a distance of 25 km?

(v) A fraction becomes $\frac{9}{11}$, if 2 is added to both the numerator and the denominator. If, 3 is added to both the numerator and the denominator it becomes $\frac{5}{6}$. Find the fraction.

(vi) Five years hence, the age of Jacob will be three times that of his son. Five years ago, Jacob's age was seven times that of his son. What are their present ages?

◎ **Thinking Process** For part (ii) Two angles will be supplementary if sum of those angles equals to 180°.

Sol.

(i) Let the two numbers be x and $y (x > y)$.

We are given that, $x - y = 26$ and $x = 3y$

The linear equations are $x - y = 26$ ...(i)

and $x = 3y$ ...(ii)

On substituting $x = 3y$ from Eq. (ii) in Eq. (i), we get

$$3y - y = 26$$
$$\Rightarrow 2y = 26$$
$$\Rightarrow y = 13$$

From Eq. (ii), $x = 3 \times 13 = 39 \Rightarrow x = 39$

Hence, the two numbers are 39 and 13.

Mistake Alert Smaller number will be multiply 3 times to be equal to the larger number and not *vice-versa*.

(ii) Let the supplementary angles be $x°$ and $y° \; (x° > y°)$

Now, we are given that

$$x° + y° = 180° \quad \text{...(i)}$$

and $x° - y° = 18°$ ...(ii)

From Eq. (ii), $y° = x° - 18°$ ...(iii)

On substituting $y° = x° - 18°$ from Eq. (iii) in Eq. (i), we get

$$x° + x° - 18° = 180°$$
$$\Rightarrow 2x° = 198°$$
$$\Rightarrow x° = 99°$$

Then, from Eq. (iii), $y° = 99° - 18° = 81° \Rightarrow y° = 81°$

Hence, the angles are 99° and 81°.

(iii) Let cost of one bat = ₹ x

Cost of one ball = ₹ y

We are given that,

Cost of 7 bats and 6 balls = ₹ 3800, *i.e.*, $7x + 6y = 3800$ ...(i)

Cost of 3 bats and 5 balls = ₹ 1750, *i.e.*, $3x + 5y = 1750$ ...(ii)

From Eq. (ii), $5y = 1750 - 3x \Rightarrow y = \dfrac{1750 - 3x}{5}$ ...(iii)

On substituting the value of y from Eq. (iii) in Eq. (i), we get

$$7x + 6 \times \frac{(1750 - 3x)}{5} = 3800$$

On multiplying by 5, we get

$$35x + 6 \times (1750 - 3x) = 5 \times 3800$$
$$\Rightarrow \quad 35x + 10500 - 18x = 19000$$
$$\Rightarrow \quad 35x - 18x = 19000 - 10500$$
$$\Rightarrow \quad 17x = 8500$$
$$\Rightarrow \quad x = 500$$

On putting the value $x = 500$ in Eq. (iii), we get

$$y = \frac{1750 - 3 \times 500}{5}$$
$$= \frac{1750 - 1500}{5}$$
$$= \frac{250}{5}$$
$$\Rightarrow \quad y = 50$$

Hence, cost of one bat = ₹ 500

Cost of one ball = ₹ 50

(iv) Let fixed charge be ₹ x and charge per km be ₹ y.

Then, by given conditions,

$$x + 10y = 105 \quad \text{...(i)}$$
and
$$x + 15y = 155 \quad \text{...(ii)}$$

From Eq. (i), $x = (105 - 10y)$ ...(iii)

On substituting $x = 105 - 10y$ from Eq. (iii) in Eq. (ii), we get

$$105 - 10y + 15y = 155$$
$$\Rightarrow \quad 5y = 155 - 105 = 50$$
$$\Rightarrow \quad y = 10$$

On putting $y = 10$ In Eq. (iii), we get

$$x = 105 - 10 \times 10 = 105 - 100$$
$$\Rightarrow \quad x = 5$$

Hence, fixed charges = ₹ 5

Rate per kilometre = ₹ 10

So, Amount to be paid for travelling 25 km = $x + 25y = 5 + 10 \times 25$

= 5 + 250 = ₹ 255

(v) Let $\frac{x}{y}$ be the fraction where x and y are positive integers.

Then, by given conditions,

$$\frac{x+2}{y+2} = \frac{9}{11} \text{ and } \frac{x+3}{y+3} = \frac{5}{6}$$

and $6 \times (x + 3) = 5 \times (y + 3)$

$\Rightarrow$ $11x + 22 = 9y + 18$

and $6x + 18 = 5y + 15$

$\Rightarrow$ $11x - 9y + 4 = 0$ ...(i)

and $6x - 5y + 3 = 0$ ...(ii)

From Eq. (ii), $5y = 6x + 3$

or $y = \frac{6x + 3}{5}$ ...(iii)

On substituting the value of y from Eq. (iii) in Eq. (i), we get

$$11x - 9 \times \left(\frac{6x + 3}{5}\right) + 4 = 0$$

$\Rightarrow$ $55x - 9 \times (6x + 3) + 20 = 0$

$\Rightarrow$ $55x - 54x - 27 + 20 = 0$

$\Rightarrow$ $x = 7$

On putting $x = 7$ in Eq. (iii), we get

$$y = \frac{6 \times 7 + 3}{5}$$

$\Rightarrow$ $y = \frac{42 + 3}{5} = \frac{45}{5}$

$\Rightarrow$ $y = 9$

Hence, the required fraction is $\frac{7}{9}$.

(vi) Let x (in year) be the present age of Jacob's son and y (in year) be the present age of Jacob. Five years hence, it has relation by given condition,

$$(y + 5) = 3(x + 5)$$

$\Rightarrow$ $y + 5 = 3x + 15$

$\Rightarrow$ $3x - y + 10 = 0$ ...(i)

Five years ago, it has relation

$$(y - 5) = 7(x - 5)$$

$\Rightarrow$ $7x - y - 30 = 0$ ...(ii)

From Eq. (i), $y = 3x + 10$ ...(iii)

On substituting y from Eq. (iii) in Eq. (ii),

$$7x - (3x + 10) - 30 = 0$$

$\Rightarrow$ $4x - 40 = 0$

$\Rightarrow$ $4x = 40$

$\Rightarrow$ $x = 10$

On substituting $x = 10$ in Eq. (iii), we get

$$y = 3 \times 10 + 10$$

$\Rightarrow$ $y = 40$

Hence, the present age of Jacob is 40 yr and present age of his son is 10 yr.

Exercise 3.3

Question 1 Solve the following pair of linear equations by the elimination method and the substitution method.

(i) $x+y=5$ and $2x-3y=4$

(ii) $3x+4y=10$ and $2x-2y=2$

(iii) $3x-5y-4=0$ and $9x=2y+7$

(iv) $\frac{x}{2}+\frac{2y}{3}=-1$ and $x-\frac{y}{3}=3$

Sol.

(i) **Solution by elimination method**

We have, $x+y=5$ ...(i)

and $2x-3y=4$ ...(ii)

On multiplying Eq. (i) by 3 and Eq. (ii) by 1 and adding them we get

$$3(x+y)+1(2x-3y)=3\times5+1\times4$$

$$\Rightarrow \quad 3x+3y+2x-3y=15+4$$

$$\Rightarrow \quad 5x=19$$

$$\Rightarrow \quad x=\frac{19}{5}$$

From Eq. (i), substituting $x=\frac{19}{5}$ in Eq. (i), we get

$$\frac{19}{5}+y=5$$

$$\Rightarrow \quad y=5-\frac{19}{5}$$

$$\Rightarrow \quad y=\frac{25-19}{5}=\frac{6}{5}$$

Hence, $x=\frac{19}{5}$ and $y=\frac{6}{5}$

Solution by substitution method

We have, $x+y=5$ ...(i)

and $2x-3y=4$ ...(ii)

From Eq. (i), $y=5-x$ ...(iii)

On substituting y from Eq. (iii) in Eq. (ii), we get

$$2x-3(5-x)=4$$

$$\Rightarrow \quad 2x-15+3x=4$$

$$\Rightarrow \quad 5x=19$$

$$\Rightarrow \quad x=\frac{19}{5}$$

Then, from Eq. (iii), substituting $x=\frac{19}{5}$,

$$y=5-\frac{19}{5}$$

$\Rightarrow \quad y = \frac{25 - 19}{5} = \frac{6}{5}$

Hence, $\quad x = \frac{19}{5}$ and $y = \frac{6}{5}$

(ii) **Solution by elimination method**

We have, $\quad 3x + 4y = 10 \quad$ ...(i)

and $\quad 2x - 2y = 2 \quad$ ...(ii)

On multiplying Eq. (i) by 1 and Eq. (ii) by 2 and adding them, we get

$$1(3x + 4y) + 2(2x - 2y) = 1 \times 10 + 2 \times 2$$

$\Rightarrow \quad 3x + 4y + 4x - 4y = 10 + 4$

$\Rightarrow \quad 7x = 14$

$\Rightarrow \quad x = 2$

From Eq. (i), substituting $x = 2$ in Eq. (i), we get

$$3 \times 2 + 4y = 10$$

$\Rightarrow \quad 4y = 4$

$\Rightarrow \quad y = 1$

Hence, $\quad x = 2$ and $y = 1$

Solution by substitution method

We have, $\quad 3x + 4y = 10 \quad$ ...(i)

and $\quad 2x - 2y = 2 \quad$ ...(ii)

From Eq. (ii), $\quad 2y = 2x - 2$

$\Rightarrow \quad y = x - 1 \quad$ (Divide by 2)...(iii)

On substituting y from Eq. (iii) in Eq. (i), we get

$$3x + 4(x - 1) = 10$$

$\Rightarrow \quad 3x + 4x - 4 = 10$

$\Rightarrow \quad 7x = 14$

$\Rightarrow \quad x = 2$

On substituting $x = 2$ in Eq. (iii), we get

$$y = 2 - 1$$

$\Rightarrow \quad y = 1$

Hence, $\quad x = 2$ and $y = 1$

Mistake Alert When using elimination method be ensure that you are using correct multipliers.

(iii) **Solution by elimination method**

We have, $\quad 3x - 5y = 4 \quad$ ...(i)

and $\quad 9x = 2y + 7 \quad$ ...(ii)

On multiplying Eq. (i) by 3, we get

$$9x - 15y = 12 \quad \text{...(iii)}$$

and $\quad 9x - 2y = 7 \quad$ ...(iv)

On subtracting Eq. (iv) from Eq. (iii), we get

$$(9x - 15y) - (9x - 2y) = 12 - 7$$

$$\Rightarrow \quad -15y + 2y = 5$$
$$\Rightarrow \quad -13y = 5$$
$$\Rightarrow \quad y = -\frac{5}{13}$$

From Eq. (i), substituting $y = -\frac{5}{13}$, we get

$$3x - 5\left(-\frac{5}{13}\right) = 4$$
$$\Rightarrow \quad 39x + 25 = 52$$
$$\Rightarrow \quad 39x = 27 \Rightarrow x = \frac{9}{13}$$

Hence, $\quad x = \frac{9}{13}$ and $y = -\frac{5}{13}$

Solution by substitution method

We have, $\quad 3x - 5y = 4 \quad$ ...(i)

$9x = 2y + 7 \quad$ ...(ii)

From Eq. (ii) $2y = 9x - 7$ or $y = \frac{9x-7}{2} \quad$ ...(iii)

Substituting y from Eq. (iii) in Eq. (i), we get

$$3x - 5 \times \left(\frac{9x-7}{2}\right) = 4$$
$$\Rightarrow \quad 6x - 45x + 35 = 8$$
$$\Rightarrow \quad -39x = -27 \Rightarrow x = \frac{9}{13}$$

From Eq. (iii), substituting $x = \frac{9}{13}$, we get

$$y = \frac{9 \times \frac{9}{13} - 7}{2} = \frac{81-91}{2 \times 13} = -\frac{10}{26}$$
$$\Rightarrow \quad y = -\frac{5}{13}$$

Hence, $\quad x = \frac{9}{13}$ and $y = -\frac{5}{13}$

(iv) **Solution by elimination method**

We have, $\quad \frac{x}{2} + \frac{2y}{3} = -1 \quad$ ...(i)

and $\quad x - \frac{y}{3} = 3 \quad$ ...(ii)

On multiplying Eq. (ii) by 2, we get

and $\quad 2x - \frac{2y}{3} = 6 \quad$ ...(iii)

On adding Eq. (i) and Eq. (iii), we get

$$\frac{x}{2} + 2x = -1 + 6 \Rightarrow \frac{5}{2}x = 5 \Rightarrow x = 2$$

Now, substituting $x = 2$ in Eq. (ii), we get

$$2 - \frac{y}{3} = 3 \Rightarrow -\frac{y}{3} = 1 \Rightarrow y = -3$$

Hence, $x = 2$ and $y = -3$

Solution by substitution method

We have, $\frac{x}{2} + \frac{2y}{3} = -1$ ...(i)

and $x - \frac{y}{3} = 3$ ...(ii)

From Eq. (ii), $\frac{y}{3} = x - 3$

$\Rightarrow$ $y = 3(x - 3)$ ...(iii)

On substituting $y = 3(x - 3)$ in Eq. (i), we get

$$\frac{x}{2} + \frac{2}{3} \times 3\,(x - 3) = -1$$

$\Rightarrow$ $\frac{x}{2} + 2(x - 3) = -1$

$\Rightarrow$ $x + 4(x - 3) = -2$

$\Rightarrow$ $5x - 12 = -2$

$\Rightarrow$ $5x = 10 \Rightarrow x = 2$

Now, on substituting $x = 2$ in Eq. (iii), we get

$$y = 3(2 - 3) = -3$$

Hence, $x = 2$ and $y = -3$

Question 2 Form the pair of linear equations in the following problems and find their solutions (if they exist) by the elimination method

(i) If we add 1 to the numerator and subtract 1 from the denominator, a fraction reduces to 1. It becomes $\frac{1}{2}$, if we only add 1 to the denominator. What is the fraction?

(ii) Five years ago, Nuri was thrice as old as Sonu. Ten years later, Nuri will be twice as old as Sonu. How old are Nuri and Sonu?

(iii) The sum of the digits of a two digit number is 9. Also, nine times this number is twice the number obtained by reversing the order of the digits. Find the number.

(iv) Meena went to a bank to withdraw ₹ 2000. She asked the cashier to give her ₹ 50 and ₹ 100 notes only. Meena got 25 notes in all. Find how many notes of ₹ 50 and ₹ 100 she received.

(v) A lending library has a fixed charge for the first three days and an additional charge for each day thereafter. Saritha paid ₹ 27 for a book kept for seven days, while Susy paid ₹ 21 for the book she kept for five days. Find the fixed charge and the charge for each extra day.

Sol. (i) Let the fraction be $\frac{x}{y}$.

According to the given conditions,

$$\frac{x+1}{y-1} = 1; \frac{x}{y+1} = \frac{1}{2}$$

$\Rightarrow$ $x + 1 = y - 1; 2x = y + 1$

$\Rightarrow$ $x - y = -2$ ...(i)

and $2x - y = 1$ ...(ii)

On subtracting Eq. (i) from Eq. (ii), we get

$$(2x - y) - (x - y) = 1 + 2$$

$\Rightarrow$ $x = 3$

On substituting $x = 3$ in Eq. (i), $3 - y = -2$

$\Rightarrow$ $y = 5$

Hence, the fraction is $\frac{3}{5}$.

(ii) Let present age of Nuri = x (in years). Present age of Sonu = y (in years)

According to the given conditions,

Five years ago, $x - 5 = 3(y - 5) \Rightarrow x - 3y = -10$ ...(i)

Ten years later, $x + 10 = 2(y + 10) \Rightarrow x - 2y = 10$ ...(ii)

On subtracting Eq. (i) from Eq. (ii), we get

$$(x - 2y) - (x - 3y) = 10 + 10$$

$\Rightarrow$ $-2y + 3y = 20 \Rightarrow y = 20$

On substituting $y = 20$ in Eq. (ii), we get

$\Rightarrow$ $x - 2 \times 20 = 10$

$\Rightarrow$ $x = 2 \times 20 + 10$

$\Rightarrow$ $x = 50$

Therefore, present age of Nuri = 50 yr

and present age of Sonu = 20 yr

(iii) Let x be the digit at unit's place and y be the digit at ten's place of the value of the number.

According to given condition,

$$x + y = 9$$ ...(i)

Value of the number = $x + 10y$

When we reverse the digits, the value of the new number = $y + 10x$

We are given that $9 \times (x + 10y) = 2 \times (y + 10x)$

$\Rightarrow$ $9x + 90y = 2y + 20x$

$$\Rightarrow \quad 88y = 11x$$

$$\Rightarrow \quad x = 8y \quad \text{...(ii)}$$

On substituting $x = 8y$ from Eq. (ii) in Eq. (i), we get

$$8y + y = 9$$

$$\Rightarrow \quad 9y = 9$$

$$\Rightarrow \quad y = 1$$

Then, from Eq. (ii), $x = 8 \times 1$

$$\Rightarrow \quad x = 8$$

Hence, the number is

$$x + 10y = 8 + 10 \times 1 = 8 + 10 = 18$$

(iv) Let number of ₹ 50 notes $= x$

Number of ₹ 100 notes $= y$

By given condition, $x + y = 25$ ...(i)

Also, $50 \times x + 100 \times y = 2000$

or $x + 2y = 40$ (Divide by 50)...(ii)

Subtracting Eq. (i) from Eq. (ii), we get

$$(x + 2y) - (x + y) = 40 - 25$$

$$\Rightarrow \quad y = 15$$

On substituting $y = 15$ in Eq. (i), we get

$$x + 15 = 25$$

$$\Rightarrow \quad x = 25 - 15$$

$$\Rightarrow \quad x = 10$$

Hence, Number of ₹ 50 notes = 10

Number of ₹ 100 notes = 15

(v) Let the fixed charges for the first three days be ₹ x.

Let the additional charge per day be ₹ y.

Saritha paid for 7 days = ₹ 27

By given condition, $x + 4 \times y = 27$

($\because$ ₹ $4y$ are to be paid for 4 extra days)

$$\Rightarrow \quad x + 4y = 27 \quad \text{...(i)}$$

and in the case of Susy, $x + 2y = 21$ ...(ii)

On subtracting Eq. (ii) from Eq. (i), we get

$$2y = 27 - 21$$

$$\Rightarrow \quad y = 3$$

On substituting $y = 3$ in Eq. (i), we get

$$x + 4 \times 3 = 27$$

$$\Rightarrow \quad x = 15$$

Fixed charge for first three days = ₹ 15

Addition charge per extra day = ₹ 3

DIKSHA APP Questions

☐ Multiple Choice Questions

Q.1 For two lines in a plane, which possibility is false.

(a) The two lines will intersect at one point
(b) The two lines will intersection at two points
(c) The two lines will not intersect
(d) The two lines will be coincident

Sol. (b) We know for any two lines $a_1x + b_1y + c_1 = 0$ and $a_2x + b_2y + c_2 = 0$ one of the following 3 possibilities hold.

(i) The lines will intersect at one point when $\frac{a_1}{a_2} \neq \frac{b_1}{b_2}$.

(ii) The lines will be parallel when $\frac{a_1}{a_2} = \frac{b_1}{b_2} \neq \frac{c_1}{c_2}$.

(iii) The lines will be coincident when $\frac{a_1}{a_2} = \frac{b_1}{b_2} = \frac{c_1}{c_2}$.

Q.2 Fill in the blank, If $\frac{a_1}{a_2} = \frac{b_1}{b_2} = \frac{c_1}{c_2}$ for two straight lines in a plane, then the lines

(a) Parallel (b) Intersecting
(c) Coincident (d) None of these

Sol. (c) For two straight lines in a plane, $a_1x + b_1y + c_1 = 0$ and $a_2x + b_2y + c_2 = 0$ when $\frac{a_1}{a_2} = \frac{b_1}{b_2} = \frac{c_1}{c_2}$, then the lines are coincident.

Q.3 Represent the following pair of lines graphically. How many solutions are possible for the following pair of lines?

$$4x + 3y = 3, 12x + 9y = 20$$

(a) one (unique) solution (b) Infinite solutions
(c) No solution (d) Exactly two solution

Sol. (c) Given pair of equations are

$$4x + 3y = 3 \quad \ldots(i)$$

and $$12x + 9y = 20 \quad \ldots(ii)$$

Table for $4x + 3y = 3$

x	0	3
$y = \frac{3-4x}{3}$	1	–3
Points	A	B

Table for $12x + 9y = 20$

x	0	1.67
$y = \frac{20 - 12x}{9}$	2.22	0
Points	C	D

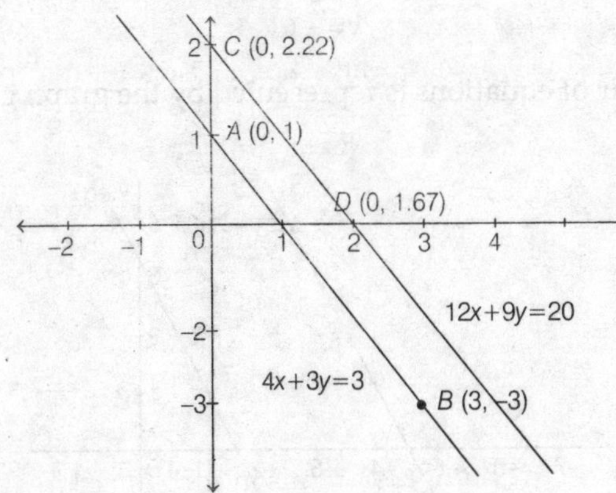

Now, consider the Eqs. (i) and (ii) and comparing with

$$ax + by + c = 0, \text{ we get}$$

$\Rightarrow$ $a_1 = 4, a_2 = 12, b_1 = 3, b_2 = 9, c_1 = -3, c_2 = -20$

$$\Rightarrow \quad \frac{a_1}{a_2} = \frac{1}{3} = \frac{b_1}{b_2}, \frac{c_1}{c_2} = \frac{-3}{-20}$$

$$\Rightarrow \quad \frac{a_1}{a_2} = \frac{b_1}{b_2} \neq \frac{c_1}{c_2}$$

$\Rightarrow$ The lines are parallel.

Hence, given pair of lines has no solution.

Q.4 For what value of k, do the equations $5x - 2y + 8 = 0$ and $15x + ky = -24$ represent coincident lines?

(a) $k = 6$ (b) $k = -6$ (c) $k \neq 6$ (d) $k \neq -6$

Sol. (b) Given equations are

$$5x - 2y + 8 = 0 \quad \text{...(i)}$$

$$15x + ky = -24$$

$$\text{or} \quad 15x + ky + 24 = 0 \quad \text{...(ii)}$$

On comparing Eqs. (i) and (ii) with $ax + by + c = 0$, we get

$$a_1 = 5, a_2 = 15$$

$$b_1 = -2, b_2 = k$$

$$c_1 = 8, c_2 = 24$$

For lines to be coincident, we have

$$\frac{a_1}{a_2} = \frac{b_1}{b_2} = \frac{c_1}{c_2}$$

$$\Rightarrow \quad \frac{a_1}{a_2} = \frac{5}{15} = \frac{1}{3} = \frac{b_1}{b_2}$$

$$\Rightarrow \quad \frac{1}{3} = -\frac{2}{k}$$

$$\Rightarrow \quad k = -6$$

Q.5 Which pair of equations is represented by the graph given below ?

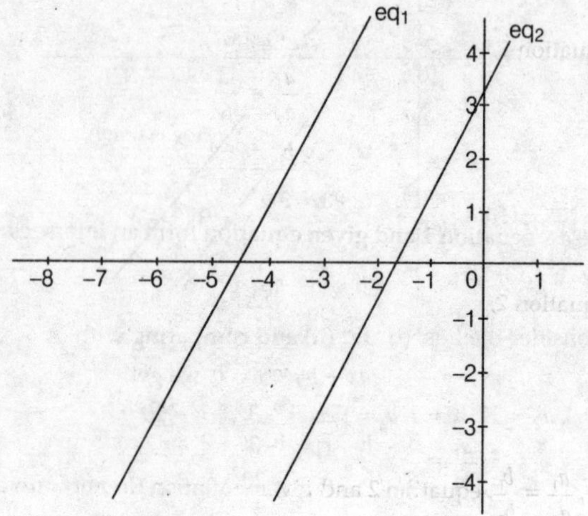

(a) $6x - 3y + 10 = 0, 2x - y + 9 = 0$
(b) $6x - 3y + 12 = 0, 2x - y + 4 = 0$
(c) Both of the above
(d) None of the above

Sol. (a) The graph represents a pair of parallel lines and we know that two lines are parallel if $\frac{a_1}{a_2} = \frac{b_1}{b_2} \neq \frac{c_1}{c_2}$.

For option (a) $\frac{a_1}{a_2} = \frac{6}{2} = 3, \frac{b_1}{b_2} = \frac{-3}{-1} = 3$

and $\frac{c_1}{c_2} = \frac{10}{9}$

Q.6 Given the liner equation $12x - 4y = 20$, which of the following linear equations in two variables is such that the geometrical representation of the pair formed is two intersecting lines.

1. $6x + 4y = 10$ 2. $6x - 2y = 10$

(a) 1 (b) 2

(c) 1 and 2 both (d) Neither

Sol. (a) Given, Equation is $12x - 4y = 20$

If the other line has to be intersecting, then

$$\frac{a_1}{a_2} \neq \frac{b_1}{b_2}$$

For equation 1,

$$\frac{a_1}{a_2} = \frac{12}{6} = 2$$

$$\frac{b_1}{b_2} = \frac{-4}{4} = -1$$

Therefore, equation 1 and given equation form an intersecting pair of lines.

For equation 2,

$$\frac{a_1}{a_2} = \frac{12}{6} = 2$$

$$\frac{b_1}{b_2} = \frac{-4}{-2} = 2$$

Since, $\frac{a_1}{a_2} = \frac{b_1}{b_2}$, equation 2 and given equation do not form an intersecting pair of lines.

Q.7 Represent the following pair of lines graphically. How many solutions are possible for the following pair of lines?

$5x - y = 7$

$x - y = -1$

(a) One (unique) solution (b) Infinite solutions

(c) No solution (d) Exactly two solutions

Sol. (a) The given pair of equations is

$$5x - y = 7$$

and

$$x - y = -1$$

Table for $5x - y = 7$ ...(i)

x	0	1
$y = 5x - 7$	−7	−2
Points	A	B

Table for $x - y = -1$

x	0	-1
$y = x + 1$	1	0
Points	C	D

Clearly, from the graph, it can be seen that the two lines intersect at a point. Hence the pair of equations has a unique solution.

Q.8 Fill in the blanks.

In the Elimination Method, if after eliminating one variable we get a true statement involving no variable then the original pair of equations is .... and has ....

(a) Inconsistent, No solution

(b) Consistent, Infinitely many solutions

(c) Inconsistent, Infinitely many solutions

(d) Consistent, One (Unique) solution

Sol. (b) After eliminating one variable in the elimination method, if we get a true statement involving no variable, the original pair of equations is consistent and has infinitely many solutions.

Q.9 Solve the following pair of equations by the elimination method.

$$3x - 4y = -7$$
$$5x - 2y = 0$$

(a) $x = -1, y = 1$ (b) $x = 1, y = \frac{5}{2}$

(c) $x = \frac{7}{2}, y = \frac{35}{4}$ (d) None of these

Sol. (b) The given pair of equations is

$$3x - 4y = -7 \quad \text{...(i)}$$
$$5x - 2y = 0 \quad \text{...(ii)}$$

On multiplying Eq. (ii) by 2, we get

$$10x - 4y = 0 \quad \text{...(iii)}$$

On subtracting Eq. (i) from Eq. (iii), we get

$$(10x - 4y) - (3x - 4y) = 0 - (-7)$$
$$\Rightarrow \quad 7x = 7$$
$$\Rightarrow \quad x = 1$$

Substituting $x = 1$ in Eq. (i), we get

$$3 - 4y = -7$$
$$\Rightarrow \quad -4y = -7 - 3$$
$$\Rightarrow \quad -4y = -10$$
$$\Rightarrow \quad y = \frac{-10}{-4} = \frac{5}{2}$$

Hence, $x = 1$ and $y = \frac{5}{2}$

Q.10 On solving pairs of linear equations, the solutions obtained are given below. Indicate in which case the use of graphical method for solution would not have been convenient.

(a) $x = 0, y = -1$

(b) $x = \frac{15}{19}, y = \frac{17}{19}$

(c) $x = -2, y = 3$

(b) $x = -16, y = -22$

Sol. (b) The graphical method is not convenient in cases when the point representing the solution of the linear equations has non-integral coordinates like $(\sqrt{3}, 2\sqrt{7})$, $(-1.75, 3.3)$, $(4/13, 1/13)$, etc. There is every possibility of making mistakes while reading such coordinates.

Q.11 $3x - 2y + 1 = 0$ and $6x - 4y + 2 = 0$ the two equations in graphical method ....

(a) Intersect (b) Parallel
(c) Coincides (d) No relation

Sol. (c) $\frac{a_1}{a_2} = \frac{3}{6} = \frac{1}{2}, \frac{b_1}{b_2} = \frac{-2}{-4} = \frac{1}{2}$ and $\frac{c_1}{c_2} = \frac{1}{2}$. Hence, $\frac{a_1}{a_2} = \frac{b_1}{b_2} = \frac{c_1}{c_2}$

Q.12 $2x - 6y + 1 = 0$ and $5x - 15y + 5 = 0$. These equations have .... solutions.

(a) Infinite (b) unique
(c) no solutions (d) two

Sol. (c) $\frac{a_1}{a_2} = \frac{2}{5}, \frac{b_1}{b_2} = \frac{-6}{-15} = \frac{2}{5}$ and $\frac{c_1}{c_2} = \frac{1}{5}$. Hence, $\frac{a_1}{a_2} = \frac{b_1}{b_2} \neq \frac{c_1}{c_2}$

Hence, the lines represent parallel lines.

Q.13 The system $kx - y = 2$ and $6x - 2y = 3$ has a unique solution only when

(a) $k = 0$ (b) $k \neq 0$
(c) $k = 3$ (d) $k \neq 3$

Sol. (d) The pair of lines have a unique solution if $\frac{a_1}{a_2} \neq \frac{b_1}{b_2}$

So, $\frac{b_1}{b_2} = \frac{-1}{-2} = \frac{1}{2}$

$\frac{a_1}{a_2} = \frac{k}{6},$

Then, $\frac{a_1}{a_2} \neq \frac{b_1}{b_2} \Rightarrow \frac{k}{6} \neq \frac{1}{2}$

$\Rightarrow$ $k \neq 3$

Hence, (d) is correct.

Q.14 The value of 'k' so that the system of equation $3x - y - 5 = 0$ and $6x - 2y - k = 0$ have infinitely many solutions is

(a) $k = -10$ (b) $k = 10$
(c) $k = -8$ (d) $k = 8$

Sol. (b) We have, system of equations

$$3x - y - 5 = 0 \quad \text{...(i)}$$
$$6x - 2y - k = 0 \quad \text{...(ii)}$$

Since, system of equations have infinitely many solution

$$\therefore \quad \frac{a_1}{a_2} = \frac{b_1}{b_2} = \frac{c_1}{c_2}$$

One comparing Eq. (i) and Eq. (ii) with $ax + by + c = 0$ we get,

$$a_1 = 3, b_1 = -1, c = -5$$
$$a_2 = 6, b_2 = -2, c_2 = -k$$

Now, $$\frac{a_1}{a_2} = \frac{b_1}{b_2} = \frac{c_1}{c_2} \Rightarrow \frac{3}{6} = \frac{-1}{-2} = \frac{-5}{-k}$$

$$\Rightarrow \quad \frac{-1}{-2} = \frac{-5}{-k}$$

$$\Rightarrow \quad k = 10$$

Hence, $k = 10$

Q.15 The solution of $px + py = p - q$ and $qx - py = p + q$ is

(a) $x = -1$ and $y = 1$ (b) $x = 1$ and $y = 1$
(c) $x = 0$ and $y = 0$ (d) $x = 1$ and $y = -1$

Sol. (d) Given,

$$px + qy = p - q \quad \ldots(i)$$
$$qx - py = p + q \quad \ldots(ii)$$

On multiplying Eq. (i) by p and Eq. (ii) by q and adding, we get

$$p^2x + q^2x = p^2 + q^2$$
$$\Rightarrow \quad x(p^2 + q^2) = p^2 + q^2$$
$$\Rightarrow \quad x = 1$$

One substituting $x = 1$ in Eq. (i), we get

$$p + qy = p - q$$
$$\Rightarrow \quad qy = -q$$
$$\Rightarrow \quad y = -1$$

Hence, $x = 1, y = -1$

Q.16 A system of two given, equations in two variables is consistent, if their graphs

(a) do not intersect at any point
(b) coincide
(c) cut the X-axis
(d) intersect only at a point or they coincide with each other.

Sol. (d) We are given pair of linear equation is consistent

$\therefore$ Either lines will intersect each other at a point or they coincide with each other.

Q.17 A pair of linear equation in two variables which has a common point *i.e.,* which has only one solution is called

(a) Consistent pair (b) Inconsistent pair
(c) Dependent pair (d) None of these

Sol. (a) We know, pair of linear equation in two variable is called consistent if either lines intersect with each other at a common point or they coincide with each other.

Q.18 If a pair of equations is consistent then the graphs of these equation are

(a) Parallel (b) Coincident
(c) Intersecting (d) either intersecting or coincident

Sol. (d) If pair of equations is consistent there the graph of these equation are either intersecting or coincident.

Q.19 The lines $3x - 4y = 9$ and $y = 0$ meet at

(a) $(-3, 0)$ (b) $(3, 0)$ (c) $\left(\frac{9}{4}, 0\right)$ (d) $\left(\frac{3}{2}, 0\right)$

Sol. (b) We are given

$$3x - 4y = a \quad \text{...(i)}$$
$$y = 0 \quad \text{...(ii)}$$

One substituting $y = 0$ from Eq. (ii) in Eq. (i), we get

$$3x - 0 = 9$$
$$\Rightarrow \quad 3x = 9 \Rightarrow x = 3$$

Hence, lines $3x - 4y = 9$ and $y = 0$ meet at $(3, 0)$

Q.20 The pair of linear equations $2x + 3y - 5 = 0$ and $3x - 2y + 5 = 0$

(a) Unique solution (b) No solution
(c) Two solution (d) Infinite solution

Sol. (a) We are given,

$$2x + 3y - 5 = 0 \quad \text{...(i)}$$
$$3x - 2y + 5 + 0 \quad \text{...(ii)}$$

One comparing Eq. (i) and Eq. (ii) with $ax + by + c = 0$, we get

$$a_1 = 2, b_1 = 3, c_1 = -5$$
$$a_2 = 3, b_2 = -2, c_2 = 5$$

as $$\frac{a_1}{a_2} \neq \frac{b_1}{b_2} \Rightarrow \frac{2}{3} \neq \frac{3}{-2}$$

$\therefore$ Linear intersect with each other

Hence, there exists a unique solution.

☐ Subjective Type Questions

Q.1 In a right angled triangle, one of the acute angles exceeds the other by 20 Degrees. If the larger angle is x and smaller angle is y, form the pair of linear equations and find the larger and smaller angles using elimination method.

Sol. In a triangle, the sum of three angles = 180°

as one angle in a right angled triangle, is 90°

Then, according to given condition,

$$x + y = 90° \quad \text{...(i)}$$

As one angle is greater than the other by 20° and x is the larger angle,

i.e., $$x - y = 20° \quad \text{...(ii)}$$

Adding Eq. (ii) to Eq. (i), we get,

$$x + y = 90°$$

$$\Rightarrow \quad x - y = 20°$$

$$2x = 110°$$

$$\Rightarrow \quad x = 55°$$

Substituting the value of x in Eq. (i), we get,

$$55° + y = 90°$$

$$\Rightarrow \quad y = 90° - 55° = 35°$$

Q.2 The sum of a two digit number and the number obtained by reversing the digits is 110. The difference between the digits is 4. Find the number if the tens digits is x and the units digit is y. Use elimination method.

Sol. Let the tens digit = x

Let the units digit = y

Then, the number = $10x + y$

Then, after reversing digits, number will be $10y + x$.

According to given condition,

$$10x + y + 10y + x = 110$$

$$\Rightarrow \quad 11x + 11y = 110 \quad \text{...(i)}$$

and $$x - y = 4 \quad \text{...(ii)}$$

On multiplying the Eq. (ii) with by 11, we get

$$11x - 11y = 44 \quad \text{...(iii)}$$

On adding Eqs. (i) and (iii), we get

$$22x = 154$$

$$\Rightarrow \quad x = 7$$

On substituting the value of x in Eq. (ii), we get

$$7 - y = 4$$

$$\Rightarrow \quad y = 3$$

Hence, the number is $10 \times 7 + 3 = 73$.

Q.3 Use substitution method to solve the following equations

$$3x + 4y = -4$$
$$x + 2y = 2$$

Sol. The given pair of equations is

$$3x + 4y = -4 \quad \text{...(i)}$$
$$x + 2y = 2 \quad \text{...(ii)}$$

From Eq. (ii), we get

$$x = 2 - 2y \quad \text{...(iii)}$$

On substituting from Eq. (iii) $x = 2 - 2y$ in Eq (i), we get

$$3(2 - 2y) + 4y = -4$$
$$\Rightarrow \quad 6 - 6y + 4y = -4$$
$$\Rightarrow \quad -2y = -4 - 6$$
$$\Rightarrow \quad -2y = -10$$
$$\Rightarrow \quad y = 5$$

On substituting the value of y in Eq. (iii), we get

$$x = 2 - 2(5) = 2 - 10 = -8$$

Hence, $x = -8$ and $y = 5$

Q.4 Use substitution method to solve the following equations

$$4x + 3y = -3$$
$$8x + 6y + 6 = 0$$

Sol. The given pair of equations is

$$4x + 3y = -3 \quad \text{...(i)}$$
$$8x + 6y = -6 \quad \text{...(ii)}$$

From Eq. (i), we get

$$3y = -3 - 4x$$
$$\Rightarrow \quad y = \frac{-3 - 4x}{3} \quad \text{...(iii)}$$

On substituting from Eq. (iii) $y = \frac{-3 - 4x}{3}$ in Eq. (ii), we get

$$8x + 6\left(\frac{-3 - 4x}{3}\right) = -6$$
$$\Rightarrow \quad 8x + 2(-3 - 4x) = -6$$
$$\Rightarrow \quad 8x - 6 - 8x = -6$$
$$\Rightarrow \quad -6 = -6$$

Hence, this is a true statement without variables.

Hence, the given equations have infinitely many solutions.

Q.5 The larger of two complementary angles exceeds the smaller by 22 degrees. If y is the larger angle and x is the smaller angle, find the angles.

◎ *Thinking Process* Two angles are complementary if sum of those two angles equals to 90°.

Sol. We are given that x is the smaller angle and y is the larger angle.

Since, x and y are complementary angles, we have

$$x + y = 90° \quad \text{...(i)}$$

According to the given condition

$$y = x + 22° \quad \text{...(ii)}$$

On substituting from Eq. (ii) $y = x + 22°$ in Eq. (i), we get,

$$x + x + 22 = 90°$$

$$\Rightarrow \quad 2x = 68°$$

$$\Rightarrow \quad x = 34°$$

Substituting the value of x in Eq. (ii), we get

$$y = 34° + 22°$$

$$= 56°$$

Hence, $x = 34°$ and $y = 56°$.

Q.6 The perimeter of an isosceles triangle is 24 cm. The length of it's congruent sides is 13 cm less than twice the length of the base. Find the length of base and the length of congruent side.

Sol. Let each of the congruent side be x cm.

Let base be y cm.

Then, the perimeter of the triangle is

$$x + x + y = 24$$

$$\Rightarrow \quad 2x + y = 24 \quad \text{...(ii)}$$

According to the condition

$$x = 2y - 13 \quad \text{...(ii)}$$

On substituting from Eq. (ii) $x = 2y - 13$ in Eq. (i), we get

$$2(2y - 13) + y = 24$$

$$\Rightarrow \quad 4y - 26 + y = 24$$

$$\Rightarrow \quad 5y = 50$$

$$\Rightarrow \quad y = 10$$

On substituting $y = 10$ in Eq. (ii) we get,

$$x = 2 \times 10 - 13 = 20 - 13$$

$$\Rightarrow \quad x = 7$$

Hence, length of congruent sides is 7cm and base of triangle is 10 cm.

Q.7 Solve the equations by graphical method : $x + y - 10 = 0$ and
$$x - y - 2 = 0$$

Sol. The given pair of equations is
$$x + y - 10 = 0$$
$$x - y - 2 = 0 \quad \ldots(i)$$

Table for $x + y - 10 = 0$

x	0	10
$y = 10 - x$	10	0
Points	A	B

Table for

x	0	2
$y = x - 2$	−2	0
Points	C	D

Now, we plot the point and join both the lines to find the solution.

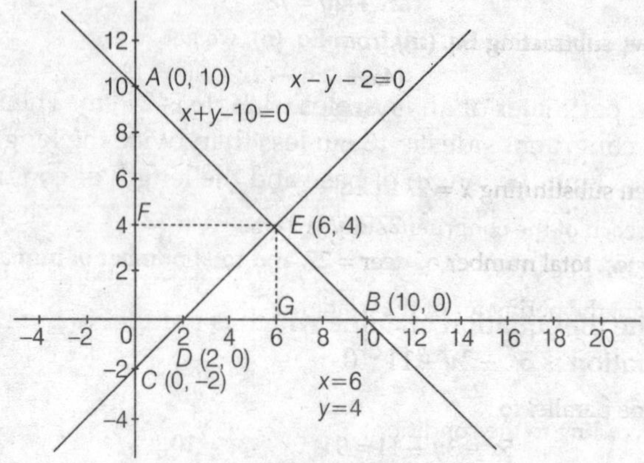

Clearly, the lines intersect at the point $E(6, 4)$. Hence, $x = 6$ and $y = 4$ is the required solution.

Q.8 In an election contested between A and B, A obtained votes equal to twice the number of persons on the electoral roll who did not cast their votes and this later number was equal to twice his majority over B. If there were 18000 persons on the electoral roll. How many voted for B.

Sol. Let x and y be the number of votes for A and B respectively.

The number of persons who did not vote = $(18000 - x - y)$

According to question, $x = 2(18000 - x - y)$

$\Rightarrow \quad 3x + 2y = 36000 \quad$ ...(i)

and $\quad (18000 - x - y) = (2)(x - y)$

$\Rightarrow \quad 3x - y = 18000 \quad$ ...(ii)

On solving Eq. (i) and (ii), we get, $y = 6000$ and $x = 8000$

Hence, vote for $B = 6000$

Q.9 At a certain time in a deer park, the number of heads and the number of legs of deer and human visitors were counted and it was found there were 39 heads & 132 legs. Find the number of deer and human visitors in the park.

Sol. Let the number of deers be x.

Let the number of humans be y.

Then, According to the condition.

$$x + y = 39 \quad \text{...(i)}$$

$$4x + 2y = 132 \quad \text{...(ii)}$$

Multiply Eq. (i) by 2, we get

$$2x + 2y = 78 \quad \text{...(iii)}$$

Now, subtracting Eq. (iii) from Eq. (ii), we get

$$(4x + 2y) - (2x + 2y) = 132 - 78$$

$\Rightarrow \quad 2x = 54$

$\Rightarrow \quad x = 27$

Then substituting $x = 27$ in Eq. (i), we get

$$27 + y = 39 \quad \Rightarrow \quad y = 12$$

Hence, total number of deer = 27, and total number of human = 12

Q.10 Write the equation of a line which is parallel to the line whose equation is $5x - 3y + 11 = 0$

Sol. A line parallel to

$$5x - 3y + 11 = 0 \text{ is } 5x - 3y = 10$$

(Change is required in the constant term only)

Q.11 Solve the equations by graphical method: $x - 2y = 10$ and $2x + 5y = 20$

Sol. The given pair of equations is

$$x - 2y = 10, \qquad 2x + 5y = 20$$

Table for $x - 2y = 10$

x	0	10
$y = \dfrac{x - 10}{2}$	-5	0
Points	A	B

Table for $2x + 5y = 20$

x	0	10
$y = \frac{2x-20}{5}$	4	0
Points	C	D

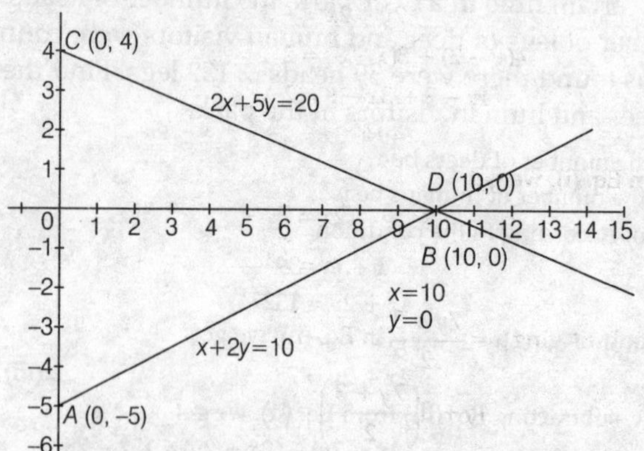

Q.12 A fraction becomes $\frac{1}{3}$ when '1' is subtracted from the numerator, and it becomes $\frac{1}{4}$ when '8' is added to its denominator. Find the fraction.

Sol. Let $\frac{x}{y}$ be a fraction

Then, according to question, $\frac{x-1}{y} = \frac{1}{3} \Rightarrow 3(x-1) = y$

$\Rightarrow \quad 3x - 3 = y \quad$ ...(i)

and, $\quad \frac{x}{y+8} = \frac{1}{4} \quad \Rightarrow \quad 4x = y + 8 \quad$ ...(ii)

On substituting the values of Eq. (i) in Eq. (ii), we get

$$4x = 3x - 3 + 8$$

$\Rightarrow \quad 4x = 3x + 5$

$\Rightarrow \quad x = 5$

On substituting with $x = 5$ in Eq.(i), we get

$$y = 3 \times 5 - 3 = 12$$

Hence, the fraction is $\frac{5}{12}$.

Q.13 Solve the following equations,

$$7(y+3)-2(x+2)=14 \quad ...(i)$$
$$4(y-2)+3(x-3)=2 \quad ...(ii)$$

Sol. The given equations are

$$7(y + 3) - 2(x + 2) = 14$$

or $\quad 7y + 21 - 2x - 4 = 14$

$\Rightarrow \quad 7y - 2x = -3 \quad ...(i)$

and $\quad 4(y - 2) + 3(x - 3) = 2$

or $\quad 4y - 8 + 3x - 9 = 2$

$\quad 4y + 3x = 19 \quad ...(ii)$

From Eq. (i), we get

$$2x = 7y - 3$$

$\Rightarrow \quad x = \dfrac{7y + 3}{2} \quad ...(iii)$

On substituting $x = \dfrac{7y+3}{2}$ in Eq. (ii), we get

$$4y + 3\left(\frac{7y + 3}{2}\right) = 19$$

$\Rightarrow \quad 8y + 21y + 9 = 38$

$\Rightarrow \quad 29y = 29$

$\Rightarrow \quad y = 1$

On substituting $y = 1$ in Eq. (iii), we get

$$x = \frac{7 \times 1 + 3}{2} = 5$$

Hence, $\quad x = 5$ and $y = 1$

Q.14 Sum of two numbers is 35 and their difference is 13. Find the numbers.

Sol. Let the larger number be x and smaller be y

Given, $\quad x + y = 35 \Rightarrow x - y = 13$

On adding both the equations, we get

or $\quad (x + y) + (x - y) = 35 + 13$

$\Rightarrow \quad 2x = 48 \Rightarrow x = 24$

On substituting $x = 24$ in Eq. (i), we get

$$24 + y = 35$$

$\Rightarrow \quad y = 35 - 24$

$\Rightarrow \quad y = 11$

Hence, number are 24 and 11.

Quadratic Equations

CHAPTER 04

Important Points

01 Quadratic Equation An equation of the form $ax^2 + bx + c = 0$, where a, b and c are real numbers and $a \neq 0$ is called a quadratic equation in the variable x.

02 Roots of a Quadratic Equation A real number α is called a root of the quadratic equation $ax^2 + bx + c = 0$ and $a \neq 0$, if $a\alpha^2 + b\alpha + c = 0$. We say that $x = \alpha$ is a solution of the quadratic equation.

The zeroes of the quadratic polynomial $ax^2 + bx + c$ are same as the roots of the quadratic equation $ax^2 + bx + c = 0$.

Note A quadratic equation has two and only two root which may be (I) real and distinct (ii) real and coincident (iii) imaginary.

03 Solution of.a Quadratic Equation by Factorisation Let the quadratic equation be $ax^2 + bx + c = 0$.

Let the factors of $ax^2 + bx + c$ be $(px + q)$ and $(rx + s)$, then

$$ax^2 + bx + c = (px + q)(rx + s)$$

We find the factors by splitting the middle term method *i.e.*, we find 2 numbers such that their sum $= b$ and Product $= ac$

Now, $$ax^2 + bx + c = 0$$

$$\Rightarrow \quad (px + q)(rx + s) = 0$$

$$\Rightarrow \quad px + q = 0 \quad \text{or} \quad rx + s = 0$$

$$\Rightarrow \quad x = -\frac{q}{p}$$

or $$x = -\frac{s}{r}$$

So, $-\frac{q}{p}$ and $-\frac{s}{r}$ are the roots of the quadratic equation $ax^2 + bx + c = 0$.

04 The equation $ax^2 + bx + c = 0$ has two roots α and β given by

$$\alpha = \frac{-b + \sqrt{b^2 - 4ac}}{2a} \text{ and } \beta = \frac{-b - \sqrt{b^2 - 4ac}}{2a}$$

05 Discriminant For the equation $ax^2 + bx + c = 0$, the expression $(b^2 - 4ac)$ is called the discriminant and is denoted by D.

So, the roots of $ax^2 + bx + c = 0$ are given by

$$\alpha = \frac{-b + \sqrt{D}}{2a} \text{ and } \beta = \frac{-b - \sqrt{D}}{2a}$$

Since, the square root of a negative number is imaginary, therefore the roots of $ax^2 + bx + c = 0$ are real, if $D \geq 0$. *i.e.*, $b^2 - 4ac \geq 0 \Rightarrow b^2 \geq 4ac$.

Note Imaginary Numbers (complex numbers) are the numbers that are not real numbers you will learn about these numbers in higher classes.

06 Nature of Roots of a Quadratic Equation

Discriminant of the quadratic equation $ax^2 + bx + c = 0$	Nature of roots of $ax^2 + bx + c = 0$	Values of roots of $ax^2 + bx + c = 0$
$D > 0$ *i.e.*, $b^2 - 4ac > 0$	Real and distinct	$\frac{-b \pm \sqrt{b^2 - 4ac}}{2a}$
$D = 0$ *i.e.*, $b^2 - 4ac = 0$	Real and equal	$\frac{-b}{2a}, \frac{-b}{2a}$
D *i.e.*, $(b^2 - 4ac)$ is a perfect square and a, b and c are rational	Both roots are rational	$\frac{-b \pm \sqrt{b^2 - 4ac}}{2a}$
D *i.e.*, $b^2 - 4ac < 0$	No real root *i.e.*, imaginary roots	No real value *i.e.*, imaginary value

07 Algebraic Identities

(i) $(a+b)^2 = a^2 + 2ab + b^2$ (ii) $(a-b)^2 = a^2 - 2ab + b^2$

(iii) $a^2 - b^2 = (a-b)(a+b)$ (iv) $(x+a)(x+b) = x^2 + (a+b)x + ab$

(v) $(a+b)^3 = a^3 + b^3 + 3a^2b + 3ab^2$

(vi) $a^3 + b^3 = (a+b)(a^2 + b^2 - ab)$

(vii) $a^3 - b^3 = (a-b)(a^2 + b^2 + ab)$

Exercise 4.1

Question 1 Check whether the following are quadratic equations.

Thinking Process An equation which is of the form $ax^2 + bx + c = 0, a \neq 0$ is called quadratic equation. So, simplify each part of the equation and check whether it is in the form of $ax^2 + bx + c = 0,\ a \neq 0$ or not.

(i) $(x+1)^2 = 2(x-3)$ (ii) $x^2 - 2x = (-2)(3-x)$

(iii) $(x-2)(x+1) = (x-1)(x+3)$ (iv) $(x-3)(2x+1) = x(x+5)$

(v) $(2x-1)(x-3) = (x+5)(x-1)$ (vi) $x^2 + 3x + 1 = (x-2)^2$

(vii) $(x+2)^3 = 2x(x^2-1)$ (viii) $x^3 - 4x^2 - x + 1 = (x-2)^3$

Sol. (i) Given equation is

$$(x+1)^2 = 2(x-3)$$

$\Rightarrow \quad x^2 + 2x + 1 = 2x - 6 \quad [\because (a+b)^2 = a^2 + 2ab + b^2]$

$\Rightarrow \quad x^2 + 1 + 6 = 0$

$\Rightarrow \quad x^2 + 7 = 0$

which is of the form $ax^2 + bx + c = 0$, where $a \neq 0$

Thus, $(x+1)^2 = 2(x-3)$ is a quadratic equation.

(ii) Given equation is

$$x^2 - 2x = (-2)(3-x)$$

$\Rightarrow \quad x^2 - 2x = -6 + 2x$

$\Rightarrow \quad x^2 - 2x - 2x + 6 = 0 \quad \Rightarrow x^2 - 4x + 6 = 0$

which is of the form $ax^2 + bx + c = 0$, where $a \neq 0$

Thus, $x^2 - 2x = (-2)(3-x)$ is a quadratic equation.

Mistake Alert $2x$ has alternative signs on either side of the equal side. So, they are not supposed to nullify each other. Rather they are getting added when taken to one side of the equation.

(iii) Given equation is

$$(x-2)(x+1) = (x-1)(x+3)$$

$\Rightarrow \quad x^2 - 2x + x - 2 = x^2 - x + 3x - 3$

$\Rightarrow \quad x^2 - 2x + x - 2 - x^2 + x - 3x + 3 = 0$

$\Rightarrow \quad$ [illegible] $1 = 0$

which is [illegible] form $ax^2 + bx + c = 0$, where $a \neq 0$ and b and c are any real [illegible]bers.

[illegible] not a quadratic equation.

Mistake Alert Even though at first glance it seems like a quadratic equation but after simplifying it becomes a linear equation.
Hence, do not judge the equations before solving especially in MCQ's type of questions.

(iv) Given equation is

$$(x-3)(2x+1) = x(x+5)$$

$\Rightarrow$ $2x^2 - 6x + x - 3 = x^2 + 5x$

$\Rightarrow$ $2x^2 - 6x + x - 3 - x^2 - 5x = 0$

$\Rightarrow$ $x^2 - 10x - 3 = 0$

which is of the form $ax^2 + bx + c = 0$, where $a \neq 0$

Thus, $(x-3)(2x+1) = x(x+5)$ is a quadratic equation.

(v) Given equation is

$$(2x-1)(x-3) = (x+5)(x-1)$$

$\Rightarrow$ $2x^2 - x - 6x + 3 = x^2 + 5x - x - 5$

$\Rightarrow$ $2x^2 - x - 6x + 3 - x^2 - 5x + x + 5 = 0$

$\Rightarrow$ $x^2 - 11x + 8 = 0$

which is of the form $ax^2 + bx + c = 0$, where $a \neq 0$

Thus, $(2x-1)(x-3) = (x+5)(x-1)$ is a quadratic equation.

(vi) Given equation is

$$x^2 + 3x + 1 = (x-2)^2$$

$\Rightarrow$ $x^2 + 3x + 1 = x^2 + 4 - 4x$ $[\because (a-b)^2 = a^2 - 2ab + b^2]$

$\Rightarrow$ $x^2 + 3x + 1 - x^2 - 4 + 4x = 0$

$\Rightarrow$ $7x - 3 = 0$

which is not of the form $ax^2 + bx + c = 0$, where $a \neq 0$ and b, c are any real numbers.

$\therefore$ It is not a quadratic equation.

(vii) Given equation is

$$(x+2)^3 = 2x(x^2 - 1)$$

$\Rightarrow$ $x^3 + 8 + 3x^2(2) + 3x(2)^2 = 2x^3 - 2x$

$[\because (a+b)^3 = a^3 + b^3 + 3ab^2 + 3a^2b]$

$\Rightarrow$ $x^3 + 8 + 6x^2 + 12x = 2x^3 - 2x$

$\Rightarrow$ $x^3 + 8 + 6x^2 + 12x - 2x^3 + 2x = 0$

$\Rightarrow$ $-x^3 + 6x^2 + 14x + 8 = 0$

which is not of the form $ax^2 + bx + c = 0$, $a \neq 0$

Thus, $(x+2)^3 = 2x(x^2 - 1)$ is not a quadratic equation.

(viii) Given equation is

$$x^3 - 4x^2 - x + 1 = (x-2)^3$$

$\Rightarrow$ $x^3 - 4x^2 - x + 1 = x^3 - 3(x^2)2 + 3x(2)^2 - (2)^3$

$[\because (a-b)^3 = a^3 - b^3 + 3ab^2 - 3a^2b]$

$\Rightarrow$ $x^3 - 4x^2 - x + 1 = x^3 - 6x^2 + 12x - 8$

$\Rightarrow$ $x^3 - 4x^2 - x + 1 - x^3 + 6x^2 - 12x + 8 = 0$

$\Rightarrow$ $2x^2 - 13x + 9 = 0$

which is of the form $ax^2 + bx + c = 0$, $a \neq 0$

Thus, $x^3 - 4x^2 - x + 1 = (x-2)^3$ is a quadratic equation.

Question 2 Represent the following situations in the form of quadratic equations

(i) The area of a rectangular plot is 528 m^2. The length of the plot (in metre) is one more than twice its breadth. We need to find the length and breadth of the plot.

(ii) The product of two consecutive positive integers is 306. We need to find the integers.

(iii) Rohan's mother is 26 years older than him. The product of their ages (in years) 3 years from now will be 360. We would like to find Rohan's present age.

(iv) A train travels a distance of 480 km at a uniform speed. If the speed had been 8 kmh^{-1} less, then it would have taken 3 hours more to cover the same distance. We need to find the speed of the train.

Sol. (i) Let the breadth of the plot = x m

Then, the length of the plot = $(2x + 1)$ m (By condition)

Area of the rectangular plot = 528 m^2 (Given)

$\because$ Area of the rectangular plot = Length × Breadth

$\therefore$ $(2x + 1)\,x = 528$

$\Rightarrow$ $2x^2 + x = 528$

$\Rightarrow$ $2x^2 + x - 528 = 0$

Since, it is of the form $ax^2 + bx + c = 0, a \neq 0$. Thus, it represents the required quadratic equation.

(ii) Let the two consecutive positive integers be x and $x + 1$.

Then, according to the question,

Product of two consecutive integers = 306

$\therefore$ $x\,(x + 1) = 306$

$\Rightarrow$ $x^2 + x = 306$

or $x^2 + x - 306 = 0$

Since, it is of the form $ax^2 + bx + c = 0, a \neq 0$. Thus, it represents the required quadratic given condition,

(iii) Let the age of Rohan = x yr

Then, his mother's age = $(x + 26)$ yr (By conditions)

After three years,

Rohan's age = $(x + 3)$ yr

Rohan's mother's age = $[(x + 26) + 3]$ yr = $(x + 29)$ yr

According to the given condition,

$(x + 3)(x + 29) = 360$

$\Rightarrow$ $x^2 + 29x + 3x + 87 = 360$

$\Rightarrow$ $x^2 + 32x - 273 = 0$

Since, it is of the form $ax^2 + bx + c = 0, a \neq 0$. Thus, it represents the required quadratic equation.

(iv) Let the speed of the train = x km/h

Distance travelled by the train = 480 km

Therefore, time taken for travelling 480 km = $\frac{480}{x}$ h $\left(\because \text{Speed} = \frac{\text{Distance}}{\text{Time}}\right)$

If the speed had been 8 km/h less *i.e.*, $(x - 8)$ km/h, then

Time taken for travelling 480 km = $\frac{480}{x-8}$ h

According to the given condition,

$$\Rightarrow \quad \frac{480}{x-8} - \frac{480}{x} = 3$$

$$\Rightarrow \quad \frac{480\,x - 480\,(x-8)}{x\,(x-8)} = 3$$

$$\Rightarrow \quad 480x - 480x + 3840 = 3x\,(x-8)$$

$$3840 = 3x^2 - 24x$$

$$\Rightarrow \quad 3x^2 - 24x - 3840 = 0$$

$$\Rightarrow \quad 3\,(x^2 - 8x - 1280) = 0$$

$$\Rightarrow \quad x^2 - 8x - 1280 = 0$$

Since, it is of the form $ax^2 + bx + c = 0, a \neq 0$. Thus, it represents the required quadratic equation.

Exercise 4.2

Question 1 Find the roots of the following quadratic equations by factorisation

(i) $x^2 - 3x - 10 = 0$

(ii) $2x^2 + x - 6 = 0$

(iii) $\sqrt{2}\,x^2 + 7x + 5\sqrt{2} = 0$

(iv) $2x^2 - x + \frac{1}{8} = 0$

(v) $100x^2 - 20x + 1 = 0$

Thinking Process If any coefficient of the quadratic equation of the form $ax^2 + bx + c = 0$ is in the fractional form, then make all the coefficient in the general form, then use factorisation method i.e., by splitting the middle term, we get the required roots of the given quadratic equation.

Sol. (i) Given equation is

$$x^2 - 3x - 10 = 0 \quad \text{[By splitting middle term]}$$

$$\Rightarrow \quad x^2 - (5x - 2x) - 10 = 0$$

$$\Rightarrow \quad x^2 - 5x + 2x - 10 = 0$$

$$\Rightarrow \quad x\,(x-5) + 2\,(x-5) = 0$$

$$\Rightarrow \quad (x-5)\,(x+2) = 0$$

Now, $x - 5 = 0 \Rightarrow x = 5$

and $x + 2 = 0 \Rightarrow x = -2$

Hence, the roots of the equation $x^2 - 3x - 10 = 0$ are -2 and 5.

(ii) Given equation is

$$2x^2 + x - 6 = 0 \quad \text{[By splitting the middle term]}$$

$$\Rightarrow \quad 2x^2 + (4x - 3x) - 6 = 0$$

$$\Rightarrow \quad 2x^2 + 4x - 3x - 6 = 0$$

$$\Rightarrow \quad 2x(x + 2) - 3(x + 2) = 0$$

$$\Rightarrow \quad (x + 2)(2x - 3) = 0$$

Now, $x + 2 = 0 \Rightarrow x = -2$

and $2x - 3 = 0 \Rightarrow x = \frac{3}{2}$

Hence, the roots of the equation $2x^2 + x - 6 = 0$ are -2 and $\frac{3}{2}$.

(iii) Given equation is

$$\sqrt{2}x^2 + 7x + 5\sqrt{2} = 0$$

$$\sqrt{2}x^2 + (5x + 2x) + 5\sqrt{2} = 0 \quad \text{[By splitting the middle term]}$$

$$\Rightarrow \quad \sqrt{2}x^2 + 5x + 2x + 5\sqrt{2} = 0$$

$$\Rightarrow \quad x(\sqrt{2}x + 5) + \sqrt{2}(\sqrt{2}x + 5) = 0$$

$$\Rightarrow \quad (\sqrt{2}x + 5)(x + \sqrt{2}) = 0$$

Now, $\sqrt{2}x + 5 = 0 \Rightarrow x = -\frac{5}{\sqrt{2}}$

and $x + \sqrt{2} = 0 \Rightarrow x = -\sqrt{2}$

Hence, the roots of the equation $\sqrt{2}x^2 + 7x + 5\sqrt{2} = 0$ are $-\frac{5}{\sqrt{2}}$ and $-\sqrt{2}$.

(iv) Given equation is $2x^2 - x + \frac{1}{8} = 0$

On multiplying on both sides by 8, we get

$$\Rightarrow \quad 16x^2 - 8x + 1 = 0$$

$$\Rightarrow \quad 16x^2 - (4x + 4x) + 1 = 0 \quad \text{[By splitting the middle term]}$$

$$\Rightarrow \quad 16x^2 - 4x - 4x + 1 = 0$$

$$\Rightarrow \quad 4x(4x - 1) - 1(4x - 1) = 0$$

$$\Rightarrow \quad (4x - 1)(4x - 1) = 0$$

Now, $4x - 1 = 0 \Rightarrow x = \frac{1}{4}$

and $4x - 1 = 0 \Rightarrow x = \frac{1}{4}$

Hence, the roots of the equation $2x^2 - x + \frac{1}{8} = 0$ are $\frac{1}{4}$ and $\frac{1}{4}$.

(v) Given equation is

$$100x^2 - 20x + 1 = 0$$

$$\Rightarrow \quad 100x^2 - (10x + 10x) + 1 = 0 \quad \text{[By splitting the middle term]}$$

$\Rightarrow \quad 100x^2 - 10x - 10x + 1 = 0$

$\Rightarrow \quad 10x(10x - 1) - 1(10x - 1) = 0$

$\Rightarrow \quad (10x - 1)(10x - 1) = 0$

Now, $10x - 1 = 0 \Rightarrow x = \frac{1}{10}$

and $10x - 1 = 0 \Rightarrow x = \frac{1}{10}$

Hence, the roots of the equation $100x^2 - 20x + 1 = 0$ are $\frac{1}{10}$ and $\frac{1}{10}$.

Question 2. Solve the following quadratic equations

(i) $x^2 - 45x + 324 = 0$ (ii) $x^2 - 55x + 750 = 0$

Sol.

(i) Given equation is

$$x^2 - 45x + 324 = 0$$

$\Rightarrow \quad x^2 - (36x + 9x) + 324 = 0$ [By splitting the middle term]

$\Rightarrow \quad x^2 - 36x - 9x + 324 = 0$

$\Rightarrow \quad x(x - 36) - 9(x - 36) = 0$

$\Rightarrow \quad (x - 36)(x - 9) = 0$

Now, $x - 36 = 0 \Rightarrow x = 36$

and $x - 9 = 0 \Rightarrow x = 9$

Hence, the roots of the equation $x^2 - 45x + 324 = 0$ are 9 and 36.

(ii) Given equation is

$$x^2 - 55x + 750 = 0$$

$\Rightarrow \quad x^2 - (30x + 25x) + 750 = 0$ [By splitting the middle term]

$\Rightarrow \quad x^2 - 30x - 25x + 750 = 0$

$\Rightarrow \quad x(x - 30) - 25(x - 30) = 0$

$\Rightarrow \quad (x - 30)(x - 25) = 0$

Now, $x - 30 = 0 \Rightarrow x = 30$

and $x - 25 = 0 \Rightarrow x = 25$

Hence, the roots of the equation $x^2 - 55x + 750 = 0$ are 25 and 30.

Question 3 Find two numbers whose sum is 27 and product is 182.

Sol. Let the numbers be x and y.

According to the given condition,

Sum of the numbers $= x + y = 27$ ...(i)

Product of the numbers $= xy = 182$ ...(ii)

$\Rightarrow \qquad y = \dfrac{182}{x}$

On substituting $y = \dfrac{182}{x}$ in Eq. (i), we get

$$x + \frac{182}{x} = 27$$

On multiplying both sides by x, we get

$\Rightarrow \qquad x^2 + 182 = 27x$

$\Rightarrow \qquad x^2 - 27x + 182 = 0$

$x^2 - (14x + 13x) + 182 = 0$ [By splitting the middle term]

$\Rightarrow \qquad x^2 - 14x - 13x + 182 = 0$

$\Rightarrow \qquad x(x - 14) - 13(x - 14) = 0$

$\Rightarrow \qquad (x - 14)(x - 13) = 0$

Now, $\qquad x - 14 = 0 \Rightarrow x = 14$

and $\qquad x - 13 = 0 \Rightarrow x = 13$

$\therefore \qquad x = 13, 14$

On substituting $x = 13$ in Eq. (i), we get $y = 14$

On substituting $x = 14$ in Eq. (i), we get $y = 13$

Therefore, in both cases, the numbers are 13 and 14.

Question 4 Find two consecutive positive integers, sum of whose squares is 365.

Sol. Let the two consecutive positive integers be x and $x + 1$.

According to the given condition,

Sum of the squares of two consecutive positive integers = 365

$x^2 + (x + 1)^2 = 365$

$\Rightarrow \qquad x^2 + x^2 + 2x + 1 = 365 \qquad [\because (a + b)^2 = a^2 + 2ab + b^2]$

$\Rightarrow \qquad 2x^2 + 2x - 364 = 0$

$\Rightarrow \qquad x^2 + x - 182 = 0$

$\Rightarrow \qquad x^2 + (14x - 13x) - 182 = 0$ [By splitting the middle term]

$\Rightarrow \qquad x^2 + 14x - 13x - 182 = 0$

$\Rightarrow \qquad x(x + 14) - 13(x + 14) = 0$

$\Rightarrow \qquad (x + 14)(x - 13) = 0$

Now, $\qquad x + 14 = 0 \Rightarrow x = -14$

and $\qquad x - 13 = 0 \Rightarrow x = 13$

$\therefore \qquad x = -14, 13$

Since, x is a positive integer

So, $x = -14$ cannot be possible therefore, $x = 13$ will be the required value.

Hence, the two consecutive positive integers are 13 and 14.

Question 5 The altitude of a right triangle is 7 cm less than its base. If the hypotenuse is 13 cm, find the other two sides.

Sol. Given that, hypotenuse of right triangle = 13 cm

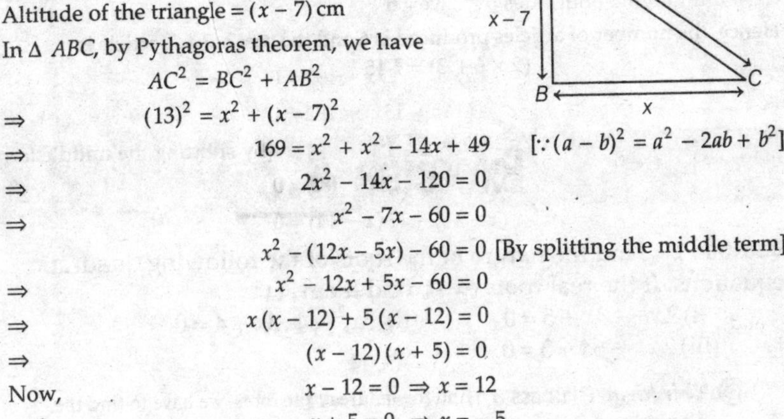

Let the base of the right triangle = x

According to the given condition,

Altitude of the triangle = $(x - 7)$ cm

In Δ ABC, by Pythagoras theorem, we have

$$AC^2 = BC^2 + AB^2$$

$\Rightarrow$ $(13)^2 = x^2 + (x - 7)^2$

$\Rightarrow$ $169 = x^2 + x^2 - 14x + 49$ $[\because (a - b)^2 = a^2 - 2ab + b^2]$

$\Rightarrow$ $2x^2 - 14x - 120 = 0$

$\Rightarrow$ $x^2 - 7x - 60 = 0$

$x^2 - (12x - 5x) - 60 = 0$ [By splitting the middle term]

$\Rightarrow$ $x^2 - 12x + 5x - 60 = 0$

$\Rightarrow$ $x(x - 12) + 5(x - 12) = 0$

$\Rightarrow$ $(x - 12)(x + 5) = 0$

Now, $x - 12 = 0 \Rightarrow x = 12$

and $x + 5 = 0 \Rightarrow x = -5$

Since, base of the triangle cannot be negative, So, $x = -5$ cannot be possible

Hence, base of the triangle = 12 cm and altitude of the triangle = 12 − 7 = 5 cm

Question 6 A cottage industry produces a certain number of pottery articles in a day. It was observed on a particular day that the cost of production of each article (in ₹) was 3 more than twice the number of articles produced on that day. If the total cost of production on that day was ₹ 90, find the number of articles produced and the cost of each article.

Sol. Let the number of pottery articles produced on a particular day = x

$\therefore$ Cost of production of each article = $2x + 3$ (By given condition)

So, the total cost of production = Number of pottery articles × Cost of production of each article

$$= x(2x + 3)$$

According to the given condition,

$x(2x + 3) = 90$

$\Rightarrow$ $2x^2 + 3x = 90$

$\Rightarrow$ $2x^2 + 3x - 90 = 0$

$\Rightarrow$ $2x^2 + (15x - 12x) - 90 = 0$ [By splitting the middle term]

$\Rightarrow$ $2x^2 + 15x - 12x - 90 = 0$

$\Rightarrow$ $x(2x + 15) - 6(2x + 15) = 0$

$\Rightarrow$ $(2x + 15)(x - 6) = 0$

Now, $2x + 15 = 0 \Rightarrow x = -\frac{15}{2}$

and $x - 6 = 0 \Rightarrow x = 6$

$\therefore$ $x = -\frac{15}{2}$ and 6

But x cannot be negative. *i.e.*, number of pottery articles should be positive.

$\therefore$ $x = 6$

Hence, the number of articles produced is 6 and the cost of each article is

$(2 \times 6 + 3) = ₹\, 15$

Exercise 4.3

Question 1 Find the nature of the roots of the following quadratic equations. If the real roots exist, find them

(i) $2x^2 - 3x + 5 = 0$ (ii) $3x^2 - 4\sqrt{3}x + 4 = 0$

(iii) $2x^2 - 6x + 3 = 0$

Thinking Process To find the nature of the roots, we have to find the, discriminant $D = b^2 - 4ac$ first.

- If $D = b^2 - 4ac > 0$ then roots with be real and distinct.
- If $D = b^2 - 4ac = 0$ then roots will be real and equal.

Sol.

(i) Given equation is

$$2x^2 - 3x + 5 = 0$$

On comparing with $ax^2 + bx + c = 0$, we get

$$a = 2, b = -3 \text{ and } c = 5$$

$\therefore$ Discriminant, $D = b^2 - 4ac = (-3)^2 - 4(2)(5)$

$$= 9 - 40 = -31 < 0$$

Therefore, the equation $2x^2 - 3x + 5 = 0$ has no real roots *i.e.*, imaginary roots.

(ii) Given equation is

$$3x^2 - 4\sqrt{3}x + 4 = 0 \quad \text{...(i)}$$

On comparing with $ax^2 + bx + c = 0$, we get

$$a = 3, b = -4\sqrt{3} \text{ and } c = 4$$

$\therefore$ Discriminant, $D = b^2 - 4ac = (-4\sqrt{3})^2 - 4 \times 3(4)$

$$= 48 - 48 = 0$$

Therefore, the equation $3x^2 - 4\sqrt{3}x + 4 = 0$ has two equal and real roots.

Eq. (i) can be written as $(\sqrt{3}x)^2 - 2(\sqrt{3}x)(2) + (2)^2 = 0$

$\Rightarrow$ $(\sqrt{3}x - 2)^2 = 0$ $[\because a^2 - 2ab + b^2 = (a - b)^2]$

$\therefore \qquad (\sqrt{3}x-2)(\sqrt{3}x-2)=0$

$\Rightarrow \qquad x=\frac{2}{\sqrt{3}},\frac{2}{\sqrt{3}}$

Therefore, the equal roots are $\frac{2}{\sqrt{3}}$ and $\frac{2}{\sqrt{3}}$.

(iii) Given equation is

$$2x^2-6x+3=0$$

On comparing with $ax^2+bx+c=0$, we get
$a=2, b=-6$ and $c=3$

$\therefore$ Discriminant, $D=b^2-4ac$

$$=(-6)^2-4(2)(3)$$
$$=36-24=12>0$$

Therefore, the equation $2x^2-6x+3=0$ has two distinct real roots.

$$\therefore \qquad x=\frac{-b\pm\sqrt{D}}{2a}=\frac{6\pm\sqrt{12}}{4}$$

$$=\frac{6\pm2\sqrt{3}}{4}=\frac{3\pm\sqrt{3}}{2}$$

Hence, the real roots are $\frac{3+\sqrt{3}}{2}$ and $\frac{3-\sqrt{3}}{2}$.

Question 2 Find the values of k for each of the following quadratic equations so that they have two equal roots

(i) $2x^2+kx+3=0$ (ii) $kx(x-2)+6=0$

Thinking Process If any quadratic equation *i.e.*, $ax^2+bx+c=0$, $a\neq0$ has two equal real roots, then its discriminant should be equal to zero *i.e.*, $D=b^2-4ac=0$.

Sol.

(i) The given equation is

$$2x^2+kx+3=0$$

On comparing with $ax^2+bx+c=0$, we get $a=2, b=k$ and $c=3$

$\therefore$ Discriminant, $D=b^2-4ac=(k)^2-4\times2\times3$

$$=k^2-24$$

For equal roots, $D=0 \Rightarrow k^2-24=0$

$\Rightarrow \qquad k^2=24$

$\Rightarrow \qquad k=\pm\sqrt{24}=\pm2\sqrt{6}$

$\therefore \qquad k=\pm2\sqrt{6}$

(ii) The given equation is

$$kx(x-2)+6=0 \qquad \text{...(i)}$$

Eq. (i) can be written as $kx^2-2kx+6=0 \qquad$ ...(ii)

On comparing Eq. (ii) with equation $ax^2 + bx + c = 0$, we get

$$a = k,\ b = -2k \text{ and } c = 6$$

$\therefore$ Discriminant, $D = b^2 - 4ac$

$$= (-2k)^2 - 4 \times k \times 6$$

$$= 4k^2 - 24k = 4k(k-6)$$

For equal roots, $D = 0 \Rightarrow 4k(k-6) = 0$

$\Rightarrow$ $k = 0$ or $k = 6$

Hence, the required valeus of k are 0 and 6.

Question 3 Is it possible to design a rectangular mango grove whose length is twice its breadth and the area is 800 m^2? If so, find its length and breadth.

Sol. Let breadth of a rectangular mango grove = x metre

$\therefore$ Length of a rectangular mango grove = $2x$ metre (By given condition)

Area of rectangular mango grove = 800 m^2 [Given]

$\Rightarrow$ Length $\times$ Breadth = $2x(x) = 800$

[$\because$ Area of rectangle = length $\times$ breadth]

$\Rightarrow$ $2x^2 = 800 \Rightarrow x^2 = 400$

$\Rightarrow$ $x = \pm 20$

Since, negative sign is not possible because breadth can't be negative.

$\therefore$ Length = $2x$ = 40 m and Breadth = 20 m

Question 4 Is the following situation possible? If so, determaine their present ages. The sum of the ages of two friends is 20 years. Four years ago, the product of their ages in years was 48.

Sol. Let age of one of two friends = x yr

Then, age of other friend = $(20 - x)$ yr

($\because$ The sum of the ages of two friends is 20 yr)

4 yr ago age of one of two friends = $(x - 4)$ yr

4 yr ago age of the other friend = $(20 - x - 4)$ yr = $(16 - x)$ yr

According to the given condition,

$$(x-4)(16-x) = 48$$

$\Rightarrow$ $16x - x^2 - 64 + 4x = 48$

$\Rightarrow$ $x^2 - 20x + 112 = 0$

On comparing the above equation with $ax^2 + bx + c = 0$, we get

$$a = 1,\ b = -20 \text{ and } c = 112$$

$\therefore$ Discriminant, $D = b^2 - 4ac = (-20)^2 - 4 \times 1 \times 112$

$$= 400 - 448 = 48 < 0$$

which implies that the real roots are not possible because this condition represents an imaginary roots. So, the solution does not exist.

Question 5 Is it possible to design a rectangular park of perimeter 80 m and area 400 m^2? If so, find its length and breadth.

Sol. Let the breadth fo the park = x metre

According to the given condition.

$$\text{Perimeter of a rectangular park} = 80 \text{ m}$$

$$\Rightarrow \quad 2(\text{Length} + \text{Breadth}) = 80 \text{ m}$$

[∵perimeter of rectangle = 2(length +breadth)]

$$\Rightarrow \quad \text{Length} + \text{Breadth} = 40 \text{ m}$$

$$\Rightarrow \quad \text{Length} = (40 - x)\text{m}$$

∴ Area of a rectangular park = Length × Breadth = $(40 - x)x$ m^2

But according to the question,

Area of the rectangular park is = 400 m^2.

$$\therefore \quad (40 - x)\,x = 400 \quad [\because \text{area of rectangle} = \text{length} \times \text{breadth}]$$

$$\Rightarrow \quad x^2 - 40x + 400 = 0$$

$$\Rightarrow \quad x^2 - 2x \times 20 + (20)^2 = 0$$

$$\Rightarrow \quad (x - 20)^2 = 0 \quad [\because a^2 - 2ab + b^2 = (a - b)^2]$$

$$\Rightarrow \quad x = 20$$

Thus, breadth of the park = 20 m

and length of the park = (40 – 20) m = 20 m

So, it is possible to design the rectangular park having equal length and breadth *i.e.*, 20 m.

DIKSHA APP Questions

☐ Multiple Choice Questions

Q.1 The roots of the quadratic equation $(2x + 1)(3x - 5) = 0$ are

(a) $\frac{-1}{2}, \frac{5}{3}$
(b) $\frac{1}{2}, \frac{-5}{3}$
(c) $\frac{1}{2}, \frac{5}{3}$
(d) $\frac{-1}{2}, \frac{-5}{3}$

Sol. (a) Given equation is $(2x + 1)(3x - 5) = 0$

So, this equation is zero when either $2x + 1 = 0$ or $3x - 5 = 0$

So, $\quad 2x + 1 = 0 \Rightarrow x = \frac{-1}{2}$

and, $\quad 3x - 5 = 0 \Rightarrow x = \frac{5}{3}$

Q.2 Find the root of the given equation $2x^2 + 5x + 5 = 0$

(a) Distinct and real
(b) Two equal real roots
(c) Two distinct real
(d) No real roots

Sol. (d) The given equation is

$$2x^2 + 5x + 5 = 0 \quad \text{...(i)}$$

On comparing Eq. (i) with $ax^2 + bx + c = 0$, we get

$$a = 2, b = 5, c = 5$$

$\therefore$ Discriminant,

$$D = b^2 - 4ac$$
$$= (5)^2 - 4 \times 2 \times 5$$
$$= 25 - 40 = -15 < 0$$

Therefore, the equation has no real roots.

Q.3 If the equation $x^2 - bx + 1 = 0$ does not possess real roots, then

(a) $-3 < b < 3$
(b) $-2 < b < 2$
(c) $b > 2$
(d) $b < -2$

Sol. (b) The given equation is

$$x^2 - bx + 1 = 0$$

On comparing with $ax + by + c = 0$, we get $a = 1, b = -b, c = 1$

An equation doesn't possess real roots when

Discriminant, $D = b^2 - 4ac < 0$

$\Rightarrow$ $(-b)^2 - 4 < 0$

$\Rightarrow$ $b^2 - 4 < 0$

$\Rightarrow$ $b^2 < 4$

$\Rightarrow$ $-2 < b < 2$

Q.4 The sum of the reciprocals of the roots of the equation $x^2 + px + q = 0$ is

(a) $\frac{p}{q}$
(b) $\frac{-p}{q}$
(c) $\frac{q}{p}$
(d) $\frac{-q}{p}$

Sol. (b) The given equation is

$$x^2 + px + q = 0$$

On comparing with $ax^2 + bx + c = 0$, we get

$$a = 1, b = p, c = a$$

$\therefore$ Discriminant, $D = b^2 - 4ac = p^2 - 4q$

So, the roots are $x = \dfrac{-p \pm \sqrt{p^2 - 4q}}{2}$

reciprocals of the roots $\dfrac{2}{-p + \sqrt{p^2 - 4q}}, \dfrac{2}{-p - \sqrt{p^2 - 4q}}$

Sum $\Rightarrow \dfrac{2}{-p + \sqrt{p^2 - 4q}} + \dfrac{2}{-p - \sqrt{p^2 - 4q}}$

$\Rightarrow = \dfrac{2[-p - \sqrt{p^2 - 4q}] + 2[-p + \sqrt{p^2 - 4q}]}{(-p)^2 - (\sqrt{p^2 - 4q})^2}$

$\Rightarrow = \dfrac{-2p - 2p}{p^2 - p^2 + 4q} = \dfrac{-4p}{4q} = \dfrac{-p}{q}$

Q.5 The roots of the equation $x^2 + 2\sqrt{3}x + 3 = 0$ are

(a) real and equal
(b) rational and equal
(c) imaginary
(d) rational and unequal

Sol. (a) The given equation is

$$x^2 + 2\sqrt{3}x + 3 = 0$$

$\Rightarrow \quad x^2 + 2 \times \sqrt{3} \times x + (\sqrt{3})^2 = 0$

$\Rightarrow \quad (x + \sqrt{3})^2 = 0 \quad [\because (a + b)^2 = a^2 + b^2 + 2ab]$

$\Rightarrow \quad (x + \sqrt{3})(x + \sqrt{3}) = 0$

$\Rightarrow \quad x = -\sqrt{3}, -\sqrt{3}$

On comparing the equation with

$ax^2 + bx + c = 0$, we get

$$a = 1; b = 2\sqrt{3}; c = 3$$

$\therefore$ Discriminant $\quad D = b^2 - 4ac$

$\Rightarrow \quad = (2\sqrt{3})^2 - 4 \times 1 \times 3 = 12 - 12 = 0$

as $\quad D = 0$

$\therefore$ The roots are real and equal.

Q.6 The equation $x^2 + 4x + k = 0$ has real roots when

(a) $k \geq 4$
(b) $k \leq 4$
(c) $k \leq 0$
(d) $k \geq 0$

Sol. (b) The given equation is,

$$x^2 + 4x + k = 0$$

The equation has real roots

$\Rightarrow$ Discriminant, $D = b^2 - 4ac \geq 0$

On comparing with $ax^2 + bx + c = 0$, we get

$$a = 1, b = 4, c = k$$

we have,

$$b^2 - 4ac \geq 0$$

$\Rightarrow$ $(4)^2 - 4 \times 1 \times k \geq 0$

$\Rightarrow$ $16 - 4k \geq 0$

$\Rightarrow$ $16 \geq 4k$

$\Rightarrow$ $k \leq 4$

Hence, option (b) is correct.

Q.7 A polygon of n sides has $n(n-3)/2$ diagonals Number of sides of a polygon with 54 diagonals is

(a) 12 (b) 9

(c) 10 (d) 8

Sol. (a) Given n sided polygon,

Number of diagonals = 54

$\Rightarrow$ $\frac{n(n-3)}{2} = 54$ [Given]

$\Rightarrow$ $n^2 - 3n = 108$

$\Rightarrow$ $n^2 - 3n - 108 = 0$

$\Rightarrow$ $n(n-12) + 9(n-12) = 0$ [By splitting the middle term]

$\Rightarrow$ $(n+9)(n-12) = 0$

$\Rightarrow$ $n + 9 = 0 \Rightarrow n = -9$

or $n - 12 = 0 \Rightarrow n = 12$

As sides of a polygon cannot be negative.

So, $n = 12$.

Q.8 The value of k such that the quadratic equation $x^2 - 2kx + (7k - 12) = 0$ has equal roots is

(a) $k = 4, 5$

(b) $k = 3, 1$

(c) $k = 3, 4$

(d) $k = 7$

Sol. (c) The given equation is

$$x^2 - 2kx + (7k - 12) = 0 \quad \ldots(i)$$

The equation has equal roots

So, discriminant, $D = b^2 - 4ac = 0$

On comparing the equation (i) with $ax^2 + bx + c = 0$, we get

$$a = 1, b = -2k, c = 7k - 12$$

Now, $D = (-2k)^2 - 4 \times 1 \times (7k - 12) = 0$

$\Rightarrow \quad 4k^2 - 28k + 48 = 0$

$\Rightarrow \quad k^2 - 7k + 12 = 0$ [divide by 4]

$\Rightarrow \quad k^2 - 3k - 4k + 12 = 0$ [By splitting the middle term]

$\Rightarrow \quad k(k - 3) - 4(k - 3) = 0$

Now, $(k - 4)(k - 3) = 0$

$\Rightarrow \quad k - 4 = 0 \Rightarrow k = 4$

or $k - 3 = 0 \Rightarrow k = 3$

Hence, roots are 3 and 4.

Q.9 The quadratic equation whose roots are 3 and –3 is

(a) $x^2 - 9 = 0$ (b) $x^2 - 3x - 3 = 0$
(c) $x^2 - 2x + 2 = 0$ (d) $x^2 + 9 = 0$

Sol. (a) Roots of the quadratic equation are 3 and –3.

$\Rightarrow \quad x = 3 \Rightarrow x - 3 = 0$

and $x = -3 \Rightarrow x + 3 = 0.$

The quadratic equation is

$$(x - 3)(x + 3) = 0$$

$\Rightarrow \quad x^2 - 9 = 0$ $[\because (x - a)(x + a) = x^2 - a^2]$

Q.10 Which of the following have real root

(a) $2x^2 + x + 1 = 0$
(b) $x^2 + x + 1 = 0$
(c) $x^2 - 6x + 6 = 0$
(d) $2x^2 + 15x + 30$

Sol. (c)

(a) The given equation is $2x^2 + x + 1 = 0$
On comparing with $ax^2 + bx + c = 0$, we get
$$a = 2, b = 1, c = 1$$
$\therefore$ Discriminant, $D = b^2 - 4ac$
$$= 1 - 4 \times 2 = 1 - 8 = -7 < 0$$
Hence, $2x^2 + x + 1 = 0$, has no real roots

(b) The given equation is $x^2 + x + 1 = 0$
On comparing with $ax^2 + bx + c = 0$, we get $a = 1, b = 1, c = 1$
$\therefore$ Discriminant, $D = b^2 - 4ac$
$$= 1 - 4 = -3 < 0$$
Hence, $x^2 + x + 1 = 0$, has no real roots,

(c) The given equation is $x^2 - 6x + 6 = 0$
On comparing with $ax^2 + bx + c = 0$, we get
$$a = 1, b = -6, c = 6$$

$\therefore$ Discriminant, $D = b^2 - 4ac$

$$= (-6)^2 - 4 \times 6$$
$$= 36 - 24 = 12 > 0$$

Hence, $x^2 - 6x + 6 = 0$, has real roots.

(d) The given equation is $2x^2 + 15x + 30 = 0$

On comparing with $ax^2 + bx + c = 0$, we get

$$a = 2, b = 15, c = 30$$

$\therefore$ Discriminant, $D = b^2 - 4ac = (15)^2 - 4 \times 2 \times 30$

$$= 225 - 240 < 0$$

Hence, $2x^2 + 15x + 30 = 0$, has no real roots.

Q.11 Which of the following equation has 2 as a root ?

(a) $2x^2 - 7x + 6 = 0$ (b) $3x^2 - 6x + 3 = 0$
(c) $x^2 - 4x + 5 = 0$ (d) $x^2 + 3x - 12 = 0$

◎ ***Thinking Process*** If α is one of the root of any quadratic equation *i.e.*, $ax^2 + bx + c = 0$, then $x = \alpha$ *i.e.*, α satisfies the equation $a\alpha^2 + b\alpha + c = 0$.

Sol. (a) The equation has 2 as a root if $x = 2$ reduces the equation to zero.

(a) The given equation is $2x^2 - 7x + 6 = 0$

On substituting $x = 2$ in $2x^2 - 7x + 6$, we get

$$2(2)^2 - 7(2) + 6 = 8 - 14 + 6 = 0$$

(b) The given equation is $3x^2 - 6x + 3 = 0$

On substituting $x = 2$ in $3x^2 - 6x + 3$, we get

$$3(2)^2 - 6(2) + 3 = 12 - 12 + 3 = 3 \neq 0$$

(c) The given equation is $x^2 - 4x + 5 = 0$

On substituting $x = 2$ in $x^2 - 4x + 5$, we get

$$(2)^2 - 4(2) + 5 = 4 - 8 + 5 = 1 \neq 0$$

(d) The given equation in $x^2 + 3x - 12 = 0$

On substituting $x = 2$ is $x^2 + 3x - 12$, we get

$$2^2 + 3 \times 2 - 12 = 4 + 6 - 12 = -2 \neq 0$$

So, $x = 2$ is not a root of $x^2 + 3x - 12 = 0$

Q.12 Which of the following are quadratic equations ?

(i) $(x - 1)^2 + 2 = 5x + 3$ (ii) $x(5x + 3) = x^2 - 1$
(a) Both (i) and (ii) (b) Only (i)
(c) Only (ii) (d) Neither

Sol. (a) (i) The given equation is $(x - 1)^2 + 2 = 5x + 3$

$\Rightarrow$ $x^2 - 2x + 1 + 2 - 5x - 3 = 0$ $[\because (a - b)^2 = a^2 - 2ab + b^2]$

$\Rightarrow$ $x^2 - 7x = 0$

Which is a form of quadratic equation *i.e.*, $ax^2 + bx + c = 0, a \neq 0$

Thus, $(x - 1)^2 + 2 = 5x + 3$ is a quadratic equation.

(ii) The given equation is $x(5x + 3) = x^2 - 1$

$\Rightarrow \quad 5x^2 + 3x - x^2 + 1 = 0 \Rightarrow 4x^2 + 3x + 1 = 0$

Which is a form of quadratic equation *i.e.*, $ax^2 + bx + c = 0, a \neq 0$

Thus $x(5x + 3) = x^2 - 1$ is a quadratic equation.

Q.13 The product of two consecutive integers is 168. Which of the following quadratic equations correctly represents this situation ?

(a) $x^2 + 2x - 168 = 0$ (b) $x^2 + x + 168 = 0$

(c) $x^2 + x - 168 = 0$ (d) None of these

Sol. (c) Let the two consecutive integers be x and $x + 1$

According to the given condition,

$$x(x + 1) = 168$$

$$\Rightarrow \quad x^2 + x = 168$$

$$\Rightarrow \quad x^2 + x - 168 = 0$$

Q.14 State which of the following statements is true.

(i) Every quadratic equation has exactly one root.

(ii) Every quadratic equation has at least two roots.

(iii) Every quadratic equation has at most two roots.

(a) All of them (b) Only statement (i)

(c) Only statement (ii) (d) Only statement (iii)

Sol. (d) As we know, Number of root equals to the degree of an algebraic equation So, a quadratic equation can have at most two roots.

Q.15 Which of the following quadratic equations has 3 as a root ?

(i) $x^2 + 6x - 12 = 0$ (ii) $x^2 - 4x + 5 = 0$

(iii) $x^2 - 4x + 3 = 0$

(a) Only equation (ii)

(b) Only equation (i)

(c) Only equation (iii)

(d) Both equation (i) and equation (iii)

Sol. (c) The given equation is $x^2 + 6x - 12 = 0$. On substituting $x = 3$ in $x^2 + 6x - 12$, we get

$$9 + 18 - 12 = 15 \neq 0$$

So, $x = 3$ is not a root of equation $x^2 + 6x - 12 = 0$

The given equation is $x^2 - 4x + 5 = 0$

On substituting $x = 3$ in $x^2 - 4x + 5$, we get

$$2(3)^2 - 4(3) + 5 = 9 - 12 + 5 = 2 \neq 0$$

So, $x = 3$ is not a root of equation $x^2 - 4x + 5 = 0$.
The given equation is $x^2 - 4x + 3 = 0$
On substituting $x = 3$ is $x^2 - 4x + 5$ we get,

$$(3)^2 - 4(3) + 3 - 9 - 12 + 3 = 0$$

So, $x = 3$ is a root of equation $x^2 - 4x + 3 = 0$

Q.16 Which of the following is a solution of the equation $2x^2 + x - 6 = 0$?

(a) $x = 2$ (b) $x = -12$
(c) $x = \frac{3}{2}$ (d) $x = -3$

Sol. (c) The given equation is $2x^2 + x - 6 = 0$, on substituting $x = 2$ in the given equation, we get

$$\text{LHS} = 2(2)^2 + (2) - 6 = 16 + 2 - 6 = 12 \neq 0$$

So, $x = 2$ is not a solution of the given equation.
On substituting $x = -12$ in the given equation, we get

$$\text{LHS} = 2(-12)^2 + (-12) - 6 = 288 - 12 - 6 = 270 \neq 0$$

So, $x = -12$ is not a solution of the given equation.
On substituting $x = \frac{3}{2}$ in the given equation, we get

$$\text{LHS} = 2(3/2)^2 + (3/2) - 6 = 9/2 + 3/2 - 6 = (12 - 12)/2 = 0.$$

So, $x = 3/2$ is a solution of the given equation
On substituting $x = -3$ in the given equation, we get.

$$\text{LHS} = 2(-3)^2 + (-3) - 6 = 18 - 3 - 6 = 9 \neq 0$$

So, $x = -3$ is not a solution of the given equation.

Q.17 Find the roots of $-7x - x^2 = 12$ using the factorisation method and choose the correct option.

(a) $x = 3, x = 4$ (b) $x = -3, x = -4$
(c) Cannot be solved (d) $x = -12, x = 5$

The given equation is $-7x - x^2 = 12$

Sol. (b) On rearranging the quadratic equation in the standard form, we get

$$x^2 + 7x + 12 = 0$$

$\Rightarrow \quad x^2 + 4x + 3x + 12 = 0$ [By splitting the middle term]

$\Rightarrow \quad x(x + 4) + 3(x + 4) = 0$

$\Rightarrow \quad (x + 3)(x + 4) = 0$

$\Rightarrow \quad x = -3, x = -4$

Hence, the roots of the given equation $-7x^2 - x^2 = 12$, are -3 and -4.

Q.18 The difference between the square of a natural number and the number itself is 110. Find the number and choose the correct option.

(a) $x = 11$ (b) $x = -10$
(c) $x = 10$ (d) $x = -11$

Sol. (a) Let the number be x.
According to the given condition, $x^2 - x = 110$

$$x^2 - x - 110 = 0$$
$\Rightarrow$ $x^2 - 11x + 10x - 110 = 0$ [By splitting the middle term]
$\Rightarrow$ $x(x - 11) + 10(x - 11) = 0$
$\Rightarrow$ $(x - 11)(x + 10) = 0$
$\Rightarrow$ $x = 11, x = -10$

Since, the number is a natural so, $x = -10$ can't be possible.
Hence, the required number is 11.

Q.19 Which of the following are not quadratic equations ?

(i) $x(x + 2) = (x + 3)(x - 6)$ (ii) $(x + 1)^3 = x^3 - 6$
(a) Both (i) and (ii) (b) Only (i)
(c) Only (ii) (d) Neither

Sol. (b) (i) The given equation is $x(x + 2) = (x + 3)(x - 6)$
$\Rightarrow$ $x^2 + 2x = x^2 - 6x + 3x - 18$
$\Rightarrow$ $2x = -3x - 18$
$\Rightarrow$ $5x + 18 = 0$

It is a linear equation and not a quadratic equation.
(ii) The given equation is $(x + 1)^3 = x^3 - 6$
$\Rightarrow$ $x^3 + 3x^2 + 3x + 1 = x^3 - 6$
$\Rightarrow$ $3x^2 + 3x + 7 = 0$

Hence, $3x^2 + 3x + 7 = 0$ .... is a quadratic equation.

Q.20 Find the roots of $x^2 - 12x + 35 = 0$ using the factorisation method and choose the correct option.

(a) $x = -5, x = -7$ (b) $x = 5, x = 7$
(c) $x = -5, x = 7$ (d) $x = 5, x = -7$

Sol. (b) The given equation is $x^2 - 12x + 35 = 0$
On splitting the middle term, we get.

$$x^2 - 7x - 5x + 35 = 0$$
$\Rightarrow$ $x(x - 7) - 5(x - 7) = 0$
$\Rightarrow$ $(x - 7)(x - 5) = 0$
$\Rightarrow$ $x = 7, x = 5$

Hence, $x = 7$ and $x = 5$ are the roots of given equation $x^2 - 12x + 35 = 0$

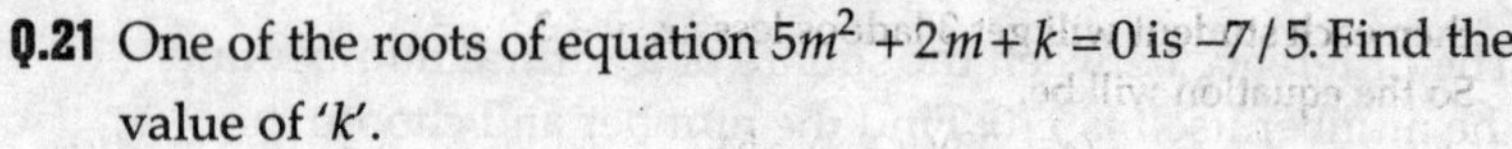

Q.21 One of the roots of equation $5m^2+2m+k=0$ is $-7/5$. Find the value of 'k'.

(a) -7 (b) $\frac{1}{7}$

(c) 7 (d) $\frac{-1}{7}$

Sol. (a) The given equation is $5m^2+2m+k=0$. If $\frac{-7}{5}$ is a root of the given equation, then

$$5(49/25)+2(-7/5)+k=0$$
$$\Rightarrow \quad 49/5-14/5+k=0$$
$$\Rightarrow \quad 35/5+k=0$$
$$\Rightarrow \quad 7+k=0$$
$$\Rightarrow \quad k=-7$$

Q.22 The value of the discriminant of the equation $x^2-10x-24=0$ is

(a) -196 (b) 4

(c) 196 (d) -4

Sol. (c) The given equation is $x^2-10x-24=0$

On comparing the given quadratic equation with its standard form, *i.e.*, $ax^2+bx+c=0, a\neq 0$
we get,

$$a=1, b=-10, c=-24$$

$\therefore$ Discriminant, $D=b^2-4ac$

So, $D=(-10)^2-4(1)(-24)$

$=100+96=196$

Q.23 Shweta was to distribute 540 ladoos equally among some students. If there were 30 students more, each would get 3 ladoos less. Find the number of students and the number of ladoos that each would get from Shweta.

(a) Number of students = 60
Number of ladoos = 9

(b) Number of students = 90
Number of ladoos = 6

(c) Number of students = 9
Number of ladoos = 60

(d) Number students = 6
Number of ladoos = 90

Sol. (a) Let number of students $=x$

Number of ladoos given to each student $=y$

So, $xy=540$ or $y=540/x$ ... (i)

If number of students were more *i.e.*, $x+30$,

then each student will get 3 ladoos less *i.e.*, $y - 3$

So the equation will be,

$$(x+30)(y-3) = 540 \quad \text{...(ii)}$$

On substituting $y = 540/x$ from Eq. (i) in Eq. (ii), we get

$$(x+30)(540/x-3) = 540$$

$$\Rightarrow \quad 540 - 3x - 90 + (16200/x) = 540$$

On multiplying both the sides by x, we get

$$540x - 3x^2 - 90x + 16200 = 540x$$

$$\Rightarrow \quad -3x^2 - 90x + 16200 = 0 \text{ or } 3x^2 + 90x - 16200 = 0$$

On dividing both sides by 3, we get

$$x^2 + 30x - 5400 = 0 \quad \text{...(iii)}$$

On splitting the middle term of Eq. (iii), we get.

$$x^2 + 90x - 60x - 5400 = 0$$

$$\Rightarrow \quad x(x+90) - 60(x+90) = 0$$

$$(x-60)(x+90) = 0; x = 60, \text{ or } x = -90$$

Number of students cannot be negative so, $x = -90$ can't be possible.

Hence, the required number of student will be $x = 60$

So, if $x = 60$, then Number of ladoos that each get $= \dfrac{540}{60} = 9$

Q.24 If $a+b+c=0$ and a, b, c are rationals then the roots of the equation $(b+c-a)x^2 + (c+a-b)x + (a+b+c) = 0$ are

(a) Equal (b) Rational

(c) Irrational (d) Imaginary

Sol. (b) The given equation is

$$(b+c-a)x^2 + (c+a-b)x + (a+b-c) = 0 \quad \text{...(i)}$$

and $a+b+c=0$

On comparing Eq. (i) with $Ax^2 + Bx + C = 0$, we get

$$A = b + c - a,$$

$$B = c + a - b$$

and $$C = a + b - c$$

$$\therefore \quad A + B + C = b + c - a + c + a - b + a + b - c$$

$$A + B + C = b + c + a$$

Therefore, $A + B + C = a + b + c = 0$

Now, Discriminant $D = B^2 - 4AC$

$$= (A+C)^2 - 4AC$$

$$= A^2 + C^2 + 2AC - 4AC$$

$$= A^2 + C^2 - 2AC = (A-C)^2$$

Therefore D is perfect square and A, B, C are rational numbers, therefore roots are rational.

Q.25 If the equation $(a^2 + b^2)x^2 - 2(ac + bd)x + c^2 + d^2 = 0$ has equal roots, then

(a) $ad = bc$ (b) $ab = cd$

(c) $ad = \sqrt{bc}$ (d) $ab = \sqrt{cd}$

Sol. (a) The given equation is

$$(a^2 + b^2)x^2 - 2(ac + bd)x + c^2 + d^2 = 0 \quad \ldots(i)$$

On comparing Eq. (i) with $Ax^2 + Bx + C = 0$, we get

$$A = a^2 + b^2,$$

$$B = -2(ac + bd)$$

and $$C = c^2 + d^2$$

We are given that Eq. (i) has equal roots

$\therefore$ Discriminant, $D = B^2 - 4AC = 0$

$\Rightarrow$ $$[-2(ac + bd)]^2 - 4(a^2 + b^2)(c^2 + d^2) = 0$$

$\Rightarrow$ $$4[a^2c^2 + b^2d^2 + 2abcd] - 4[a^2c^2 + a^2d^2 + b^2c^2 + b^2d^2] = 0$$

$\Rightarrow$ $$[a^2c^2 + b^2d^2 + 2abcd - a^2c^2 - a^2d^2 - b^2c^2 - b^2d^2] = 0$$

$\Rightarrow$ $$2abcd - a^2d^2 - b^2c^2 = 0$$

$\Rightarrow$ $$a^2d^2 + b^2c^2 - 2abcd = 0$$

$\Rightarrow$ $$(ad)^2 + (bc)^2 - (2abcd) = 0$$

$\Rightarrow$ $$(ad - bc)^2 = 0$$

$\Rightarrow$ $$ad = bc$$

☐ Subjective Type Questions

Q.1 Out of a group of swans, $\frac{7}{2}$ times the square root of the total number are playing on the shore of a tank. The two remaining ones are playing, with amorous fight, in the water. What is the total number of swans ?

Sol. Let the total numbers of swans = x

Numbers of swans playing on the shore = $\frac{7}{2}\sqrt{x}$

Remaining swans = 2

According to given condition,

$$x = 7/2\sqrt{x} + 2$$

$\Rightarrow$ $$x - 2 = \frac{7}{2}\sqrt{x}$$

$\Rightarrow$ $$2(x - 2) = 7\sqrt{x}$$

$\Rightarrow$ $$4(x - 2)^2 = 49x$$

$\Rightarrow$ $$4(x^2 - 4x + 4) = 49x \quad [\because (a - b)^2 = a^2 - 2ab + b^2]$$

$$\Rightarrow \quad 4x^2 - 65x + 16 = 0$$
$$\Rightarrow \quad (x - 16)(4x - 1) = 0$$
$$\Rightarrow \quad x - 16 = 0$$
or $$4x - 1 = 0$$
$$\Rightarrow \quad x = 16$$
or $$x = 1/4$$

Since, the number of swans cannot be in fraction.

$\therefore \quad x = \frac{1}{4}$ can not be possible

Hence, the total number of swans = 16

Q.2 A two digit number is such that product of its digits is 18. When 63 is subtracted from the number, the digits interchange their places. Find the number.

Sol. Let the two digit number be $10x + y$

We are given $x \times y = 18$ ...(i)

According to the condition, we have

$$\Rightarrow \quad 10x + y - 63 = 10y + x$$
$$\Rightarrow \quad 9x - 9y - 63 = 0$$
$$\Rightarrow \quad 9x - 9y = 63$$
$$\Rightarrow \quad x - y = 7$$
$$\Rightarrow \quad x = 7 + y \quad \text{...(ii)}$$

On substituting the value of $x = (7 + y)$ in Eq. (i), we get

$$\Rightarrow \quad (7 + y) \cdot y = 18$$
$$\Rightarrow \quad y^2 + 7y = 18$$
$$\Rightarrow \quad y^2 + 7y - 18 = 0$$
$$\Rightarrow \quad y^2 + 9y - 2y - 18 = 0$$
$$\Rightarrow \quad y(y + 9) - 2(y + 9) = 0$$
$$\Rightarrow \quad (y + 9)(y - 2) = 0$$
$$\Rightarrow \quad y = -9, y = 2$$

Although $y = -9$ can't be possible

Hence required value of $y = 2$

Now, On substituting the value of $y = 2$ in Eq. (ii), we get.

$$x = 7 + 2 = 9$$

Therefore, the required two digit number is $10(9) + 2 = 92$

Q.3 If 2 is a root of the equation $x^2 + bx + 12 = 0$ and the equation $x^2 + bx + q = 0$ has equal roots, then find the value of q.

Sol. The given equation is $x^2 + bx + 12 = 0$

Since, 2 is the root of the equation $x^2 + bx + 12 = 0$

$\therefore \quad 2^2 + b(2) + 12 = 0$

$\Rightarrow \quad 4 + 2b + 12 = 0$

$\Rightarrow \quad 2b = -16$

$\Rightarrow \quad b = -8$

On substituting $b = -8$ in the equation $x^2 + bx + q = 0$

i.e., $\quad x^2 - 8x + q = 0$

On comparing with $ax^2 + bx + c = 0$, we get

$$a = 1, b = -8, c = q$$

Since equation has equal roots

$\therefore$ Discriminant, $\quad D = b^2 - 4ac = 0$

$\Rightarrow \quad (-8)^2 - 4 \times 1 \times q = 0$

$\Rightarrow \quad 64 - 4q = 0$

$\Rightarrow \quad q = 16$

Hence, the value of q is 16.

Q.4 If I had walked 1 km per hour faster, I would have taken 10 minutes less to walk 2 km. Find the rate of my walking.

Sol. Distance = 2 km

Let the speed be x km/hr

New speed = $(x + 1)$ km/hr

Time taken with normal speed $= \frac{2}{x}$ hr $\quad \left[\because \text{Time} = \frac{\text{Distance}}{\text{Speed}}\right]$

Time taken with new speed $= \frac{2}{x+1}$ hr

According to given condition

$\frac{2}{x} - \frac{2}{x+1} = \frac{10}{60} \Rightarrow \frac{2x + 2 - 2x}{x^2 + x} = \frac{1}{6} \quad \left[\because 1 \text{ minute} = \frac{1}{60} \text{ hour}\right]$

$\Rightarrow \quad x^2 + x = 12$

$\Rightarrow \quad x^2 + x - 12 = 0$

$\Rightarrow \quad x(x + 4) - 3(x + 4) = 0$

$\Rightarrow \quad (x + 4)(x - 3) = 0$

$\Rightarrow \quad x = -4$ or $x = 3$

Since, speed can not be negative.

So, $x = -4$ can not be possible

So, speed is $x = 3$ km/hr

Q.5 $\dfrac{1}{p+q+x}=\dfrac{1}{p}+\dfrac{1}{q}+\dfrac{1}{x}$ solve by factorization method.

Sol. $\dfrac{1}{p+q+x}=\dfrac{1}{p}+\dfrac{1}{q}+\dfrac{1}{x}$

$\Rightarrow \quad \dfrac{1}{p+q+x}-\dfrac{1}{x}=\dfrac{1}{p}+\dfrac{1}{q}$

$\Rightarrow \quad \dfrac{x-p-q-x}{x^2+px+qx}=\dfrac{p+q}{pq}$

$\Rightarrow \quad \dfrac{-(p+q)}{x^2+px+qx}=\dfrac{p+q}{pq}$

$\Rightarrow \quad \dfrac{-1}{x^2+px+qx}=\dfrac{1}{pq}$

$\Rightarrow \quad x^2+px+qx=-pq$

$\Rightarrow \quad x^2+px+qx+pq=0$

$\Rightarrow \quad x(x+p)+q(x+p)=0$

$\Rightarrow \quad (x+p)(x+q)=0$

$\Rightarrow \quad x=-p$ or $x=-q$

Q.6 If –4 is a root of the quadratic equation $x^2+px-4=0$ and the quadratic equation $x^2+px+k=0$ has equal root, find the value of k.

Sol. The given quadratic equation is $x^2+px-4=0$ and –4 is root of $x^2+px-4=0$

$\therefore \quad (-4)^2+p(-4)-4+0$

$\Rightarrow \quad 16-4p-4=0$

$\Rightarrow \quad -4p=-12$

$\Rightarrow \quad p=3$

Now, $\quad x^2+px+k=0$ (Given)

$\Rightarrow \quad x^2+3x+k=0$ [Putting $p=3$]

$D=b^2-4ac$

$\Rightarrow \quad 0=(3)^2-4\times 1\times k$ [For equation roots $D=0$]

$\Rightarrow \quad 4k=9$

$\Rightarrow \quad k=\dfrac{9}{4}$

Q.7 Value of x for $x^2 - 8x + 15 = 0$ is

Sol. The given equation is

$$x^2 - 8x + 15 = 0$$

$\Rightarrow$ $x^2 - 5x - 3x + 15 = 0$ [By splitting the middle term]

$\Rightarrow$ $x(x-5) - 3(x-5) = 0$

$\Rightarrow$ $(x-3)(x-5) = 0$

$\Rightarrow$ $x = 3, 5$

Hence, the value of x are 3 or 5.

Q.8 If –5 is a root of the quadratic equation $2x^2 + px - 15 = 0$ and the quadratic equation $p(x^2 + x) + k = 0$ has equal roots, find the value of k.

Sol. The given quadratic equation is $2x^2 + px - 15 = 0$

$\because$ –5 is the root of the given quadratic equation

$\therefore$ $2(-5)^2 + p(-5) - 15 = 0$

$\Rightarrow$ $50 - 5p - 15 = 0$

$\Rightarrow$ $35 - 5p = 0$

$\Rightarrow$ $5p = 35$

$\Rightarrow$ $p = 7$

Now, given that equation $p(x^2 + x) + k = 0$ has equal roots

i.e., $7(x^2 + x) + k = 0$ has equal roots

i.e., $7x^2 + 7x + k = 0$

On comparing the quadratic equation $7x^2 + 7x + k = 0$ with $ax^2 + bx + c = 0, a \neq 0$, we get $a = 7, b = 7, c = k$

Now, for equal roots,

$$D = 0$$

$\Rightarrow$ $b^2 - 4ac = 0$

$\Rightarrow$ $49 - 4 \times 7 \times k = 0$

$\Rightarrow$ $7(7 - 4k) = 0$

$\therefore$ $k = \frac{7}{4}$

Q.9 A two digit number is four times the sum of the digits. it is also equal to 3 times the product of digits. Find the number.

Sol. Let ones digit of number = x

Let tens digit of number = y

$\therefore$ Number = $10y + x$

According to given condition,

$\Rightarrow$ $$10y + x = 4(x + y)$$

$\Rightarrow$ $$10y + x = 4x + 4y$$

$$x - 2y = 0 \Rightarrow x = 2y \quad ...(i)$$

and $$10y + x = 3xy \quad ...(ii)$$

On substituting $x = 2y$ from Eqs. (i) in (ii), we get

$$10y + 2y = 3(2y)y$$

$\Rightarrow$ $$12y = 6y^2$$

$\Rightarrow$ $$6y^2 - 12y = 0$$

$\Rightarrow$ $$y(y - 2) = 0$$

$$y = 0 \text{ and } y = 2$$

Since, $y = 0$ can't positive

So, $y = 2$

On substituting $y = 2$ in Eq. (i) we get

$$x = 2 \times 2 \Rightarrow x = 4$$

Hence the required number $= 10y + x = 10(2) + 4 = 20 + 4 = 24$.

Q.10 The following picture shows the shape of a certain grass patch. If the area of the patch is 80 cm^2, find k.

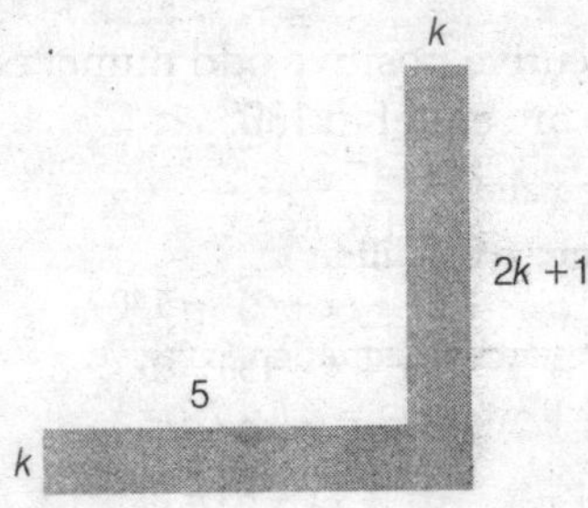

Sol. The total area $= 5k + k(2k + 1)$ [$\because$ Area of rectangle = length $\times$ breadth]

$$= 5k + 2k^2 + k$$

$$= 2k^2 + 6k$$

Since, the area is 80 m^2

$\therefore$ $$2k^2 + 6k = 80$$

$\Rightarrow$ $$2k^2 + 6k - 80 = 0$$

$$(2k - 10)(k + 8) = 0$$

$\Rightarrow$ $$k = 5 \text{ or } k = -8$$

Since, the length cannot be negative, So $k = -8$ cannot be possible.

Hence, the required value of k is 5.

Q.11 Find two numbers that sum to 21 and the sum of the squares is 261.

Sol. Let the numbers be x and y

According to the given condition

$$x + y = 21 \quad \Rightarrow \quad x = 21 - y \quad \text{...(i)}$$

and $$x^2 + y^2 = 261 \quad \text{...(ii)}$$

On substituting $x = 21 - y$ from Eq. (i) in Eq. (ii), we get

$\Rightarrow$ $$(21 - y)^2 + y^2 = 261$$

$\Rightarrow$ $$441 - 42y + y^2 + y^2 = 261$$

$\Rightarrow$ $$2y^2 - 42y + 180 = 0$$

$\Rightarrow$ $$y^2 - 21y + 90 = 0$$

$\Rightarrow$ $$y^2 - 15y - 6y + 90 = 0 \quad \text{[By splitting the middle form]}$$

$\Rightarrow$ $$y(y - 15) - 6(y - 15) = 0$$

$\Rightarrow$ $$(y - 15)(y - 6) = 0$$

$\Rightarrow$ $$y = 15 \text{ and } y = 6$$

On substituting $y = 15$ and $y = 6$ in Eq. (i), we get

$$x = 21 - 15 = 6$$

and $$x = 21 - 6 = 15$$

Hence, the required numbers are 6 and 15.

Q.12 Find two consecutive positive odd numbers such that the sum of their squares are equal to 130.

Sol. Let the number be x and $x + 2$

According to the given condition

$$x^2 + (x + 2)^2 = 130$$

$\Rightarrow$ $$x^2 + x^2 + 4x + 4 - 130 = 0$$

$\Rightarrow$ $$2x^2 + 4x - 126 = 0$$

$\Rightarrow$ $$x^2 + 2x - 63 = 0$$

$\Rightarrow$ $$x^2 + 9x - 7x - 63 = 0$$

$\Rightarrow$ $$x(x + 9) - 7(x + 9) = 0$$

$\Rightarrow$ $$(x + 9)(x - 7) = 0$$

$\Rightarrow$ $$x + 9 = 0$$

or $$x - 7 = 0$$

$\Rightarrow$ $$x = -9 \text{ or } x = 7$$

Since, $x = -9$ can not be possible

So, $x = 7$

So, required numbers $x = 7$ and $x + 2$

i.e., $7 + 2 = 9$

Hence, the numbers are 7 and 9.

Q.13 Find the values of k for quadratic equation $2x^2 + kx + 3 = 0$, so that they have two equal roots.

Sol. The given equation is $2x^2 + kx + 3 = 0$

On comparing with $ax^2 + bx + c = 0$, we get $a = 2, b = k, c = 3$

If equation has two equal real roots then, Discriminant $D = 0$

$$b^2 - 4ac = D$$

On substituting $D = 0$, we get

$$b^2 - 4ac = 0$$

$\Rightarrow$ $k^2 - 4(2)(3) = 0 \quad \Rightarrow k^2 - 24 = 0$

$\Rightarrow$ $k^2 = 24 \quad \Rightarrow k = \pm\sqrt{24}$

$\Rightarrow$ $k = \sqrt{4 \times 6} \quad \Rightarrow k = \pm 2\sqrt{6}$

Hence in the equation value of k is $\pm 2\sqrt{6}$.

Q.14 Solve quadratic equation by using formula method $x^2 - 5x + 6 = 0$

Sol. The given equation $x^2 - 5x + 6 = 0$ is in the standard form.

On comparing with $ax^2 + bx + c = 0$, we get

$$a = 1, b = -5, c = 6$$

$\because$ $$x = \frac{-b \pm \sqrt{b^2 - 4ac}}{2a}$$

$\Rightarrow$ $$x = \frac{-(-5) \pm \sqrt{(-5)^2 - 4(1)(6)}}{2(1)}$$

$\Rightarrow$ $$x = \frac{5 \pm \sqrt{25 - 24}}{2}$$

$\Rightarrow$ $$x = \frac{5 \pm \sqrt{1}}{2} \Rightarrow x = \frac{5+1}{2}, x = \frac{5-1}{2}$$

$\Rightarrow$ $$x = \frac{6}{2}, x = \frac{4}{2} \Rightarrow x = 3, x = 2$$

Hence, roots are 3 and 2.

Q.15 Find the nature of the roots of equation $x^2 - 2x + 3 = 0$.

Sol. The given equation is $x^2 - 2x + 3 = 0$

On comparing with $ax^2 + bx + c = 0$, we get

$$a = 1, b = -2, c = 3$$

$\because$ Discriminant, $D = b^2 - 4ac$,

$\Rightarrow$ $= (-2)^2 - 4(1)(3)$

$\Rightarrow$ $= 4 - 12 \Rightarrow = -8 < 0$

Since, discriminant $D < 0$.

So, the given equation has no real roots.

Q.16 Write the equation in the standard form $x(2x+3) = x^2 + 1$

Sol. The given equation is $x(2x + 3) = x^2 + 1$

$\Rightarrow \quad 2x^2 + 3x = x^2 + 1$

$\Rightarrow \quad 2x^2 + 3x - x^2 - 1 = 0 \Rightarrow x^2 + 3x - 1 = 0$

This equation is in standard form .

Q.17 There are three consecutive positive integers such that the sum of the square of the first and the product of the other two is 154. Find the integers.

Sol. Let the three consecutive positive integers be x, $x + 1$, $x + 2$.

According to given condition

$$x^2 + (x + 1)(x + 2) = 154$$

$\Rightarrow \quad x^2 + (x^2 + 3x + 2) = 154$

$\Rightarrow \quad 2x^2 + 3x - 152 = 0$

$\Rightarrow \quad 2x^2 - 16x + 19x - 152 = 0$

$\Rightarrow \quad 2x(x - 8) + 19(x - 8) = 0$

$$(x - 8)(2x + 19) = 0$$

$$x - 8 = 0 \quad \Rightarrow x = 8$$

and $x + 19 = 0 \Rightarrow x = \dfrac{-19}{2}$

$\Rightarrow \quad x = 8 \text{ or } -\dfrac{19}{2}$

Since, x is a positive integer, So, $x = \dfrac{-19}{2}$ can not be possible.

Therefore, the required value of x is 8.

Thus, the numbers are 8, 9, 10.

Q.18 A piece of cloth costs ₹ 200. If the piece was 5 m longer and each metre of cloth cost ₹ 2 less, the cost of the the piece would have remained unchanged. How long is the piece and what is the oringinal rate per metre ?

Sol. Let the length of piece of cloth is x metre and it original costs ₹ y/metre.

Total cost of the piece of cloth = ₹ 200

Then, cost of per metre, $y = \dfrac{200}{x}$

$\Rightarrow \quad xy = 200 \quad \ldots \text{(i)}$

and $\quad (x + 5)(y - 2) = 200$

$\Rightarrow \quad xy + 5y - 2x - 10 = 200$

$\Rightarrow \quad 200 + 5y - 2x - 10 = 200$

$\Rightarrow \quad 5y - 2x - 10 = 0$

$$\Rightarrow \quad 5y = 2x + 10$$

$$\Rightarrow \quad y = (2x + 10)/5$$

On substituting $y = \frac{(2x+10)}{5}$ in Eq. (i), we get

$$\Rightarrow \quad x(2x + 10)/5 = 200$$

$$\Rightarrow \quad x(2x + 10) = 200 \times 5$$

$$\Rightarrow \quad 2x^2 + 10x = 1000$$

$$\Rightarrow \quad x^2 + 5x - 500 = 0$$

$$\Rightarrow \quad x^2 + 25x - 20x - 500 = 0 \quad \text{[By splitting the middle term]}$$

$$\Rightarrow \quad x(x + 25) - 20(x + 25) = 0$$

$$\Rightarrow \quad (x + 25)(x - 20) = 0$$

either, $x + 25 = 0 \Rightarrow x = -25$

or $x - 20 = 0 \Rightarrow x = 20$

Since, the length of the cloth can not be negative, So, $x = -25$ can not be possible.

$\therefore$ $x = 20$ metre

On substituting $x = 20$ in Eq. (i), we get

$$20y = 200 \quad \Rightarrow y = 10$$

Thus, cloth is 20 m long and the original rate of piece of cloth is ₹ 10/m.

Q.19 The diagonals of a rectangular field is 60 metres more than the shorter side. If the longer side is 30 metres more than the shorter side, find the sides of the field.

Sol. Let the length of the shorter side be x m

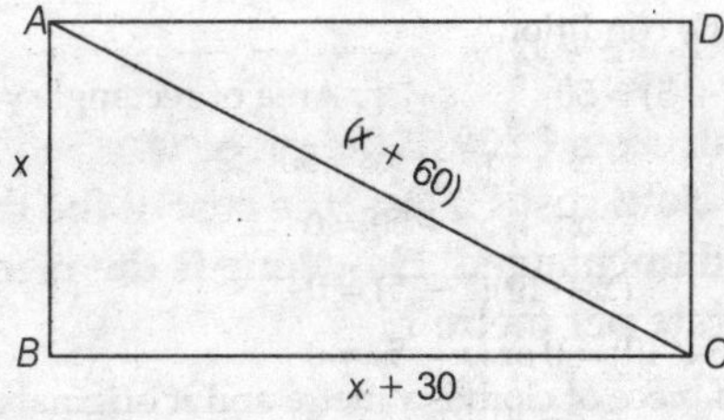

$\therefore$ Longer side be = $(x + 30)$ metres

Diagonal of the rectangular field = $(x + 60)$ metres

By using Pythagoras theorem, we get

$$AB^2 + BC^2 = AC^2$$

$$\Rightarrow \quad x^2 + (x + 30)^2 = (x + 60)^2$$

$$\Rightarrow \quad x^2 + x^2 + 60x + 900 = x^2 + 120x + 3600$$

$$\Rightarrow \quad x^2 - 60x - 2700 = 0$$

On comparing the equation $x^2 - 60x - 2700 = 0$ with $ax^2 + bx + c = 0$, $a \neq 0$, we get

$$a = 1, b = -60, c = -2700$$

Using formula method,

$$x = \frac{-b \pm \sqrt{b^2 - 4ac}}{2a}$$

$$\Rightarrow \quad x = \frac{-60 \pm \sqrt{(-60)^2 - 4 \times 1 \times (-2700)}}{2 \times 1}$$

$$\Rightarrow \quad x = \frac{60 \pm \sqrt{3600 + 10800}}{2} \Rightarrow x = \frac{60 \pm \sqrt{14400}}{2}$$

$$\Rightarrow \quad x = \frac{60 \pm 120}{2}$$

$$\Rightarrow \quad x = \frac{60 + 120}{2}, x = \frac{60 - 120}{2} \Rightarrow x = \frac{180}{2}, x = \frac{-60}{2}$$

$$\Rightarrow \quad x = 90, x = -30$$

Since, length can not be in negative, So, $x = -30$ can not be possible

Hence, $x = 90$

Shorter side = 90

Longer side = 90 + 30 = 120

Thus sides of the rectangular field are 120 m and 90 m.

Q.20 The length of a rectangle is 5 cm more than its width and the area is 50 cm^2. Find the length, width and the perimeter.

Sol. Let the width be x. Then, the length = $x + 5$.

According to the condition,

$$x(x + 5) = 50 \qquad [\because \text{Area of rectangle} = \text{length} \times \text{breadth}]$$

$$\Rightarrow \quad x^2 + 5x = 50$$

$$\Rightarrow \quad x^2 + 5x - 50 = 0$$

$$\Rightarrow \quad (x + 10)(x - 5) = 0$$

$$\Rightarrow \quad (x + 10) = 0 \text{ or } (x - 5) = 0$$

$$\Rightarrow \quad x = -10 \text{ or } x = 5$$

$x = -10$ is impossible to be a width

Thus width = 5 cm; So, the length = 10 cm.

Perimeter of rectangle = 2 (length + breadth)

$$\Rightarrow \quad = 2(10 + 5) = 2 \times 15 = 30 \text{ cm}$$

Hence, perimeter = 30 cm.

Arithmetic Progressions

CHAPTER 05

Important Points

01 **Sequence** An arrangement of number in a definite order according to some rule, is called as a sequence.

e.g., 1, 2, 3, 4, 5, 6, ...
2, 4, 6, 8, 10, ...

Each of the numbers in the sequence is called a term.

A sequence is said to be finite or infinite, according to the number of finite or infinite terms it contains.

Consider a sequence $a_1, a_2, a_3, a_4, ...$

Then, the first term is a_1, the second term is a_2, the third term is a_3 and so on.

02 **Arithmetic Progression** A succession of numbers is said to be an Arithmetic Progression (AP), if each term of the sequence can be obtained by adding a fixed number, d to the preceding term except the first term a. The fixed number d may be positive, negative or zero and it is called the common difference of AP.

$a, a + d, a + 2d, a + 3d, ...$ represents an arithmetic progression, where a is the first term and d is the common difference. This is the general form of an AP.

Examples

(i) 3,7, 11, 15, 19, ...

(ii) 15, 12, 9, 6, 3, ...

(iii) 2, 2, 2, 2, ...

(iv) –2.5, – 3, – 3.5, – 4, ...

Note • A given list of numbers $a_1, a_2, a_3, a_4, \ldots$ is an AP, if the differences $a_2 - a_1, a_3 - a_2, a_4 - a_3, \ldots$ gives the same value which is common difference, d.

- For any given AP, d is found by subtracting any term from its succeeding term.
- In general for an AP, $a_1, a_2, a_3, a_4, \ldots$ and $d = a_{k+1} - a_k$. where, a_{k+1} and a_k are the $(k+1)$th and the kth terms respectively. This follows even if the $(k+1)$th term is smaller.

03 Finite AP An AP with finite number of terms is called a finite AP. Every finite AP has a last term

Examples

(i) Natural numbers from 1 to 10.

1, 2, 3, 4, 5, 6, 7, 8, 9, 10.

Here, first term is 1, common difference is 1 and the last term is 10.

(ii) The set of odd natural numbers less than 11.

1,3, 5, 7, 9.

Here, the first term is 1, the common difference is 2 and the last term is 9.

04 Infinite AP An AP with infinitely many terms is called an infinite AP. These APs do not have a last term.

Examples

(i) 1, 2, 3, 4, ... (ii) –1, – 2, –3, –4, ...

05 *n*th term of an AP The nth term a_n (or the general term) of an AP is $a_n = a + (n-1)d$, where a is the first term and d is the common difference.

The last term, if it exists, is sometimes also denoted by l.

Note n is always a positive integer as n dentoes the position of a term.

06 *n*th term of an AP from the End The nth term a_n of an AP from the end is $a_n = l - (n-1)d$, where l is the last term and d is the common difference.

07 Sum of *n* terms of an AP The sum S_n of the first n terms of an AP is given by

$$S_n = \frac{n}{2}[2a + (n-1)d]$$

where n is the number of terms, a is the first term and d is the common difference.

(i) If l is the last term of the finite AP, say the nth term, then the sum of all terms of the AP is given by

$$S_n = \frac{n}{2}(a + l)$$

(ii) The nth term of an AP is the difference of the sum to first n terms and the sum to first $(n-1)$ terms of it, *i.e.*,

$$a_n = S_n - S_{n-1}$$

(iii) Sum of first n positive integers is given by

$$S_n = \frac{n(n+1)}{2}$$

(iv) Sum of first n odd positive integers is given by $S_n = n^2$

(iv) Sum of first n even positive integers is given by

$$S_n = n(n+1)$$

Exercise 5.1

Question 1 In which of the following situations, does the list of numbers involved make an arithmetic progression and why?

(i) The taxi fare after each km, when the fare is ₹ 15 for the first km and ₹ 8 for each additional km.

(ii) The amount of air present in a cylinder when a vacuum pump removes $\frac{1}{4}$ of the air remaining in the cylinder at a time.

(iii) The cost of digging a well after every metre of digging, when it costs ₹ 150 for the first metre and rises by ₹ 50 for each subsequent metre.

(iv) The amount of money in the account every year, when ₹ 10000 is deposited at compound interest at 8% per annum.

Sol. According to the question,

Taxi fare after the first km *i.e.*, 1 km = ₹15

Taxi fare after the second km *i.e.*, 2 km = ₹15 + 8 = ₹23

Taxi fare after the third km *i.e.*, 3 km = ₹23 + 8 = ₹31 and so on

i.e., 15, 23, 31, 39, ...

Here, each term is obtained by adding 8 to the preceding term except first term. So, it is an AP.

(ii) Let the amount of air present in the cylinder be y units.

So, $a_1 = y$

After the first removal, $a_2 = y - \frac{y}{4} = \frac{3y}{4}$

After the second removal, $a_3 = \frac{3y}{4} - \frac{1}{4}\left(\frac{3}{4}y\right)$

$= \frac{3y}{4} - \frac{3y}{16} = \frac{9y}{16}$

After the third removal, $a_4 = \frac{9y}{16} - \frac{1}{4}\left(\frac{9y}{16}\right)$

$= \frac{9y}{16} - \frac{9y}{64} = \frac{27}{64}y$

and i.e., on is the sequence becomes, $y, \frac{3y}{4}, \frac{9y}{16}, \frac{275}{64}, \ldots$

Here, $a_2 - a_1 = \frac{3y}{4} - y = -\frac{y}{4}$

and $a_3 - a_2 = \frac{9y}{16} - \frac{3y}{4} = \frac{9y - 12y}{16} = -\frac{3y}{16}$

$\Rightarrow \frac{3y}{4} - y \neq \frac{9y}{16} - \frac{3y}{4}$

$\Rightarrow$ It does not form an AP, because common difference is not same.

(iii) According to the question,

Cost of digging the well for 1 metre, = ₹ 150

Cost of digging the well for 2 metres, a_2 = ₹ 150 + 50 = ₹ 200

cost of digging the well for 3 metres, a_3 = ₹ 200 + 50 = ₹ 250

i.e., 150, 200, 250 ....

Here, each term is obtained by adding 50 to the preceding term except first term. So, it is an AP.

(iv) Amount deposited initially is ₹ 10,000(a_1)

$\text{Amount} = \left[P\left(1 + \frac{r}{100}\right)^t\right]$

Where, P = ₹ 10,000, $r = 8\%$ p.a.

At the end of first year, $a_2 = 10000\left(1 + \frac{8}{100}\right) = 10000\left(\frac{108}{100}\right)$

At the end of second year, $a_3 = 10000\left(1 + \frac{8}{100}\right)^2 = 10000\left(\frac{108}{100}\right)^2$

At the end of third year, $a_4 = 10000\left(\frac{108}{100}\right)^3$

and so on *i.e.*, the sequence becomes,

$10000, 10000\left(\frac{108}{100}\right), 10000\left(\frac{108}{100}\right)^2, 10000\left(\frac{108}{100}\right)^3 \ldots\ldots\ldots$

i.e., 10,000, 10800, 11664, ...

Now, $(a_2 - a_1) = 10800 - 10000 = 800$
and $(a_3 - a_2) = 11664 - 10800 = 864$
$\therefore$ $800 \neq 864$

Since, the common difference are not same.

So, it does not form an AP.

Question 2 Write first four terms of the AP, when the first term a and the common difference d are given as follows

(i) $a = 10, d = 10$ (ii) $a = -2, d = 0$

(iii) $a = 4, d = -3$ (iv) $a = -1, d = \frac{1}{2}$

(v) $a = -1.25, d = -0.25$

Sol. (i) Given, $a = 10$, $d = 10$

$a_1 = a, a_2 = a + d, a_3 = a + 2d, a_4 = a + 3d$, ... represents an AP.

Now, $a_1 = 10, a_2 = 10 + 10 = 20, a_3 = 10 + 2 \times 10 = 30,$
$a_4 = 10 + 3 \times 10 = 40$

Thus, the first four terms of the AP are 10, 20, 30, 40.

(ii) Given, $a = -2$, $d = 0$

Now, $a_1 = a, a_2 = a + d, a_3 = a + 2d, a_4 = a + 3d$ represent first four terms of an AP.

i.e., $a_1 = -2, a_2 = -2 + 0 = -2, a_3 = -2 + 2(0) = -2, a_4 = -2 + 3(0) = -2$

Thus, the first four terms of the AP are –2, – 2, – 2, – 2.

(iii) Given, $a = 4$, $d = -3$

Now, $a_1 = a, a_2 = a + d, a_3 = a + 2d, a_4 = a + 3d$ represent first four terms of an AP.

i.e., $a_1 = 4, a_2 = 4 - 3 = 1, a_3 = 4 + 2(-3) = 4 - 6 = -2$

and $a_4 = 4 + 3(-3) = 4 - 9 = -5$

Thus, the first four terms of the AP are 4, 1, –2, – 5.

(iv) Given, $a = -1$, $d = \frac{1}{2}$

Now $a_1 = a, a_2 = a + d, a_3 = a + 2d, a_4 = a + 3d$ represent first four terms of an AP.

i.e., $a_1 = -1, a_2 = -1 + \frac{1}{2} = -\frac{1}{2}, a_3 = -1 + 2\left(\frac{1}{2}\right) = 0, a_4 = -1 + 3\left(\frac{1}{2}\right) = \frac{1}{2}$

Thus, the first four terms of the AP are $-1, -\frac{1}{2}, 0, \frac{1}{2}$.

(v) Given, $a = -1.25$, $d = -0.25$

Now, $a_1 = a, a_2 = a + d, a_3 = a + 2d, a_4 = a + 3d$ represent first four terms of an AP.

i.e., $a_1 = -1.25, a_2 = -1.25 - 0.25 = -1.50, a_3 = -1.25 + 2(-0.25)$

$= -1.25 - 0.50$

$= -1.75$

and $a_4 = -1.25 + 3(-0.25)$

$= -1.25 - 0.75$

$= -2.00$

Thus, the first four terms of the AP are – 1.25, – 1.50, – 1.75, – 2.00.

Question 3 For the following APs, write the first term and the common difference

(i) 3, 1, –1, –3,... (ii) – 5, – 1, 3, 7, ...

(iii) $\frac{1}{3}, \frac{5}{3}, \frac{9}{3}, \frac{13}{3}, \ldots$ (iv) 0.6, 1.7, 2.8, 3.9, ...

Sol. (i) First term $a = a_1 = 3$,

Common difference, d = 2nd term – 1st term

$= 1 - 3 = -2$

(ii) First term $a = -5$

Common difference, d = 2nd term – 1st term $= -1 - (-5) = -1 + 5 = 4$

(iii) First term $a = \frac{1}{3}$

Common difference, d = 2nd term – 1st term $= \frac{5}{3} - \frac{1}{3} = \frac{4}{3}$

(iv) First term $a = 0.6$

Common difference, d = 2nd term – 1st term $= 1.7 - 0.6 = 1.1$

Question 4 Which of the following are APs ? If they form an AP, find the common difference d and write three more terms.

(i) 2, 4, 8, 16, ... (ii) $2, \frac{5}{2}, 3, \frac{7}{2}, \ldots$

(iii) – 1.2, – 3.2, – 5.2, – 7.2, ... (iv) – 10, – 6, – 2, 2, ...

(v) $3, 3+\sqrt{2}, 3+2\sqrt{2}, 3+3\sqrt{2}, \ldots$

(vi) 0.2, 0.22, 0.222, 0.2222, ... (vii) 0, – 4, – 8, – 12, ...

(viii) $-\frac{1}{2}, -\frac{1}{2}, -\frac{1}{2}, -\frac{1}{2}, \ldots$ (ix) 1, 3, 9, 27, ...

(x) $a, 2a, 3a, 4a, \ldots$ (xi) $a, a^2, a^3, a^4, \ldots$

(xii) $\sqrt{2}, \sqrt{8}, \sqrt{18}, \sqrt{32}, \ldots$ (xiii) $\sqrt{3}, \sqrt{6}, \sqrt{9}, \sqrt{12}, \ldots$

(xiv) $1^2, 3^2, 5^2, 7^2, \ldots$ (xv) $1^2, 5^2, 7^2, 73, \ldots$

Sol.

(i) Here, $a_1 = 2, a_2 = 4, a_3 = 8, a_4 = 16$

$$a_2 - a_1 = 4 - 2 = 2$$
$$a_3 - a_2 = 8 - 4 = 4$$
$$a_4 - a_3 = 16 - 8 = 8$$

Clearly $\quad a_2 - a_1 \neq a_3 - a_2$

Hence, the given list of numbers does not form an AP, because the common difference is not the same.

(ii) Here, $a_1 = 2, a_2 = \frac{5}{2}, a_3 = 3, a_4 = \frac{7}{2}, ...$

$$a_2 - a_1 = \frac{5}{2} - 2 = \frac{5-4}{2} = \frac{1}{2}$$
$$a_3 - a_2 = 3 - \frac{5}{2} = \frac{6-5}{2} = \frac{1}{2}$$
$$a_4 - a_3 = \frac{7}{2} - 3 = \frac{7-6}{2} = \frac{1}{2}$$

Clearly, the difference of successive terms is constant, therefore list of numbers form an AP. So, common difference, $d = \frac{1}{2}$.

Next three terms of AP are

$$a_5 = a_4 + d = \frac{7}{2} + \frac{1}{2} = \frac{7+1}{2} = \frac{8}{2} = 4$$
$$a_6 = a_5 + d = 4 + \frac{1}{2} = \frac{8+1}{2} = \frac{9}{2} = 4.5$$
$$a_7 = a_6 + d = \frac{9}{2} + \frac{1}{2} = \frac{9+1}{2} = \frac{10}{2} = 5$$

(iii) Here, $a_1 = -1.2, a_2 = -3.2, a_3 = -5.2, a_4 = -7.2$

$$a_2 - a_1 = -3.2 - (-1.2) = -3.2 + 1.2 = -2$$
$$a_3 - a_2 = -5.2 - (-3.2) = -5.2 + 3.2 = -2$$
$$a_4 - a_3 = -7.2 - (-5.2) = -7.2 + 5.2 = -2$$

Clearly, the difference of successive terms is constant, therefore list of numbers form an AP. So, common difference, $d = -2$.

Next three terms of AP are

$$a_5 = a_4 + d = -7.2 + (-2) = -9.2$$
$$a_6 = a_5 + d = -9.2 + (-2) = -11.2$$
$$a_7 = a_6 + d = -11.2 + (-2) = -13.2$$

(iv) $-10, -6, -2, 2, ...$

Here, $\quad a_1 = -10, a_2 = -6, a_3 = -2, a_4 = 2$

$$a_2 - a_1 = -6 - (-10) = -6 + 10 = 4$$
$$a_3 - a_2 = -2 - (-6) = -2 + 6 = 4$$
$$a_4 - a_3 = 2 - (-2) = 2 + 2 = 4$$

Clearly, the difference of successive terms is constant, therefore list of numbers form an AP. So, common difference, $d = 4$.

Next three terms of AP are

$$a_5 = a_4 + d = 2 + 4 = 6$$
$$a_6 = a_5 + d = 6 + 4 = 10$$
$$a_7 = a_6 + d = 10 + 4 = 14$$

(v) $3, 3+\sqrt{2}, 3+2\sqrt{2}, 3+3\sqrt{2}, ...$

Here, $a_1 = 3, a_2 = 3+\sqrt{2}, a_3 = 3+2\sqrt{2}, a_4 = 3+3\sqrt{2}$

$$a_2 - a_1 = 3 + \sqrt{2} - 3 = \sqrt{2}$$
$$a_3 - a_2 = 3 + 2\sqrt{2} - (3+\sqrt{2}) = \sqrt{2}$$
$$a_4 - a_3 = 3 + 3\sqrt{2} - (3+2\sqrt{2}) = \sqrt{2}$$

Clearly, the difference of successive terms is constant, therefore list of numbers form an AP. So, common difference, $d = \sqrt{2}$.

Next three terms of AP are

$$a_5 = a_4 + d = 3 + 3\sqrt{2} + \sqrt{2} = 3 + 4\sqrt{2}$$
$$a_6 = a_5 + d = 3 + 4\sqrt{2} + \sqrt{2} = 3 + 5\sqrt{2}$$
$$a_7 = a_6 + d = 3 + 5\sqrt{2} + \sqrt{2} = 3 + 6\sqrt{2}$$

(vi) 0.2, 0.22, 0.222, 0.2222, ...

Here, $a_1 = 0.2, a_2 = 0.22, a_3 = 0.222, a_4 = 0.2222$

$$a_2 - a_1 = 0.22 - 0.2 = 0.02$$
$$a_3 - a_2 = 0.222 - 0.22 = 0.002$$
$$a_4 - a_3 = 0.2222 - 0.222 = 0.0002$$

Clearly $a_2 - a_1 \neq a_3 - a_2$

Hence, the given list of numbers does not form an AP, because the common difference is not the same.

(vii) 0, – 4, – 8, – 12, ...

Here, $a_1 = 0, a_2 = -4, a_3 = -8, a_4 = -12$

$$a_2 - a_1 = -4 - 0 = -4$$
$$a_3 - a_2 = -8 - (-4) = -8 + 4 = -4$$
$$a_4 - a_3 = -12 - (-8) = -12 + 8 = -4$$

Clearly, the difference of successive terms is constant, therefore list of numbers form an AP. So, common difference, $d = -4$.

Next three terms of AP are

$$a_5 = a_4 + d = -12 + (-4) = -16$$
$$a_6 = a_5 + d = -16 + (-4) = -20$$
$$a_7 = a_6 + d = -20 + (-4) = -24$$

(viii) Here, $a_1 = -\frac{1}{2}, a_2 = -\frac{1}{2}, a_3 = -\frac{1}{2}, a_4 = -\frac{1}{2}$

$$a_2 - a_1 = -\frac{1}{2} - \left(-\frac{1}{2}\right) = -\frac{1}{2} + \frac{1}{2} = 0$$
$$a_3 - a_2 = -\frac{1}{2} - \left(-\frac{1}{2}\right) = -\frac{1}{2} + \frac{1}{2} = 0$$
$$a_4 - a_3 = -\frac{1}{2} - \left(-\frac{1}{2}\right) = -\frac{1}{2} + \frac{1}{2} = 0$$

Clearly, difference of successive terms is constant, therefore list of numbers form an AP. So, common difference, $d = 0$.

Next three terms of AP are

$$a_5 = a_4 + d = -\frac{1}{2} + 0 = -\frac{1}{2}$$

$$a_6 = a_5 + d = -\frac{1}{2} + 0 = -\frac{1}{2}$$

$$a_7 = a_6 + d = -\frac{1}{2} + 0 = -\frac{1}{2}$$

(ix) 1, 3, 9, 27, ...

Here, $a_1 = 1, a_2 = 3, a_3 = 9, a_4 = 27$

$$a_2 - a_1 = 3 - 1 = 2$$

$$a_3 - a_2 = 9 - 3 = 6$$

$$a_4 - a_3 = 27 - 9 = 18$$

Clearly, $a_2 - a_1 \neq a_3 - a_2$

Hence, the given list of numbers does not form an AP, because the common difference is not the same.

(x) $a, 2a, 3a, 4a, ...$

Here, $a_1 = a, a_2 = 2a, a_3 = 3a, a_4 = 4a$

$$a_2 - a_1 = 2a - a = a$$

$$a_3 - a_2 = 3a - 2a = a$$

$$a_4 - a_3 = 4a - 3a = a$$

Clearly, difference of successive terms is constant, therefore list of numbers form an AP. So, common difference, $d = a$.

Next three terms of AP are

$$a_5 = a_4 + d = 4a + a = 5a$$

$$a_6 = a_5 + d = 5a + a = 6a$$

$$a_7 = a_6 + d = 6a + a = 7a$$

(xi) $a, a^2, a^3, a^4, ...$

Here, $a_1 = a, a_2 = a^2, a_3 = a^3, a_4 = a^4$

$$a_2 - a_1 = a^2 - a = a(a-1)$$

$$a_3 - a_2 = a^3 - a^2 = a^2(a-1)$$

$$a_4 - a_3 = a^4 - a^3 = a^3(a-1)$$

Clearly, $a_2 - a_1 \neq a_3 - a_2$

Hence, the given list of numbers does not form an AP, because the common difference is not the same.

(xii) $\sqrt{2}, \sqrt{8}, \sqrt{18}, \sqrt{32}, ...$

Here, $a_1 = \sqrt{2}, a_2 = \sqrt{8} = 2\sqrt{2}, a_3 = \sqrt{18} = 3\sqrt{2}$

$$a_4 = \sqrt{32} = 4\sqrt{2}$$

$$a_2 - a_1 = 2\sqrt{2} - \sqrt{2} = \sqrt{2}$$

$$a_3 - a_2 = 3\sqrt{2} - 2\sqrt{2} = \sqrt{2}$$

$$a_4 - a_3 = 4\sqrt{2} - 3\sqrt{2} = \sqrt{2}$$

Clearly, difference of successive terms is constant, therefore list of numbers form an AP. So, common difference, $d = \sqrt{2}$.

Next three terms of AP are

$$a_5 = a_4 + d = 4\sqrt{2} + \sqrt{2} = 5\sqrt{2} = \sqrt{50}$$
$$a_6 = a_5 + d = 5\sqrt{2} + \sqrt{2} = 6\sqrt{2} = \sqrt{72}$$
$$a_7 = a_6 + d = 6\sqrt{2} + \sqrt{2} = 7\sqrt{2} = \sqrt{98}$$

(xiii) $\sqrt{3}, \sqrt{6}, \sqrt{9}, \sqrt{12}, \ldots$

Here, $a_1 = \sqrt{3}, a_2 = \sqrt{6}, a_3 = \sqrt{9}, a_4 = \sqrt{12}$

$$a_2 - a_1 = \sqrt{6} - \sqrt{3} = \sqrt{3 \times 2} - \sqrt{3} = \sqrt{3}(\sqrt{2} - 1)$$

and $$a_3 - a_2 = \sqrt{9} - \sqrt{6} = 3 - \sqrt{3 \times 2} = \sqrt{3}(\sqrt{3} - \sqrt{2})$$

$$a_4 - a_3 = \sqrt{12} - \sqrt{9}$$
$$= \sqrt{4 \times 3} - \sqrt{9}$$
$$= 2\sqrt{3} - 3$$
$$= \sqrt{3}(2 - \sqrt{3})$$

Clearly, $a_2 - a_1 \neq a_3 - a_2$

Hence, the given list of numbers does not form an AP, because the common difference is not same.

(xiv) $1^2, 3^2, 5^2, 7^2, \ldots$

Here, $a_1 = 1^2 = 1, a_2 = 3^2 = 9,$

$$a_3 = 5^2 = 25, a_4 = 7^2 = 49$$
$$a_2 - a_1 = 9 - 1 = 8$$
$$a_3 - a_2 = 25 - 9 = 16$$
$$a_4 - a_3 = 49 - 25 = 24$$

Clearly, $a_2 - a_1 \neq a_3 - a_2$

Hence, the given list of numbers does not form an AP, because the common difference is not the same.

(xv) $1^2, 5^2, 7^2, 73, \ldots\ldots$

Here, $a_1 = 1^2 = 1, a_2 = 5^2 = 25, a_3 = 7^2 = 49, a_4 = 73$

$$a_2 - a_1 = 25 - 1 = 24$$
$$a_3 - a_2 = 49 - 25 = 24$$
$$a_4 - a_3 = 73 - 49 = 24$$

Clearly, difference of successive terms is constant, therefore list of numbers form an AP. So, common difference, $d = 24$.

Next three terms of AP are

$$a_5 = a_4 + d = 73 + 24 = 97$$
$$a_6 = a_5 + d = 97 + 24 = 121$$
$$a_7 = a_6 + d = 121 + 24 = 145$$

Exercise 5.2

Question 1 Fill in the blanks in the following table, given that a is the first term, d the common difference and a_n the nth term of the AP.

Thinking Process Use the formula of the a_n the nth term of AP that is $a_n = a + (n-1)d$ and determine the unknown values in all points.

	a	d	n	a_n
(i)	7	3	8	...
(ii)	– 18	...	10	0
(iii)	...	–3	18	–5
(iv)	– 18.9	2.5	...	3.6
(v)	3.5	0	105	...

Sol.

(i) The nth term of an AP is $a_n = a + (n-1)d$

$$= 7 + (8-1)3 = 7 + 7 \times 3 = 7 + 21 = 28$$

(ii) The nth term of an AP is $a_n = a + (n-1)d$

$$\Rightarrow \quad 0 = -18 + (10-1)d$$

$$\Rightarrow \quad 18 = 9d \Rightarrow d = \frac{18}{9} = 2$$

(iii) The nth term of an AP is $a_n = a + (n-1)d$

$$\Rightarrow \quad -5 = a + (18-1)(-3)$$

$$\Rightarrow \quad -5 = a + 17(-3) \Rightarrow -5 = a - 51$$

$$\Rightarrow \quad a = -5 + 51 = 46$$

(iv) The nth term of an AP is $a_n = a + (n-1)d$

$$\Rightarrow \quad 3.6 = -18.9 + (n-1)2.5$$

$$3.6 + 18.9 = (n-1)2.5$$

$$\Rightarrow \quad 22.5 = (n-1)2.5$$

$$\Rightarrow \quad n - 1 = \frac{22.5}{2.5} \Rightarrow n - 1 = 9$$

$$\Rightarrow \quad n = 9 + 1 = 10$$

(v) The nth term of an AP is $a_n = a + (n-1)d = 3.5 + (105-1) \times 0$

$$= 3.5 + 0 = 3.5$$

Question 2 Choose the correct choice in the following and justify.

(i) 30th term of the AP 10, 7, 4, ..., is

(a) 97 (b) 77 (c) – 77 (d) – 87

(ii) 11th term of the AP $-3, -\frac{1}{2}, 2, \ldots$ is

(a) 28 (b) 22

(c) – 38 (d) $-48\frac{1}{2}$

Sol.

(i) (c) Here, first term $a = 10$, common difference, $d = 7 - 10 = -3$, number of terms $n = 30$

Since, the nth term of an AP is $a_n = a + (n-1)d$

$$\Rightarrow \quad a_{30} = 10 + (30-1)(-3)$$
$$= 10 + 29(-3) = 10 - 87 = -77$$

Hence, option (c) is correct.

(ii) (b) Here, $a = -3$, $d = -\frac{1}{2} - (-3) = -\frac{1}{2} + 3 = \frac{-1+6}{2} = \frac{5}{2}$, number of terms $n = 11$

Since, the nth term of an AP is

$$a_n = a + (n-1)d$$
$$\therefore \quad a_{11} = -3 + (11-1)\frac{5}{2}$$
$$= -3 + 10 \times \frac{5}{2} = -3 + 25 = 22$$

Hence, option (b) is correct.

Question 3 In the following APs, find the missing terms in the boxes.

(i) 2, □, 26

(ii) □, 13, □, 3

(iii) 5, □, □, $9\frac{1}{2}$

(iv) – 4, □, □, □, □, 6

(v) □, 38, □, □, □, – 22

Sol. (i) Let 2, □, 26 be a, $a + d$ and $a + 2d$, respectively are in AP.

$$\therefore \quad a = 2 \text{ and } a + 2d = 26$$
$$\Rightarrow \quad 2 + 2d = 26 \quad (\because a = 2)$$
$$\Rightarrow \quad 2d = 26 - 2 = 24$$
$$\Rightarrow \quad d = \frac{24}{2} = 12$$

Hence, the missing term $= a + d = 2 + 12 = 14$

(ii) Let □, 13, □, 3 be a, $a + d$, $a + 2d$ and $a + 3d$, respectively are in AP.

$$\therefore \quad a + d = 13 \quad \text{...(i)}$$
$$\text{and} \quad a + 3d = 3 \quad \text{...(ii)}$$

On subtracting Eq. (i) from Eq. (ii), we get

$$2d = -10 \Rightarrow d = -5$$

Put, $d = -5$ in Eq. (ii), we get

$$a + 3(-5) = 3$$
$$a - 15 = 3$$
$$\Rightarrow \quad a = 3 + 15 = 18$$

Hence, the missing term are $a = 18$ and $a + 2d = 18 + 2(-5)$

$$= 18 - 10 = 8$$

(iii) Let 5, □, □, $9\frac{1}{2}$ be a, $a+d$, $a+2d$ and $a+3d$, respectively are in AP.

$\therefore$ $$a = 5 \quad \text{...(i)}$$

and $$a + 3d = 9\frac{1}{2} = \frac{19}{2} \quad \text{...(ii)}$$

On subtracting Eq. (i) from Eq. (ii), we get

$$3d = \frac{19}{2} - 5 = \frac{19-10}{2} = \frac{9}{2}$$

$\Rightarrow$ $$3d = \frac{9}{2}$$

$\Rightarrow$ $$d = \frac{1}{3} \times \frac{9}{2} = \frac{3}{2}$$

Hence, the missing terms are $a + d = 5 + \frac{3}{2} = \frac{10+3}{2} = \frac{13}{2} = 6\frac{1}{2}$

and $$a + 2d = 5 + 2 \times \frac{3}{2} = 5 + 3 = 8$$

(iv) Let – 4, □, □, □, □, 6 be a, $a+d$, $a+2d$, $a+3d$, $a+4d$ and $a+5d$, respectively are in AP.

$\therefore$ $$a = -4 \quad \text{...(i)}$$

and $$a + 5d = 6 \quad \text{...(ii)}$$

On putting $a = -4$ in Eq. (ii), we get

$$-4 + 5d = 6$$

$\Rightarrow$ $$5d = 6 + 4 = 10$$

$\Rightarrow$ $$d = \frac{10}{5} = 2$$

Hence, the missing terms are

$$a + d = -4 + 2 = -2$$

$$a + 2d = -4 + 2 \times 2 = -4 + 4 = 0$$

$$a + 3d = -4 + 3 \times 2 = -4 + 6 = 2$$

and $$a + 4d = -4 + 4 \times 2 = -4 + 8 = 4$$

(v) Let □, 38, □, □, □, – 22 be a, $a+d$, $a+2d$, $a+3d$, $a+4d$ and $a+5d$, respectively are in AP.

$\therefore$ $$a + d = 38 \quad \text{...(i)}$$

and $$a + 5d = -22 \quad \text{...(ii)}$$

On subtracting Eq. (i) from Eq. (ii), we get

$$4d = -60 \Rightarrow d = -\frac{60}{4} = -15$$

On putting $d = -15$ in Eq. (i), we get

$$a + (-15) = 38$$

$\Rightarrow$ $$a - 15 = 38$$

$\Rightarrow$ $$a = 38 + 15 = 53$$

Hence, the missing terms are $a = 53$

$$a + 2d = 53 + 2 \times (-15) = 53 - 30 = 23$$
$$a + 3d = 53 + 3 \times (-15) = 53 - 45 = 8$$

and $$a + 4d = 53 + 4 \times (-15) = 53 - 60 = -7$$

Question 4 Which term of the AP 3, 8, 13, 18, ... is 78 ?

Sol. Let nth term be 78.

Given, 3, 8, 13, 18 .... are in AP.

First term, $a = 3$, common difference, $d = 8 - 3 = 5$

$\because$ nth term $a_n = 78$

$\therefore$ $a + (n-1)d = 78$

$\Rightarrow$ $3 + (n-1)5 = 78$

$\Rightarrow$ $(n-1)5 = 78 - 3$

$\Rightarrow$ $5(n-1) = 75$

$\Rightarrow$ $n - 1 = 15$

$\Rightarrow$ $n = 15 + 1$

$\Rightarrow$ $n = 16$

Hence, 16th term be 78.

Question 5 Find the number of terms in each of the following APs

(i) 7, 13, 19, ..., 205 (ii) $18, 15\frac{1}{2}, 13, \ldots, -47$

Sol.

(i) Suppose, there are n terms in the given AP. Then, nth term $a_n = 205$, first term $a = 7$, common difference $d = 13 - 7 = 6$

$\because$ $a + (n-1)d = a_n$

$\Rightarrow$ $7 + (n-1)6 = 205$

$\Rightarrow$ $6(n-1) = 205 - 7$

$\Rightarrow$ $6(n-1) = 198$

$\Rightarrow$ $n - 1 = \frac{198}{6} = 33$

$\Rightarrow$ $n = 33 + 1 = 34$

Hence, the given AP contains 34 terms.

(ii) Suppose, there are n terms in the given AP.

Given, first term $a = 18$, common difference $d = 15\frac{1}{2} - 18 = \frac{31}{2} - 18$

$$= \frac{31 - 36}{2} = \frac{-5}{2}$$

Then, nth term $a_n = -47$

$\Rightarrow$ $a + (n-1)d = a_n$

$\Rightarrow$ $18 + (n-1)\left(\frac{-5}{2}\right) = -47$

$\Rightarrow \quad \left(\frac{-5}{2}\right)(n-1) = -47 - 18 = -65$

$\Rightarrow \quad (n-1) = -65 \times \frac{-2}{5} = -13 \times -2 = 26$

$\Rightarrow \quad n = 26 + 1 = 27$

Hence, the given AP contains 27 terms.

Question 6 Check whether – 150 is a terms of the AP 11, 8, 5, 2, ...

Sol. Here, $a_1 = 11, a_2 = 8, a_3 = 5, a_4 = 2$

$$a_2 - a_1 = 8 - 11 = -3$$
$$a_3 - a_2 = 5 - 8 = -3$$
$$a_4 - a_3 = 2 - 5 = -3$$

Clearly, the successive difference of terms is constant. So, the list of numbers are in AP. Hence, common difference $d = -3$.

Let –150 be the nth term of the given AP.

We know that, the nth term of an AP is $a_n = a_1 + (n-1)\,d$

$\Rightarrow \quad -150 = 11 + (n-1)(-3)$

$\Rightarrow \quad -3(n-1) = -150 - 11 = -161$

$\Rightarrow \quad n - 1 = \frac{161}{3}$

$\Rightarrow \quad n = \frac{161}{3} + 1 = \frac{164}{3}$

But n should be positive integer. So, our assumption was wrong and so – 150 is not a term of the given AP.

Question 7 Find the 31st term of an AP whose 11th term is 38 and the 16th term is 73.

Sol. Let a be the first term and d the common difference of an AP.

Now, the nth term of an AP is $a_n = a + (n-1)\,d$

$a_{11} = a + 10\,d = 38 \quad [\because a_{11} = 38 \text{ (Given)}] \quad \ldots\text{(i)}$

and $a_{16} = a + 15\,d = 73 \quad [\because a_{16} = 73 \text{ (Given)}] \quad \ldots\text{(ii)}$

On subtracting Eq. (i) from Eq. (ii), we get

$$5d = 35 \Rightarrow d = \frac{35}{5} = 7$$

From Eq. (i), $a + 10 \times 7 = 38$

$\Rightarrow \quad a = 38 - 70 = -32$

$\therefore$ The 31st term of an AP $a_{31} = a + 30\,d$

$= -32 + 30 \times 7$

$= -32 + 210 = 178$

Hence, 31st term of an AP is 178.

Question 8 An AP consists of 50 terms of which 3rd term is 12 and the last term is 106. Find the 29th term.

Sol Let a be the first term and d the common difference.

Now, the nth term of an AP, $a_n = a + (n-1)d$

$\therefore$ $a_3 = a + 2d = 12$ $[\because a_3 = 12 \text{ (Given)}]$ ...(i)

and $a_{50} = a + 49d = 106$ $[\because a_{50} = 106 \text{ (Given)}]$ ...(ii)

On subtracting Eq. (i) from Eq. (ii), we get

$$47d = 94$$

$\Rightarrow$ $$d = \frac{94}{47} = 2$$

From Eq. (i) $a + 2 \times 2 = 12$

$\Rightarrow$ $a = 12 - 4 = 8$

$\therefore$ The 29th term of an AP $a_{29} = a + (29-1)d$

$$= 8 + 28 \times 2$$

$$= 8 + 56 = 64$$

Hence, 29th term of an AP is 64.

Question 9 If the 3rd and 9th terms of an AP are 4 and -8. respectively, which term of this AP is zero?

Sol Let a be the first term and d the common difference of an AP.

$\because$ The n th term of an AP is

$$a_n = a + (n-1)d$$

$\therefore$ $a_3 = a + 2d = 4$ $[\because a_3 = 4 \text{ (Given)}]$ ...(i)

and $a_9 = a + 8d = -8$ $[\because a_9 = -8 \text{ (Given)}]$ ...(ii)

On subtracting Eq. (i) from Eq. (ii), we get

$$6d = -12 \Rightarrow d = \frac{-12}{6} = -2$$

From Eq. (i), $a + 2 \times (-2) = 4$

$\Rightarrow$ $a - 4 = 4 \Rightarrow a = 4 + 4 = 8$

Let the nth term of an AP is zero.

Then, $a_n = 0 \Rightarrow a + (n-1)d = 0$

$\Rightarrow$ $8 + (n-1)(-2) = 0$

$\Rightarrow$ $(n-1)(-2) = -8$

$\Rightarrow$ $$n - 1 = \frac{-8}{-2} = 4$$

$\Rightarrow$ $n = 4 + 1 = 5$

Hence, 5th term of an AP is zero.

Question 10 The 17th term of an AP exceeds its 10th term by 7. Find the common difference.

Sol. Let a be the first term and d the common difference of an AP.

Given, $a_{17} - a_{10} = 7$

$\Rightarrow$ $(a + 16d) - (a + 9d) = 7$ $[\because a_n = a + (n-1)d]$

$\Rightarrow$ $7d = 7 \Rightarrow d = 1$

Hence, the common difference of an AP is 1.

Question 11 Which term of the AP 3, 15, 27, 39, ... will be 132 more than its 54th term?

Sol. Here, first term $a = 3$, common difference $d = 15 - 3 = 12$

Then, $a_{54} = a + 53\,d = 3 + 53 \times 12$ $[\because a_n = a + (n-1)d]$

$= 3 + 636 = 639$

Let a_n be 132 more than its 54th term.

Then, $a_n = a_{54} + 132$ (By given condition)

$\Rightarrow$ $a_n = 639 + 132$

$\Rightarrow$ $a_n = 771$

$\Rightarrow$ $a + (n-1)\,d = 771$ $[\because a_n = a + (n-1)d]$

$\Rightarrow$ $3 + (n-1)\,12 = 771$

$\Rightarrow$ $12\,(n-1) = 771 - 3$

$\Rightarrow$ $12\,(n-1) = 768$

$\Rightarrow$ $n - 1 = \dfrac{768}{12} = 64$

$\Rightarrow$ $n = 65$

Hence, 65th term is 132 more than its 54th term of an AP.

Question 12 Two APs have the same common difference. The difference between their 100th terms is 100, what is the difference between their 1000th terms?

Sol. Let the two APs be $a_1, a_2, a_3, \ldots.. a_n$ and $b_1, b_2, b_3, \ldots. b_n$

Also, let d be the same common difference of two APs, then

the nth term of first AP $a_n = a_1 + (n-1)\,d$

and the nth term of second AP $b_n = b_1 + (n-1)\,d$

Now, $a_n - b_n = [a_1 + (n-1)\,d] - [b_1 + (n-1)\,d]$

$\Rightarrow$ $a_n - b_n = a_1 - b_1 \ \forall\, n \in N$

$\Rightarrow$ $a_{100} - b_{100} = a_1 - b_1 = 100$ (Given)

$\therefore$ $a_{1000} - b_{1000} = a_1 - b_1$

$\Rightarrow$ $a_{1000} - b_{1000} = 100$ $[\because a_1 - b_1 = 100]$

Hence, the difference between their 1000th terms is also 100 for all $n \in N$.

Question 13 How many three digit numbers are divisible by 7?

Sol. We know that, 105 is the first and 994 is the last 3 digit number divisible by 7. Thus, we have to determine the number of terms in the list 105, 112, 119, ... ,994.

Clearly, the successive difference of terms is constant with common difference

$$d = 112 - 105 = 7$$

So, it forms an AP.

Let there be n terms in the AP, then nth term = 994

$$\because \quad a_n = a + (n-1)d$$

$$\Rightarrow \quad 105 + (n-1)\,7 = 994$$

$$\Rightarrow \quad 7\,(n-1) = 994 - 105$$

$$\Rightarrow \quad 7\,(n-1) = 889$$

$$\Rightarrow \quad n - 1 = \frac{889}{7} = 127$$

$$\Rightarrow \quad n = 127 + 1 = 128$$

So, there are 128 numbers of three digit which are divisible by 7.

Question 14 How many multiples of 4 lie between 10 and 250?

Sol. We see that 12 is the first integer between 10 and 250, which is a multiple of 4. Also, when we divide 250 by 4, the remainder is 2. Therefore, 250 – 2 = 248 is the greatest integer divisible by 4 and lying between 10 and 250. Thus, we have to find the number of terms in an AP whose first term = 12, last term = 248 and common difference = 4.

Let the n term of the AP, is

$$a_n = 248$$

$$\Rightarrow \quad 12 + (n-1)\,4 = 248 \qquad [\because a_n = a + (n-1)\,d]$$

$$\Rightarrow \quad 4\,(n-1) = 248 - 12$$

$$\Rightarrow \quad 4\,(n-1) = 236$$

$$\Rightarrow \quad n - 1 = \frac{236}{4} = 59$$

$$\Rightarrow \quad n = 59 + 1 = 60$$

Hence, there are 60 multiples of 4 lie between 10 and 250.

Question 15 For what value of n, are the nth terms of the AP's 63, 65, 67, ... and 3, 10, 17, ... are equal?

Sol. Given, nth terms of the AP's 63, 65, 67, ... and 3, 10, 17, ... are equal.

Here, first term of first AP $(a_1) = 63$

Common difference of first AP $(d_1) = 65 - 63 = 2$

and first term of second AP $(b_1) = 3$

Common difference of second AP $(d_2) = 10 - 3 = 7$

Then, by condition nth term of both AP's are equal.

$\therefore \quad 63 + (n-1)\,2 = 3 + (n-1)\,7 \qquad [\because a_n = a + (n-1)\,d]$

$\Rightarrow \quad 7\,(n-1) - 2\,(n-1) = 63 - 3$

$\Rightarrow \quad (n-1)(7-2) = 60 \Rightarrow 5\,(n-1) = 60$

$\Rightarrow \quad (n-1) = \dfrac{60}{5} = 12$

$\Rightarrow \quad n = 12 + 1 = 13$

Hence, the 13th terms of the two given AP's are same.

Question 16 Determine the AP whose third term is 16 and the 7th term exceeds the 5th term by 12.

Sol. Let a be the first term and d be the common difference of an AP.

Given that, the third term of the AP, $a_3 = 16$

$\Rightarrow \quad a + 2d = 16 \qquad [\because a_n = a + (n-1)\,d] \quad \ldots(\text{i})$

and 7th term of an AP = 12 + 5th term of an AP

$\therefore \quad a_7 = 12 + a_5$

$\Rightarrow \quad a_7 - a_5 = 12$

$\Rightarrow \quad (a + 6d) - (a + 4d) = 12 \Rightarrow 2d = 12$

$\Rightarrow \quad d = 6 \qquad \ldots(\text{ii})$

On putting $d = 6$ in Eq. (i), we get

$a + 2 \times 6 = 16$

$\Rightarrow \quad a = 16 - 12 = 4$

Since, the terms of an AP in the form $a, a + d, a + 2d, a + 3d, \ldots$

Then, the AP is $4, 4 + 6, 4 + 2 \times 6, 4 + 3 \times 6, \ldots$

i.e., 4, 10, 16, 22, ...

Question 17 Find the 20th term from the last term of the AP 3, 8, 13, ... 253.

Sol. Given, l = last term = 253

and common difference, $d = 8 - 3 = 5$

$\therefore$ 20th term from the end $= l - (20-1)\,d = l - 19\,d = 253 - 19 \times 5$

$[\because a_n = l - (n-1)d]$

$= 253 - 95 = 158$

Hence, the 20th term from the last is 158.

Question 18. The sum of the 4th and 8th terms of an AP is 24 and the sum of the 6th and 10th terms is 44. Find the first three terms of the AP.

Sol. Let a be the first term and d the common difference of an AP.

Given, $\quad a_4 + a_8 = 24 \qquad$ (By condition)

$\Rightarrow \quad (a + 3d) + (a + 7d) = 24 \qquad [\because a_n = a + (n-1)\,d]$

$\Rightarrow \quad 2a + 10d = 24$

$\Rightarrow \quad a + 5d = 12 \qquad \ldots(\text{i})$

and $a_6 + a_{10} = 44$ (By condition)

$\Rightarrow (a + 5d) + (a + 9d) = 44$

$\Rightarrow 2a + 14d = 44$

$\Rightarrow a + 7d = 22$ ...(ii)

On subtracting Eq. (i) from Eq. (ii), we get

$$2d = 10 \Rightarrow d = 5$$

$\therefore$ From Eq. (i), we get $a + 5 \times 5 = 12$

$\Rightarrow a + 25 = 12$

$\Rightarrow a = -13$

Hence, the first three terms are

$$a_1 = a = -13$$

$$a_2 = a + d = -13 + 5 = -8$$

$$a_3 = a + 2d = -13 + 2 \times 5 = -3$$

Question 19 Subba Rao started work in 1995 at an annual salary of ₹ 5000 and received an increment of ₹ 200 each year. In which year did his income reach ₹ 7000 ?

Sol. The annual salary received by Subba Rao in the years 1995, 1996, 1997 etc., is ₹ 5000, ₹ 5200, ₹ 5400, ..., ₹ 7000

Hence, the list of numbers 5000, 5200, 5400, ..., 7000 forms an AP

$\because a_2 - a_1 = a_3 - a_2 = 200$

Then, the nth term of the AP is $a_n = 7000$

$\Rightarrow 7000 = a + (n - 1) d$ $[\because a_n = a + (n - 1) d]$

$\Rightarrow 7000 = 5000 + (n - 1)(200)$

$\Rightarrow 200 (n - 1) = 7000 - 5000 = 2000$

$\Rightarrow n - 1 = \frac{2000}{200} = 10 \Rightarrow n = 10 + 1 = 11$

Thus, in 11th year of his service or in 2005, Subba Rao received an annual salary of ₹ 7000.

Question 20 Ramkali saves ₹ 5 in the first week of a year and then increased her weekly savings by ₹ 1.75. If in the *n*th week, her weekly saving becomes ₹ 20.75. Find *n*.

Sol. Ramkali's savings in the subsequent weeks are respectively ₹ 5, ₹ 5 + ₹ 1.75, ₹ 5 + 2 × ₹ 1.75, ₹ 5 + 3 × ₹ 1.75, ...

In the *n*th week, her savings become, a_n = ₹ 20.75

$\Rightarrow 5 + (n - 1) \times 1.75 = 20.75$

$[\because a_n = a + (n - 1)d$ and $d = 5 + 1.75 - 5 = 1.75]$

$\Rightarrow (n - 1) \times 1.75 = 20.75 - 5 = 15.75$

$\Rightarrow n - 1 = \frac{15.75}{1.75} = 9$

$\Rightarrow n = 9 + 1 = 10$

Hence, the required number of weeks for Ramkali's savings to be ₹ 20.75 is 10.

Exercise 5.3

Question 1 Find the sum of the following AP's

(i) 2, 7, 12, ..., to 10 terms

(ii) $-37, -33, -29, \ldots$, to 12 terms

(iii) 0.6, 1.7, 2.8, ... to 100 terms

(iv) $\frac{1}{15}, \frac{1}{12}, \frac{1}{10}, \ldots$, to 11 terms

◎ ***Thinking Process*** To find the sum of the following AP's series use formula $S_n = \frac{n}{2}[2a + (n-1)d]$.

Sol.

(i) Let a be the first term and d be the common difference of the given AP.

Then, we have $a = 2$ and $d = 7 - 2 = 5$ and $n = 10$

Since, sum of n terms of an AP, $S_n = \frac{n}{2}[2a + (n - 1)\, d]$

Putting $a = 2$, $d = 5$, $n = 10$, we get

$$S_{10} = \frac{10}{2}[2 \times 2 + (10 - 1)\, 5] = 5\,(4 + 9 \times 5)$$
$$= 5\,(4 + 45) = 5 \times 49 = 245$$

(ii) Let a be the first term and d be the common difference of the given AP.

Then, we have $a = -37$, $d = -33 - (-37) = -33 + 37 = 4$ and $n = 12$

Since, Sum of n terms of an AP, $S_n = \frac{n}{2}[2a + (n - 1)\, d]$, we get

$$S_{12} = \frac{12}{2}[2 \times (-37) + (12 - 1)\, 4]$$
$$= 6\,(-74 + 11 \times 4)$$
$$= 6\,(-74 + 44)$$
$$= 6 \times (-30) = -180$$

(iii) Let a be the first term and d be the common difference of the given AP.

Then, we have $a = 0.6$, $d = 1.7 - 0.6 = 1.1$ and $n = 100$

Since, Sum of n terms of an AP, $S_n = \frac{n}{2}[2a + (n - 1)\, d]$, we get

$$S_{100} = \frac{100}{2}[2 \times 0.6 + (100 - 1)\, 1.1]$$
$$= 50\,(1.2 + 99 \times 1.1)$$
$$= 50\,(1.2 + 108.9) = 50 \times 110.1 = 5505$$

(iv) Let a be the first term and d be the common difference of the given AP.

Then, we have $a = \frac{1}{15}$, $d = \frac{1}{12} - \frac{1}{15} = \frac{5 - 4}{60} = \frac{1}{60}$

Putting, $a = \frac{1}{15}$, $d = \frac{1}{60}$, $n = 11$ in $S_n = \frac{n}{2}[2a + (n - 1)\, d]$, we get

Sum of 11 terms of an AP, $S_{11} = \frac{11}{2}\left[2 \times \frac{1}{15} + (11-1)\frac{1}{60}\right]$

$$= \frac{11}{2}\left(\frac{2}{15} + 10 \times \frac{1}{60}\right)$$

$$= \frac{11}{2}\left(\frac{2}{15} + \frac{1}{6}\right)$$

$$= \frac{11}{2} \times \frac{4+5}{30} = \frac{11}{2} \times \frac{9}{30} = \frac{33}{20}$$

Question 2 Find the sums given below

(i) $7 + 10\frac{1}{2} + 14 + \ldots + 84$ (ii) $34 + 32 + 30 + \ldots + 10$

(iii) $-5 + (-8) + (-11) + \ldots + (-230)$

Sol.

(i) $7 + 10\frac{1}{2} + 14 + \ldots + 84$

Since, the last term is given.

Here, first term $a = 7$, common difference $d = 10\frac{1}{2} - 7 = 3\frac{1}{2} = \frac{7}{2}$

and last term $l = a_n = 84$

$\therefore$ $84 = a + (n-1)\,d$ $[\because a_n = a + (n-1)\,d]$

$\Rightarrow$ $84 = 7 + (n-1)\frac{7}{2}$

$\Rightarrow$ $\frac{7}{2}(n-1) = 84 - 7$

$\Rightarrow$ $\frac{7}{2}(n-1) = 77$

$\Rightarrow$ $n - 1 = 77 \times \frac{2}{7}$

$\Rightarrow$ $n - 1 = 22$

$\Rightarrow$ $n = 23$

$\because$ Sum of n terms of an AP, $S_n = \frac{n}{2}(a + l)$

$\Rightarrow$ $S_{23} = \frac{23}{2}(7 + 84)$

$$= \frac{23}{2} \times 91 = \frac{2093}{2} = 1046\frac{1}{2}$$

(ii) $34 + 32 + 30 + \ldots + 10$

Since, the last term is given.

Here, first term $a = 34$, common difference $d = 32 - 34 = -2$,

last term $l = a_n = 10$

$\therefore$ $10 = a + (n-1)\,d$ $[\because a_n = a + (n-1)\,d]$

$\Rightarrow$ $10 = 34 + (n-1)(-2)$

$\Rightarrow$ $(-2)(n-1) = 10 - 34$

$\Rightarrow \quad (-2)(n-1) = -24$

$\Rightarrow \quad n-1 = 12$

$\Rightarrow \quad n = 12 + 1 = 13$

By sum of n terms of an AP, $S_n = \frac{n}{2}(a + l)$, we get

$$\Rightarrow \quad S_{13} = \frac{13}{2}(34 + 10)$$

$$= \frac{13}{2} \times 44 = 13 \times 22 = 286$$

(iii) $-5 + (-8) + (-11) + \dots + (-230)$

Since, the last term is given.

Here, first term $a = -5$, common difference $d = -8 - (-5)$ $= -8 + 5 = -3$, last term $l = a_n = -230$

$\therefore \quad -230 = a + (n-1)d \qquad [\because a_n = a + (n-1)d]$

$\Rightarrow \quad -230 = -5 + (n-1)(-3)$

$\Rightarrow \quad (-3)(n-1) = -230 + 5$

$\Rightarrow \quad (-3)(n-1) = -225$

$\Rightarrow \quad n - 1 = \frac{-225}{-3}$

$\Rightarrow \quad n - 1 = 75 \Rightarrow n = 75 + 1 = 76$

$\therefore$ By sum of n terms of an AP, $S_n = \frac{n}{2}(a + l)$, we get

$$\Rightarrow \quad S_{76} = \frac{76}{2}(-5 - 230) = 38 \times -235 = -8930$$

Question 3 In an AP

(i) given $a = 5, d = 3, a_n = 50$, find n and S_n.

(ii) given $a = 7, a_{13} = 35$, find d and S_{13}.

(iii) given $a_{12} = 37, d = 3$, find a and S_{12}.

(iv) given $a_3 = 15, S_{10} = 125$, find d and a_{10}.

(v) given $d = 5, S_9 = 75$, find a and a_9.

(vi) given $a = 2, d = 8, S_n = 90$, find n and a_5.

(vii) given $a = 8, a_n = 62, S_n = 210$, find n and d.

(viii) given $a_n = 4, d = 2, S_n = -14$, find n and a.

(ix) given $a = 3, n = 8, S = 192$, find d.

(x) given $l = 28, S = 144$, and there are total 9 terms, find a.

Sol. (i) Here, $a = 5$, $d = 3$ and $a_n = 50$

$\Rightarrow \quad a + (n-1)d = 50 \qquad [\because a_n = a + (n-1)d]$

$\Rightarrow \quad 5 + (n-1)3 = 50$

$$\Rightarrow \quad (n-1) = \frac{45}{3} = 15$$

$$\Rightarrow \quad n = 15 + 1 = 16$$

On putting, $n = 16$, $a = 5$ and $l = a_n = 50$ in $S_n = \frac{n}{2}(a + l)$, we get

$$S_{16} = \frac{16}{2}(5 + 50)$$

$$= 8 \times 55 = 440$$

Hence, $n = 16$ and $S_{16} = 440$

(ii) Here, $a = 7$ and $a_{13} = 35$

Let d be the common difference of the given AP.

Then, $a_{13} = 35 \Rightarrow a + 12d = 35$ $\quad [\because a_n = a + (n-1)d]$

$\Rightarrow \quad 7 + 12d = 35$ $\quad (\because a = 7)$

$\Rightarrow \quad 12d = 35 - 7 = 28$

$\Rightarrow \quad d = \frac{28}{12} = \frac{7}{3}$

On putting, $n = 13$, $a = 7$ and $l = a_{13} = 35$ in $S_n = \frac{n}{2}(a + l)$, we get

$$S_{13} = \frac{13}{2}(7 + 35) = \frac{13}{2} \times 42$$

$$= 13 \times 21 = 273$$

Hence, $d = \frac{7}{3}$ and $S_{13} = 273$

(iii) Here, $a_{12} = 37$, $d = 3$

Let a be the first term of given AP, then

$$a_{12} = 37$$

$\Rightarrow \quad a + 11d = 37$ $\quad [\because a_n = a + (n-1)d]$

$\Rightarrow \quad a + 11(3) = 37$ $\quad (\because d = 3)$

$\Rightarrow \quad a = 37 - 33 = 4$

On putting, $n = 12$, $a = 4$ and $l = a_{12} = 37$ in $S_n = \frac{n}{2}(a + l)$, we get

$$S_{12} = \frac{12}{2}(4 + 37) = 6 \times 41 = 246$$

Hence, $a = 4$

and $S_{12} = 246$

(iv) Here, $a_3 = 15$, $S_{10} = 125$

Let a be the first term and d be the common difference of the given AP.

Then,

$a + 2d = 15$ $\quad [\because a_n = a + (n-1)d]$ ...(i)

and $\frac{10}{2}[2a + (10-1)d] = 125$ $\quad \left[\because S_n = \frac{n}{2}[2a + (n-1)d\right]$

$$\Rightarrow \quad 5(2a + 9d) = 125$$

$$\Rightarrow \quad 2a + 9d = 25 \qquad \text{...(ii)}$$

On multiplying Eq. (i) by 2 and subtracting from Eq. (ii), we get

$$2(a + 2d) - (2a + 9d) = 2 \times 15 - 25$$

$$\Rightarrow \quad 4d - 9d = 30 - 25$$

$$\Rightarrow \quad -5d = 5$$

$$\Rightarrow \quad d = -\frac{5}{5} = -1$$

$$\therefore \quad a_{10} = a + 9d = (a + 2d) + 7d$$

$$= 15 + 7(-1) \qquad \text{[From Eq. (i)]}$$

$$= 15 - 7 = 8$$

Hence, $d = -1, a_{10} = 8$

(v) Here, $d = 5$, $S_9 = 75$

Let a be the first term of the given AP. Then,

$$\frac{9}{2}[2a + (9 - 1)5] = 75 \qquad \left[\because S_n = \frac{n}{2}[2a + (n - 1)d]\right]$$

$$\Rightarrow \quad \frac{9}{2}(2a + 40) = 75$$

$$\Rightarrow \quad 9a + 180 = 75 \Rightarrow 9a = 75 - 180$$

$$\Rightarrow \quad 9a = -105$$

$$\Rightarrow \quad a = \frac{-105}{9} = \frac{-35}{3}$$

So, $a_9 = a + 8d$

$$= \frac{-35}{3} + 8 \times 5 \qquad [\because a_n = a + (n - 1)d]$$

$$= \frac{-35 + 120}{3} = \frac{85}{3}$$

Hence, $a = \frac{-35}{3}$ and $a_9 = \frac{85}{3}$

(vi) Here, first term $a = 2$, common difference $d = 8$, sum of n terms $S_n = 90$

$$S_n = 90$$

$$\Rightarrow \quad \frac{n}{2}[2 \times 2 + (n - 1)8] = 90 \qquad \left[\because S_n = \frac{n}{2}[2a + (n - 1)d]\right]$$

$$\Rightarrow \quad \frac{n}{2}(4 + 8n - 8) = 90$$

$$\Rightarrow \quad \frac{n}{2}(8n - 4) = 90$$

$$\Rightarrow \quad n(4n - 2) = 90$$

$$\Rightarrow \quad 4n^2 - 2n - 90 = 0$$

$\therefore \quad n = \dfrac{-(-2) \pm \sqrt{(-2)^2 - 4 \times 4 \times (-90)}}{2 \times 4}$

$\left(\because \text{By quadratic formula } x = \dfrac{-b \pm \sqrt{b^2 - 4ac}}{2a}\right)$

$= \dfrac{2 \pm \sqrt{4 + 1440}}{8} = \dfrac{2 \pm \sqrt{1444}}{8}$

$= \dfrac{2 \pm 38}{8} = \dfrac{40}{8}, \dfrac{-36}{8} = 5, \dfrac{-9}{2}$

Since, n cannot be negative.

$\therefore \quad n = 5$

$\because \quad a_n = a + (n-1)d$

$\therefore \quad a_5 = 2 + (5-1)8 = 2 + 32 = 34$

Hence, $\quad n = 5$ and $a_5 = 34$

Quick Solution

To find the value of n, $4n^2 - 2n - 90 = 0$

$\Rightarrow \quad 2n^2 - n - 45 = 0$

$\Rightarrow \quad 2n^2 - 10n + 9n - 45 = 0$

$\Rightarrow \quad 2n(n-5) + 9(n-5) = 0$

$\Rightarrow \quad (2n+9)(n-5) = 0$

$\Rightarrow \quad n = \dfrac{-9}{2}$ or 5

(vii) Here, $a = 8$, $l = a_n = 62$, $S_n = 210$

Let d be the common difference of the given AP.

Since, $\quad S_n = 210$

$\therefore \quad \dfrac{n}{2}(a + l) = 210 \qquad \left[\because S_n = \dfrac{n}{2}(a + l)\right]$

$\Rightarrow \quad \dfrac{n}{2}(8 + 62) = 210 \qquad (\because a = 8, l = a_n = 62)$

$\Rightarrow \quad \dfrac{n}{2} \times 70 = 210$

$\Rightarrow \quad n = 210 \times \dfrac{2}{70} = 3 \times 2 = 6$

and $\quad a_n = 62 \Rightarrow a_6 = 62$

$\Rightarrow \quad a + 5d = 62 \qquad [\because a_n = a + (n-1)d]$

$\Rightarrow \quad 8 + 5d = 62 \qquad (\because a = 8)$

$\Rightarrow \quad 5d = 62 - 8 = 54$

$\Rightarrow \quad d = \dfrac{54}{5}$

Hence, $\quad d = \dfrac{54}{5}$ and $n = 6$

(viii) Here, $l = a_n = 4$, $d = 2$, $S_n = -14$

Let a be the first term of the given AP. Then,

$$a_n = 4$$

$\Rightarrow$ $a + (n-1)2 = 4$ $(\because d = 2)$ $[\because a_n = a + (n-1)d]$

$\Rightarrow$ $a = 4 - 2(n-1)$ ...(i)

and $S_n = -14$

$\Rightarrow$ $\frac{n}{2}(a + l) = -14$ $\left[\because S_n = \frac{n}{2}(a + l)\right]$

$\Rightarrow$ $n(a + 4) = -28$ $(\because l = a_n)$

$\Rightarrow$ $n[4 - 2(n-1) + 4] = -28$ [From Eq. (i)]

$\Rightarrow$ $n(4 - 2n + 2 + 4) = -28$

$\Rightarrow$ $n(-2n + 10) = -28$

$\Rightarrow$ $n(-n + 5) = -14$

$\Rightarrow$ $-n^2 + 5n = -14$

$\Rightarrow$ $n^2 - 5n - 14 = 0$

$\Rightarrow$ $n^2 - 7n + 2n - 14 = 0$ (By factorisation method)

$\Rightarrow$ $n(n-7) + 2(n-7) = 0$

$\Rightarrow$ $(n-7)(n+2) = 0$

$\Rightarrow$ $n = 7$ or $n = -2$

Since, n cannot be negative.

$\therefore$ $n = 7$

Putting $n = 7$ in Eq. (i), we get

$$a = 4 - 2(7-1) = 4 - 2 \times 6$$

$$= 4 - 12 = -8$$

Hence, $n = 7$ and $a = -8$

(ix) Here, $a = 3$, $n = 8$, $S_n = 192$

Let d be the common difference of the given AP.

$\because$ $S_n = \frac{n}{2}[2a + (n-1)d]$

$\therefore$ $192 = \frac{8}{2}[2 \times 3 + (8-1)d]$

$\Rightarrow$ $192 = 4(6 + 7d)$

$\Rightarrow$ $48 = 6 + 7d$

$\Rightarrow$ $7d = 48 - 6 = 42$

$\Rightarrow$ $d = \frac{42}{7} = 6$

Hence, $d = 6$

(x) Here, last term $l = 28$, sum of n terms $S_n = 144$, total number of terms $n = 9$

Let a be the first term of given AP.

$$\because \quad S_n = 144$$

$$\therefore \quad \frac{n}{2}(a + l) = 144 \qquad \left[\because S_n = \frac{n}{2}(a + l)\right]$$

$$\Rightarrow \quad \frac{9}{2}(a + 28) = 144$$

$$\Rightarrow \quad a + 28 = 144 \times \frac{2}{9}$$

$$\Rightarrow \quad a + 28 = 32$$

$$\Rightarrow \quad a = 32 - 28 = 4$$

Hence, $a = 4$

Question 4 How many term of the AP 9, 17, 25 ... must be taken to give a sum of 636?

Sol. Let a, d and n are first term, common difference and number of terms of the A.P., respectively.

$\therefore \quad a = 9$ and $d = 17 - 9 = 8$

$$\because \quad S_n = 636$$

$$\therefore \quad \frac{n}{2}[2a + (n - 1)d] = 636$$

$$\Rightarrow \quad \frac{n}{2}[2 \times 9 + (n - 1) 8] = 636$$

$$\Rightarrow \quad \frac{n}{2}(18 + 8n - 8) = 636$$

$$\Rightarrow \quad \frac{n}{2}(8n + 10) = 636$$

$$\Rightarrow \quad n(4n + 5) = 636$$

$$\Rightarrow \quad 4n^2 + 5n - 636 = 0$$

$$\therefore \quad n = \frac{-5 \pm \sqrt{(5)^2 - 4 \times 4 \times (-636)}}{2(4)}$$

$$\left(\text{By quadratic formula, } x = \frac{-b \pm \sqrt{b^2 - 4ac}}{2a}\right)$$

$$= \frac{-5 \pm \sqrt{25 + 10176}}{8}$$

$$= \frac{-5 \pm \sqrt{10201}}{8} = \frac{-5 \pm 101}{8}$$

$$= \frac{96}{8}, \frac{-106}{8} = 12, \frac{-53}{4}$$

Since, n cannot be negative.

$\therefore$ $$n = 12$$

Hence, the sum of 12 terms is 636.

Note Sometimes n has two values and both are positive. Both the answer are valid. This is possible when a is positive and d is negative.

Question 5. The first term of an AP is 5, the last term is 45 and the sum is 400. Find the number of terms and the common difference.

Sol. Let a be the first term and d be the common difference of an AP.

Given, first term $a = 5$, last term $l = 45$ and sum of n terms $S_n = 400$

$\because$ $$S_n = \frac{n}{2}(a + l)$$

$\Rightarrow$ $$400 = \frac{n}{2}(5 + 45)$$

$\Rightarrow$ $$400 \times 2 = 50n$$

$\Rightarrow$ $$n = \frac{400 \times 2}{50} = 8 \times 2 = 16$$

and $$l = 45$$

$\Rightarrow$ $$5 + (16 - 1)d = 45 \qquad [\because l = a_n = a + (n-1)d]$$

$\Rightarrow$ $$15d = 45 - 5 = 40$$

$\Rightarrow$ $$d = \frac{40}{15} = \frac{8}{3}$$

$\therefore$ The number of terms is 16 and the common difference is $\frac{8}{3}$.

Question 6 The first and the last terms of an AP are 17 and 350, respectively. If the common difference is 9, how many terms are there and what is their sum?

Sol. Let a be the first term and d be the common difference.

Given, first term $a = 17$, last term $l = a_n = 350$, common difference $d = 9$

$\because$ $$l = a_n = 350$$

$\Rightarrow$ $$17 + (n-1)9 = 350 \qquad [\because l = a_n = a + (n-1)d]$$

$\Rightarrow$ $$9(n-1) = 350 - 17 = 333$$

$\Rightarrow$ $$n - 1 = \frac{333}{9} = 37$$

$\Rightarrow$ $$n = 37 + 1 = 38$$

Putting $a = 17$, $l = 350$, $n = 38$

$\because$ Sum of n terms, $S_n = \frac{n}{2}(a + l)$, we get

$\Rightarrow$ $$S_{38} = \frac{38}{2}(17 + 350) = 19(367) = 6973$$

So, there are 38 terms in the AP having their sum as 6973.

Question 7 Find the sum of first 22 terms of an AP in which $d = 7$ and 22nd term is 149.

Sol. Let a be the first term and d the common difference of the given AP. Then, $d = 7$ and $a_{22} = 149$

$\Rightarrow \quad a + (22 - 1)\, d = 149 \quad [\because a_n = a + (n-1)\, d]$

$\Rightarrow \quad a + 21 \times 7 = 149$

$\Rightarrow \quad a = 149 - 147 = 2$

Put $a = 2$, $n = 22$ and $d = 7$ in

Sum of n terms, $S_n = \frac{n}{2}[2a + (n-1)\, d]$, we get

$$S_{22} = \frac{22}{2}[2 \times 2 + (22 - 1)\, 7] = 11\,(4 + 21 \times 7)$$

$$= 11\,(4 + 147) = 11 \times 151 = 1661$$

Hence, the sum of first 22 terms is 1661.

Question 8 Find the sum of first 51 terms of an AP whose second and third terms are 14 and 18, respectively.

Sol. Let a be the first term and d be the common difference of the given AP.
Given that, second term $a_2 = 14$ and third term $a_3 = 18$

$\Rightarrow \quad a + d = 14 \quad [\because a_n = a + (n-1)\, d] \quad \ldots(i)$

and $\quad a + 2d = 18 \quad \ldots(ii)$

On subtracting Eq. (i) from Eq. (ii), we get

$$d = 4$$

Put $d = 4$ in Eq. (i), we get

$$a + 4 = 14$$

$\Rightarrow \quad a = 14 - 4 = 10$

$\because \quad$ Sum of n terms, $S_n = \frac{n}{2}[2a + (n-1)\, d]$, we get

$\therefore \quad S_{51} = \frac{51}{2}[2 \times 10 + (51 - 1) \times 4]$

$$= \frac{51}{2}[20 + 50 \times 4]$$

$$= \frac{51}{2}(20 + 200)$$

$$= \frac{51}{2} \times 220$$

$$= 51 \times 110 = 5610$$

Hence, the sum of first 51 terms is 5610.

Question 9 If the sum of 7 terms of an AP is 49 and that of 17 terms is 289, find the sum of n terms.

Sol. Given, sum of 7 terms $S_7 = 49$ and sum of 17 terms $S_{17} = 289$. Let a be the first term and d be the common difference of the given AP.

$$\therefore \quad S_7 = \frac{7}{2}[2a + (7-1)d] = 49 \qquad \left[\because S_n = \frac{n}{2}[2a + (n-1)d]\right]$$

$$\Rightarrow \quad \frac{7}{2}(2a + 6d) = 49$$

$$\Rightarrow \quad a + 3d = 7 \qquad \text{...(i)}$$

and $$S_{17} = \frac{17}{2}[2a + (17-1)d] = 289$$

$$\Rightarrow \quad \frac{17}{2}(2a + 16d) = 289$$

$$\Rightarrow \quad a + 8d = 17 \qquad \text{...(ii)}$$

On subtracting Eq. (i) from Eq. (ii), we get

$$5d = 10 \Rightarrow d = 2$$

Put, $d = 2$ in Eq. (i), we get

$$a + 3(2) = 7$$

$$\Rightarrow \quad a + 6 = 7 \Rightarrow a = 1$$

$$\therefore \quad \text{Sum of } n \text{ terms, } S_n = \frac{n}{2}[2a + (n-1)d]$$

$$= \frac{n}{2}[2 \times 1 + (n-1)2]$$

$$= \frac{n}{2}(2 + 2n - 2) = \frac{n}{2} \times 2n = n^2$$

Hence, the required sum of first n terms is n^2.

Question 10 Show that $a_1, a_2, \ldots, a_n, \ldots$ form an AP, where a_n is defined as below (i) $a_n = 3 + 4n$ (ii) $a_n = 9 - 5n$. Also, find the sum of the first 15 terms in each case.

Sol.

(i) Given, $a_n = 3 + 4n$

Put $n = 1, 2, 3, 4, \ldots$, we get

7, 11, 15, 19, ... $(3 + 4n)$ which is an AP with common difference 4.

Here, first term $a = 7$, common difference $d = 4$ and number of terms $n = 15$

$$\text{Sum of } n \text{ terms,} \quad S_n = \frac{n}{2}[2a + (n-1)d], \text{ we get}$$

$$\Rightarrow \quad S_{15} = \frac{15}{2}[2 \times 7 + (15-1)4]$$

$$= \frac{15}{2}(14 + 14 \times 4) = \frac{15}{2}(14 + 56)$$

$$= \frac{15}{2} \times 70 = 15 \times 35 = 525$$

Hence, the sum of the first 15 terms is 525.

(ii) Given, $a_n = 9 - 5n$
Putting, $n = 1, 2, 3, 4, \ldots$, we get,
the sequence $4, -1, -6, -11, \ldots, (9 - 5n)$ which is an AP with common difference -5.
Here, first term $a = 4$, common difference $d = -5$
and number of terms $n = 15$,

$$S_n = \frac{n}{2}[2a + (n-1)d], \text{ we get}$$

$$\Rightarrow \quad S_{15} = \frac{15}{2}[2 \times 4 + (15-1)(-5)]$$

$$= \frac{15}{2}[(8 + 14(-5)] = \frac{15}{2}(8 - 70)$$

$$= \frac{15}{2} \times (-62) = 15 \times (-31) = -465$$

Hence, the sum of the first 15 terms is -465.

Question 11 If the sum of the first n terms of an AP is $4n - n^2$, what is the first term (that is S_1)? What is the sum of first two terms? What is the second term? Similarly, find the 3rd, the 10th and the nth terms.

Sol. Given, the sum of first n terms, $S_n = 4n - n^2$

Put $n = 1$, $\quad S_1 = 4 \times 1 - 1^2 = 4 - 1 = 3$

$\Rightarrow$ First term $= 3$ $\quad [\because S_1 = a_1 = a]$

Put, $n = 2$, we get

$$S_2 = 4 \times 2 - 2^2 = 8 - 4 = 4$$

$\because$ The nth term of an AP, $a_n = S_{n+1} - S_n$

$\therefore$ Second term $= S_2 - S_1 = 4 - 3 = 1$

Put $n = 3$, $\quad S_3 = 4 \times 3 - 3^2 = 12 - 9 = 3$

Sum of first two terms $S_2 = 4$

$\therefore$ Third term $= S_3 - S_2 = 3 - 4 = -1$

Put $n = 9$, $\quad S_9 = 4 \times 9 - 9^2 = 36 - 81 = -45$

and put $n = 10$, $\quad S_{10} = 4 \times 10 - 10^2$

$$= 40 - 100 = -60$$

$\therefore$ Tenth term $= S_{10} - S_9$

$$= -60 - (-45) = -60 + 45 = -15$$

Also, $\quad S_n = 4n - n^2$ (Given)

Put $n = n - 1$, $\quad S_{n-1} = 4(n-1) - (n-1)^2$

$\therefore$ nth term $= S_n - S_{n-1} = (4n - n^2) - 4(n-1) + (n-1)^2$

$$= 4n - n^2 - (-n^2 + 6n - 5)$$

$$= 4n - n^2 + n^2 - 6n + 5 = 5 - 2n$$

Hence, the first term is 3, sum of first two term is 4, 2nd term is 1, 3rd term is -1, 10th term is -15 and the nth term is $5 - 2n$.

Question 12 Find the sum of the first 40 positive integers divisible by 6.

Sol. The first 40 positive integers divisible by 6 are 6, 12, 18, ...

Clearly, it is an AP with first term $a = 6$ and common difference $d = 6$

$\because$ Sum of n terms, $$S_n = \frac{n}{2}[2a + (n-1)d]$$

$$\therefore \quad S_{40} = \frac{40}{2}[2 \times 6 + (40-1)6]$$
$$= 20(12 + 39 \times 6)$$
$$= 20(12 + 234)$$
$$= 20 \times 246 = 4920$$

Hence, the sum of the first 40 positive integers divisible by 6 is 4920.

Question 13 Find the sum of the first 15 multiples of 8.

Sol. The first 15 multiples of 8 are $8 \times 1, 8 \times 2, 8 \times 3, \ldots, 8 \times 15$.

i.e., 8, 16, 24, ..., 120 are in AP.

Here, first term $a = 8$, last term, $l = 120$ and number of terms $n = 15$

$\because$ Sum of n terms, $$S_n = \frac{n}{2}(a + l)$$

$$\therefore \quad S_{15} = \frac{15}{2}(8 + 120)$$
$$= \frac{15}{2} \times 128 = 15 \times 64 = 960$$

Hence, the sum of the first 15 multiples of 8 is 960.

Question 14 Find the sum of the odd numbers between 0 and 50.

Sol. The odd numbers between 0 and 50 are 1, 3, 5,..., 49.

Here, first term $a = 1$ and last term, $l = 49$

Let n be the number of term and the common difference $d = 3 - 1 = 2$

$\because$ nth term $a_n = a + (n-1)d = l$

$$\therefore \quad 1 + (n-1)(2) = 49$$
$$\Rightarrow \quad 2(n-1) = 48$$
$$\Rightarrow \quad n - 1 = 24 \Rightarrow n = 25$$

Now, sum of n terms, $$S_n = \frac{n}{2}(a + l)$$

$$\therefore \quad S_{25} = \frac{25}{2}(1 + 49)$$
$$= \frac{25}{2} \times 50 = 25 \times 25 = 625$$

Hence, the sum of odd numbers between 0 and 49 is 625.

Question 15 A contract on construction job specifies a penalty for delay of completion beyond a certain date as follows : ₹ 200 for the first day, ₹ 250 for the second day, ₹ 300 for the third day etc., the penalty for each succeeding day being ₹ 50 more than for the preceding day. How much money the contractor has to pay as penalty, if he has delayed the work by 30 days?

Sol. Since, the penalty for each succeeding day is ₹ 50 more than the preceding day, therefore the penalties for the first day, the second day, the third day, etc. will form an AP.

Let us denote the penalty for the nth day by a_n, then

$$a_1 = ₹\ 200, \quad a_2 = ₹\ 250, \quad a_3 = ₹\ 300$$

Here, $a = 200$, $d = ₹\ 250 - ₹\ 200 = ₹\ 50$ and $n = 30$

$\therefore$ The money the contractor has to pay as penalty, if he has delayed the work by 30 days.

$$\because \quad S_n = \frac{n}{2}[2a + (n-1)d]$$

$$\Rightarrow \quad S_{30} = \frac{30}{2}[2 \times 200 + (30-1)50] = 15(400 + 29 \times 50)$$

$$= 15(400 + 1450) = 15 \times 1850 = 27750$$

So, contractor has to pay ₹ 27750 for delay of 30 days.

Question 16 A sum of ₹ 700 is to be used to give seven cash prizes to students of a school for their overall academic performance. If each prize is ₹ 20 less than its preceding prize, find the value of each of the prizes.

Sol. Here, ₹ 700 is to be used to give 7 cash prizes.

Let the value of first prize be ₹ a. Then, value of second prize ₹$(a - 20)$, value of third prize be ₹$[(a - 20) - 20]$ and so on.

Thus, we get an AP where first term is a and common difference is -20.

Since, $$S_7 = 700$$

$$\therefore \quad \frac{7}{2}[2a + (7-1)(-20)] = 700 \qquad \left[\because S_n = \frac{n}{2}[2a + (n-1)d\right]$$

$$\Rightarrow \quad a - 60 = 100$$

$$\Rightarrow \quad a = 160$$

Hence, value of 1st prize = ₹ 160

Value of 2nd prize = ₹ 160 – ₹ 20 = ₹ = 140

Value of 3rd prize = ₹ 140 – ₹ 20 = ₹ 120

Value of 4th prize = ₹ 120 – ₹ 20 = ₹ 100

Value of 5th prize = ₹ 100 – ₹ 20 = ₹ 80

Value of 6th prize = ₹ 80 – ₹ 20 = ₹ 60

Value of 7th prize = ₹ 60 – ₹ 20 = ₹ 40

Question 17 In a school, students thought of planting trees in and around the school to reduce air pollution. It was decided that the number of trees, that each section of each class will plant, will be the same as the class, in which they are studying, *e.g.*, a section of class I will plant 1 tree, a section of class II will plant 2 trees and, so on till class XII. There are three sections of each class. How many trees will be planted by the students?

Sol. According to question, there are three sections of each class, so the number of trees that each section planted *i.e.*, Class I, Class II, Class III,..., Class XII are $1 \times 3, 2 \times 3, 3 \times 3, \ldots, 12 \times 3$, respectively.

3, 6, 9, ... 36. Clearly, it form an AP.

Here, the first term, $a = 3$, common difference, $d = 6 - 3 = 3$

and the last term, $l = 36$

Now, the nth term of an AP, $a_n = a + (n-1)d = l$

$$\Rightarrow \quad 3 + (n-1)(3) = 36$$

$$\Rightarrow \quad (n-1)3 = 33$$

$$\Rightarrow \quad n - 1 = 11 \Rightarrow n = 12$$

Hence, the total number of the trees planted by the students

$$S_{12} = \frac{12}{2}(3 + 36) \qquad \left[\because S_n = \frac{n}{2}(a + l)\right]$$

$$= 6 \times 39 = 234$$

Question 18 A spiral is made up of successive semi-circles, with centres alternately at A and B, starting with centre at A, of radii 0.5 cm, 1.0 cm, 1.5 cm, 2.0 cm, ... as shown in figure. What is the total length of such a spiral made up of thirteen consecutive semi-circles? $\left(\text{Take, } \pi = \frac{22}{7}\right)$

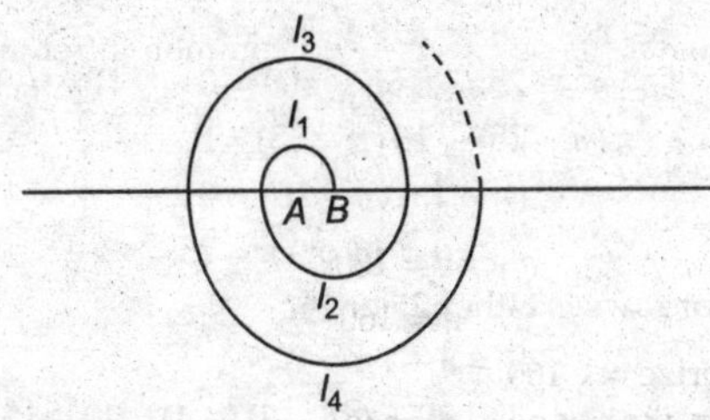

◎ ***Thinking Process*** Length of successive semicircles is $l_1, l_2, l_3, l_4, \ldots$ with centres at A, B, A, B, respectively.

Sol. Length of spiral made up of thirteen consecutive semi-circles

$$= (\pi \times 0.5 + \pi \times 1.0 + \pi \times 1.5 + \pi \times 2.0 + \ldots + \pi \times 6.5)$$

[∵ Circumference or length of semicircle is πr.]

$$= \pi \times 0.5(1 + 2 + 3 + \ldots + 13)$$

which form an AP with first term, $a = 1$, common difference, $d = 2 - 1 = 1$ and number of term, $n = 13$

$\because$ Sum of n terms $= \frac{n}{2}[2a + (n-1)d]$

$$= \pi \times 0.5 \times \frac{13}{2}[2 \times 1 + (13-1) \times 1]$$

$$= \frac{22}{7} \times \frac{5}{10} \times \frac{13}{2} \times 14 = 143 \text{ cm}$$

Question 19 200 logs are stacked in the following manner : 20 logs in the bottom row, 19 in the next row, 18 in the row next to it and, so on (see figure). In how many rows are the 200 logs placed and how many logs are in the top row?

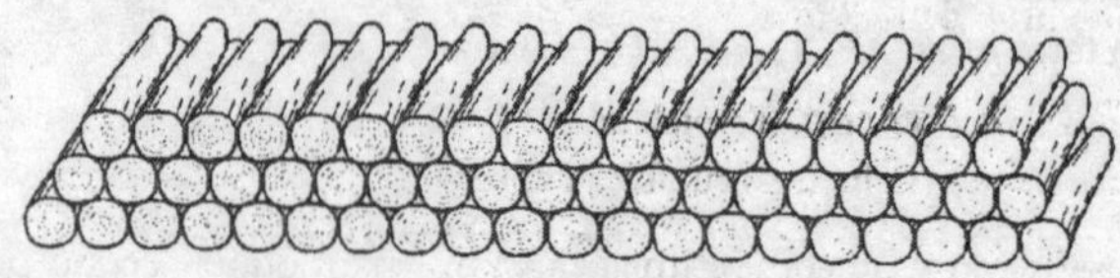

Sol. Since, logs are stacked in each row form a series 20 + 19 + 18 + 17 +....
Clearly, it is an AP with first term, $a = 20$ and common difference,
$d = 19 - 20 = -1$

Suppose, $S_n = 200$

$\because$ $S_n = \frac{n}{2}[2a + (n-1)d]$

$\therefore$ $200 = \frac{n}{2}[2 \times 20 + (n-1)(-1)]$

$\Rightarrow$ $400 = n(40 - n + 1)$

$\Rightarrow$ $400 = n(41 - n)$

$\Rightarrow$ $n^2 - 41n + 400 = 0$

$\Rightarrow$ $n^2 - 25n - 16n + 400 = 0$ (By factorisation method)

$\Rightarrow$ $n(n-25) - 16(n-25) = 0$

$\Rightarrow$ $(n-25)(n-16) = 0$

$\Rightarrow$ $n = 16$ or $n = 25$

Hence, the number of rows is either 25 or 16.

When $n = 16$, $a_n = a + (n-1)d$

$$= 20 + (16-1)(-1) = 20 - 15 = 5$$

When $n = 25$, $a_n = a + (n-1)d$

$$= 20 + (25-1)(-1) = 20 - 24$$

$$= -4$$ (Not possible)

Hence, the number of row is 16 and number of logs in the top row = 5.

Question 20 In a potato race, a bucket is placed at the starting point, which is 5 m from the first potato, and the other potatoes are placed 3 m apart in a straight line. There are ten potatoes in lines (see figure) A competitor starts from the bucket, picks up the nearest potato, runs back with it, drops it in the bucket, runs back to pick up the next potato, runs to the bucket to drop it in, and she continues in the same way until all the potatoes are in the bucket. What is the total distance the competitor has to run?

◎ *Thinking Process* To pick up the first potato and the second potato, the total distance (in metres) run by a competitor is $2 \times 5 + 2 \times (5 + 3)$].

Sol. The distance run by competitor to pickup first potato, second potato, third potato,...... are, respectively

$2 \times 5, 2 \times (5 + 3), 2 \times (5 + 3 + 3), 2 \times (5 + 3 + 3 + 3)$...... *i.e.*, 10, 16, 22, 28, ...

Clearly, it is an AP with first term, $a = 10$ and common difference, $d = 16 - 10 = 6$

$\because$ The sum of n terms, $S_n = \frac{n}{2}[2a + (n - 1)d]$

$\therefore$ The sum of 10 terms, $S_{10} = \frac{10}{2}[2 \times 10 + (10 - 1) \times 6]$ $[\because n = 10$ (Given)]

$= 5(20 + 54)$

$= 5 \times 74$

$= 370$

Hence, the total distance the competitor has to run is 370 m.

Exercise 5.4 (Optional)

Question 1 Which term of the AP 121, 117, 113, ... is its first negative term?

Thinking Process Find n for $a_n < 0$.

Sol. Given, first term, $a = 121$, common difference, $d = 117 - 121 = -4$

Since, nth term of an AP, $a_n = a + (n-1)d$

$$= 121 + (n-1) \times (-4)$$

$$= 121 - 4n + 4 = 125 - 4n$$

For first negative term, $a_n < 0$

$\Rightarrow$ $125 - 4n < 0$

$\Rightarrow$ $125 < 4n$

$\Rightarrow$ $4n > 125$

$\Rightarrow$ $n > \frac{125}{4}$

$\Rightarrow$ $n > 31\frac{1}{4}$

Least integral value of $n = 32$,

Hence, 32nd term of the given AP is the first negative term.

Question 2 The sum of the third and the seventh terms of an AP is 6 and their product is 8. Find the sum of first sixteen terms of the AP.

Sol. Let the first term and the common difference of the AP be a and d, respectively.

According to the question,

$$a_3 + a_7 = 6$$

$\Rightarrow$ $[a + (3-1)d] + [a + (7-1)d] = 6$ $\quad [\because a_n = a + (n-1)d]$

$\Rightarrow$ $(a + 2d) + (a + 6d) = 6$

$\Rightarrow$ $2a + 8d = 6$

$\Rightarrow$ $a + 4d = 3$ $\quad$ ...(i)

Also it is given that $(a_3) \times (a_7) = 8$

$\Rightarrow$ $(a + 2d)(a + 6d) = 8$

$\Rightarrow$ $\{(a + 4d) - 2d\}\{(a + 4d) + 2d\} = 8$

$\Rightarrow$ $(3 - 2d)(3 + 2d) = 8$ $\quad$ [Using Eq. (i)]

$$\Rightarrow \quad 9 - 4d^2 = 8 \qquad [\because (a-b)(a+b) = a^2 - b^2]$$

$$\Rightarrow \quad 4d^2 = 9 - 8$$

$$\Rightarrow \quad d^2 = \frac{1}{4}$$

$$\Rightarrow \quad d = \pm \frac{1}{2}$$

On putting $d = \frac{1}{2}$, in Eq. (i), we get

$$a + 4\left(\frac{1}{2}\right) = 3$$

$$\Rightarrow \quad a + 2 = 3$$

$$\Rightarrow \quad a = 3 - 2$$

$$\Rightarrow \quad a = 1$$

$\therefore$ Sum of first sixteen terms of the AP = S_{16}

$$\because \quad S_n = \frac{n}{2}[2a + (n-1)d]$$

$$\therefore \quad S_{16} = \frac{16}{2}\left[2(1) + (16-1)\frac{1}{2}\right]$$

$$= 8\left[2 + 15\left(\frac{1}{2}\right)\right]$$

$$= 8\left(\frac{19}{2}\right) = 76$$

On putting $d = -\frac{1}{2}$, in Eq. (i), we get

$$a + 4\left(-\frac{1}{2}\right) = 3$$

$$\Rightarrow \quad a - 2 = 3$$

$$\Rightarrow \quad a = 5$$

$\therefore$ Sum of first sixteen terms of the AP = S_{16}

$$S_{16} = \frac{16}{2}[2a + (16-1)d] \qquad \left[\because S_n = \frac{n}{2}\{2a + (n-1)d\}\right]$$

$$= 8\left[2(5) + 15\left(-\frac{1}{2}\right)\right]$$

$$= 8\left(10 - \frac{15}{2}\right) = 8\left(\frac{5}{2}\right) = 20$$

Hence, the sum of first sixteen terms of the AP are 20 or 76.

Question 3 A ladder has rungs 25 cm apart (see figure). The rungs decrease uniformly in length from 45 cm at the bottom to 25 cm at the top. If the top and the bottom rungs are $2\frac{1}{2}$ m apart, what is the length of the wood required for the rungs?

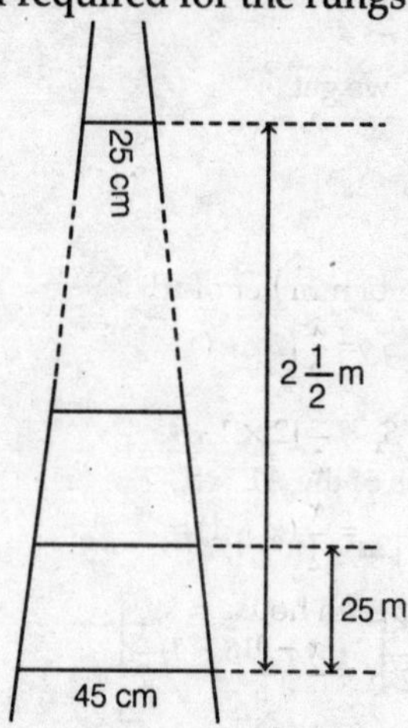

◎ ***Thinking Process*** Number of rungs $= \frac{250}{25} + 1$.

Sol. Total distance between the top and bottom rungs $= 2\frac{1}{2}$ m

$$= \frac{5}{2} \text{ m} = \frac{5}{2} \times 100 \text{ cm} = \frac{500}{2} = 250 \text{ cm}$$

Distance between two runs = 25 cm

$\therefore$ Total number of rungs $= \frac{250}{25} + 1 = 11$

Now, as the lengths of the rungs decrease uniformly, they will be in an AP.
Length of top rung = 25 cm
Length of the bottom rungs = 45 cm
Thus, this forms are AP where

The first term $a = 45$

The last term $l = 25$

and the number of terms $n = 11$

Thus, the required length of the wood is

$$S_n = \frac{n}{2}(a + l) = \frac{11}{2}(45 + 25)$$

$$= \frac{11}{2}(70) = 11 \times 35 = 385 \text{ cm}$$

Question 4 The houses of a row are numbered consecutively from 1 to 49. Show that there is a value of x such that the sum of the numbers of the houses preceding the house numbered x is equal to the sum of the numbers of the houses following it. Find this value of x.

◎ *Thinking Process* $S_{x-1} = S_{49} - S_x$

Sol. The consecutive numbers on the houses of a row are 1, 2, 3, ...49. Clearly, this list of number forming an AP.

Here, $a = 1, d = 2 - 1 = 1$

Let us assume that the sum of number of xth house is S_x.

$$\because \quad S_x = \frac{x}{2}[2a + (x-1)d] \qquad \left[\because S_n = \frac{n}{2}[2a + (n-1)d]\right]$$

$$\Rightarrow \quad S_x = \frac{x}{2}[2 \times 1 + (x-1) \times 1]$$

$$= \frac{x}{2}(x+1) = \frac{x^2 + x}{2}$$

Sum of number of preceding xth house $= S_{x-1}$

$$\therefore \quad S_{x-1} = \frac{x-1}{2}[2 \times 1 + (x - 1 - 1) \times 1]$$

$$= \frac{x-1}{2}(2 + x - 2)$$

$$= \frac{(x-1)x}{2} = \frac{x^2 - x}{2}$$

and
$$S_{49} = \frac{49}{2}[2 \times 1 + (49 - 1) \times 1]$$

$$= \frac{49}{2}[2 + 48] = \frac{49}{2} \times 50 = 49 \times 25$$

According to given condition,
$$S_{x-1} = S_{49} - S_x$$

$$\frac{x^2 - x}{2} = 49 \times 25 - \frac{x^2 + x}{2}$$

$$\Rightarrow \quad \frac{x^2 - x}{2} + \frac{x^2 + x}{2} = 49 \times 25$$

$$\Rightarrow \quad \frac{x^2 - x + x^2 + x}{2} = 49 \times 25$$

$$\Rightarrow \quad x^2 = 49 \times 25$$

$$\Rightarrow \quad x = \pm (7 \times 5) = \pm 35$$

Since, x is a counting number.

$\therefore$ Taking positive sign, we get

$$x = 35$$

Hence, house number 35 is such that the sum of the number of houses preceding the house numbered 35 is equal to the sum of the numbers of the houses following it.

Question 5 A small terrace at a football ground comprises of 15 steps each of which is 50 m long and built of solid concrete. Each step has a rise of $\frac{1}{4}$ m and a tread of $\frac{1}{2}$ m (see figure). Calculate the total volume of concrete required to build the terrace.

Thinking Process Volume of concrete required to build the first step

$$= \frac{1}{4} \times \frac{1}{2} \times 50 \text{ m}^3$$

Sol. Since, the volume of concrete required to build the first step, second step, third step,... are $\frac{1}{4} \times \frac{1}{2} \times 50, \left(2 \times \frac{1}{4}\right) \times \frac{1}{2} \times 50, \left(3 \times \frac{1}{4}\right) \times \frac{1}{2} \times 50, \ldots,$ $\left(15 \times \frac{1}{4}\right) \times \frac{1}{2} \times 50$

i.e., $$\frac{50}{8}, 2 \times \frac{50}{8}, 3 \times \frac{50}{8}, \ldots, \left(15 \times \frac{50}{8}\right)$$

So, the total volume of concrete required

$$= \frac{50}{8} + 2 \times \frac{50}{8} + 3 \times \frac{50}{8} + \ldots + 15 \times \frac{50}{8}$$

$$= \frac{50}{8} [1 + 2 + 3 + \ldots 1 + 15]$$

which forms an AP with first term, $a = 1$, common difference, $d = 2 - 1 = 1$ and number of term, $n = 15$

$$= \frac{50}{8} \times \left[\frac{15}{2} [2 \times 1 + (15 - 1) \times 1]\right]$$

$$\left[\because S_n = \frac{n}{2} \{2a + (n - 1)\}\right]$$

$$= \frac{50}{8} \times \frac{15}{2} \times (2 + 14) = \frac{25 \times 15}{8} \times 16$$

$$= 750 \text{ m}^3$$

Hence, the volume of concrete required to build the terrace is 750 m^3.

DIKSHA APP Questions

☐ Multiple Choice Questions

Q.1 The sum of first n odd natural number is

(a) n (b) n^2

(c) $n+1$ (d) $n+2$

Sol. (b) The odd number numbers are 1, 3, 5, 7, ...
where the first term $a = 1$

common difference, $d = 3 - 1 = 2$

$\therefore$ Sum of first n odd natural numbers is

$$S_n = \frac{n}{2}[2 \times 1 + (n-1)2] \quad \left[\because S_n = \frac{n}{2}[2a + (n-1)d]\right]$$

$$= \frac{n}{2}[2 + 2n - 2] = \frac{2n^2}{2} = n^2$$

Q.2 The list of numbers $-12, -9, -6, -3, 0, \ldots\ldots$ forms ....

(a) No AP (b) An AP with $d = 3$

(c) An AP with $d = -3$ (d) An AP with $d = 0$

Sol. (b) The given list of numbers is $-12, -9, -6, -3, 0, \ldots$

Here, $a_1 = -12, a_2 = -9, a_3 = -6, a_4 = -3,$

$$a_2 - a_1 = -9 - (-12) = -9 + 12 = 3$$

$a_3 - a_2 = -6 - (-9) = -6 + 9 = 3$

$a_4 - a_3 = -3 - (-6) = -3 + 6 = 3$

Since, the difference is same.

Therefore, this is an AP with $d = 3$

Q.3 In an AP, $S_5 = 30$ and $S_4 = 20$, then the value of a_5 is

(a) 10

(b) 50

(c) 20

(d) 9

Sol. (a) Given $S_5 = 30$ and $S_4 = 20$

Then, we know,

$$a_5 = S_5 - S_4 = 30 - 20 = 10 \quad [\because a_n = S_n - S_{(n-1)}]$$

Q.4 The sum of first 50 odd natural number is

(a) 250 (b) 500

(c) 2500 (d) 5000

Sol. (c) The series of first odd natural number are 1, 3, 5, 7.........

Here $a = 1$ and common difference $d = 3 - 1 = 2$

Now, $S_{50} = \frac{50}{2}[2 \times 1 + (50 - 1)2]$ $\left[\because S_n = \frac{n}{2}[2a + (n-1)d]\right]$

$= 25[2 + 49 \times 2]$

$= 25[2 + 98]$

$= 25 \times 100$

$= 2500$

Quick Solution

We know sum of first n odd natural numbers is n^2.

Here, $n = 50$

So, the required sum is $S_{50} = 50^2 = 2500$

Q.5 The first and last terms of an AP are 1 and 11 respectively. If the sum of its terms is 36, the number of terms is

(a) 8 (b) 7

(c) 4 (d) 6

Sol. (d) The first term of an AP, $a = 1$

The last term of the AP, $l = 11$

Sum of the terms $S_n = 36$

We know, $S_n = \frac{n}{2}(a + l)$

$\Rightarrow$ $36 = \frac{n}{2}(1 + 11)$

$\Rightarrow$ $36 = \frac{n}{2}(12)$

$\Rightarrow$ $36 = 6n$

$\Rightarrow$ $n = 6$

Q.6 Which term of the AP 5, 8, 11, 14, ... is 320 ?

(a) 64th

(b) 104th

(c) 105th

(d) 106th

Sol. (d) In the given AP, the first term, $a = 5$

and Common difference, $d = 8 - 5 = 3$

Let nth term of this AP is 320.

So, $l = 320$

$$\Rightarrow \quad 5 + (n-1)3 = 320 \quad [\because a_n = a + (n-1)d]$$
$$\Rightarrow \quad 3(n-1) = 315$$
$$\Rightarrow \quad (n-1) = \frac{315}{3}$$
$$\Rightarrow \quad (n-1) = 105$$
$$\Rightarrow \quad n = 106$$

Q.7 The 6th and 8th terms of an AP are 12 and 22 respectively. Its second term is

(a) 8 (b) –8 (c) 6 (d) –3

Sol. (b) Given, 6th term of the AP is 12

i.e., $a_6 = 12$

$$\Rightarrow \quad a + (6-1)d = 12$$
$$\Rightarrow \quad a + 5d = 12 \quad \ldots\text{(i)}$$

and 8th term of the AP is 22

i.e., $a_8 = 22$

$$\Rightarrow \quad a + 7d = 22 \quad \ldots\text{(ii)}$$

On subtracting Eq. (i) from Eq. (ii), we get

$$2d = 10$$
$$\Rightarrow \quad d = 5$$

On substituting $d = 5$ in Eq. (i), we get

$$a + 5 \times 5 = 12$$
$$\Rightarrow \quad a + 25 = 12$$
$$a = 12 - 25$$
$$\Rightarrow \quad a = -13$$

So, the second term is, $a_2 = a + d = -13 + 5 = -8$

Q.8 The 11th term of the AP $-3, \frac{-1}{2}, 2, \ldots$ is

(a) 21 (b) 22

(c) 23 (d) None of these

Sol. (b) The first term is $a = -3$,

The common difference is

$$\frac{-1}{2} - (-3) = \frac{-1}{2} + 3 = \frac{5}{2}$$

$\therefore$ 11th term is $a_{11} = a + 10d$

$$= -3 + 10\left(\frac{5}{2}\right) = -3 + 25 = 22 \quad [\because a_n = a + (n-1)d]$$

Q.9 Which term of the AP 19, $18\frac{1}{5}, 17\frac{2}{5}$, ... is the first negative term ?

(a) 20th (b) 23rd
(c) 25th (d) 18th

Sol. (c) In the given AP,

the first term; $a = 19$

common difference, $d = 18\frac{1}{5} - 19 = \frac{91}{5} - 19 = \frac{-4}{5}$

Let the first negative term be the *n*th term, *an*.

i.e., $a_n = a + (n-1)d$

$\Rightarrow \quad a_n = 19 + (n-1)\left(\frac{-4}{5}\right)$

Now, $a_n < 0$

$\Rightarrow \quad 19 + (n-1)\left(\frac{-4}{5}\right) < 0$

$\Rightarrow \quad \frac{-4}{5}(n-1) < -19$

$\Rightarrow \quad n - 1 > \frac{95}{4}$

$\Rightarrow \quad n > \frac{95}{4} + 1$

$\Rightarrow \quad n > \frac{99}{4}$

$\Rightarrow \quad n > 24.75$

$\Rightarrow \quad n = 25$

Q.10 The *n*th term of the AP in 2, 5, 8 ...... is

(a) $3n - 1$ (b) $2n - 1$
(c) $3n - 2$ (d) $2n - 3$

Sol. (a) The first term, $a = 2$

The common difference, $d = 5 - 2 = 3$

So, the *n*th term of the AP is

$$\begin{aligned} a_n &= a + (n-1)d \\ &= 2 + (n-1)3 \\ &= 2 + 3n - 3 \\ &= 3n - 1 \end{aligned}$$

Q.11 If the 10th term of an AP is 0, then find the ratio of the 27th term and the 15th term of the AP.

(a) 1:1 (b) 17:5
(c) 1:3 (d) 3:1

Sol. (b) Given that the 10th term of the AP is 0

i.e., $a_{10} = 0$

$\Rightarrow \quad a + 9d = 0 \quad$ ...(i) $\quad [\because a_n = a + (n-1)d]$

Now, 27th term of the AP is

$$a_{27} = a + 26d = a + 9d + 17d = 17d \quad \text{[from Eq. (i)]}$$

And 15th term of the AP is

$$a_{15} = a + 14d = a + 9d + 5d = 5d \quad \text{[from Eq. (i)]}$$

Hence, the required ratio is $\frac{a_{27}}{a_{15}} = \frac{17d}{5d} = \frac{17}{5}$

Q.12 If a, b, c, d, e and f are in A.P, then $e - c$ is equal to

(a) $2(c-a)$ (b) $2(f-d)$
(c) $2(d-c)$ (d) $d-c$

Sol. (c) a, b, c, d, e and f are in A.P Let d_1 be the common difference

Here, $a_1 = a, a_2 = b, a_3 = c, a_4 = d, a_5 = e, a_6 = f$

Then, $\quad e - c = a_5 - a_3 = a_1 + 4d_1 - (a_1 + 2d_1)$

$= a_1 + 4d_1 - a_1 - 2d_1$

$\Rightarrow \quad e - c = 2d_1 \quad$ ...(i)

Now, $\quad 2(c-a) = 2(a_3 - a_1) = 2(a_1 + 2d_1 - a_1) = 4d_1 \quad$ ...(ii)

$2(f-d) = 2(a_6 - a_4) = 2(a_1 + 5d_1 - a_1 - 3d_1) = 4d_1 \quad$ ...(iii)

$2(d-c) = 2(a_4 - a_3) = 2(a_1 + 3d_1 - a_1 - 2d_1) = 2d_1 \quad$ ...(iv)

From Eq. (i) and (iv), we get $e = c = 2(d-c) = 2d_1$

Q.13 Which of the following is finite A.P ?

(i) 90, 80, 70, 60, … (ii) $a, a-2, a-3, a-4$
(iii) 3, 5, 7, 9, 11, 13

(a) All (b) (ii) and (iii)
(c) Only (iii) (d) (i) and (iii)

Sol. (c) (i) 90, 80, 70, 60 ……

$a_2 - a_1 = 80 - 90 = -10$

$a_3 - a_2 = 70 - 80 = -10$

$a_4 - a_3 = 60 - 70 = -10$

This is an A.P. but it is an infinite A.P. as we don't know the last term of the A.P.

(ii) $a, a-2, a-3, a-4$

$$a_2 - a_1 = -2$$
$$a_3 - a_2 = -1$$
$$a_4 - a_3 = -1$$

Since, $a_2 - a_1 \neq a_3 - a_2$, so this is not an AP.

(iii) 3, 5, 7, 9, 11, 13

$$a_2 - a_1 = 2$$
$$a_3 - a_2 = 2$$
$$a_4 - a_3 = 2$$

Since, the common difference is 2, this is an A.P. and it is a Finite A.P. as the last term is given as 13.

So, the correct option is option (c).

Q.14 A farmer borrows ₹ 10,000 from a friend and promises to pay back 10% of the balance every month. Make a list of the money that he repays every month and state which of the following statements are true ?

(a) It is an A.P. with common difference of ₹ –1000.

(b) It is an A.P. with common difference of ₹ –100.

(c) It is an A.P. with common difference of ₹ 1000.

(d) It is not an A.P.

Sol. (d) Sum borrowed = ₹ 10000

Amount paid back in first month = 10% of ₹ 10000 = ₹ 1000

Now the, Balance = ₹ 9000

Amount paid back in second month = 10% of ₹ 9000 = ₹ 900

Balance = ₹ 8100

Amount paid back in third month = 10% of ₹ 8100 = ₹ 810

Balance = ₹ 7290

Amount paid back in fourth month = 10% of ₹ 7290 = ₹ 729

List of numbers (money paid back every month) is 1000, 900, 810 , 729,...

$$a_2 - a_1 = 900 - (1000) = -100$$
$$a_3 - a_2 = 810 - (900) = -90$$
$$a_4 - a_3 = 729 - (810) = -81$$

Since $a_3 - a_2 \neq a_4 - a_3$

So, this is not an A.P.

Q.15 The first four terms of an AP, whose first term is –6 and the common difference is 6, are

(a) –6, 0, 6, 12 (b) –6, – 12, – 18, – 24

(c) –6, 0, 6, – 12 (d) –6, – 12, – 24, – 48

Sol. (a) In the given A.P., $a = -6$, $d = 6$

First term $= a = -6$

Second term $= a + d = -6 + 6 = 0$

Third term $= a + 2d = -6 + 12 = 6$

Fourth term $= a + 3d = -6 + 18 = 12$

Q.16 Find x, y and z such that the following numbers are in AP : $x, 10, y, 16, z$.

(a) $x = 15, y = 5, z = 0$ (b) $x = 5, y = 15, z = 20$

(c) $x = 7, y = 13, z = 19$ (d) $x = 6, y = 12, z = 18$

Sol. (c) The given A.P. is x, 10, y, 16, z.

$$a = x, d = 10 - x$$

The fourth term is 16

$\therefore$ $a_4 = 16$

$\Rightarrow$ $16 = a + (4-1)d$ $[\because a_n = a + (n-1)d]$

$\Rightarrow$ $16 = x + 3(10 - x)$

$\Rightarrow$ $16 = x + 30 - 3x$

$\Rightarrow$ $2x = 30 - 16 = 14$

$\Rightarrow$ $x = 7$

i.e., $a = 7, d = 10 - 7 = 3$

$y = 7 + (3-1)3 = 13$ $[\because y = a_3]$

$z = 7 + (5-1)3 = 19$ $[\because z = a_5]$

Q.17 The 11th and 13th terms of an AP are 35 and 41 respectively. The common difference of the A.P. is

(a) 38 (b) 5

(c) 6 (d) 3

Sol. (d) 11th term is $a_{11} = a + (11-1)d = 35$ $[\because a_n = a + (n-1)d]$

$\Rightarrow$ $a + 10d = 35$

$\Rightarrow$ $a = 35 - 10d$ ... (i)

13th term is $a_{13} = a + (13-1)d = 41$

$\Rightarrow$ $a + 12d = 41$ ... (ii)

On substituting value of a from Eq. (i), we get

$$35 - 10d + 12d = 41$$

$\Rightarrow$ $2d = 41 - 35$ ... (iii)

$\Rightarrow$ $2d = 6$ ... (iv)

$\Rightarrow$ $d = 3$

☐ Subjective Type Questions

Q.1 Is 68 a term of the A.P. 7, 10, 13, ...?

Sol. We know that *n*th term of an A.P., $= a + (n-1)d$

Here, $a = 7$ and $d = `3$

Let *n*th term is 68.

$\Rightarrow \quad 68 = 7 + (n-1)3$

$\Rightarrow \quad 68 - 7 = (n-1)3$

$\Rightarrow \quad 61/3 = n - 1$

$\Rightarrow \quad n = \dfrac{64}{3}$

$\because n$ is not a natural number.

$\therefore$ 68 is not a term of the given AP.

Q.2 The sum of the 5th and the 7th terms of an AP is 52 and the 10th term is 46. Find the AP.

Sol. Let the first term and common difference of AP are a and d, respectively.

According to the question,

$a_5 + a_7 = 52$

$\Rightarrow \quad a + (5-1)d + a + (7-1)d = 52 \quad [\because a_n = a + (n-1)d]$

$\Rightarrow \quad a + 4d + a + 6d = 52$

$\Rightarrow \quad 2a + 10d = 52$

$\Rightarrow \quad a + 5d = 26 \quad \ldots(i)$

Now, $\quad a_{10} = 46 \quad$ (given)

$\Rightarrow \quad a + (10-1)d = 46$

$\Rightarrow \quad a + 9d = 46 \quad \ldots(ii)$

On subtracting Eq. (i) from Eq. (ii), we get

$4d = 20$

$\Rightarrow \quad d = 5$

On substituting $d = 5$ in Eq. (i), we get

$a + 25 = 26$

$\Rightarrow \quad a = 1$

The AP is $a, a + d, a + 2d, a + 3d$ ....

Hence, the AP is 1, 6, 11, 16,.........

Q.3 Find the value of the middle term of the following AP
$-6, -2, 2, \ldots\ldots, 58$

Sol. The given AP is –6, –2, 2, ..., 58

So, the first term, the common difference and the *n*th term are,

$a = -6$, $d = 4$, $a_n = 58$, respectively.

Now, $58 = -6 + (n-1)4$ $\quad [\because a_n = a + (n-1)d]$

$\Rightarrow \quad 64 = (n-1)4$

$\Rightarrow \quad 16 = n - 1$

$\Rightarrow \quad n = 17$

Middle term $= \left[\dfrac{(n+1)}{2}\right]$th term = 9 th term

$\therefore$ Middle term $a_9 = -6 + 8 \times 4 = 26$ $\quad [\because a_9 = a + 8d]$

Q.4 Find the sum of first 100 natural numbers.

Sol. The first natural numbers are 1, 2, 3, ... 100

Here, $a = 1$ and $d = 1$, and $a_n = l = 100$

Now, $S_{100} = \dfrac{100}{2}[2 \times 1 + (100 - 1)1]$ $\quad \left[\because S_n = \dfrac{n}{2}[2a + (n-1)d]\right]$

$= 50[2 + 99]$

$= 50 \times 101$

$= 5050.$

Q.5 The common difference between the terms of two AP's is same. If the difference between their 50th terms is 100, what is the difference between their 100th terms?

Sol. Let A and a be their first terms and d be their common difference which is same, difference between their 50th terms is 100.

$\therefore (A + 49d) - (a + 49d) = 100$ $\quad [\because a_n = a + (n-1)d]$

$A - a = 100$ $\quad$ ...(i)

Difference between their 100th terms is

$(A + 99d) - (a + 99d) = A - a = 100$ $\quad$ [From Eq. (i)]

The difference between their 100th terms is also same *i.e.*, 100.

Q.6 How many terms of the A.P. $20, 19\frac{1}{3}, 18\frac{2}{3}, \ldots$ should be taken, so that their sum is 300. Explain the double answer.

Sol. Here, $a = 20$

$$d = 19\frac{1}{3} - 20 = \frac{58}{3} - 20 = \frac{-2}{3}$$

Let the sum of n terms be 300.

$S_n = 300$

$\Rightarrow \quad 300 = \dfrac{n}{2}\left[2 \times 20 + (n-1)\left(-\dfrac{2}{3}\right)\right]$ $\quad \left[\because S_n = \dfrac{n}{2}[2a + (n-1)d]\right]$

$$\Rightarrow \quad 600 = n\left[40 - \frac{2n}{3} + \frac{2}{3}\right]$$

$$\Rightarrow \quad 600 = n\left[\frac{-2n}{3} + \frac{122}{3}\right]$$

$$\Rightarrow \quad 600 = \frac{-2n^2}{3} + \frac{122n}{3}$$

$$\Rightarrow \quad 1800 = -2n^2 + 122n$$

$$\Rightarrow \quad n^2 - 61n + 900 = 0$$

$$\Rightarrow \quad n^2 - 36n - 25n + 900 = 0$$

$$\Rightarrow \quad n(n-36) - 25(n-36) = 0$$

$$\Rightarrow \quad (n-36)(n-25)$$

$$\Rightarrow \quad n = 25 \text{ or } 36$$

Sum of first 25 terms = Sum of first 36 terms = 300

$\Rightarrow$ sum of all terms from 25th to 36th term is zero.

Q.7 Sum of first six terms of an AP is 42. The ratio of its 10th terms to its 30th term is 1:3. Calculate the first term and the 13th term of the AP.

Sol. The sum of first 6 terms of the AP is 42.

$$\Rightarrow \quad S_6 = 42$$

$$\Rightarrow \quad \frac{n}{2}[2a + (n-1)d] = 42$$

$$\Rightarrow \quad \frac{6}{2}[2a + 5d] = 42$$

$$\Rightarrow \quad 2a + 5d = 14 \quad \text{...(i)}$$

Ratio of the 10th term to its 30th term is 1 : 3 *i.e.*,

$$\frac{a_{10}}{a_{30}} = \frac{a + 9d}{a + 29d} = \frac{1}{3}$$

$$\Rightarrow \quad 3a + 27d = a + 29d$$

$$\Rightarrow \quad 2a - 2d = 0 \quad \text{...(ii)}$$

On subtracting Eq. (ii) from Eq. (i), we get

$$(2a + 5d) - (2a - 2d) = 14 - 0$$

$$\Rightarrow \quad 7d = 14$$

$$\Rightarrow \quad d = 2$$

On substituting $d = 2$ in Eq. (i), we get

$$2a + 10 = 14$$

$$\Rightarrow \quad a = 2$$

Now, $\quad a_{13} = a + 12d = 2 + 12 \times 2 = 26$

Hence, the first term of the AP is 2 and 13th term is 26.

Q.8 A factory produced 1100 cars in 3rd year and 2700 cars in 11th year. Assuming that the production increase by a fixed amount every year, find the production of cars in 20th year and total cars produced in 20 years.

Sol. Since, the factory produced 1100 cars in 3rd year and 2700 cars in the 11th year.

$\therefore \quad a_3 = 1100$ and $a_{11} = 2700$

$a + 2d = 1100 \quad [\because a_n = a + (n-1)d] \quad ...(i)$

and $a + 10d = 2700 \quad ...(ii)$

Subtracting Eq. (i) from Eq. (ii), we get

$8d = 1600$

$\Rightarrow \quad d = 200$

On putting the value of d in Eq. (ii), we get

$a = 700$

Number of cars produced in 20th year $= a_{20} = a + 19d$

$= 700 + 19 \times 200 = 4500$

Total cars produced in 20 years $= S_{20} = \frac{n}{2}[a + l]$

$= \frac{20}{2}(700 + 4500) = 52000 \quad [\because a_{20} = l]$

Q.9 The sum of the fourth and eight terms of an arithmetic progression is 24 and the sum of the sixth and tenth terms is 44. Find the first three terms of the Arithmetic progression.

Sol. According to the question,

$a_4 + a_8 = 24$

$\Rightarrow \quad a + 3d + a + 7d = 24 \quad [\because a_n = a + (n-1)d]$

$\Rightarrow \quad 2a + 10d = 24$

$\Rightarrow \quad a + 5d = 12 \quad ...(i)$

and $a_6 + a_{10} = 44 \quad$ [Given]

$\Rightarrow \quad a + 5d + a + 9d = 44$

$\Rightarrow \quad 2a + 14d = 44$

$\Rightarrow \quad a + 7d = 22 \quad ...(ii)$

On subtracting Eq. (i) from Eq. (ii), we get

$2d = 10$

$\Rightarrow \quad d = \frac{10}{2}$

$\Rightarrow \quad d = 5$

Substitute $d = 5$ in Eq. (i), we get

$$a + 5(5) = 12$$
$$\Rightarrow \quad a + 25 = 12$$
$$\Rightarrow \quad a = 12 - 25$$
$$\Rightarrow \quad a = -13$$

$\therefore$ Three terms of Arithmetic progression are

$$= a, a + d\ a + 2d$$
$$= -13, -13 + 5, -13 + 10$$
$$= -13, -8, -3$$

Q.10 A line segment is divided into four parts forming an arithmetic progression. The sum of the lengths of 3rd and 4th parts is three times the sum of the lengths of first two parts. If the length of fourth part is 14 cm, find the total length of the line segment.

Sol. Let the four parts of the line segment be

$$a - 3d, a - d, a + d, a + 3d$$

According to the question

$$(a + d + a + 3d) = 3(a - 3d + a - d)$$
$$\Rightarrow \quad 2a + 4d = 3(2a - 4d)$$
$$\Rightarrow \quad 2(a + 2d) = 3 \times 2(a - 2d)$$
$$\Rightarrow \quad a + 2d = 3a - 6d$$
$$\Rightarrow \quad 2d + 6d = 3a - a$$
$$\Rightarrow \quad 2a = 8d$$
$$\Rightarrow \quad a = \frac{8d}{2}$$
$$\Rightarrow \quad a = 4d \quad \text{...(i)}$$
$$\Rightarrow \quad a + 3d = 14 \quad [\because a_4 = 14]$$
$$\Rightarrow \quad 4d + 3d = 14 \quad [\text{From Eq. (i)}]$$
$$\Rightarrow \quad 7d = 14$$
$$\Rightarrow \quad d = \frac{14}{7}$$
$$\Rightarrow \quad d = 2$$

Put the value of d in Eq. (i), we get

$$a = 4 \times 2$$
$$\Rightarrow \quad a = 8$$

$\therefore$ Length of the line segment

$$= a - 3d + a - d + a + d + a + 3d = 4a$$
$$= 4 \times 8 = 32 \text{ cm.} \quad [\because a = 8]$$

Q.11 The seventh term of an arithmetic progression is four times its second term and twelfth term is 2 more than three times of its fourth term. Find the arithmetic progression.

Sol. $\because a_7 = 4a_2$

$\Rightarrow \quad a + 6d = 4(a + d) \qquad [\because a_n = a + (n-1)d]$

$\Rightarrow \quad a + 6d = 4a + 4d$

$\Rightarrow \quad 6d - 4d = 4a - a$

$\Rightarrow \quad 2d = 3a \qquad \ldots(i)$

Now, $\quad a_{12} = 3a_4 + 2$

$\Rightarrow \quad a + 11d = 3(a + 3d) + 2 \qquad [\because a_n = a + (n-1)d]$

$\Rightarrow \quad a + 11d = 3a + 9d + 2$

$\Rightarrow \quad 11d - 9d = 3a - a + 2$

$\Rightarrow \quad 2d = 2a + 2 \qquad \ldots(ii)$

On substituting, Eqs. (i) and (ii), we get

$3a = 2a + 2$

$\Rightarrow \quad 3a - 2a = 2 \Rightarrow a = 2$

Put the value of a in Eq. (i), we get

$2d = 3a$

$\Rightarrow \quad 2d = 3 \times 2$

$\Rightarrow \quad 2d = 6$

$\Rightarrow \quad d = \frac{6}{2} \Rightarrow d = 3$

$\therefore$ The required sequence

$a, a + d, a + 2d, \ldots\ldots\ldots$

i.e., $\quad 2, 2 + 3, 2 + 2 \times 3, \ldots\ldots\ldots$

The required sequence 2, 5, 8, ...

Q.12 An A.P consist of 37 terms. The sum of the three middle most term is 225 and the sum of the last three terms is 429. Find AP.

Sol. We are given that the AP contains 37 terms.

$\therefore \quad n = 37$

The middle most term is $\frac{n+1}{2}$ th term $= \frac{37+1}{2}$ th term = 19 th term

So, three middle terms are 18th term 19th term and 20th term.

The sum of three middle most term is 225.

$\Rightarrow \quad a_{18} + a_{19} + a_{20} = 225$

$\Rightarrow \quad a + 17d + a + 18d + a + 19d = 225$

$\Rightarrow \quad 3a + 54d = 225$

$\Rightarrow \quad a + 18d = 75 \qquad \ldots(i)$

and sum of last 3 terms is 429

$\Rightarrow \quad a_{35} + a_{36} + a_{37} = 429$

$\Rightarrow \quad a + 34d + a + 35d + a + 36d = 429$

$\Rightarrow \quad 3a + 105d = 429$

$\Rightarrow \quad a + 35d = 143 \quad \text{...(ii)}$

On subtracting Eq. (i) from Eq. (ii), we get

$35d - 18d = 143 - 75$

$\Rightarrow \quad 17d = 68$

$\Rightarrow \quad d = 4$

On substituting $d = 4$ in Eq. (i), we get

$a + 18 \times 4 = 75$

$\Rightarrow \quad a = 75 - 72 = 3$

Then, the required A.P is 3, 7, 11, 15, ...

Q.13 The digits of a positive number, having three digits are in A.P. and their sum is 15. The number obtained by reversing the digits is 594 less than the original number. Find the number.

Sol. Let the digit at the hundredth place of the number be $(a + d)$.

Digit at the tens place be a.

Digit at the ones place be $(a - d)$.

Sum of the digits = 15

$\Rightarrow \quad a + d + a + a - d = 15$

$\Rightarrow \quad 3a = 15 \Rightarrow a = 5$

The number formed by the digits

$= 100(5 + d) + 10(5) + (5 - d)$

$= 555 + 99d$

The number formed by reversing the digits

$= 100(5 - d) + 10(5) + (5 + d)$

$= 555 - 99d$

Given that the number formed by reversing the digits is 594 less than the original number

$(555 + 99d) - (555 - 99d) = 594$

$\Rightarrow \quad 198d = 594$

$\Rightarrow \quad d = 3$

Now, $\quad a + d = 5 + 3 = 8 \Rightarrow a = 5$

$a - d = 5 - 3 = 2$

Hence, the number formed by the digits

$= 100(8) + 10(5) + 1(2) = 852$

Triangles

CHAPTER 06

Important Points

01 Similar Figures Two figures are said to be similar, if they have the same shape but it may differ in size.

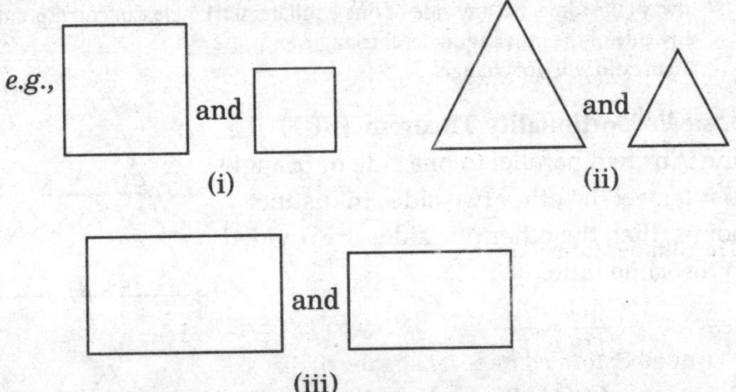

02 Congruency of Figures Two figures are said to be congruent, if they have the same shape and the same size.

Note 1. Congruent figures are always similar, whereas similar figures are not necessarily congruent.

2. Two polygons of the same number of sides are similar, if
   (i) their corresponding angles are equal.
   (ii) their corresponding sides are in the same ratio (or proportion).

03 Similar Triangle Two triangles are said to be similar, if their corresponding angles are equal and corresponding sides are proportional (*i.e.*, the ratios of the lengths of the corresponding sides are equal).

e.g. If, in $\Delta\, ABC$ and ΔPQR

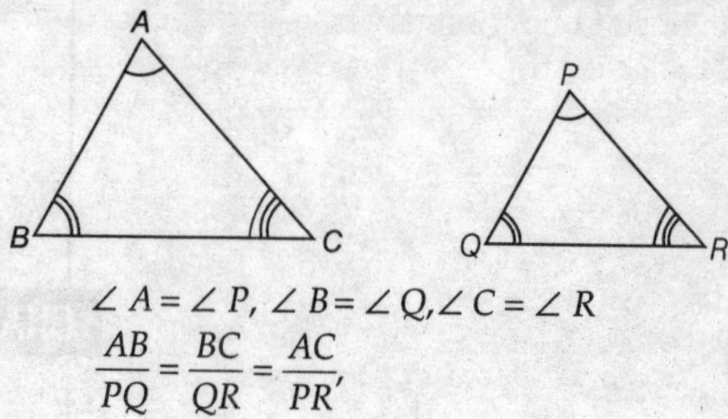

$$\angle A = \angle P,\ \angle B = \angle Q, \angle C = \angle R$$

and $$\frac{AB}{PQ} = \frac{BC}{QR} = \frac{AC}{PR},$$

Then, $\Delta\, ABC \sim \Delta\, PQR$; where symbol ~ is read as, 'is similar to'.

04 Conversely If $\Delta\, ABC$ is similar to $\Delta\, PQR$, then

$$\angle A = \angle P; \angle B = \angle Q; \angle C = \angle R \text{ and } \frac{AB}{PQ} = \frac{BC}{QR} = \frac{AC}{PR}$$

Note The ratio of any two corresponding sides of two equilateral triangles is always the same. i.e. any side of one equilateral triangle can correspond to any side of the other equilateral triangle and their ratio will not change.

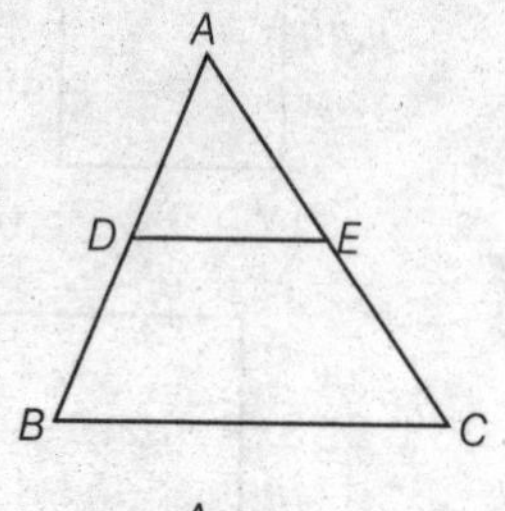

05 Basic Proportionality Theorem (BPT) If a line is drawn parallel to one side of triangle to intersect the other two sides in distinct points, then the other two sides are divided in the same ratio.

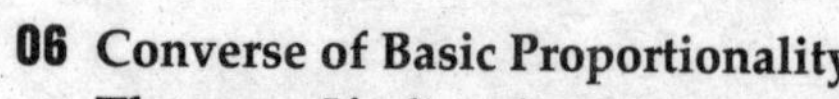

i.e., $$\frac{AD}{DB} = \frac{AE}{EC}$$

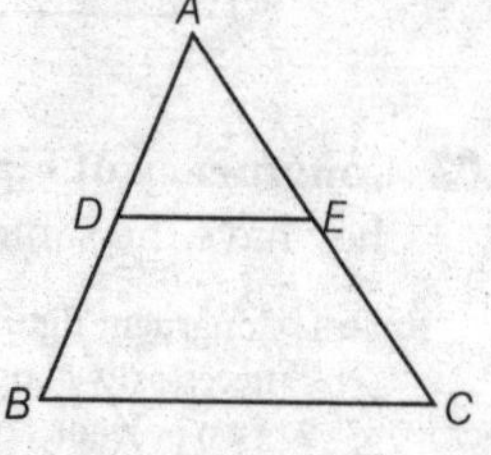

06 Converse of Basic Proportionality Theorem If a line divides any two sides of a triangle in the same ratio, then the line must be parallel to the third side. *i.e.,*

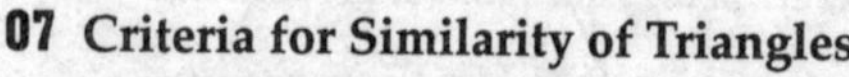

If $$\frac{AD}{DB} = \frac{AE}{EC}$$

Then, $DE \parallel BC$

07 Criteria for Similarity of Triangles

(i) **AAA** (AA) **Similarity** If in two triangles, corresponding angles are equal, then their corresponding sides are in the same ratio, *i.e.,* they are proportional and hence the two triangles are similar.

or

If two angles of one triangle are respectively equal to two angles of another triangle, then the two triangles are similar.

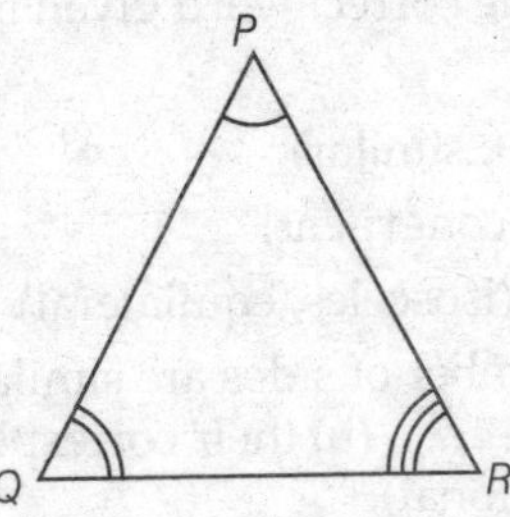

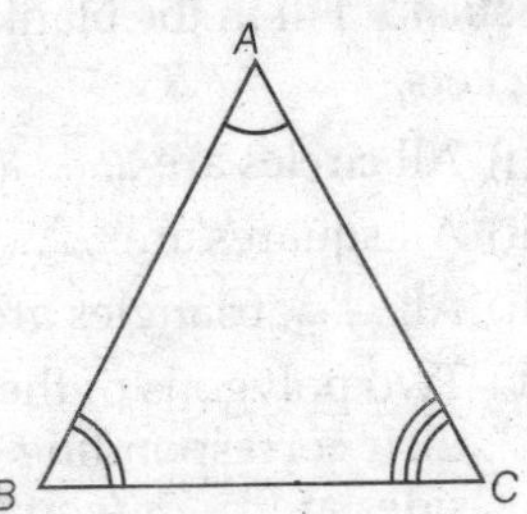

(ii) **SSS Similarity** If in two triangles, sides of one triangle are proportional to (*i.e.*, in the same ratio as) the sides of the other triangle, then their corresponding angles are equal and hence the two triangles are similar.

In ΔPQR and ΔABC, $\Delta PQR \sim \Delta ABC$, if $\frac{PQ}{AB} = \frac{QR}{BC} = \frac{PR}{AC}$

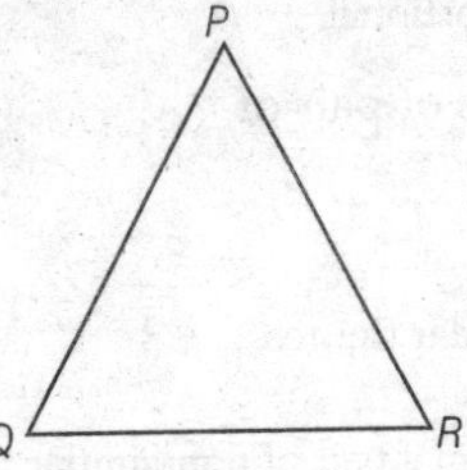

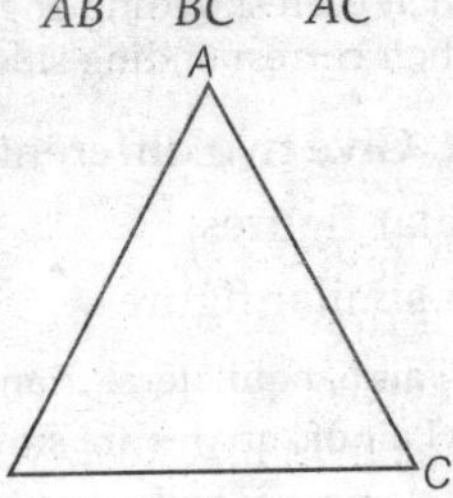

(iii) **SAS Similarity** If one angle of a triangle is equal to one angle of the other triangle and the sides including these angles are proportional, then the two triangles are similar.

In, ΔPQR and ΔABC, $\Delta PQR \sim \Delta ABC$, if $\frac{PQ}{AB} = \frac{PR}{AC}$ and $\angle P = \angle A$.

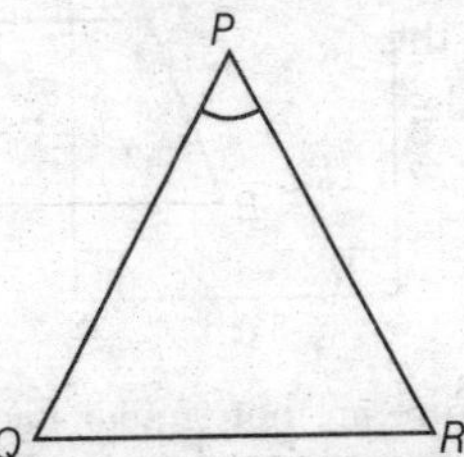

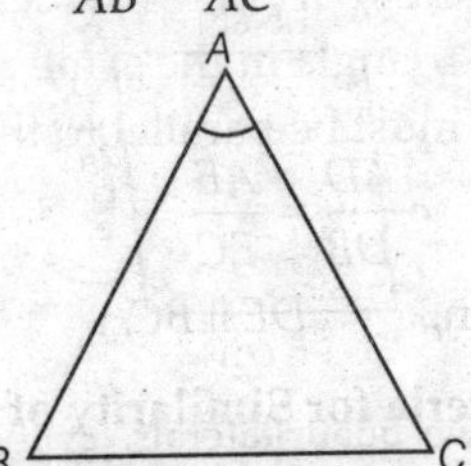

08 RHS Criterion If in two triangles, hypotenuse and one side of one triangle are proportional to the hypotenuse and one side of the other triangle, then the two triangles are similar.

Exercise 6.1

Question 1 Fill in the blanks using the correct word given in brackets.

(i) All circles are ....(congruent, similar)

(ii) All squares are ....(similar, congruent)

(iii) All .... triangles are similar. (isosceles, equilateral)

(iv) Two polygons of the same number of sides are similar, if (a) their corresponding angles are .... (b) their corresponding sides are ....(equal, proportional).

Sol. (i) All circles are similar because they have same shape but not same size.

(ii) All squares are similar because they have same shape but not same size.

(iii) All equilateral triangles are similar because they have same shape but not same size.

(iv) Two polygons of the same number of sides are similar, if
(a) their corresponding angles are equal.
(b) their corresponding sides are proportional.

Question 2 Give two different examples of pair of

(i) similar figures.

(ii) non-similar figures.

Sol. (i) (a) Pair of equilateral triangle are similar figures.
(b) Pair of squares are similar figures.

(ii) (a) A triangle and a quadrilateral form a pair of non-similar figures.
(b) A square and a trapezium form a pair of non-similar figures.

Question 3 State whether the following quadrilaterals are similar or not.

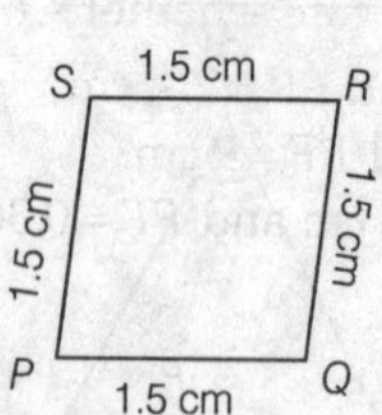

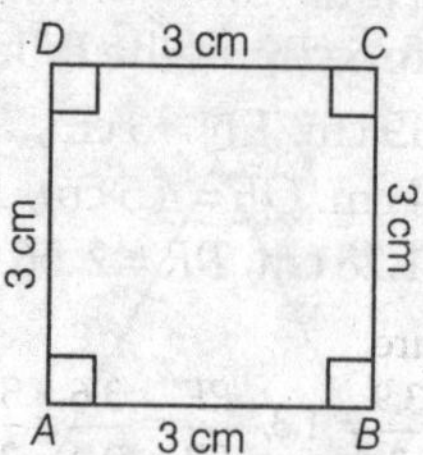

Sol. The two quadrilaterals, in the given figure are not similar because their corresponding angles are not equal even though their corresponding sides are proportional. It is clear from the figure that, $\angle A$ is 90° but $\angle P$ is not 90°.

Note Both of the conditions of the similar figures should be satisfied. If one of the two conditions is not satisfied, then the figures fails to be similar.

Exercise 6.2

Question 1 In figures (i) and (ii), $DE \parallel BC$. Find EC in figure (i) and AD in figure (ii).

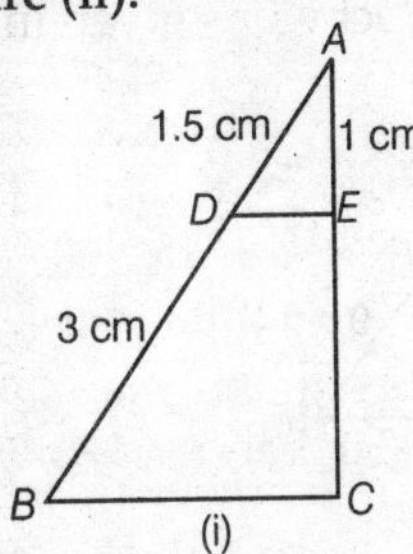

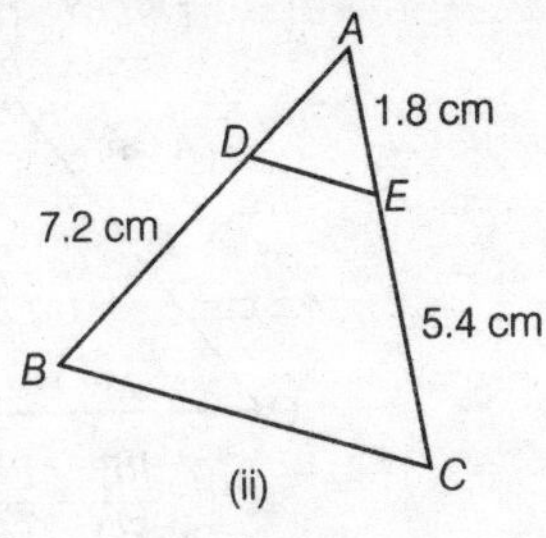

Thinking Process Use the basic proportionality theorem to find the required value.

Sol. (i) In figure (i), $DE \parallel BC$ (Given)

$\therefore \quad \frac{AD}{DB} = \frac{AE}{EC}$ (By basic proportionality theorem)

$\Rightarrow \quad \frac{1.5}{3} = \frac{1}{EC}$

($\because AD = 1.5$ cm, $DB = 3$ cm and $AE = 1$ cm, given)

$\Rightarrow \quad EC = \frac{3}{1.5} = 2$ cm

(ii) In figure (ii), $DE \parallel BC$ (Given)

$\therefore \quad \frac{AD}{DB} = \frac{AE}{EC}$ (By basic proportionality theorem)

$\Rightarrow \quad \frac{AD}{7.2} = \frac{1.8}{5.4}$ ($\because AE = 1.8$ cm, $EC = 5.4$ cm and $BD = 7.2$ cm, given)

$\Rightarrow \quad AD = \frac{1.8 \times 7.2}{5.4} = 2.4$ cm

Question 2 E and F are points on the sides PQ and PR, respectively of a ΔPQR, for each of the following cases, state whether $EF \parallel QR$.

(i) $PE = 3.9$ cm, $EQ = 3$ cm, $PF = 3.6$ cm and $FR = 2.4$ cm.

(ii) $PE = 4$ cm, $QE = 4.5$ cm, $PF = 8$ cm and $RF = 9$ cm.

(iii) $PQ = 1.28$ cm, $PR = 2.56$ cm, $PE = 0.18$ cm and $PF = 0.36$ cm.

Sol. (i) In figure,

$\frac{PE}{EQ} = \frac{3.9}{3} = 1.3, \quad \frac{PF}{FR} = \frac{3.6}{2.4} = \frac{3}{2} = 1.5$

$\because \quad \frac{PE}{EQ} \neq \frac{PF}{FR}$

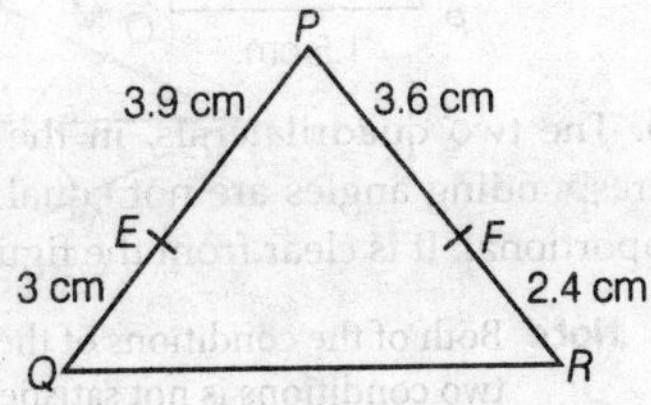

$\therefore EF$ is not parallel to QR because the converse of the basic proportionality theorem is not satisfied.

(ii) In figure, $\frac{PE}{EQ} = \frac{4}{4.5} = \frac{40}{45} = \frac{8}{9}$

and $\frac{PF}{FR} = \frac{8}{9}$

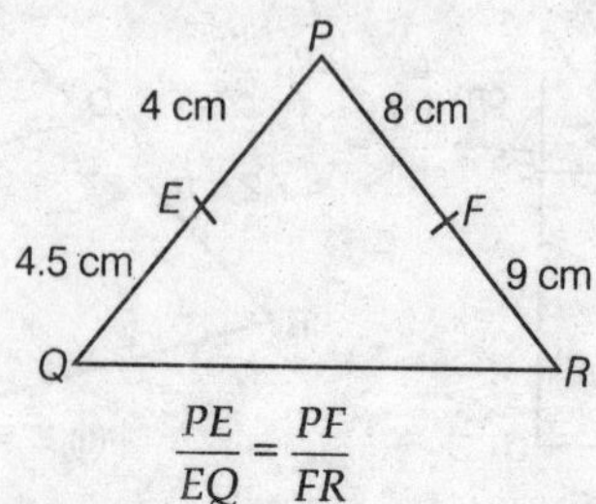

$\because$ $\frac{PE}{EQ} = \frac{PF}{FR}$

$\therefore EF \parallel QR$ because the converse of the basic proportionality theorem is satisfied.

(iii) In figure, $\frac{PE}{EQ} = \frac{PE}{PQ - PE} = \frac{0.18}{1.28 - 0.18} = \frac{0.18}{1.10} = \frac{9}{55}$

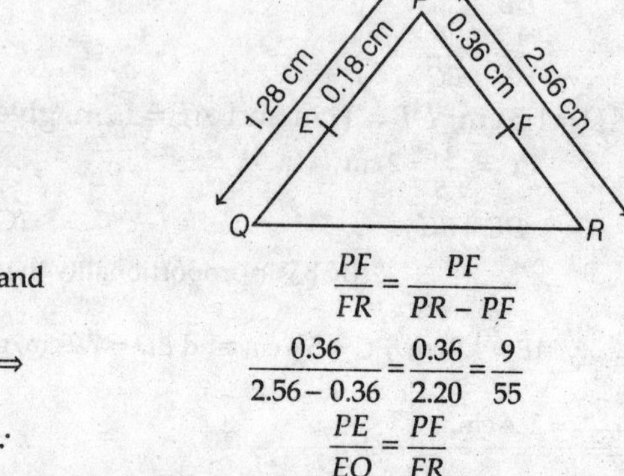

and $\frac{PF}{FR} = \frac{PF}{PR - PF}$

$\Rightarrow$ $\frac{0.36}{2.56 - 0.36} = \frac{0.36}{2.20} = \frac{9}{55}$

$\because$ $\frac{PE}{EQ} = \frac{PF}{FR}$

$\therefore EF \parallel QR$ because the converse of the basic proportionality theorem is satisfied.

Question 3 In figure, if $LM \parallel CB$ and $LN \parallel CD$, prove that $\frac{AM}{AB} = \frac{AN}{AD}$.

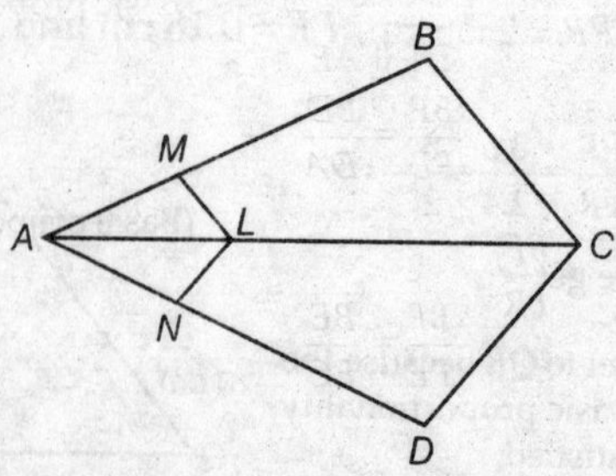

Sol. In Δ ACB, $LM \parallel CB$ (Given)

$$\Rightarrow \frac{AM}{MB} = \frac{AL}{LC} \quad \text{...(i)}$$

(Basic proportionality theorem)

In Δ ACD, $LN \parallel CD$ (Given)

$$\Rightarrow \frac{AN}{ND} = \frac{AL}{LC} \quad \text{...(ii)}$$

(Basic proportionality theorem)

From Eqs. (i) and (ii), we get

$$\frac{AM}{MB} = \frac{AN}{ND} \Rightarrow \frac{MB}{AM} = \frac{ND}{AN}$$

$$\frac{MB}{AM} + 1 = \frac{ND}{AN} + 1 \quad \text{(Adding 1 to both the sides)}$$

$$\Rightarrow \frac{MB + AM}{AM} = \frac{ND + AN}{AN}$$

$$\Rightarrow \frac{AM}{AM + MB} = \frac{AN}{AN + ND}$$

$$\Rightarrow \frac{AM}{AB} = \frac{AN}{AD}$$

Hence Proved.

Question 4 In figure, $DE \parallel AC$ and $DF \parallel AE$. Prove that $\frac{BF}{FE} = \frac{BE}{EC}$.

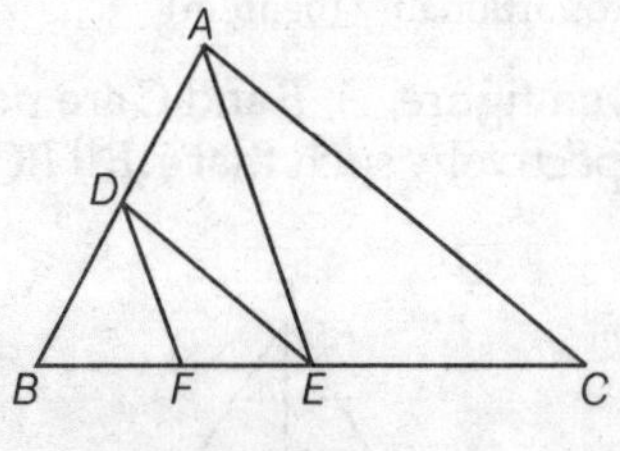

Sol. In Δ BAC, $DE \parallel AC$ (Given)

$$\Rightarrow \frac{BE}{EC} = \frac{BD}{DA} \quad \text{...(i)}$$

(Basic proportionality theorem)

In Δ BAE, $DF \parallel AE$ (Given)

$$\Rightarrow \frac{BF}{FE} = \frac{BD}{DA} \quad \text{...(ii)}$$

(Basic proportionality theorem)

From Eqs. (i) and (ii), we get

$$\frac{BF}{FE} = \frac{BE}{EC}$$

Hence Proved.

Question 5 In figure, $DE \parallel OQ$ and $DF \parallel OR$. Show that $EF \parallel QR$.

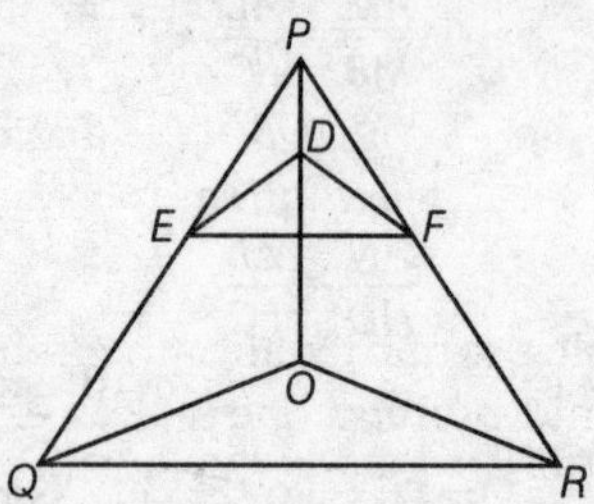

Sol. In figure, $DE \parallel OQ$ and $DF \parallel OR$, then by basic proportionality theorem,

In $\Delta\, PQO$, we have, $$\frac{PE}{EQ} = \frac{PD}{DO} \quad \ldots(i)$$

and in $\Delta\, POR$,

$$\frac{PF}{FR} = \frac{PD}{DO} \quad \ldots(ii)$$

From Eqs. (i) and (ii), we get $$\frac{PE}{EQ} = \frac{PF}{FR}$$

Now, in $\Delta\, PQR$, we have proved that

$$\frac{PE}{EQ} = \frac{PF}{FR}$$

$\therefore$ $$EF \parallel QR$$

(By converse of basic proportionality theorem) **Hence Proved.**

Question 6 In the given figure, A, B and C are points on OP, OQ and OR, respectively, such that $AB \parallel PQ$ and $AC \parallel PR$. Show that $BC \parallel QR$.

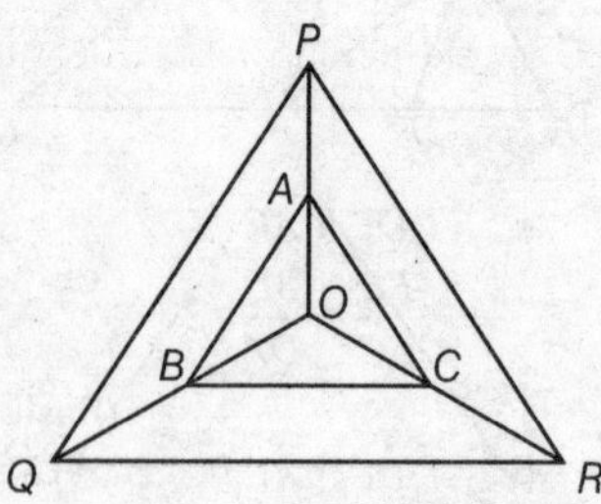

Sol. In ΔPQO, $AB \parallel PQ$ (Given)

$\Rightarrow$ $$\frac{OA}{AP} = \frac{OB}{BQ} \quad \ldots(i)$$

(Basic proportionality theorem)

Also, in ΔPOR, $AC \parallel PR$ (Given)

$\Rightarrow$ $$\frac{OA}{AP} = \frac{OC}{CR} \quad \ldots(ii)$$

(Basic proportionality theorem)

From Eqs. (i) and (ii), we get

$$\frac{OB}{BQ} = \frac{OC}{CR}$$

$\therefore$ $BC \parallel QR$

(Converse of basic proportionality theorem)

Hence Proved

Question 7 Using basic proportionality theorem, prove that a line drawn through the mid-point of one side of a triangle parallel to another side bisects the third side. (recall that you have proved it in Class IX).

Sol. Let, in ΔABC, D be the mid-point of AB.

i.e., $$\frac{AD}{DB} = 1 \quad \text{...(i)}$$

The line drawn through D is parallel to BC *i.e.*, $l \parallel BC$.

The line l meets AC at E.

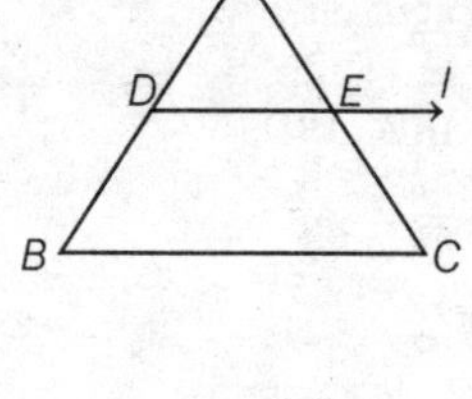

By using basic proportionality theorem, we get

$$\frac{AD}{DB} = \frac{AE}{EC}$$

$\Rightarrow$ $\frac{AE}{EC} = 1$ [From Eq. (i)]

$\Rightarrow$ $AE = EC$

Therefore, E is the mid-point of AC. **Hence Proved.**

Question 8 Using converse of basic proportionality theorem, prove that the line joining the mid-points of any two sides of a triangle is parallel to the third side. (recall that you done it in Class IX).

Sol. Let in ΔABC, D and E be mid-points of side AB and AC, respectively.

$\therefore$ $AD = DB$ and $AE = EC$

$\Rightarrow$ $\frac{AD}{DB} = 1$ and $\frac{AE}{EC} = 1$

$\Rightarrow$ $\frac{AD}{DB} = \frac{AE}{EC}$

$\therefore$ $DE \parallel BC$

(By converse of basic proportionality theorem)

Question 9 $ABCD$ is a trapezium in which $AB \parallel DC$ and its diagonals intersect each other at the point O. Show that $\dfrac{AO}{BO} = \dfrac{CO}{DO}$.

Sol. Given, $ABCD$ is a trapezium and diagonals AC and BD intersect each other at the point O. Draw a line EF passing through O such that,

$$EF \parallel AB$$

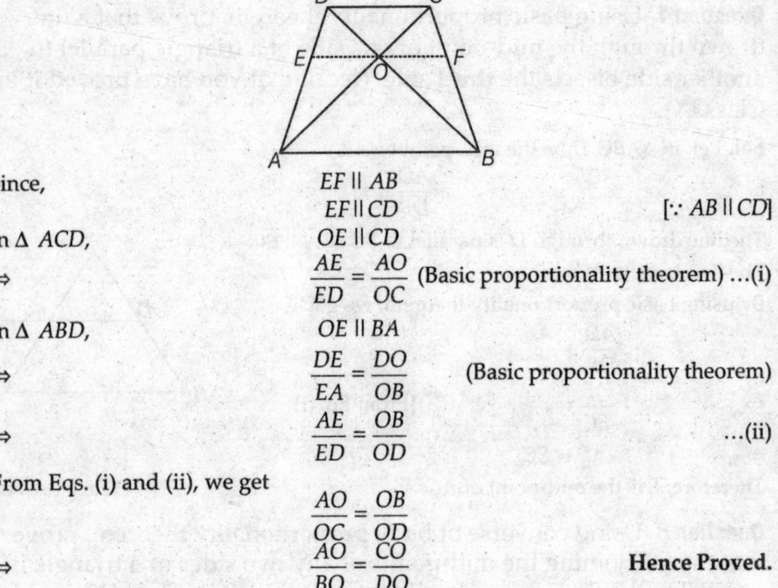

Since,
$$EF \parallel AB$$
$$EF \parallel CD \qquad [\because AB \parallel CD]$$

In $\Delta\, ACD$,
$$OE \parallel CD$$
$$\Rightarrow \quad \frac{AE}{ED} = \frac{AO}{OC} \quad \text{(Basic proportionality theorem) ...(i)}$$

In $\Delta\, ABD$,
$$OE \parallel BA$$
$$\Rightarrow \quad \frac{DE}{EA} = \frac{DO}{OB} \quad \text{(Basic proportionality theorem)}$$
$$\Rightarrow \quad \frac{AE}{ED} = \frac{OB}{OD} \quad \text{...(ii)}$$

From Eqs. (i) and (ii), we get
$$\frac{AO}{OC} = \frac{OB}{OD}$$
$$\Rightarrow \quad \frac{AO}{BO} = \frac{CO}{DO}$$

Hence Proved.

Question 10 The diagonals of a quadrilateral $ABCD$ intersect each other at the point O such that $\dfrac{AO}{BO} = \dfrac{CO}{DO}$. Show that $ABCD$ is a trapezium.

Sol. Given, $ABCD$ is a quadrilateral and diagonals AC and BD intersect each other at the point O.

In figure,
$$\frac{AO}{BO} = \frac{CO}{DO} \quad \text{(Given)}$$
$$\Rightarrow \quad \frac{AO}{OC} = \frac{BO}{OD} \quad \text{(Given) ...(i)}$$

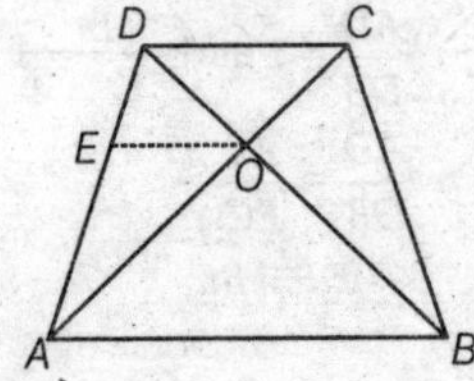

Through O, draw a line that meets AD at E such that, $OE \parallel BA$

In Δ DAB, $EO \parallel AB$

$\Rightarrow \quad \dfrac{DE}{EA} = \dfrac{DO}{OB}$ (Basic proportionality Theorem)

$\Rightarrow \quad \dfrac{AE}{ED} = \dfrac{BO}{OD}$ ...(ii)

From Eqs. (i) and (ii), we get

$$\frac{AO}{OC} = \frac{AE}{ED}$$

$\Rightarrow \quad OE \parallel CD$

(By converse of basic proportionality theorem)

Now, we have

$$BA \parallel OE \text{ and } OE \parallel CD \Rightarrow AB \parallel CD$$

$\therefore$ Quadrilateral $ABCD$ is a trapezium. **Hence Proved.**

Exercise 6.3

Question 1 State which pairs of triangles in the given figure are similar. Write the similarity criterion used by you for answering the question and also write the pairs of similar triangles in the symbolic form.

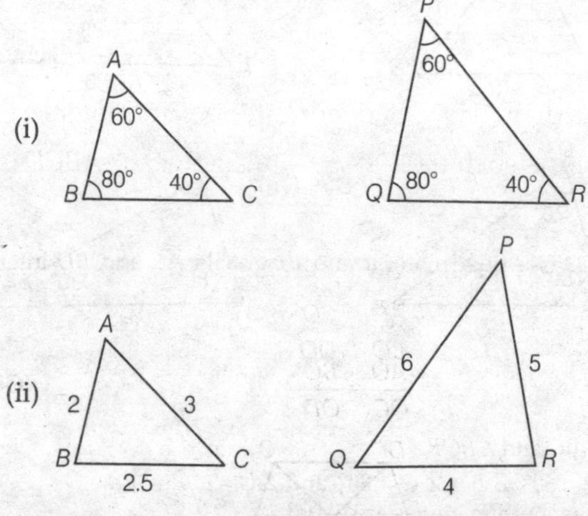

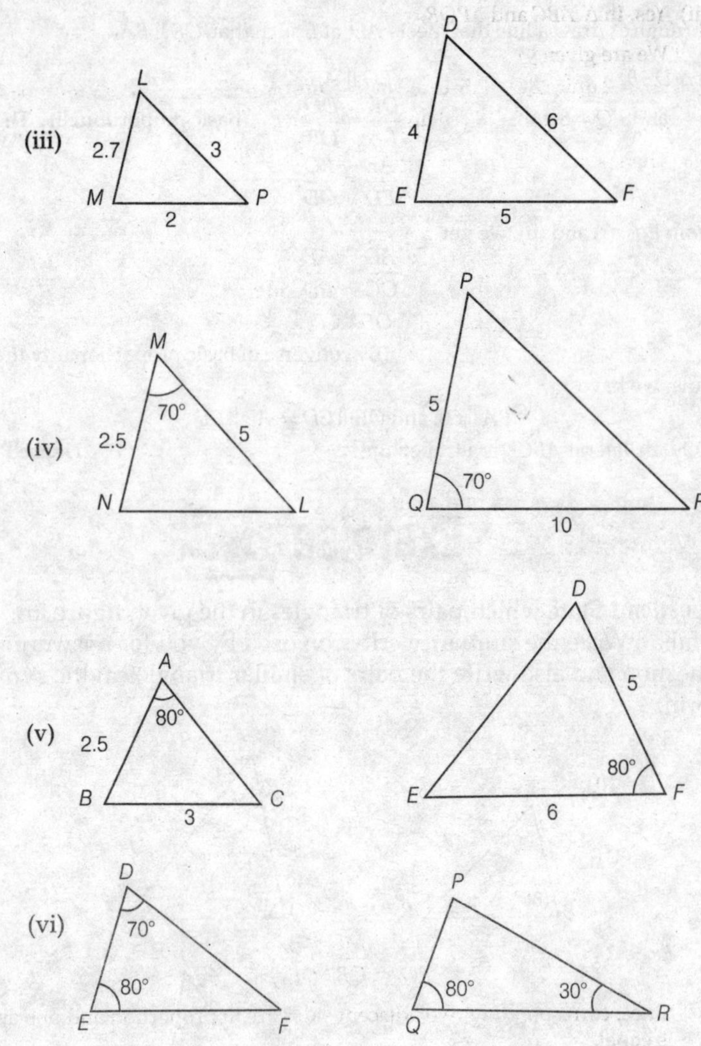

Sol.

(i) Yes. In $\Delta\, ABC$ and $\Delta\, PQR$,

$\angle A = \angle P = 60°$, $\angle B = \angle Q = 80°$ and $\angle C = \angle R = 40°$

Since, corresponding angles are equal.

$\therefore\ \Delta ABC \sim \Delta\ PQR$ (By AAA similarity criterion)

(ii) Yes. In Δ ABC and ΔPQR,

We are given,

$AB = 2$ unit, $BC = 2.5$ unit, $AC = 3$ unit

and $PQ = 6$ unit, $QR = 4$ unit, $PR = 5$ unit

Then, $$\frac{AB}{QR} = \frac{2}{4} = \frac{1}{2}, \frac{BC}{RP} = \frac{2.5}{5} = \frac{1}{2}$$

and $$\frac{CA}{PQ} = \frac{3}{6} = \frac{1}{2}$$

Since, all the corresponding sides are equal in proportion .

Therefore, their corresponding angles are also equal.

Hence, $\Delta ABC \sim \Delta QRP$ (By SSS similarity criterion)

(iii) No. In ΔLMP and ΔDEF

We are given, $LM = 2.7$ unit, $MP = 2$ unit, $LP = 3$ unit and $DE = 4$ unit, $EF = 5$ unit, $DF = 6$ unit.

Then, $\frac{MP}{DE} = \frac{2}{4} = \frac{1}{2}, \frac{LP}{DF} = \frac{3}{6} = \frac{1}{2}$ and $\frac{LM}{EF} = \frac{2.7}{5} \neq \frac{1}{2}$

i.e., $$\frac{MP}{DE} = \frac{LP}{DF} \neq \frac{LM}{EF}$$

Since, all the corresponding sides are not equal in proportion.

Thus, the two triangles are not similar.

(iv) Yes. In ΔLMN and ΔPQR

We are given, $MN = 2.5$ unit, $ML = 5$ unit and $\angle M = 70°$ and $PQ = 5$ unit, $QR = 10$ unit and $\angle Q = 70°$

$$\angle M = \angle Q = 70°, \frac{MN}{PQ} = \frac{2.5}{5} = \frac{1}{2}$$

and $$\frac{ML}{QR} = \frac{5}{10} = \frac{1}{2}$$

i.e., $$\frac{MN}{PQ} = \frac{ML}{QR}$$

Since, corresponding two adjacent sides are in proportion and one angle is equal.

Therefore, $\Delta MNL \sim \Delta QPR$ (By SAS similarity criterion)

Mistake Alert Here, if you consider $\frac{ML}{PQ} = \frac{5}{5} = 1$

Then, you won't get a second corresponding side for the SAS criteria of similarity.

(v) No. in $\Delta ABC, \angle A$ is given but the included side AC is not given.

(vi) Yes. in $\Delta DEF, \angle D = 70°, \angle E = 80°$, then $\angle F = 30°$

($\because$ In $\Delta DEF, \angle D + \angle E + \angle F = 180°$)

In $\Delta PQR, \angle Q = 80°, \angle R = 30°$, then $\angle P = 70°$

($\because$ In $\Delta QPR, \angle Q + \angle P + \angle R = 180°$).

Since, $\angle D = \angle P, \angle E = \angle Q, \angle F = \angle R$

$\therefore$ $\Delta DEF \sim \Delta PQR$ (By AAA similarity criterion)

Question 2 In given figure, $\Delta ODC \sim \Delta OBA, \angle BOC = 125°$ and $\angle CDO = 70°$. Find $\angle DOC, \angle DCO$ and $\angle OAB$.

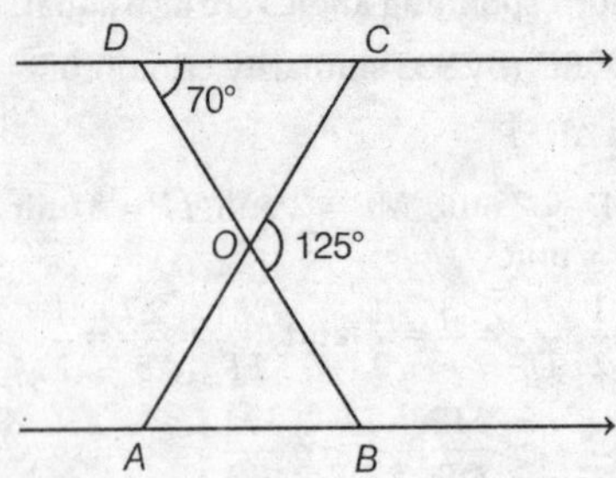

Sol. We are given, $\Delta ODC \sim \Delta OBA, \angle BOC = 125°$ and $\angle CDO = 70°$

We know, $\angle DOC + \angle BOC = 180° \Rightarrow \angle DOC + 125° = 180°$

[$\because$ Linear pair of angles]

$\Rightarrow$ $\angle DOC = 180° - 125° = 55°$

In ΔOCD,

$\angle DCO + \angle CDO + \angle DOC = 180°$ (Angle sum property of triangle)

$\Rightarrow$ $\angle DCO + 70° + 55° = 180°$

$\Rightarrow$ $\angle DCO + 125° = 180°$

$\Rightarrow$ $\angle DCO = 180° - 125° = 55°$

Now, we are given that, $\Delta ODC \sim \Delta OBA$. (Similar triangle)

$\Rightarrow$ $\angle OCD = \angle OAB$

$\Rightarrow$ $\angle OAB = \angle OCD$

$\Rightarrow$ $\angle OAB = 55°$

Hence, we have $\angle DOC = 55°, \angle DCO = 55°$ and $\angle OAB = 55°$.

Question 3 Diagonals AC and BD of a trapezium $ABCD$ with $AB \parallel DC$ intersect each other the point O. Using a similarity criterion for two triangles, show that $\dfrac{OA}{OC} = \dfrac{OB}{OD}$.

Sol. Draw $ABCD$ is a trapezium and AC and BD are diagonals intersect at O.

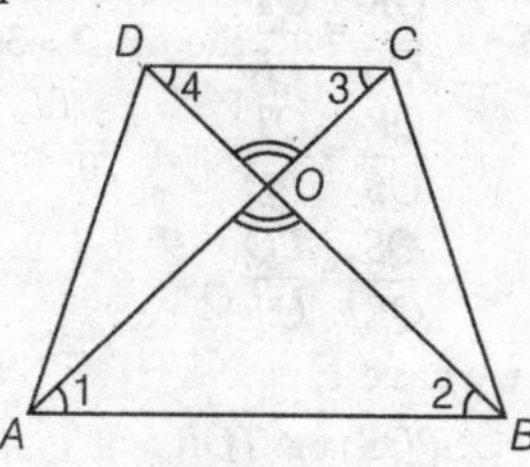

In the figure, $AB \parallel DC$ (Given)

$\Rightarrow$ $\angle 1 = \angle 3, \angle 2 = \angle 4$ (Alternate interior angles)

Also, $\angle DOC = \angle BOA$ (Vertically opposite angles)

Therefore, $\Delta OCD \sim \Delta OAB$ (By AAA similarity criterion)

$\therefore$ $$\frac{OC}{OA} = \frac{OD}{OB}$$

(Ratios of the corresponding sides of the similar triangles are equal)

$\Rightarrow$ $$\frac{OA}{OC} = \frac{OB}{OD}$$ (Taking reciprocals)

Hence proved.

Mistake Alert Whenever the figure is not given in the question. Always label the vertices either in clockwise or in anti clockwise.

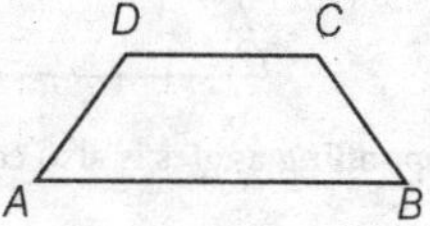

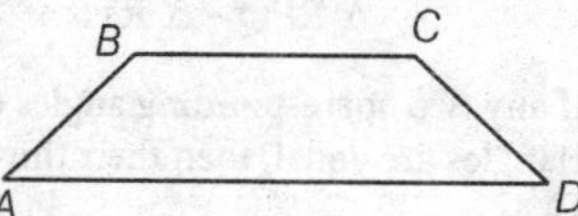

Question 4 In the figure, $\frac{QR}{QS} = \frac{QT}{PR}$ and $\angle 1 = \angle 2$, show that $\Delta PQS \sim \Delta TQR$.

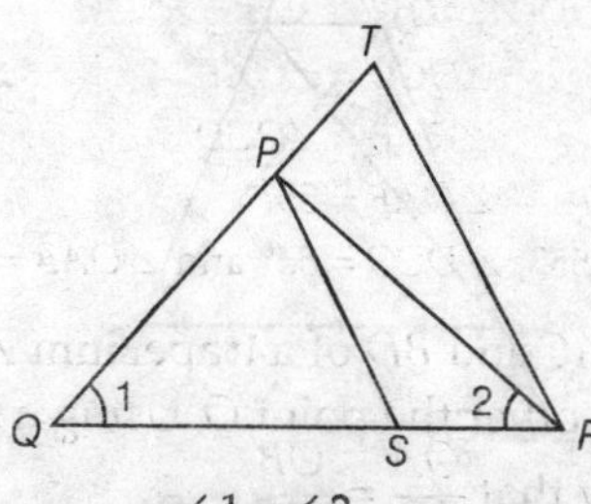

Sol. In the ΔPQR, $\angle 1 = \angle 2$ (Given)

$\Rightarrow$ $PQ = PR$

(Sides opposite to equal angles are also equal)

We are given that,

$$\frac{QR}{QS} = \frac{QT}{PR}$$

$$\Rightarrow \quad \frac{QR}{QS} = \frac{QT}{PQ} \qquad (\because PQ = PR)$$

$$\Rightarrow \quad \frac{QS}{QR} = \frac{PQ}{QT} \qquad \text{(Taking reciprocals) ...(i)}$$

Now, in $\Delta\ PQS$ and $\Delta\ TQR$, we have

$$\angle PQS = \angle TQR \qquad (\text{Each} = \angle 1)$$

and

$$\frac{QS}{QR} = \frac{PQ}{QT} \qquad \text{[By Eq. (i)]}$$

Therefore, by SAS similarity criterion, we have $\Delta PQS \sim \Delta TQR$.

Question 5 S and T are points on sides PR and QR of $\Delta\, PQR$ such that $\angle P = \angle RTS$. Show that $\Delta\, RPQ \sim \Delta\, RTS$.

Sol. Draw a $\Delta\, PQR$ such that S and T are points on PR and QR, respectively and joining them.

In figure, we have $\Delta\ RPQ$ and $\Delta\ RTS$ in which

$$\angle RPQ = \angle RTS \qquad \text{(Given)}$$

$$\angle PRQ = \angle SRT \text{ (common angle)}$$

Hence, by AA similarity criterion, we have

$$\Delta\ RPQ \sim \Delta\ RTS$$

Note If any two corresponding angles of two triangles are equal, then their third corresponding angles is also equal by AAA.

Question 6 In the figure, if $\Delta\, ABE \cong \Delta\, ACD$, show that $\Delta\, ADE \sim \Delta\, ABC$.

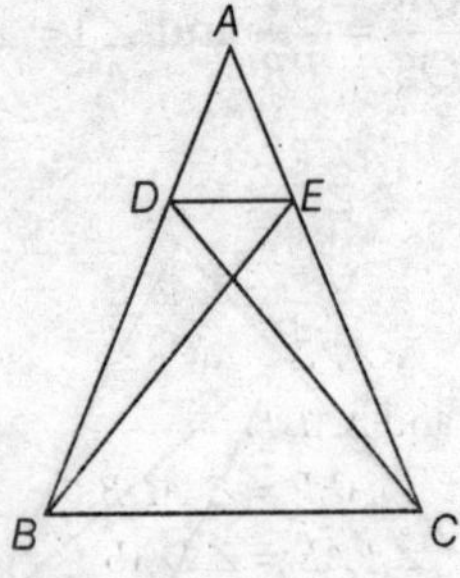

Sol. In the figure, $\Delta ABE \cong \Delta ACD$ (Given)

$$\Rightarrow \quad AB = AC \text{ and } AE = AD \qquad \text{(CPCT)}$$

$$\Rightarrow \quad \frac{AB}{AC} = 1 \text{ and } \frac{AD}{AE} = 1$$

$\Rightarrow$ $$\frac{AB}{AC} = \frac{AD}{AE}$$ (Each = 1)

Now, in ΔADE and ΔABC, we have

$$\frac{AD}{AE} = \frac{AB}{AC}$$ **Hence Proved.**

$\Rightarrow$ $$\frac{AD}{AB} = \frac{AE}{AC}$$

And also, $\angle DAE = \angle BAC$ (Common angle)

Therefore, $\Delta ADE \sim \Delta ABC$ (By SAS similarity criterion)

Hence Proved.

Question 7 In the figure, altitudes AD and CE of $\Delta\ ABC$ intersect each other at the point P. Show that

(i) $\Delta\ AEP \sim \Delta\ CDP$ (ii) $\Delta\ ABD \sim \Delta\ CBE$

(iii) $\Delta\ AEP \sim \Delta\ ADB$ (iv) $\Delta\ PDC \sim \Delta\ BEC$

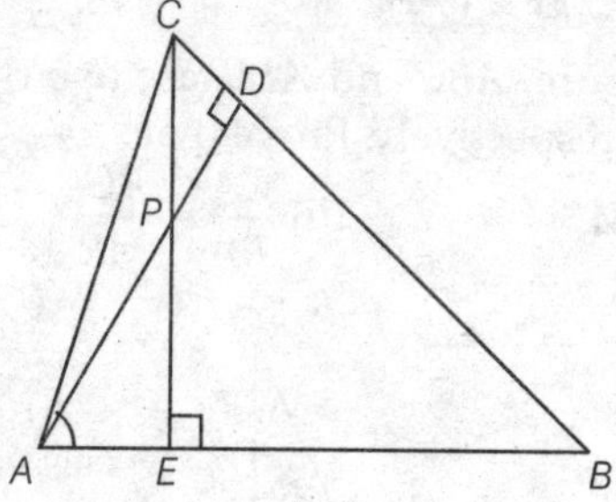

Sol. (i) In the figure, in ΔAEP and ΔCDP,

$\angle AEP = \angle CDP$ (Each = 90°)

and $\angle APE = \angle CPD$ (Vertically opposite angles)

$\Rightarrow$ $\angle\ AEP \sim \Delta\ CDP$ (By AA similarity criterion)

(ii) In the figure, in ΔABD and ΔCBE,

$\angle\ ADB = \angle\ CEB$ (Each = 90°)

and $\angle\ ABD = \angle\ CBE$ (Common angle)

$\Rightarrow$ $\Delta\ ABD \sim \Delta\ CBE$ (By AA similarity criterion)

(iii) In the figure, in ΔAEP and ΔADB,

$\angle\ AEP = \angle\ ADB$ (Each = 90°)

and $\angle\ PAE = \angle\ DAB$ (Common angle)

$\Rightarrow$ $\Delta\ AEP \sim \Delta\ ADB$ (By AA similarity criterion)

(iv) In figure, in ΔPDC and ΔBEC

$\angle\ PDC = \angle\ BEC$ (Each = 90°)

and $\angle\ PCD = \angle\ BCE$ (Common angle)

$\Rightarrow$ $\Delta\ PDC \sim \Delta\ BEC$ (By AA similarity criterion)

Question 8 E is a point on the side AD produced of a parallelogram $ABCD$ and BE intersects CD at F. Show that $\Delta\ ABE \sim \Delta\ CFB$.

Sol. Draw a parallelogram $ABCD$ and produce the line AD to AE and joining BE.

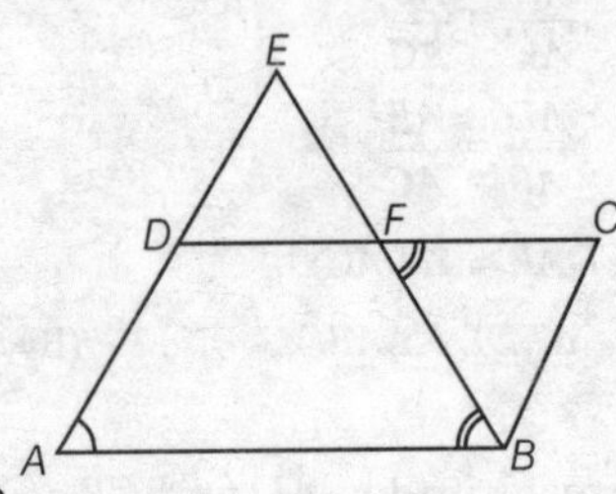

In parallelogram $ABCD$,

$$\angle A = \angle C \quad \text{...(i) [}\because \text{Opposite angles]}$$

Now, for ΔABE and ΔCFB, we have

$\angle EAB = \angle BCF$ [From Eq. (i)]

$\angle ABE = \angle BFC$ (Alternate interior angles as $AB \parallel FC$)

Therefore, $\Delta\ ABE \sim \Delta\ CFB$ (By AA similarity)

Question 9 In the figure, ABC and AMP are two right triangles, right angled at B and M, respectively. Prove that

(i) $\Delta\ ABC \sim \Delta\ AMP$ (ii) $\dfrac{CA}{PA} = \dfrac{BC}{MP}$

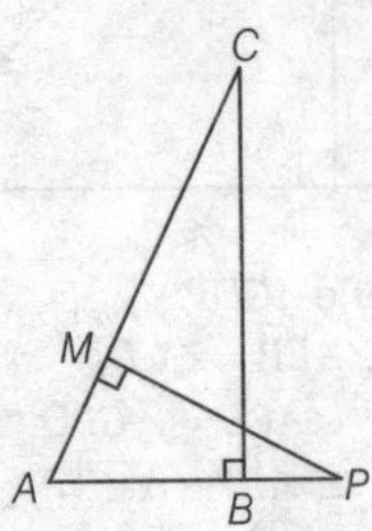

Sol. (i) Given, ΔABC and ΔAMP two right angle triangle.
In the figure, for ΔABC and ΔAMP, we have
$\angle ABC = \angle AMP$ (Each $= 90°$)

and $\angle BAC = \angle PAM$ (Common angle $\angle A$)

Therefore, $\Delta ABC \sim \Delta AMP$ (By AA similarity criterion)

(ii) As $\Delta\ ABC \sim \Delta\ AMP$,

$\Rightarrow$ $$\frac{AC}{AP} = \frac{BC}{MP}$$

(Ratio of the corresponding sides of similar triangles)

Therefore, $$\frac{CA}{PA} = \frac{BC}{MP}$$ **Hence Proved.**

Question 10 CD and GH are respectively the bisectors of $\angle ACB$ and $\angle EGF$ such that D and H lie on sides AB and FE of ΔABC and ΔEFG, respectively. If $\Delta ABC \sim \Delta FEG$. Show that

(i) $\dfrac{CD}{GH} = \dfrac{AC}{FG}$ (ii) $\Delta DCB \sim \Delta HGE$ (iii) $\Delta DCA \sim \Delta HGF$

Sol. Draw two ΔABC and ΔEFG along that draw two bisectors CD and GH of $\angle ACB$ and $\angle EGF$.

$\angle BCD = \angle ACD = \frac{1}{2}\angle ACB$ and $\angle EGH = \angle FGH = \angle FGE$

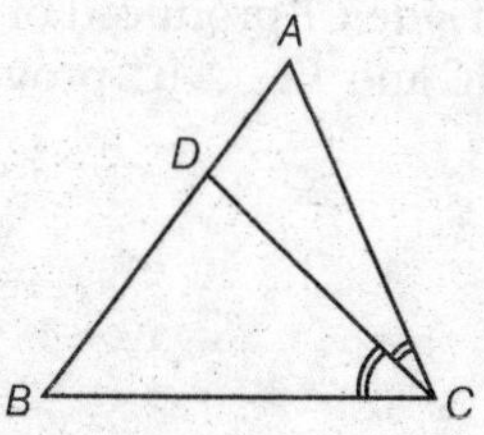

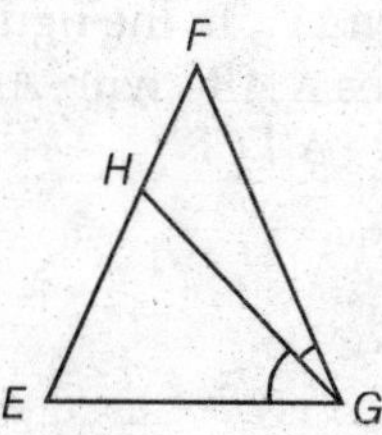

Since, $\Delta ABC \sim \Delta FEG$

Therefore, $\angle A = \angle F, \angle B = \angle E$ and $\angle ACB = \angle FGE$ ...(i)

(i) In ΔACD and ΔFGH

$$\angle CAD = \angle GFH \quad \text{[From Eq. (i)]}$$

$$\angle ACD = \angle FGH \quad \text{...(ii)}$$

$$\left[\begin{array}{l}\because \angle ACB = \angle FGE \\ \therefore \frac{1}{2}\angle ACB = \frac{1}{2}\angle FGE\end{array}\right]$$

$\Rightarrow$ $\angle ACD = \angle FGH$

Therefore,

$$\Delta ACD \sim \Delta FGH \quad \text{(By AA similarity criterion)}$$

$\therefore$ $\dfrac{CD}{GH} = \dfrac{AC}{FG}$

($\because$ Corresponding sides of two similar triangles are proportional)

(ii) In ΔDCB and ΔHGE,

$$\angle DBC = \angle HEG \quad \text{[From Eq. (i)]}$$

$$\angle DCB = \angle HGE$$

$\because$ $\angle ACB = \angle FGE$

$\therefore$ $\frac{1}{2}\angle ACB = \frac{1}{2}\angle FGE$

$\Rightarrow$ $\angle DCB = \angle HGE$

Therefore, $\Delta DCB \sim \Delta HGE$ (By AA similarity criterion)

(iii) In ΔDCA and ΔHGF,

$\angle DAC = \angle HFG$ [From Eq. (i)]

$\angle DCA = \angle HGF$ $\left[\begin{array}{l} \because \angle ACB = \angle FGE \\ \therefore \frac{1}{2}\angle ACB = \frac{1}{2}\angle FGE \\ \Rightarrow \angle DCA = \angle HGF \end{array}\right]$

Therefore, $\Delta DCA \sim \Delta HGF$ (By AA similarity criterion)

Question 11 In the figure, E is a point on side CB produced of an isosceles ΔABC with $AB = AC$. If $AD \perp BC$ and $EF \perp AC$, prove that $\Delta ABD \sim \Delta ECF$.

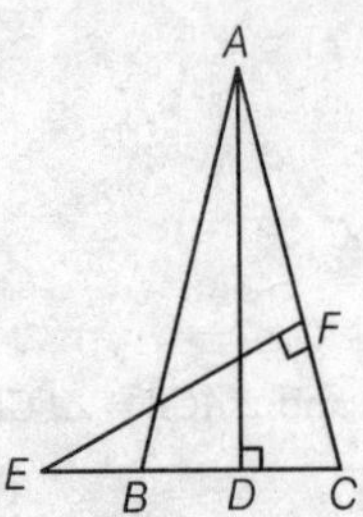

Sol. Given that ΔABC is an isosceles triangle.

And $AB = AC \Rightarrow \angle B = \angle C$ ...(i)

In ΔABD and ΔECF, we have

$\angle ABD = \angle ECF$ [From Eq. (i)]

and $\angle ADB = \angle EFC$ [Each = 90°]

Therefore, $\Delta ABD \sim \Delta ECF$ (By AA similarity criterion)

Question 12 Sides AB and BC and median AD of a ΔABC are respectively proportional to sides PQ and QR and median PM of ΔPQR. Show that $\Delta ABC \sim \Delta PQR$.

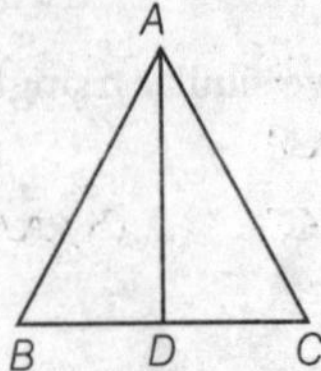

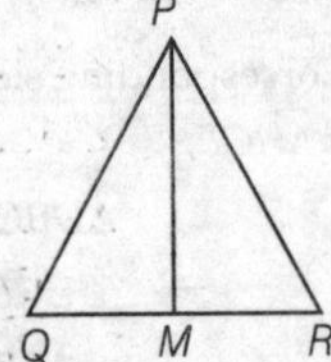

Sol. Given, for ΔABC and ΔPQR, AD and PM are the medians for ΔABC and ΔPQR, respectively.

Also, $\frac{AB}{PQ} = \frac{BC}{QR} = \frac{AD}{PM}$

$\because$ vertex D bisects BC and vertex M bisects QR.

$\therefore$
$$\frac{AB}{PQ} = \frac{2BD}{2QM} = \frac{AD}{PM}$$

$(\because BC = BD + DC = 2BD, QR = QM + MR = 2QM)$

$\Rightarrow$
$$\frac{AB}{PQ} = \frac{BD}{QM} = \frac{AD}{PM}$$

$\therefore$ By SSS similarly criterion, we have $\Delta ABD \sim \Delta PQM$

$\Rightarrow$ The corresponding angles are equal

$\Rightarrow$ $\angle ABD = \angle PQM$ [CPCT]

i.e. $\angle ABC = \angle PQR$

In ΔABC and ΔPQR,

$$\frac{AB}{PQ} = \frac{BC}{QR} \text{ and } \angle ABC = \angle PQR$$

Therefore, By SAS similarity crilterion

$$\Delta ABC \sim \Delta PQR$$

Question 13 D is point on the side BC of a $\Delta\ ABC$ such that $\angle\ ADC = \angle\ BAC$. Show that $CA^2 = CB \cdot CD$.

Sol. Draw a $\Delta\ ABC$ such that D is a point on BC and join AD.

We are given $\angle ADC = \angle BAC$

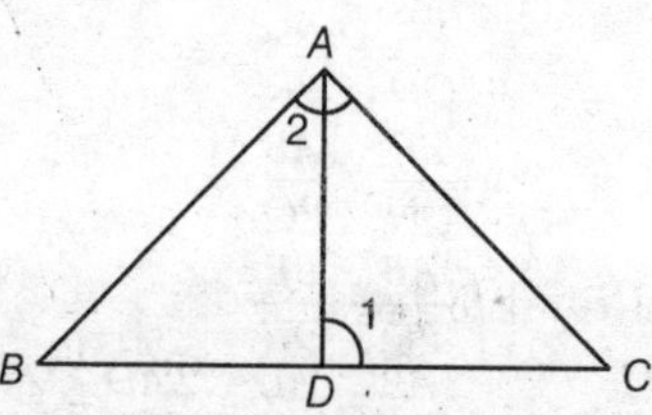

In $\Delta\ ABC$ and $\Delta\ DAC$, we have

$\angle\ BAC = \angle\ ADC$ (Given)

and $\angle\ ACB = \angle\ DCA$ (Common $\angle\ C$)

Therefore, $\Delta\ ABC \sim \Delta\ DAC$ (By AA similarity criterion)

$\therefore$ $\dfrac{CA}{CD} = \dfrac{CB}{CA}$ [CPCT]

$\Rightarrow$ $CA \times CA = CB \times CD$

$\Rightarrow$ $CA^2 = CB \times CD$ **Hence Proved.**

Question 14 Sides AB and AC and median AD of a $\Delta\ ABC$ are respectively proportional to sides PQ and PR and median PM of another $\Delta\ PQR$. Show that $\Delta\ ABC \sim \Delta\ PQR$.

Sol. Given, in $\Delta\ ABC$ and $\Delta\ PQR$,

AD and PM are their medians, respectively.

Also, $$\frac{AB}{PQ} = \frac{AC}{PR} = \frac{AD}{PM} \quad \text{...(i)}$$

Construction Produce AD to E such that $AD = DE$ and produce PM to N such that $PM = MN$. Join BE, CE, QN and RN.

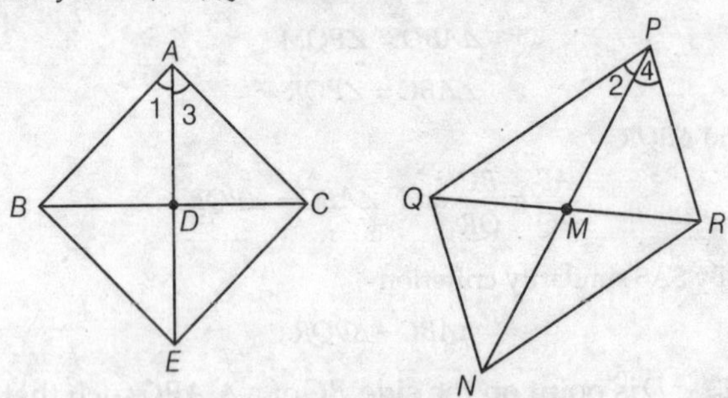

Proof Quadrilaterals $ABEC$ and $PQNR$ are parallelograms because their diagonals bisect each other at D and M, respectively.

$$\Rightarrow \quad BE = AC \quad \text{and} \quad QN = PR$$

$$\Rightarrow \quad \frac{BE}{QN} = \frac{AC}{PR}$$

$$\Rightarrow \quad \frac{BE}{QN} = \frac{AB}{PQ} \quad \text{[By Eq. (i)]}$$

i.e., $$\frac{AB}{PQ} = \frac{BE}{QN} \quad \text{...(ii)}$$

From Eq. (i), $$\frac{AB}{PQ} = \frac{AD}{PM} = \frac{2AD}{2PM} = \frac{AE}{PN}$$

($\because$ Diagonals are bisect each other)

i.e., $$\frac{AB}{PQ} = \frac{AE}{PN} \quad \text{...(iii)}$$

From Eqs. (ii) and (iii), we have

$$\frac{AB}{PQ} = \frac{BE}{QN} = \frac{AE}{PN}$$

$$\Rightarrow \quad \Delta\ ABE \sim \Delta\ PQN$$

$$\Rightarrow \quad \angle 1 = \angle 2 \quad \text{...(iv)}$$

Similarly, we can prove that

$$\Delta\ ACE \sim \Delta\ PRN$$

$$\Rightarrow \quad \angle 3 = \angle 4 \quad \text{...(v)}$$

On adding Eqs. (iv) and (v), we get

$$\angle 1 + \angle 3 = \angle 2 + \angle 4$$

$\Rightarrow$ $$\angle A = \angle P$$

In ΔABC and ΔPQR

$$\frac{AB}{PQ} = \frac{AC}{PR} \quad \text{[From Eq. (i)]}$$

And $$\angle A = \angle P$$

Therefore, $$\Delta ABC \sim \Delta PQR \quad \text{(By SAS similarity criterion)}$$

Question 15 A vertical pole of length 6 m casts a shadow 4 m long on the ground and at the same time a tower casts a shadow 28 m long. Find the height of the tower.

Sol. In figure (i), suppose that AB is a pole and behind it the sun is risen which casts a shadow of length $BC = 4$ m and makes an angle θ to the horizontal and in figure (ii) PM is a tower and behind it the [same elevation in both the cases as both shadous are cast at the same time] Sun risen which casts a shadow of length, $NM = 28$ m.

Let the height of tower, PM is h

In Δ ACB and ΔPNM, we have $\angle C = \angle N = \theta$

and $$\angle ABC = \angle PMN = 90°$$

$\therefore$ $$\Delta ABC \sim \Delta PMN \quad \text{(AA similarity criterion)}$$

$\Rightarrow$ $$\frac{AB}{PM} = \frac{BC}{MN} \Rightarrow \frac{AB}{BC} = \frac{PM}{MN}$$

$\Rightarrow$ $$\frac{6}{4} = \frac{h}{28} \Rightarrow h = \frac{6 \times 28}{4} = 42 \text{ m}$$

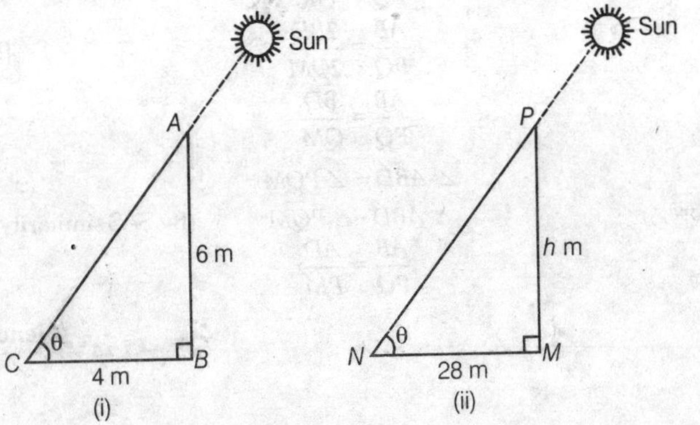

(i) (ii)

Hence, the required height of the tower is 42m.

Question 16 If AD and PM are medians of $\Delta\ ABC$ and $\Delta\ PQR$, respectively, where $\Delta ABC \sim \Delta PQR$, prove that $\frac{AB}{PQ} = \frac{AD}{PM}$.

Sol. Draw two $\Delta\ ABC$ and ΔPQR taking D and M points on BC and QR such that AD and PM are the medians of the ΔABC and ΔPQR.

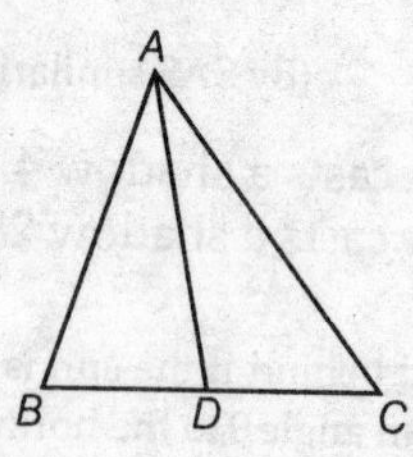

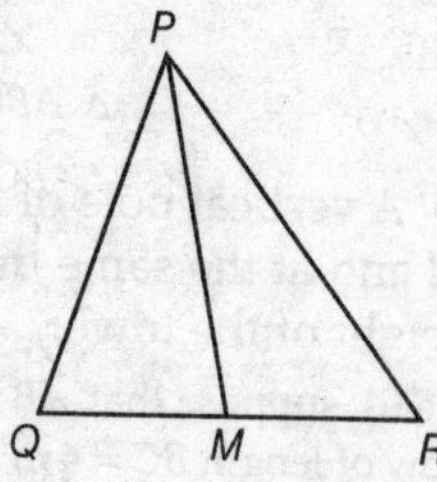

$$\Delta ABC \sim \Delta PQR \quad \text{(Given)}$$

$\therefore$ $$\frac{AB}{PQ} = \frac{BC}{QR} = \frac{AC}{PR} \text{ and } \angle A = \angle P, \angle B = \angle Q, \angle C = \angle R \quad \text{...(i)}$$

Since, AD and PM are medians of ΔABC and ΔPQR, respectively.

Therefore, $$BD = CD = \frac{1}{2} BC$$

and $$QM = RM = \frac{1}{2} QR \quad \text{...(ii)}$$

($\because D$ is mid-point of BC and M is mid-point of QR)

From Eq. (i); we get $$\frac{AB}{PQ} = \frac{BC}{QR}$$

$\Rightarrow$ $$\frac{AB}{PQ} = \frac{2BD}{2QM} \quad \text{[By Eq. (ii)]}$$

$\Rightarrow$ $$\frac{AB}{PQ} = \frac{BD}{QM}$$

and $$\angle ABD = \angle PQM \quad (\because \angle B = \angle Q)$$

Therefore, $$\Delta\ ABD \sim \Delta\ PQM \quad \text{(By SAS similarity criterion)}$$

$\Rightarrow$ $$\frac{AB}{PQ} = \frac{AD}{PM}$$

Hence Proved.

DIKSHA APP Questions

Q.1 If $\Delta ABC \sim \Delta DEF$ such that $2AB = DE$ and $BC = 8$ cm then $EF = ?$

(a) 16 cm (b) 12 cm
(c) 8 cm (d) 4 cm

Sol. (a) We have,

$$\Delta ABC \sim \Delta DEF$$

$$\therefore \quad \frac{AB}{DE} = \frac{BC}{EF} = \frac{AC}{DF} \quad \text{...(i)}$$

Since, $2AB = DE$

$$\Rightarrow \quad \frac{AB}{DE} = \frac{1}{2}$$

$$\Rightarrow \quad \frac{BC}{EF} = \frac{1}{2} \quad \text{(From Eq. (i))}$$

$$\Rightarrow \quad \frac{8}{EF} = \frac{1}{2} \Rightarrow EF = 16 \text{ cm} \quad [\because BC = 8 \text{ cm}]$$

Q.2 In a triangle ABC if DE is parallel to BC and $AD = 4x - 3$, $DB = 3x - 1$, $AE = 8x - 7$, $EC = 5x - 3$ then the value of x is

(a) 1 (b) 2
(c) 3 (d) 4

◎ ***Thinking Process*** Use basic propertionality theorem to get required value of x.

Sol. (a) Given that, in ΔABC

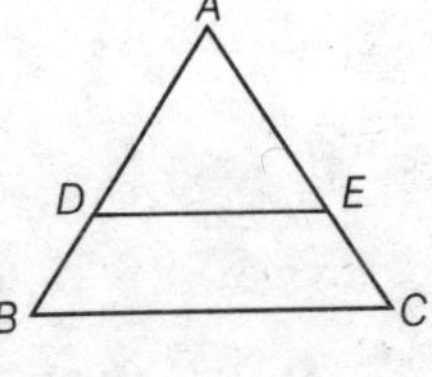

$$DE \parallel BC$$

and
$$AD = 4x - 3,$$
$$DB = 3x - 1,$$
$$AE = 8x - 7$$
$$EC = 5x - 3$$

We know that if a line is drawn parallel to one side of a triangle to intersect the other two sides in distinct points, then the other two sides are divided in the same ration.

i.e.,
$$\frac{AD}{DB} = \frac{AE}{EC}$$

$$\Rightarrow \quad \frac{4x - 3}{3x - 1} = \frac{8x - 7}{5x - 3}$$

$$\Rightarrow \quad (4x - 3)(5x - 3) = (8x - 7)(3x - 1)$$

$$\Rightarrow \quad (20x^2 - 12x - 15x + 9 = 24x^2 - 8x - 21x + 7)$$

$$\Rightarrow \quad -4x^2 + 2x + 2 = 0$$
$$\Rightarrow \quad -2x^2 + x + 1 = 0$$
$$\Rightarrow \quad -2x^2 + 2x - x + 1 = 0$$
$$\Rightarrow \quad -2x(x-1) - 1(x-1) = 0$$
$$\Rightarrow \quad (-2x-1)(x-1) = 0$$

Now, $x - 1 = 0 \Rightarrow x = 1$

or $-2x - 1 = 0 \Rightarrow x = \frac{-1}{2}$

Hence, $x = 1$, or $\frac{-1}{2}$

Since, length can not be negative. Therefore, $x = 1$.

Q.3 $ABCD$ is a trapezium such that $BC \parallel AD$ and $AD = 4$ cm. If the diagonals AC and BD intersect at O such that $\frac{OA}{OC} = \frac{OD}{OB} = \frac{1}{2}$, then BC?

(a) 7 cm (b) 8 cm

(c) 9 cm (d) 6 cm

Sol. (b) Given, $ABCD$ is a trapezium such that $BC \parallel AD$

and $AD = 4$ cm

Also, given $\frac{OA}{OC} = \frac{OD}{OB} = \frac{1}{2}$

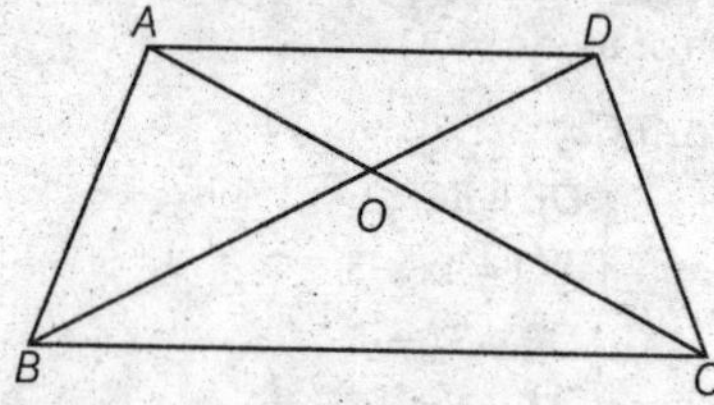

Now, in ΔAOD and ΔCOB, we have

$\angle OAD = \angle OCB$ (Alternate interior angle)

$\angle ODA = \angle OBC$ (Alternate interior angle)

So, $\Delta AOD \sim \Delta COB$ (By AA similarity)

Therefore, $\frac{OA}{OC} = \frac{OD}{OB} = \frac{AD}{BC} = \frac{1}{2}$ (Corresponding sides of similar triangles)

$$\Rightarrow \quad \frac{AD}{BC} = \frac{1}{2}$$

$$\Rightarrow \quad \frac{4}{BC} = \frac{1}{2} \Rightarrow BC = 8 \text{ cm} \qquad [\because AD = 4 \text{ cm}]$$

Q.4 In a parallelogram $ABCD$, AC is the diagonal, which of the following is true ?

(a) $\Delta ABC \sim \Delta CDA$ (b) $\Delta ABC \sim \Delta DAC$
(c) $\Delta ABC \sim \Delta ACD$ (d) $\angle B \neq \angle D$

Sol. (a) Given, in a parallelogram $ABCD$,

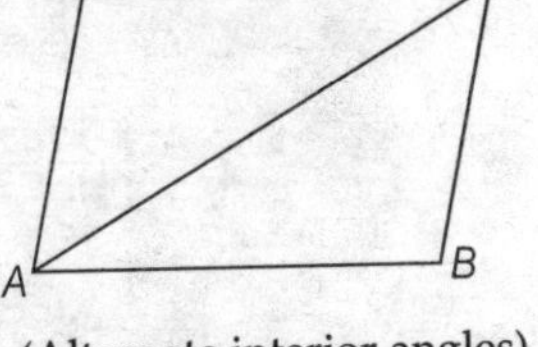

AC is the diagonal.

Then, in ΔADC and ΔCBA,

$$\angle ADC = \angle CBA$$

(Opposite angles of a parallel)

$$\angle DAC = \angle BCA \quad \text{(Alternate interior angles)}$$

Hence, by AA criterion of similarity, we get

$$\Delta ABC \sim \Delta CDA$$

Q.5 At a certain time of the day, a man 6 ft tall casts his shadow 8 ft long. At the same time the length of the shadow cast by a building 45 feet high, next to him is

(a) 90 ft (b) 60 ft.
(c) 45 ft (d) 54 ft.

Thinking Process Firstly, draw a figure according to the given conditions, then show that both triangles are similar by AAA similarly criterion, then use ratio of sides of both triangles to get required length or we can use converse of basic proportionality theorem to get the required value.

Sol. (b) Let the length of the shadow of the building = x ft

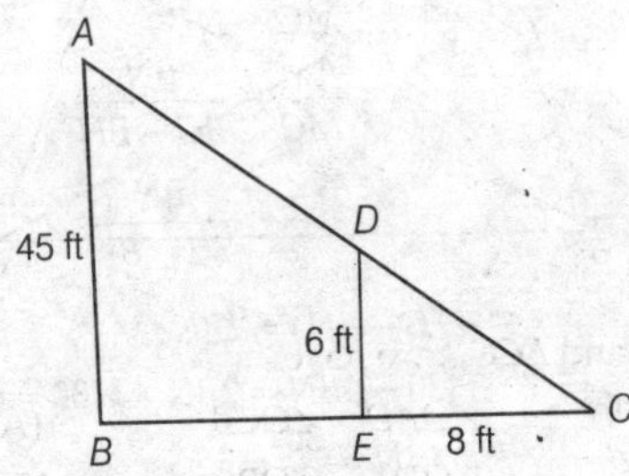

In ΔABC, we have $AB \parallel DE$.

By using of BPT, we get

$$\Rightarrow \quad \frac{AB}{DE} = \frac{BC}{EC}$$

$$\Rightarrow \quad \frac{45}{6} = \frac{x}{8} \Rightarrow x = \frac{45 \times 8}{6} = 60 \text{ ft}$$

$\therefore$ The length of shadow casted by the building is 60 ft.

Quick Solution

In ΔABC and DEC, we have

$\angle B = \angle E$ [∵ Each 90°]

$\angle ACB = \angle DCE$ [Common]

$\therefore \Delta ABC \sim \Delta DEC$ [By *AA* similarity criterion]

$$\Rightarrow \quad \frac{AB}{DE} = \frac{AC}{DC} = \frac{BC}{CE}$$

$$\Rightarrow \quad \frac{AB}{DE} = \frac{BC}{CE}$$

$$\Rightarrow \quad \frac{45}{6} = \frac{x}{8}$$

$$\Rightarrow \quad x = 60 \text{ ft.}$$

Q.6 In figure, $MN \parallel AB$, $BC = 7.5$ cm, $AM = 4$ cm and $MC = 2$ cm. Find the length BN.

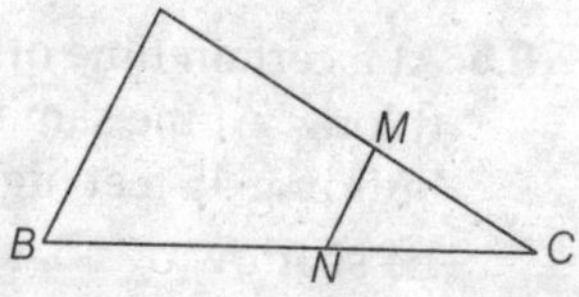

(a) 6 cm (b) 7 cm

(c) 5 cm (d) 4 cm

Sol. (c) Given, $MN \parallel AB$

and $BC = 7.5$ cm, $AM = 4$ cm, $MC = 2$ cm

In ΔABC,

By propertionality theorem, we get

$$\Rightarrow \quad \frac{AM}{MC} = \frac{BN}{NC}$$

$$\Rightarrow \quad \frac{AM}{MC} = \frac{BN}{BC - BN}$$

$$\Rightarrow \quad \frac{4}{2} = \frac{BN}{7.5 - BN}$$

$$\Rightarrow \quad 4(7.5 - BN) = 2BN$$

$$\Rightarrow \quad 30 - 4BN = 2BN \Rightarrow 30 = 6BN$$

$$\Rightarrow \quad BN = \frac{30}{6} = 5$$

$\therefore BN$ is 5 cm.

Mistake Alert Remember that Basic proportionality theorem applies only if a line is parallel to one side of triangle and intersect with two other side.

Q.7 In figure, $DE \parallel BC$ in triangle ABC such that $BC = 8$ cm, $AB = 6$ cm and $DA = 1.5$ cm. Find DE.

(a) 2 cm (b) 3 cm

(c) 4 cm (d) 5 cm

Sol. (a) Given, in ΔABC, $DE \parallel BC$

and $BC = 8$ cm, $AB = 6$ cm, $DA = 1.5$ cm

Since, $BC \parallel DE$,

$\angle CBA = \angle EDA$ (Corresponding angles)

and $\angle BCA = \angle DEA$

By AA criterion of similarity, we get

$$\Delta ABC \sim \Delta ADE$$

$$\therefore \quad \frac{AB}{AD} = \frac{BC}{DE} \Rightarrow \frac{6}{1.5} = \frac{8}{DE}$$

$$\Rightarrow \quad DE = \frac{8 \times 1.5}{6} = 2 \text{ cm}$$

Q.8 The shadow of a 5 m long stick is 2 m. At the same time the length of the shadow of a 12.5 m high tree (in m) is

(a) 6.3 m (b) 5.4 m (c) 7.2 m (d) 5 m

Sol. (d) Let DE be 5 m long stick and BC be 12.5 m high tree, then DA and BA are the shadows of stick and tree, respectively.

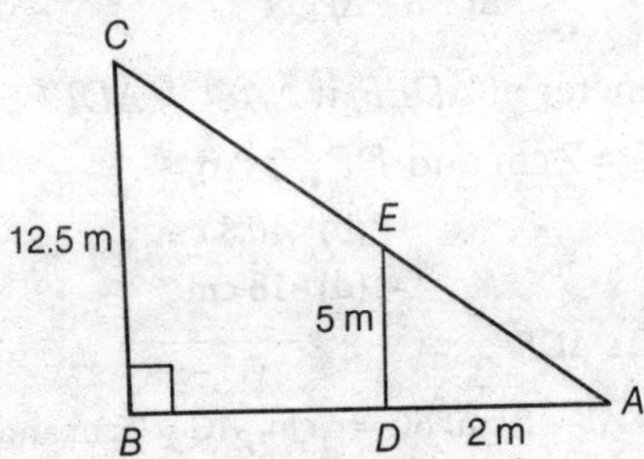

Now, in ΔABC and ΔADE, we have

$\angle B = \angle D$ [Each 90°]

$\angle BCA = \angle DEA$ ($\because$ Corresponding angles)

$\angle A = \angle A$ (Common)

$\therefore$ By AA criterion of similarity, we get

$$\Delta ABC \sim \Delta ADE$$

$$\Rightarrow \quad \frac{AD}{AB} = \frac{DE}{BC} \Rightarrow \frac{2}{AB} = \frac{5}{12.5}$$

$$\Rightarrow \quad AB = \frac{12.5 \times 2}{5} = 5 \text{ m}$$

Q.9 If in triangles ABC and DEF, $\frac{AB}{DE} = \frac{BC}{FD}$, then the two triangles will be similar, when

(a) $\angle B = \angle E$
(b) $\angle A = \angle D$
(c) $\angle B = \angle D$
(d) $\angle A = \angle F$

Sol. (c) Since ratios of two corresponding sides are equal, then according to the SAS similarity criterion. The angle made at the vertex joining the two sides should be equal.

i.e., B is the vertex joining AB and BC and D is the vertex joining ED and FD.

Hence, $\angle B = \angle D$

Q.10 If in two triangles ABC and PQR, $\frac{AB}{QR} = \frac{BC}{PR} = \frac{CA}{PQ}$, then

(a) $\Delta CAB \sim \Delta PQR$
(b) $\Delta ABC \sim \Delta PQR$
(c) $\Delta CBA \sim \Delta PQR$
(d) $\Delta BCA \sim \Delta PQR$

Sol. (a) When similarity is expressed symbolically, correct correspondence of the vertices is important, Hence, as

$$\frac{AB}{QR} = \frac{BC}{PR}$$

This implies that vertex B and vertex R are the corresponding vertices.

Similarly, C and P are the corresponding vertices and, A and Q are the corresponding vertices.

Hence, $\Delta CAB \sim \Delta PQR$

Q.11 Find the perimeter of ΔDEF, if $\Delta ABC \sim \Delta DEF$, $AB = 5$ cm, $BC = 6$ cm. $AC = 7$ cm and $DE = 3$ cm.

(a) 30 cm
(b) 10.8 cm
(c) 21.6 cm
(d) 18 cm

Sol. (b) Given, $\Delta ABC \sim \Delta DEF$,

And $AB = 5$ cm, $BC = 6$ cm, $AC = 7$ cm and $DE = 3$ cm

Therefore, $\frac{AB}{DE} = \frac{BC}{EF} = \frac{AC}{DF} = \frac{5}{3}$ [$\because AB = 5$ cm and $DE = 3$ cm]

Perimeter of $\Delta ABC = AB + BC + AC = 5 + 6 + 7 = 18$ cm

Perimeter of $\Delta DEF = DE + EF + DF$

$$= \frac{3}{5}AB + \frac{3}{5}BC + \frac{3}{5}AC$$

$$= \frac{3}{5}[AB + BC + AC] = \frac{3}{5} \times 18$$

$$= 10.8 \text{ cm.}$$

Q.12 Which pairs of triangles in the given figure are similar ?

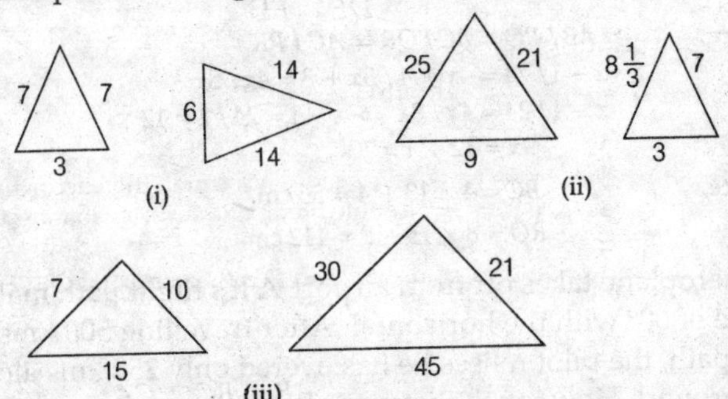

(a) All (b) (i) and (ii) (c) (ii) and (iii) (d) Only (ii)

Sol. (a) Observe that in each part, the corresponding sides of the triangles are proportional by SSS criterion.

Q.13 ΔEFG and ΔQRS are similar. The length of the sides of ΔEFG are 144, 128, 112. The length of the smallest side of $\Delta QRS = 280$. What is the length of the largest side of ΔQRS?

(a) 320 (b) 760 (c) 360 (d) None of these

Sol. (c) Since the two triangles are similar by the SSS rule,

$$EF / QR = FG / RS = EG / QS$$

Or we can say,
largest side of ΔEFG /largest side of ΔQRS will be qual to smallest side of ΔEFG /smallest side of $\Delta QRS \Rightarrow 144 / x = 112 / 280$

$\Rightarrow$ $$x = (144 \times 280) / 112 = 360$$

Mistake Alert In word problems involving similar triangles, carefully read to identify which sides are corresponding before writing the proportion.

Q.14 In the given figure, $\Delta ABC \sim \Delta PQR$, and the sides are of length (in cm) as marked along them. Find the lengths of side BC and side RQ.

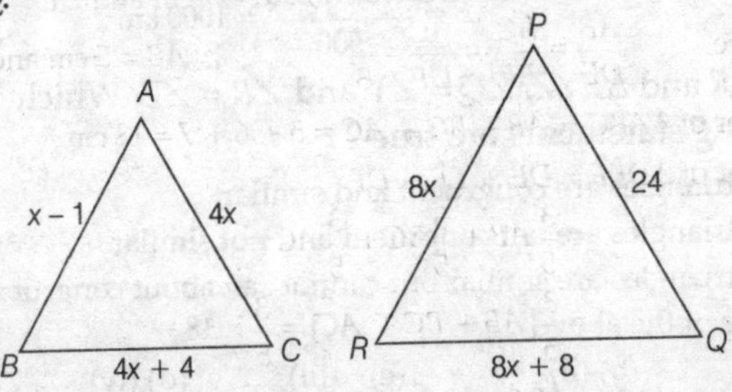

(a) $BC = 9.28$ cm, $RQ = 18.56$ cm (b) $BC = 56$ cm, $RQ = 112$ cm
(c) Cannot be determined (d) $BC = 10$ cm, $RQ = 20$ cm

Sol. (b) $\Delta ABC \sim \Delta PQR$,

Hence, $AB / PQ = BC / QR = AC / PR$

$\Rightarrow$ $x - 1 / 24 = 4x + 4 / 8x + 8 = 4x / 8x$

$\Rightarrow$ $x - 1 / 24 = 4x / 8x \Rightarrow x - 1 = 24 / 2 = 12$

So, $x = 12 + 1 = 13$

Hence, $BC = 4 \times 13 + 4 = 56$ cm.

and $RQ = 8 \times 13 + 8 = 112$ cm.

Q.15 An aeroplane takes off from airport A. It's flight path makes an angle of 60° with the horizontal. After travelling 500 kms on this path, the pilot relises he has overed only 250 kms along the ground. How much distance along the ground would have been covered after flying 2000 kms along the flight path, assuming there is no change in the flight path or in the speed of the plane ? Solve with help of a diagram.

(a) 2000 km (b) 1000 km (c) 500 km (d) 250 km

Sol. (b) In ΔABD and ΔACE, $\angle A$ is common.

If the filight path and speed of the plane does not change. It measns AC and AB and AD and AE will be in proportion.

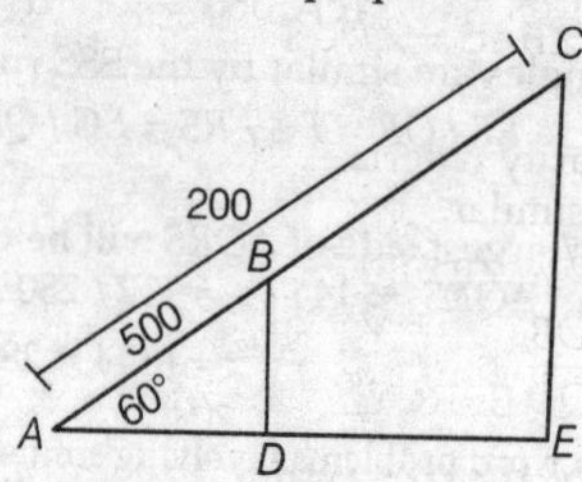

This means ΔABD and ΔACE are similar.

So, $$\frac{500}{250} = \frac{2000}{AE}$$

$$AE = \frac{2000 \times 250}{500} = 1000 \text{ km}$$

Q.16 In ΔPQR and ΔXYZ, $\angle Q = \angle Y$ and $\angle R = \angle Z$. Which of the following statements are true ?

(i) The triangles are congruent and similar

(ii) The triangles are not congruent and not similar

(iii) The triangles are similar but cannot say about congruency

(vi) None of the above

(a) (i) (b) (ii) (c) (iii) (d) (iv)

Sol. (c) As two equal corresponding angles are given, then by AA similarity criterion, the two triangles are similar and the corresponding sides are proportional.

But nothing is mentioned about the corresponding sides of the triangles. So, we cannot say anything about the congruency.

Q.17 $ABCD$ is a trapezium in which $AB \parallel CD$. Its diagonals intersect at point O. Which of the following statements are true ?

(a) $AO/OD = BO/OC$ (b) $AO/OC = BO/OD$

(c) $AO/OD = AB/CD$

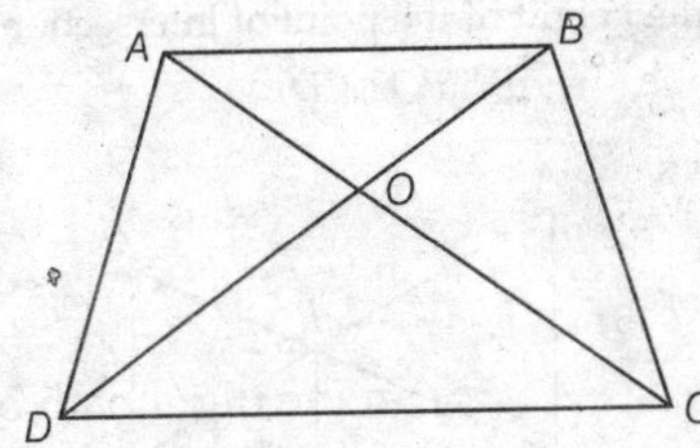

Sol. (b) Given, $ABCD$ is a trapezium

And $AB \parallel CD$,

$\angle ABD = \angle BDC$

and $\angle BAC = \angle DCA$,

In ΔAOB and ΔCOD, $\angle ABD = \angle BDC$. (Alternate angles)

$\angle BAC = \angle DCA$ (Alternate angles)

and $\angle AOB = \angle COD$ (Vertically opposite angles)

Hence, by AAA similarity criteria,

ΔAOB and ΔCOD are similar.

i.e., $\Delta AOB \sim \Delta COD$

$\therefore \quad \frac{AO}{CO} = \frac{OB}{OD}$

Q.18 Identity the pairs of figures which are similar but not congruent.

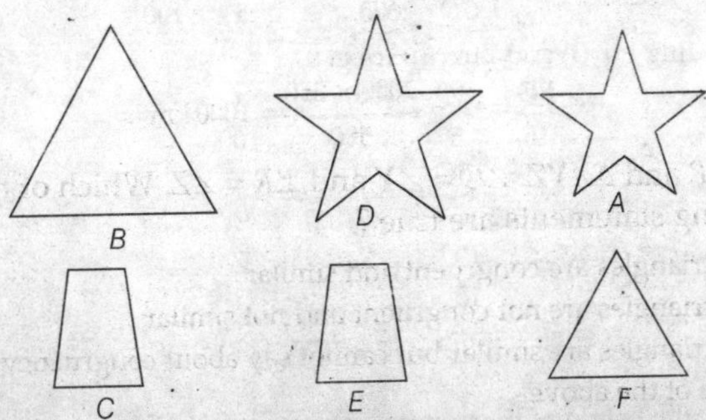

(a) A and D, B and F (b) All

(c) A and D, C and E (d) C and E, B and F

Sol. (a) The pair C and E are congruent. The other two pairs are similar.

□ Subjective Type Questions

Q.1 If two poles 5 m and 15 m high are 100 m apart, then find the height of the point of intersection of the line joining the top of each pole to the foot of the opposite pole.

Sol. Given, $AB = 15$ m and $CD = 5$ m

Now, let PQ be the height of the point of intersection.

$\Rightarrow \quad AB \parallel PQ \parallel CD$

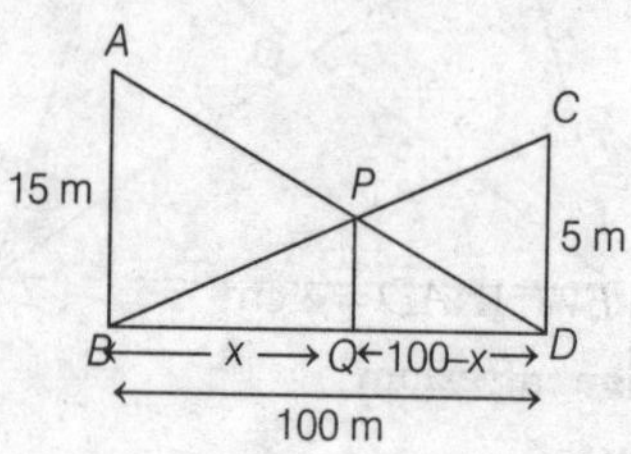

Now, in ΔABD and ΔPQD

$$\angle B = \angle Q = 90°$$

$$\angle BAC = \angle QPD \quad \text{(Corresponding angles)}$$

Hence, by AA criterion of similarity

$$\Delta ABD \sim \Delta PQD$$

$$\Rightarrow \quad \frac{PQ}{AB} = \frac{QD}{BD}$$

$$\Rightarrow \quad \frac{PQ}{15} = \frac{100 - x}{100} \quad \text{...(i)}$$

Similarly, $\Delta CDB \sim \Delta PQB$ by AA criterion of similarity.

Therefore, $\frac{PQ}{CD} = \frac{BQ}{BD} \Rightarrow \frac{PQ}{5} = \frac{x}{100}$ ...(ii)

On adding Eq. (i) and Eq. (ii), we get

$$\frac{PQ}{15} + \frac{PQ}{5} = \frac{100 - x}{100} + \frac{x}{100}$$

$$\Rightarrow \quad \frac{PQ + 3PQ}{15} = \frac{100 - x + x}{100}$$

$$\Rightarrow \quad \frac{4PQ}{15} = 1$$

$$\Rightarrow \quad PQ = \frac{15}{4} = 3.75$$

Hence, the height of the point of intersection is 3.75 m.

Q.2 If $\Delta ABC \sim \Delta RPQ$, $AB = 3$ cm, $BC = 5$ cm, $AC = 6$ cm, $RP = 6$ cm and $PQ = 10$ cm, then find QR

Sol. Given, $AB = 3$ cm, $BC = 5$ cm, $AC = 6$ cm

$RP = 6$ cm, $PQ = 10$ cm.

And $\qquad \Delta ABC \sim \Delta RPQ$

$\therefore \frac{AB}{RP} = \frac{BC}{PQ} = \frac{AC}{RQ}$ (Proportional sides of similar triangles)

$\Rightarrow \qquad \frac{3}{6} = \frac{5}{10} = \frac{6}{QR}$

$\Rightarrow \qquad \frac{1}{2} = \frac{1}{2} = \frac{6}{QR}$

$\Rightarrow \qquad QR = 12$ cm

Q.3 In ΔDEW, $AB \parallel EW$. If $AD = 4$ cm, $DE = 12$ cm and $DW = 24$ cm, then find the value of DB.

Sol. In ΔDEW, $AB \parallel EW$

So, by basic proportionality theorem, we have

$\frac{DA}{AE} = \frac{DB}{BW} \Rightarrow \frac{AE}{AD} = \frac{BW}{BD}$

On adding 1 in numberatar and denominator, we get

$\Rightarrow \frac{AE}{AD} + 1 = \frac{BW}{BD} + 1 \Rightarrow \frac{AE + AD}{AD} = \frac{BW + BD}{BD}$

$\Rightarrow \frac{DE}{AD} = \frac{DW}{BD}$

$\Rightarrow \qquad \frac{AD}{DE} = \frac{DB}{DW}$

$\Rightarrow \qquad \frac{4}{12} = \frac{DB}{24} \Rightarrow DB = 8$ cm

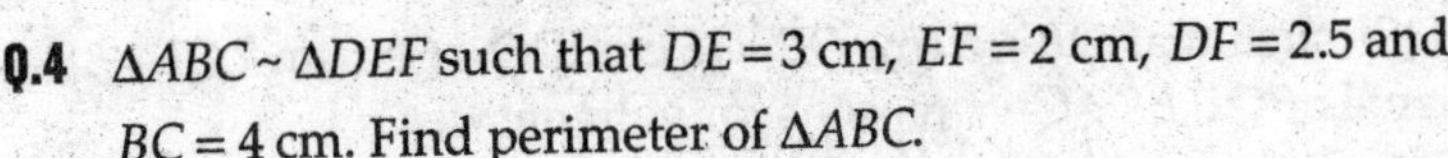

Q.4 $\Delta ABC \sim \Delta DEF$ such that $DE = 3$ cm, $EF = 2$ cm, $DF = 2.5$ and $BC = 4$ cm. Find perimeter of ΔABC.

Sol. We are given two triangles ΔABC and ΔDEF such that $\Delta ABC \sim \Delta DEF$

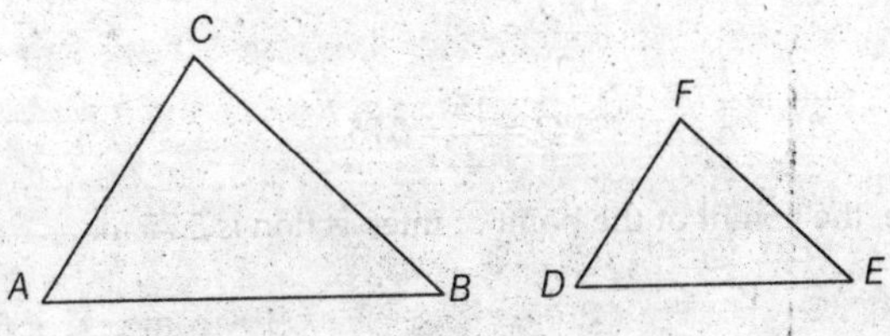

$DE = 3$ cm, $EF = 2$ cm, $DF = 2.5$ and $BC = 4$ cm

Since, $\Delta ABC \sim \Delta DEF$

Therefore, $\frac{AC}{DF} = \frac{AB}{DE} = \frac{BC}{EF} = \frac{4}{2} = 2$

Hence, $AC = 5$ cm and $AB = 6$ cm

$\therefore$ Perimeter of $\Delta ABC = 4 + 6 + 5 = 15$ cm

Q.5 In triangle ABC, $DE \parallel BC$ and $\frac{AD}{DB} = \frac{3}{5}$. If $AC = 4.8$ cm. Find AE.

Sol. Given, in a ΔABC, $DE \parallel BC$

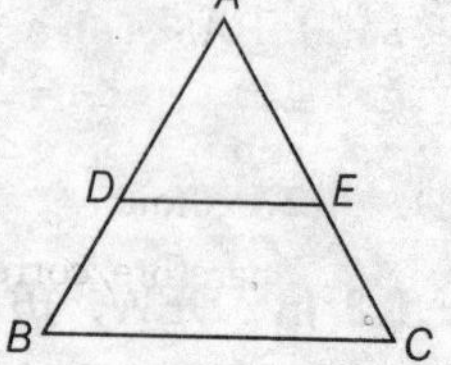

$$\frac{AD}{DB} = \frac{3}{5}$$

and $AC = 4.8$ cm

As $DE \parallel BC$,

By basic proportionality theorem, we have

$$\frac{AD}{DB} = \frac{AE}{EC}$$

$$\Rightarrow \quad \frac{AD}{DB} = \frac{AE}{AC - AE}$$

$$\Rightarrow \quad \frac{3}{5} = \frac{AE}{4.8 - AE}$$

$$\Rightarrow \quad 3(4.8 - AE) = 5AE$$

$$\Rightarrow \quad 14.4 - 3AE = 5AE$$

$$\Rightarrow \quad 8AE = 14.4$$

$$\Rightarrow \quad AE = \frac{14.4}{8} = 1.8 \text{ cm}$$

Hence, $AE = 1.8$ cm

Q.6 P and Q are the points on the sides DE and DF of a triangle DEF such that $DP = 5$ cm, $DE = 15$ cm, $DQ = 6$ cm and $QF = 18$ cm. Is $PQ \parallel EF$? Give reasons for your answer.

Sol. $\frac{DP}{PE} = \frac{5}{15 - 5} = \frac{1}{2}$

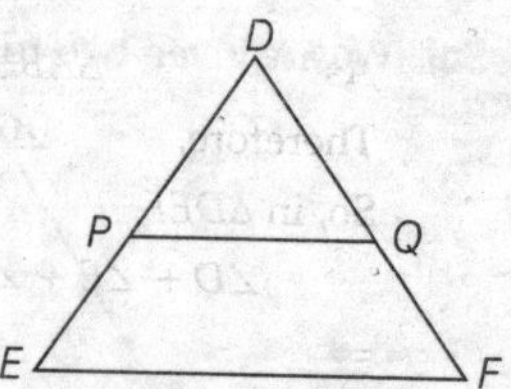

and $\frac{DQ}{QF} = \frac{6}{18} = \frac{1}{3}$

As $\frac{DP}{PE} \neq \frac{DQ}{QF}$,

[By converse of BPT theorem]

Therefore PQ is not parallel to EF.

Q.7 In the given figure, $DE \parallel BC$, $AB = 6$ cm, $BD = 3.5$ cm and $BC = 12$ cm, find DE.

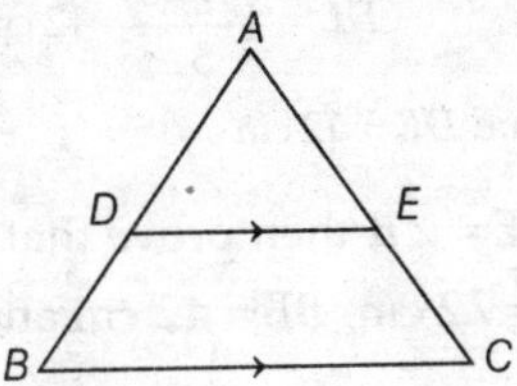

Sol. In ΔABC and ΔADE, we have

$\angle A = \angle A$ (Common angle)

and $\angle ABC = \angle ADE$ (Corresponding angles)

Therefore, $\Delta ABC \sim \Delta ADE$ [By AA similarity criterion]

Therefore, corresponding sides are proportional

$$\Rightarrow \quad \frac{AD}{AB} = \frac{DE}{BC}$$

$$\Rightarrow \quad \frac{AB - BD}{AB} = \frac{DE}{12} \Rightarrow \frac{2.5}{6} = \frac{DE}{12}$$

$$\Rightarrow \quad DE = 2.5 \times 2 = 5 \text{ cm}$$

Hence, $DE = 5$ cm

Q.8 If $\Delta ABC \sim \Delta DFE$, $\angle A = 30°$, $\angle C = 50°$, $AB = 5$ cm, $AC = 8$ cm and $DF = 7.5$ cm, find DE and $\angle F$.

Sol. Given, $\Delta ABC \sim \Delta DFE$

$\angle A = 30°$, $\angle C = 50°$

$AB = 5$ cm, $AC = 8$ cm

$DF = 7.5$ cm

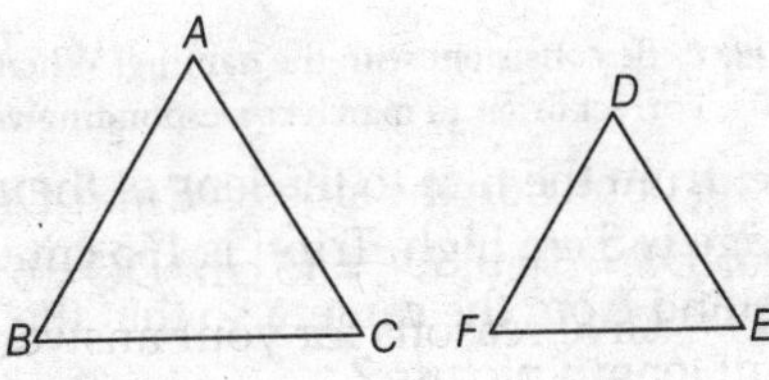

As $\Delta ABC \sim \Delta DFE$,

Therefore, $\angle A = \angle D = 30°$, $\angle C = \angle E = 50°$

So, in ΔDEF,

$\angle D + \angle E + \angle F = 180°$ [Angle sum property of triangle]

$$\Rightarrow \quad 30 + 50 + \angle F = 180°$$

$$\Rightarrow \quad \angle F = 180° - 80° = 100°$$

Also, $$\frac{AB}{DF} = \frac{AC}{DE}$$

$$\Rightarrow \qquad \frac{5}{7.5} = \frac{8}{DE}$$

$$\Rightarrow \qquad DE = \frac{8 \times 7.5}{5} = 12 \text{ cm}$$

Hence, $\angle F = 100°$ and $DE = 12$ cm

Q.9 In ΔABC, if $\angle ADE = \angle B$, then prove that $\Delta ADE \sim \Delta ABC$. Also if $AD = 7.6$ cm, $AE = 7.2$ cm, $BE = 4.2$ cm and $BC = 8.4$ cm, then find DE.

Sol. Given, $\angle ADE = \angle B$, i.e. $\angle 1 = \angle 2$

$AD = 7.6$ cm

$AE = 7.2$ cm

$BE = 4.2$ cm

$BC = 8.4$ cm

In ΔADE and ΔABC, we have

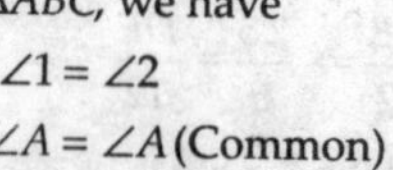

$$\angle 1 = \angle 2$$

$$\angle A = \angle A \text{ (Common)}$$

So, By AA similarity criterion $\Delta ADE \sim \Delta ABC$

Therefore, $\qquad \frac{AD}{AB} = \frac{DE}{BC}$

$$\Rightarrow \qquad \frac{7.6}{7.2 + 4.2} = \frac{DE}{8.4} \qquad \{\because AB = AE + BE = 7.2 + 4.2\}$$

$$\Rightarrow \qquad \frac{7.6}{11.4} = \frac{DE}{8.4} \Rightarrow DE = \frac{7.6 \times 8.4}{11.4} = 5.6$$

Hence, $DE = 5.6$ cm

Mistake Alert Be consistent with the naming! When stating that triangles are similar, use correct order to match corresponding vertices.

Q.10 The distance from the film to the lens of the camera is 10 cm. The film image is 5 cm high. Tripti is 165 cm tall. How far should she stand from the camera so that the photographer can take a full length picture ?

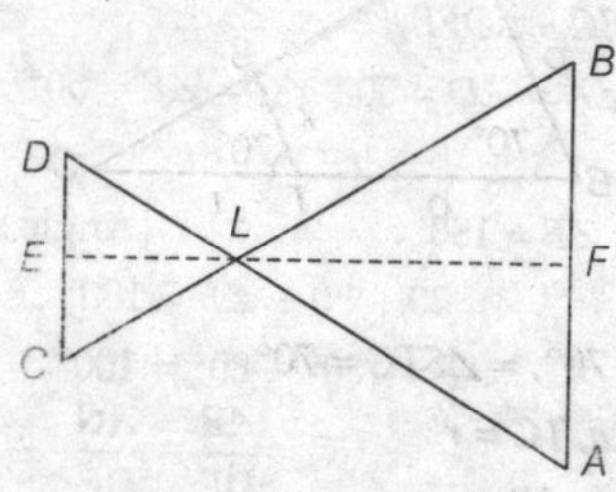

Sol. With reference to the figure, AB is Tripti's height = 165 cm, CD the height of the film image = 5 cm, L is the position of the lens, LE = 10 cm.
Let, x is distance that Tripti has to stand for a full length photo.

Since $AB \parallel CD$,

$$\angle DCL = \angle ABL \quad \text{(Alternate interior angles)}$$
$$\angle DLC = \angle ALB \quad \text{(Vertically opposite angles)}$$
$$\Delta DLC \sim \angle ALB$$

So, By AA similarity criterion

LE and LF are altitudes of similar triangles.

If two triangles are similar, then the measures of the corresponding altitudes are proportional to measures of corresponding sides.

$$\frac{AB}{CD} = \frac{LF}{LE}$$

$$\Rightarrow \quad \frac{165}{5} = \frac{LF}{10}$$

$$\Rightarrow \quad LF = 165 \times \frac{10}{5} = 330 \text{ cm}$$

Q.11 If $\Delta ABC \sim \Delta RPQ$, $AB = 3$ cm, $BC = 5$ cm. $AC = 6$ cm, $RP = 6$ cm and $PQ = 10$ cm. The find QR.

Sol. We have, AB = 3 cm, BC = 5 cm, AC = 6 cm, RP = 6 cm and PQ = 10 cm

and $\qquad \Delta ABC \sim \Delta RPQ,$

Therefore, corresponding sides of ΔABC and ΔPPQ are in the same ratio

i.e., $$\frac{AB}{RP} = \frac{BC}{PQ} = \frac{AC}{RQ} \quad \ldots\text{(i)}$$

$$\Rightarrow \quad \frac{3}{6} = \frac{5}{10} = \frac{6}{QR}$$

$$\Rightarrow \quad QR = \frac{10 \times 6}{5} = 12 \text{ cm.}$$

Q.12 In the given figure, find x in terms of p, q and

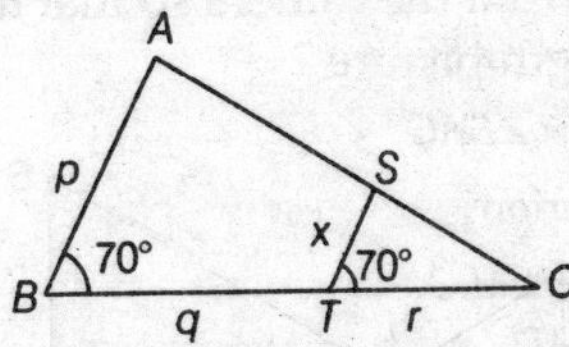

Sol. We have,

$$\angle B = 70°, = \angle STC = 70°$$
$$BT = q, TC = r$$
$$ST = x, AB = p$$

In ΔABC and ΔSTC, we have

$$\angle ABC = \angle STC = 70°$$

and $\angle ACB = \angle SCT$ [∵ Common angle]

Hence, By AA similarity criterion,

$$\Delta ABC \sim \Delta STC$$

Therefore, $\frac{TC}{BC} = \frac{ST}{AB}$

$\Rightarrow \quad \frac{r}{q+r} = \frac{x}{p}$

$\Rightarrow \quad x = \frac{rp}{q+r}$

Hence, the required value of $x = \frac{rp}{q+r}$

Q.13 In the given figure, $AC \perp BD$ and $CE \perp AD$ prove that $AC^2 = DA \cdot AE$

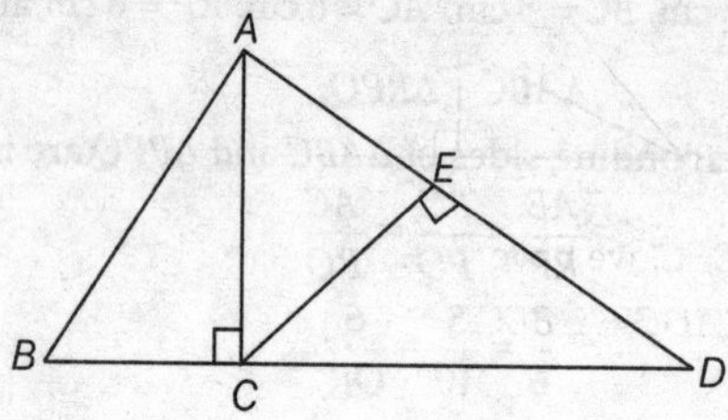

Sol. Given, in the figure

$$AC \perp BD \text{ and } CE \perp AD$$

In ΔACD and ΔACE, we have

$\angle ACD = \angle AEC$ [∵ Each 90°]

$\angle DAC = \angle EAC$ [∵ Common angle]

By AA similarity criterion

$$\Delta ACD \sim \Delta AEC$$

Therefore, $\frac{AC}{AE} = \frac{AD}{AC}$

$\Rightarrow \quad AC^2 = AD \cdot AE$

$\Rightarrow \quad AC^2 = DA \cdot AE$ **Hence Proved.**

Q.14 R and S are points on the sides DE and EF, respectively, of ΔDEF that $ER = 5$ cm, $RD = 2.5$ cm, $SE = 1.5$ cm and $FS = 3.5$ cm. Find whether $RS \parallel DF$ or not.

Sol. We have,

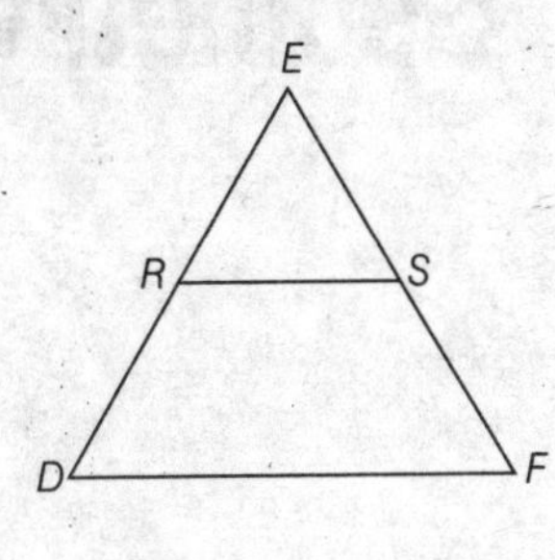

$$ER = 5 \text{ cm}, RD = 2.5 \text{ cm}$$

$$SE = 1.5 \text{ cm}, FS = 3.5 \text{ cm}$$

Now, $\dfrac{ER}{RD} = \dfrac{5}{2.5} = \dfrac{50}{25} = \dfrac{2}{1}$

and $\dfrac{ES}{FS} = \dfrac{1.5}{3.5} = \dfrac{15}{35} = \dfrac{3}{7}$

As $\dfrac{ER}{RD} \neq \dfrac{ES}{FS}$

Therefore, RS is not parallel to DF. [$\because$ Converse of BPT]

Q.15 In ΔABC, from A and B altitudes AD and BE are drawn. Prove that $\Delta ADC \sim \Delta BEC$. Is $\Delta ADB \sim \Delta AEB$ and $\Delta ADB \sim \Delta ADC$.

Sol. Given, AD are BE are altitudes from A and B, respectively.

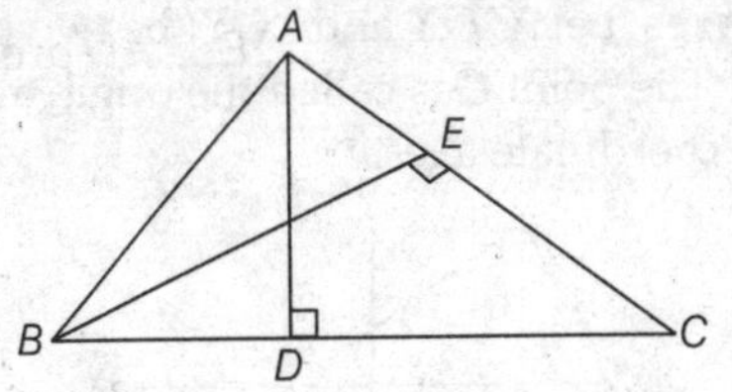

In ΔADC and ΔBEC, we have

$\angle ADC = \angle BEC$ [$\because$ Each 90°]

$\angle ACD = \angle BCE$ [$\because$ Common angles]

By AA similarity criterion.

$$\Delta ADC \sim \Delta BEC$$

Now, in ΔADB and ΔAEB

$\angle ADB = \angle AEB$ [$\because$ Each of 90°]

ΔADB is not similar to ΔAEB because they are not equiangular *i.e.*, there are no other angles which satisfy the AA similarity criterion.

Also ΔADB is not similar to ΔADC because they are not equiangular *i.e.*, there are no angles in ΔADB and ΔADC which satisfy the AA similarity criterion.

Coordinate Geometry

CHAPTER 07

Important Points

01 Coordinate Geometry Coordinate geometry is the branch of mathematics which deals with the position of an object lying in a plane, dercribed with the help of two mutually perpendicular lines.

02 Coordinate Axes Let $X'OX$ and YOY' be two perpendicular lines intersect at O. The point O is called the origin and $X'OX$ and YOY' are called the coordinate axes.

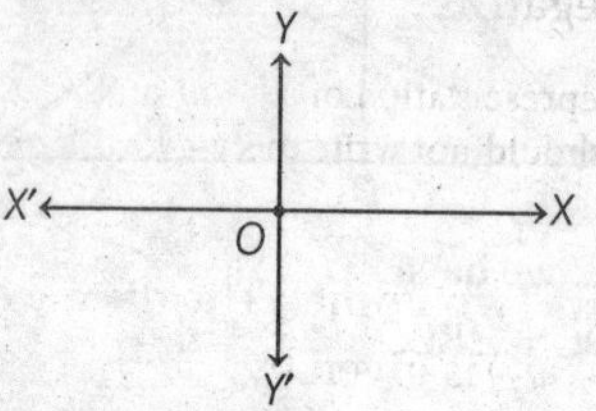

03 Coordinates of a Point Let P be any point in a plane. The distance of a point P from Y-axis is x and the distance of point P from X-axis is y. Thus, the coordinates of a point P are (x, y) *i.e.*, x is called the x-coordinate or **abscissa** and y is called the y-coordinate or **ordinate**.

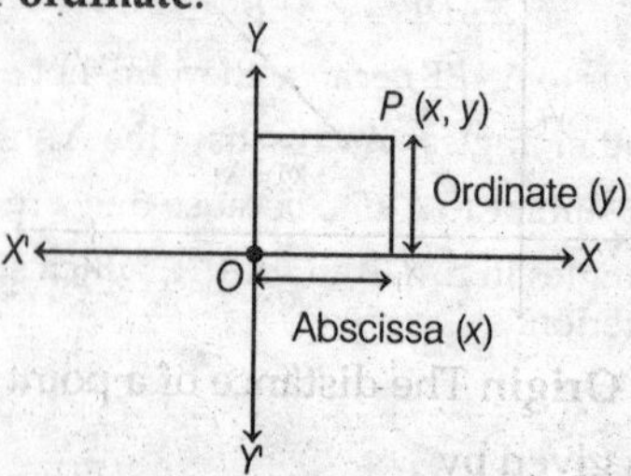

Note The abscissa of every point on Y-axis is zero.
The ordinate of every point on X-axis is zero.

04 Quadrant The X-axis and Y-axis divides the cartesian plane into four parts. Each part is called quadrant.

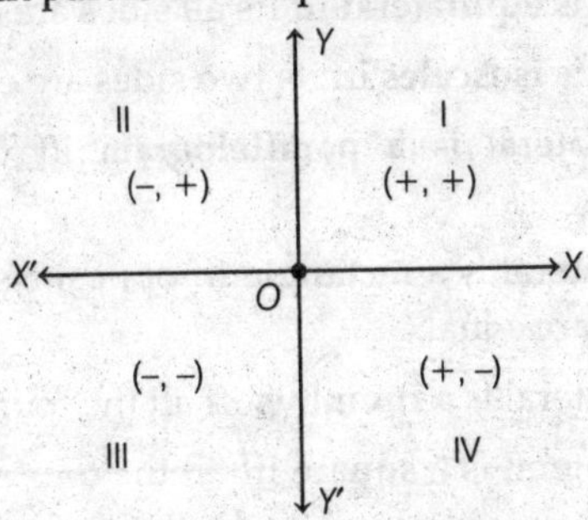

In the first quadrant (I), both x and y-coordinates are positive.

In the second quadrant (II), the x-coordinate is negative and the y-coordinate is positive.

In the third quadrant (III), both x and y-coordinates are negative.

In the fourth quadrant (IV), the x-coordinate is positive and y-coordinate is negative.

Note The correct representation of a point on the cartesian plane, symbolically, is (x, y). One should not write the y-coordinate first and then x-coordinate.

05 Distance between Two Points The distance between two points $A(x_1, y_1)$ and $B(x_2, y_2)$ is given by

$$AB = \sqrt{(x_2 - x_1)^2 + (y_2 - y_1)^2}$$

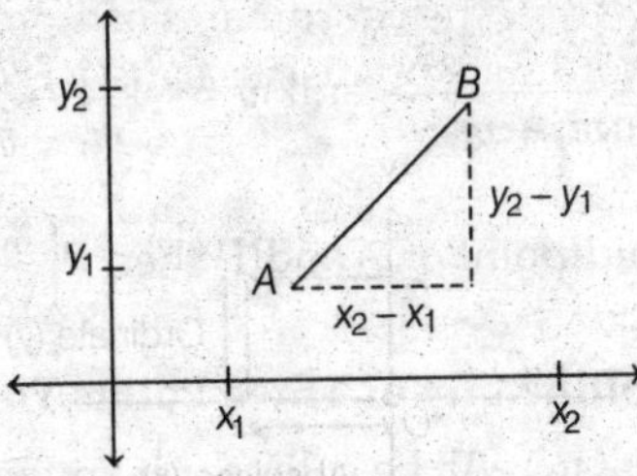

06 Distance from Origin The distance of a point $A(x, y)$ from the origin $O(0, 0)$ is given by

$$AO = \sqrt{(x-0)^2 + (y-0)^2} = \sqrt{x^2 + y^2}$$

07 Some Useful Results

(i) A triangle is **equilateral** iff its all sides are equal.

(ii) A triangle is **isosceles** iff its two sides are equal.

(iii) A quadrilateral is a **parallelogram** iff opposite sides are equal.

(iv) A quadrilateral is a **rectangle** iff opposite sides are equal and diagonals are equal.

(v) A quadrilateral is a **rhombus** iff all the four sides are equal.

(vi) A quadrilateral is a **square** iff all the four sides are equal and the diagonals are equal and all the four angles are right angles.

(vii) A rectangle is a parallelogram whose diagonals are equal.

(viii) A square is a rhombus whose diagonals are equal and all the four angles are right angles.

(ix) In parallelogram, rectangle, square and rhombus all have diagonals bisecting each other.

(x) A square is a rectangle with all sides equal.

08 Section Formulae

(i) If $P(x, y)$ divides the line segment joining $A(x_1, y_1)$ and $B(x_2, y_2)$ internally in the ratio $m_1 : m_2$, then

$$x = \frac{m_1 x_2 + m_2 x_1}{m_1 + m_2} \text{ and } y = \frac{m_1 y_2 + m_2 y_1}{m_1 + m_2}$$

(ii) If P divides AB externally in the ratio $m_1 : m_2$, then

$$x = \frac{m_1 x_2 - m_2 x_1}{m_1 - m_2} \text{ and } y = \frac{m_1 y_2 - m_2 y_1}{m_1 - m_2}$$

(iii) If P is the mid-point of A and B, then $P\left(\frac{x_1 + x_2}{2}, \frac{y_1 + y_2}{2}\right)$.

09 Condition of Collinearity of Three Points Three points $A(x_1, y_1)$, $B(x_2, y_2)$ and $C(x_3, y_3)$ will be collinear if and only if distance between A and C = Distance between A and B + Distance between B and C *i.e.*, $AC = AB + BC$

Exercise 7.1

Question 1 Find the distance between the following pairs of points.

(i) (2, 3), (4, 1) (ii) (– 5, 7), (– 1, 3)

(iii) $(a, b), (-a, -b)$

◎ **Thinking Process** The distance between two points (x_1, y_1) and (x_2, y_2) is $\sqrt{(x_2-x_1)^2+(y_2-y_1)^2}$, use this formula and simplify all parts.

Sol.

(i) Let $A(2, 3)$ and $B(4, 1)$ be the given points.

Here, $x_1 = 2, y_1 = 3$ and $x_2 = 4, y_2 = 1$

$$\therefore \quad AB = \sqrt{(x_2-x_1)^2+(y_2-y_1)^2}$$
$$= \sqrt{(4-2)^2+(1-3)^2}$$
$$= \sqrt{(2)^2+(-2)^2} = \sqrt{4+4} = \sqrt{8} = 2\sqrt{2}$$

(ii) Let $A(-5, 7)$ and $B(-1, 3)$ be the given points.

Here, $x_1 = -5, y_1 = 7$ and $x_2 = -1, y_2 = 3$

$$\therefore \quad AB = \sqrt{(x_2-x_1)^2+(y_2-y_1)^2}$$
$$= \sqrt{(-1+5)^2+(3-7)^2}$$
$$= \sqrt{(4)^2+(-4)^2} = \sqrt{16+16} = \sqrt{32} = 4\sqrt{2}$$

(iii) Let $A(a, b)$ and $B(-a, -b)$ be the given points.

Here, $x_1 = a, y_1 = b$ and $x_2 = -a, y_2 = -b$

$$\therefore \quad AB = \sqrt{(x_2-x_1)^2+(y_2-y_1)^2}$$
$$= \sqrt{(-a-a)^2+(-b-b)^2} = \sqrt{(-2a)^2+(-2b)^2}$$
$$= \sqrt{4a^2+4b^2} = 2\sqrt{a^2+b^2}$$

Question 2 Find the distance between the points (0, 0) and (36, 15). Can you now find the distance between the two towns A and B?

Sol. Let $M(0, 0)$ and $N(36, 15)$ be the given points.

Here, $x_1 = 0, y_1 = 0$ and $x_2 = 36, y_2 = 15$

$$\therefore \quad MN = \sqrt{(x_2-x_1)^2+(y_2-y_1)^2} = \sqrt{(36-0)^2+(15-0)^2}$$
$$= \sqrt{(36)^2+(15)^2}$$
$$= \sqrt{1296+225} = \sqrt{1521} = 39$$

Since, the position of towns A and B are given (0, 0) and (36, 15), respectively. So, the distance between them is 39 km.

Question 3 Determine if the points (1, 5), (2, 3) and (– 2, – 11) are collinear.

◎ ***Thinking Process*** For the condition of collinearity first find distance between three points.
i.e., *AB*, *BC* and *CA* by using distance formula and check that the sum of distance two sides is equal to third distance or not.

Sol. Let $A(1, 5)$, $B(2, 3)$ and $C(-2, -11)$ be the given points.

Then, $AB = \sqrt{(2-1)^2 + (3-5)^2}$

$$[\because \text{Distance} = \sqrt{(x_2 - x_1)^2 + (y_2 - y_1)^2}]$$

$$= \sqrt{1^2 + (-2)^2} = \sqrt{1+4} = \sqrt{5}$$

$$BC = \sqrt{(-2-2)^2 + (-11-3)^2}$$

$$= \sqrt{(-4)^2 + (-14)^2} = \sqrt{16 + 196} = \sqrt{212}$$

$$= \sqrt{4 \times 53} = 2\sqrt{53}$$

$$AC = \sqrt{(-2-1)^2 + (-11-5)^2}$$

$$= \sqrt{(-3)^2 + (-16)^2}$$

$$= \sqrt{9 + 256} = \sqrt{265}$$

Now, $AB + AC = \sqrt{5} + \sqrt{265} \neq \sqrt{212}$

$\therefore$ $AB + AC \neq BC$

Similarly, $AB \neq BC + AC$

and $AC \neq AB + BC$

Hence, *A*, *B* and *C* are non-collinear.

Question 4 Check whether $(5, -2), (6, 4)$ and $(7, -2)$ are the vertices of an isosceles triangle.

◎ ***Thinking Process*** As we know that in isosceles triangle two sides are equal, so find distance between the three vertices and check whether two distance are of equal length.

Sol Let $P(5, -2), Q(6, 4)$ and $R(7, -2)$ be the given points.

Then, by distance formula, $d = \sqrt{(x_2 - x_1)^2 + (y_2 - y_1)^2}$

$$PQ = \sqrt{(6-5)^2 + (4+2)^2}$$

$$= \sqrt{(1)^2 + (6)^2}$$

$$= \sqrt{1+36} = \sqrt{37}$$

$$QR = \sqrt{(7-6)^2 + (-2-4)^2}$$

$$= \sqrt{(1)^2 + (-6)^2}$$

$$= \sqrt{1+36} = \sqrt{37}$$

$$PR = \sqrt{(7-5)^2 + (-2+2)^2} = \sqrt{(2)^2 + 0^2} = \sqrt{4} = 2$$

$\because$ $PQ = QR$

Hence, ΔPQR is an isosceles triangle.

Question 5 In a classroom, 4 friends are seated at the points *A*, *B*, *C* and *D* as shown in figure. Champa and Chameli walk into the class and after observing for a few minutes Champa asks Chameli, "Don't you think *ABCD* is a square?" Chameli disagrees. Using distance formula, find which of them is correct.

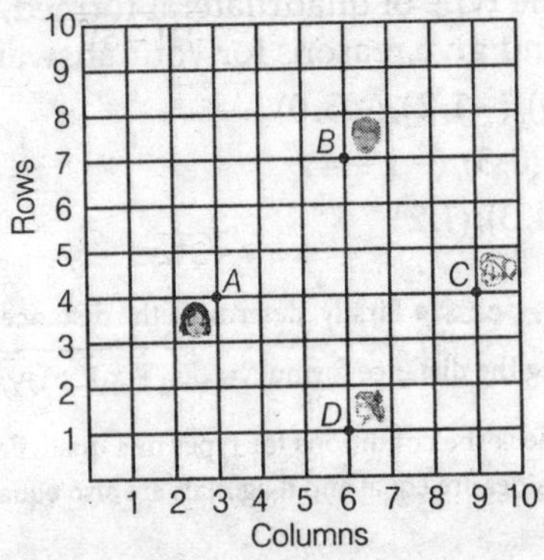

Sol. From the given figure, the coordinates of the points *A*, *B*, *C* and *D* are (3, 4), (6, 7), (9, 4) and (6, 1), respectively.

$\therefore$ $$AB = \sqrt{(6-3)^2 + (7-4)^2}$$

$$\left[\because \text{Distance} = \sqrt{(x_2 - x_1)^2 + (y_2 - y_1)^2}\,\right]$$

$$= \sqrt{3^2 + 3^2}$$

$$= \sqrt{9+9} = \sqrt{18} = 3\sqrt{2}$$

$$BC = \sqrt{(9-6)^2 + (4-7)^2}$$

$$= \sqrt{3^2 + (-3)^2}$$

$$= \sqrt{9+9} = \sqrt{18} = 3\sqrt{2}$$

$$CD = \sqrt{(6-9)^2 + (1-4)^2}$$

$$= \sqrt{(-3)^2 + (-3)^2}$$
$$= \sqrt{9+9} = \sqrt{18} = 3\sqrt{2}$$

and $$DA = \sqrt{(3-6)^2 + (4-1)^2}$$
$$= \sqrt{(-3)^2 + 3^2}$$
$$= \sqrt{9+9} = \sqrt{18} = 3\sqrt{2}$$

Now, $$AC = \sqrt{(9-3)^2 + (4-4)^2}$$
$$= \sqrt{36+0} = 6$$

and $$BD = \sqrt{(6-6)^2 + (1-7)^2}$$
$$= \sqrt{0+36} = \sqrt{36} = 6$$

Here, $$AB = BC = CD = DA$$
and $$AC = BD = 6$$

Since, the four sides are equal and diagonals are also equal. Hence, $ABCD$ is a square. So, Champa is correct.

Question 6 Name the type of quadrilateral formed, if any, by the following points and give reasons for your answer :

(i) $(-1,-2),(1,0),(-1,2),(-3,0)$

(ii) $(-3,5),(3,1),(0,3),(-1,-4)$

(iii) $(4,5),(7,6),(4,3),(1,2)$

Thinking Process ◆ Firstly, determine the distances AB, BC, CD, DA, AC and BD by using the distance formula $= \sqrt{(x_2 - x_1)^2 + (y_2 - y_1)^2}$.

◆ Secondly, check the conditions for types of a quadrilaterals

(a) If all four sides are equal and diagonals are also equal, then quadrilateral is a square.

(b) If opposite sides are equal and diagonals are not equal, then quadrilateral is a parallelogram.

Sol. (i) Let $A(-1,-2)$, $B(1,0)$, $C(-1,2)$ and $D(-3,0)$ be the given points.

Then, $$AB = \sqrt{(1+1)^2 + (0+2)^2} = \sqrt{2^2 + 2^2}$$
$$\left[\because \text{distance} = \sqrt{(x_2 - x_1)^2 + (y_2 - y_1)^2}\right]$$
$$= \sqrt{4+4} = \sqrt{8} = 2\sqrt{2}$$
$$BC = \sqrt{(-1-1)^2 + (2-0)^2} = \sqrt{(-2)^2 + 2^2}$$
$$= \sqrt{4+4} = \sqrt{8} = 2\sqrt{2}$$
$$CD = \sqrt{(-3+1)^2 + (0-2)^2} = \sqrt{(-2)^2 + (-2)^2}$$
$$= \sqrt{4+4} = \sqrt{8} = 2\sqrt{2}$$

$$DA = \sqrt{(-1+3)^2 + (-2-0)^2} = \sqrt{(2)^2 + (-2)^2}$$
$$= \sqrt{4+4} = \sqrt{8} = 2\sqrt{2}$$

Now, $AC = \sqrt{(-1+1)^2 + (2+2)^2} = \sqrt{0+4^2} = 4$

and $BD = \sqrt{(-3-1)^2 + (0-0)^2} = \sqrt{(-4)^2 + 0} = 4$

Here, $AB = BC = CD = DA$

and $AC = BD$

Since, the four sides AB, BC, CD and DA are equal and the diagonals AC and BD are also equal.

$\therefore$ The quadrilateral $ABCD$ is a square.

(ii) Let $A(-3, 5)$, $B(3, 1)$, $C(0, 3)$ and $D(-1, -4)$ be the given points.

Then, $AC = \sqrt{(0+3)^2 + (3-5)^2} = \sqrt{3^2 + (-2)^2}$

$[\because \text{Distance} = \sqrt{(x_2 - x_1)^2 + (y_2 - y_1)^2}]$

$$= \sqrt{9+4} = \sqrt{13}$$

$$AB = \sqrt{(3+3)^2 + (1-5)^2} = \sqrt{6^2 + (-4)^2} = \sqrt{36+16} = \sqrt{52} = 2\sqrt{13}$$

$$BC = \sqrt{(0-3)^2 + (3-1)^2} = \sqrt{9+4} = \sqrt{13}$$

$\because$ $AB = BC + AC$

Hence, they are collinear and cannot form a quadrilateral.

(iii) Let $A(4, 5)$, $B(7, 6)$, $C(4, 3)$ and $D(1, 2)$ be the given points.

Then, $AB = \sqrt{(7-4)^2 + (6-5)^2} = \sqrt{3^2 + 1^2} = \sqrt{9+1} = \sqrt{10}$

$[\because \text{Distance} = \sqrt{(x_2 - x_1)^2 + (y_2 - y_1)^2}]$

$$BC = \sqrt{(4-7)^2 + (3-6)^2} = \sqrt{(-3)^2 + (-3)^2} = \sqrt{9+9} = \sqrt{18}$$

$$CD = \sqrt{(1-4)^2 + (2-3)^2} = \sqrt{(-3)^2 + (-1)^2} = \sqrt{9+1} = \sqrt{10}$$

$$DA = \sqrt{(4-1)^2 + (5-2)^2} = \sqrt{3^2 + (3)^2} = \sqrt{9+9} = \sqrt{18}$$

$$AC = \sqrt{(4-4)^2 + (3-5)^2} = \sqrt{0 + (-2)^2} = 2$$

and $BD = \sqrt{(1-7)^2 + (2-6)^2} = \sqrt{(-6)^2 + (-4)^2} = \sqrt{36+16} = \sqrt{52}$

Since, $AB = CD$, $BC = DA$

and $AC \neq BD$

Since, opposite sides are equal.

$\therefore$ The quadrilateral $ABCD$ is a parallelogram.

Question 7 Find the point on the X-axis which is equidistant from $(2, -5)$ and $(-2, 9)$.

Thinking Process On X-axis the coordinates of any point is $(x, 0)$ *i.e.*, y-coordinate is 0 on X-axis.

Sol. Since, the point is on the X-axis.

$\therefore$ It's ordinate = 0

Let, $A(x, 0)$ is any point on the X-axis.

Since, $A(x, 0)$ is equidistant from $B(2, -5)$ and $C(-2, 9)$.

$$\therefore \quad AB = AC$$

$$\Rightarrow \quad \sqrt{(x-2)^2 + (0+5)^2} = \sqrt{(x+2)^2 + (0-9)^2}$$

On squaring both sides, we get $\quad [\because \text{Distance} = \sqrt{(x_2 - x_1)^2 + (y_2 - y_1)^2}\,]$

$$\Rightarrow \quad x^2 - 4x + 4 + 25 = x^2 + 4x + 4 + 81 \quad [\because (a-b)^2 = a^2 + b^2 - 2ab]$$

$$\Rightarrow \quad -4x - 4x = 81 - 25 \quad [(a+b)^2 = a^2 + b^2 + 2ab]$$

$$\Rightarrow \quad -8x = 56$$

$$\Rightarrow \quad x = -\frac{56}{8} = -7$$

So, the point equidistant from given points on the X-axis is $(-7, 0)$.

Question 8 Find the values of y for which the distance between the points $P(2, -3)$ and $Q(10, y)$ is 10 units.

Sol. According to the question,

$$PQ = 10$$

$$\Rightarrow \quad \sqrt{(10-2)^2 + (y+3)^2} = 10 \quad [\because \text{Distance} = \sqrt{(x_2 - x_1)^2 + (y_2 - y_1)^2}\,]$$

$$\Rightarrow \quad \sqrt{(8)^2 + (y+3)^2} = 10$$

$$\Rightarrow \quad \sqrt{64 + y^2 + 9 + 6y} = 10$$

$$\Rightarrow \quad \sqrt{y^2 + 6y + 73} = 10$$

On squaring both sides, we get

$$y^2 + 6y + 73 = 100$$

$$\Rightarrow \quad y^2 + 6y - 27 = 0$$

$$\Rightarrow \quad y^2 + 9y - 3y - 27 = 0$$

$$\Rightarrow \quad y(y+9) - 3(y+9) = 0$$

$$\Rightarrow \quad (y+9)(y-3) = 0$$

$$\Rightarrow \quad y = -9 \text{ or } y = 3$$

Question 9 If $Q(0, 1)$ is equidistant from $P(5, -3)$ and $R(x, 6)$, find the values of x. Also, find the distance QR and PR.

Sol. Since, the point $Q(0, 1)$ is equidistant from $P(5, -3)$ and $R(x, 6)$.

$$\therefore \quad QP = QR$$

$$\Rightarrow \quad \sqrt{(5-0)^2 + (-3-1)^2} = \sqrt{(x-0)^2 + (6-1)^2}$$

$$[\because \text{Distance} = \sqrt{(x_2 - x_1)^2 + (y_2 - y_1)^2}\,]$$

On squaring the both sides, we get

$$\Rightarrow \quad 5^2 + (-4)^2 = x^2 + 5^2$$

$$\Rightarrow \quad 25 + 16 = x^2 + 25$$

$$\Rightarrow \quad x^2 = 16$$

$$\Rightarrow \quad x = \pm 4$$

Thus, R is (4, 6) or (– 4, 6).

Now, QR = Distance between $Q(0, 1)$ and $R(4, 6)$

$$= \sqrt{(4-0)^2 + (6-1)^2}$$

$$= \sqrt{4^2 + 5^2}$$

$$= \sqrt{16+25} = \sqrt{41}$$

Also, QR = Distance between $Q(0, 1)$ and $R(-4, 6)$

$$= \sqrt{(-4-0)^2 + (6-1)^2}$$

$$= \sqrt{(-4)^2 + 5^2}$$

$$= \sqrt{16+25} = \sqrt{41}$$

and PR = Distance between $P(5, -3)$ and $R(4, 6)$

$$= \sqrt{(4-5)^2 + (6+3)^2}$$

$$= \sqrt{(-1)^2 + 9^2}$$

$$= \sqrt{1+81} = \sqrt{82}$$

Also, PR = Distance between $P(5, -3)$ and $R(-4, 6)$

$$= \sqrt{(-4-5)^2 + (6+3)^2}$$

$$= \sqrt{(-9)^2 + 9^2} = 9\sqrt{1+1}$$

$$= 9\sqrt{2}$$

Mistake Alert Not forget to find the distance of QR and PR with the two coordinates of R.

Question 10 Find a relation between x and y such that the point (x, y) is equidistant from the points (3, 6) and (– 3, 4).

Sol. Let the point $A(x, y)$ be equidistant from the points $B(3, 6)$ and $C(-3, 4)$.

$$\therefore \quad AB = AC$$

$$\Rightarrow \quad \sqrt{(x-3)^2 + (y-6)^2} = \sqrt{(x+3)^2 + (y-4)^2}$$

$$\left[\because \text{Distance} = \sqrt{(x_2 - x_1)^2 + (y_2 - y_1)^2}\right]$$

On squaring both sides, we get

$$\Rightarrow \quad x^2 - 6x + 9 + y^2 - 12y + 36 = x^2 + 6x + 9 + y^2 - 8y + 16$$

$$\Rightarrow \quad -6x - 6x - 12y + 8y + 36 - 16 = 0$$

$$\Rightarrow \quad -12x - 4y + 20 = 0$$

$$\Rightarrow \quad -4(3x + y - 5) = 0$$

$$\Rightarrow \quad 3x + y - 5 = 0$$

Exercise 7.2

Question 1 Find the coordinates of the point which divides the join of $(-1, 7)$ and $(4, -3)$ in the ratio 2 : 3.

Sol. Let the coordinates of a point are (x, y).

We have, $x_1 = -1, y_1 = 7,$

$x_2 = 4, y_2 = -3$

and $m_1 = 2, m_2 = 3$

$\therefore$ By using section formula,

$$x = \frac{m_1x_2 + m_2x_1}{m_1 + m_2} = \frac{2(4) + 3(-1)}{2 + 3} = \frac{8 - 3}{5} = \frac{5}{5} = 1$$

and
$$y = \frac{m_1y_2 + m_2y_1}{m_1 + m_2} = \frac{2(-3) + 3(7)}{2 + 3}$$

$$= \frac{-6 + 21}{5} = \frac{15}{5} = 3$$

Hence, coordinates of the point are (1, 3).

Question 2 Find the coordinates of the points of trisection of the line segment joining $(4, -1)$ and $(-2, -3)$.

Sol. Let $A(4, -1)$ and $B(-2, -3)$ be the end points of line end points of rgtsegments and points of trisection of the line segment be P and Q.
Then,

$$AP = PQ = BQ = k \quad \text{(Say)}$$

$\therefore$ $PB = PQ + QB = 2k$

and $AQ = AP + PQ = 2k$

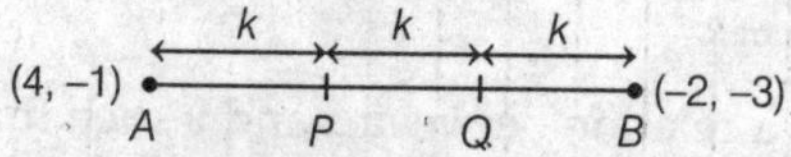

$\Rightarrow$ $AP : PB = k : 2k = 1 : 2$

and $AQ : QB = 2k : k = 2 : 1$

Since, P divides AB internally in the ratio 1 : 2. So, the coordinate of P are

$$\left[\text{By using}\left(\frac{m_1x_2 + m_2x_1}{m_1 + m_2}, \frac{m_1y_2 + m_2y_1}{m_1 + m_2}\right)\right]$$

$$= \left(\frac{1 \times (-2) + 2 \times 4}{1 + 2}, \frac{1 \times (-3) + 2 \times (-1)}{1 + 2}\right)$$

$$= \left(\frac{-2 + 8}{3}, \frac{-3 - 2}{3}\right)$$

$$= \left(\frac{6}{3}, \frac{-5}{3}\right) = \left(2, -\frac{5}{3}\right)$$

and Q divides AB internally in the ratio 2 : 1.

So, the coordinates of Q are $\left[\text{By using}\left(\dfrac{m_1x_2 + m_2x_1}{m_1 + m_2}, \dfrac{m_1y_2 + m_2y_1}{m_1 + m_2}\right)\right]$

$$= \left(\frac{2 \times (-2) + 1 \times 4}{2 + 1}, \frac{2 \times (-3) + 1 \times (-1)}{2 + 1}\right)$$

$$= \left(\frac{-4 + 4}{3}, \frac{-6 - 1}{3}\right)$$

$$= \left(0, -\frac{7}{3}\right)$$

So, the two points of trisection are $\left(2, -\dfrac{5}{3}\right)$ and $\left(0, -\dfrac{7}{3}\right)$.

Question 3 To conduct Sports Day activities, in your rectangular shaped school ground $ABCD$, lines have been drawn with chalk powder at a distance of 1 m each. 100 flower pots have been placed at a distance of 1 m from each other along AD, as shown in figure. Niharika runs $\dfrac{1}{4}$th the distance AD on the 2nd line and posts a green flag. Preet runs $\dfrac{1}{5}$th the distance AD on the eighth line and posts a red flag. What is the distance between both the flags? If Rashmi has to post a blue flag exactly halfway between the line segment joining the two flags, where should she post her flag?

Sol. From the above figure, the position of green flag posted by Niharika is $M\left(2, \frac{1}{4} \times 100\right)$ i.e., $M(2, 25)$ and position of red flag posted by Preet is $N\left(8, \frac{1}{5} \times 100\right)$ i.e., $N(8, 20)$.

Now, $$MN = \sqrt{(8-2)^2 + (20-25)^2}$$
$$= \sqrt{(6)^2 + (-5)^2} = \sqrt{36+25} = \sqrt{61}$$

Hence, the distance between flags $= \sqrt{61}$ m

Let P be the position of the blue flag posted by Rashmi in the halfway of line segment MN.

M (2, 25) P N (8, 20)

$\therefore$ $$P \text{ is given by} = \left(\frac{x_1 + x_2}{2}, \frac{y_1 + y_2}{2}\right) = \left(\frac{2+8}{2}, \frac{25+20}{2}\right)$$
$$= \left(\frac{10}{2}, \frac{45}{2}\right) = (5, 22.5)$$

Hence, the blue flag is on the fifth line at a distance of 22.5 m along AD.

Question 4 Find the ratio in which the line segment joining the points (–3, 10) and (6, – 8) is divided by (– 1, 6).

Sol. Let the point $A(-1, 6)$ divide the line joining $B(-3, 10)$ and $C(6, -8)$ in the ratio $k : 1$. Then, the coordinates of A are $\left(\frac{6k-3}{k+1}, \frac{-8k+10}{k+1}\right)$

$$\left[\because \text{Internally ratio} = \left(\frac{m_1x_2 + m_2x_1}{m_1 + m_2}, \frac{m_1y_2 + m_2y_1}{m_1 + m_2}\right)\right]$$

But the coordinates of A are given by $(-1, 6)$.

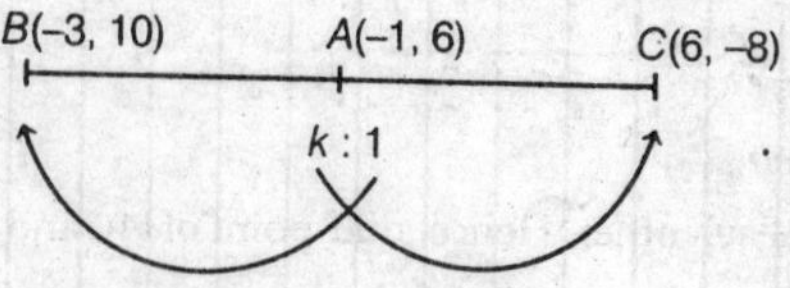

On comparing coordinates, we get
$$\frac{6k-3}{k+1} = -1 \text{ and } \frac{-8k+10}{k+1} = 6$$
$\Rightarrow$ $$6k - 3 = -k - 1 \text{ and } -8k + 10 = 6k + 6$$
$\Rightarrow$ $$6k + k = -1 + 3 \text{ and } -8k - 6k = 6 - 10$$
$\Rightarrow$ $$7k = 2 \text{ and } -14k = -4$$
$\Rightarrow$ $$k = \frac{2}{7}$$

So, the point A divides BC in the ratio 2 : 7.

Question 5 Find the ratio in which the line segment joining $A(1, -5)$ and $B(-4, 5)$ is divided by the x-axis. Also, find the coordinates of the point of division.

Sol. Let the required ratio be $k : 1$. So, the coordinates of the point M of division $A(1, -5)$ and $B(-4, 5)$ are $\left(\frac{kx_2 + 1 \cdot x_1}{k+1}, \frac{ky_2 + 1 \cdot y_1}{k+1}\right)$ i.e., $\left(\frac{-4k+1}{k+1}, \frac{5k-5}{k+1}\right)$.

But according to the question, the line segment joining $A(1, -5)$ and $B(-4, 5)$ is divided by the x-axis. So, y-coordinates must be zero.

$$\therefore \quad \frac{5k-5}{k+1} = 0$$

$$\Rightarrow \quad 5k - 5 = 0$$

$$\Rightarrow \quad 5k = 5$$

$$\Rightarrow \quad k = 1$$

So, the required ratio is $1 : 1$ and the point of division M is $\left(\frac{-4(1)+1}{1+1}, \frac{5(1)-5}{1+1}\right)$

i.e., $\left(-\frac{3}{2}, 0\right)$.

Question 6 If $(1, 2), (4, y), (x, 6)$ and $(3, 5)$ are the vertices of a parallelogram taken in order, find x and y.

Sol. Let $A(1, 2)$, $B(4, y)$, $C(x, 6)$ and $D(3, 5)$ be the vertices of a parallelogram.

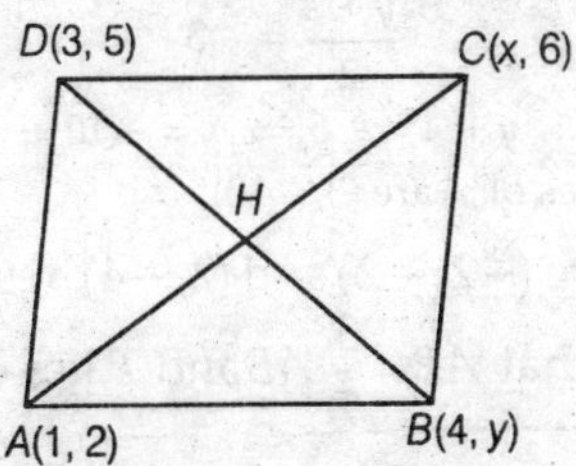

Since, $ABCD$ is a parallelogram.

$\therefore$ AC and BD will bisect each other. Hence, mid-point of AC and mid-point of BD are same point.

$\therefore$ Mid-point of AC is $\left(\frac{1+x}{2}, \frac{2+6}{2}\right)$ = Mid-point of BD is $\left(\frac{4+3}{2}, \frac{y+5}{2}\right)$

$$\left[\because \text{Mid-point} = \left(\frac{x_1+x_2}{2}, \frac{y_1+y_2}{2}\right)\right]$$

$$\therefore \quad \frac{1+x}{2} = \frac{4+3}{2} \text{ and } \frac{2+6}{2} = \frac{5+y}{2}$$

$$\Rightarrow \quad 1 + x = 7 \text{ and } 8 = 5 + y$$

$$\therefore \quad x = 6 \text{ and } y = 3$$

Question 7 Find the coordinates of a point A, where AB is the diameter of a circle whose centre is $(2, -3)$ and B is $(1, 4)$.

Sol. Let $C(2, -3)$ be the centre of circle and the coordinates of end point are $A(x, y)$ and $B(1, 4)$.

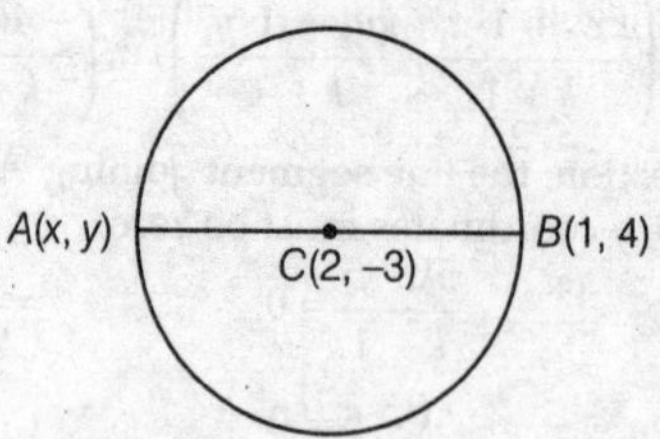

Since, AB is diameter.

$\therefore C$ is the mid-point of AB.

The coordinates of C are $\left(\frac{x+1}{2}, \frac{y+4}{2}\right)$.

$$\left[\because \text{Coordinate of mid-point} = \left(\frac{x_1 + x_2}{2}, \frac{y_1 + y_2}{2}\right)\right]$$

But it is given that the coordinates of C are $(2, -3)$.

$$\therefore \quad \frac{x+1}{2} = 2$$

$$\Rightarrow \quad x + 1 = 4 \Rightarrow x = 3$$

$$\text{and} \quad \frac{y+4}{2} = -3$$

$$\Rightarrow \quad y + 4 = -6 \Rightarrow y = -10$$

So, the required coordinates of A are $(3, -10)$.

Question 8 If A and B are $(-2, -2)$ and $(2, -4)$, respectively, find the coordinates of P such that $AP = \frac{3}{7} AB$ and P lies on the line segment AB.

Sol. According to the question,

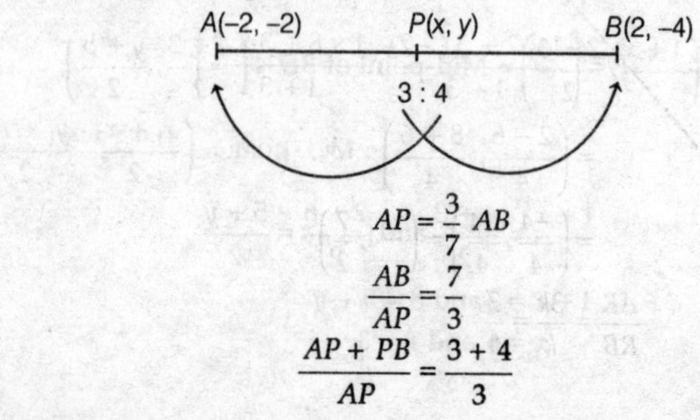

$$AP = \frac{3}{7} AB$$

$$\Rightarrow \quad \frac{AB}{AP} = \frac{7}{3}$$

$$\Rightarrow \quad \frac{AP + PB}{AP} = \frac{3+4}{3}$$

$$\Rightarrow \quad 1+\frac{PB}{AP}=1+\frac{4}{3}$$

$$\Rightarrow \quad \frac{PB}{AP}=\frac{4}{3} \Rightarrow \frac{AP}{PB}=\frac{3}{4}$$

$$\Rightarrow \quad AP:PB=3:4$$

Now, $P(x, y)$ be the point which divides the line segment joining the points $A(-2,-2)$ and $B(2,-4)$ in the ratio 3 : 4.

$$\therefore \quad x=\frac{3\times 2+4\times(-2)}{3+4}=\frac{6-8}{7}=\frac{-2}{7} \quad \left(\because x=\frac{m_1x_2+m_2x_1}{m_1+m_2}\right)$$

and
$$y=\frac{3\times(-4)+4\times(-2)}{3+4} \quad \left(\because y=\frac{m_1y_2+m_2y_1}{m_1+m_2}\right)$$

$$=\frac{-12-8}{7}=\frac{-20}{7}$$

Hence, the required coordinates of the point P are $\left(-\frac{2}{7},-\frac{20}{7}\right)$.

Mistake Alert Students take wrong internal ratio while applying section formula, so be careful and take that particular ratio in which point divides the line segment.

Question 9 Find the coordinates of the points which divide the line segment joining $A(-2,2)$ and $B(2,8)$ into four equal parts.

Sol. Let P, Q and R be the points on line segment AB such that

$$AP=PQ=QR=RB$$

Let
$$AP=PQ=QR=RB=k$$

k k k k
(–2, 2) A P Q R B (2, 8)

Now,
$$\frac{AP}{PB}=\frac{k}{3k}=\frac{1}{3}$$

Therefore, P divides AB internally in the ratio 1 : 3.

$$\left[\because \text{Internally ratio}=\left(\frac{m_1x_2+m_2x_1}{m_1+m_2},\frac{m_1y_2+m_2y_1}{m_1+m_2}\right)\right]$$

$$\therefore \quad P=\left(\frac{1\times 2+3(-2)}{1+3},\frac{1\times 8+3\times 2}{1+3}\right)$$

$$=\left(\frac{2-6}{4},\frac{8+6}{4}\right)$$

$$=\left(\frac{-4}{4},\frac{14}{4}\right)=\left(-1,\frac{7}{2}\right)$$

Again,
$$\frac{AR}{RB}=\frac{3k}{k}=\frac{3}{1}$$

Therefore, R divides AB internally in the ratio 3 : 1.

$$\therefore \quad R = \left(\frac{3 \times 2 + 1 \times (-2)}{3+1}, \frac{3 \times 8 + 1 \times 2}{3+1}\right)$$

$$= \left(\frac{6-2}{4}, \frac{24+2}{4}\right)$$

$$= \left(\frac{4}{4}, \frac{26}{4}\right) = \left(1, \frac{13}{2}\right)$$

Also, $$\frac{AQ}{QB} = \frac{2k}{2k} = \frac{1}{1}$$

$\therefore Q$ is the mid-point of AB.

$$\therefore \quad Q = \left(\frac{-2+2}{2}, \frac{2+8}{2}\right) \Rightarrow Q = \left(\frac{0}{2}, \frac{10}{2}\right) = (0, 5)$$

$$\left[\because \text{Mid-point} = \left(\frac{x_1 + x_2}{2}, \frac{y_1 + y_2}{2}\right)\right]$$

So, required points are $\left(-1, \frac{7}{2}\right)$, $(0, 5)$ and $\left(1, \frac{13}{2}\right)$.

Question 10 Find the area of a rhombus if its vertices are (3, 0), (4, 5), (–1, 4) and (–2, –1) taken in order.

[**Hint** Area of a rhombus = $\frac{1}{2}$ (Product of its diagonals)]

◎ ***Thinking Process*** First find the diagonals of the rhombus by using distance formula and apply the formula of area of rhombus.

Sol. Let $A(3, 0)$, $B(4, 5)$, $C(-1, 4)$ and $D(-2, -1)$ be the vertices of the rhombus $ABCD$.

A(3, 0)
D(–2, –1)
B(4, 5)
C(–1, 4)

$$\therefore \quad \text{Diagonal, } AC = \sqrt{(-1-3)^2 + (4-0)^2}$$

$$\left[\because \text{Distance} = \sqrt{(x_2 - x_1)^2 + (y_2 - y_1)^2}\right]$$

$$= \sqrt{(-4)^2 + 4^2}$$

$$= \sqrt{16 + 16} = \sqrt{32} = 4\sqrt{2}$$

Diagonal, $BD = \sqrt{(-2-4)^2 + (-1-5)^2}$
$= \sqrt{(-6)^2 + (-6)^2}$
$= \sqrt{36+36} = \sqrt{72} = 6\sqrt{2}$

Now, area of the rhombus $ABCD = \frac{1}{2} \times AC \times BD$
$= \frac{1}{2} \times 4\sqrt{2} \times 6\sqrt{2}$
$= 24$ sq units

DIKSHA APP Questions

☐ Multiple Choice Questions

Q.1 The point which lies on the Y-axis is......

(a) (−3, 0) (b) (1, 0)
(c) (0, 2) (d) (2, 3)

Sol. (c) Since the point lies on the Y-axis, hence its abscissa is zero. So, the point is of the form $(0, y)$.

Hence, the only point is (0, 2)

Q.2 Distance between the point $P(x, y)$ and the origin is ....

(a) $\sqrt{x^2 - y^2}$
(b) $\sqrt{x^2 + y^2}$
(c) $\sqrt{x + y}$
(d) $\sqrt{x - y}$

◎ ***Thinking Process*** Coordinate of origin is (0, 0).

Sol. (b) The distance between the point $P(x, y)$ and the origin $O(0, 0)$ is given by $OP = \sqrt{x^2 + y^2}$

Q.3 The distance of Y-axis from the point (4,3) is ...

(a) 3 units
(b) 4 units
(c) 7 units
(d) 1 unit

Sol. (b) In the given figure, the distance of $P(4, 3)$, from Y-axis will be calculated from $Q(0, 3)$ because that will be the shortest distance between P and Y-axis.

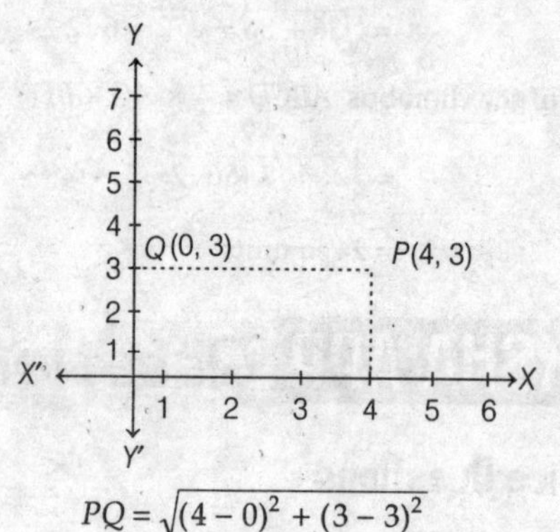

$\Rightarrow$ $$PQ = \sqrt{(4-0)^2 + (3-3)^2}$$

$$= \sqrt{4^2} = 4 \quad \text{(As distance is not negative)}$$

Quick Solution

Distance between the point P and Y-axis = abscissa of the point P

= 4 units.

Q.4 Distance between the points $(4, 6)$ and $(6, 8)$ is

(a) $\sqrt{2}$ units
(b) 2 units
(c) $2\sqrt{2}$ units
(d) 4 units

Sol. (c) Let $P(4, 6)$ and $Q(6, 8)$ be the given points.

So, the distance between $P(4, 6)$ and $Q(6, 8)$ is

$$PQ = \sqrt{(6-4)^2 + (8-6)^2} \quad \left[\because \text{Distance} = \sqrt{(x_2 - x_1)^2 + (y_2 - y_1)^2}\right]$$

$$= \sqrt{2^2 + 2^2} = \sqrt{4+4}$$

$$= \sqrt{8} = 2\sqrt{2} \text{ units}$$

Q.5 The ordinate and abscissa of a point P are $\frac{6}{5}$ and $-\frac{5}{2}$, respectively, then the point P lies in

(a) I quadrant
(b) II quadrant
(c) III quadrant
(d) IV quadrant

Sol. (b) Since the ordinate is $\frac{6}{5}$ and abscissa is $\frac{-5}{2}$, so the point is $\left(\frac{-5}{2}, \frac{6}{5}\right)$.

So, x-coordinate is on the negative X-axis any y-coordinate is on the positive Y-axis.
Hence, the point is in the second quadrant.

Q.6 If the origin is the mid-point of the line segment joined by the points $(2,3)$ and (x, y), then (x, y) is

(a) (2, 3) (b) (–2, 3)
(c) (–2, – 3) (d) (2, – 3)

Sol. (c) The origin is the mid-point of the line segment joined by the points (2, 3) and (x, y).

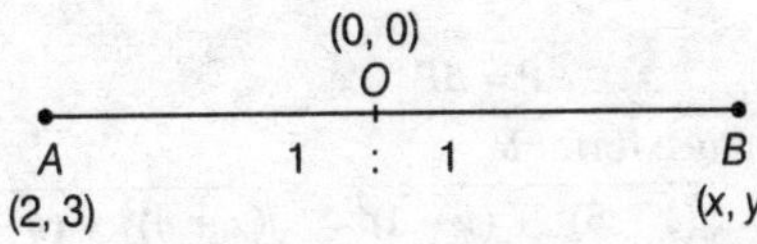

Mid-point is obtained by the formula, $\left(\frac{x_1 + x_2}{2}, \frac{y_1 + y_2}{2}\right)$.

Let $A(2, 3)$ and $B(x, y)$ be the given points.

Then, $O(0, 0) = \left(\frac{2 + x}{2}, \frac{3 + y}{2}\right)$

Equating the corresponding coordinates, we get

$$0 = \frac{2 + x}{2} \text{ and } 0 = \frac{3 + y}{2}$$

$\Rightarrow$ $2 + x = 0$ and $3 + y = 0$

$\Rightarrow$ $x = -2$ and $y = -3$

The coordinates of B is $(-2, -3)$.

Q.7 The distance of the point $P(2,3)$ from the X-axis is

(a) 2 (b) 3 (c) 1 (d) 4

Sol. (b) In the given figure, the distance of point $P(2, 3)$, from X-axis will be calculated from $Q(2, 0)$ because that will be the shortest distance between P and X-axis.

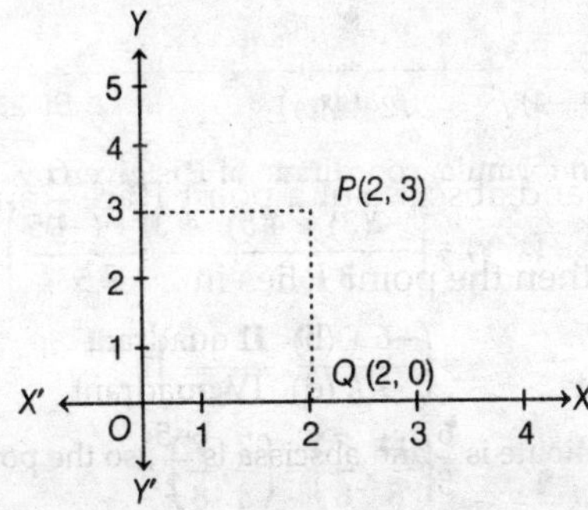

$\Rightarrow$ $PQ = \sqrt{(2 - 2)^2 + (3 - 0)^2} = \sqrt{0 + 3^2} = 3$ units

Q.8 If the distance of $P(x, y)$ from $A(5, 1)$ and $B(-1, 5)$ are equal, then which is true ?

(a) $x = 2y$ (b) $3x = 2y$

(c) $2x = 3y$ (d) $2x = y$

Sol. (b) Given, the two points $A(5, 1)$ and $B(-1, 5)$ are equidistant from the point $P(x, y)$.

$$\therefore \quad AP = BP$$

Then, by distance formula,

$$\sqrt{(x-5)^2 + (y-1)^2} = \sqrt{(x+1)^2 + (y-5)^2}$$

On squaring the both sides, we get

$$\Rightarrow \quad x^2 + 25 - 10x + y^2 + 1 - 2y = x^2 + 1 + 2x + y^2 + 25 - 10y$$

$$\Rightarrow \quad 25 - 10x + 1 - 2y = 1 + 2x + 25 - 10y$$

$$\Rightarrow \quad -10x - 2x - 2y + 10y = 0 \Rightarrow -12x + 8y = 0$$

$$\Rightarrow \quad -3x + 2y = 0$$

$$\Rightarrow \quad 2y = 3x$$

Q.9 Find the co-ordinates of a point which divide the segment AB in the ratio $3:5$ internally, where $A(4, -1)$ and $B(-2, 4)$.

(a) $\left(\frac{7}{2}, \frac{7}{4}\right)$ (b) $\left(\frac{7}{4}, \frac{7}{8}\right)$

(c) $\left(\frac{7}{4}, \frac{7}{6}\right)$ (d) None of these

Sol. (b) Let $P(x, y)$ be the point which divides the line segment AB in the ratio $3:5$ internally, where $A(4, -1)$ and $B(-2, 4)$.

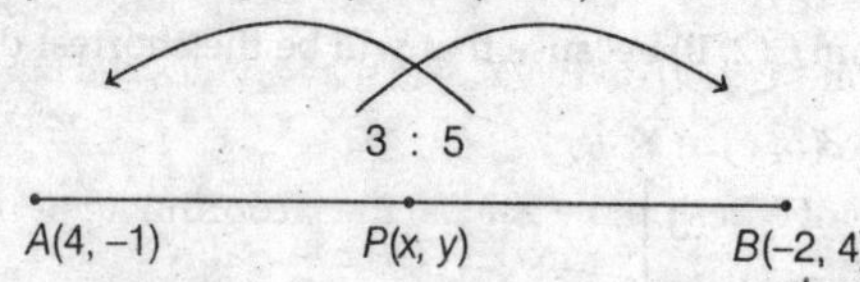

Then, by section formula, coordinate of P is given by

$$P(x, y) = \left(\frac{-2(3) + 4(5)}{3+5}, \frac{4(3) + (-1)5}{3+5}\right)$$

$$= \left(\frac{-6 + 20}{8}, \frac{12 - 5}{8}\right)$$

$$= \left(\frac{14}{8}, \frac{7}{8}\right) = \left(\frac{7}{4}, \frac{7}{8}\right)$$

Q.10 The point which lies on the perpendicular bisector of the line segment joining the points $A(-2, -5)$ and $B(2, 5)$ and the line segment is

(a) (0, 0) (b) (0, 2)
(c) (2, 0) (d) (−2, 0)

Sol. (a) Let $P(x, y)$ be the point which lies on the perpendicular bisector of the line segment joining the points $A(-2, -5)$ and $B(2, 5)$ and the line segment.

Since, the point P lies on perpendicular bisector and the line segment.

∴ P is the intersection point.

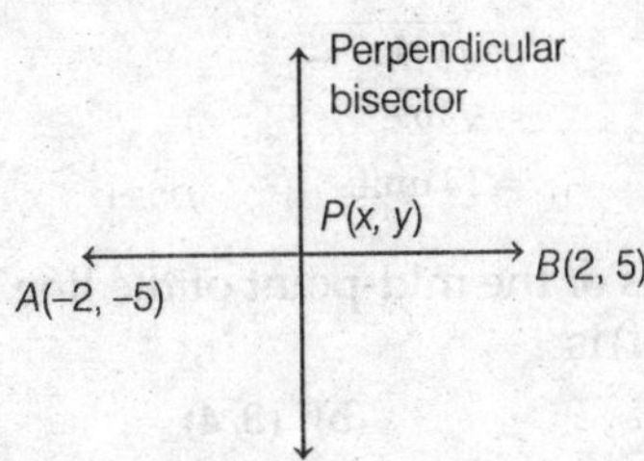

Then, P divides the line segment AB in the ratio 1: 1
i.e., P is the mid-point of AB.

By mid-point formula, we have $(x, y) = \left(\frac{-2+2}{2}, \frac{-5+5}{3}\right) = (0, 0)$

Hence, origin represents the point P.

Q.11 In what ratio does the X-axis divide the line segment joining the points $A(2, -3)$ and $B(5, 6)$ is

(a) 1 : 2 (b) 2 : 3 (c) 3 : 2 (d) 4 : 3

Sol. (a) Let the point $P(x, y)$ on the X-axis that divides the line segment joining $A(2, -3)$ and $B(5, 6)$ in k: 1.

Since, the point P lies on the X-axis, the y-coordinate of the point is 0.

Now, by section formula,

$$(x, y) = \left(\frac{kx_2 + x_1}{k+1}, \frac{ky_2 + y_1}{k+1}\right)$$

$$\Rightarrow \quad (x, 0) = \left(\frac{k(5) + 2}{k+1}, \frac{k(6) - 3}{k+1}\right)$$

$$\Rightarrow \quad 0 = \frac{6k - 3}{k+1} \Rightarrow 6k - 3 = 0$$

$$\Rightarrow \quad k = \frac{3}{6} = \frac{1}{2}$$

Hence, the ratio is 1 : 2.

Q.12 Distance between the points $(5, -8)$ and $(-7, -3)$ is

(a) 15 units (b) 10 units
(c) 13 units (d) 5 units

Sol. (c) Let P and Q represent the points $(5, -8)$ and $(-7, -3)$ respectively.

$\therefore$ The distance $PQ = \sqrt{(-7-5)^2 + (-3+8)^2}$

$$\left[\because d = \sqrt{(x_2 - x_1)^2 + (y_2 - y_1)^2}\right]$$

$$= \sqrt{(-12)^2 + (5)^2}$$
$$= \sqrt{144 + 25}$$
$$= \sqrt{169}$$
$$= 13 \text{ units}$$

Q.13 The coordinates of the mid-point of the line joining the points $(11, 5)$ and $(5, 11)$ is

(a) (4, 8) (b) (8, 4)
(c) (8, 8) (d) (0, 8)

Sol. (c) Let $P(x, y)$ denote the mid-point of the line joining the points (11, 5) and (5, 11)

Then, mid-point formula is given by

$$(x, y) = \left(\frac{x_1 + x_2}{2}, \frac{y_1 + y_2}{2}\right)$$

$$= \left(\frac{11+5}{2}, \frac{5+11}{2}\right) = \left(\frac{16}{2}, \frac{16}{2}\right) = (8, 8)$$

Q.14 The mid-point of the line joining $(3a, 4)$ and $(-2, 2b)$ is $(2, 2a+2)$, then the values of a and b are

(a) $a = 4, b = 4$ (b) $a = 2, b = 4$
(c) $a = 2, b = 2$ (d) $a = 1, b = 4$

Sol. (b) Let $A(3a, 4)$, $B(-2, 2b)$ and $C(2, 2a + 2)$ represent given points.

Since, C is the mid-point of the line AB.

$$\therefore (2, 2a+2) = \left(\frac{3a-2}{2}, \frac{4+2b}{2}\right) \quad \left[\because \text{mid point, } (x, y) = \left(\frac{x_1 + x_2}{2}, \frac{y_1 + y_2}{2}\right)\right]$$

Equating the corresponding coordinates, we get

$$2 = \frac{3a-2}{2} \text{ and } 2a + 2 = \frac{4+2b}{2}$$

$$\Rightarrow \quad 4 = 3a - 2$$

$$\Rightarrow \quad 3a = 6 \quad \Rightarrow a = 2$$

On substituting $a = 2$ in the other equation, we get

$$2 \times 2 + 2 = \frac{4 + 2b}{2}$$

$$\Rightarrow \quad 12 = 4 + 2b$$

$$\Rightarrow \quad 2b = 8$$

$$\Rightarrow \quad b = 4$$

Q.15 Find the distance between the points $A(a+b, a-b)$ and $B(a-b, a+b)$.

(a) $2\sqrt{2}b$ units

(b) $2\sqrt{2}a$ units

(c) $\sqrt{2}b$ units

(d) 2 units

Sol. (a) Given, point $A(a+b, a-b)$ and $B(a-b, a+b)$

$$\therefore \quad AB = \sqrt{(a+b-(a-b))^2 + (a-b-(a+b))^2}$$

$$\left[\because \text{distance} = \sqrt{(x_2 - x_1)^2 + (y_2 - y_1)^2}\right]$$

$$= \sqrt{(a+b-a+b)^2 + (a-b-a-b)^2}$$

$$= \sqrt{(2b)^2 + (-2b)^2}$$

$$= \sqrt{4b^2 + 4b^2}$$

$$= \sqrt{8b^2} = 2\sqrt{2}b \text{ units}$$

Q.16 If $P\left(\frac{a}{2}, 4\right)$ is the mid-point of the line segment joining the points $A(-6, 5)$ and $B(-2, 3)$, then the value of a is

(a) -8

(b) 3

(c) -4

(d) 4

Sol. (a) $P\left(\frac{a}{2}, 4\right)$ is the mid-point of the line segment joining the points $A(-6, 5)$ and $B(-2, 3)$, then by mid-point formula,

$$\left(\frac{a}{2}, 4\right) = \left(\frac{-6-2}{2}, \frac{5+3}{2}\right) \qquad \left[\because (x, y) = \left(\frac{x_1 + x_2}{2}, \frac{y_1 + y_2}{2}\right)\right]$$

$$\Rightarrow \quad \frac{a}{2} = \frac{-8}{2}$$

$$\Rightarrow \quad a = -8$$

Q.17 The distance of the point $(a\cos\alpha, a\sin\alpha)$ from the origin is

(a) 1 unit (b) $a\sin\alpha$ units

(c) $a\cos\alpha$ units (d) a units

Sol. (d) The coordinates of origin are (0, 0).

The distance between points $(a\cos\alpha, a\sin\alpha)$ and (0, 0) is

$= \sqrt{(a\cos\alpha - 0)^2 + (a\sin\alpha - 0)^2}$ $[\because \text{distance} = \sqrt{(x_2 - x_1)^2 + (y_2 - y_1)^2}]$

$= \sqrt{(a\cos\alpha)^2 + (a\sin\alpha)^2}$

$= \sqrt{a^2\cos^2\alpha + a^2\sin^2\alpha} = \sqrt{a^2(\cos^2\alpha + \sin^2\alpha)}$

$= \sqrt{a^2}$ $[\because \cos^2\theta + \sin^2\theta = 1]$

$= a$ units.

☐ Subjective Type Questions

Q.1 Prove that the points (3, 0), (6, 4) and (−1, 3) are the vertices of a right angled isosceles triangle.

Sol. Let the triangle be ΔABC as shown in figure.
Distances are

$$AB = \sqrt{(3-6)^2 + (0-4)^2} = 5$$

$$BC = \sqrt{(6+1)^2 + (4-3)^2} = 5\sqrt{2}$$

and $$CA = \sqrt{(-1-3)^2 + (3-0)^2} = 5$$

A(3, 0)
B(6, 4) C(−1, 3)

Here, $AB = AC \Rightarrow \Delta ABC$ is isosceles triangle.

Consider,

$AB^2 + AC^2 = (5)^2 + (5)^2 = 25 + 25 = 50$

$\Rightarrow$ and $BC^2 = (5\sqrt{2})^2 = 50$

Here, $AB^2 + AC^2 = BC^2$

So, ΔABC is a right angled triangle.

Q.2 The x-coordinate of a point P is twice its y-coordinate. If P is equidistant from $Q(2, -5)$ and $R(-3, 6)$, find the coordinates of P.

Sol. Given, point-P is equidistant from $Q(2, -5)$ and $R(-3, 6)$.

Let the coordinates of point P are (x, y)

$\because$ $x = 24$ (Given)

$\therefore$ $(x, y) = (24, 4)$

Now, $PQ = PR \Rightarrow \sqrt{(2y-2)^2 + (y+5)^2} = \sqrt{(2y+3)^2 + (y-6)^2}$

$\because$ distance $= \sqrt{(x_2 - x_1)^2 + (y_2 - y_1)^2}$

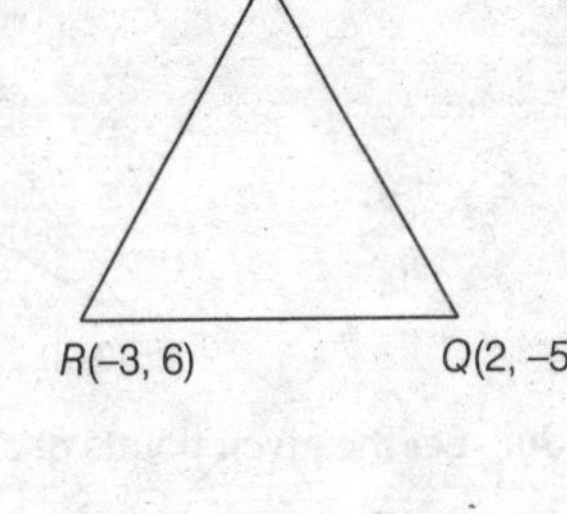

On squaring both sides, we get

$4y^2 + 4 - 8y + y^2 + 10y + 25$
$= 4y^2 + 9 + 12y + y^2 + 36 - 12y$

$\Rightarrow \quad 2y + 29 = 45,$

$\Rightarrow \quad 2y = 45 - 29$

$\Rightarrow \quad 2y = 16$

$\Rightarrow \quad y = 8$

$\because \quad x = 2y$

$\therefore \quad = 2 \times 8 = 16$

Hence, coordinates of P are (16, 8).

Q.3 Find the ratio in which Y-axis divides the line segment joining the points $A(5, -6)$ and $B(-1, -4)$ and find the point.

◎ ***Thinking Process*** On Y-axis the coordinate of any point is $(0, y)$ or $(0, -y)$.

Sol. Let the point on Y-axis be $P(0, y)$ and $AP : PB = k : 1$.

$\therefore$ Co-ordinates of P given by : $\left(\frac{mx_2 + nx_1}{m+n}, \frac{my_2 + ny_1}{m+n}\right)$

$\Rightarrow \quad x = \frac{k(-1) + 1(5)}{k+1}$

But points lies on Y-axis so, x-coordinate is zero.

$\Rightarrow \quad \frac{5-k}{k+1} = 0 \Rightarrow k = 5$

Hence, the required ratio is 5 : 1.

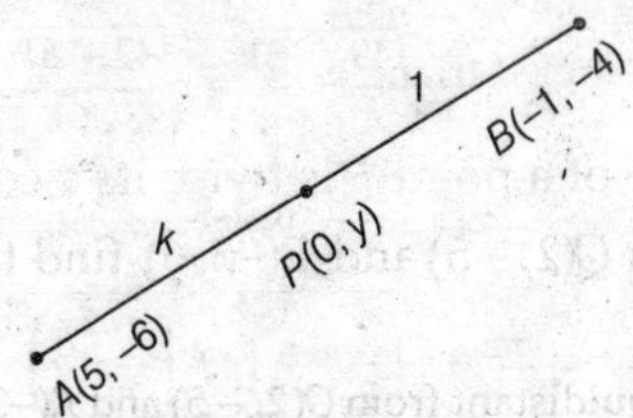

Now, $y = \frac{(-4)(5) + (-6)(1)}{5+1} = \frac{-13}{3}$

Hence, point on Y-axis is $\left(0, \frac{-13}{3}\right)$.

Q.4 Find the lengths of medians of triangle whose vertices are $(1, -1)$, $(0, 4)$ and $(-5, 3)$.

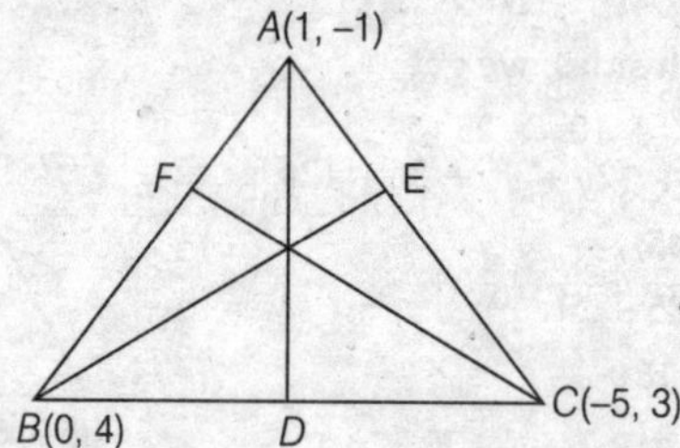

Sol. Let the given points of a triangle be $A(1, -1)$, $B(0, 4)$ and $C(-5, 3)$.

Let D, E, F be the mid-points of the sides BC, CA and AB, respectively. Then, the coordinates of D are

$$= D\left(\frac{0-5}{2}, \frac{4+3}{2}\right) = D\left(\frac{-5}{2}, \frac{7}{2}\right)$$

The coordinates of E are

$$= E\left(\frac{-5+1}{2}, \frac{3-1}{2}\right) = E\left(\frac{-4}{2}, \frac{2}{2}\right) = E(-2, 1)$$

The coordinates of F are

$$= F\left(\frac{0+1}{2}, \frac{4-1}{2}\right) = F\left(\frac{1}{2}, \frac{3}{2}\right)$$

Now,

$$AD = \sqrt{\left(\frac{-5}{2} - 1\right)^2 + \left(\frac{7}{2} + 1\right)^2}$$

$$= \sqrt{\left(\frac{-5-2}{2}\right)^2 + \left(\frac{7+2}{2}\right)^2}$$

$$= \sqrt{\left(\frac{-7}{2}\right)^2 + \left(\frac{9}{2}\right)^2}$$

$$= \sqrt{\frac{49}{4} + \frac{81}{4}} = \sqrt{\frac{49+81}{4}} = \sqrt{\frac{130}{4}}$$

$$= \frac{\sqrt{130}}{2} \text{ units.}$$

and

$$CF = \sqrt{\left(\frac{1}{2} + 5\right)^2 + \left(\frac{3}{2} - 3\right)^2}$$

$$= \sqrt{\left(\frac{1+10}{2}\right)^2 + \left(\frac{3-6}{2}\right)^2} = \sqrt{\left(\frac{11}{2}\right)^2 + \left(\frac{-3}{2}\right)^2}$$

$$= \sqrt{\left(\frac{121}{4} + \frac{9}{4}\right)} = \sqrt{\frac{121+9}{4}} = \sqrt{\frac{130}{4}} = \frac{\sqrt{130}}{2} \text{ units}$$

$$BE = \sqrt{(0+2)^2 + (4-1)^2}$$
$$= \sqrt{(2)^2 + (3)^2} = \sqrt{4+9} = \sqrt{13} \text{ units.}$$

Hence, the lengths of medians are $AD = \frac{\sqrt{130}}{2}$ units,

$$BE = \sqrt{13} \text{ units and } \quad CF = \frac{\sqrt{130}}{2} \text{ units.}$$

Q.5 The line segment joining the points $(3, -4)$ and $(1, 2)$ is trisected at the points P and Q. If coordinates of P and Q are $(p, -2)$ and $\left(\frac{5}{3}, q\right)$ respectively, find the value of p and q.

Sol. Let, AB is the line segment joining the points $A(3, -4)$ and $B(1, 2)$.

Then, P and Q trisects AB

i.e., $AP = PQ = QB = k$ (say)

A(3, –4) P Q B(1, 2)

Then, $PB = PQ + QB = 2k$

and $\qquad AQ = AP + PQ = 2k$

$\Rightarrow \qquad AP : PB = k : 2k = 1 : 2$

and $\qquad AQ : QB = 2k : k : 2 : 1$

Since, P divides AB internally in the ratio $1 : 2$.

So, by section formula the coordinates of P are

$$(p, -2) = \left(\frac{1(1) + 2(3)}{1+2}, \frac{1(2) + 2(-4)}{1+2}\right) = \left(\frac{1+6}{3}, \frac{2-8}{3}\right)$$

$$= \left(\frac{7}{3}, -2\right) \quad \left(\because \text{Using section formula} = \frac{m_1x_2 + m_2x_1}{m_1 + m_2}, \frac{m_1y_2 + m_2y_1}{m_1 + m_2}\right)$$

On comparing x-co-ordinate of both sides, we get

$$p = \frac{7}{3}$$

Similarly, Q divide AB internally in the ratio $2 : 1$.

$$\text{Then, } \left(\frac{5}{3}, q\right) = \left(\frac{2(1) + 1(3)}{2+1}, \frac{2(2) + 1(-4)}{2+1}\right) = \left(\frac{5}{3}, \frac{4-4}{3}\right) = \left(\frac{5}{3}, 0\right)$$

On comparing y-co-ordinate of both sides, we get

$$q = 0$$

Hence, $\qquad p = \frac{7}{3}$ and $q = 0$

Q.6 If two vertices of an equilateral triangle are $(0,0)$, $(3\sqrt{3})$, find the third vertex.

Sol. Let (x, y) be the coordinates of the third vertex.

Again let point P be $(0, 0)$, $R(x, y)$ and $Q(3, \sqrt{3})$.

Then, PQR form an equilateral triangle.

Using distance formula, $PQ = \sqrt{(3-0)^2 + (\sqrt{3}-0)^2}$

$$= \sqrt{(3)^2 + (\sqrt{3})^2} = \sqrt{9+3} = \sqrt{12}$$

$\because$ All sides are equal in equilatenal triangle.

$\therefore \quad PQ = QR = PR = \sqrt{12}$ units ...(i)

Now, using distance formula

$$QR = \sqrt{(3-x)^2 + (\sqrt{3}-y)^2}$$

$$\sqrt{12} = \sqrt{(3-x)^2 + (\sqrt{3}-y)^2}$$

On squaring both sides, we get

$$12 = (3-x)^2 + (\sqrt{3}-y)^2 \quad \text{[Using Eq. (i)]}$$

$$\Rightarrow \quad 12 = 9 + x^2 - 6x + 3 + y^2 - 2\sqrt{3}y$$

$$\Rightarrow \quad x^2 + y^2 - 6x - 2\sqrt{3}y = 0 \quad \text{...(ii)}$$

Now, $PR = \sqrt{(x-0)^2 + (y-0)^2}$

$$\Rightarrow \quad \sqrt{x^2 + y^2} = \sqrt{12} \quad \text{[Using Eq. (i)]}$$

$$\therefore \quad x^2 + y^2 = 12 \quad \text{...(iii)}$$

Put the value of $x^2 + y^2$ in Eq. (ii), we get

$$-6x - 2\sqrt{3}y = -12$$

$$\Rightarrow \quad 6x + 2\sqrt{3}y = 12$$

$$\Rightarrow \quad 6x = 12 - 2\sqrt{3}y \Rightarrow 3x = 6 - \sqrt{3}y$$

$$\Rightarrow \quad x = 2 - \frac{1}{\sqrt{3}}y \quad \text{...(iv)}$$

Put the value of x in Eq. (iii), we get

$$\left(2 - \frac{1}{\sqrt{3}}y\right)^2 + y^2 = 12$$

$$4 + \frac{1}{3}y^2 - \frac{4}{\sqrt{3}}y + y^2 = 12$$

$$\Rightarrow \quad \frac{4}{3}y^2 - \frac{4}{\sqrt{3}}y = 8$$

$$\Rightarrow \quad \frac{4}{3}y^2 - \frac{4\sqrt{3}}{3}y = 8$$

$$\Rightarrow \quad 4y^2 - 4\sqrt{3}y = 24$$

$$\Rightarrow \quad y^2 - \sqrt{3}y - 6 = 0$$

$$\Rightarrow \quad y^2 - 2\sqrt{3}y + \sqrt{3}y - 6 = 0$$

$$\Rightarrow \quad y(y-2\sqrt{3})+\sqrt{3}(y-2\sqrt{3})=0 \Rightarrow y=2\sqrt{3},-\sqrt{3}$$

When $\quad y=2\sqrt{3}$

the value of x is $=2-\frac{1}{\sqrt{3}}(2\sqrt{3})=2-2=0$

When $\quad y=-\sqrt{3}$

$\therefore$ The value of x is $=2-\frac{1}{\sqrt{3}}(-\sqrt{3})=2+1=3$

So, third vertex is $(0, 2\sqrt{3})$ or $(3, -\sqrt{3})$.

Q.7 If $P(2,-1), Q(3,4), R(-2,3)$ and $S(-3,-2)$ be four points in a plane, show that $PQRS$ is a rhombus but not a square.

Sol. Given the points $P(2,-1)$, $Q(3, 4)$, $R(-2, 3)$ and $S(-3,-2)$ are the plane.

Then, we have the distance formula for the points $A(x_1, y_1)$ and $B(x_2, y_2)$ as

$$AB=\sqrt{(x_2-x_1)^2+(y_2-y_1)^2}$$

So,
$$PQ=\sqrt{(3-2)^2+(4+1)^2}=\sqrt{1^2+5^2}=\sqrt{26}$$

$$QR=\sqrt{(-2-3)^2+(3-4)^2}=\sqrt{(-5)^2+(-1)^2}=\sqrt{26}$$

$$RS=\sqrt{(-3+2)^2+(-2-3)^2}=\sqrt{(-1)^2+(-5)^2}=\sqrt{26}$$

$$PS=\sqrt{(-3-2)^2+(-2+1)^2}=\sqrt{(-5)^2+(-1)^2}=\sqrt{26}$$

Now, for diagonal,

$$PR=\sqrt{(-2-2)^2+(3+1)^2}=\sqrt{(-4)^2+4^2}=\sqrt{32}=4\sqrt{2}$$

$$QS=\sqrt{(-3-3)^2+(-2-4)^2}=\sqrt{(-6)^2+(-6)^2}+\sqrt{72}=6\sqrt{2}$$

$\because \quad PQ=QR=RS=PS$

and $\quad PR \neq QS$

Hence, $PQRS$ forms a rhombus.

Note A quadrilateral is a square iff all the four sides are equal and the diagonals are also equal.

Q.8 The points $(3,-4)$ and $(6,-5)$ are the endpoints of a diagonal of a parallelogram. If one of the endpoints of the second diagonal is $(-2,1)$. Find the other points.

Sol. Let $ABCD$ be the parallelogram and AC and BD are the two diagonals.

According to question one diagonal has endpoint *i.e.*, $A(3,-4)$ and $C(6,-5)$ and second diagonal has endpoints *i.e.*, $B(-2, 1)$ and $D(x, y)$.

We know that the diagonals of a parallelogram bisect each other.

$\therefore$ Mid-Point of AC = Mid-point of BD

$$\Rightarrow \quad \left(\frac{3+6}{2}, \frac{-4-5}{2}\right) = \left(\frac{-2+x}{2}, \frac{1+y}{2}\right)$$

On comparing the x and y co-ordinate, we get

$$-2 + x = 9 \text{ and } 1 + y = -9$$

$$\Rightarrow \quad x = 9 + 2 \text{ and } y = -9 - 1$$

$$\Rightarrow \quad x = 11 \quad \text{and } y = -10$$

So, the fourth vertex is $D(11, -10)$.

Q.9 In what ratio does Y-axis divides the line segment joining the point $p(-4, 5)$ and $q(3, -7)$.

Sol. Let $A(x, y)$ be the point on the Y-axis that divides the line segment joining the point $p(-4, 5)$ and $q(3, -7)$ in $k : 1$.

As A lies on Y-axis, its abscissa is zero.
Then, by section formula, we have

$$(x, y) = \left(\frac{3k-4}{k+1}, \frac{-7k+5}{k+1}\right)$$

$$\Rightarrow \quad (0, y) = \left(\frac{3k-4}{k+1}, \frac{-7k+5}{k+1}\right)$$

Equating the x-coordinates, we get

$$\frac{3k-4}{k+1} = 0 \Rightarrow 3k - 4 = 0 \Rightarrow k = \frac{4}{3}$$

Q.10 If the point $C(-1, 2)$ divides internally the line segment joining the points $A(2, 5)$ and $B(x, y)$ in the ratio $3 : 4$, find the value of $x^2 + y^2$.

Sol. Using section formula,

$$-1 = \frac{3 \times x + 4 \times 2}{3 + 4}$$

C(−1, 2)

A(2, 5) 3 : 4 B(x, y)

$$\Rightarrow \quad -1 = \frac{3x + 8}{7}$$

$$\Rightarrow \quad 3x + 8 = -7 \Rightarrow 3x = -15 \Rightarrow x = -5$$

Similarly, $\quad 2 = \dfrac{3 \times y + 4 \times 5}{3 + 4}$

$$\Rightarrow \quad 14 = 3y + 20 \Rightarrow 3y = -6 \Rightarrow y = -2$$

Hence, $\quad x^2 + y^2 = (-5)^2 + (-2)^2 = 25 + 4 = 29$

Q.11 Find the ratio in which the point $(-3, k)$ divides the line segment joining the points $(-5, -4)$ and $(-2, 3)$. Also find the value of k.

Sol. Let A, B, C be the points representing the coordinates $(-5, -4)$, $(-2, 3)$ and $(-3, k)$, respectively.

$A(-5, -4)$ $C(-3, k)$ $B(-2, 3)$

Let C divides AB internally in the ratio $m : 1$.

Then, by section formula,

$$(-3, k) = \left(\frac{-2(m) - 5}{m + 1}, \frac{3(m) + (-4)(1)}{m + 1}\right)$$

$$\Rightarrow \quad (-3, k) = \left(\frac{-2m - 5}{m + 1}, \frac{3m - 4}{m + 1}\right)$$

Equating the coordinates, we get

$$\frac{-2m - 5}{m + 1} = -3$$

$$\Rightarrow \quad -2m - 5 = -3(m + 1) \Rightarrow -2m - 5 = -3m - 3$$

$$\Rightarrow \quad -2m + 3m = -3 + 5$$

$$m = 2 \quad \text{...(i)}$$

and

$$\frac{3m - 4}{m + 1} = k$$

$$\Rightarrow \quad \frac{3(2) - 4}{2 + 1} = k \quad \text{[From Eq. (i)]}$$

$$\Rightarrow \quad \frac{6 - 4}{3} = k \Rightarrow k = \frac{2}{3}$$

Hence, the point $(-3, k)$ divides the line segment joining the points $(-5, -4)$ and $(-2, 3)$ in $2 : 1$ and the value of k is $\frac{2}{3}$.

Q.12 Let P and Q be the points of trisection of the line segment joining the points $A(2, -2)$ and $B(-7, 4)$ such that P is nearer to A. Find the coordinates of P and Q.

Sol. Given, P and Q be the points of trisection of the line segment joining the points $A(2, -2)$ and $B(-7, 4)$.

$A(2, -2)$ P Q $B(-7, 4)$

$$\Rightarrow \quad AP = PQ = QB = k \text{ (say)}$$

Then, $AQ = AP + PQ = 2k$

and $PB = PQ + QB = 2k$

$\therefore$ $AP : PB = 1 : 2$

and $AQ : QB = 2 : 1$

Now, P divides AB internally in the ratio $1 : 2$.

So, by section formula, the coordinates of P are

$$= \left(\frac{1(-7)+2(2)}{1+2}, \frac{1(4)+2(-2)}{1+2}\right)$$

$$= \left(\frac{-7+4}{3}, \frac{4-4}{3}\right) = \left(\frac{-3}{3}, 0\right) = (-1, 0)$$

Similarly, Q divides AB internally in the ratio $2:1$.

$\therefore$ Coordinates of point $Q \left(\frac{2(-7)+1(2)}{2+1}, \frac{2(4)+1(-2)}{2+1}\right)$

$$= \left(\frac{-14+2}{3}, \frac{8-2}{3}\right) = \left(\frac{-12}{3}, \frac{6}{3}\right) = (-4, 2)$$

Hence, the coordinates of P is $(-1, 0)$ and Q is $(-4, 2)$.

Q.13 Find a relation between x and y such that the point (x, y) is equidistant from the points $(7, 1)$ and $(3, 5)$.

Sol. Let $P(x, y)$ be equidistant from the points $A(7, 1)$ and $B(3, 5)$.

$\therefore$ $AP = BP$

By distance formula, $\sqrt{(x-7)^2 + (y-1)^2} = \sqrt{(x-3)^2 + (y-5)^2}$

On squaring both sides, we get

$\Rightarrow$ $x^2 + 49 - 14x + y^2 + 1 - 2y = x^2 + 9 - 6x + y^2 + 25 - 10y$

$\Rightarrow$ $-14x - 2y + 50 = -6x - 10y + 34$

$\Rightarrow$ $-14x + 6x - 2y + 10y = 34 - 50 \Rightarrow -8x + 6y = -16$

$\Rightarrow$ $8x - 8y = 16 \Rightarrow x - y = 2$

Q.14 Find the coordinates of the point R on the line segment joining the points $P(-1, 3)$ and $Q(2, 5)$ such that $PR = \frac{3}{5}PQ$.

(x, y)

P(–1, 3) 3 R 2 Q(2,5)

Sol. We have $\frac{PR}{PQ} = \frac{3}{5} \Rightarrow \frac{PQ}{PR} = \frac{5}{3}$

$\Rightarrow$ $\frac{PR + RQ}{PR} = \frac{5}{3} \Rightarrow 1 + \frac{RQ}{PR} = \frac{5}{3} \Rightarrow \frac{RQ}{PR} = \frac{5}{3} - 1 = \frac{2}{3}$

$\therefore$ $RQ : PR = 2 : 3$ or $PR : RQ = 3 : 2$

i.e., R divides PQ internally in the ratio $3 : 2$.

So, by section formula, the coordinates of R are

$$= \left(\frac{3(2)+2(-1)}{3+2}, \frac{3(5)+2(3)}{3+2}\right) = \left(\frac{6-2}{5}, \frac{15+6}{5}\right) = \left(\frac{4}{5}, \frac{21}{5}\right)$$

Hence, the required coordinates of the point R is $\left(\frac{4}{5}, \frac{21}{5}\right)$.

Introduction to Trigonometry

CHAPTER 08

Important Points

01 Meaning of Trigonometry The word 'trigonometry' is derived from the Greek word 'tri' meaning three, 'gon' meaning sides and 'metron meaning measure.

02 Concept of Perpendicular, Base and Hypotenuse in a Right Angled Triangle For any acute angle (which is also known as the angle of reference) in a right angled triangle; the side opposite to the acute angle is called the perpendicular; the side adjacent to it is called the base and side opposite to the right angle is called the hypotenuse.

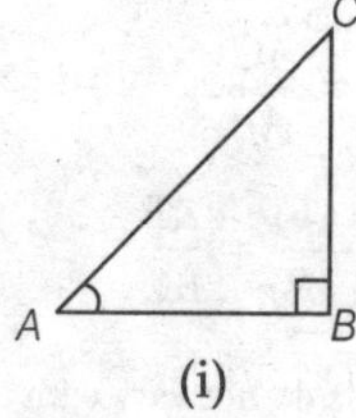

(i)

Angle of reference = $\angle A$
Perpendicular = BC
Base = AB
Hypotenuse = AC

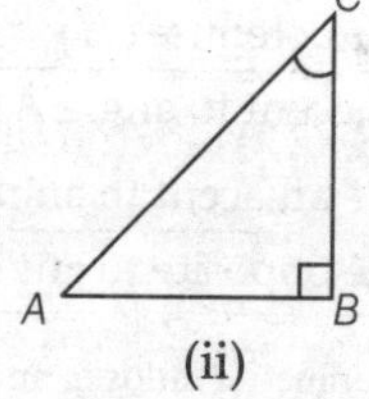

(ii)

Angle of reference = $\angle C$
Perpendicular = AB
Base = BC
Hypotenuse = AC

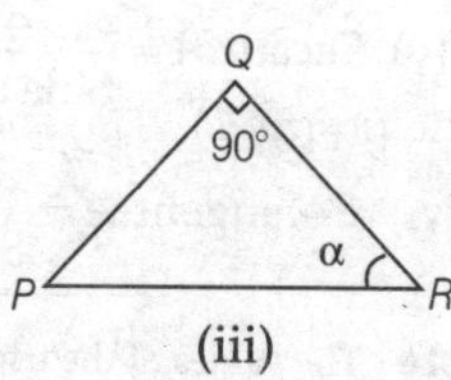

(iii)

Angle of reference = $\angle R$
Perpendicular = PQ
Base = QR
Hypotenuse = PR

03 Trigonometric Ratio The ratios of the sides of a right angled triangle with respect to its acute angles, are called trigonometric ratio.

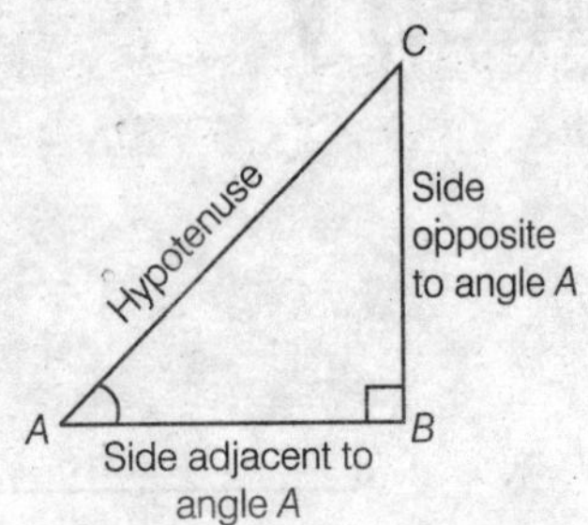

Trigonometric ratios of the $\angle A$ in right angled ΔABC are defined as follows

(i) $\text{Sine } A = \dfrac{\text{Side opposite to angle } A\,(P)}{\text{Hypotenuse}\,(H)} = \dfrac{BC}{AC}$

(ii) $\text{Cosine } A = \dfrac{\text{Side adjacent to angle } A\,(B)}{\text{Hypotenuse}\,(H)} = \dfrac{AB}{AC}$

(iii) $\text{Tangent } A = \dfrac{\text{Side opposite to angle } A\,(P)}{\text{Side adjacent to angle } A\,(B)} = \dfrac{BC}{AB}$

(iv) $\text{Cosecant } A = \dfrac{\text{Hypotenuse}\,(H)}{\text{Side opposite to angle } A\,(P)} = \dfrac{AC}{BC}$

(v) $\text{Secant } A = \dfrac{\text{Hypotenuse}\,(H)}{\text{Side adjacent to angle } A\,(B)} = \dfrac{AC}{AB}$

(vi) $\text{Cotangent } A = \dfrac{\text{Side adjacent to angle } A\,(B)}{\text{Side opposite to angle } A\,(P)} = \dfrac{AB}{BC}$

Note The values of the trigonometric ratios of an angle do not vary with the lengths of the sides of the triangle, if the angle remains the same.

04 Reciprocal Relations Trigonometric ratio and the reciprocal relations between them are as below

(i) $\sin A = \dfrac{1}{\operatorname{cosec} A}$; $\operatorname{cosec} A = \dfrac{1}{\sin A}$

(ii) $\cos A = \dfrac{1}{\sec A}$; $\sec A = \dfrac{1}{\cos A}$

(iii) $\tan A = \dfrac{1}{\cot A}$; $\cot A = \dfrac{1}{\tan A}$

Note

Term	sine	cosine	tangent	cotangent	secant	cosecant
In short	sin	cos	tan	cot	sec	cosec

05 Quotient Relation

(i) $\tan A = \dfrac{\sin A}{\cos A}$ (ii) $\cot A = \dfrac{\cos A}{\sin A}$

Note
- Each trigonometric ratio is a real number and has no unit.
- $\sin\theta$ is used as an abbreviation for 'the sine of the angle θ'. $\sin\theta$ is not the product of sin and θ.
- Trigonometric ratios are also written as *t*-ratios.
- If one of the trigonometric ratios of an acute angle is known the remaining trigonometric ratios of angle can be easily determined.

Trigonometric Ratios of Some Specific Angles

Angles	0°	30°	45°	60°	90°	180°	270°	360°
Degrees	0°	30°	45°	60°	90°	180°	270°	360°
Radians	0	$\frac{\pi}{6}$	$\frac{\pi}{4}$	$\frac{\pi}{3}$	$\frac{\pi}{2}$	π	$\frac{3\pi}{2}$	2π
$\sin\theta$	0	$\frac{1}{2}$	$\frac{1}{\sqrt{2}}$	$\frac{\sqrt{3}}{2}$	1	0	-1	0
$\cos\theta$	1	$\frac{\sqrt{3}}{2}$	$\frac{1}{\sqrt{2}}$	$\frac{1}{2}$	0	-1	0	1
$\tan\theta$	0	$\frac{1}{\sqrt{3}}$	1	$\sqrt{3}$	∞	0	∞	0
$\text{cosec}\,\theta$	∞	2	$\sqrt{2}$	$\frac{2}{\sqrt{3}}$	1	∞	-1	∞
$\sec\theta$	1	$\frac{2}{\sqrt{3}}$	$\sqrt{2}$	2	∞	-1	∞	1
$\cot\theta$	∞	$\sqrt{3}$	1	$\frac{1}{\sqrt{3}}$	0	∞	0	∞

∞ = Undefined

Note
- The values of $\sin\theta$ and $\cos\theta$ always lie between 0 and 1.
- Division by 0 is not allowed, hence $\frac{1}{0}$ is not defined or infinity.
- In the case of $\tan\theta$, the values increase from 0 to ∞.
- In the case of $\cot\theta$, the values decrease from ∞ to 0.
- In the case of $\text{cosec}\,\theta$, the values decrease from ∞ to 1.
- In the case of $\sec\theta$, the values increase from 1 to ∞.
- If one of the sides and any other part (either an acute angle or any side) of a right triangle is known, the remaining sides and angles of the triangle can be determined.

06 Fundamental Trigonometric Identities An equation involving trigonometric ratios of an angle is called a trigonometric identity, if it is true for all values of the angle θ.

(i) $\sin^2\theta + \cos^2\theta = 1$ or $\sin^2\theta = 1 - \cos^2\theta$ or $\cos^2\theta = 1 - \sin^2\theta$

(ii) $1 + \tan^2\theta = \sec^2\theta$ or $\sec^2\theta - 1 = \tan^2\theta$ or $\sec^2\theta - \tan^2\theta = 1$ for $0° \le A < 90°$

(iii) $1 + \cot^2\theta = \text{cosec}^2\theta$ or $\text{cosec}^2\theta - \cot^2\theta = 1$ or $\cot^2\theta = \text{cosec}^2\theta - 1$ for $0° < A \le 90°$

Note • $\sin^2\theta = (\sin\theta)^2$

But $\sin\theta^2 \neq (\sin\theta)^2$

• $\sin^{-1}\theta \neq \frac{1}{\sin\theta}$, $(\sin\theta)^{-1} = \frac{1}{\sin\theta} = \text{cosec}\theta$

Exercise 8.1

Question 1 In ΔABC, right angled at B, $AB = 24$ cm, $BC = 7$ cm. Determine

(i) $\sin A$, $\cos A$ (ii) $\sin C$, $\cos C$

Thinking Process First find the hypotenuse that is side AC by using Pythagoras theorem, then find the respective values and simplify the function.

Sol. (i) In right angled ΔABC, using the Pythagoras theorem, we have

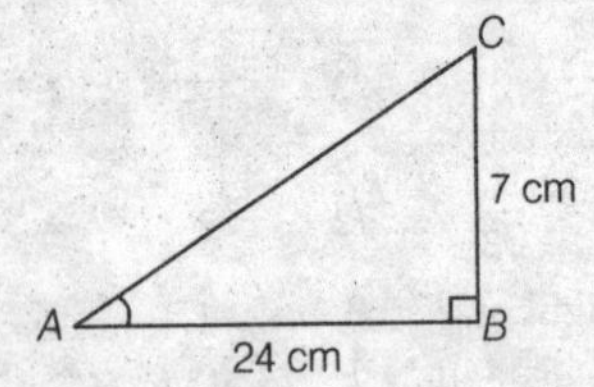

$$AC^2 = AB^2 + BC^2 = (24)^2 + (7)^2$$

$$= 576 + 49 = 625$$

$\therefore$ $AC = 25$ cm (∵ Side cannot be –ve)

(i) $\sin A = \frac{P}{H} = \frac{CB}{AC} = \frac{7}{25}$

and $\cos A = \frac{B}{H} = \frac{AB}{AC} = \frac{24}{25}$

(ii) $\sin C = \frac{P}{H} = \frac{AB}{AC} = \frac{24}{25}$ and $\cos C = \frac{B}{H} = \frac{CB}{AC} = \frac{7}{25}$

Question 2 In figure, find $\tan P - \cot R$.

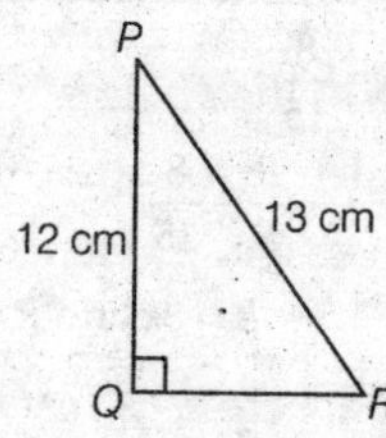

Sol. In right angled ΔPQR, $PQ^2 + QR^2 = PR^2$ (By Pythagoras theorem)

$\Rightarrow$ $(12)^2 + QR^2 = (13)^2 \Rightarrow 144 + QR^2 = 169$

$\Rightarrow$ $QR^2 = 169 - 144 = 25$

$\therefore$ $QR = 5\text{ cm}$ ($\because$ Side cannot be –ve)

$$\tan P = \frac{P}{B} = \frac{QR}{PQ} = \frac{5}{12}$$

and $$\cot R = \frac{B}{P} = \frac{QR}{PQ} = \frac{5}{12}$$

$\therefore$ $$\tan P - \cot R = \frac{5}{12} - \frac{5}{12} = 0$$

Question 3 If $\sin A = \frac{3}{4}$, then calculate $\cos A$ and $\tan A$.

Sol. Given, $\sin A = \frac{3}{4} \Rightarrow \frac{P}{H} = \frac{3}{4}$

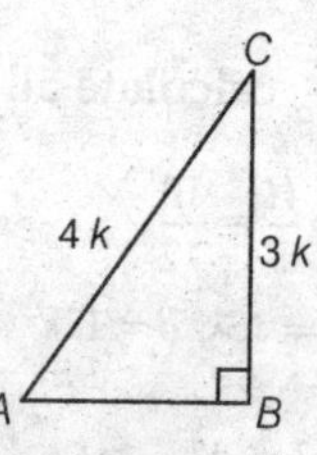

Let $P = 3k$ and $H = 4k$. In right angled ΔABC,

$P^2 + B^2 = H^2$ (By Pythagoras theorem)

$\Rightarrow$ $(3k)^2 + B^2 = (4k)^2$

$\Rightarrow$ $9k^2 + B^2 = 16k^2$

$\Rightarrow$ $B^2 = 16k^2 - 9k^2 = 7k^2$

$\therefore$ $B = k\sqrt{7}$ ($\because$ Base cannot be –ve)

Now, $$\cos A = \frac{B}{H} = \frac{k\sqrt{7}}{4k} = \frac{\sqrt{7}}{4}$$

and $$\tan A = \frac{P}{B} = \frac{3k}{k\sqrt{7}}$$

$$\tan A = \frac{3}{\sqrt{7}} \times \frac{\sqrt{7}}{\sqrt{7}} = \frac{3\sqrt{7}}{7}$$

Question 4 Given 15 cot $A = 8$, find sin A and sec A.

Sol. Given, $15 \cot A = 8 \Rightarrow \cot A = \frac{8}{15}$

$\Rightarrow$ $\frac{B}{P} = \frac{8}{15}$ $\left[\cot A = \frac{\text{Base}}{\text{Perpendicular}}\right]$

Let $B = 8k$ and $P = 15k$

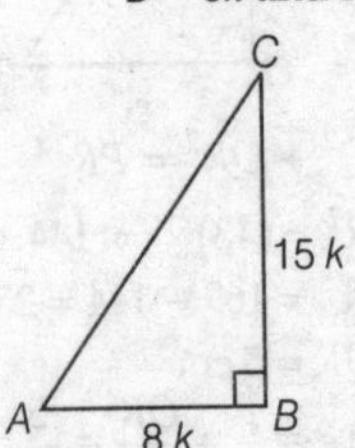

In right angled ΔABC,

$$H^2 = B^2 + P^2 \quad \text{(By Pythagoras theorem)}$$
$$= (8k)^2 + (15k)^2$$
$$= 64k^2 + 225k^2 = 289k^2$$

$\therefore$ $H = 17k$ ($\because$ Side cannot be – ve)

Now, $\sin A = \frac{P}{H} = \frac{15k}{17k} = \frac{15}{17}$

and $\sec A = \frac{H}{B} = \frac{17k}{8k} = \frac{17}{8}$

Question 5 Given $\sec\theta = \frac{13}{12}$, calculate all other trigonometric ratios.

Sol. Given, $\sec \theta = \frac{13}{12} \Rightarrow \frac{H}{B} = \frac{13}{12}$

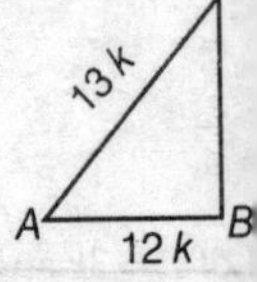

Let $H = 13k$, $B = 12k$

In right angled ΔABC,

$$P^2 + B^2 = H^2$$

(By Pythagoras theorem)

$\Rightarrow$ $P^2 + (12k)^2 = (13k)^2$

$\Rightarrow$ $P^2 + 144k^2 = 169k^2$

$\Rightarrow$ $P^2 = 169k^2 - 144k^2 = 25k^2$

$\Rightarrow$ $P = 5k$ ($\because$ Side cannot be – ve)

Now, $\sin\theta = \frac{P}{H} = \frac{5k}{13k} = \frac{5}{13}$, $\cos\theta = \frac{B}{H} = \frac{12k}{13k} = \frac{12}{13}$

$\tan\theta = \frac{P}{B} = \frac{5k}{12k} = \frac{5}{12}$, $\text{cosec}\ \theta = \frac{1}{\sin\theta} = \frac{13}{5}$

and $\cot\theta = \frac{1}{\tan\theta} = \frac{12}{5}$

Question 6 If $\angle A$ and $\angle B$ are acute angles such that $\cos A = \cos B$, then show that $\angle A = \angle B$.

Sol. In the given triangle,

$$\cos A = \cos B \qquad \text{(Given)}$$

B

A C

$$\cos A = \frac{B}{H} = \frac{AC}{B} \text{ and } \cos B = \frac{B}{H} = \frac{BC}{AB}$$

$\therefore$ $$\frac{AC}{AB} = \frac{BC}{AB} \Rightarrow AC = BC$$

$\Rightarrow$ $$\angle A = \angle B$$

($\because$ Angles opposite to equal sides are also equal)

Question 7 If $\cot\theta = \frac{7}{8}$, then evaluate

(i) $\frac{(1+\sin\theta)(1-\sin\theta)}{(1+\cos\theta)(1-\cos\theta)}$ (ii) $\cot^2\theta$

Sol. Given, $\cot\theta = \frac{7}{8} \Rightarrow \frac{B}{P} = \frac{7}{8}$

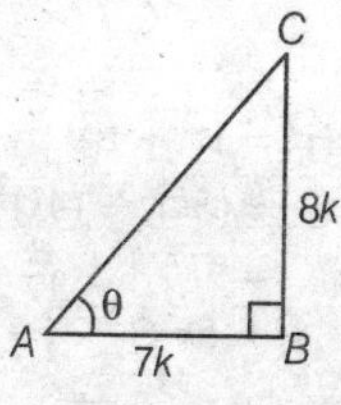

Let $$B = 7k, P = 8k$$

In a right angled ΔABC,

$$H^2 = B^2 + P^2 \qquad \text{(By Pythagoras theorem)}$$
$$= 49k^2 + 64k^2$$
$$= 113k^2$$
$$H = k\sqrt{113} \qquad (\because \text{Side cannot be} -\text{ve})$$

Now, $$\sin\theta = \frac{P}{H} = \frac{8k}{k\sqrt{113}} = \frac{8}{\sqrt{113}}$$

and $$\cos\theta = \frac{B}{H} = \frac{7k}{k\sqrt{113}} = \frac{7}{\sqrt{113}}$$

(i) $\dfrac{(1+\sin\theta)(1-\sin\theta)}{(1+\cos\theta)(1-\cos\theta)} = \dfrac{1^2 - \sin^2\theta}{1^2 - \cos^2\theta}$ $[\because (a+b)(a-b) = a^2 - b^2]$

$$= \frac{1-\left(\frac{8}{\sqrt{113}}\right)^2}{1-\left(\frac{7}{\sqrt{113}}\right)^2}$$

$$= \frac{1-\frac{64}{113}}{1-\frac{49}{113}} = \frac{\frac{113-64}{113}}{\frac{113-49}{113}} = \frac{49}{64}$$

(ii) $\cot^2\theta = \left(\dfrac{7}{8}\right)^2 = \dfrac{49}{64}$ $\left(\because \text{Given } \cot\theta = \dfrac{7}{8} \text{ and } \cot\theta = \dfrac{B}{P}\right)$

Question 8 If $3\cot A = 4$, check whether $\dfrac{1-\tan^2 A}{1+\tan^2 A} = \cos^2 A - \sin^2 A$ or not.

Sol. Given, $3\cot A = 4 \Rightarrow \cot A = \dfrac{4}{3} \Rightarrow \dfrac{B}{P} = \dfrac{4}{3}$

Let $B = 4k, P = 3k$

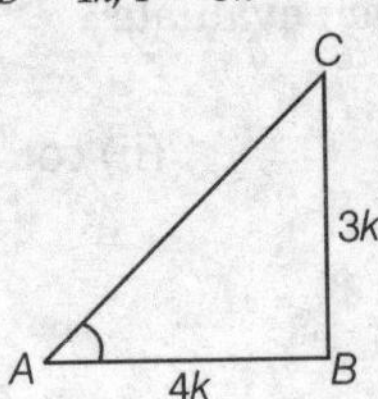

In right angled ΔABC,

$$H^2 = P^2 + B^2$$ (By Pythagoras theorem

$$= (3k)^2 + (4k)^2$$

$$= 9k^2 + 16k^2 = 25k^2$$

$\therefore$ $H = 5k$ $(\because$ Side cannot be –ve

Now, $\tan A = \dfrac{1}{\cot A} = \dfrac{3}{4}$ $\left(\because \cot A = \dfrac{4}{3}\right.$

$$\cos A = \frac{B}{H} = \frac{4}{5}$$

and $\sin A = \dfrac{P}{H} = \dfrac{3}{5}$

Now, $\text{LHS} = \dfrac{1-\tan^2 A}{1+\tan^2 A}$

$$= \frac{1-\left(\frac{3}{4}\right)^2}{1+\left(\frac{3}{4}\right)^2} = \frac{\frac{16-9}{16}}{\frac{16+9}{16}} = \frac{7}{25}$$ ...

and $$\text{RHS} = \cos^2 A - \sin^2 A = \left(\frac{4}{5}\right)^2 - \left(\frac{3}{5}\right)^2$$

$$= \frac{16-9}{25} = \frac{7}{25} \quad \text{...(ii)}$$

From Eqs. (i) and (ii), we get LHS = RHS

Question 9 In ΔABC, right angled at B, if $\tan A = \frac{1}{\sqrt{3}}$, find the value of

(i) $\sin A \cos C + \cos A \sin C$ (ii) $\cos A \cos C - \sin A \sin C$

Thinking Process We know that $\tan\theta = \frac{\text{Perpendicular}}{\text{Base}}$

Now using pythagoras theorem, get the value of hypotenuse, *i.e.*, $(H)^2 = B^2 + P^2$ and then find the value of trigonometric ratios $\sin A$ and $\cos A$, $\sin C$ and $\cos C$ and get the desired result.

Sol. Given, $$\tan A = \frac{1}{\sqrt{3}}$$

$\Rightarrow$ $$\frac{P}{B} = \frac{1}{\sqrt{3}}$$

Let $$P = 1k,\ B = \sqrt{3}k$$

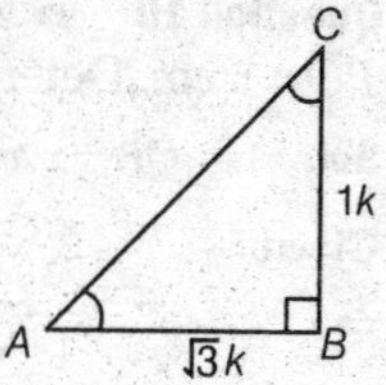

In right angled ΔABC

$$B^2 + P^2 = H^2 \quad \text{(Pythagoras theorem)}$$

$\Rightarrow$ $$(\sqrt{3}k)^2 + (1k)^2 = H^2$$

$\Rightarrow$ $$3k^2 + k^2 = H^2$$

$\Rightarrow$ $$H^2 = 4k^2$$

$\therefore$ $$H = 2k \quad (\because \text{Side cannot be} -\text{ve})$$

(i) $$\sin A \cos C + \cos A \sin C = \left(\frac{P}{H}\right)\left(\frac{B}{H}\right) + \left(\frac{B}{H}\right)\left(\frac{P}{H}\right)$$

$$= \left(\frac{BC}{AC}\right)\left(\frac{BC}{AC}\right) + \left(\frac{AB}{AC}\right)\left(\frac{AB}{AC}\right)$$

$$= \left(\frac{1k}{2k}\right)\left(\frac{1k}{2k}\right) + \left(\frac{\sqrt{3}k}{2k}\right)\left(\frac{\sqrt{3}k}{2k}\right)$$

$$= \frac{1k^2}{4k^2} + \frac{3k^2}{4k^2} = \frac{4k^2}{4k^2} = \frac{4}{4}$$

$$= 1$$

(ii) $\cos A \cos C - \sin A \sin C = \left(\frac{B}{H}\right)\left(\frac{B}{H}\right) - \left(\frac{P}{H}\right)\left(\frac{P}{H}\right)$

$$= \left(\frac{AB}{AC}\right)\left(\frac{BC}{AC}\right) - \left(\frac{BC}{AC}\right)\left(\frac{AB}{AC}\right)$$

$$= \left(\frac{\sqrt{3}k}{2k}\right)\left(\frac{1\,k}{2k}\right) - \left(\frac{1\,k}{2k}\right)\left(\frac{\sqrt{3}k}{2k}\right)$$

$$= \frac{1}{2} \times \frac{\sqrt{3}}{2} - \frac{\sqrt{3}}{2} \times \frac{1}{2}$$

$$= \frac{\sqrt{3}}{4} - \frac{\sqrt{3}}{4} = 0$$

Mistake Alert Students remember that the values of the trigonometric ratio are change if the reference angle taken is different. If taken angle is A, then the corresponding base is AB and perpendicular is BC and if taken angle is C, then the corresponding base is BC and perpendicular is AB.

Question 10 In ΔPQR, right angled at Q, $PR + QR = 25$ cm and $PQ = 5$ cm. Determine the values of $\sin P$, $\cos P$ and $\tan P$.

Sol. Let $QR = x$ and $PR = y$

Given, $PR + QR = 25$

$\Rightarrow$ $y + x = 25$

$\Rightarrow$ $y = (25 - x)$ ...(i)

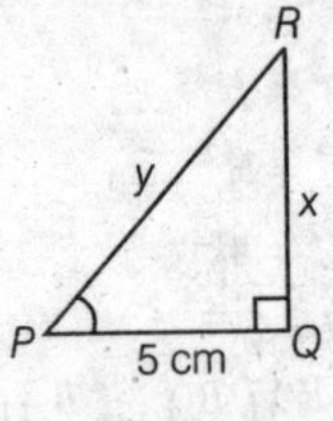

In right angled ΔPQR,

$x^2 + (5)^2 = y^2$ (By Pythagoras theorem)

$\Rightarrow$ $x^2 + 25 = (25 - x)^2$ [Put the value of y from Eq. (i)]

$\Rightarrow$ $x^2 + 25 = 625 + x^2 - 50x$

$\Rightarrow$ $x^2 - x^2 + 50x = 625 - 25 \Rightarrow 50x = 600$

$\therefore$ $x = \frac{600}{50} = 12$ cm

From Eq. (i), we get $y = 25 - 12 = 13$ cm,

Now, $\sin P = \frac{x}{y} = \frac{12}{13}, \cos \frac{PQ}{PR} = \frac{5}{13}$ and $\frac{QR}{PQ} = \frac{12}{5}$

Question 11 State whether the following are true or false. Justify your answer.

(i) The value of $\tan A$ is always less than 1.

(ii) $\sec A = \frac{12}{5}$ for some value of $\angle A$.

(iii) $\cos A$ is the abbreviation used for the cosecant of $\angle A$.

(iv) $\cot A$ is the product of cot and A.

(v) $\sin\theta = \frac{4}{3}$ for some angle θ.

Sol.

(i) False, because the value of $\tan A$ increase from 0 to ∞. Also, $\tan 45° = 1$.

(ii) True, because the value of $\sec A$ increase from 1 to ∞.

(iii) False, $\cos A$ is the abbreviation used for the cosine of $\angle A$.

(iv) False, because $\cot A$ is one symbol. We cannot separate cot and A. 'cot' alone has no, meaning

(v) False, because the value of $\sin\theta$ always lies between 0 and 1. Here, $\sin\theta = \frac{4}{3}$ which is greater than 1. So, it is not possible.

Exercise 8.2

Question 1 Evaluate the following.

(i) $\sin 60° \cos 30° + \sin 30° \cos 60°$

(ii) $2\tan^2 45° + \cos^2 30° - \sin^2 60°$

(iii) $\dfrac{\cos 45°}{\sec 30° + \operatorname{cosec} 30°}$

(iv) $\dfrac{\sin 30° + \tan 45° - \operatorname{cosec} 60°}{\sec 30° + \cos 60° + \cot 45°}$

(v) $\dfrac{5\cos^2 60° + 4\sec^2 30° - \tan^2 45°}{\sin^2 30° + \cos^2 30°}$

Thinking Process Put all the values from the trigonometric ratio table and simplify all parts.

Sol

(i) $\sin 60° \cos 30° + \sin 30° \cos 60°$

$$= \frac{\sqrt{3}}{2} \times \frac{\sqrt{3}}{2} + \frac{1}{2} \times \frac{1}{2} = \frac{3}{4} + \frac{1}{4} = \frac{3+1}{4} = \frac{4}{4} = 1$$

(ii) $2\tan^2 45° + \cos^2 30° - \sin^2 60°$

$$= 2(1)^2 + \left(\frac{\sqrt{3}}{2}\right)^2 - \left(\frac{\sqrt{3}}{2}\right)^2 = 2(1) + \frac{3}{4} - \frac{3}{4} = 2$$

(iii) $\dfrac{\cos 45°}{\sec 30° + \operatorname{cosec} 30°} = \dfrac{\frac{1}{\sqrt{2}}}{\frac{2}{\sqrt{3}} + \frac{2}{1}} = \dfrac{\frac{1}{\sqrt{2}}}{\frac{2+2\sqrt{3}}{\sqrt{3}}} = \dfrac{1}{\sqrt{2}} \times \dfrac{\sqrt{3}}{(2+2\sqrt{3})}$

$$= \frac{\sqrt{3}}{2\sqrt{2}+2\sqrt{6}} \times \frac{2\sqrt{2}-2\sqrt{6}}{2\sqrt{2}-2\sqrt{6}}$$

(Multiply by the conjugate of $2\sqrt{2} + 2\sqrt{6}$ in numerator and denominator both to make denominator free from radical sign.)

$$= \frac{2\sqrt{6}-2\sqrt{18}}{(2\sqrt{2})^2-(2\sqrt{6})^2} = \frac{2\sqrt{6}-2(3\sqrt{2})}{8-24} \qquad (\because \sqrt{18} = \sqrt{9\times 2} = 3\sqrt{2})$$

$[\because a^2 - b^2 = (a+b)(a-b)]$

$$= \frac{-2(3\sqrt{2})+2\sqrt{6}}{-16} = \frac{-2(3\sqrt{2}-\sqrt{6})}{-16} = \frac{3\sqrt{2}-\sqrt{6}}{8}$$

(iv) $\dfrac{\sin 30° + \tan 45° - \operatorname{cosec} 60°}{\sec 30° + \cos 60° + \cot 45°}$

$$= \frac{\frac{1}{2}+\frac{1}{1}-\frac{2}{\sqrt{3}}}{\frac{2}{\sqrt{3}}+\frac{1}{2}+1} = \frac{\frac{\sqrt{3}+2\sqrt{3}-4}{2\sqrt{3}}}{\frac{4+\sqrt{3}+2\sqrt{3}}{2\sqrt{3}}}$$

$$= \frac{3\sqrt{3}-4}{4+3\sqrt{3}} \times \frac{4-3\sqrt{3}}{4-3\sqrt{3}}$$

(Multiply by the conjugate of $4 + 3\sqrt{3}$ in numerator and denominator both)

$$= \frac{12\sqrt{3}-27-16+12\sqrt{3}}{16-27} = \frac{24\sqrt{3}-43}{-11}$$

$$= \frac{-(43-24\sqrt{3})}{-11} = \frac{43-24\sqrt{3}}{11}$$

(v) $\dfrac{5\cos^2 60° + 4\sec^2 30° - \tan^2 45°}{\sin^2 30° + \cos^2 30°}$

$$= \frac{5\left(\frac{1}{2}\right)^2 + 4\left(\frac{2}{\sqrt{3}}\right)^2 - (1)^2}{\left(\frac{1}{2}\right)^2 + \left(\frac{\sqrt{3}}{2}\right)^2} = \frac{5\left(\frac{1}{4}\right)+4\left(\frac{4}{3}\right)-1}{\frac{1}{4}+\frac{3}{4}}$$

$$= \frac{\frac{(15+64-12)}{12}}{\left(\frac{1+3}{4}\right)}$$

$$= \frac{67}{12} \times \frac{4}{4} = \frac{67}{12}$$

Question 2 Choose the correct option and justify your choice

(i) $\dfrac{2\tan 30^\circ}{1+\tan^2 30^\circ}=$

(a) $\sin 60^\circ$ (b) $\cos 60^\circ$ (c) $\tan 60^\circ$ (d) $\sin 30^\circ$

(ii) $\dfrac{1-\tan^2 45^\circ}{1+\tan^2 45^\circ}=$

(a) $\tan 90^\circ$ (b) 1 (c) $\sin 45^\circ$ (d) 0

(iii) $\sin 2A = 2\sin A$ is true when $A=$

(a) 0° (b) 30° (c) 45° (d) 60°

(iv) $\dfrac{2\tan 30^\circ}{1-\tan^2 30^\circ}=$

(a) $\cos 60^\circ$ (b) $\sin 60^\circ$ (c) $\tan 60^\circ$ (d) $\sin 30^\circ$

Sol. (i) (a) $\dfrac{2\tan 30^\circ}{1+\tan^2 30^\circ} = \dfrac{2\left(\frac{1}{\sqrt{3}}\right)}{1+\left(\frac{1}{\sqrt{3}}\right)^2} = \dfrac{\frac{2}{\sqrt{3}}}{\left(1+\frac{1}{3}\right)}$

$$= \frac{\frac{2}{\sqrt{3}}}{\left(\frac{3+1}{3}\right)} = \frac{2}{\sqrt{3}} \times \frac{3}{4} = \frac{\sqrt{3}}{2} = \sin 60^\circ$$

(ii) (d) $\dfrac{1-\tan^2 45^\circ}{1+\tan^2 45^\circ} = \dfrac{1-(1)^2}{1+(1)^2} = \dfrac{1-1}{1+1} = \dfrac{0}{2} = 0$

(iii) (a) Given, $\sin 2A = 2\sin A$

When $A = 0^\circ$, $\sin(2\times 0^\circ) = 2\sin(0^\circ) \Rightarrow \sin(0^\circ) = 2(0)$

$\therefore$ $0 = 0$, True

(iv) (c) $\dfrac{2\tan 30^\circ}{1-\tan^2 30^\circ} = \dfrac{2\left(\frac{1}{\sqrt{3}}\right)}{1-\left(\frac{1}{\sqrt{3}}\right)^2} = \dfrac{2\left(\frac{1}{\sqrt{3}}\right)}{1-\frac{1}{3}} = \dfrac{\frac{2}{\sqrt{3}}}{\frac{3-1}{3}}$

$$= \frac{2}{\sqrt{3}} \times \frac{3}{2} = \frac{3}{\sqrt{3}} = \sqrt{3} = \tan 60^\circ$$

Question 3 If $\tan(A+B) = \sqrt{3}$ and $\tan(A-B) = \dfrac{1}{\sqrt{3}}$;

$0^\circ < A+B \leq 90^\circ$; $A > B$, then find A and B.

Thinking Process First analysis the trigonometry ratio table to get that angle in which the value of $\tan\theta$ is $\sqrt{3}$ and $\dfrac{1}{\sqrt{3}}$ and form two equations.

Sol. We have, $\tan(A+B)=\sqrt{3} \Rightarrow \tan(A+B)=\tan 60^\circ$

$\therefore \quad A+B=60^\circ \Rightarrow A=60^\circ-B \quad \ldots(i)$

and $\quad \tan(A-B)=\dfrac{1}{\sqrt{3}} \Rightarrow \tan(A-B)=\tan 30^\circ$

$\therefore \quad A-B=30^\circ$

$\Rightarrow \quad 60^\circ-B-B=30^\circ$ [Put the value of A from Eq. (i)]

$\Rightarrow \quad 2B=60^\circ-30^\circ \Rightarrow 2B=30^\circ$

$\Rightarrow \quad B=\dfrac{30^\circ}{2}$

$\Rightarrow \quad B=15^\circ \quad \ldots(ii)$

Now, from Eqs. (i) and (ii), we get

$$A=60^\circ-15^\circ=45^\circ$$

Hence, $\quad A=45^\circ$ and $B=15^\circ$

Question 4 State whether the following are true or false. Justify your answer.

(i) $\sin(A+B)=\sin A+\sin B$

(ii) The value of $\sin\theta$ increases as θ increases.

(iii) The value of $\cos\theta$ increases as θ increases.

(iv) $\sin\theta=\cos\theta$ for all values of θ.

(v) $\cot A$ is not defined for $A=0^\circ$.

Sol. (i) False, because

when $A=60^\circ$ and $B=30^\circ$.

$$\sin(A+B)=\sin(60^\circ+30^\circ)=\sin 90^\circ=1$$

and $\quad \sin A+\sin B=\sin 60^\circ+\sin 30^\circ$

$$=\frac{\sqrt{3}}{2}+\frac{1}{2}=\frac{\sqrt{3}+1}{2}$$

So, $\quad \sin(A+B)\neq\sin A+\sin B$

(ii) True, because it is clear from the table below that the $\sin\theta$ increase as θ increases.

θ	0°	30°	45°	60°	90°
$\sin\theta$	0	$\frac{1}{2}$	$\frac{1}{\sqrt{2}}$	$\frac{\sqrt{3}}{2}$	1

(iii) False, because it is clear from the table below that the $\cos\theta$ does not increase as θ increases.

θ	0°	30°	45°	60°	90°
$\cos\theta$	1	$\frac{\sqrt{3}}{2}$	$\frac{1}{\sqrt{2}}$	$\frac{1}{2}$	0

(iv) False, because it is true only for $\theta=45^\circ$ $\quad \left(\because \sin 45^\circ=\dfrac{1}{\sqrt{2}}=\cos 45^\circ\right)$

(v) True, since for $A=0^\circ$, $\tan A=\tan 0^\circ=0$

$$\therefore \quad \cot A=\frac{1}{\tan A}=\frac{1}{0}=\text{not defined}$$

Exercise 8.3

Question 1 Express the trigonometric ratios sin A, sec A and tan A in terms of cot A.

Sol. (i) We know that $\operatorname{cosec}^2 A = 1 + \cot^2 A \Rightarrow \operatorname{cosec} A = \sqrt{1 + \cot^2 A}$

Now, $$\sin A = \frac{1}{\operatorname{cosec} A} = \frac{1}{\sqrt{1 + \cot^2 A}} \qquad \left(\because \sin A = \frac{1}{\operatorname{cosec} A}\right)$$

(ii) $$\tan A = \frac{1}{\cot A} \qquad \left(\because \tan A = \frac{1}{\cot A}\right)$$

(iii) We know that, $\sec^2 A = 1 + \tan^2 A \Rightarrow \sec A = \sqrt{1 + \tan^2 A}$

$$= \sqrt{1 + \left(\frac{1}{\cot A}\right)^2} = \sqrt{1 + \frac{1}{\cot^2 A}} \qquad \left(\because \tan A = \frac{1}{\cot A}\right)$$

$$= \sqrt{\frac{\cot^2 A + 1}{\cot^2 A}} = \frac{\sqrt{1 + \cot^2 A}}{\cot A}$$

Question 2 Write all the other trigonometric ratios of $\angle A$ in terms of sec A.

◎ *Thinking Process* First apply the fundamental trigonometric identities $\sin^2 A + \cos^2 A = 1$ and $\sec^2 A = 1 + \tan^2 A$ to write all ratio in terms of sec A.

Sol (i) We know that $\sin^2 A + \cos^2 A = 1 \Rightarrow \sin^2 A = 1 - \cos^2 A$

$$\Rightarrow \qquad \sin A = \sqrt{1 - \cos^2 A}$$

$$= \sqrt{1 - \frac{1}{\sec^2 A}} \qquad \left(\because \cos A = \frac{1}{\sec A}\right)$$

$$= \sqrt{\frac{\sec^2 A - 1}{\sec^2 A}} = \frac{\sqrt{\sec^2 A - 1}}{\sec A}$$

(ii) $$\cos A = \frac{1}{\sec A} \qquad \left(\because \cos A = \frac{1}{\sec A}\right)$$

(iii) We know that $\sec^2 A = 1 + \tan^2 A$

$$\Rightarrow \qquad \tan^2 A = \sec^2 A - 1$$

$$\Rightarrow \qquad \tan A = \sqrt{\sec^2 A - 1}$$

(iv) $$\cot A = \frac{1}{\tan A} = \frac{1}{\sqrt{\sec^2 A - 1}}$$ [By using part (iii)]

(v) $$\operatorname{cosec} A = \frac{1}{\sin A} = \frac{\sec A}{\sqrt{\sec^2 A - 1}}$$ [By using part (i)]

Question 3 Choose the correct option. Justify your choice.

(i) $9\sec^2 A - 9\tan^2 A =$

(a) 1 (b) 9 (c) 8 (d) 0

(ii) $(1+\tan\theta+\sec\theta)(1+\cot\theta-\text{cosec}\,\theta) =$

(a) 0 (b) 1 (c) 2 (d) -1

(iii) $(\sec A+\tan A)(1-\sin A) =$

(a) $\sec A$ (b) $\sin A$ (c) $\text{cosec } A$ (d) $\cos A$

(iv) $\dfrac{1+\tan^2 A}{1+\cot^2 A} =$

(a) $\sec^2 A$ (b) -1 (c) $\cot^2 A$ (d) $\tan^2 A$

Sol. (i) (b) $9\sec^2 A - 9\tan^2 A = 9(\sec^2 A - \tan^2 A)$

$$= 9 \times 1 \quad (\because \sec^2 A - \tan^2 A = 1)$$

$$= 9$$

(ii) (c) $(1+\tan\theta+\sec\theta)(1+\cot\theta-\text{cosec}\,\theta)$

$$= \left(1+\frac{\sin\theta}{\cos\theta}+\frac{1}{\cos\theta}\right)\left(1+\frac{\cos\theta}{\sin\theta}-\frac{1}{\sin\theta}\right)$$

$$\left[\because \tan\theta = \frac{\sin\theta}{\cos\theta}, \cot\theta = \frac{\cos\theta}{\sin\theta}, \sec\theta = \frac{1}{\cos\theta}, \text{cosec}\,\theta = \frac{1}{\sin\theta}\right]$$

$$= \left(\frac{(\cos\theta+\sin\theta)+(1)}{\cos\theta}\right)\times\left(\frac{(\sin\theta+\cos\theta)-(1)}{\sin\theta}\right)$$

$$= \frac{(\cos\theta+\sin\theta)^2-(1)^2}{\cos\theta\cdot\sin\theta} \quad [\because (a+b)(a-b) = a^2-b^2]$$

$$= \frac{\cos^2\theta+\sin^2\theta+2\cos\theta\sin\theta-1}{\cos\theta\sin\theta} \quad [\because (a+b)^2 = a^2+b^2+2ab]$$

$$= \frac{1+2\cos\theta\sin\theta-1}{\cos\theta\sin\theta} \quad (\because \cos^2\theta+\sin^2\theta = 1)$$

$$= \frac{2\cos\theta\sin\theta}{\cos\theta\sin\theta} = 2$$

(iii) (d) $(\sec A+\tan A)(1-\sin A)$

$$= \left(\frac{1}{\cos A}+\frac{\sin A}{\cos A}\right)(1-\sin A) \quad \left[\because \sec A = \frac{1}{\cos A}; \tan A = \frac{\sin A}{\cos A}\right]$$

$$= \frac{(1+\sin A)(1-\sin A)}{\cos A}$$

$$= \frac{1-\sin^2 A}{\cos A} \quad [\because (a+b)(a-b) = a^2-b^2]$$

$$= \frac{\cos^2 A}{\cos A} \quad (\because \sin^2 A+\cos^2 A = 1)$$

$$= \cos A$$

(iv) (d) $\dfrac{1+\tan^2 A}{1+\cot^2 A}=\dfrac{\sec^2 A}{\text{cosec}^2 A}=\dfrac{\dfrac{1}{\cos^2 A}}{\dfrac{1}{\sin^2 A}}$ $\left(\begin{array}{l}\because 1+\tan^2 A=\sec^2 A\\ 1+\cot^2 A=\text{cosec}^2 A\end{array}\right)$

$=\dfrac{1}{\cos^2 A}\times\dfrac{\sin^2 A}{1}$ $\left[\because \tan A=\dfrac{\sin A}{\cos A}\right]$

$=\tan^2 A$

Question 4 Prove the following identities, where the angles involved are acute angles for which the expressions are defined.

(i) $(\text{cosec}\,\theta-\cot\theta)^2=\dfrac{1-\cos\theta}{1+\cos\theta}$

(ii) $\dfrac{\cos A}{1+\sin A}+\dfrac{1+\sin A}{\cos A}=2\sec A$

(iii) $\dfrac{\tan\theta}{1-\cot\theta}+\dfrac{\cot\theta}{1-\tan\theta}=1+\sec\theta\cos\theta$

[**Hint** Write the expression in terms of $\sin\theta$ and $\cos\theta$]

(iv) $\dfrac{1+\sec A}{\sec A}=\dfrac{\sin^2 A}{1-\cos A}$

[**Hint** Simplify LHS and RHS separately]

(v) $\dfrac{\cos A-\sin A+1}{\cos A+\sin A-1}=\text{cosec}\,A+\cot A,$

using the identity $\text{cosec}^2 A=1+\cot^2 A$

(vi) $\sqrt{\dfrac{1+\sin A}{1-\sin A}}=\sec A+\tan A$

(vii) $\dfrac{\sin\theta-2\sin^3\theta}{2\cos^3\theta-\cos\theta}=\tan\theta$

(viii) $(\sin A+\text{cosec}\,A)^2+(\cos A+\sec A)^2=7+\tan^2 A+\cot^2 A$

(ix) $(\text{cosec}\,A-\sin A)(\sec A-\cos A)=\dfrac{1}{\tan A+\cot A}$

[**Hint** Simplify LHS and RHS separately]

(x) $\left(\dfrac{1+\tan^2 A}{1+\cot^2 A}\right)=\left(\dfrac{1-\tan A}{1-\cot A}\right)^2=\tan^2 A$

Sol. (i) LHS $= (\operatorname{cosec}\theta - \cot\theta)^2 = \left(\frac{1}{\sin\theta} - \frac{\cos\theta}{\sin\theta}\right)^2 = \left(\frac{1-\cos\theta}{\sin\theta}\right)^2$

$$= \frac{(1-\cos\theta)^2}{\sin^2\theta} = \frac{(1-\cos\theta)^2}{1-\cos^2\theta} \qquad (\because \sin^2\theta + \cos^2\theta = 1)$$

$$= \frac{(1-\cos\theta)(1-\cos\theta)}{(1+\cos\theta)(1-\cos\theta)} \qquad [\because a^2 - b^2 = (a+b)(a-b)]$$

$$= \frac{1-\cos\theta}{1+\cos\theta} = \text{RHS}$$

(ii) LHS $= \frac{\cos A}{1+\sin A} + \frac{1+\sin A}{\cos A} = \frac{\cos^2 A + (1+\sin A)^2}{(1+\sin A)\cdot\cos A}$

$$= \frac{\cos^2 A + \sin^2 A + 1 + 2\sin A}{(1+\sin A)\cdot\cos A} \qquad [\because (a+b)^2 = a^2 + b^2 + 2ab]$$

$$= \frac{1+1+2\sin A}{(1+\sin A)\cdot\cos A} \qquad (\because \sin^2 A + \cos^2 A = 1)$$

$$= \frac{2+2\sin A}{(1+\sin A)\cdot\cos A} = \frac{2(1+\sin A)}{(1+\sin A)\cos A}$$

$$= \frac{2}{\cos A} = 2\sec A = \text{RHS} \qquad \left[\therefore \frac{1}{\cos A} = \sec A\right]$$

(iii) LHS $= \frac{\tan\theta}{1-\cot\theta} + \frac{\cot\theta}{1-\tan\theta} = \frac{\frac{\sin\theta}{\cos\theta}}{1-\frac{\cos\theta}{\sin\theta}} + \frac{\frac{\cos\theta}{\sin\theta}}{1-\frac{\sin\theta}{\cos\theta}}$

$$= \frac{\frac{\sin\theta}{\cos\theta}}{\frac{\sin\theta-\cos\theta}{\sin\theta}} + \frac{\frac{\cos\theta}{\sin\theta}}{\frac{\cos\theta-\sin\theta}{\cos\theta}} \qquad \left(\because \tan\theta = \frac{\sin\theta}{\cos\theta} \text{ and } \cot\theta = \frac{\cos\theta}{\sin\theta}\right)$$

$$= \frac{\sin\theta}{\cos\theta} \times \frac{\sin\theta}{\sin\theta-\cos\theta} + \frac{\cos\theta}{\sin\theta} \times \frac{\cos\theta}{\cos\theta-\sin\theta}$$

$$= \frac{\sin^2\theta}{\cos\theta(\sin\theta-\cos\theta)} - \frac{\cos^2\theta}{\sin\theta(\sin\theta-\cos\theta)}$$

$$= \frac{\sin^3\theta - \cos^3\theta}{\cos\theta\cdot\sin\theta(\sin\theta-\cos\theta)}$$

$$= \frac{(\sin\theta-\cos\theta)\cdot(\sin^2\theta+\cos^2\theta+\sin\theta\cos\theta)}{\cos\theta\cdot\sin\theta\cdot(\sin\theta-\cos\theta)}$$

$$[\because x^3 - y^3 = (x-y)(x^2+y^2+xy)]$$

$$= \frac{1+\sin\theta\cos\theta}{\cos\theta\sin\theta} \qquad (\because \sin^2\theta + \cos^2\theta = 1)$$

$$= \frac{1}{\cos\theta\cdot\sin\theta} + \frac{\sin\theta\cdot\cos\theta}{\sin\theta\cdot\cos\theta} = \frac{1}{\cos\theta\cdot\sin\theta} + 1$$

$$= 1 + \sec\theta\cdot\operatorname{cosec}\theta = \text{RHS} \qquad \left[\because \frac{1}{\cos\theta} = \sec\theta, \frac{1}{\sin\theta} = \operatorname{cosec}\theta\right]$$

(iv) $$\text{LHS} = \frac{1+\sec A}{\sec A} = \frac{1+\dfrac{1}{\cos A}}{\dfrac{1}{\cos A}} = \frac{\dfrac{\cos A+1}{\cos A}}{\dfrac{1}{\cos A}} \qquad \left(\because \sec A = \frac{1}{\cos A}\right)$$

$$= \frac{\cos A+1}{\cos A} \times \frac{\cos A}{1} = \cos A + 1$$

$$\text{LHS} = 1 + \cos A \qquad \ldots\text{(i)}$$

Now, $$\text{RHS} = \frac{\sin^2 A}{1-\cos A} = \frac{1-\cos^2 A}{1-\cos A} \qquad (\because \sin^2 A + \cos^2 A = 1)$$

$$= \frac{(1+\cos A)(1-\cos A)}{(1-\cos A)} \qquad [\because a^2 - b^2 = (a+b)(a-b)]$$

$$= 1 + \cos A \qquad \ldots\text{(ii)}$$

From Eqs. (i) and (ii), we get LHS = RHS

(v) $$\text{LHS} = \frac{\cos A - \sin A + 1}{\cos A + \sin A - 1}$$

◎ ***Thinking Process*** First divide by $\sin A$ in numerator and denominator to convert the expression into $\cot A$ and $\operatorname{cosec} A$ because RHS is *i.e.*, also in $\cot A$ and $\operatorname{cosec} A$ form

On dividing numerator and denominator by $\sin A$, we get

$$\text{LHS} = \frac{\dfrac{\cos A}{\sin A} - \dfrac{\sin A}{\sin A} + \dfrac{1}{\sin A}}{\dfrac{\cos A}{\sin A} + \dfrac{\sin A}{\sin A} - \dfrac{1}{\sin A}} = \frac{\cot A - 1 + \operatorname{cosec} A}{\cot A + 1 - \operatorname{cosec} A}$$

$$= \frac{\cot A + \operatorname{cosec} A - 1}{\cot A + 1 - \operatorname{cosec} A} = \frac{(\cot A + \operatorname{cosec} A) - (\operatorname{cosec}^2 A - \cot^2 A)}{\cot A + 1 - \operatorname{cosec} A}$$

$$(\because 1 = \operatorname{cosec}^2 A - \cot^2 A)$$

$$= \frac{(\cot A + \operatorname{cosec} A) - [(\operatorname{cosec} A + \cot A)(\operatorname{cosec} A - \cot A)]}{\cot A + 1 - \operatorname{cosec} A}$$

$$[\because (a^2 - b^2) = (a+b)(a-b)]$$

$$= \frac{(\cot A + \operatorname{cosec} A)[1 - (\operatorname{cosec} A - \cot A)]}{\cot A + 1 - \operatorname{cosec} A}$$

$$= \frac{(\cot A + \operatorname{cosec} A)[1 - \operatorname{cosec} A + \cot A]}{\cot A + 1 - \operatorname{cosec} A} = \cot A + \operatorname{cosec} A = \text{RHS}$$

◎ ***Thinking Process*** First rationalisation the denomination and apply formula $(a-b)(a+b) = a^2 - b^2$ to prove the equation.

(vi) LHS $= \sqrt{\dfrac{1+\sin A}{1-\sin A}} = \sqrt{\dfrac{1+\sin A}{1-\sin A} \times \dfrac{1+\sin A}{1+\sin A}}$

(Rationalisation and the denomination)

$$= \sqrt{\frac{(1+\sin A)^2}{1-\sin^2 A}} = \sqrt{\frac{(1+\sin A)^2}{\cos^2 A}} \quad (\because \sin^2 A + \cos^2 A = 1)$$

$$= \frac{1+\sin A}{\cos A} = \frac{1}{\cos A} + \frac{\sin A}{\cos A}$$

$$= \sec A + \tan A = \text{RHS}$$

(vii) LHS $= \dfrac{\sin\theta - 2\sin^3\theta}{2\cos^3\theta - \cos\theta} = \dfrac{\sin\theta(1-2\sin^2\theta)}{\cos\theta(2\cos^2\theta - 1)}$

$$= \frac{\sin\theta[1-2(1-\cos^2\theta)]}{\cos\theta(2\cos^2\theta - 1]} \quad (\because \sin^2\theta + \cos^2\theta = 1)$$

$$= \frac{\sin\theta[1-2+2\cos^2\theta]}{\cos\theta[2\cos^2\theta - 1]}$$

$$= \frac{\sin\theta(2\cos^2\theta - 1)}{\cos\theta(2\cos^2\theta - 1)} = \frac{\sin\theta}{\cos\theta} = \tan\theta = \text{RHS}$$

(viii) LHS $= (\sin A + \operatorname{cosec} A)^2 + (\cos A + \sec A)^2$

$$= \sin^2 A + \operatorname{cosec}^2 A + 2\sin A \operatorname{cosec} A + \cos^2 A + \sec^2 A + 2\cos A \sec A$$

$$[\because (a+b)^2 = a^2 + b^2 + 2ab]$$

$$= (\sin^2 A + \cos^2 A) + (1 + \cot^2 A)$$

$$+ 2\sin A \cdot \frac{1}{\sin A} + (1 + \tan^2 A) + 2\cos A \cdot \frac{1}{\cos A}$$

$$(\because 1 + \cot^2 A = \operatorname{cosec}^2 A \text{ and } \sec^2 A = 1 + \tan^2 A)$$

$$= 1 + 1 + \cot^2 A + 2 + 1 + \tan^2 A + 2 \quad (\because \sin^2 A + \cos^2 A = 1)$$

$$= 7 + \tan^2 A + \cot^2 A = \text{RHS}$$

(ix) LHS $= (\operatorname{cosec} A - \sin A)(\sec A - \cos A)$

$$= \left(\frac{1}{\sin A} - \frac{\sin A}{1}\right)\left(\frac{1}{\cos A} - \frac{\cos A}{1}\right)$$

$$= \left(\frac{1-\sin^2 A}{\sin A}\right)\left(\frac{1-\cos^2 A}{\cos A}\right) = \frac{\cos^2 A}{\sin A} \times \frac{\sin^2 A}{\cos A} \quad (\because \sin^2 A + \cos^2 A = 1)$$

$$= \cos A \sin A \qquad \ldots(i)$$

Now, $$\text{RHS} = \frac{1}{\tan A + \cot A} = \frac{1}{\left(\dfrac{\sin A}{\cos A} + \dfrac{\cos A}{\sin A}\right)}$$

$$= \frac{1}{\left(\dfrac{\sin^2 A + \cos^2 A}{\cos A \sin A}\right)} = \frac{1}{\dfrac{1}{\cos A \sin A}} \quad (\because \sin^2 A + \cos^2 A = 1)$$

$$= 1 \times \frac{\cos A \sin A}{1} = \cos A \sin A \quad \text{...(ii)}$$

From Eqs. (i) and (ii), we get LHS = RHS

Mistake Alert Students not to forget simplify the equation LHS and RHS separately.

(x) First part $= \left(\dfrac{1+\tan^2 A}{1+\cot^2 A}\right)$

$$= \frac{\dfrac{1}{1} + \dfrac{\sin^2 A}{\cos^2 A}}{\dfrac{1}{1} + \dfrac{\cos^2 A}{\sin^2 A}} = \frac{\dfrac{\cos^2 A + \sin^2 A}{\cos^2 A}}{\dfrac{\sin^2 A + \cos^2 A}{\sin^2 A}}$$

$$= \frac{\dfrac{1}{\cos^2 A}}{\dfrac{1}{\sin^2 A}} \quad (\because \sin^2 A + \cos^2 A = 1)$$

$$= \frac{1}{\cos^2 A} \times \frac{\sin^2 A}{1} = \frac{\sin^2 A}{\cos^2 A} = \tan^2 A = \text{Third part}$$

Second part $$\left(\frac{1-\tan A}{1-\cot A}\right)^2 = \left(\frac{1-\dfrac{\sin A}{\cos A}}{1-\dfrac{\cos A}{\sin A}}\right)^2 = \left(\frac{\dfrac{\cos A - \sin A}{\cos A}}{\dfrac{\sin A - \cos A}{\sin A}}\right)^2$$

$$= \left(\frac{\cos A - \sin A}{\cos A} \times \frac{\sin A}{\sin A - \cos A}\right)$$

$$= \left(-1 \times \frac{\sin A}{\cos A}\right)^2 = (-\tan A)^2 = \tan^2 A = \text{Third part}$$

DIKSHA APP Questions

☐ Multiple Choice Questions

Q.1 The value of $\sec^2 A - \tan^2 A$ is

(a) 0 (b) $\frac{1}{4}$ (c) $\frac{1}{2}$ (d) 1

Sol. (d) According to the trigonometric identity,

$$1 + \tan^2 A = \sec^2 A \text{ for } 0 \le A < 90°$$

$$\sec^2 A - \tan^2 A = 1 \text{ for } 0 \le A < 90°$$

Q.2 The value of $\tan^2 60°$ is

(a) $\frac{1}{2}$ (b) $\sqrt{3}$ (c) 1 (d) 3

Sol. (d) $\tan^2 60° = (\tan 60°)^2$

$$= (\sqrt{3})^2 \qquad (\because \tan 60° = \sqrt{3})$$

$$= 3$$

Q.3 If $2\cos\theta = 1$, then $\theta =$

(a) 30° (b) 45° (c) 60° (d) 90°

Sol. (c) $2\cos\theta = 1$

$\Rightarrow$ $\cos\theta = \frac{1}{2}$

We know that $\cos 60° = \frac{1}{2}$ $\left[\because \cos 60° = \frac{1}{2}\right]$

$\Rightarrow$ $\theta = 60°$

Q.4 The value of $\sin A$ is

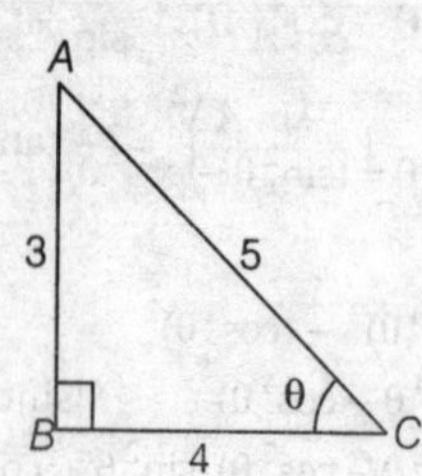

(a) $\frac{4}{5}$ (b) $\frac{3}{5}$ (c) $\frac{5}{4}$ (d) $\frac{5}{3}$

Sol. (a) By trigonometric ratios,

$$\sin A = \frac{\text{Side opposite to } \angle A}{\text{Hypotenuse}} = \frac{BC}{AC} = \frac{4}{5}$$

Q.5 If $\cot\theta = \frac{40}{9}$, then the value of $\operatorname{cosec}\theta$ is ____.

(a) $\operatorname{cosec}\theta = \frac{9}{41}$ (b) $\operatorname{cosec}\theta = \frac{41}{9}$

(c) $\operatorname{cosec}\theta = \frac{40}{9}$ (d) $\operatorname{cosec}\theta = \frac{9}{40}$

◎ ***Thinking Process*** First we will get the value of perpendicular and base with the help of $\cot\theta = \frac{40}{9}$ after that apply Pythagors theorem to find the value of $\operatorname{cosec}\theta$.

Sol. (b) Consider a right angled triangle.

If $\cot\theta = \frac{40}{9} = \frac{\text{Base}}{\text{Perpendicular}}$

Then, the side opposite to $\angle\theta = 9x$,

Adjacent side $= 40x$

Calculating Hypotenuse using Pythagoras Theorem,

$(\text{Hypotenuse})^2 = (9x)^2 + (40x)^2$

$(\text{Hypotenuse})^2 = \sqrt{1681x^2} = 41x$

Now, $\operatorname{cosec}\theta =$ Hypotenuse/side opposite to $\angle\theta$

So $\operatorname{cosec}\theta = \frac{41x}{9x} = \frac{41}{9}$

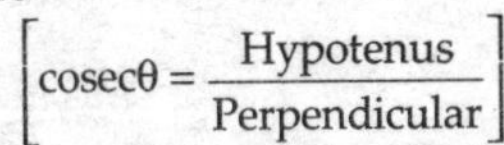

Q.6 State whether the following equation is true or false.
$\sin^8\theta - \cos^8\theta = (\sin^2\theta - \cos^2\theta)(1 - 2\sin^2\theta\cos^2\theta)$

(a) True (b) False (c) Cannot say (d)

Sol. (a) To Prove : $\sin^8\theta - \cos^8\theta = (\sin^2\theta - \cos^2\theta)(1 - 2\sin^2\theta\cos^2\theta)$

Consider LHS

$= \sin^8\theta - \cos^8\theta = (\sin^4\theta)^2 - (\cos^4\theta)^2$

$= (\sin^4\theta + \cos^4\theta)(\sin^4\theta - \cos^4\theta)$ {since, $a^2 - b^2 = (a+b)(a-b)$}

$= (\sin^4\theta + \cos^4\theta)(\sin^2\theta - \cos^2\theta)(\sin^2\theta + \cos^2\theta)$

$= (\sin^4\theta + \cos^4\theta)(\sin^2\theta - \cos^2\theta)$ {since, $\sin^2\theta + \cos^2\theta = 1$}

Now, find the value of

$$\sin^4\theta + \cos^4\theta = (\sin^2\theta + \cos^2\theta)^2 - \sin^2\theta\cos^2\theta$$
$$= 1 - 2\sin^2\theta\cos^2\theta$$

Hence, $(\sin^4\theta + \cos^4\theta)(\sin^2\theta - \cos^2\theta) = (\sin^2\theta - \cos^2\theta)(1 - 2\sin^2\theta\cos^2\theta)$

$= \text{RHS}$

Hence, the given equation is true.

Q.7 If $\sec A - \tan A = p$, then find the values of $\sec A$ and $\tan A$ in terms of p.

(a) $\sec A = \frac{1}{2}[p + 1/p]$, $\tan A = \frac{1}{2}[1/p - p]$

(b) $\sec A = \frac{1}{2}[1/p - p]$, $\tan A = \frac{1}{2}[p + 1/p]$

(c) $\sec A = p$, $\tan A = 1/p$

(d) Cannot be determined

◎ ***Thinking Process*** First multiply and divide by $(\sec A + \tan A)$ in function $\sec A - \tan A = p$

Sol. (a) We know that

$$\sec A - \tan A = p \quad \text{...(i)}$$

On multiply and divide by $(\sec A + \tan A)$, we get

$$(\sec A - \tan A)\cdot\frac{(\sec A + \tan A)}{(\sec A + \tan A)} = p$$

$$\Rightarrow \frac{\sec^2 A - \tan^2 A}{\sec A + \tan A} = p \quad [\because (a-b)\cdot(a+b) = a^2 - b^2]$$

As $1 + \tan^2 A = \sec^2 A$, so $\sec^2 A - \tan^2 A = 1$

$$\therefore \frac{1}{\sec A + \tan A} = p$$

$$\Rightarrow \sec A + \tan A = \frac{1}{p} \quad \text{...(ii)}$$

Adding Eqs. (i) and (ii), we get

$$2\sec A = p + \frac{1}{p}$$

$$\Rightarrow \sec A = \frac{1}{2}\left[p + \frac{1}{p}\right]$$

Subtracting Eq. (i) from Eq. (ii), we get

$$2\tan A = \left[\frac{1}{p} - p\right]$$

$$\Rightarrow \tan A = \frac{1}{2}\left[\frac{1}{p} - p\right]$$

Q.8 If $2\sec^2 A(1+\sin A)(1-\sin A)=k$, then find the value of k.

(a) 0 (b) 1

(c) 2 (d) $\frac{1}{2}$

Sol. (c) $2\sec^2 A(1+\sin A)(1-\sin A)=k$

$\left(\frac{2}{\cos^2 A}\right)(1-\sin^2 A)=k$ (as $\sec A=\frac{1}{\cos A}$ and $(a+b)(a-b)=a^2-b^2$)

$\left(\frac{2}{\cos^2 A}\right)(\cos^2 A)=k$ $[\because 1-\sin^2 A=\cos^2 A]$

$\Rightarrow$ $2=k \Rightarrow k=2$

Q.9 If $\sin\theta=\frac{7}{25}$ then the value of $\sec\theta$ is

(a) $\sec\theta=\frac{24}{25}$

(b) $\sec\theta=\frac{25}{24}$

(c) $\sec\theta=\frac{25}{7}$

(d) $\sec\theta=\frac{24}{7}$

Sol. (b) Let us draw a right angled ΔABC right angled at B.

$\because$ $\sin\theta=\frac{7}{25}$ (Given)

Then, the side opposite to $\angle A = BC = 7x$,

Hypotenuse $= 25x$

Side adjacent to $\angle A = AB$

Calculating adjacent side using Pythagoras theorem,

$$AC^2 = BC^2 + AB^2$$

$$\Rightarrow (25x)^2 = (7x)^2 + AB^2$$

$$\Rightarrow AB^2 = 625x^2 - 49x^2 = 576x^2$$

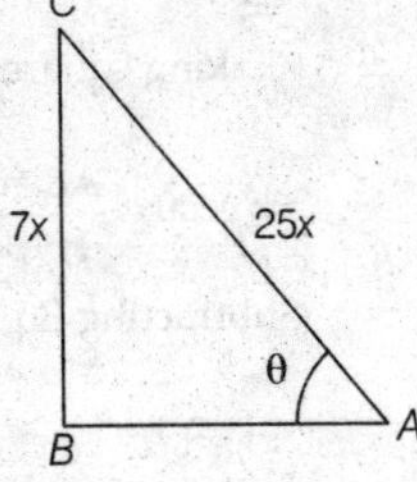

Taking square roots on both sides, we get

$$AB = 24x$$

$\because$ $\sec\theta=\frac{\text{Hypotenuse}}{\text{Adjacent side to } \angle A}$

$$\Rightarrow \sec\theta=\frac{25x}{24x}$$

$$\Rightarrow \sec\theta=\frac{25}{24}$$

Q.10 Which of the following statements are true ?

(i) $\sin A = \frac{15}{8}$ is for some $\angle A$

(ii) The value of $\sin A$ (or $\cos A$) is always less than or equal to 1.

(iii) $\tan A$ is the product of tan and A.

(a) Only Statement (i) (b) Only Statement (ii)

(c) Only Statement (iii) (d) All the three statements

Sol. (b) $\sin A$ = Side opposite to $\angle A$/Hypotenuse

$\cos A$ = Side adjacent to $\angle A$/Hypotenuse

Since, the hypotenuse is the longest side in a right triangle and it is in the denominator, so the value of sin and cos is always less than equal to 1.

So, Statement (i) is not true.

Also, $\tan A$ is the abbreviation of tangent of the $\angle A$, or its one term.

So, Statement (iii) is also incorrect.

Q.11 If $\operatorname{cosec} \theta = 61/11$, find the value of $\cos \theta$.

(a) 11/60 (b) 61/60 (c) 60/61 (d) 11/61

Sol. (c) Let us draw right angled ΔABC right angled at B.

$\operatorname{cosec} \theta = 61/11$ (Given)

Let $\angle A = \theta$

Then, the side opposite to $\angle A = BC = 11x$,

Hypotenuse $= 61x$

Side adjacent to $\angle A = AB$

Calculating adjacent side using Pythagoras theorem,

$$AC^2 = BC^2 + AB^2$$

$$\Rightarrow \quad (61x)^2 = (11x)^2 + AB^2$$

$$\Rightarrow \quad AB^2 = 3721x^2 - 121x^2 = 3600x^2$$

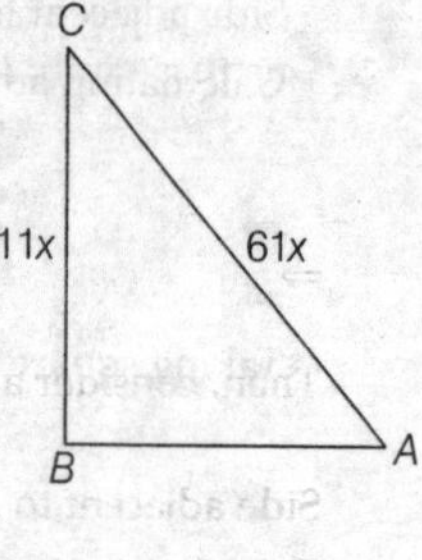

Taking square roots on both sides, we get

$$AB = 60x$$

$$\because \cos\theta = \frac{\text{Adjacent side}}{\text{Hypotenuse}} \text{ to } \angle A$$

$$\Rightarrow \quad \cos\theta = \frac{60x}{61x}$$

$$\Rightarrow \quad \cos\theta = \frac{60}{61}$$

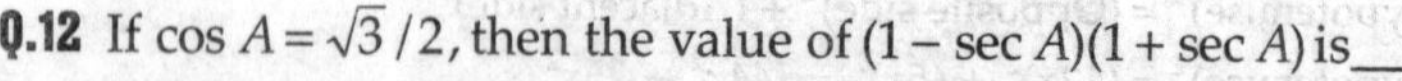

Q.12 If $\cos A = \sqrt{3}/2$, then the value of $(1 - \sec A)(1 + \sec A)$ is__.

(a) $\frac{-1}{3}$ (b) $\frac{1}{4}$ (c) $\frac{-1}{\sqrt{3}}$ (d) -3

Sol. (a) $\cos A = \frac{\sqrt{3}}{2}$

So as $\sec A = \frac{1}{\cos A}$

$\therefore \quad \sec A = \frac{2}{\sqrt{3}}$

Now, $(1 - \sec A)(1 + \sec A) = 1^2 \sec^2 A \qquad [\because (a+b)(a-b) = a^2 - b^2]$

$$= 1 - \left(\frac{2}{\sqrt{3}}\right)^2 = 1 - \frac{4}{3} = \frac{-1}{3}$$

Q.13 If $5\sec\theta - 12\text{cosec}\,\theta = 0$, then find the values of $\tan\theta$, $\cos\theta$ and $\sin\theta$.

(a) $\tan\theta = \frac{12}{5}$, $\sin\theta = \frac{12}{5}$, $\cos\theta = \frac{5}{12}$

(b) $\tan\theta = \frac{5}{12}$, $\sin\theta = \frac{5}{13}$, $\cos\theta = \frac{12}{13}$

(c) $\tan\theta = \frac{12}{5}$, $\sin\theta = \frac{12}{13}$, $\cos\theta = \frac{5}{13}$

(d) $\tan\theta = \frac{12}{5}$, $\sin\theta = \frac{12}{5}$, $\cos\theta = \frac{13}{5}$

◎ *Thinking Process* First solve the given equation to evaluate the value of $\tan\theta$ by converting $\sec\theta$ and $\text{cosec}\,\theta$ into $\cos\theta$ and $\sin\theta$ respectively.

Sol. (c) Given, $5\sec\theta - 12\text{cosec}\,\theta = 0$

$$5\sec\theta = 12\,\text{cosec}\,\theta$$

as $\sec\theta = \frac{1}{\cos\theta}$ and $\text{cosec}\,\theta = \frac{1}{\sin\theta}$

$\therefore \quad \frac{5}{\cos\theta} = \frac{12}{\sin\theta}$

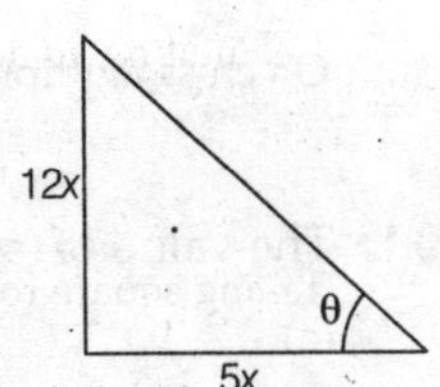

On cross multiplication, we get

$$\frac{\sin\theta}{\cos\theta} = \frac{12}{5}$$

$\Rightarrow \quad \tan\theta = \frac{12}{5}$

Then, consider a triangle, let side opposite to $\angle\theta = 12x$,

Side adjacent to $\angle\theta = 5x$

Calculating Hypotenuse using Pythagoras theorem,

$(\text{Hypotenuse})^2 = (\text{Opposite side})^2 + (\text{Adjacent side})^2$

$(\text{Hypotenuse})^2 = (12x)^2 + (5x)^2 = 144x^2 + 25x^2$

Hypotenuse $= \sqrt{169x^2} = 13x$

$\therefore$ $$\cos\theta = \frac{5x}{13x} = \frac{5}{13} \text{ and } \sin\theta = \frac{12x}{13x} = \frac{12}{13}$$

Q.14 In ΔPQR right angled at Q, $QR = 5$ cm and $\angle PRQ = 60°$. Determine the length of side PR.

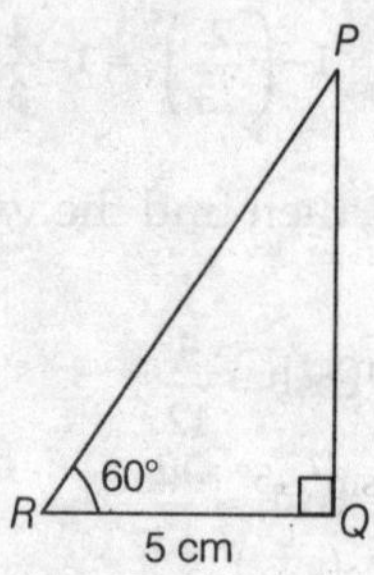

(a) $5\sqrt{3}$ cm (b) 5 cm

(c) 10 cm (d) Cannot be determined

Sol. (c) To find the length of the side PR, we will choose the trigonometric ratio involving PR and the given side QR. Since, QR is the side adjacent to angle R and PR is the side hypotenuse. Therefore

$$\cos R = \frac{QR}{PR}$$

i.e., $$\cos 60° = \frac{QR}{PR}$$

$\Rightarrow$ $$\frac{1}{2} = \frac{5}{PR} \qquad \left[\because \cos 60° = \frac{1}{2}\right]$$

On cross multiplication, we get

$$PR = 10 \text{ cm}$$

Q.15 The value of $(\sin 30° + \cos 30°) = (\sin 60° - \cos 60°)$ is

(a) 0 (b) $1 - \sqrt{3}$ (c) $1 + \sqrt{3}$ (d) 1

Sol. (a) We know that

$$\sin 30° = \frac{1}{2}, \sin 60° = \frac{\sqrt{3}}{2} \Rightarrow \cos 30° = \frac{\sqrt{3}}{2}, \cos 60° = \frac{1}{2}$$

So, $$(\sin 30° + \cos 30°) - (\sin 60° + \cos 60°) = \left(\frac{1}{3} + \frac{\sqrt{3}}{2}\right) - \left(\frac{\sqrt{3}}{2} + \frac{1}{2}\right) = 0$$

Q.16 The value of $(2 \tan 45° - 2 \sin 30°)$ is

(a) 2 (b) 1 (c) 1/2 (d) 3/4

Sol. (b) We know that, $\tan 45° = 1$ and $\sin 30° = 1/2$,

$\therefore$

$$2\tan 45° - 2\sin 30°$$
$$= 2(1) - 2\left(\frac{1}{2}\right) = 2 - 1 = 1$$

Q.17 The value of $(2\sin^2 45° - \tan^2 30° - \sin^2 60°)$ is

(a) $\frac{-1}{6}$ (b) $\frac{-11}{4}$ (c) $\frac{-1}{12}$ (d) $\frac{-13}{12}$

Sol. (c) We know,

$$\sin 45° = \frac{1}{\sqrt{2}}$$
$$\sin 60° = \frac{\sqrt{3}}{2} \text{ and } \tan 30° = \frac{1}{\sqrt{3}},$$

So,

$$2\sin^2 45° - \tan^2 30° - \sin^2 60°$$
$$= 2\left(\frac{1}{\sqrt{2}}\right)^2 - \left(\frac{1}{\sqrt{3}}\right)^2 - \left(\frac{\sqrt{3}}{2}\right)^2 = 2\left(\frac{1}{2}\right) - \frac{1}{3} - \frac{3}{4}$$
$$= 1 - \frac{1}{3} - \frac{3}{4} = \frac{(12-4-9)}{12} = -\frac{1}{12}$$

☐ Subjective Type Questions

Q.1 If $4\tan\theta = 3$, then find the value of $\frac{4\sin\theta - \cos\theta + 1}{4\sin\theta + \cos\theta - 1}$.

Sol. Given, $4\tan\theta = 3$

$\Rightarrow$ $$\tan\theta = \frac{3}{4} = \frac{\text{Perpendicular}}{\text{Base}}$$

In ΔABC

$$\angle ABC = 90° \text{ and } \angle ACB = \theta \text{ and } BA = 3, BC = 4$$

By using pythagoras theorem, we get

$$AC = \sqrt{AB^2 + BC^2} = \sqrt{3^2 + 4^2} = \sqrt{9 + 16} = \sqrt{25}$$

$\therefore$ $$AC = 5$$

$\therefore$ $$\sin\theta = \frac{AB}{AC} = \frac{3}{5} \text{ and } \cos\theta = \frac{BC}{AC} = \frac{4}{5}$$

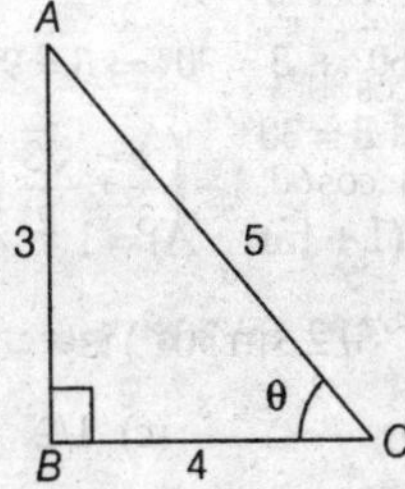

Now, $= \dfrac{4\sin\theta - \cos\theta + 1}{4\sin\theta + \cos\theta - 1} = \dfrac{4 \times \frac{3}{5} - \frac{4}{5} + 1}{4 \times \frac{3}{5} + \frac{4}{5} - 1}$

$$= \dfrac{\frac{12}{5} - \frac{4}{5} + 1}{\frac{12}{5} + \frac{4}{5} - 1} = \dfrac{\frac{12 - 4 + 5}{5}}{\frac{12 + 4 - 5}{5}} = \frac{13}{11}$$

Q.2 Prove that $\sec A(1 - \sin A)(\sec A + \tan A) = 1$

Sol. Take LHS $= \sec A(1 - \sin A)(\sec A + \tan A)$

$$= \left[\frac{1}{\cos A} \cdot (1 - \sin A)\left(\frac{1}{\cos A} + \frac{\sin A}{\cos A}\right)\right] \quad \left[\because \sec A = \frac{1}{\cos A}, \tan A = \frac{\sin A}{\cos A}\right]$$

$$= \left(\frac{1 - \sin A}{\cos A}\right) \cdot \frac{(1 + \sin A)}{\cos} \quad [(a - b)(a + b) = a^2 - b^2]$$

$$= \frac{1 - \sin^2 A}{\cos^2 A} = \frac{\cos^2 A}{\cos^2 A} = 1 \quad [\because 1 - \sin^2 A = \cos^2 A]$$

$= \text{RHS}$

Hence, $\sec(1 - \sin A)(\sec A + \tan A) = 1$

Q.3 If $\cos(A + B) = 0$ and $\sin(A - B) = \frac{1}{2}$, then find the value of A and B.

Sol. $\cos(A + B) = 0 = \cos 90°$

$\Rightarrow \quad A + B = 90° \quad \text{...(i)}$

and $\quad \sin(A - B) = \frac{1}{2} = \sin 30°$

$\Rightarrow \quad A - B = 30° \quad \text{...(ii)}$

On adding Eq. (i) and (ii),

$$A + B + A - B = 90 + 30$$

$\Rightarrow \quad 2A = 120 \Rightarrow A = 60°$

Substituting the value of A in Eq. (i), we get

$$A + B = 90°$$

$\Rightarrow \quad 60° + B = 90° \Rightarrow B = 90° - 60° \Rightarrow B = 30°$

The value of $A = 60°$ and $B = 30°$

Q.4 Prove that $(1 - \sin^2 A)(1 + \tan^2 A) = 1$

Sol. LHS $(1 - \sin^2 A)(1 + \tan^2 A) = 1 = \cos^2 A \cdot \sec^2 A$

Since, $1 - \sin^2 A = \cos^2 A$,

$$1+\tan^2 A = \sec^2 A$$

$$= \cos^2 A \cdot \frac{1}{\cos^2 A} \qquad \left[\because \sec A = \frac{1}{\cos A}\right]$$

$$= 1$$

Q.5 Prove that $\cos^2\theta = \dfrac{1}{1+\tan^2\theta}$

Sol. LHS $= \cos^2\theta$

$$= \frac{1}{\sec^2\theta} \qquad \left[\because \cos A = \frac{1}{\sec A}\right]$$

$$= \frac{1}{1+\tan^2\theta} = \text{RHS} \qquad [\sec^2 A = 1+\tan^2 A]$$

Q.6 Find the value of $[\sin\theta + \cos\theta)]^2 + [\sin\theta - \cos\theta]^2$

Sol. $[\sin\theta + \cos\theta)]^2 + [\sin\theta - \cos\theta]^2$

$$= \{\sin^2\theta + 2\sin\theta\cdot\cos\theta + \cos^2\theta\} + \{\sin^2\theta - 2\sin\theta\cdot\cos\theta + \cos^2\theta\}$$

$$[\because (a+b)^2 = a^2 + b^2 + 2ab, (a-b)^2 = a^2 + b^2 - 2ab]$$

$$= \{\sin^2\theta + \cos^2\theta + 2\sin\theta\cdot\cos\theta\} + \{\sin^2\theta + \cos^2\theta - 2\sin\theta\cdot\cos\theta\}$$

$$= 1 + 2\sin\theta\cdot\cos\theta + 1 - 2\sin\theta\cdot\cos\theta = 2$$

Q.7 Prove that $\tan A \sin A + \cos A = \sec A$

Sol. LHS $\tan A \sin A + \cos A$

$$= \frac{\sin A}{\cos A}\cdot \sin A + \cos A$$

$$= \frac{\sin^2 A}{\cos A} + \cos A = \frac{\sin^2 A + \cos^2 A}{\cos A}$$

$$= \frac{1}{\cos A} = \sec A \qquad [\because \sin^2 A + \cos^2 A = 1]$$

Q.8 If $\angle A = 60°$ and $\angle B = 30°$, then prove that

$$\cos(A+B) = \cos A \cos B - \sin A \sin B$$

Sol. LHS $= \cos(A+B) = \cos(60° + 30°) = \cos 90° = 0$

RHS $\cos A \cos B - \sin A \sin B$

$$= \cos 60°\cdot\cos 30° - \sin 60° \sin 30°$$

$$= \frac{1}{2}\cdot\frac{\sqrt{3}}{2} - \frac{\sqrt{3}}{2}\cdot\frac{1}{2} = \frac{\sqrt{3}}{4} - \frac{\sqrt{3}}{4} = 0$$

Hence, LHS = RHS

Hence, $\cos(A+B) = \cos A \cos B - \sin A \sin B$ **Hence Proved.**

Q.9 Find the value of $\tan^2 60° + 2\tan^2 45°$.

Sol. $\tan^2 60° + 2\tan^2 45°$

$$= (\sqrt{3})^2 + 2(\sqrt{1})^2 \quad [\because \tan 60° = \sqrt{3} \text{ and } \tan 45° = 1]$$
$$= 3 + 2(1) = 3 + 2 = 5$$

Q.10 If $\cos\theta = \frac{24}{25}$, then find $\tan\theta$.

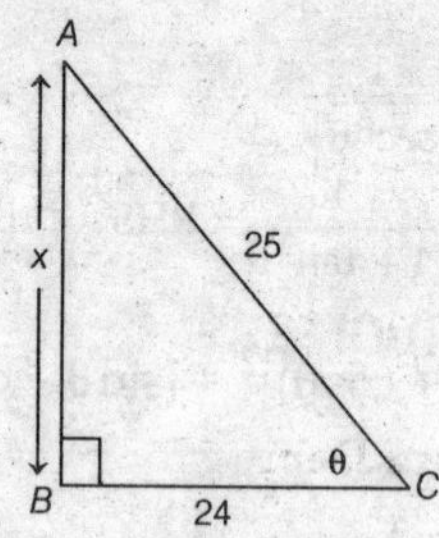

Sol. In ΔABC, $\angle B = 90°$, $\angle C = \theta$ and let $AB = x$

$$\because \cos\theta = \frac{24}{25} = \frac{\text{Base}}{\text{Hypotenus}}$$

$\therefore$ $AB^2 = AC^2 - BC^2$ [Pythagoras theorem]

$\Rightarrow$ $x^2 = 25^2 - 24^2$

$\Rightarrow$ $x^2 = 625 - 576$

$\Rightarrow$ $x^2 = 49$

$\Rightarrow$ $x = \sqrt{49}$

$\Rightarrow$ $x = 7$

Now, $\tan\theta = \frac{\text{Perpendicular}}{\text{Base}} = \frac{AB}{BC} = \frac{7}{24}$

Some Applications of Trigonometry

CHAPTER 09

Important Points

01 Angle of Elevation and Depression

Let BP and OA be two horizontal lines. If an observer is at point O and the point P is under consideration, then line OP is called the line of sight of he point P and $\angle AOP$ is known as the angle of elevation.

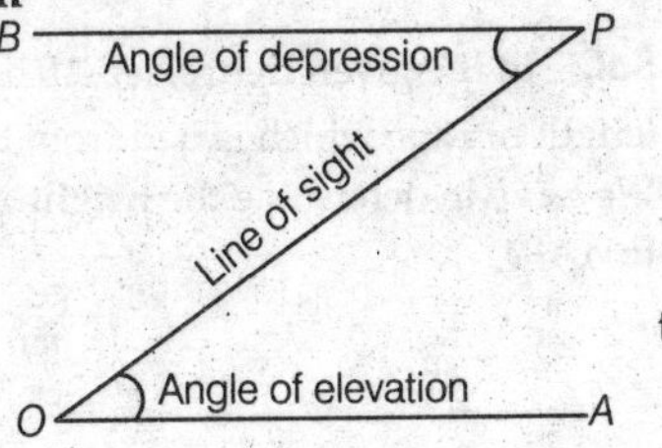

Suppose, if an observer is at point P and the point O is under consideration, then $\angle BPO$ is known as angle of depression.

Note The angle of elevation of a point P as seen from a point O is always equal to the angle of depression of O as seen from P.

02 If the angle of elevation moves towards the perpendicular line (tower/building), then it increases and if the angle of elevation moves away from the perpendicular line (tower/building), then it decreases.

03 If height of tower is doubled and the distance between the observer and foot of the tower is also doubled, then angle of elevation remains same.

04 If the angle of elevation of the sun decreases, then the shadow of the tower increases.

Exercise 9.1

Question 1 A circus artist is climbing a 20 m long rope, which is tightly stretched and tied from the top of a vertical pole to the ground. Find the height of the pole, if the angle made by the rope with the ground level is 30°(see figure).

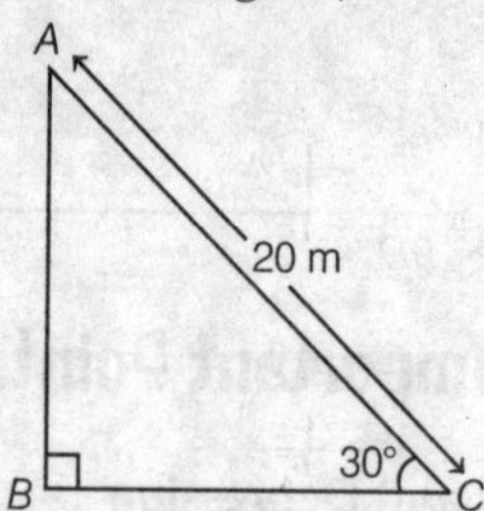

Sol. In the given figure, let AB be the height of the pole and $AC = 20$ m be the length of rope which is tied from the top of the pole.

We have to determine the height AB ____ .

In ΔABC,

$$\sin 30° = \frac{AB}{AC} = \frac{AB}{20} \quad \left[\because \sin\theta = \frac{\text{Perpendicular}}{\text{Hypotenuse}}\right]$$

$$\Rightarrow \quad \frac{1}{2} = \frac{AB}{20}$$

$$\Rightarrow \quad AB = \frac{20}{2} = 10 \text{ m} \quad \left[\because \sin 30° = \frac{1}{2}\right]$$

Hence, the height of the pole is 10 m.

Question 2 A tree breaks due to storm and the broken part bends so that the top of the tree touches the ground, making an angle 30° with it. The distance between the foot of the tree to the point where the top touches the ground is 8 m. Find the height of the tree.

◎ ***Thinking Process*** First the draw a right angle triangle from the given information in the question.

Now, apply the suitable trigonometric ratio corresponding to given sides in the triangle get the required value of which we need.

Sol. Let the initial height of the tree be AC. When the storm come, the tree broke from point B. The broken part of the tree BC touches the ground at point D, making an angle 30° on the ground.

Also given, $AD = 8$ m

In right ΔBAD, $\left[\therefore \tan\theta = \frac{\text{Perpendicular}}{\text{Base}}\right]$

$$\tan 30° = \frac{AB}{AD}$$

$$\Rightarrow \quad \frac{1}{\sqrt{3}} = \frac{AB}{8}$$

$$\Rightarrow \quad AB = \frac{8}{\sqrt{3}} \text{ m}$$

Again, in ΔBAD,

$$\cos 30° = \frac{AD}{BD} \Rightarrow \frac{\sqrt{3}}{2} = \frac{8}{BD} \qquad \left[\because \cos\theta = \frac{\text{Base}}{\text{Hypotenuse}}\right]$$

$$\Rightarrow \quad BD = \frac{16}{\sqrt{3}}$$

$$\therefore \quad AC = AB + BC = AB + BD \qquad [\because BC = BD]$$

$$= \frac{8}{\sqrt{3}} + \frac{16}{\sqrt{3}} = \frac{24}{\sqrt{3}} + \frac{\sqrt{3}}{\sqrt{3}} = 8\sqrt{3} \text{ m}$$

Hence, the height of the tree is $8\sqrt{3}$ m.

Question 3 A contractor plans to install two slides for the children to play in a park, for the children below the age of 5 yr, she prefers to have a slide whose top is at a height of 1.5 m and is inclined at an angle of 30° to the ground, where as for elder children, she wants to have a steep slide at a height of 3 m, and inclined at an angle of 60° to the ground. What should be the length of the slide in each case?

Thinking Process First draw two cases separately of two slides of below the age of 5 year children and elder children then apply respective trigonometric ratios to find the length of the slide is each case.

Sol. (i) In Figure. (a), it is the slide for the children below the age of 5 yr.

Let $BC = 1.5$ m be the height of the slide and slide AC is inclined at $\angle CAB = 30°$ to the ground.

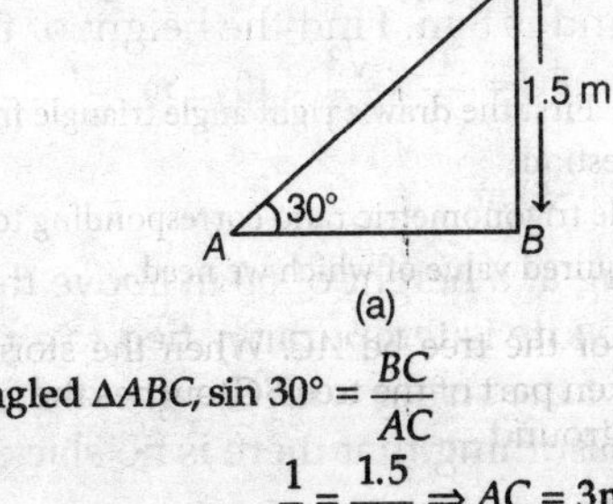

(a)

In right angled ΔABC, $\sin 30° = \frac{BC}{AC}$

$$\Rightarrow \quad \frac{1}{2} = \frac{1.5}{AC} \Rightarrow AC = 3\text{m}$$

(ii) In figure. (b), it is the slide for the elder children. Let $RQ = 3$ m be the height of the slide and slide PR is inclined at an $\angle RPQ = 60°$ to the ground.

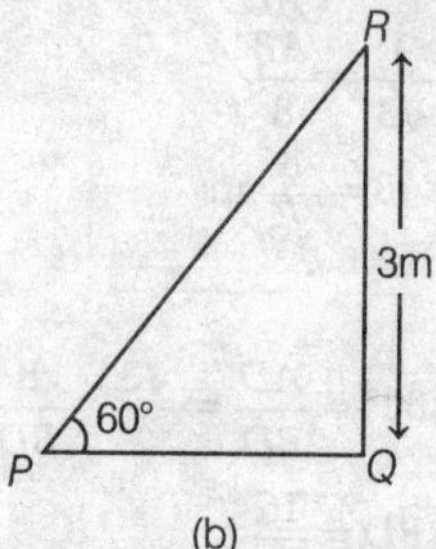

(b)

In right angled ΔPQR,

$$\sin 60° = \frac{RQ}{PR} \Rightarrow \frac{\sqrt{3}}{2} = \frac{3}{PR}$$

$$\Rightarrow \qquad PR = \frac{3 \times 2}{\sqrt{3}} = 2\sqrt{3} \text{ m}$$

Hence, lengths of the slides in each case are 3 m and $2\sqrt{3}$ m.

Question 4 The angle of elevation of the top of a tower from a point on the ground, which is 30 m away from the foot of the tower, is 30°. Find the height of the tower.

Sol. Let BC be the height of the tower which is standing on the ground AB. Let A be a point on the ground which makes an elevation of the top of the tower.

Also, $\qquad AB = 30$ m

In right angled ΔABC,

$$\tan 30° = \frac{BC}{AB}$$

$$\Rightarrow \qquad \frac{1}{\sqrt{3}} = \frac{BC}{30}$$

$$\Rightarrow \qquad BC = \frac{30}{\sqrt{3}} \times \frac{\sqrt{3}}{\sqrt{3}} = 10\sqrt{3} \text{ m}$$

Hence, height of the tower is $10\sqrt{3}$ m.

Question 5 A kite is flying at a height of 60 m above the ground. The string attached to the kite is temporarily tied to a point on the ground. The inclination of the string with the ground is 60°. Find the length of the string, assuming that there is no slack in the string.

Sol. Let C be the position of the kite and AC be the length of the string which makes an angle of 60° on the ground. The height of the kite from the ground is $BC = 60$ m.

In right angled ΔABC,

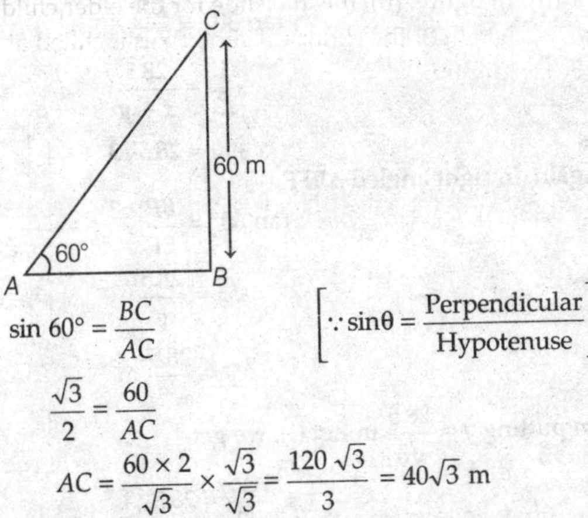

$$\sin 60° = \frac{BC}{AC} \qquad \left[\because \sin\theta = \frac{\text{Perpendicular}}{\text{Hypotenuse}}\right]$$

$$\Rightarrow \quad \frac{\sqrt{3}}{2} = \frac{60}{AC}$$

$$\Rightarrow \quad AC = \frac{60 \times 2}{\sqrt{3}} \times \frac{\sqrt{3}}{\sqrt{3}} = \frac{120\sqrt{3}}{3} = 40\sqrt{3} \text{ m}$$

Hence, length of the string is $40\sqrt{3}$ m.

Mistake Alert Students using the wrong triangle on failing to recognize the correct right angled triangle in word problems.

Question 6 A 1.5 m tall boy is standing at some distance from a 30 m tall building. The angle of elevation from his eyes to the top of the building increases from 30° to 60° as he walks towards the building. Find the distance, he walked towards the building.

Thinking Process First draw a clear, labelled diagram representing the problem which include proper angle of elevation between the boy's eye and the top of the building and placing the proper heigh and distances.

Sol. Let $AB = 30$ m be the height of the building, $DC = 1.5$ m be the height of the man and the point D be the man's eyes. The angles of elevations are $\angle BDF = 30°$ and $\angle BEF = 60°$.

Let $\qquad DE = x$ and $EF = y$

Now, $\qquad BF = AB - AF = 30 - 1.5 = 28.5$m $\qquad [\because CD = AF]$

In right angled ΔBFD,

$$\tan 30° = \frac{BF}{DF}$$

$$\Rightarrow \quad \frac{1}{\sqrt{3}} = \frac{28.5}{x + y}$$

$$\Rightarrow \quad x + y = 28.5\sqrt{3} \quad \text{...(i)}$$

Again, in right angled ΔBFE,

$$\tan 60° = \frac{BF}{EF}$$

$$\Rightarrow \quad \sqrt{3} = \frac{28.5}{y}$$

$$\Rightarrow \quad y = \frac{28.5}{\sqrt{3}} \text{ m} \quad \text{...(ii)}$$

On putting $y = \frac{28.5}{\sqrt{3}}$ in Eq. (i), we get

$$x + \frac{28.5}{\sqrt{3}} = 28.5\sqrt{3}$$

$$\Rightarrow \quad x = 28.5\left(\sqrt{3} - \frac{1}{\sqrt{3}}\right) = 28.5\left(\frac{3-1}{\sqrt{3}}\right)$$

$$\Rightarrow \quad x = \frac{28.5 \times 2}{\sqrt{3}} \times \frac{\sqrt{3}}{\sqrt{3}} = \frac{57\sqrt{3}}{3} = 19\sqrt{3} \text{ m}$$

Hence, the distance between the two elevations is $19\sqrt{3}$ m.

Question 7 From a point on the ground, the angles of elevations of the bottom and the top of a transmission tower fixed at the top of a 20 m high building are 45° and 60°, respectively. Find the height of the tower.

Sol. Let $BC = 20$ m be the height of the building and $DC = h$ m be height of the tower, which is fixed at the top of the building. Let A be a fixed point on the ground. From a fixed point A, the angles of elevations of the bottom and the top of the transmission tower are

$$\angle BAC = 45° \text{ and } \angle BAD = 60°$$

Also, let $AB = x$

In right angled ΔABC,

$$\tan 45° = \frac{BC}{AB} \Rightarrow 1 = \frac{20}{x} \Rightarrow x = 20 \text{ m} \quad \text{...(i)}$$

Again, in right angled ΔABD,

$$\tan 60° = \frac{BD}{AB}$$

$$\Rightarrow \quad \sqrt{3} = \frac{20 + h}{x}$$

$$\Rightarrow \quad \sqrt{3} = \frac{20 + h}{20} \quad \text{[From Eq. (i), } x = 20 \text{ m]}$$

$$\Rightarrow \quad 20 + h = 20\sqrt{3} \Rightarrow h = 20(\sqrt{3} - 1) \text{ m}$$

Hence, the height of the tower is $20(\sqrt{3} - 1)$ m.

Mistake Alert Students took wrong trigonometric ratio which include hypotenuse that is $\sin \theta$, $\cos \theta$.

Question 8 A statue, 1.6 m tall, stands on the top of a pedestal. From a point on the ground, the angle of elevation of the top of the statue is 60° and from the same point, the angle of elevation of the top of the pedestal is 45°. Find the height of the pedestal.

Sol. Let $BC = h$ metre be the height of the pedestal and $CD = 1.6$ m be the height of the statue, which is standing on the pedestal. Let A be a fixed point on the ground. From the point A, the angles of elevations of the top of the statue and bottom of the statue are

$$\angle DAB = 60° \text{ and } \angle CAB = 45°$$

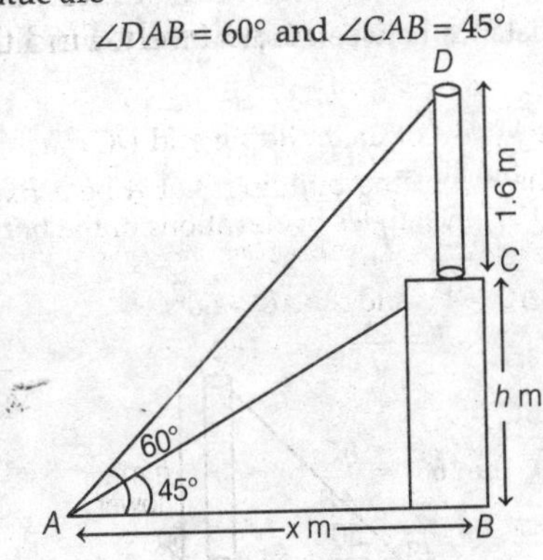

Also, let $AB = x$ metre.

In right angled ΔABD, $\tan 60° = \frac{BD}{AB}$

$$\Rightarrow \quad \sqrt{3} = \frac{CD + CB}{x}$$

$$\Rightarrow \quad \sqrt{3} = \frac{1.6 + h}{x} \quad [\because CD = 1.6, CB = h]$$

$$\Rightarrow \quad h = \sqrt{3}\,x - 1.6 \quad \text{...(i)}$$

In right angled ΔABC,

$$\tan 45° = \frac{BC}{AB} \Rightarrow 1 = \frac{h}{x}$$

$$\Rightarrow \quad x = h$$

On putting $x = h$ in Eq. (i), we get

$$h = \sqrt{3}\,h - 1.6$$

$$\Rightarrow \quad h(\sqrt{3} - 1) = 1.6$$

$$\Rightarrow \quad h = \frac{1.6}{(\sqrt{3} - 1)} \times \frac{\sqrt{3} + 1}{\sqrt{3} + 1} \quad \text{[Rationalize the denominator]}$$

$$= \frac{1.6}{2}(\sqrt{3} + 1) = 0.8(\sqrt{3} + 1)\,\text{m}$$

Hence, the height of the pedestal is $0.8(\sqrt{3} + 1)$ m.

Question 9 The angle of elevation of the top of a building from the foot of the tower is 30° and the angle of elevation of the top of the tower from the foot of the building is 60°. If the tower is 50 m high, then find the height of the building.

Sol. Let $BC = 50$ m be the height of the tower and $AD = h$ metre be the height of the building and angles of elevations from the bottom of building and tower as well are

$$\angle BAC = 60° \text{ and } \angle ABD = 30°$$

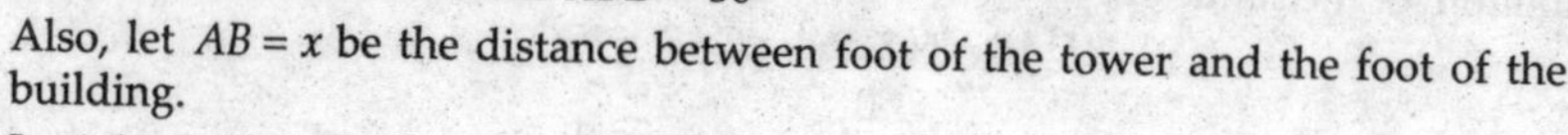

Also, let $AB = x$ be the distance between foot of the tower and the foot of the building.

In right angled ΔBAD,

$$\tan 30° = \frac{AD}{AB}$$

$$\Rightarrow \quad \frac{1}{\sqrt{3}} = \frac{h}{x}$$

$$\Rightarrow \quad h = \frac{x}{\sqrt{3}} \quad \text{...(i)}$$

Again, in right angled ΔABC,

$$\tan 60° = \frac{BC}{AB}$$

$$\Rightarrow \quad \sqrt{3} = \frac{50}{x} \Rightarrow x = \frac{50}{\sqrt{3}}\,\text{m}$$

On putting $x = \frac{50}{\sqrt{3}}$ in Eq. (i), we get

$$h = \frac{50}{\sqrt{3}} \times \frac{1}{\sqrt{3}} = \frac{50}{3} = 16\frac{2}{3}\,\text{m}$$

Hence, the height of the building is $16\frac{2}{3}$ m.

Question 10 Two poles of equal heights are standing opposite each other on either side of the road, which is 80 m wide. From a point between them on the road, the angles of elevation of the top of the poles are 60° and 30°, respectively. Find the height of the poles and the distances of the point from the poles.

Sol. Let $AB = 80$ m be the width of the road. On both sides of the road poles $AE = BD = h$ metre are standing. Let C be any point on AB such that point C makes elevations are $\angle BCD = 60°$ and $\angle ACE = 30°$.

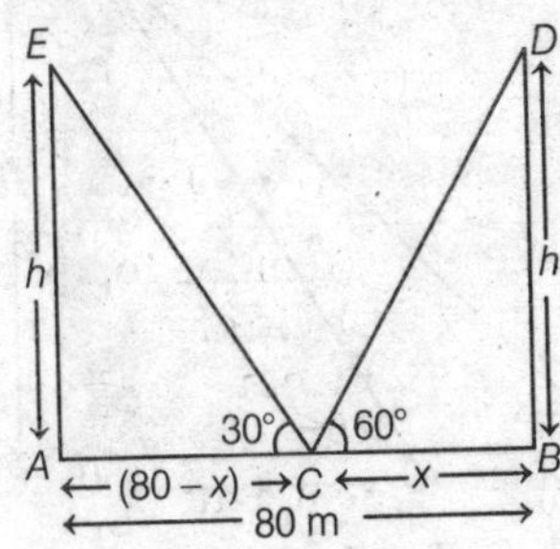

Let $BC = x$. Then, $AC = AB - BC = (80 - x)$ m.

In right angled ΔEAC,

$$\tan 30° = \frac{AE}{AC}$$

$$\Rightarrow \quad \frac{1}{\sqrt{3}} = \frac{h}{80 - x}$$

$$\Rightarrow \quad 80 - x = h\sqrt{3}$$

$$\Rightarrow \quad h\sqrt{3} + x = 80 \quad \text{...(i)}$$

Again, in right angled ΔCBD,

$$\tan 60° = \frac{BD}{BC}$$

$$\Rightarrow \quad \sqrt{3} = \frac{h}{x} \Rightarrow h = \sqrt{3}\,x \quad \text{...(ii)}$$

On putting $h = \sqrt{3}x$ in Eq. (i), we get

$$\sqrt{3}x \times (\sqrt{3}) + x = 80$$

$$\Rightarrow \quad 3x + x = 80$$

$$\Rightarrow \quad 4x = 80$$

$$\Rightarrow \quad x = 20 \text{ m}$$

On putting $x = 20$ in Eq. (ii), we get

$$h = 20\sqrt{3} \text{ m}$$

Also, $AC = 80 - x = 80 - 20 = 60$ m

Hence, the height of the poles is $20\sqrt{3}$ m and the distance of the point is 20 m and 60 m from the poles.

Question 11 A TV tower stands vertically on a bank of a canal. From a point on the other bank directly opposite the tower, the angle of elevation of the top of the tower is 60°. From another point 20 m away from this point on the line joining this point to the foot of the tower, the angle of elevation of the top of the tower is 30° (see figure). Find the height of the tower and the width of the canal.

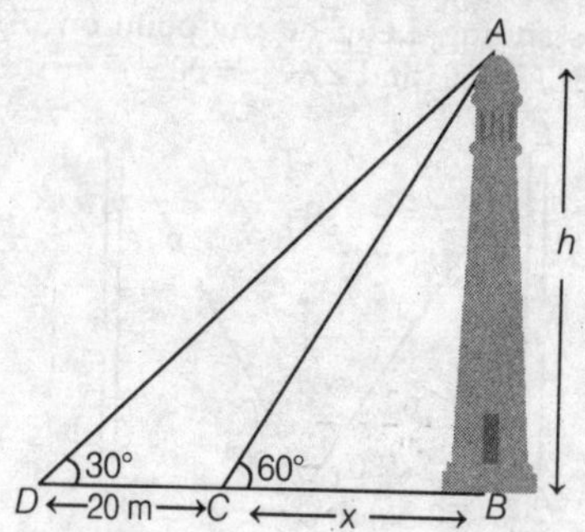

Sol. Let $BC = x$ metre be the width of the canal and $AB = h$ metre be the height of the tower and angle of elevations from the top of the tower are $\angle ADB = 30°$ and $\angle ACB = 60°$.

In right angled ΔABD,

$$\tan 30° = \frac{AB}{DB}$$

$$\Rightarrow \quad \frac{1}{\sqrt{3}} = \frac{h}{DC + CB}$$

$$\Rightarrow \quad \frac{1}{\sqrt{3}} = \frac{h}{20 + x} \quad [\because DC = 20\text{ m}, CB = x]$$

$$\Rightarrow \quad 20 + x = \sqrt{3}\,h \quad \text{...(i)}$$

Again, in right angled ΔABC,

$$\tan 60° = \frac{AB}{BC}$$

$$\Rightarrow \quad \sqrt{3} = \frac{h}{x}$$

$$\Rightarrow \quad h = \sqrt{3}x \quad \text{...(ii)}$$

On putting $h = \sqrt{3}x$ in Eq. (i), we get

$$20 + x = \sqrt{3}\,(\sqrt{3}\,x)$$

$$\Rightarrow \quad 20 + x = 3x$$

$$\Rightarrow \quad 2x = 20$$

$$\Rightarrow \quad x = 10\text{ m}$$

On putting $x = 10$ m in Eq. (ii), we get

$$h = \sqrt{3}\,(10) \Rightarrow h = 10\sqrt{3}\text{ m}$$

Hence, the height of the tower is $10\sqrt{3}$ m and width of the canal is 10 m.

Question 12 From the top of a 7 m high building, the angle of elevation of the top of a cable tower is 60° and the angle of depression of its foot is 45°. Determine the height of the tower.

Sol. Let $AD = 7$ m be the height of the building and $BC = h$ metre be the height of the cable tower. From the top of the building D, the angles of elevation and depression are $\angle CDE = 60°$ and $\angle EDB = 45°$.

From the point D, a perpendicular line DE is drawn on BC.

As $$DE \parallel AB$$

$\therefore$ $$\angle EDB = \angle ABD = 45° \quad \text{[Alternative interior angles]}$$

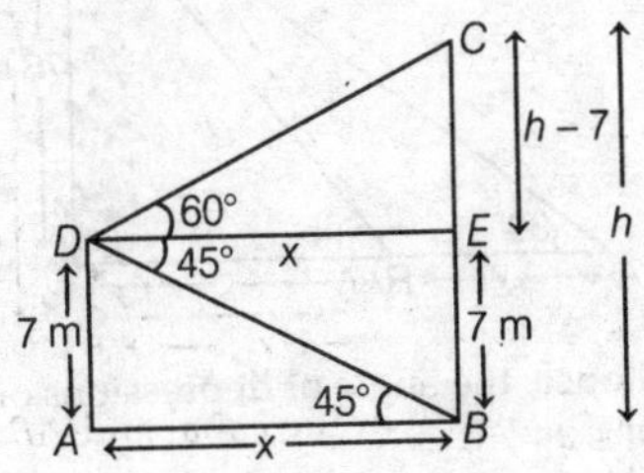

Also, let $AB = DE = x$ metre be the distance between building and tower.

In right angled ΔBAD,

$$\tan 45° = \frac{AD}{AB} \Rightarrow 1 = \frac{7}{x}$$

$\Rightarrow$ $$x = 7 \text{ m} \quad \text{...(i)}$$

In right angled ΔCED,

$$\tan 60° = \frac{CE}{DE}$$

$\Rightarrow$ $$\sqrt{3} = \frac{h-7}{x} \quad [\because CE = BC - BE \Rightarrow h - 7]$$

$\Rightarrow$ $$h - 7 = x\sqrt{3}$$

$\Rightarrow$ $$h = x\sqrt{3} + 7$$

$\Rightarrow$ $$h = 7\sqrt{3} + 7 \quad \text{[from Eq. (i), } x = 7 \text{ m]}$$

$\Rightarrow$ $$h = 7(\sqrt{3} + 1) \text{ m}$$

Hence, the height of the tower is $7(\sqrt{3} + 1)$ m.

Mistake Alert Students might confuse between the angle of elevation with the angle of depression.

Question 13 As observed from the top of a 75 m high lighthouse from the sea-level, the angles of depression of two ships are 30° and 45°. If one ship is exactly behind the other on the same side of the lighthouse then find the distance between the two ships.

Sol. Let $CD = 75$ m be the height of the lighthouse from the sea-level AC. Let A and B be the positions of two ships on the sea-level.

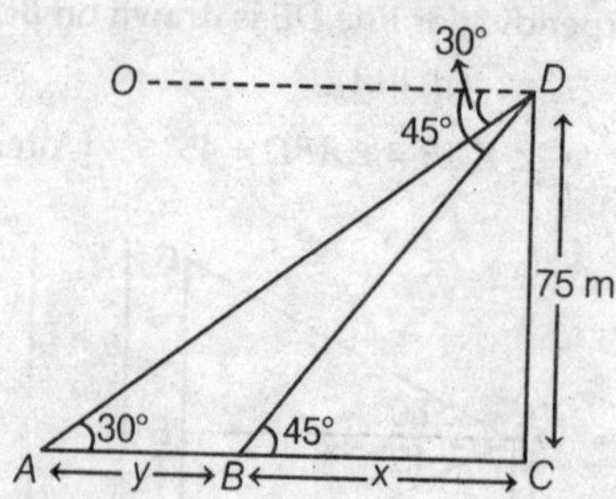

From point D of a lighthouse, the angle of depressions of two ships A and B are $\angle ODA = 30°$ and $\angle ODB = 45°$

$\Rightarrow \angle CAD = 30°$ and $\angle CBD = 45°$ (alternates interior angle as $OD \parallel AC$)

Let distance between two ships $AB = y$ metre and $BC = x$ metre.

In right angled ΔACD,

$$\tan 30° = \frac{CD}{AC} \Rightarrow \frac{1}{\sqrt{3}} = \frac{75}{AB + BC}$$

$$\Rightarrow \quad \frac{1}{\sqrt{3}} = \frac{75}{y + x} \quad [\because AB = y, BC = x]$$

$$\Rightarrow \quad x + y = 75\sqrt{3} \quad \ldots(i)$$

In right angled ΔBCD,

$$\tan 45° = \frac{CD}{BC}$$

$$\Rightarrow \quad 1 = \frac{75}{x}$$

$$\Rightarrow \quad x = 75 \text{ m}$$

On putting $x = 75$ in Eq.(i), we get

$$75 + y = 75\sqrt{3}$$

$$\Rightarrow \quad y = 75(\sqrt{3} - 1) \text{ m}$$

Hence, the distance between the two ships is $75(\sqrt{3} - 1)$ m.

Note If two lines are parallel and cut by the transversal, then their alternate interior angles are equal.

Question 14 A 1.2 m tall girl spots a balloon moving with the wind in a horizontal line at a height of 88.2 m from the ground. The angle of elevation of the balloon from the eyes of the girl at any instant is 60°. After some time, the angle of elevation reduces to 30°(see figure). Find the distance travelled by the balloon during the interval.

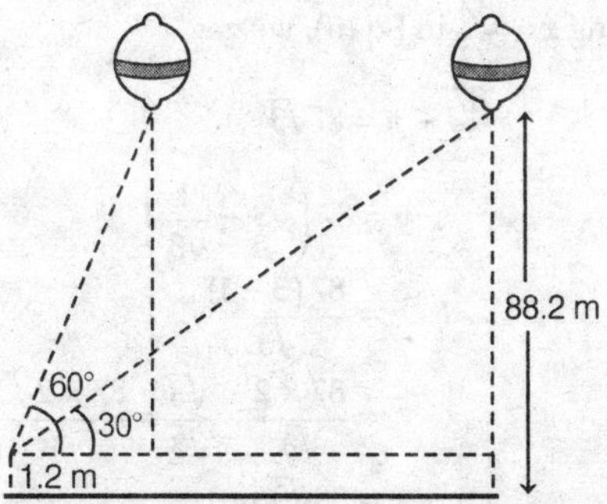

Sol. Let $AD = 1.2$ m be the tall girl standing on the horizontal line AB.

Let $FH = EB = 88.2$ m be the height of balloon from the line AB. At the eye of the girl D, the angles of elevations are $\angle FDC = 60°$ and $\angle EDC = 30°$.

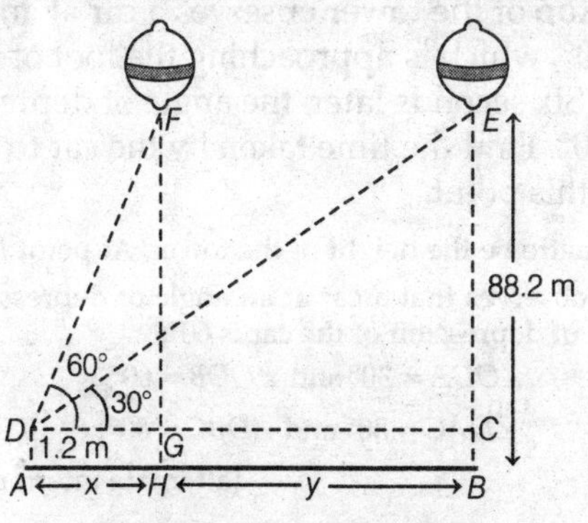

Now, $FG = EC = 88.2 - 1.2 = 87$ m $[\because AD = BC]$

Let the distance travelled by the balloons $HB = y$ metre and $AH = x$ metre.

$\therefore$ $DG = x$ metre and $GC = y$ metre

In right angled ΔDGF,

$$\tan 60° = \frac{FG}{DG}$$

$$\Rightarrow \quad \sqrt{3} = \frac{87}{x}$$

$$\Rightarrow \quad x = \frac{87}{\sqrt{3}} \quad \text{...(i)}$$

In right angled ΔDCE,

$$\tan 30° = \frac{EC}{DC}$$

$$\Rightarrow \quad \frac{1}{\sqrt{3}} = \frac{87}{DG + GC}$$

$$\Rightarrow \quad x + y = 87\sqrt{3} \quad \text{...(ii)}$$

$\therefore$ From Eq. (i), putting $x = \frac{87}{\sqrt{3}}$ in Eq (ii), we get

$$\frac{87}{\sqrt{3}} + y = 87\sqrt{3}$$

$$\Rightarrow \quad y = 87\left(\sqrt{3} - \frac{1}{\sqrt{3}}\right)$$

$$= \frac{87\,(3-1)}{\sqrt{3}}$$

$$= \frac{87 \times 2}{\sqrt{3}} \times \frac{\sqrt{3}}{\sqrt{3}} = \frac{87 \times 2\sqrt{3}}{3} = 29 \times 2\sqrt{3}$$

$$= 58\sqrt{3} \text{ m}$$

Hence, the distance between the two balloons is $58\sqrt{3}$ m.

Question 15 A straight highway leads to the foot of a tower. A man standing at the top of the tower observes a car at an angle of depression of 30°, which is approaching the foot of the tower with a uniform speed. Six seconds later, the angle of depression of the car is found to be 60°. Find the time taken by the car to reach the foot of the tower from this point.

Sol. Let $CD = h$ metre be the height of the tower. At point D, a man is standing on the tower and observes that a car at an angle of depression of 30°. After six seconds, the angle of depression of the car is 60°.

i.e., $\angle ODA = 30°$ and $\angle ODB = 60°$

$\Rightarrow$ $\angle DAC = 30°$ and $\angle DBC = 60°$

[alternate interior angles as $OD \parallel AC$]

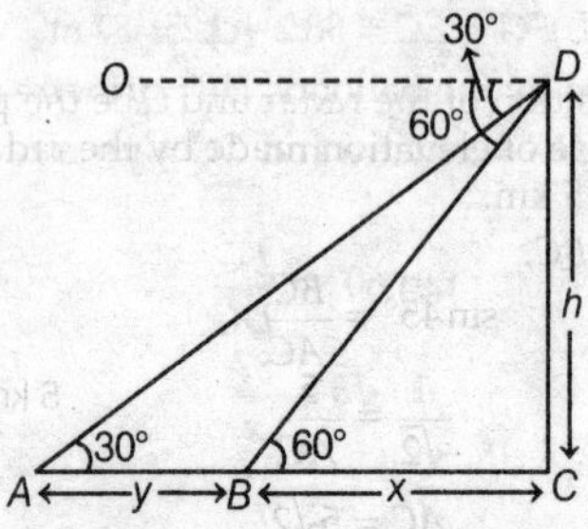

Let $AB = y$ and $BC = x$

In right angled ΔBCD,

$$\tan 60° = \frac{CD}{BC} \Rightarrow \sqrt{3} = \frac{h}{x}$$

$$\Rightarrow \quad h = \sqrt{3}\,x \quad \text{...(i)}$$

In right angled ΔACD,

$$\tan 30° = \frac{CD}{AC} \Rightarrow \frac{1}{\sqrt{3}} = \frac{h}{x+y}$$

$$\Rightarrow \quad x + y = h\sqrt{3}$$

$$\Rightarrow \quad x + y = \sqrt{3}x(\sqrt{3}) \quad \text{[from Eq. (i)]}$$

$$\Rightarrow \quad x + y = 3x \quad \text{...(ii)}$$

It is given that car moves from point A to point B in six seconds.
Let its speed be k km/s.

$$\therefore \quad \text{Time} = \frac{\text{Distance}}{\text{Speed}}$$

$$\Rightarrow \quad 6 = \frac{y}{k} \Rightarrow y = 6k \quad \text{[Distance from point } A \text{ to point } B \text{ is } y]$$

On putting $y = 6K$ in Eq (ii), we get

$$x + 6k = 3x$$

$$\Rightarrow \quad 6k = 2x \Rightarrow x = 3k$$

Hence, the distance of BC is half of AB. Thus, the time taken is also half.
Hence, the car moves from point B to point C in 3 s.

Note The line of sight is the line drawn from the eye of on observer to the point in the object viewed by the observer

DIKSHA APP Questions

☐ Multiple Choice Questions

Q.1 A radar detects an aeroplane in the sky at an altitude of 5 km, at an angle of elevation of 45°. Find the distance of the aeroplane from the radar.

(a) $5\sqrt{2}$ (b) 4 (c) 5 (d) 6

Sol. (a) Let A be the position of the radar and C be the position of the aeroplane. The angle of elevation made by the radar is 45° and the height of the aeroplane is 5 km.

In right angled ΔABC,

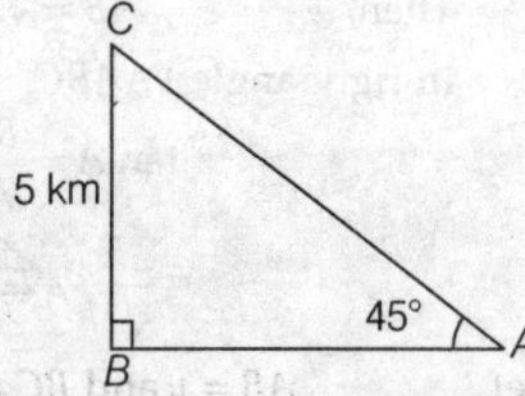

$$\sin 45° = \frac{BC}{AC}$$

$$\Rightarrow \quad \frac{1}{\sqrt{2}} = \frac{5}{AC}$$

$$\Rightarrow \quad AC = 5\sqrt{2}$$

The distance of the aeroplane from the radar is $5\sqrt{2}$ km

Q.2 A kite is flying at an angle of elevation of 60°, the kite is tied with a string of 60 m. find the height of the kite.

(a) 30 m (b) 40 m (c) $30\sqrt{3}$ m (d) $40\sqrt{3}$ m

Sol. (c) Let C be the position of the kite and AC be the length of the string that is $AC = 60$ m.

The angle of elevation is 60°.

In right angled ΔABC,

$$\sin 60° = \frac{BC}{AC}$$

$$\Rightarrow \quad \frac{\sqrt{3}}{2} = \frac{BC}{60}$$

$$\Rightarrow \quad BC = \frac{60\sqrt{3}}{2} = 30\sqrt{3} \text{ m}$$

Hence, the height of the kite is $30\sqrt{3}$ m.

Q.3 A pole cast a shadow of length 20 m on the ground, when the sun's elevation is 60°. Find the height of pole.

(a) 30 m (b) 40 m (c) 50 m (d) $20\sqrt{3}$ m

Sol. (d) Let AB be the shadow of the pole. The elevation of the sun is 60°.

In right angled ΔABC,

$$\tan 60° = \frac{BC}{AB} \qquad \left[\because \tan\theta = \frac{\text{Perpendicular}}{\text{Base}}\right]$$

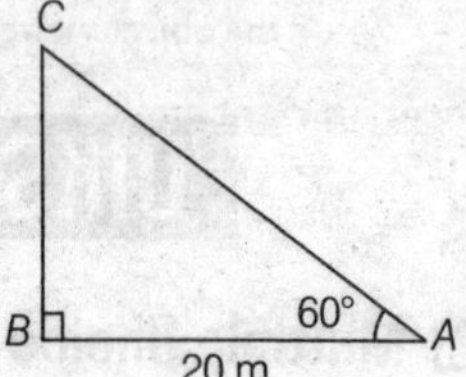

$$\Rightarrow \quad \sqrt{3} = \frac{BC}{20}$$

$$\Rightarrow \quad 20\sqrt{3} \text{ m} = BC$$

Hence, the height of the pole is $20\sqrt{3}$ m.

Q.4 The shadow of a tree is $\sqrt{3}$ times its height, the angle of elevation of the sun is

(a) 45° (b) 30° (c) 60° (d) 90°

Sol. (b) Let BC be the height of the tree and AB be the shadow of the tree.

Let $BC = h$ metre

Then, $AB = \sqrt{3}h$ metre

In right angled ΔABC,

$$\tan A = \frac{BC}{AB}$$

$$= \frac{h}{\sqrt{3}h} = \frac{1}{\sqrt{3}}$$

$$\Rightarrow \quad \tan A = \frac{1}{\sqrt{3}}$$

$$\Rightarrow \quad \tan A = \tan 30^\circ$$

$$\Rightarrow \quad A = 30^\circ$$

Hence, the angle of elevation of the sum is 30°.

Q.5 The angles of elevations of the top of a tower from two points distant x and $y (x > y)$ from its foot are 30° and 60° respectively, then the height of the tower is

(a) $\sqrt{x+y}$ (b) $\sqrt{xy}$ (c) $\sqrt{x-y}$ (d) $\sqrt{\frac{x}{y}}$

Sol. (b) BC is the tower and the two points be A and D having angles of elevations 30° and 60° respectively.

$$AB = x \text{ units}$$

and $$DB = y \text{ units}$$

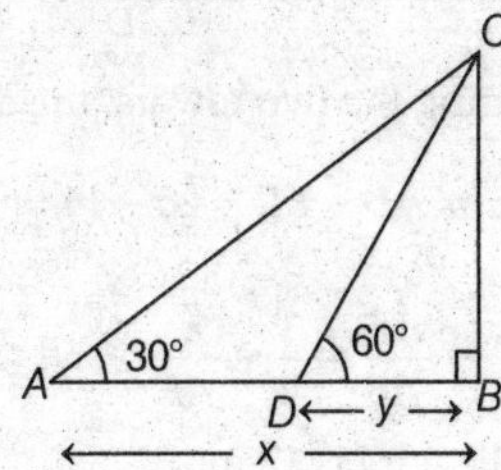

In right angled ΔABC,

$$\tan 30^\circ = \frac{BC}{AB}$$

$$\Rightarrow \quad \frac{1}{\sqrt{3}} = \frac{BC}{x}$$

$$\Rightarrow \quad \frac{x}{\sqrt{3}} = BC \qquad \text{...(i)}$$

Also, in right angled ΔDBC,

$$\tan 60^\circ = \frac{BC}{DB}$$

$$\Rightarrow \quad \sqrt{3} = \frac{BC}{y}$$

$$\Rightarrow \quad \sqrt{3}y = BC \qquad \text{...(ii)}$$

On multiplying Eqs. (i) and (ii), we get

$$\frac{x}{\sqrt{3}} \times \sqrt{3}y = BC^2$$

$$\Rightarrow \quad BC^2 = xy$$

$$BC = \sqrt{xy} \text{ units}$$

Q.6 The tops of two poles of heights 20 m and 14 m are connected by a wire. If the wire makes an angle of 30° with the horizontal, then the length of the wire is

(a) 12 m (b) 10 m (c) 8 m (d) 4 m

Sol. (a) Let BC and AD be the two tqwers with heights 14 m and 20 m, respectively.

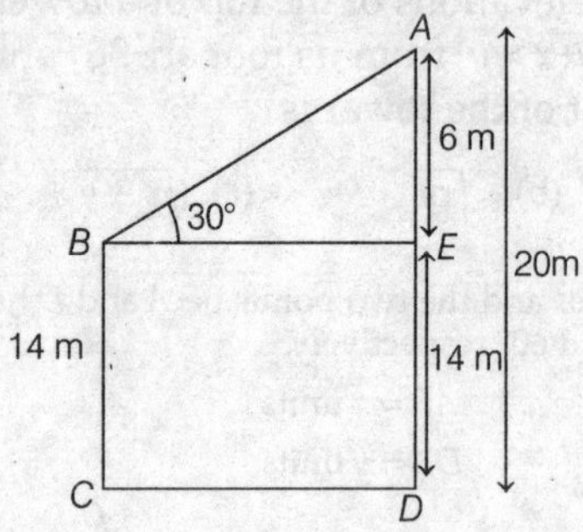

Let AB be the wire joining the two towers, the angle of elevation is 30°. *i.e.*, $\angle ABE = 30°$

$$AE = AD - ED = 20 - 14 = 6 \text{ m}$$

In right angled ΔAEB,

$$\sin 30° = \frac{AE}{AB} \Rightarrow \frac{1}{2} = \frac{6}{AB} \Rightarrow AB = 12 \text{ m}$$

Hence, the length of the wire is 12 m.

Q.7 The angle of elevation of top of a tower at a point 100 m from its foot on the horizontal plane is 45°. The height of tower is

(a) 50 m (b) 75 m (c) 100 m (d) 125 m

Sol. (c) Let BC be the height of the tower and $AB = 100$ m be the distance of the angle of elevation from the foot of the tower.

The angle of elevation is 45°.

In right angled ΔABC,

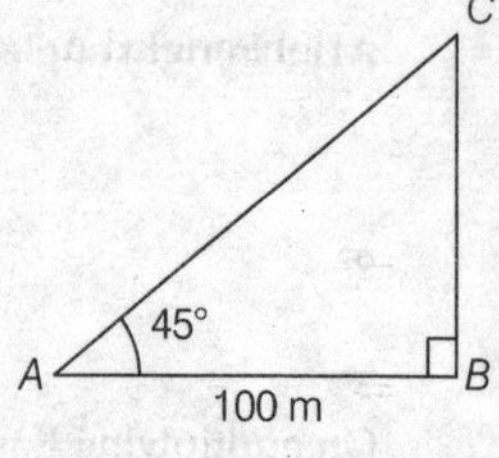

$$\tan 45° = \frac{BC}{AB}$$

$$\Rightarrow \quad 1 = \frac{BC}{100}$$

$$\Rightarrow \quad BC = 100 \text{ m}$$

Hence, the height of the tower is 100 m.

Note Whenever the angle is 45°, the base and perpendicular are the same. Hence, height of the tower will be directly 100 m.

Q.8 The height of a tower is 10 m. Find the length of its shadow, when sun's altitude is 45°.

(a) 10 m (b) 20 m (c) 30 m (d) 40 m

Sol. (a) Let $BC = 10$ m be the height of the tower and AB be the shadow of the tower.

The angle of elevation is 45°.

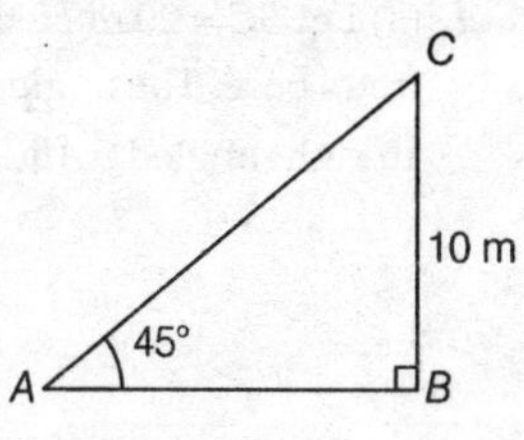

In right angled ΔABC,

$$\tan 45° = \frac{BC}{AB}$$

$$\Rightarrow \quad 1 = \frac{10}{AB}$$

$$\Rightarrow \quad AB = 10 \text{ m}$$

Hence, the length of the shadow is 10 m.

Q.9 A ladder 12 m long just reaches the top of a vertical wall. If the ladder makes an angle of 60° with the ground, then the height of the wall is

(a) $12\sqrt{3}$ m (b) $6\sqrt{3}$ m

(c) 6 m (d) Cannot be determined

Sol. (b) Let $AC = 12$ m be the length of the ladder.

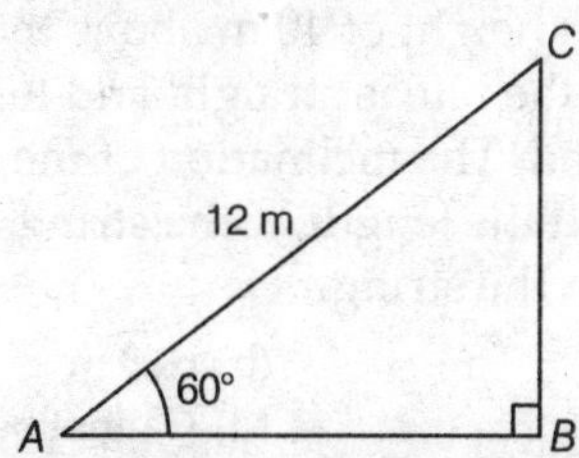

Let BC be the height of the wall. The angle of elevation is 60°.

In right angled ΔABC,

$$\sin 60° = \frac{BC}{AC}$$

$$\Rightarrow \quad \frac{\sqrt{3}}{2} = \frac{BC}{12}$$

$$\Rightarrow \quad BC = \frac{12\sqrt{3}}{2} = 6\sqrt{3} \text{ m}$$

Hence, the height of the wall is $6\sqrt{3}$ m.

Q.10 The angle of elevation of the top of a tree from a point on the ground, which is 20 m away from the base of the tree, is 30°. Find the height of the tree.

(a) $\frac{20\sqrt{3}}{3}$ m (b) $20\sqrt{3}$ m (c) 10 m (d) Cannot be determined

Sol. (a) Let $BC = 20$ m be the distance between the angle of elevation and the tree's base. The angle of elevation is 30° and BA is the height of tree

In right angled ΔABC,

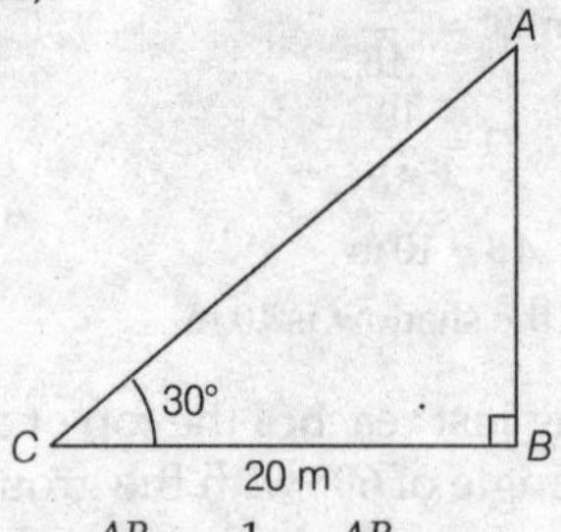

$$\tan 30° = \frac{AB}{BC} \Rightarrow \frac{1}{\sqrt{3}} = \frac{AB}{20} \Rightarrow AB = \frac{20}{\sqrt{3}} \text{ m}$$

The height of the tree $= \frac{20}{\sqrt{3}}$ m $= \frac{20\sqrt{3}}{3}$ m.

Q.11 A kite is flying at a height of 40 m above the ground. The string attached to the kite is straight and temporarily tied to a point on the ground. The inclination of the string with the ground is 45°. Find the length of the string, assuming that there is no slack in the string.

(a) $40\sqrt{2}$ m (b) $6\sqrt{3}$ m

(c) 6 m (d) Cannot be determined

Sol. (a) Let $AB = 40$ m be the kite's height and AC be the string tied to the string. The angle of elevation is 45°.

In right angled ΔABC,

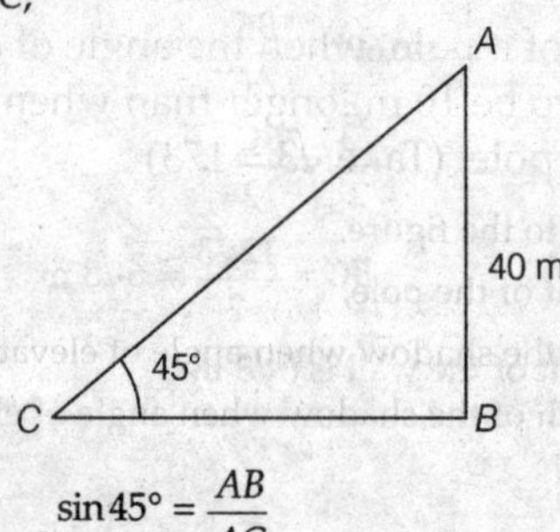

$$\sin 45° = \frac{AB}{AC}$$

$$\Rightarrow \qquad \frac{1}{\sqrt{2}} = \frac{40}{AC}$$

$$\Rightarrow \qquad AC = 40\sqrt{2} \text{ m}$$

The length of the string $= 40\sqrt{2}$ m.

Q.12 If the height of a pole is 6 m and it casts a shadow $2\sqrt{3}$ m long on the ground, then the angle of elevation of the sun is

(a) 30° (b) 60° (c) 90° (d) 45°

Sol. (b) In the figure, BC is height of the pole = 6 m and AB is length of shadow that is $AB = 2\sqrt{3}$ m.

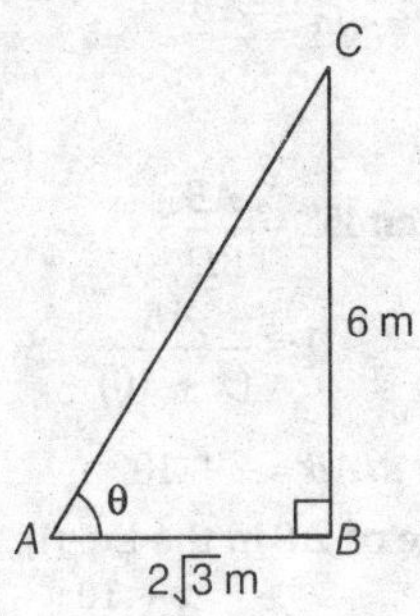

The elevation of the sun will be $\angle CAB = \theta$.

In right angled ΔABC,

$$\tan\theta = \frac{BC}{AB} = \frac{6}{2\sqrt{3}} = \sqrt{3}$$

$$\Rightarrow \qquad \tan\theta = \sqrt{3}$$

$$\Rightarrow \qquad \tan\theta = \tan 60°$$

Hence, $\theta = 60°$.

The angle of elevation of the sun is 60°.

☐ Subjective Type Questions

Q.1 The shadow of a pole, when the angle of elevation of sun is 45° is found to be 10 m longer than when it is 60°. Find the height of the pole. (Take $\sqrt{3} = 1.73$)

Sol. With reference to the figure,

Let AB = height of the pole,

BC = length of the shadow when angle of elevation is $60° = x$

and BD = length of the shadow when angle of elevation is $45° = x + 10$.

In right ΔABC,

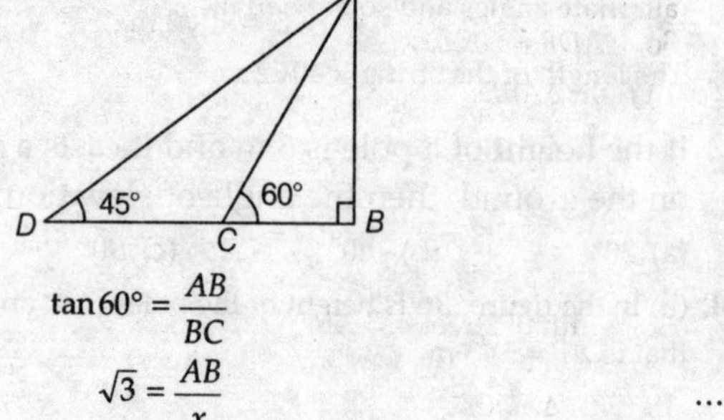

$$\tan 60° = \frac{AB}{BC}$$

$$\Rightarrow \quad \sqrt{3} = \frac{AB}{x} \quad \text{...(i)}$$

In right ΔABD,

$$\tan 45° = \frac{AB}{BD}$$

$$\Rightarrow \quad 1 = \frac{AB}{(x+10)} \quad \text{...(ii)}$$

$$\Rightarrow \quad AB = x + 10$$

On substituting the value of AB in the Eq. (i), we get

$$\sqrt{3} = \frac{x+10}{x}$$

$$\Rightarrow \quad \sqrt{3}x = x + 10$$

$$\Rightarrow \quad \sqrt{3}x - x = 10$$

$$\Rightarrow \quad 1.73x - x = 10 \quad [\text{Taking } \sqrt{3} = 1.73]$$

$$\Rightarrow \quad 0.73x = 10$$

$$\Rightarrow \quad x = \frac{10}{0.73} \approx 13.7 \text{ m}$$

Hence, height of the pole is 13.7 m.

Q.2 A window in a building is 10 m above the ground. From this window, the angles of elevation and depression of the top and foot of another house across the street are $30°$ and $60°$, respectively. Find the height of the second house and the width of the street.

Sol. With reference to the figure,

let AB = height of the window = 10 m,

BD = width of street

and CD = height of second house

Angle of elevation of top $(\angle CAO) = 30°$

and angle of depression at bottom $(\angle OAD) = 60°$

Since, AD is a transversal to the parallel lines AO and BD. Therefore, $\angle OAD$ and $\angle ADB$ are alternate angles and so are equal.
So, $\angle ADB = 60°$.

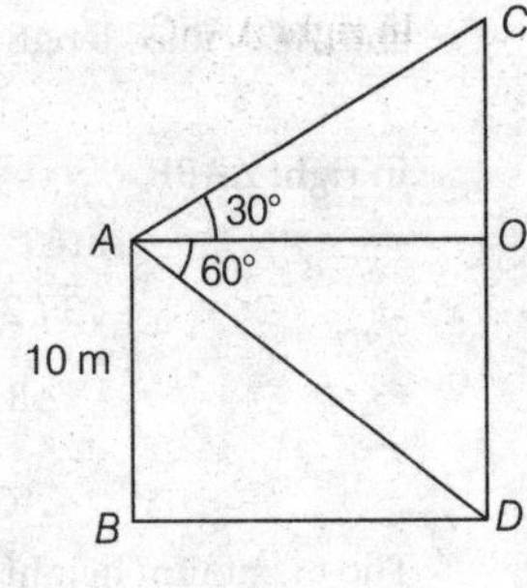

In right ΔABD,

$$\tan 60° = \frac{AB}{BD}$$

$$\Rightarrow \quad \sqrt{3} = \frac{10}{BD} \text{ or } BD = \frac{10}{\sqrt{3}} \text{ m}$$

So, width of street $= \frac{10}{\sqrt{3}}$ m.

In right ΔAOC,

$$\tan 30° = \frac{OC}{AO} \quad \left[\text{as } AO = BD = \frac{10}{\sqrt{3}} \text{ m}\right]$$

$$\Rightarrow \quad \frac{1}{\sqrt{3}} = \frac{OC}{\left(\frac{10}{\sqrt{3}}\right)} \Rightarrow \frac{1}{\sqrt{3}} = \frac{\sqrt{3}OC}{10}$$

$$\Rightarrow \quad OC = \frac{10}{3} = 3.33 \text{ m}$$

$$\Rightarrow \quad OC = 10/3 = 3.33 \text{ m}$$

Hence, height of second house $= CD = OD + OC$

$$= 10 + 3.33 = 13.33 \text{ m}$$

Q.3 A ladder on the truck of the fire brigade can be elevated to an angle of 60° maximum. The length of the ladder can be extended to 25 m. If the platform of the truck is 5 m above the ground, then find the maximum height that the ladder can attain above the ground. (take $\sqrt{3} = 1.73$)

Sol. With reference to the figure,

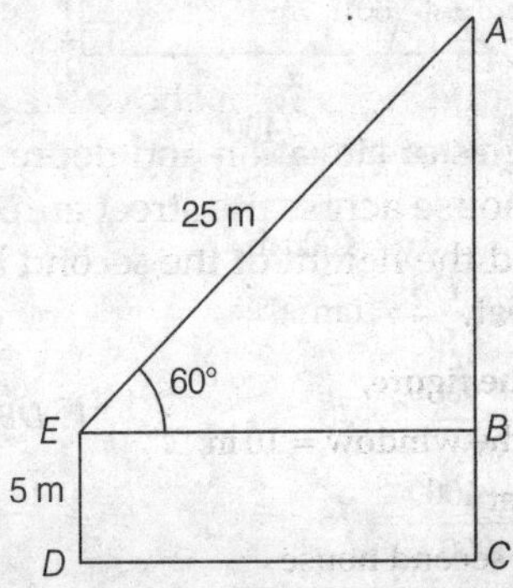

Let ED = height of the platform $= BC$,

AC = maximum height from the ground that ladder can reach $= AB + BC$

and AE = max. length of ladder = 25 m

$$\angle AEB = 60°$$

In right ΔABE,

$$\sin 60° = AB / AE = AB / 25$$

$$\Rightarrow \quad \sqrt{3}/2 = AB/25$$

$$\Rightarrow \quad AB = \frac{25\sqrt{3}}{2} = 21.625 \text{ m}$$

$$\therefore \quad AC = AB + BC = 21.625 + 5 = 26.625 \text{ m}$$

The maximum height that ladder can reach is 26.625 m.

Q.4 An aeroplane, when flying at a height of 4000 m from the ground passes vertically above another aeroplane at an instant when the angles of elevations of the two planes from the same point on the ground are 60° and 45°, respectively. Find the vertical distance between the aeroplanes at that instant.

Sol. Let y be the vertical distance between the aeroplanes and BA = 4000 m, $CB = x$ that distance from the ground.

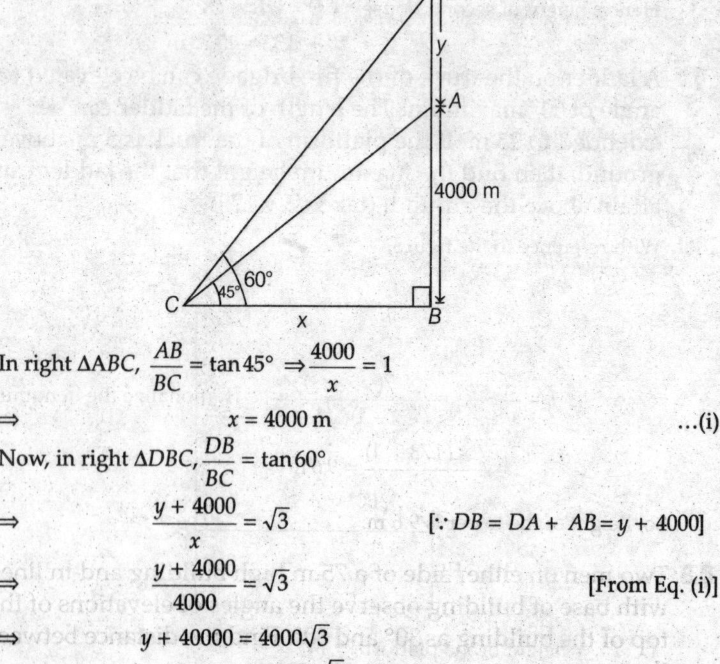

In right ΔABC, $\frac{AB}{BC} = \tan 45° \Rightarrow \frac{4000}{x} = 1$

$$\Rightarrow \quad x = 4000 \text{ m} \quad \text{...(i)}$$

Now, in right ΔDBC, $\frac{DB}{BC} = \tan 60°$

$$\Rightarrow \quad \frac{y + 4000}{x} = \sqrt{3} \quad [\because DB = DA + AB = y + 4000]$$

$$\Rightarrow \quad \frac{y + 4000}{4000} = \sqrt{3} \quad \text{[From Eq. (i)]}$$

$$\Rightarrow \quad y + 40000 = 4000\sqrt{3}$$

$$\Rightarrow \quad y = 4000(\sqrt{3} - 1)$$

$$y = 4000(1.73 - 1)$$

$\Rightarrow$ $$y = 4000 \times 0.73 \Rightarrow y = 2920 \text{ m}$$

So, vertical distance between the aeroplanes is 2920 m.

Q.5 A 7 m long flagtaff is fixed on the top of a tower standing on the horizontal plane. From a point on the ground, the angles of elevations of the top and bottom of the flagstaff are 60° and 45°, respectively. Find the height of the tower correct to one place of decimal.

Sol. Let AB be the tower of height h, DA be the flagstaff of height 7 m and $BC = x$.

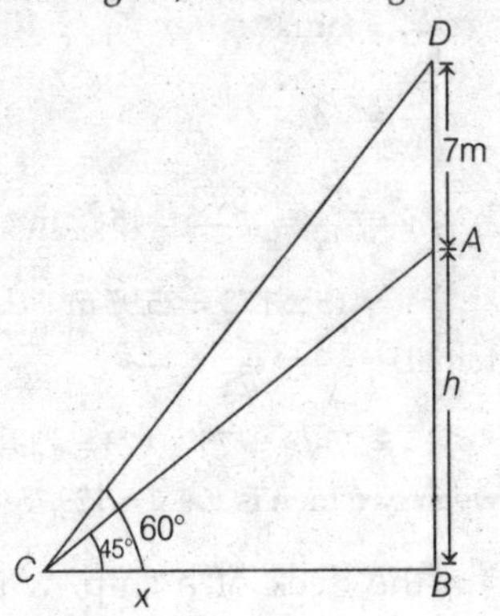

In right ΔABC, $\dfrac{AB}{BC} = \tan 45°$

$\Rightarrow$ $$\frac{h}{x} = 1 \Rightarrow h = x \quad \text{...(i)}$$

Now, in ΔDBC, $\dfrac{DB}{BC} = \tan 60° \Rightarrow \dfrac{h+7}{x} = \sqrt{3}$ $[\because DB = DA + AB = h + 7]$

$\Rightarrow$ $$h + 7 = \sqrt{3}h \quad [\because \text{Using Eq. (i)}]$$

$\Rightarrow$ $$(\sqrt{3} - 1)h = 7$$

$\Rightarrow$ $$h = \frac{7}{\sqrt{3} - 1} = \frac{7(\sqrt{3} + 1)}{(\sqrt{3} - 1)(\sqrt{3} + 1)} \quad \text{[Rationalize the denominator]}$$

$$= \frac{7 \times (1.73 + 1)}{2} = 9.6 \text{ m}$$

So, height of the tower is 9.6 m.

Q.6 Two men on either side of a 75 m high building and in line with base of building observe the angles of elevations of the top of the building as 30° and 60°. Find the distance between the two men.

Sol. Let C and D be the positions of two men and AB is the height of building

Let $CB = y$ and $BD = x$

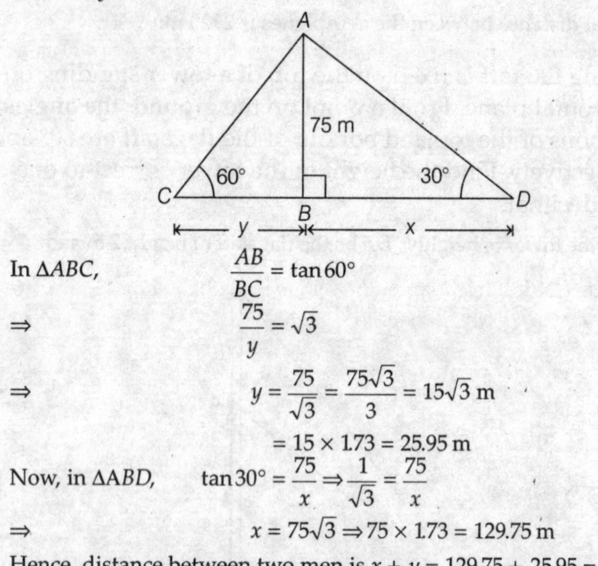

In ΔABC, $\frac{AB}{BC} = \tan 60°$

$\Rightarrow$ $\frac{75}{y} = \sqrt{3}$

$\Rightarrow$ $y = \frac{75}{\sqrt{3}} = \frac{75\sqrt{3}}{3} = 15\sqrt{3}$ m

$= 15 \times 1.73 = 25.95$ m

Now, in ΔABD, $\tan 30° = \frac{75}{x} \Rightarrow \frac{1}{\sqrt{3}} = \frac{75}{x}$

$\Rightarrow$ $x = 75\sqrt{3} \Rightarrow 75 \times 1.73 = 129.75$ m

Hence, distance between two men is $x + y = 129.75 + 25.95 = 155.7$ m

Q.7 A man standing on the deck of a ship, which is 10 m above water level, observes the angle of elevation of the top of a hill as 60° and the angle of depression of the base of hill as 30°. Find the distance of the hill from the ship and the height of the hill.

Sol. Let AB be the water level, DA be the height of ship = 10 m and BC be the hill of height h from water level and $\angle CDE = 60°$, $\angle BDE = 30°$

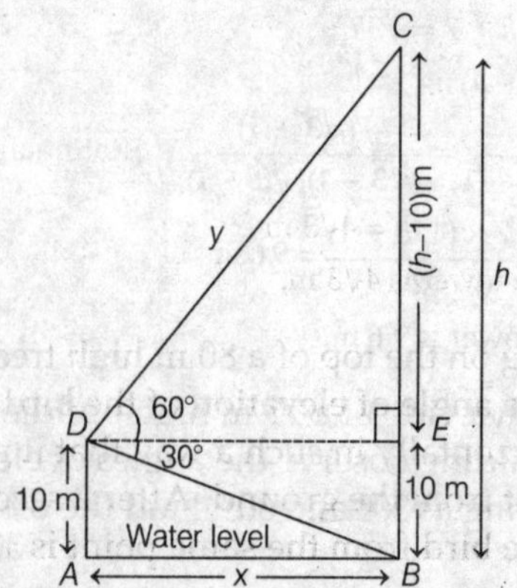

Let $AB = x$.

In right ΔDEB, $\frac{BE}{DE} = \tan 30° \Rightarrow \frac{10}{x} = \frac{1}{\sqrt{3}}$ [$\because DA = EB$]

$\Rightarrow$ $x = 10\sqrt{3}$ m ...(i)

Now, in right ΔCED, $\frac{CE}{ED} = \tan 60°$, $\frac{h-10}{x} = \sqrt{3}$

$\Rightarrow$ $\frac{h-10}{10\sqrt{3}} = \sqrt{3}$ [$\because CE = CB - EB = h - 10$]

$\Rightarrow$ $h - 10 = 30$

$\Rightarrow$ $h = 40$ m

So, distance of hill from ship = $10\sqrt{3}$ m and the height of the hill = 40 m.

Q.8 The angles of elevations of the top of a tower from two points at distances of 4 m and 9 m from the base of the tower and in the same straight line with it are 60° and 30°, respectively. Find the height of the tower.

Sol. Let AB be the tower of height h.

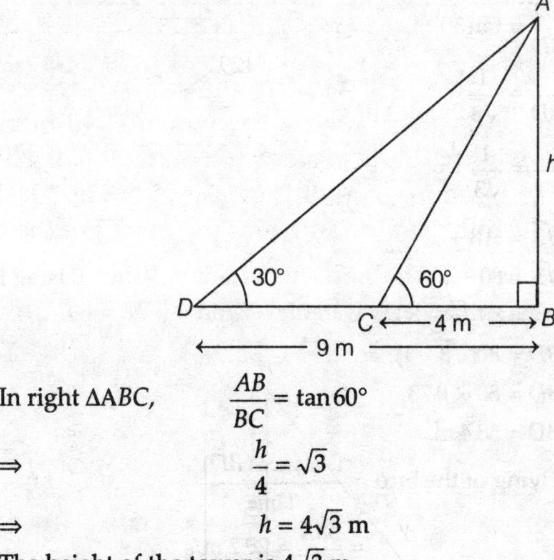

In right ΔABC, $\frac{AB}{BC} = \tan 60°$

$\Rightarrow$ $\frac{h}{4} = \sqrt{3}$

$\Rightarrow$ $h = 4\sqrt{3}$ m

The height of the tower is $4\sqrt{3}$ m.

Q.9 A bird is sitting on the top of a 80 m high tree. From a point on the ground, the angle of elevation of the bird is 45°. The bird flies away horizontally in such a way that it remained at a constant height from the ground. After 2 seconds, the angle of elevation of the bird from the same point is 30°. Find the speed of flying bird.

Sol. Let BC be the 80 m high tree.

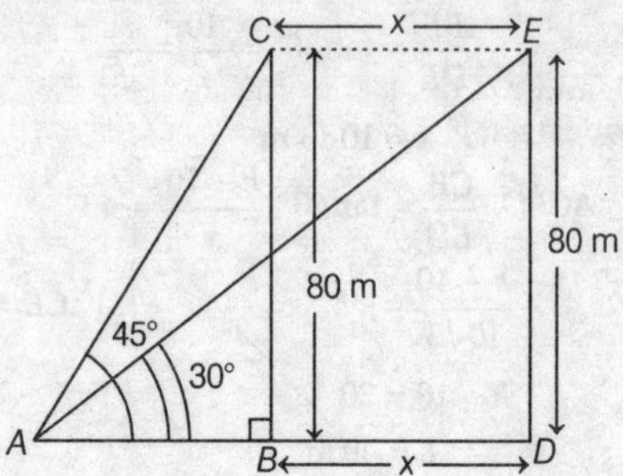

After 2 seconds, position of the bird is C.

Let $CE = x$

In right ΔCBA, $\frac{BC}{AB} = \tan 45°$

$\Rightarrow \quad \frac{80}{AB} = 1$

$\Rightarrow \quad AB = 80$ ...(i)

In right ΔEDA, $\frac{ED}{AD} = \tan 30°$

$\Rightarrow \quad \frac{80}{AB + BD} = \frac{1}{\sqrt{3}}$

$\Rightarrow \quad \frac{80}{AB + x} = \frac{1}{\sqrt{3}}$

$\Rightarrow \quad 80\sqrt{3} = AB + x$

$\Rightarrow \quad 80\sqrt{3} = 80 + x$ [Using Eq. (i)]

$\Rightarrow \quad x = 80\sqrt{3} - 80$

$\Rightarrow \quad BD = 80(\sqrt{3} - 1)$

$\Rightarrow \quad BD = 80 \times 0.73$

$\Rightarrow \quad BD = 58.4 \text{ m}$

So, the speed of flying of the bird $= \frac{\text{Distance } (BD)}{\text{Time}}$

$= \frac{58.4}{2} = 29.2 \text{ m/s}$

The speed of flying bird is 29.2 m/s.

Q.10 A vertical pedestal stands on the ground and is surmounted by a vertical flagstaff of height 5 m. At a point on the ground, the angles of elevations of the bottom and the top of the flagstaff are 30° and 60°, respectively. Find the height of the pedestal.

Sol. Let BC be the height of the pedestal and $CD = 5$ m be the height of the flagstaff.

Let $\angle DAB = 60°$ and $\angle CAB = 30°$ be the angles of elevations of the top and the bottom of the flagstaff, respectively.

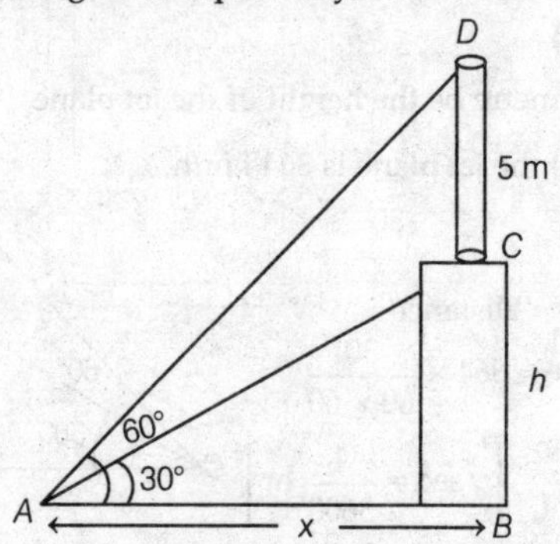

Let $BC = h$ metre

and $AB = x$ metre

In right angled ΔABC,

$$\tan 30° = \frac{BC}{AB} = \frac{h}{x}$$

$$\Rightarrow \quad \frac{1}{\sqrt{3}} = \frac{h}{x}$$

$$\Rightarrow \quad \frac{x}{\sqrt{3}} = h \quad \Rightarrow \quad x = \sqrt{3}h \quad \text{...(i)}$$

In right angled ΔABD,

$$\tan 60° = \frac{BD}{AB} = \frac{BC + CD}{AB}$$

$$\Rightarrow \quad \sqrt{3} = \frac{h + 5}{x}$$

$$\Rightarrow \quad \sqrt{3}x = h + 5 \quad \text{...(ii)}$$

On substituting the value of x from Eq. (i), in Eq. (ii) we get

$$\Rightarrow \quad \sqrt{3}(\sqrt{3}h) = h + 5$$

$$\Rightarrow \quad 3h - h = 5$$

$$\Rightarrow \quad 2h = 5$$

$$\Rightarrow \quad h = \frac{5}{2}$$

The height of the pedestal is $\frac{5}{2}$ m or 2.5 m.

Q.11 The angle of elevation of a jet plane from a point A on the ground is 60°. After a flight of 30 s, the angle of elevation changes to 30°. If the jet plane is flying at a speed of 864 km/h, then find the height at which the jet plane is flying. (use $\sqrt{3} = 1.732$)

Sol. Let $AB = DE = x$ metre be the height of the jet plane.

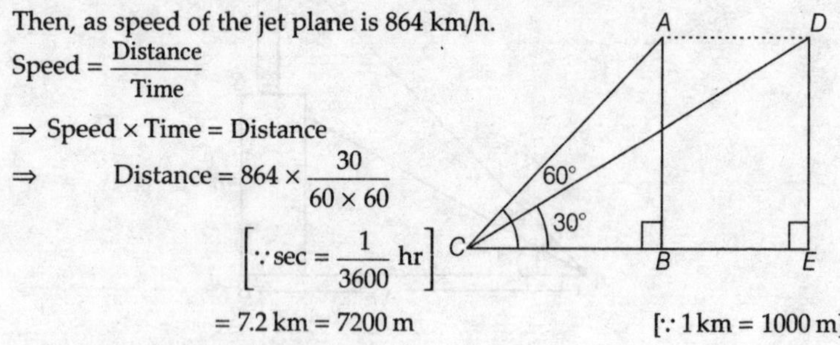

Then, as speed of the jet plane is 864 km/h.

$$\text{Speed} = \frac{\text{Distance}}{\text{Time}}$$

$\Rightarrow$ Speed × Time = Distance

$$\Rightarrow \quad \text{Distance} = 864 \times \frac{30}{60 \times 60} \qquad \left[\because \text{sec} = \frac{1}{3600}\text{ hr}\right]$$

$$= 7.2 \text{ km} = 7200 \text{ m} \qquad [\because 1 \text{ km} = 1000 \text{ m}]$$

Hence, $AD = BE = 7.2$ km = 7200 m

Now, In right angled ΔABC,

$$\tan 60° = \frac{AB}{BC}$$

$$\Rightarrow \quad \sqrt{3} = \frac{x}{BC}$$

$$\Rightarrow \quad x = \sqrt{3}BC \qquad \ldots(i)$$

Now, in right angled ΔDEC,

$$\tan 30° = \frac{DE}{CE} = \frac{DE}{BC + BE} \qquad [\because BE = 72000 \text{ m}]$$

$$\Rightarrow \quad \frac{1}{\sqrt{3}} = \frac{x}{BC + 7200}$$

$$BC + 7200 = \sqrt{3}x \qquad \ldots(ii)$$

From Eq. (i) substituting $BC = \frac{x}{\sqrt{3}}$, in Eq. (ii), we get

$$\text{So,} \quad \frac{x}{\sqrt{3}} + 7200 = \sqrt{3}x$$

$$\Rightarrow \quad \sqrt{3}x - \frac{x}{\sqrt{3}} = 7200$$

$$\Rightarrow \quad x\left(\sqrt{3} - \frac{1}{\sqrt{3}}\right) = 7200 \Rightarrow x\left(\frac{3-1}{\sqrt{3}}\right) = 7200$$

$$\Rightarrow \quad x = \frac{7200\sqrt{3}}{2}$$

$$\Rightarrow \quad x = 3600\sqrt{3} = 3600 \times 1.732 = 6235.2 \text{ m}$$

Hence, the height of the jet plane is 6235.2 m.

Q.12 The angle of elevation of a stationary cloud from a point 200 metre above the lake is 30° and the angle of depression of its reflection in the lake is found to be 60°. Find the height of the cloud.

Sol. Let A be the position of the cloud, B be the point 200 metre above the lake and F be the reflection of A in the lake.

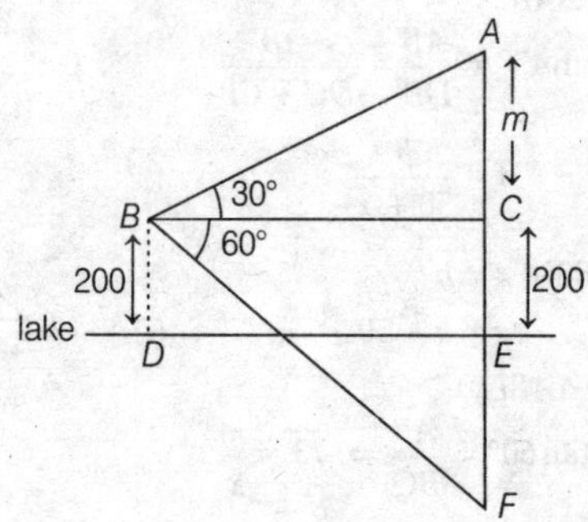

Let $AC = m$

Now, $AE = EF$

$$\Rightarrow \qquad EF = (200 + m)$$

Now, from ΔABC, we get,

$$\cot 30° = \frac{BC}{AC} = \frac{BC}{m} \qquad [\because AE = AC + CE \Rightarrow m + 200]$$

$$BC = m\cot 30° \qquad \text{...(i)}$$

In right ΔCFB,

$$CF = 200 + (200 + m) \qquad [\because CF = CE + EF]$$

$$= (400 + m) \text{ metre}$$

Now, $$\cot 60° = \frac{BC}{CF} = \frac{BC}{400 + m}$$

So, $$BC = (400 + m)\cot 60° \qquad \text{...(ii)}$$

From Eqs. (i) and (ii), we get

$$(400 + m)\cot 60° = m\cot 30°$$

$$\Rightarrow (400 + m) \times 1/\sqrt{3} = m\sqrt{3} \qquad \left[\because \cot 60° = \frac{1}{\sqrt{3}}, \cot 30° = \sqrt{3}\right]$$

$$\Rightarrow \qquad 400 + m = 3m$$

$$\Rightarrow \qquad 2m = 400$$

$$\Rightarrow \qquad m = 200$$

Hence, height of the cloud from the take is AE

$$= AE = 200 + m = 200 + 200 = 400 \text{ metres}$$

Q.13 If the sun ray's inclination increases from 45° to 60°, then the length of the shadow of a tower decreases by 50 m. Find the height of the tower (in m).

Sol. Let AB be the height of the tower. Let $\angle ADB = 45°$ and $\angle ACB = 60°$ be the two angles of elevations of the sun. Let $BC = x$ m.

In right angled ΔABD,

$$\tan 45° = \frac{AB}{DB} = \frac{AB}{DC + CB}$$

$$1 = \frac{h}{50 + x}$$

$$\Rightarrow \quad 50 + x = h$$

$$\Rightarrow \quad x = h - 50 \quad \ldots(i)$$

In right angled ΔABD,

$$\tan 60° = \frac{AB}{BC} \Rightarrow \sqrt{3} = \frac{h}{x}$$

$$\Rightarrow \quad \sqrt{3}x = h \quad \ldots(ii)$$

On substituting the value of x from Eq. (i), in Eq. (ii), we get

$$\sqrt{3}(h - 50) = h$$

$$\sqrt{3}h - h = 50$$

$$h = \frac{50}{\sqrt{3} - 1} \text{ m}$$

Hence, the height of the tower is $\frac{50}{\sqrt{3} - 1}$ m

Q.14 The angle of elevation of a plane from a point A on ground is 60°. After a flight of 15 s, the angle of elevation changes to 30°. If plane is flying at a constant height of $3600\sqrt{3}$ m, then find the speed of the plane in km/hr.

Sol. Let A be the position of plane from the ground and after 15 s it changes to B. Let $\angle AEC = 30°$ and $\angle BEC = 60°$ be the two angles of elevations of the plane.

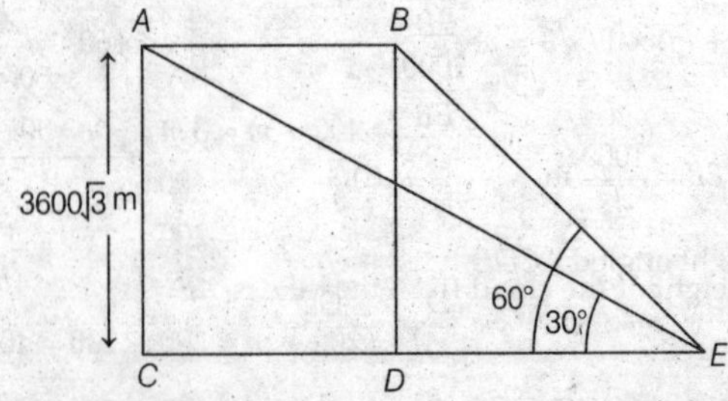

In ΔACE,

$$\cot 30° = \frac{CE}{AC} = \frac{CE}{3600\sqrt{3}}$$

$$\sqrt{3} = \frac{CE}{3600\sqrt{3}}$$

$$CE = 10800 \text{ m}$$

In ΔBED,

$$\cot 60° = \frac{DE}{BD}$$

$$\frac{1}{\sqrt{3}} = \frac{DE}{3600\sqrt{3}}$$

$$DE = \frac{3600\sqrt{3}}{\sqrt{3}}$$

$$DE = 3600 \text{ m}$$

$$CD + DE = CE$$

$$CD + 3600 = 10800$$

$$CD = 10800 - 3600 = 7200 \text{ m}$$

Distance travelled = 7200 m = CD.

Time taken = 15 s

$\because$ $$S = \frac{D}{T} = \frac{7200}{15}$$

$$S = 480 \text{ m/s}$$

$$= 480 \times \frac{18}{5} \text{ km/w} = 1728 \text{ km/hr} \qquad \left[1 \text{ m/s} = \frac{18}{5} \text{ km/hr}\right]$$

Hence, the required speed of plane is 1728 km/hr.

Q.15 An aeroplane flying horizontally 1 km above the ground is observed at an angle of 60°. After 10 s, its elevation is 30°. Find the speed of the aeroplane in km/hr.

Sol. Let E be the position on the ground and $AB = CD = 1 \text{ km} = 1000$ m be the height of the aeroplane.

Then, in right angled ΔABE,

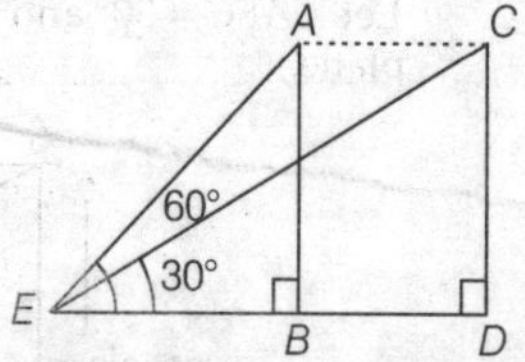

$$\tan 60° = \frac{1000}{EB}$$

$$\Rightarrow \quad \sqrt{3} = \frac{1000}{EB}$$

$$\Rightarrow \quad EB = \frac{1000}{\sqrt{3}} \text{ m} \qquad \text{...(i)}$$

Now, in right angled ΔCDE,

$$\tan 30° = \frac{CD}{ED} = \frac{CD}{EB + BD}$$

$$\Rightarrow \quad \frac{1}{\sqrt{3}} = \frac{1000}{\frac{1000}{\sqrt{3}} + BD} \qquad \text{[From Eq. (i)]}$$

$$\Rightarrow \quad \frac{1000}{\sqrt{3}} + BD = 1000\sqrt{3}$$

$$\Rightarrow \quad BD = 1000\sqrt{3} - \frac{1000}{\sqrt{3}}$$

$$\Rightarrow \quad BD = \frac{2000\sqrt{3}}{3}\text{ m}$$

Now, time taken to travel the distance BD is 10 s

$$\text{Now, speed} = \frac{\text{Distance}}{\text{Time}}$$

$$= \frac{\frac{2000\sqrt{3}}{3}}{10}$$

$$= \frac{2000\sqrt{3}}{30} = \frac{200\sqrt{3}}{3}\text{ m/s}$$

Now, $\text{Speed} = 200\frac{\sqrt{3}}{3} \times \frac{18}{5}$ km/hr.

$$= 240\sqrt{3}\text{ km/hr.} \qquad \left[1\text{ m/s} = \frac{18}{5}\text{ km/hr}\right]$$

Hence, the speed of aeroplane is $240\sqrt{3}$ km/hr.

Circles

CHAPTER 10

Important Points

01 **Circle** A circle is a collection of all points in a plane at a constant distance from a fixed point.

Or

A circle is the locus of a point that moves in a plane in such a way that its distance from a given point in the plane is always constant.

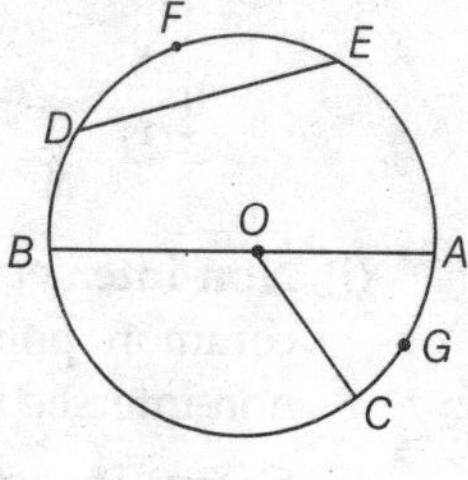

The fixed point O is the centre of the circle.

02 **Radius** The distance of any point on the circle to the centre is the radius of the circle. In the figure, OC, OA and OB are the radius.

03 **Diameter** The line joining the two points of the circle passing through the centre is the diameter of the circle. Its length is twice the radius. In the figure, AB is the diameter.

04 **Chord** A line segment joining any two points on a circle is called a chord of the circle. The maximum length of the chord is equal to the length of the diameter. In the figure, DE is a chord.

05 **Circumference** The length of the boundary of the circle is a called the circumference of the circle. It is given by the formula $C = 2\pi r$.

06 **Arc** A part of a circle joining two points on the boundary of the circle. In the figure, the curve AGC is an arc.

07 Sector An area made by an arc and the two radii of the circle is called a sector of the circle. In the figure, the area covered by *AOCG* is a sector of the circle.

08 Segment An area made by the chord and an arc (which are made by the same two points) is known as a segment. In the figure, the area covered by *DEF* is a segment.

09 Concentric Circles Circles having the same centre but different radii are said to be concentric circles.

10 Relation Between a Circle and a Line in a Plane There can be three possibilities as shown below

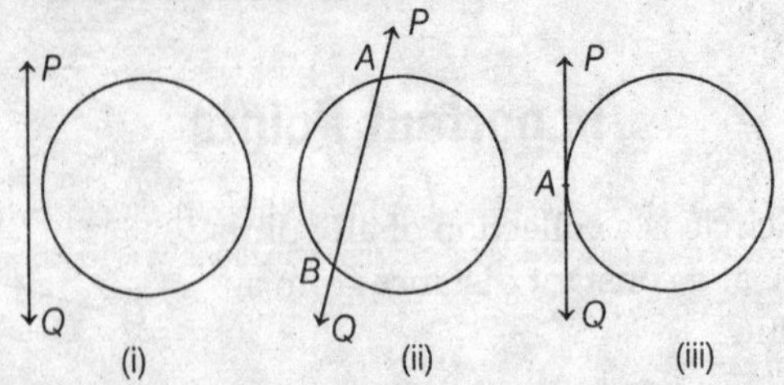

(i) **Non-intersecting** In figure (i), the line and the circle have no common point. In this case, the line *PQ* is said to be a non-intersecting line with respect to the circle.

(ii) **Secant** In figure (ii), the line and the circle intersect at two points.
In this case, the line *PQ* is said to be a secant of the circle.

(iii) **Tangent** In figure (iii), the line and the circle have only one common point. In this case, the line *PQ* is said to be a tangent of the circle.

11 Tangent to a Circle

(i) There is only one tangent at a point of the circle.

(ii) The tangent to a circle is a special case of the secant when two endpoints of its corresponding chord coincide.

(iii) The common point of the tangent and the circle is called the point of contact and the tangent is said to touch the circle at this point.

(iv) The line containing the radius through the point of contact is sometimes called the 'normal to the circle at that point.

12 Number of Tangents from a Point on a Circle.

(i) There is no tangent to a circle passing through a point lying inside the circle.

(ii) There is only one tangent at one point of contact.

(iii) There are exactly two tangents to a circle through a point that is outside of the circle.

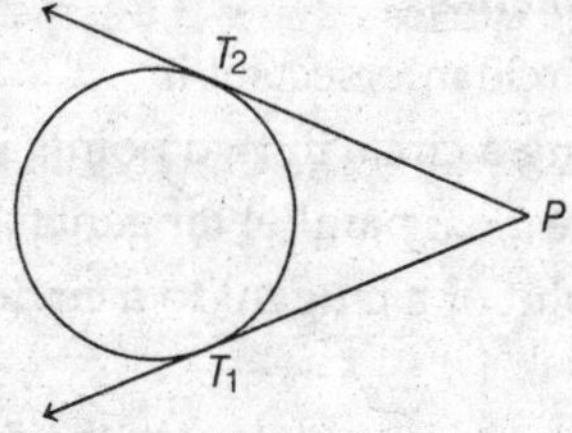

Note The length of the segment of the tangent from the external point P and the point of contact with the circle is called the length of the tangent from the point P to the circle.

13 Theorems.

(i) The tagnent at any point of a circle is perpendicular to the radius through the point of contact.

(ii) The lengths of tangents drawn from an external point to a circle are equal.

Note The centre lies on the bisector of the angle between the two tangents.

(iii) The perpendicular from the centre of a circle to a chord bisects the chord and *vice-versa*.

(iv) Sum of angles of a quadrilateral is 360°.

Exercise 10.1

Question 1 How many tangents can a circle have?

Sol. For every point of a circle, we can draw a tangent. Therefore, infinite number of tangents can be drawn.

Question 2 Fill in the blanks.

(i) A tangent to a circle intersects it in .... point(s).

(ii) A line intersecting a circle in two points is called a ....

(iii) A circle can have .... parallel tangents at the most.

(iv) The common point of a tangent to a circle and the circle is called ....

Sol. (i) One. A tangent line touches or intersects the circle only at one point.

(ii) Secant. Any line intersecting the circle at two points is called a secant.

(iii) Two. Maximum a circle can have two parallel tangents which can be drawn to the opposite side of the centre.

(iv) Point of contact.

Question 3 A tangent PQ at a point P of a circle of radius 5 cm meets a line through the centre O at a point Q, so that $OQ = 12$ cm. Length PQ is

(a) 12 cm (b) 13 cm (c) 8.5 cm (d) $\sqrt{119}$ cm

Sol. (d) Here, PQ is a tangent, which touches a point P of the circle and $OP = 5$ cm is a radius of circle. Join $OQ = 12$ cm. Since, radius of circle OP is perpendicular to the tangent PQ.

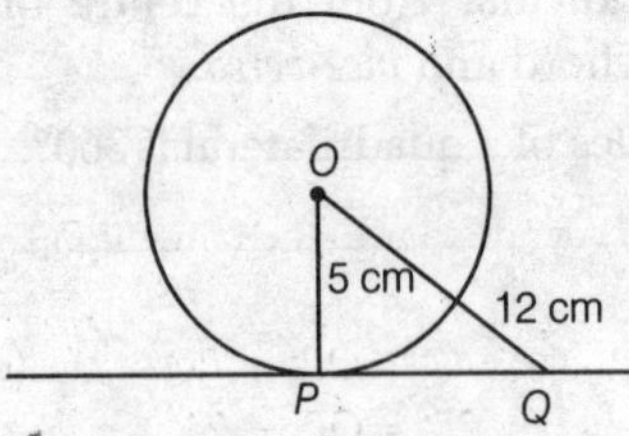

$\therefore$ In right $\Delta\, OPQ$, by Pythagoras theorem

$$OQ^2 = OP^2 + PQ^2$$

$$\Rightarrow \quad (12)^2 = (5)^2 + PQ^2$$

$$\Rightarrow \quad PQ^2 = 144 - 25 = 119$$

$$\Rightarrow \quad PQ = \sqrt{119} \text{ cm}$$

Question 4 Draw a circle and two lines parallel to a given line such that one is a tangent and the other, a secant to the circle.

Sol. Firstly draw a circle with centre O and draw a line l. Now, we draw a two parallel lines to l, such that one line m is tangent to the circle and another n is secant to the circle.

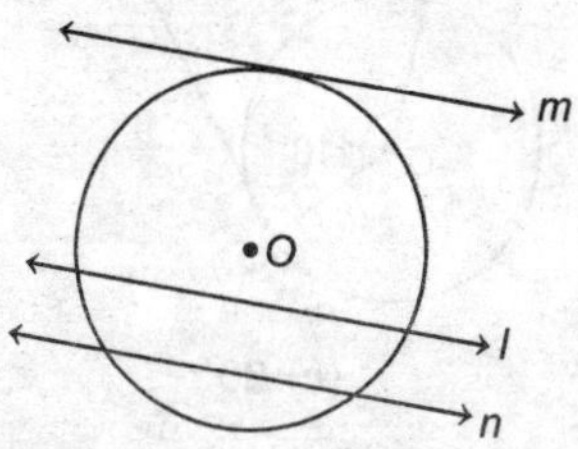

Exercise 10.2

Question 1 From a point Q, the length of the tangent to a circle is 24 cm and the distance of Q from the centre is 25 cm. The radius of the circle is

(a) 7 cm (b) 12 cm
(c) 15 cm (d) 24.5 cm

Sol. (a) Given that, the length of the tangent $QP = 24$ cm and $QO = 25$ cm.
Join OP.

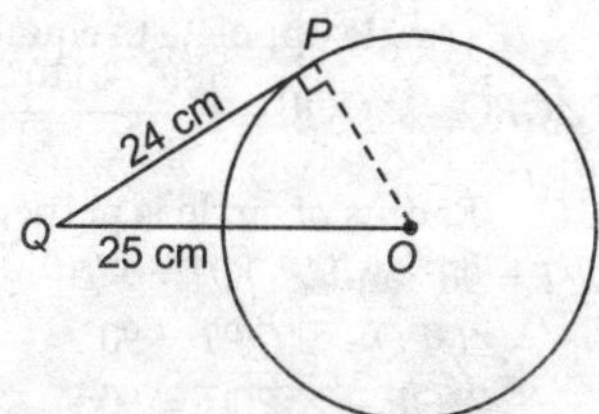

We know, radius OP is perpendicular to the tangent PQ.
In right ΔOPQ,

$$OQ^2 = OP^2 + PQ^2 \quad \text{(by Pythagoras theorem)}$$

$$\Rightarrow \quad 25^2 = OP^2 + 24^2$$

$$\Rightarrow \quad OP^2 = 625 - 576 = 49$$

$$\Rightarrow \quad OP = 7 \text{ cm}$$

Mistake Alert As length cannot be negative, so answer is never -7 cm.

Question 2 In figure, if TP and TQ are the two tangents to a circle with centre O, so that $\angle POQ = 110°$, then $\angle PTQ$ is equal to

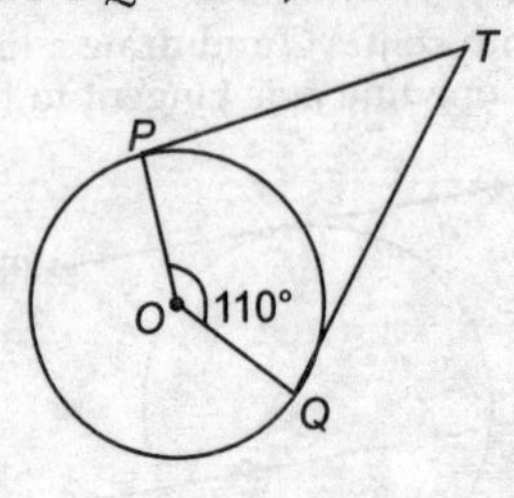

(a) 60° (b) 70° (c) 80° (d) 90°

Sol. (b) Join PQ,

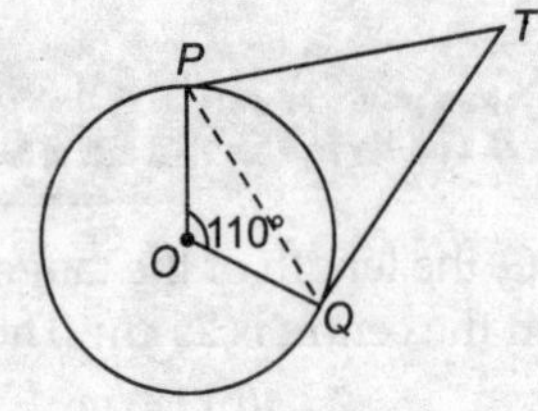

In ΔOPQ, we have

$$OP = OQ = \text{radius of circle}$$

$\therefore$ $\angle OPQ = \angle OQP$

(Angle opposite to equal sides are also equal)

$\Rightarrow$ $\angle OPQ = \angle OQP = \dfrac{180° - 110°}{2} = 35°$

Since, $OP \perp PT$ and $OQ \perp TQ$ (Radius of circle is perpendicular to the tangent)

$\therefore$ $\angle OPT = 90°$ and $\angle OQT = 90°$

$\Rightarrow$ $\angle OPQ + \angle QPT = 90°$

and $\angle OQP + \angle PQT = 90°$

$\Rightarrow$ $35° + \angle QPT = 90°$

and $35° + \angle PQT = 90°$

$\Rightarrow \angle QPT = 55°$ and $\angle PQT = 55°$

In ΔPTQ, we have

$\angle QPT + \angle PQT + \angle PTQ = 180°$ [$\because$ angle sum property of a triangle]

$\Rightarrow$ $55° + 55° + \angle PTQ = 180°$

$\Rightarrow$ $\angle PTQ = 180° - (55° + 55°) = 70°$

Question 3 If tangents PA and PB from a point P to a circle with centre O are inclined to each other at angle of 80°, then $\angle POA$ is equal to

(a) 50° (b) 60° (c) 70° (d) 80°

Sol. (a) As O is the centre of the circle and PA and PB are the two tangents from the point P.

$\therefore$ $$OA \perp PA \text{ and } OB \perp PB$$

i.e. $$\angle PAO = \angle PBO = 90°$$

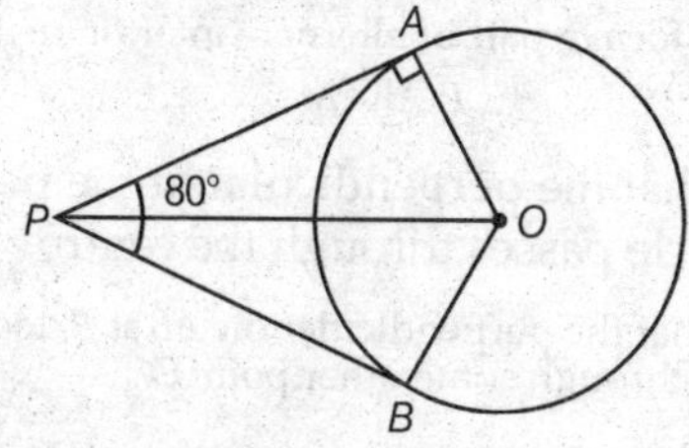

Consider the quadrilateral $PAOB$, then

$$\angle PAO + \angle AOB + \angle PBO + \angle BPA = 360°$$

(sum of angles of a quadrilateral is 360°)

$\Rightarrow$ $$90° + \angle AOB + 90° + \angle BPA = 360°$$

$\Rightarrow$ $$180° + \angle AOB + 80° = 360°$$

$\Rightarrow$ $$260° + \angle AOB = 360°$$

$\Rightarrow$ $$\angle AOB = 360° - 260° = 100° \quad \text{...(i)}$$

Now In right ΔPBO and right ΔPAO,
we have,

$$OP = OP \quad \text{(common side)}$$

$$OB = OA \quad \text{(radii of the same circle)}$$

$$PB = PA$$

[the lengths of tangents drawn from an external point to a circle are equal]

$\therefore$ By SSS congruency, $\Delta PBO \cong \Delta PAO$

$\Rightarrow$ $$\angle BOP = \angle AOP \quad \text{(CPCT)}$$

From Eq. (i), $$\angle AOB = 100°$$

$\Rightarrow$ $$2\angle POA = 100°$$

$\Rightarrow$ $$\angle POA = \frac{100}{2} = 50°$$

Question 4 Prove that the tangents drawn at the ends of a diameter of a circle are parallel.

Sol. Let AB be a diameter of a given circle and let PQ and LM be the tangent lines drawn to the circle at points A and B, respectively. Since, the tangent at a point to a circle is perpendicular to the radius through the point.

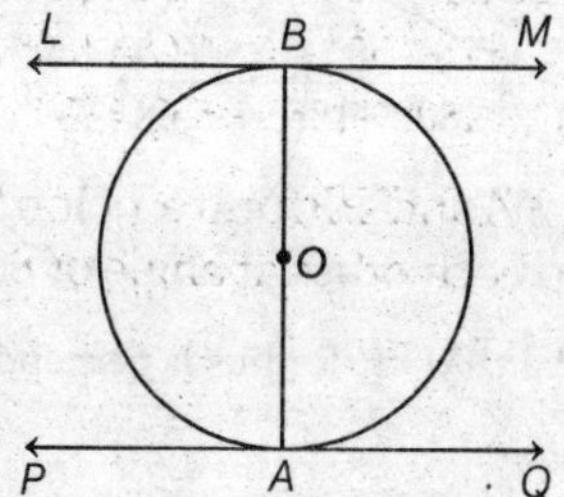

$\therefore AB \perp PQ$ and $AB \perp LM$

$\Rightarrow$ $$\angle PAB = 90^\circ$$

and $$\angle ABM = 90^\circ$$

$\Rightarrow$ $$\angle PAB = \angle ABM$$

But $\angle PAB$ and $\angle ABM$ form a pair of alternate interior angles

$\therefore$ $$PQ \parallel LM$$ **Hence proved.**

Question 5 Prove that the perpendicular at the point of contact to the tangent to a circle passes through the centre.

Sol. Let us suppose that the perpendicular on AB at P does not pass through the centre O and it passes through some other point O'.

Then, as $O'P \perp AB$

$\Rightarrow$ $$\angle O'PB = 90^\circ \quad \text{...(i)}$$

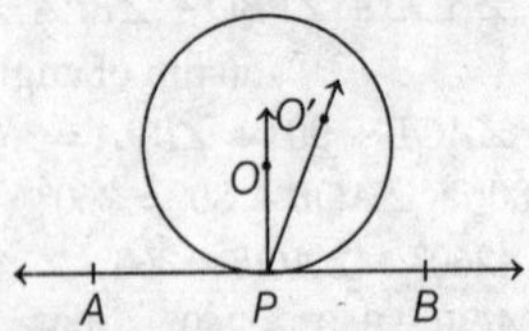

But the line joining the centre, of the circle to the point of contact of the tangent is perpendicular to the tangent.

Then, $$OP \perp AB,$$

$\Rightarrow$ $$\angle OPB = 90^\circ \quad \text{...(ii)}$$

So, from Eqs. (i) and (ii),

$$\angle O'PB = \angle OPB$$

But there cannot be two different right angles on the same side of the initial side.

$\Rightarrow \angle O'PB = \angle OPB$ is not possible unless both the angles coincide.

i.e., The line OP and $O'P$ coincide.

$\therefore$ The perpendicular to AB through P passes through centre O.

Question 6 The length of a tangent from a point A at distance 5 cm from the centre of the circle is 4 cm. Find the radius of the circle.

Sol. Given, $OA = 5\text{cm}$ and $AM = 4\text{cm}$

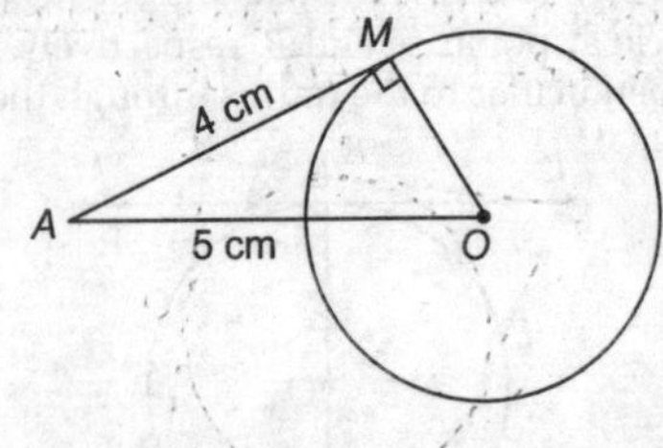

$\because$ $OM \perp AM$ ($\because$ Radius is perpendicular to the tangent AM)

In right ΔOMA, we have

$$OA^2 = OM^2 + MA^2 \quad \text{(By Pythagoras theorem)}$$

$\Rightarrow$ $$5^2 = OM^2 + 4^2$$

$\Rightarrow$ $$OM^2 = 25 - 16 = 9 \Rightarrow OM = 3 \text{ cm}$$

Hence, the radius of the circle is 3 cm.

Question 7 Two concentric circles are of radii 5 cm and 3 cm. Find the length of the chord of the larger circle which touches the smaller circle.

Sol. Here, we draw two cocentric circles C_1 and C_2 of radii $r_1 = 3$ cm and $r_2 = 5$ cm.

Now, we draw a chord AB such that it touches the circle C_1 at point D.

The centre of concentric circles is O. Since, the chord touches the circle C_1, it is tangent to the circle.

Since, OD is the radius of circle C.

$\therefore$ $OD \perp AB$ [$\because$ Radius is perpendicular to the tangent AB]

Also, radius perpendicular to a chord bisects the chord.

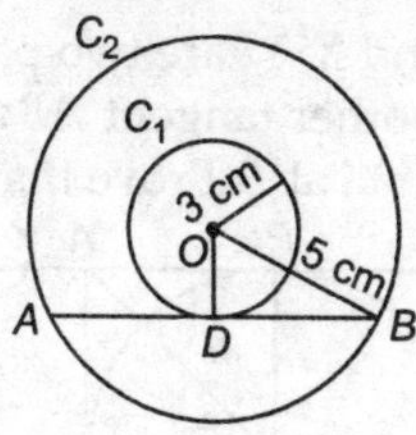

e., $AD = BD$

n right ΔOBD, we have

$$OB^2 = OD^2 + DB^2 \quad \text{(By Pythagoras theorem)}$$

$\Rightarrow$ $$5^2 = 3^2 + DB^2$$

$\Rightarrow$ $$DB^2 = 25 - 9 = 16$$

$\Rightarrow$ $$DB = 4 \text{ cm}$$

Length of chord $= AB = 2\,AD = 2 \times 4 = 8$ cm

Mistake Alert "Be careful!" cocentric circles shares the same centre but have different radii.

Question 8 A quadrilateral $ABCD$ is drawn to circumscribe a circle see figure). Prove that $AB + CD = AD + BC$.

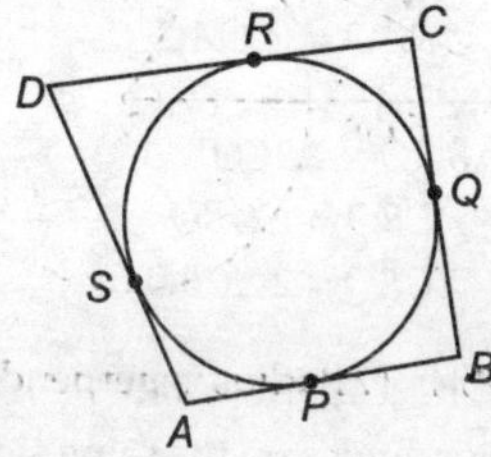

Sol. Using theorem, the lengths of tangents drawn from an external point to a circle are equal.

Since, A is an external point, then

$$AP = AS \quad \ldots(i)$$

Since, B is an external point, then

$$BP = BQ \quad \ldots(ii)$$

Since, C is an external point, then

$$RC = CQ \quad \ldots(iii)$$

Since, D is an external point, then

$$RD = SD \quad \ldots(iv)$$

On adding Eqs. (i), (ii), (iii) and (iv), we get

$$(AP + BP) + (RC + RD) = AS + BQ + CQ + SD$$

$$\Rightarrow \quad AB + CD = (AS + SD) + (BQ + CQ)$$

$$[\because AP + BP = AB \text{ and } RC + RD = CD]$$

$$\Rightarrow \quad AB + CD = AD + BC$$

$[\because AS + SD = AD$ and $BQ + CQ = BC]$ **Hence proved.**

Question 9 In figure, XY and $X'Y'$ are two parallel tangents to a circle with centre O and another tangent AB with point of contact C intersecting XY at A and $X'Y'$ at B. Prove that $\angle AOB = 90°$.

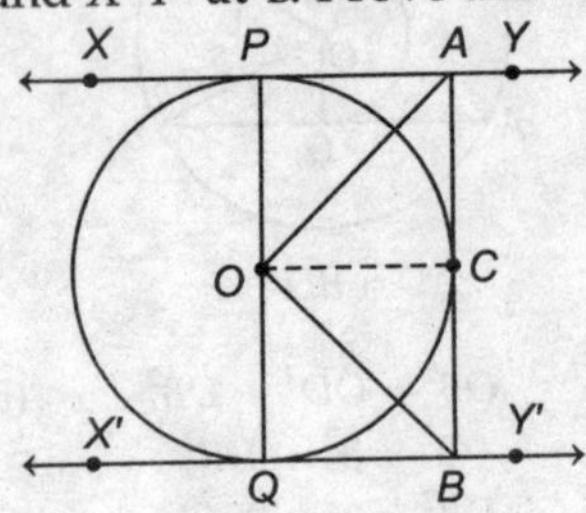

Sol. Since, tangents drawn from an external point to a circle are equal.

$$\therefore \quad AP = AC$$

Thus, in ΔAPO and ΔACO, we have

$$AP = AC$$

$$AO = AO \quad \text{(Common)}$$

$$OP = OC \quad \text{(Radius of circle)}$$

$\therefore$ By SSS criterion of congruence, we have

$$\Delta APO \cong \Delta ACO$$

$$\Rightarrow \quad \angle PAO = \angle OAC$$

$$\Rightarrow \quad \angle PAC = 2\angle CAO$$

Similarly, we can prove that $\Delta BQO \cong \Delta BCO$

$$\angle CBO = \angle OBQ$$

$$\Rightarrow \quad \angle CBQ = 2\angle CBO$$

Since, $XY \parallel X'Y'$

$$\therefore \quad \angle PAC + \angle QBC = 180°$$

(Sum of interior angles on the same side of transversal is 180°)

$$\therefore \quad 2\angle CAO + 2\angle CBO = 180° \quad \ldots(i)$$

$$\Rightarrow \quad \angle CAO + \angle CBO = 90°$$

In Δ *AOB*, we have

$$\Rightarrow \quad \angle CAO + \angle CBO + \angle AOB = 180°$$

$$\Rightarrow \quad \angle CAO + \angle CBO = 180° - \angle AOB \quad \ldots(ii)$$

$\therefore$ From Eqs. (i) and (ii), we get

$$180° - \angle AOB = 90°$$

$$\Rightarrow \quad \angle AOB = 90°$$

Question 10 Prove that the angle between the two tangents drawn from an external point to a circle is supplementary to the angle subtended by the line-segment joining the points of contact at the centre.

Sol. Let *PQ* and *PR* be two tangents drawn from an external point *P* to a circle with centre *O*.

In right ΔOQP and ΔORP, we have

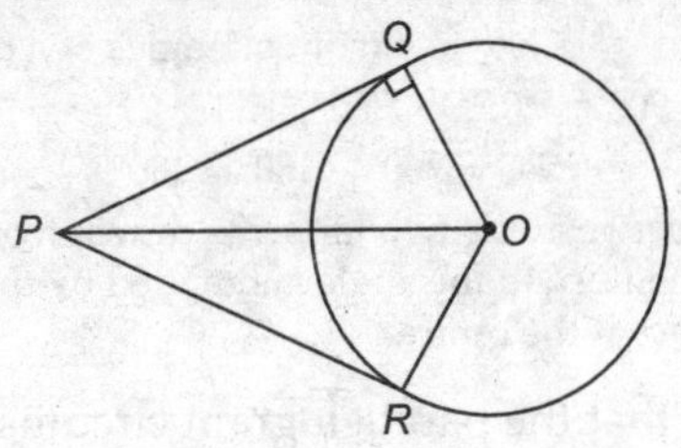

$PQ = PR$ (Tangents drawn from an external point are equal)

$OQ = OR$ (Radius of circle)

$OP = OP$ (Common)

Therefore, by SSS criterion of congruence,

$$\Delta OQP \cong \Delta ORP$$

$$\Rightarrow \quad \angle QPO = \angle RPO$$

$$\text{and} \quad \angle POQ = \angle POR$$

$$\therefore \quad \angle QPR = 2\angle OPQ$$

$$\text{and} \quad \angle QOR = 2\angle POQ \quad \ldots(i)$$

In ΔOPQ, we have

$$\angle QPO + \angle QOP + \angle PQO = 180° \quad \text{[Angle sum property of triangle]}$$

$$\Rightarrow \quad \angle QPO + \angle QOP + 90° = 180°$$

$$\angle QPO + \angle QOP = 90°$$

$$\Rightarrow \quad \angle QOP = 90° - \angle QPO$$

$$\Rightarrow \quad 2\angle QOP = 180° - 2\angle QPO \quad \text{(Multiplying both sides by 2)}$$

$$\Rightarrow \quad \angle QOR = 180° - \angle QPR \quad \text{[from Eq. (i)]}$$

$$\Rightarrow \quad \angle QOR + \angle QPR = 180°$$

Hence proved.

Quick Solution

Let PQ and PR be the two tangents drawn from an external point P to a circle with centre O.

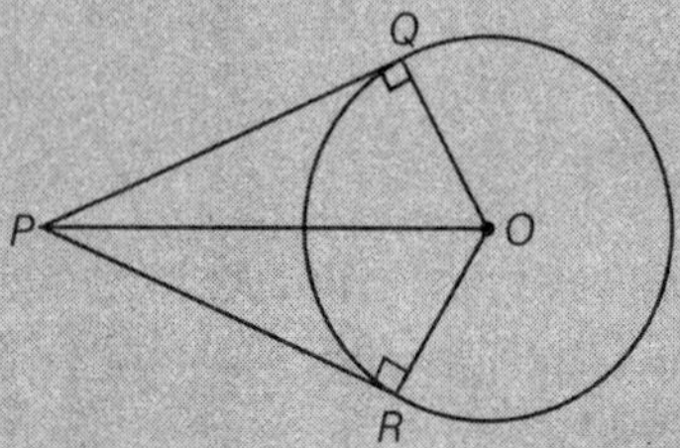

Now, we know that the line joining the centre and the point of contact of the tangent (radius) is perpendicular to the tangent.

$\therefore\ OQ \perp PQ$ and $OR \perp PR$

$\Rightarrow \angle OQP = \angle ORP = 90^\circ$

Also, In quadrilateral $PQOR$, we have

$$\angle PQO + \angle QOR + \angle ORP + \angle RPQ = 360^\circ$$

(sum of angles of a quadrilateral is 360°.)

$\Rightarrow 90^\circ + \angle QOR + 90^\circ + \angle RPQ = 360^\circ$

$\Rightarrow \quad \angle QOR + \angle RPQ = 360^\circ - 180^\circ = 180^\circ$

Hence, the angle between the two tangents drawn from on external point to a circle is supplementory to the angle subtended by the line segment joining the points of contact at the centre.

Question 11 Prove that the parallelogram circumscribing a circle is a rhombus.

◎ ***Thinking Process*** Make use of the property that tangents to a circle from an exterior point are equal in length.

Sol. Let $ABCD$ be a parallelogram circumscribing a circle. Using the property that the tangents to a circle from an external point are equal in length, we get.

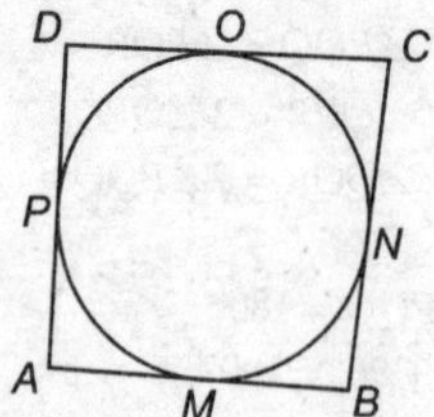

$$\therefore \quad AM = AP \text{ and } BM = BN$$

$$CO = CN \text{ and } DO = DP$$

On adding all equations, we get

$$(AM + BM) + (CO + DO) = AP + BN + CN + DP$$

$$\Rightarrow \quad AB + CD = (AP + PD) + (BN + NC) = AD + BC \quad \left\{\begin{bmatrix} \because AB = AM + MB, \\ BC = BN + NC, \\ CD = CO + OD, \\ AD = AP + PD \end{bmatrix}\right.$$

$$\Rightarrow \quad 2AB = 2BC$$

($\because ABCD$ is a parallelogram. $\therefore AB = CD$ and $BC = AD$)

$$\Rightarrow \quad AB = BC$$

$$\therefore \quad AB = BC = CD = DA$$

So, $ABCD$ is a rhombus. **Hence proved.**

Question 12 A triangle ABC is drawn to circumscribe a circle of radius 4 cm such that the segments BD and DC into which BC is divided by the point of contact D are of lengths 8 cm and 6 cm, respectively
(see figure). Find the sides AB and AC.

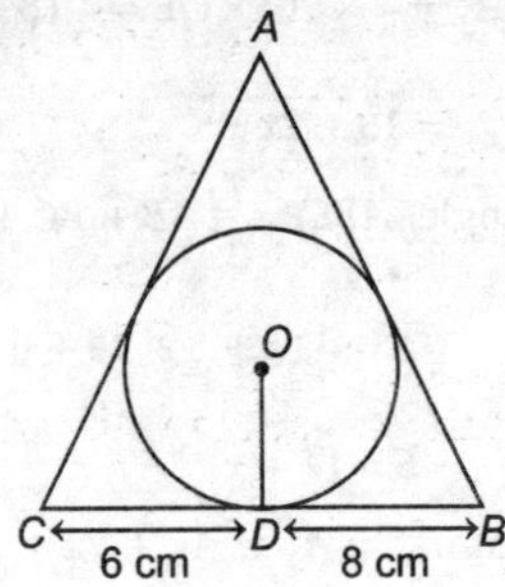

Sol. Given, $CD = 6$ cm, $BD = 8$ cm and radius $= 4$ cm

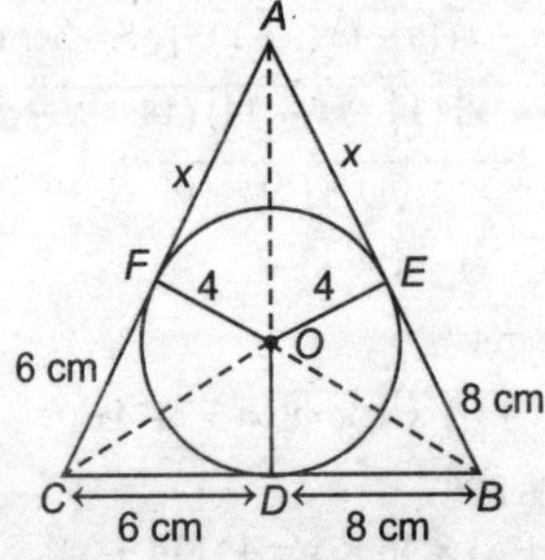

Join OC, OA and OB.

By using the property, tangents drawn from external point equal in length.

$\therefore$ $CD = CF = 6$ cm

and $BD = BE = 8$ cm

Let $AF = AE = x$ cm

In ΔOCB,

$$\text{Area of triangle, } A_1 = \frac{1}{2} \text{ Base} \times \text{Height}$$

$$\Rightarrow \quad = \frac{1}{2} \times CB \times OD$$

$$\Rightarrow \quad = \frac{1}{2} \times 14 \times 4 = 28 \text{ cm}^2$$

In ΔOCA,

$$\text{Area of triangle, } A_2 = \frac{1}{2} \times AC \times OF = \frac{1}{2}(6 + x) \times 4 = 12 + 2x$$

In ΔOBA,

$$\text{Area of triangle, } A_3 = \frac{1}{2} \times AB \times OE = \frac{1}{2}(8 + x) \times 4$$

$$\Rightarrow \quad = 16 + 2x$$

Now, semi-perimeter of triangle, $ABC = \frac{1}{2}(AB + BC + CA)$

$$S = \frac{1}{2}(x + 8 + 14 + 6 + x)$$

$$\Rightarrow \quad S = 14 + x$$

Now, $\quad$ area of $\Delta ABC = A_1 + A_2 + A_3$

$$= 28 + (12 + 2x) + (16 + 2x)$$

$$\Rightarrow \quad = 56 + 4x \qquad \ldots\text{(i)}$$

By using Heron's formula, we have

$$\text{Area of } \Delta ABC = \sqrt{s(s-a)(s-b)(s-c)} \quad [\because S = \text{Semiperimeter of traingle.}]$$

$$= \sqrt{(14 + x)(14 + x - 14)(14 + x - x - 6)(14 + x - x - 8)}$$

$$= \sqrt{(14 + x) \times (x) \times (8) \times (6)}$$

$$= \sqrt{(14 + x) \times x \times 48} \qquad \ldots\text{(ii)}$$

$\therefore$ From Eqs. (i) and (ii), we get

$$\sqrt{(14 + x) \times x \times 48} = 56 + 4x$$

On squaring both sides, we get

$$(14 + x) \times 48 \times x = 4^2 (14 + x)^2$$

$$\Rightarrow \quad 3x = 14 + x$$

$$\Rightarrow \quad 2x = 14$$

$\Rightarrow \quad x = 7$

$\therefore \quad$ Length of $AC = 6 + x = 6 + 7 = 13$ cm

and length of $AB = 8 + x = 8 + 7 = 15$ cm

Question 13 Prove that opposite sides of a quadrilateral circumscribing a circle subtend supplementary angles at the centre of the circle.

Sol. Let *ABCD* be a quadrilateral circumscribing a circle with centre *O*. A circle touches the sides of a quadrilateral at points *E*, *F*, *G* and *H*.

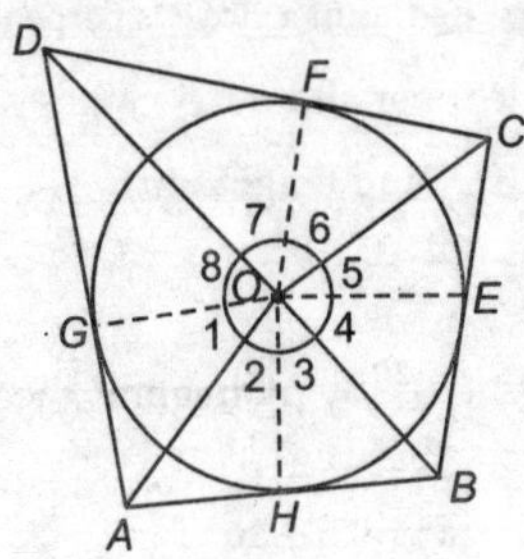

To prove $\angle AOB + \angle COD = 180^\circ$

and $\angle AOD + \angle BOC = 180^\circ$

Construction Join *OH*, *OE*, *OF* and *OG*.

Proof Using the property, two tangents drawn from an external point to a circle subtend equal angles at the centre.

$$\therefore \quad \left.\begin{aligned} \angle 1 &= \angle 2 \\ \angle 3 &= \angle 4 \\ \angle 5 &= \angle 6 \\ \angle 7 &= \angle 8 \end{aligned}\right\} \quad \ldots \text{(i)}$$

We know the sum of all angles subtended at a point *O* is 360°.

$\therefore \angle 1 + \angle 2 + \angle 3 + \angle 4 + \angle 5 + \angle 6 + \angle 7 + \angle 8 = 360^\circ$

$\Rightarrow \quad 2(\angle 2 + \angle 3 + \angle 6 + \angle 7) = 360^\circ$

or $\quad 2(\angle 1 + \angle 8 + \angle 4 + \angle 5) = 360^\circ$ [From Eq. (i)]

$\Rightarrow \quad (\angle 2 + \angle 3) + (\angle 6 + \angle 7) = 180^\circ$

or $\quad (\angle 1 + \angle 8) + (\angle 4 + \angle 5) = 180^\circ$

$\Rightarrow \quad \angle AOB + \angle COD = 180^\circ$

or $\quad \angle AOD + \angle BOC = 180^\circ$

Hence Proved.

DIKSHA APP Questions

☐ Multiple Choice Questions

Q.1 If the radii of two concentric circles are 4 cm and 5 cm, then the length of chord of one circle which is tangent to the other circle is

(a) 3 cm (b) 6 cm (c) 9 cm (d) 1 cm

◎ ***Thinking Process*** Radius of a circle is perpendicular to the tangent.

Sol. (b) Let C_1 and C_2 be the inner and outer circles of radii 4 cm and 5 cm.

Let AB be the chord of C_2 and tangent to C_1.

Then, $OD \perp AB$

So, in right ΔODB,

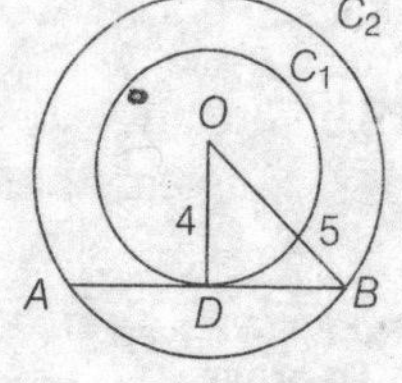

$$H^2 = P^2 + B^2 \text{ [By pythagoras theorem]}$$

$$\Rightarrow \quad 5^2 = 4^2 + B^2$$

$$\Rightarrow \quad B^2 = 25 - 16 = 9$$

$$\Rightarrow \quad B = 3 \text{ cm}$$

Since, the radius perpendicular to the chord, bisects the chord.

Therefore, $AB = 2DB = 2 \times 3 = 6$ cm

Q.2 PQ is tangent to a circle with centre O at the point P. If ΔOPQ is an isosceles triangle with P as the vertex, then $\angle OQP$ is equal to

(a) 30° (b) 60° (c) 45° (d) 90°

Sol. (c) In ΔOPQ, $OP = PQ$, ($\because \Delta OPQ$ is an isosceles triangle)

$\Rightarrow \quad \angle QOP = \angle OQP$ ...(i)

(angles opposite to equal sides are equal)

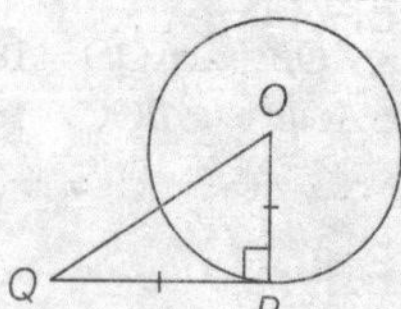

So, In ΔOPQ,

$\angle OPQ + \angle POQ + \angle OQP + 180°$ (angle sum property of triangle)

$$\Rightarrow \quad 90° + \angle POQ + \angle POQ = 180° \quad \text{[from Eq. (i)]}$$
$$\Rightarrow \quad 2\angle POQ = 90°$$
$$\Rightarrow \quad \angle POQ = 45°$$
$$\Rightarrow \quad \angle OQP = \angle POQ = 45°$$

Q.3 A line intersecting the circle in two points is called a

(a) radius (b) tangent
(c) secant (d) None of these

Sol. (c) A secant is a line that intersects the circle at two points.

Q.4 How many tangents can be drawn from an external point to a circle.

(a) 1 (b) 2 (c) 3 (d) 4

Sol. (b) Exactly two tangents can be drawn from an external point of a circle.

Q.5 The angle between two radii of a circle is 130, the angle between the tangents is

(a) 90 (b) 50 (c) 70 (d) 40

Sol. (b) Given, $\angle AOB = 130°$

We know that the angle between the two tangents and angle between the radii through the point of contact are supplementary angles.

$$\therefore \quad \angle APB + \angle AOB = 180°$$
$$\Rightarrow \quad \angle APB + 130° = 180°$$
$$\Rightarrow \quad \angle APB = 180° - 130° = 50°$$

Q.6 A point P is 13 cm from the center of a circle. Radius of the circle is 5 cm. A tangent is drawn from point P to the circle, then the length of the tangent is

(a) 10cm (b) 11cm (c) 12 cm (d) 13 cm

Sol. (c) Given, $OP = 13$ cm, $OA = 5$ cm

Now, radius is perpendicular to the tangent at the point of contact.

$$\Rightarrow \quad \angle OAP = 90°$$

$\therefore$ In right ΔOAP, we have

$OP^2 = OA^2 + AP^2$ [By pythagoras theorem]

$$\Rightarrow \quad 13^2 = 5^2 + AP^2$$
$$\Rightarrow \quad 169 - 25 = AP^2$$
$$\Rightarrow \quad AP = \sqrt{144} = 12 \text{ cm}$$

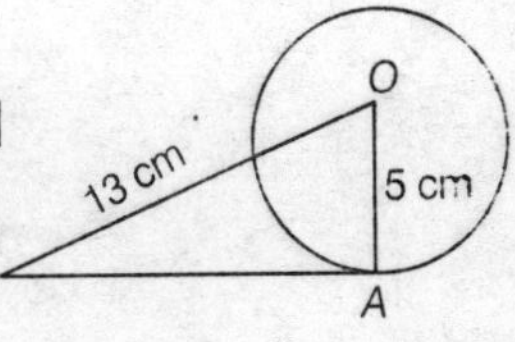

Q.7 A tangent PQ at point P of a circle of radius 12 cm meets a line through the center O to a point Q, so that $OQ = 20$ cm. Length PQ is

(a) 14 (b) 15 (c) 16 (d) 10

Sol. (c) Given, $OP = 12$ cm, $OQ = 20$ cm

We know, radius is perpendicular to the tangent at the point of contact

$\Rightarrow \quad \angle OPQ = 90°$

$\therefore$ In right ΔOPQ, we have

$$OQ^2 = OP^2 + PQ^2 \text{ [By pythagoras theorem]}$$

$$\Rightarrow \quad 20^2 = 12^2 + PQ^2$$

$$\Rightarrow \quad PQ^2 = 400 - 144 = 256$$

$$\Rightarrow \quad PQ = 16 \text{ cm}$$

P, 12 cm, Q, 20 cm, O

Q.8 Which of the following pairs of lines in a circle cannot be parallel ?

(a) Two chords (b) A chord and a tangent
(c) Two tangents (d) Two diameters

Sol. (d) Two chords are parallel when they are equidistant from the centre. A chord and a tangent can also be parallel as they do not intersect each other.

Two tangents are parallel if the point of contact of the two tangents is on either end of the diameter.

Two diameters cannot be parallel as they intersect at the centre of the circle.

Q.9 The lengths of three consecutive sides of a quadrilateral circumscribing a circle are 4 cm, 5 cm and 7 cm. Find the length of the fourth side of the quadrilateral.

(a) 7 cm (b) 6 cm (c) 8 cm (d) 9 cm

Sol. (b) Let, $AB = 7$ cm, $BC = 5$ cm and $CD = 4$ cm

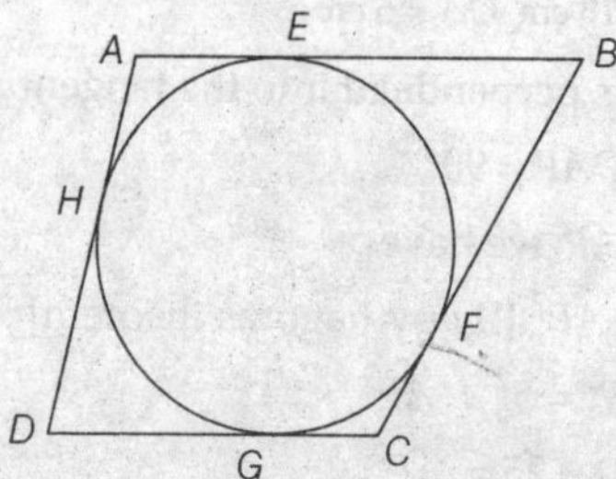

Since, lengths of tangents drawn from an external point to the circle are equal.

$\Rightarrow \quad AH = AE, BE = BF, CF = CG, DG = DH \quad$ ...(i)

Also, $\quad AB = AE + BE$

$BC = BF + CF$

$DC = CG + GD$

$AD = AH + HD$

$\Rightarrow \quad AB + CD = AE + BE + CG + GD$

$= AH + BF + CF + DH \quad$ [from Eq. (i)]

$= AD + BC \quad [\because AH + DH = AD, BF + CF = BC]$

On substituting the values of $AB = 7\text{cm}$, $CD = 4\text{cm}$, $BC = 5$, we get,

$\Rightarrow \quad 7\text{ cm} + 4\text{ cm} = AD + 5\text{ cm} \Rightarrow AD = 11\text{ cm} - 5\text{ cm} = 6\text{ cm}$

Q.10 AB and CD are two common tangents to circles which touch each other at C. If D lies on AB such that $CD = 4$ cm, then AB is equal to

(a) 4 cm (b) 6 cm (c) 8 cm (d) 12 cm

Sol. (c) Given that, $DC = 4$ cm

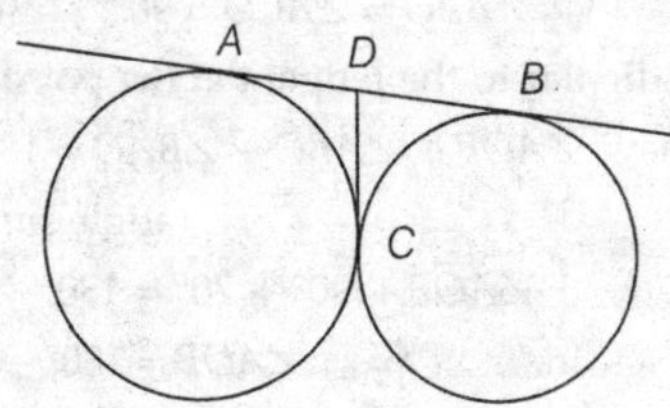

Since, lengths of tangents drawn from an external point to the circle are equal.

$\Rightarrow \quad AD = CD$ and $CD = DB$

$\Rightarrow \quad AD = DB = CD = 4$ cm

$\Rightarrow \quad AB = AD + DB = 4 + 4 = 8$ cm

Q.11 Find the distance between two parallel tangents of a circle whose radius is 3.5 cm.

(a) 7 cm (b) 3.5 cm

(c) 10 cm (d) Cannot be determined

Sol. (a) Given, radius, $r = 3.5$ cm.

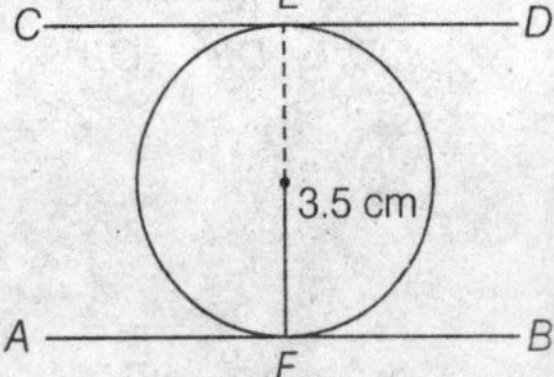

As two tangents are parallel when the point of contact of both of them is on either end of the diameter.

Hence, the distance between them is the length of the diameter.

$\Rightarrow$ diameter $= 2r = 2 \times 3.5 = 7$ cm

Q.12 If tangents AB and AC from a point A to a circle with centre O are inclined to each other at an angle of 40°, then $\angle AOB$ is

(a) 140° (b) 100° (c) 50° (d) 70°

Sol. (d) Given, $\angle BAC = 40°$

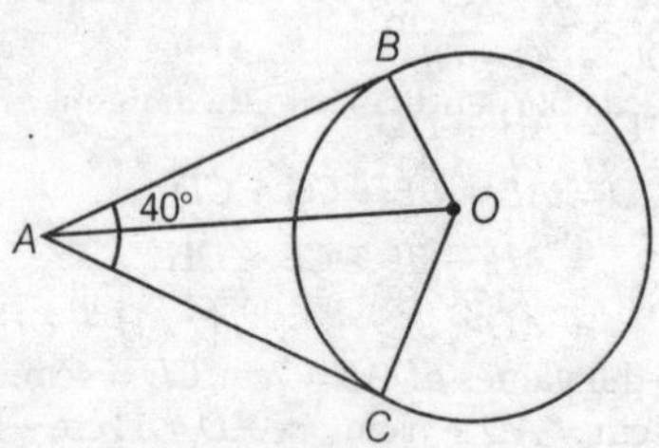

The line joining the center of circle and vertex of two tangents in the bisector of the angle between two tangents.

$\Rightarrow \quad \angle BAC = 2\angle BAO$

$\Rightarrow \quad 40° = 2\angle BAO$

$\Rightarrow \quad \angle BAO = 20° = \angle CAO$

Now, as $\quad \angle ABO = \angle ACO = 90°$

(radius is perpendicular to the tangent at the point of contact)

$\Rightarrow$ In ΔABO, we have $\angle AOB + \angle ABO + \angle BAO = 180°$

(angle sum property of triangle)

$\Rightarrow \quad \angle AOB + 90° + 20° = 180°$

$\Rightarrow \quad \angle AOB = 180° - 110° = 70°$

Q.13 If radii of the two circles are 6 cm and 10 cm, then the length of the chord of one circle which is tangent to other is

(a) 8 cm (b) 16 cm (c) 20 cm (d) 10 cm

Sol. (b) Let C_1 and C_2 be the inner and outer circles of radii 6 cm and 10 cm.

Let AB be the chord of C_2 and tangent to C_1.
Then,

$OD \perp AB$

So, in right ΔODB, we have

$OD^2 + DB^2 = OB^2$ [By pythagoras theorem]

$\Rightarrow \quad 6^2 + DB^2 = 10^2$

$\Rightarrow \quad DB^2 = 100 - 36$

$= 64$

$\Rightarrow \quad DB = 8$ cm

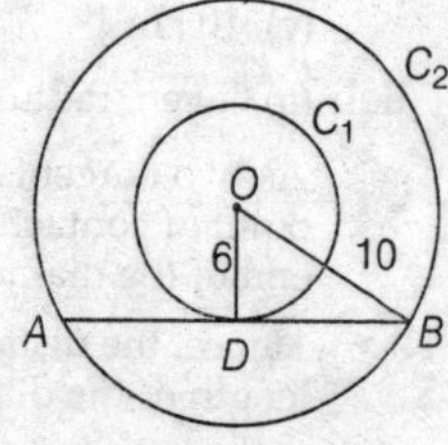

Since, the radius perpendicular to the chord, bisects the chord.

$\Rightarrow \quad AB = 2DB = 2 \times 8 = 16$ cm

Q.14 PQ a tangent at P on a circle of radius 5 cm meets a line through the centrer O at Q such that $OQ = 12$ cm, the length of PQ is

(a) 12 cm (b) 13 cm (c) 8.5 cm (d) $\sqrt{119}$ cm

Sol. (d) Given, $OP = 5$ cm, $OQ = 12$ cm

We know, the radius is perpendicular to the tangent at the point of contact.

$\Rightarrow \qquad \angle OPQ = 90°$

$\therefore$ In right ΔOPQ, we have

$$OP^2 + PQ^2 = OQ^2 \text{ [By pythagoras theorem]}$$

$$\Rightarrow \quad 5^2 + PQ^2 = 12^2$$

$$\Rightarrow \quad PQ^2 = 144 - 25$$

$$\Rightarrow \quad PQ^2 = 119$$

$$\Rightarrow \quad PQ = \sqrt{119} \text{ cm}$$

P
5 cm
Q
12 cm
O

Mistake Alert When using the pythagoras theorem involving radius and tangent in circle make sure you have correctly identified the angles and sides.

Q.15 The common point of a tangent and the circle is called

(a) Point of contact (b) Secant
(c) Centre (d) Diameter

Sol. (a) The point at which the tangent touches the circle is called the point of contact.

Q.16 The number of points at which a tangent intersect a circle is

(a) One (b) Two (c) Three (d) Infinite

Sol. (a) The tangent only touches the circle at one point known as the point of contact.

Q.17 The number of tangents a circle can have

(a) One (b) Two (c) Three (d) infinite

Sol. (d) As a circle is made up of an infinite number of points equidistant from a fixed point (radius) and there is exactly one tangent can make on each of the points on the circle, so there are infinite number of tangents that a circle can have.

Q.18 The centre of the circle lies on the bisector of angle between the two ......

(a) Chords (b) Tangents
(c) Secants (d) None of these

Sol. (b) A line joining the angle between the two tangents and the centre of the circle bisects the angle subtended by the two tangents.

Q.19 Perpendicular at the end of any radius of a circle is called

(a) Chord (b) Tangent (c) Normal (d) Radius

Sol. (b) The radius joining the point of contact of the tangent is always perpendicular to the tangent. So, at any end of the radius, a tangent is perpendicular to it.

Q.20 Length of a tangent drawn from a point which is at a distance of 12.5 cm from the centre of a circle is 12 cm, find the diameter of the circle.

(a) 3.5 cm (b) 21 cm (c) 7 cm (d) 14 cm

Sol. (c) Length of tangent = $XY = 12$ cm

Distance of X from $O = OX = 12.5$ cm

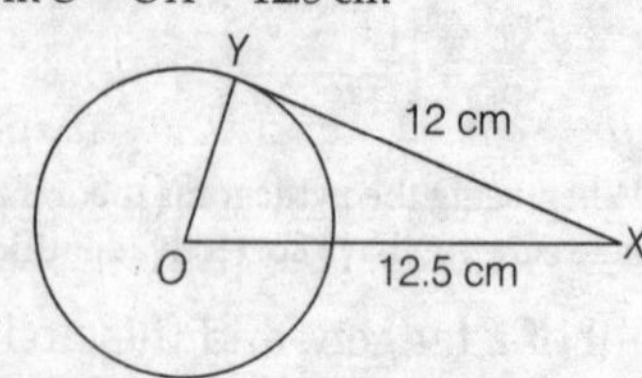

Radius of circle = OY

In ΔOYX, we have

$$\angle OYX = 90°$$

(as tangent is perpendicular to radius at point of contact)

So, By pythagoras theorem,

$$OX^2 = OY^2 + XY^2$$

$$OY^2 = 12.5^2 - 12^2 = 156.25 - 144 = 12.25$$

So, $$OY = \sqrt{12.25} = 3.5 \text{ cm}$$

So, Radius of circle = $OY = 3.5$ cm

Diameter of circle = $2 \times 3.5 = 7$ cm

☐ Subjective Type Questions

Q.1 In given figure, AP and BP are tangents to a circle with centre O, such that $AP = 5$ cm and $\angle APB = 60°$. Find the length of chord AB.

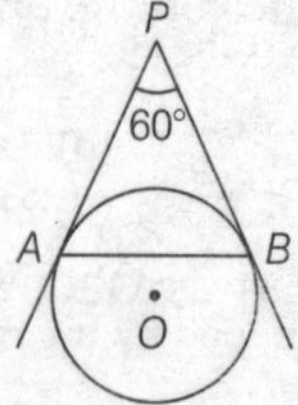

Sol. In ΔAPB we have, $AP = 5\text{cm}$ and $\angle APB = 60°$

$$AP = BP$$

[$\because$ The lengths of tangents drawn from external point to a circle are equal]

$\Rightarrow \quad \angle PAB = \angle PBA$ [Angle opposite to equal sides are also equal]

Let $\angle PAB = x$

Then, in $\Delta APB, x + x + 60° = 180°$ [angle sum property]

$\Rightarrow \quad 2x = 180° - 60° = 120°$

$\Rightarrow \quad x = 60°$

Therefore $\angle PAB = 60°, \angle PBA = 60°$

As all three angles of ΔAPB are $60°$. So, ΔAPB is an equilateral triangle.

Hence, $AB = AP = BP = 5$ cm

Q.2 In given figure, a circle is inscribed in a ΔABC, such that it touches the sides AB, BC and CA at points D, E and F respectively. If the lengths of sides AB, BC and CA are 12 cm, 8 cm and 10 cm respectively, find the lengths of AD, BE and CF.

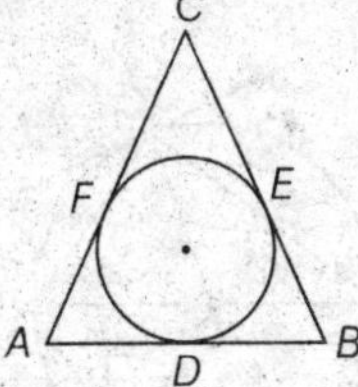

Sol. Given, $AB = 12$ cm, $CA = 10$ cm, $BC = 8$ cm

Let $\quad AD = AF = x$

[$\because$ Tangent drawn from external point to circle are equal]

$\therefore \quad DB = BE = 12 - x$ and $CF = CE = 10 - x$

$BC = BE + EC \Rightarrow 8 = 12 - x + 10 - x$

$\Rightarrow \quad x = 7$

$\therefore \quad AD = 7$ cm, $BE = 5$ cm and $CF = 3$ cm

Q.3 In given figure, AOB is a diameter of a circle with centre O and AC is a tangent to the circle at A. If $\angle BOC = 130°$, then find $\angle ACO$.

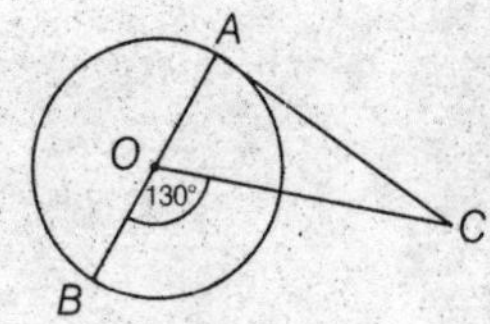

Sol. $\angle AOC + \angle BOC = 180°$ [∵ Linear Pair Axiom]

$\Rightarrow \quad \angle AOC + 130° = 180°$

$\Rightarrow \quad \angle AOC = 180° - 130°$

$\Rightarrow \quad \angle AOC = 50°$

Since, $\angle OAC = 90°$

[angle between radius OA and tangent AC is 90°]

Now, in ΔAOC,

$\angle OAC + \angle AOC + \angle ACO = 180°$

[∵ sum of all angles of a triangle is 180°]

$\Rightarrow \quad 90° + 50° + \angle ACO = 180°$

$\Rightarrow \quad \angle ACO = 180° - 140° \Rightarrow \angle ACO = 40°$

Hence, $\angle ACO = 40°$

Q.4 In given figure, PQ is a tangent at a point C to a circle with centre O. If AB is a diameter and $\angle CAB = 30°$, find $\angle PCA$.

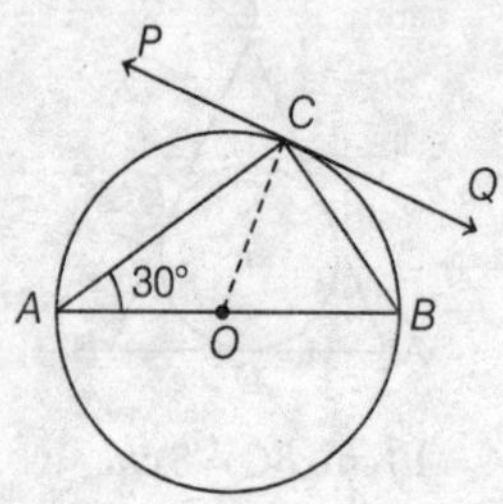

Sol. Construction Given PQ is tangent, AB is diameter $\angle CAB = 30°$.

In ΔAOC we have, $AO = CO$ [Radii]

$\therefore \quad \angle CAO = \angle OCA$ (∵ Angles opposite to equal sides are equal)

or $\quad \angle CAB = \angle OCA$

Since, $\angle CAB = 30°$

So, $\angle OCA = 30°$

Since, $OC \perp PQ$ (∵ Tangent is perpendicular to radius at point of contact)

$\Rightarrow \quad \angle PCO = 90° \Rightarrow \angle OCA + \angle PCA = 90° \Rightarrow 30° + \angle PCA = 90°$

[∵ $\angle OCA = 30°$]

$\therefore \quad \angle PCA = 60°$

Q.5 From an external point P, tangents PA and PB are drawn to a circle with centre O. If $\angle PAB = 50°$, then find $\angle AOB$.

Sol. Given, $\angle PAB = 50°$, PA and PB are two tangents drawn from an external point P.

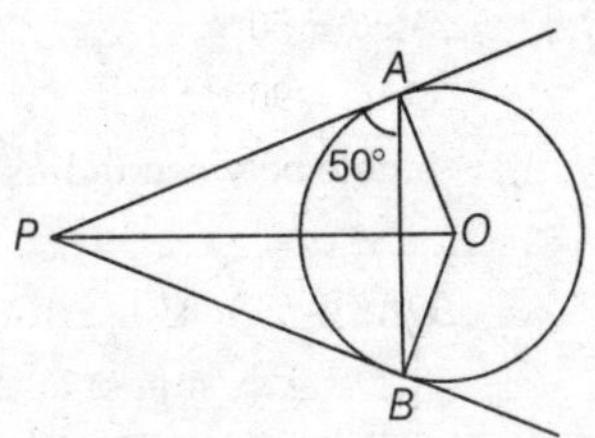

$\angle PAB + \angle OAB = 90°$

[∵ angle between radius OA and tangent PA is 90°]

$\Rightarrow$ $50° + \angle OAB = 90°$

$\Rightarrow$ $\angle OAB = 90° - 50° = 40°$

Now, $PA = PB$

[∵ tangents drawn from an external point are equal]

$\Rightarrow$ $\angle PA = PB$

$\Rightarrow$ $\angle PBA = \angle PAB$ [∵ Equal sides have corresponding equal angles]

$\Rightarrow$ $\angle PBA = 50°$

$\angle PBA + \angle OBA = 90°$

[∵ angle between radius OB and tangent PB is 180°]

$\Rightarrow$ $50° + \angle OBA = 90°$

$\Rightarrow$ $\angle OBA = 90° - 50° = 40°$

Now, in ΔAOB, we have

$OA = OB$ [Radii]

$\therefore$ $\angle OAB = \angle OBA$ [Angle opposite to equal sides are also equal]

$\therefore$ $\angle OBA = 40°$

Now, $\angle AOB + \angle ABO + \angle OAB = 180°$

[∵ sum of all angles in triangle is 180°]

$\Rightarrow$ $\angle AOB + 40° + 40° = 180°$

$\Rightarrow$ $\angle AOB = 180° - 80° = 100°$

Hence, $\angle AOB = 100°$

Q.6 The incircle of an isosceles triangle ABC, with $AB = AC$, touches the sides AB, BC and CA at D, E and F respectively. Prove that E bisects BC.

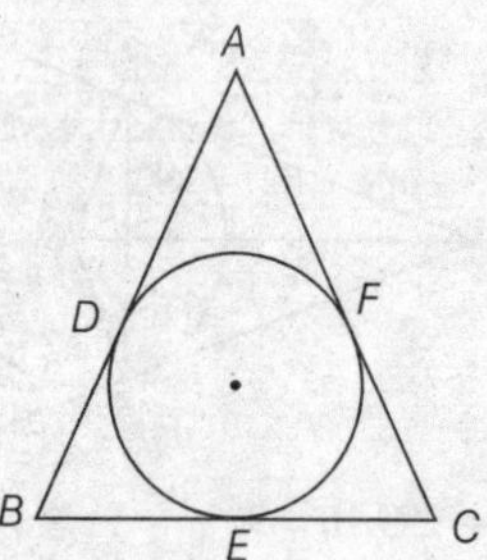

Sol. Given, ΔABC is an isosceles triangle.

$AB = AC$ ...(i)

Since, lengths of two tangents drawn from an external point are equal.

$\Rightarrow \quad AD = AF, BD = BE$ and $CE = CF$ ...(ii)

As $\quad AB = AC$

$\Rightarrow \quad AD + DB = AF + FC$

$\Rightarrow \quad DB = FC \quad$ ($AD = AF$ from Eq. (ii)) ...(iii)

$\Rightarrow \quad BE = EC \quad$ ($\because DB = BE$ and $FC = EC$ from Eq. (ii))

$\Rightarrow \quad BC = 2BE$

So, E bisects BC.

Q.7 In given figure from an external point P, two tangents PT and PS are drawn to a circles center O and radius r. If $PO = 2r$, show that $\angle OTS = \angle OST = 30$

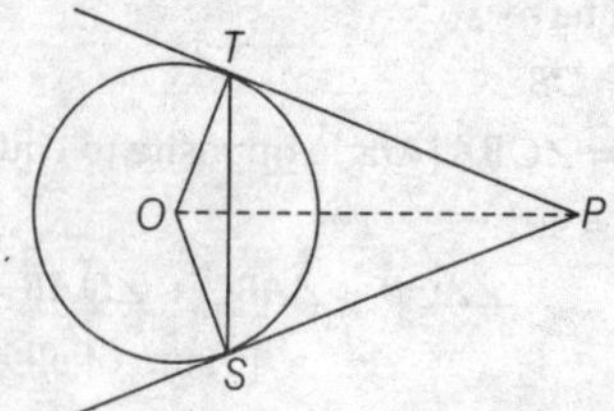

Sol. Let $\angle TOP = Q$

And $\quad \angle TOP = \angle SOP = \theta$

[A line joining the angle between the two tangents and the center of the circle bisects the angle subtended by the two radii.]

In right triangle OTP, we have

$$\cos\theta = \frac{OT}{OP} = \frac{r}{2r} = \frac{1}{2} = \cos 60^\circ$$

$\Rightarrow \quad \theta = 60^\circ$

In ΔOTS, we have, $OT = OS$ [Radii]

$\therefore$ $\angle OTS = \angle OST$

[Angle opposite to equal sides are also equal]

Now, $\angle OTS + \angle OST + \angle TOS = 180°$

[Angle sum property of triangle]

$\Rightarrow$ $\angle OTS + \angle OTS + \angle TOP + \angle SOP = 180°$

[$\because \angle OTS = \angle OST$ and $\angle TOS = \angle TOP + \angle SOP$]

$\Rightarrow$ $2\angle OTS + 60° + 60° = 180°$ [$\because \angle TOP = \angle SOP = 60°$]

$\Rightarrow$ $\angle OTS = 30°$

$\Rightarrow$ $\angle OTS = \angle OST = 30°$ **Hence Proved.**

Q.8 A circle is inscribed in the quadrilateral $ABCD$. Given, $BC = 38$ cm, $BQ = 27$ cm, $CD = 25$ cm and $\angle ADC = 90°$, find the radius of the circle.

Sol. Let the side BC touches the circle at point Q, the side CD touches the circle at point R and the side DA touches the circle at point S and side AB touches the circle at point P. Also let the center of circle be O.

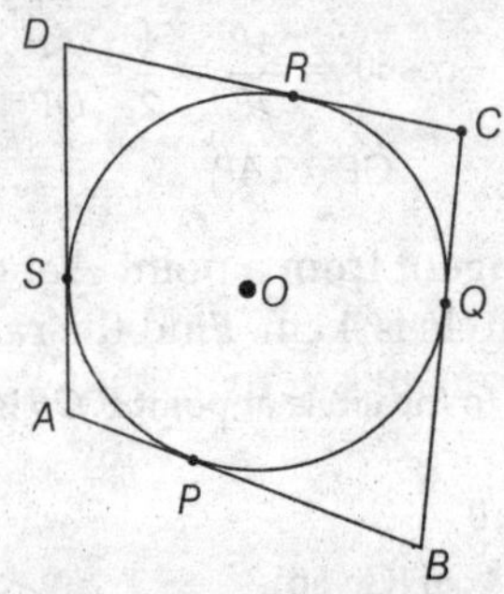

Now, $BQ = BP = 27$cm and $BC = 38$

[$\because$ Tangents drawn from external points are equal]

So, $CQ = 11$cm $= CR$

$CD = 25$, So, $DR = DS = 14$ cm

Since, $\angle ADC = 90°$ and $DR = DS$

Therefore, $DROS$ is a square.

Radius of the circle $= OR = OS = 14$ cm [$\because OR$ and OS are radii of circle]

Q.9 Two tangents PA and PB are drawn to the circle with centre O such that $\angle APB = 120$. Prove that $OP = 2\,AP$.

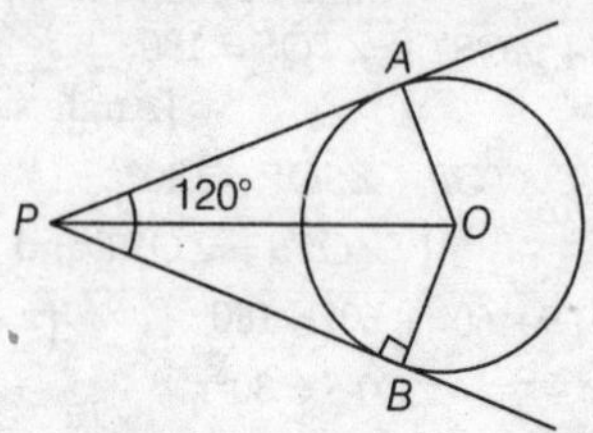

Sol. Given, $\angle APB = 120°$

Now, angle subtended by the two tangents is bisected by the line joining to its vertex and the centre of the circle.

$$\Rightarrow \quad \angle BPO = \angle APO$$

$$\Rightarrow \quad \angle BPO + \angle APO = 120°$$

$$\Rightarrow \quad \angle APO = \frac{120}{2} = 60°$$

In ΔAPO, we have

$$\cos 60° = \frac{AP}{OP} \Rightarrow \frac{1}{2} = \frac{AP}{OP}$$

$$\Rightarrow \quad OP = 2AP$$ **Hence proved.**

Q.10 The length of a tangent from a point A at distance 5 cm from the centre of the circle is 4 cm. Find the radius of the circle.

Sol. Let AB is the tangent to the circle at point B. OB is the radius at point of contact.

$\therefore \quad OB \perp AB$

$OA = 5$ cm and $AB = 4$ cm [Given]

In ΔABO, we have

$OA^2 = AB^2 + BO^2$ [Pythagoras theorem]

$\Rightarrow \quad 5^2 = 4^2 + BO^2$

$\Rightarrow \quad BO^2 = 25 - 16$

$\Rightarrow \quad BO^2 = 9 \Rightarrow BO = 3$

$\therefore$ Radius = 3 cm.

Areas Related to Circle

CHAPTER 11

Important Points

01 Circle It is a collection of all points in a plane which are at a constant distance from a fixed point.

(i) Area of circle $= \pi r^2$

(ii) Area of semi-circle $= \dfrac{\pi r^2}{2}$

(iii) Area of quadrant of circle $= \dfrac{\pi r^2}{4}$

(iv) Circumference of circle $= 2\pi r = \pi d$

where, $d = 2r =$ diameter of circle.

(v) Circumference of semi-circle $= \pi r$

(vi) Perimeter of semi-circle $= \pi r + 2r$

02 Area of Sector of Circle The circular region enclosed by two radii and corresponding arc is called a sector of the circle. The arc AB is called the length of the arc. The region OAB is called the **minor sector** and the region $OACDBO$ is called the **major sector**.

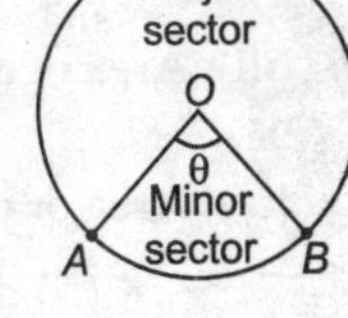

(i) Length of an arc of sector $AB = \dfrac{\theta}{360^\circ} \times 2\pi r$

(ii) Area of minor sector $OAB = \dfrac{\theta}{360^\circ} \times \pi r^2$

(iii) Area of major sector $OACDBO = \dfrac{360^\circ - \theta}{360^\circ} \times \pi r^2$

Remark Area of the circle = Area of the minor sector + Area of the major sector.

03 Area of Segment of Circle Let AB be a chord of the circle having centre O.
The region covered by the line and the curve *i.e.*, region ABC is a segment of the circle.

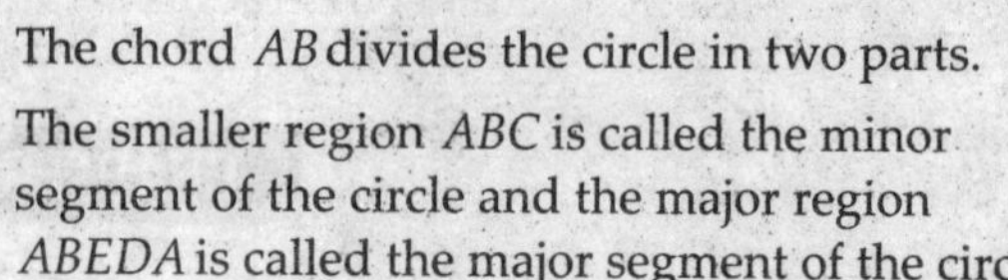

The chord AB divides the circle in two parts.
The smaller region ABC is called the minor segment of the circle and the major region $ABEDA$ is called the major segment of the circle.

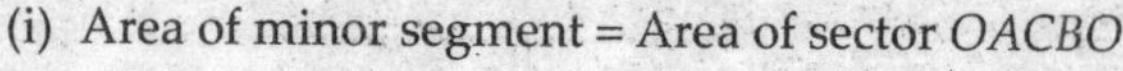

(i) Area of minor segment = Area of sector $OACBO$ – Area of ΔOAB

$$= \frac{\theta}{360^\circ} \times \pi r^2 - \text{Area of } \Delta OAB$$

(ii) Area of major segment = Area of circle – Area of minor segment(ACB)

$$= \pi r^2 - \left(\frac{\theta}{360^\circ} \times \pi r^2 - \text{Area of } \Delta OAB\right)$$

Note • The area of the sector and segment means, we have to determine the area of minor sector and minor segment.

• Area of the circle = Area of major segment + Area of minor segment.

04 Important Useful Formulae

(i) Area of square = $(\text{Side})^2$

(ii) Area of triangle = $\frac{1}{2} \times \text{Base} \times \text{Height}$

(iii) Area of an equilateral triangle = $\frac{\sqrt{3}}{4} (\text{Side})^2$

(iv) Area of trapezium = $\frac{1}{2}$ (Sum of parallel side) × Distance between two parallel sides

(v) Area of ring = $\pi (R^2 - r^2)$

where, R and r be radius of outer ring and inner ring respectively.

Exercise 11.1

Unless stated otherwise, use $\pi = \frac{22}{7}$.

Question 1 Find the area of a sector of a circle with radius 6 cm if angle of the sector is 60°.

Sol. $\because$ Area of sector $= \frac{\theta \pi r^2}{360^\circ}$

Given, $r = 6$ cm, $\theta = 60^\circ$

$$\therefore \qquad \text{Area of sector} = 60^\circ \times \frac{22}{7} \times \frac{(6)^2}{360^\circ} = \frac{132}{7} \text{ cm}^2$$

Question 2 Find the area of a quadrant of a circle whose circumference is 22 cm.

◎ ***Thinking Process*** The area of the circle is πr^2, then quadrant is one-fourth of the circle, then area is also the one fourth of the circle *i.e.*, area of quadrant $= \frac{\pi r^2}{4}$.

Sol. Let r be the radius of the circle.

Since, circumference of circle = 22 cm

$$\Rightarrow \qquad 2\pi r = 22$$

$$\Rightarrow \qquad 2 \times \frac{22}{7} \times r = 22$$

$$\therefore \qquad \text{Radius of circle, } r = \frac{7}{2}$$

$$\therefore \text{Area of a quadrant of a circle} = \frac{\pi r^2}{4} = \frac{22}{7} \times \frac{\left(\frac{7}{2}\right)^2}{4} = \frac{11}{14} \times \frac{49}{4} = \frac{77}{8} \text{ cm}^2$$

Question 3 The length of the minute hand of a clock is 14 cm. Find the area swept by the minute hand in 5 min.

Sol. Given, length of the minute hand of clock = 14 cm

It means radius of circle is $r = 14$ cm

$\because$ The angle moved by the minute hand in 30 min = 180°

$\therefore$ The angle moved by the minute hand in 1 min $= \frac{180^\circ}{30^\circ} = 6^\circ$

$\therefore$ The angle moved by the minute hand in 5 min $= 5 \times 6 = 30^\circ$

$\therefore$ Using the formula,

$$\text{Area of sector of circle} = \frac{\theta \pi r^2}{360^\circ} = 30^\circ \times \frac{22 \times (14)^2}{7 \times 360^\circ}$$

$$= \frac{22 \times 14 \times 2}{12} = \frac{616}{12} = \frac{154}{3} \text{ cm}^2$$

Question 4 A chord of a circle of radius 10 cm subtends a right angle at the centre. Find the area of the corresponding

(i) minor segment (ii) major sector. (Use $\pi = 3.14$)

Sol. Radius of the circle, $r = 10$ cm

Angle of the sector $= 90°$

$\therefore \Delta AOB$ is a right angled triangle.

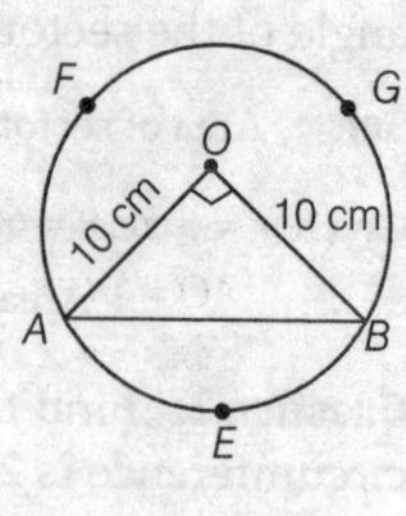

$\therefore$ Area of $\Delta AOB = \frac{1}{2} \times \text{Base} \times \text{Perpendicular}$

$= \frac{1}{2} \times 10 \times 10 = 50 \text{ cm}^2$

Area of sector $= \frac{\theta \pi r^2}{360°} = \frac{90°}{360°} \times 3.14 \times (10)^2$

$= \frac{314}{4} = 78.5 \text{ cm}^2$

(i) Area of minor segment AEB = Area of sector $OAEB$ – Area of ΔAOB

$= 78.5 - 50$

$= 28.5 \text{ cm}^2$

(ii) Area of major sector $OAFGBO$ = Area of the circle – Area of sector $OAEB$

$= \pi r^2 - 78.5 = 3.14 \times (10)^2 - 78.5$

$= 314 - 78.5 = 235.5 \text{ cm}^2$

Mistake Alert Student forget to use the value of π is 3.14. follow the instruction in the question for which value of π to use. If not mentioned, choose $\pi = \frac{22}{7}$.

Question 5 In a circle of radius 21 cm, an arc subtends an angle of 60° at the centre. Find

(i) the length of the arc.

(ii) area of the sector formed by the arc.

(iii) area of the segment formed by the corresponding chord.

Sol. Since, arc ABC subtends an angle 60° at the centre.

$\therefore$ $\theta = 60°$

and radius, $r = 21$ cm

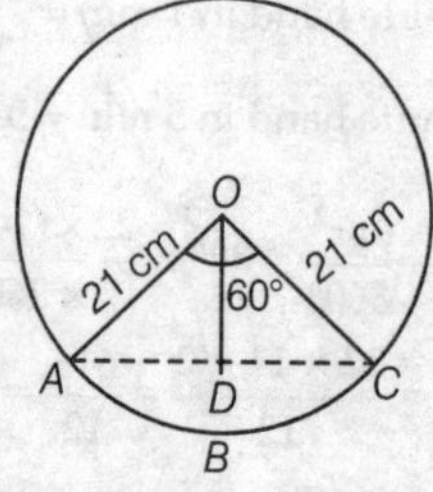

(i) Length of arc $ABC = \frac{\theta}{360°} \times 2\pi r = \frac{60°}{360°} \times 2 \times \frac{22}{7} \times 21$

$$= \frac{44}{6} \times 3 = 22 \text{ cm}$$

(ii) Area of the sector ($OABC$) formed by the arc $= \frac{\theta}{360°} \times \pi r^2$

$$= \frac{60°}{360°} \times \frac{22}{7} \times (21)^2$$

$$= \frac{22}{6 \times 7} \times 21 \times 21 = \frac{9702}{42} = 231 \text{ cm}^2$$

(iii) Now, draw a perpendicular drawn from centre of the circle to the chord.

$AO = OC$ (radius)

$\angle ODA = \angle ODC$ (each 90°)

$AD = DC$ (perpendicular dram from centre bisect the chord)

$\therefore$ $\Delta OAD \cong \Delta ODC$ (By RHS)

$\therefore$ $\angle AOD = \angle DOC = 30°$ (By CPCT)

and $AD = DC$

In right ΔAOD,

$$\sin 30° = \frac{AD}{AO} \Rightarrow \frac{1}{2} = \frac{AD}{21} \left[\because \sin\theta = \frac{P}{H}, \cos\theta = \frac{B}{H}\right]$$

$\Rightarrow$ $AD = 10.5$ cm

and $\cos 30° = \frac{OD}{AO} \Rightarrow \frac{\sqrt{3}}{2} = \frac{OD}{21}$

$\Rightarrow$ $OD = 10.5\sqrt{3}$ cm

$\therefore$ $AC = 2\ AD = 2 \times 10.5 = 21$ cm

(perpendicular drawn from the centre bisect the chord)

$\therefore$ Area of $\Delta OAC = \frac{1}{2} \times AC \times OD = \frac{1}{2} \times 21 \times 10.5\sqrt{3}$

$$= \frac{441\sqrt{3}}{4} \text{ cm}^2$$

$\therefore$ Area of the segment = Area of sector formed by the arc − Area of ΔOAC

$$= \left(231 - \frac{441\sqrt{3}}{4}\right) \text{cm}^2$$

Quick Solution

(iii) In ΔAOC,

$OA = OC = 21$cm (radius of the circle)

$\Rightarrow \angle OAC = OCA$[angles opposite to equal sides are equal]

Also, $\angle AOC = 60°$

So, in ΔAOC,

$\angle AOC + \angle OAC + \angle OCA = 180°$ (by angle sum property)

$\Rightarrow$ $60° + \angle OAC + \angle OAC = 180°$

$2\angle OAC = 180° - 60°$

$\Rightarrow$ $\angle OAC = 60°$

$\Rightarrow$ ΔAOC is an equilateral triangle.

$\therefore$ Area of $\Delta AOC = \frac{\sqrt{3}}{4} \times \text{Side}^2$

$= \frac{\sqrt{3}}{4} \times 21 \times 21 \text{ cm}^2$ $(\because OA = 21 \text{ cm})$

$= \frac{441\sqrt{3}}{4} \text{ cm}^2$

Area of the segment = area of sector formed by arc – area of ΔDAC

$= \left(231 - \frac{441\sqrt{3}}{4}\right) \text{cm}^2$

Question 6 A chord of a circle of radius 15 cm subtends an angle of 60° at the centre. Find the areas of the corresponding minor and major segments of the circle. (Use $\pi = 3.14$ and $\sqrt{3} = 1.73$)

Sol. Since, chord AB subtends an angle 60° to the centre.

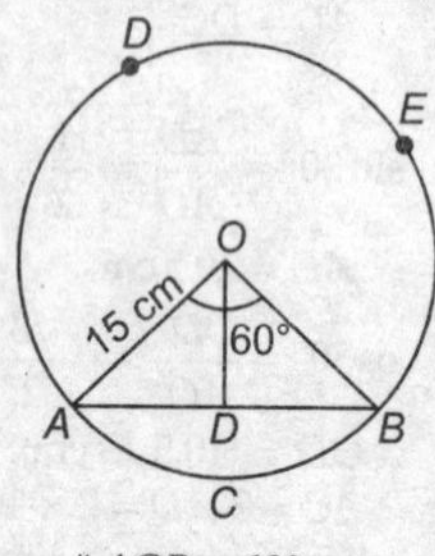

$\therefore$ $\angle AOB = 60°$

In ΔAOB,

$OA = OB = 15$ cm (radii)

$\Rightarrow$ $\angle OAB = \angle OBA$ (angles opposite to equal sides are equal)

In ΔAOB,

$\angle AOB + \angle OAB + \angle OBA = 180°$ (angle sum property)

$\Rightarrow$ $60° + 2\angle OAB = 180°$ $[\angle OAB = \angle OBA]$

$\Rightarrow$ $2\angle OAB = 180° - 60°$

$\Rightarrow$ $\angle OAB = \frac{120°}{2} = 60°$

$\Rightarrow$ $\angle OAB = \angle AOB = \angle OBA = 60°$

$\Rightarrow$ ΔAOB is an equilateral triangle.

$\Rightarrow$ Area of $\Delta AOB = \frac{\sqrt{3}}{4}(15)^2$ $(\because s = 15 \text{ cm})$

$= 97.3125 \text{ cm}^2$

Now, Area of sector $OACBO = \frac{\theta \pi r^2}{360°} = 60° \times \frac{3.14}{360°}(15)^2$

$= \frac{3.14 \times 225}{6} = \frac{706.5}{6} = 117.75 \text{ cm}^2$

$\therefore$ Area of minor segment $ACBDA$

$= \text{Area of sector } OACBO - \text{Area of } \Delta OAB$

$= 117.75 - 97.3125 = 20.4375 \text{ cm}^2$

Now, Area of major segment = Area of circle – Area of minor segment

$= \pi(15)^2 - 20.4375$ $\quad [\because \text{Area of circle} = \pi r^2]$

$= 3.14 \times 225 - 20.4375 = 706.5 - 20.4375$

$= 686.0625 \text{ cm}^2$

Question 7 A chord of a circle of radius 12 cm subtends an angle of 120° at the centre. Find the area of the corresponding segment of the circle. (Use $\pi = 3.14$ and $\sqrt{3} = 1.73$).

◎ *Thinking Process* First evaluate the area of triangle by applying trigonometric ratios, then find the area of corresponding segment of the circle.

Sol. Given, chord AB subtends an angle 120° to the centre.

i.e., $\angle AOB = 120°$

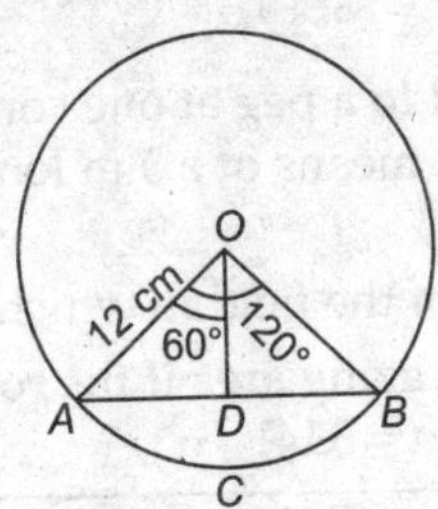

Draw $OD \perp AB$ and bisects it such that

$$AD = BD$$

$AO = BO$ (radius of circle)

$\angle ODA = \angle ODB$ (each 90°)

$\because \quad \Delta AOD \cong \Delta BOD$ (By RHS rule)

$\Rightarrow \quad \angle AOD = \angle BOD$ (By CPCT)

$\therefore \quad \angle AOD = \angle BOD = 60°$

Also, radius of circle, $r = 12$ cm

In right ΔAOD,

$$\sin 60° = \frac{AD}{AO} \Rightarrow \frac{\sqrt{3}}{2} = \frac{AD}{12}$$

$$\Rightarrow \quad AD = 6\sqrt{3} = 10.392 \text{ cm}$$

and $$\cos 60° = \frac{OD}{AO}$$

$$\Rightarrow \quad \frac{1}{2} = \frac{OD}{12}$$

$\Rightarrow \qquad OD = 6 \text{ cm}$

$\therefore$ Length of chord, $AB = 2\ AD = 2 \times 10.392 = 20.784$ cm

Now, $\qquad$ Area of $\Delta\ AOB = \frac{1}{2} \times AB \times DO$

$$= \frac{1}{2} \times 20.784 \times 6$$

$$= 62.352 \text{ cm}^2$$

Now, $\quad$ Area of sector $OACBO = \frac{\theta \pi r^2}{360°} = 120° \times \frac{3.14 \times (12)^2}{360°}$

$$= \frac{3.14 \times 144}{3}$$

$$= \frac{452.16}{3} = 150.72 \text{ cm}^2$$

$\therefore$ Area of the corresponding segment

$$= \text{Area of sector } OACBO - \text{Area of } \Delta\ AOB$$

$$= 150.72 - 62.352$$

$$= 88.368 \text{ cm}^2$$

Question 8 A horse is tied to a peg at one corner of a square shaped grass field of side 15 m by means of a 5 m long rope (see figure). Find

(i) the area of the part of the field in which the horse can graze.

(ii) the increase in the grazing area if the rope were 10 m long instead of 5 m. (Use $\pi = 3.14$)

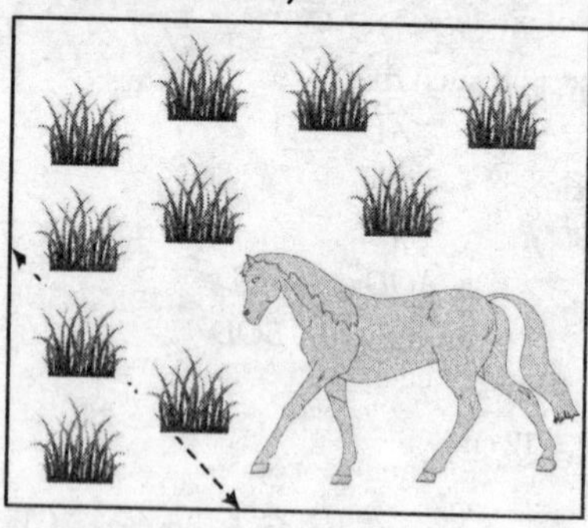

Sol. Given, side of a square = 15 m

$\therefore \qquad$ Area of square $= (15)^2 = 225 \text{ m}^2$ [$\because$ Area of square $= (\text{Side}^2)$]

Also, $\qquad$ length of rope = 5 m

$\therefore \qquad$ Radius of arc = 5 m

(i) $\therefore$ Area of the field, grazed by the horse,

$$A_1 = \frac{\theta \pi r^2}{360°} = 90° \times \frac{3.14}{360°} \times (5)^2$$

($\because$ Angle between two adjacent sides of a square is 90°)

$$= \frac{3.14 \times 25}{4} = \frac{78.5}{4} = 19.625 \text{ cm}^2$$

(ii) If length of rope = 10 m

$\therefore$ Area of field, grazed by the horse

$$A_2 = \frac{\theta \pi r^2}{360°} = \frac{90 \times 3.14 \times (10)^2}{360}$$

$$= \frac{3.14 \times 100}{4} = \frac{314}{4} = 78.5 \text{ cm}^2$$

$\therefore$ Required increase in the grazing area

$$= A_2 - A_1 = 78.5 - 19.625$$

$$= 58.875 \text{ cm}^2$$

Question 9 A brooch is made with silver wire in the form of a circle with diameter 35 mm. The wire is also used in making 5 diameters which divide the circle into 10 equal sectors as shown in figure. Find

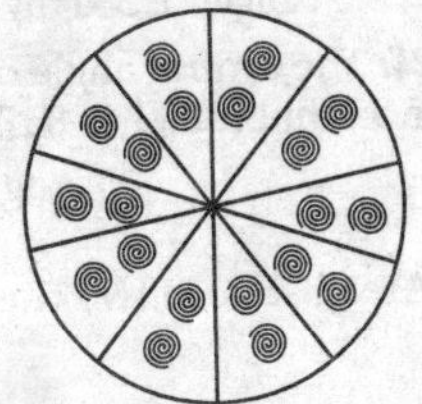

(i) the total length of the silver wire required.

(ii) the area of each sector of the brooch.

Sol. Given, diameter of circle, $d = 35$ mm

$\therefore$ Circumference of circle $= \pi d = \frac{22}{7} \times 35 = 110$ mm

Now, length of 5 diameters $= 5 \times 35 = 175$ mm

(i) The total silver wire required $= \pi d + 5d = 110 + 175 = 285$ mm

(ii) Here, we see that the whole circle is divide into 10 sector.

$\therefore$ Angle of each sector $= \frac{360°}{10} = 36°$

$\therefore$ Area of each sector of the brooch

$$= \frac{\theta\ \pi r^2}{360°} = \frac{36}{360°} \times \frac{22}{7}\left(\frac{35}{2}\right)^2 \quad \left(\because r = \frac{d}{2} = \frac{35}{2} \text{ mm}\right)$$

$$= \frac{22}{70} \times \frac{1225}{4}$$

$$= \frac{26950}{70 \times 4} = \frac{385}{4} \text{ mm}^2$$

Question 10 An umbrella has 8 ribs which are equally spaced (see figure). Assuming umbrella to be a flat circle of radius 45 cm, find the area between the two consecutive ribs of the umbrella.

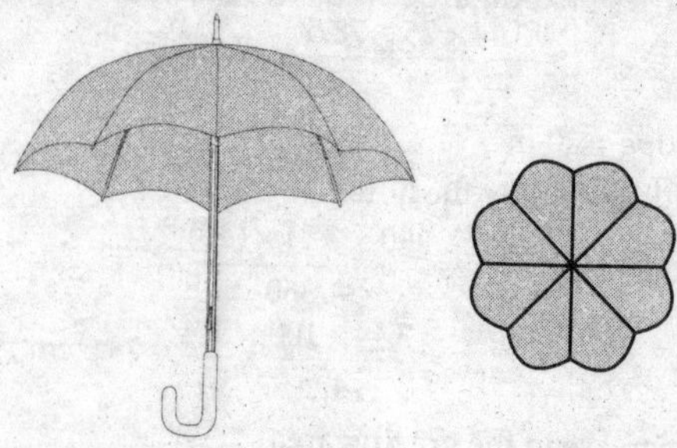

Radius of the flat circle = 45 cm

Thinking Process To find the angle between two ribs, divide the total angle *i.e.*,360° by 8 because there are 8 ribs which are equally spaced.

Sol. The central angle of an umbrella is 360°.
Since, umbrella has 8 ribs.

$\therefore$ Angle between two ribs $= \dfrac{360°}{8} = 45°$

$\therefore$ Area between two ribs = Area of one sector of an umbrella $= \dfrac{\theta \pi r^2}{360°}$

$$= 45° \times \frac{22}{7} \times \frac{(45)^2}{360°} \quad (\because r = 45, \text{ Given})$$

$$= \frac{22}{7 \times 8}(45)^2 = \frac{22275}{28} \text{ cm}^2$$

Question 11 A car has two wipers which do not overlap. Each wiper has a blade of length 25 cm sweeping through an angle of 115°. Find the total area cleaned at each sweep of the blades.

Sol. Given, length of wiper blade = 25 cm = r (say)

Angle made by this blade, $\theta = 115°$.

$\therefore$ The area cleaned by one blade = Area of sector formed by blade.

$$= \frac{\theta \pi r^2}{360°} = 115° \times \frac{22}{7 \times 360°} \times (25)^2$$

$$= \frac{23 \times 22}{7 \times 72} \times 625 = \frac{23 \times 11 \times 625}{7 \times 36} = \frac{158125}{252} \text{ cm}^2$$

$\therefore$ Total area cleaned by both blade = 2 × the area cleaned by one blade

$$= \frac{2 \times 158125}{252} = \frac{158125}{126} \text{ cm}^2$$

Mistake Alert Students forget to multiply the area cleaned by one blade by 2 to get the area cleaned by both b;ade.

Question 12 To warn ships for under water rocks, a lighthouse spreads a red coloured light over a sector of angle 80° to a distance of 16.5 km. Find the area of the sea over which the ships are warned. (Use $\pi = 3.14$)

Sol. Given, sector angle $\theta = 80°$

and distance or radius, $r = 16.5$ km

$$\therefore \quad \text{Area of sector} = \frac{\theta \pi r^2}{360°} = \frac{80° \times 3.14 \times (16.5)^2}{360°}$$

$$= \frac{2 \times 3.14 \times 272.25}{9} = \frac{1709.73}{9} = 189.97 \text{ km}^2$$

which is the required area of the sea over which the ships are warned.

Question 13 A round table cover has six equal designs as shown in figure. If the radius of the cover is 28 cm, find the cost of making the designs at the rate of ₹0.35 per cm^2. (Use $\sqrt{3} = 1.7$)

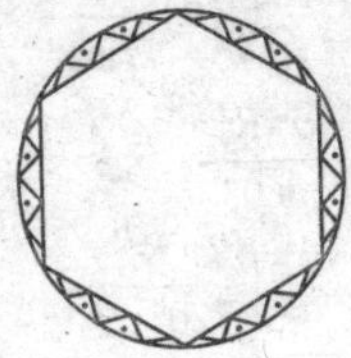

Sol. $\because$ Central angle of a circle is 360°.

$\therefore$ Angle of each sector $= \frac{360°}{6} = 60°$ ($\because$ six equal designs)

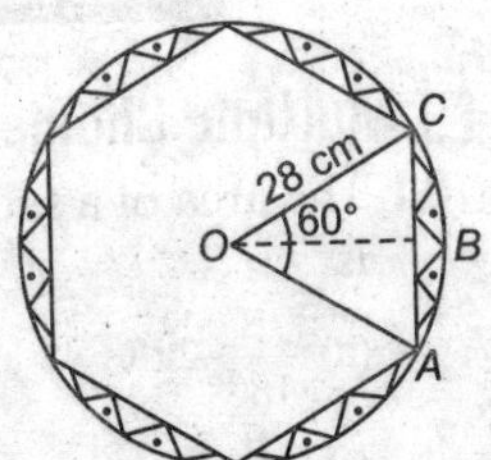

Now, we determine the area of one segment of a circle.

Here, AC is a chord of the circle.

$OA = OC$ (Radius of circle)

$\therefore \angle OAC = \angle OCA$

(angle opposite to equal sides are equal)

In ΔOAC,

$$\angle AOC + \angle OAC + \angle OCA = 180° \quad \text{(angle sum property)}$$

$$\Rightarrow \quad 60° + \angle OAC + OAC = 180°$$

$$\Rightarrow \quad 60° + 2\angle OAC = 120°$$

$$\Rightarrow \quad \angle AOC = 60°$$

$$\therefore \quad \angle OCA = 60°$$

Then, ΔAOC is equilatral triangle.

Area of equilateral ΔAOC

$$= \frac{\sqrt{3}}{4} \times (\text{Side})^2$$

$$= \frac{\sqrt{3}}{4} \times (28)^2 = \frac{1.7}{4} \times 784 = \frac{1332.8}{4} = 33.2 \text{ cm}^2$$

Now, Area of sector $OABCO = \frac{\theta \pi r^2}{360°} = 60° \times \frac{22 \times (28)^2}{7 \times 360°}$

$$= \frac{22 \times 4 \times 28}{6} = 410.67 \text{ cm}^2$$

$\therefore$ Area of segment $ABCA$ = Area of sector $OABCO$ – Area of ΔAOC

$$= 410.67 - 333.2 = 77.47 \text{ cm}^2$$

$\therefore$ Area of six segment $= 6 \times 77.47 = 464.82 \text{ cm}^2$

Since, the cost of making the design at the rate of ₹0.35 per cm^2.

$\therefore$ Total cost $= 464.82 \times 0.35 =$ ₹ 162.68

Question 14 Tick the correct answer in the following

Area of a sector of angle p (in degrees) of a circle with radius R is

(a) $\frac{p}{180°} \times 2\pi R$ (b) $\frac{p}{180°} \times \pi R^2$

(c) $\frac{p}{360°} \times 2\pi R$ (d) $\frac{p}{720°} \times 2\pi R^2$

Sol. (d) Area of sector $= \frac{\theta \pi r^2}{360°} = \frac{p \pi R^2}{360°}$ (given, $\theta = p, r = R$)

$$= \frac{p\, 2\pi R^2}{720°}$$

DIKSHA APP Questions

☐ Multiple Choice Questions

Q.1 The area of a sector of a circle with radius R and sector angle θ is

(a) $\frac{\theta}{180°} 2\pi R$ (b) $\frac{\theta}{180°} \pi R^2$

(c) $\frac{\theta}{360°} 2\pi R$ (d) $\frac{\theta}{360°} \pi R^2$

Sol. (d) As the angle at the centre of the circle is 360°, then the area of the sector of the circle with radius R and the sector angle θ is given by $\frac{\theta}{360°} \pi R^2$.

Q.2 The area of quadrant of a circle, whose circumference is 88 cm is

(a) 44 cm^2 (b) 88 cm^2

(c) 154 cm^2 (d) None of these

Sol. (c) Let r be the radius of the circle.

Given, circumference = 88 cm

$$\Rightarrow \quad 2\pi r = 88 \text{ cm} \Rightarrow r = \frac{88}{2\pi}$$

$$\Rightarrow \quad r = \frac{88 \times 7}{2 \times 22} = 2 \times 7 = 14 \text{ cm}$$

$\therefore$ Area of a quadrant of a circle $= \dfrac{\pi r^2}{4} = \dfrac{22}{7} \times \dfrac{14 \times 14}{4} = 154 \text{ cm}^2$

Q.3 If the radius of a circle is 42 cm and an arc subtends an angle of 60° at the centre, then the length of the arc is

(a) 42 cm (b) 44 cm
(c) 46 cm (d) None of these

Sol. (b) Since, the arc ABC subtends an angle of 60° at the curve.

$$\therefore \quad \theta = 60°$$

and radius = 42 cm

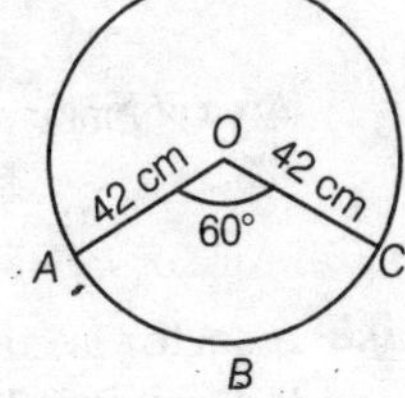

Then, the length of the arc $ABC = \dfrac{\theta}{360°} \times 2\pi r$

$$= \frac{60°}{360°} \times 2 \times \frac{22}{7} \times 42$$

$$= 44 \text{ cm}$$

Q.4 (a) Area of a sector of angle 150° of a circle with radius 21 cm is

(a) 577.5 cm^2 (b) 27.5 cm^2
(c) 55 cm^2 (d) 1155 cm^2

Sol. (a)Since arc ABC subtends an angle of 150° at the centre

$$\therefore \quad \theta = 150°$$

and radius = 21 cm

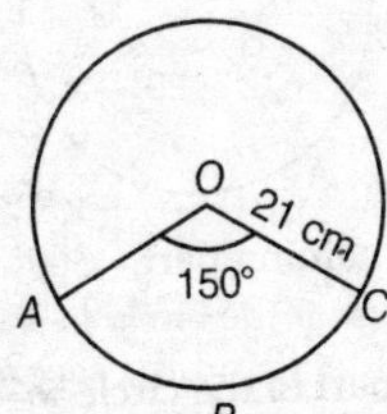

Then, area of the sector formed by the arc

$$= \frac{\theta}{360°} \times \pi r^2$$

$$= \frac{150°}{360°} \times \frac{22}{7} \times 21 \times 21 = 577.5 \text{ cm}^2$$

Q.5 (b) The radius of a circle is 10 cm. If the area of a minor sector of the circle is 100 cm^2, then the area of its corresponding major sector is (Take $\pi = 3.14$)

(a) 314 cm^2 (b) 214 cm^2
(c) 114 cm^2 (d) 100 cm^2

Sol. (b)Given, radius = 10 cm

Area of minor sector = 100 cm^2

Area of circle = πr^2

$$= \pi(10)^2 = 100\pi \text{ cm}^2$$

Area of major sector = Area of circle – Area of minor sector

$$= 100\pi - 100$$

$$= 100(3.14 - 1) = 100(2.14) = 214 \text{ cm}^2$$

Q.6 A sector is cut off from a circle of radius 21 cm. The angle of the sector is 120°. The area of the remaining part of the circle is

(a) 1386 cm^2 (b) 462 cm^2
(c) 924 cm^2 (d) 793 cm^2

Sol. (c) Given, radius of the circle, $r = 21$ cm

Sector angle = 120°

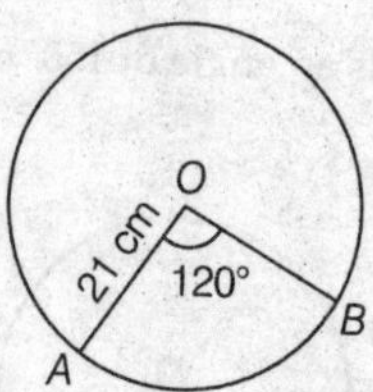

Angle measure of the remaining part = 360° – 120° = 240°

($\because$ total angle = 360°)

$\therefore$ Area of the remaining part of the circle $= \dfrac{240°}{360°} \times \pi r^2$

$$= \frac{2}{3} \times \frac{22}{7} \times 21 \times 21 = 924 \text{ cm}^2$$

Given, radius of circle π = 21 cm

Sector angle = 120°

Area of circle = πr^2

$$= \frac{22}{7} \times 21 \times 21 = 1386 \text{ cm}^2$$

Area of sector cut off $= \frac{\theta}{360°} \times \pi r^2$

$$= \frac{120°}{360°} \times \frac{22}{7} \times 21 \times 21 = 462 \text{ cm}^2$$

Area of remaining part of circle = Area of circle – Area of sector cut off

$$= 1386 \text{ cm}^2 - 462 = 924 \text{ cm}^2$$

Q.7 A circular disc of radius 6 cm is divided into three sectors with the angles of sectors measuring 170°, 100°and 90°, respectively. The ratio of the areas of these sectors is ___.

(a) 11 : 10 : 07 (b) 15 : 10 : 07
(c) 15 : 08 : 07 (d) 17 : 10 : 09

Sol. (d) Given, circular disc is divided into 3 sectors.

$$\theta_1 = 170°, \theta_2 = 100°, \theta_2 = 90°, r = 6 \text{ cm}$$

Area of minor sector $= \frac{\theta}{360°} \pi r^2$

Area of sector 1 $= \frac{170°}{360°} \times 36\pi$ $[\because r = 6 \text{ cm}]$

Area of sector 2 $= \frac{100°}{360°} \times 36\pi$

Area of sector 3 $= \frac{90°}{360°} \times 36\pi$

Hence, ratio of areas of these sectors = 170 : 100 : 90 = 17 : 10 : 9

Q.8 If the area of a sector of a circle is 3.85 cm^2 and the angle of the sector is 36°, then find the radius of the circle. (Take $\pi = 22/7$)

(a) 3.5 cm (b) 3.85 cm (c) 12.25 cm (d) 1.1 cm

Sol. (a) Given, the area of the sector = 3.85 cm^2

The angle of the sector = 36°

$\therefore$ Area of the sector $= \frac{\theta}{360°} \times \pi r^2$

$$\Rightarrow \quad 3.85 = \frac{36°}{360°} \times \frac{22}{7} \times r^2$$

$$\Rightarrow \quad r^2 = 3.85 \times \frac{360°}{36°} \times \frac{7}{22}$$

$$\Rightarrow \quad r^2 = 3.85 \times 10 \times \frac{7}{22}$$

$$\Rightarrow \quad r^2 = 12.25$$

$$\therefore \quad r = 3.5 \text{ cm}$$

Q.9 If the area of sector $OA \times BO$ of circle is 100.25 cm^2, and the area of the enclosed triangle AOB is 78 cm^2, what will be the area of the enclosed segment?

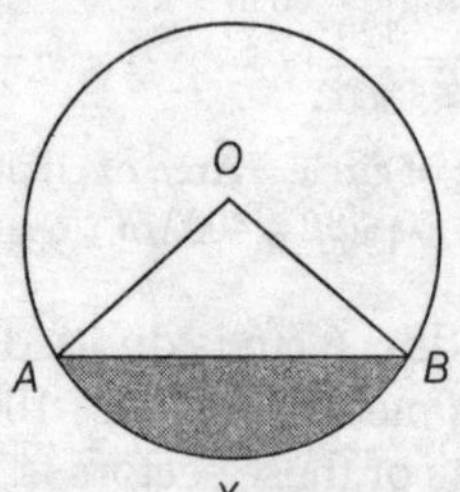

(a) 22.25 cm^2 (b) 78 cm^2
(c) 12.25 cm^2 (d) 32.25 cm^2

Sol. (a) Given, area of $OA \times BO = 100.25$ cm^2

Area of the enclosed triangle $AOB = 78$ cm^2

Now, area of the segment = Area of the sector $OA \times BO$ – Area of ΔAOB

$$= 100.25 - 78 = 22.25 \text{ cm}^2$$

Q.10 A segment of a circle is bounded by which of the following ?

(a) A chord and an arc (b) Two arcs
(c) Two chords (d) Two radii and an arc

Sol. (a) We know that, the portion (or part) of the circular region enclosed between a chord and the corresponding arc is called a segment of the circle.

☐ Subjective Type Questions

Q.1 The minute hand of a clock is 8 cm long. Find the area swept by the minute hand between 8. 30 am and 9.00 am.

Sol. Given, length of the minute hand of a clock = 8 cm

Number of minutes between 8 : 30 am to 9 : 00 am = 30 min

Angle moved by the minute hand in 30 min = $30 \times 6° = 180°$

As radius = 8 cm, we have

$$\text{Area of the sector of the circle} = \frac{\theta \pi r^2}{360°}$$

$$= \frac{180°}{360°} \times \frac{22}{7} \times 8 \times 8$$

$$= \frac{704}{7}$$

$$= 100.57 \text{ cm}^2$$

Q.2 A horse is tethered to a corner of a rectangular field 80 m by 50 m by a rope of length 7 m. Find the area over which it can graze. Also find the area beyond his reach.

Sol. Given, length of the rectangle = 80 m

Breadth of the rectangle = 50 m

$\therefore$ Area of the rectangle = $l \times b$

$$= 80 \times 50 = 4000 \text{ m}^2$$

Also, length of the rope = 7 m

$\Rightarrow$ radius of the sector = 7 cm

Area of the field grazed by the horse = $\frac{\theta}{360°} \times \pi r^2$

$$= \frac{90°}{360°} \times \frac{22}{7} \times 7 \times 7 = 38.5 \text{ m}^2$$

[$\because$ Angle in rectangular field is 90°]

Area boyond horse's reach = Area of the rectangle – Area of the field grazed by the horse

$$= 4000 - 38.5$$

$$= 3961.5 \text{ m}^2$$

Q.3 A chord of a circle of radius 6 cm is making an angle 60° at the centre. Find the length of the chord.

Sol. Radius of the circle = 6 cm

Angle made by the chord at the centre = 60°

Let the other angles in the triangle be x because the radius of the circle are equal and angles opposite to equal sides are equal.

We know that,

Sum of the angles in the triangle = 180°

$\Rightarrow \quad x + x + 60° = 180°$

$\Rightarrow \quad 2x + 60° = 180° \Rightarrow 2x = 120° \Rightarrow x = 60°$

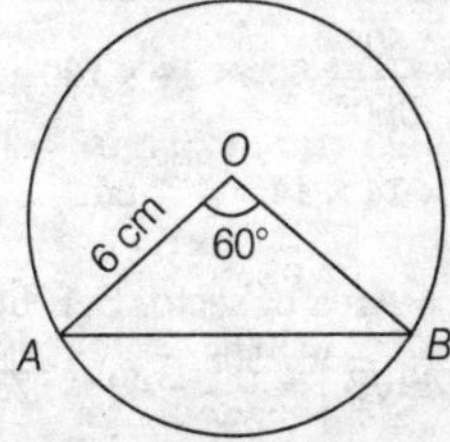

Such that given triangle is equilateral triangle.

Hence, in the equilateral triangle all sides are equal.

Hence, Chord of the circle is 6 cm.

Q.4 Find the area of the sector of a circle with radius 4 cm and of angle 30°. Also, find the area of the corresponding major sector (Use $\pi = 3.14$)

Sol. Given sector is $OAPB$.

Area of the sector $OAPB = \frac{\theta}{360°} \times \pi r^2$

$\Rightarrow \quad \frac{30°}{360°} \times 3.14 \times 4 \times 4 = \frac{12.56}{3} \approx 4.19 \text{ cm}^2$

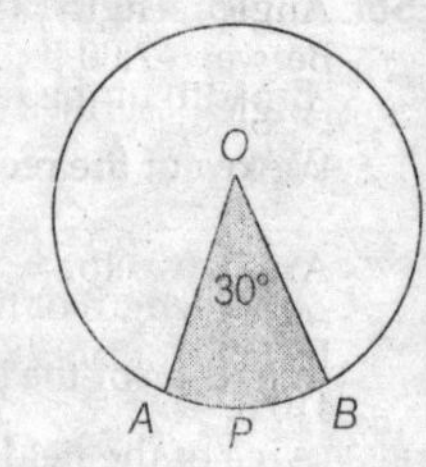

Area of the corresponding major sector

$= \pi r^2 - \text{Area of sector } OAPB = (3.14 \times 16 - 4.19) \text{ cm}^2$

$\approx 46.1 \text{ cm}^2$

Quick Solution

Area of the corresponding major sector $= \frac{360° - \theta}{360°} \times \pi r^2$

$= \frac{360° - 30°}{360°} \times 3.14 \times 4 \times 4 = 46.05 \approx 46.1 \text{ cm}^2$

Q.5 Find the area of the minor segment of a circle of radius 14 cm, when its central angle is 60°. Also find the area of the corresponding major segment

Sol. In ΔAOB, $\angle AOB = 60°$

Also $AO = BO \Rightarrow \angle OAB = \angle OBA$ (angle opposite to equal sides are equal)

In ΔAOB,

$\angle AOB + \angle OAB \mid \angle OBA = 180°$ (Angle sum property)

$\Rightarrow \quad 60° + \angle OAB + \angle OAB = 180°$ ($\because \angle OAB = \angle OBA$)

$\Rightarrow \quad 2\angle OAB = 120° \Rightarrow \angle OAB = 60° \Rightarrow \angle OBA = 60°$

$\therefore \Delta AOB$ is an equilateral triangle.

Area of equilateral triangle

$\Delta AOB = \frac{\sqrt{3}}{4} \times 14 \times 14 = 49\sqrt{3} \text{ cm}^2$

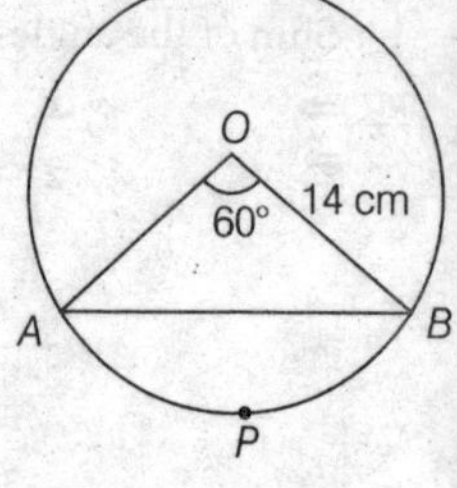

Area of sector $OAPBO = \frac{60°}{360°} \times \pi \times 14 \times 14$

$= \frac{1}{6} \times \frac{22}{7} \times 14 \times 14 = \frac{308}{3} \text{ cm}^2$

Area of minor segment = Area of sector $OAPBO$ – Area of triangle OAB

$= \left(\frac{308}{3} - 49\sqrt{3}\right) = \frac{308}{3} - 49 \times 1.732 = 17.8 \text{ cm}^2$

Area of circle $= \pi r^2 = \frac{22}{7} \times 14 \times 14 = 616 \text{ cm}^2$

Area of major segment = Area of circle – Area of minor segment

$[616 - 17.8] = 598.2 \text{ cm}^2$

Q.6 The length of the minute hand of a clock is 14 cm. The area swept by the minute hand between 7 : 00 pm to 7 : 40 pm is __.

Sol. Radius of minute hand is 14 cm.

Angle described by minute hand in 1 min. = 6°

Between 7:00 pm to 7:40 pm, there are a 40 min.

Angle described by minute hand in 40 min = 40 × 6° = 240°

We know, area of a sector $= \dfrac{\theta}{360°}\pi r^2$

Area of sector $= \dfrac{240°}{360°} \times \dfrac{22}{7} \times (14)^2 = 410.67 \text{ cm}^2$

Hence, the area swept by the minute hand between 7:00 pm to 7:40 pm is 410.67 cm^2.

Q.7 If a chord of a circle of radius 80 cm subtends an angle of 60° at the centre, then the area of the corresponding segment of the circle is ____. (Take $\pi = 3.14$)

Sol. Given, radius of the circle = 80 cm

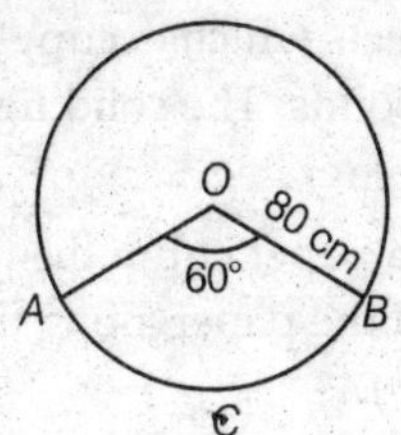

Angle of the sector = 60°

Now, as $OA = OB = 80$ cm (radius)

Then, $\angle OAB = \angle OBA$ (Angles equal to opposite sides are equal)

So, in ΔAOB,

$$\angle OAB + \angle OBA + \angle AOB = 180° \text{ (Angle sum property)}$$

$$\Rightarrow \quad 2\angle OAB + 60° = 180°$$

$$\Rightarrow \quad 2\angle OAB = 180° - 60° = 120°$$

$$\Rightarrow \quad \angle OAB = \frac{120°}{2} = 60°$$

$$\Rightarrow \quad \angle AOB = \angle OAB = \angle OBA = 60°$$

Hence, ΔOAB is an equilateral triangle.

$$\Rightarrow \quad \text{Area of } \Delta OAB = \frac{\sqrt{3}}{4}(\text{side})^2 = \frac{\sqrt{3}}{4}(80)^2$$

$$= 2771.281 \text{ cm}^2$$

Area of the sector $= \dfrac{\theta}{360°} \times \pi r^2$

$$= \frac{60°}{360°} \times 3.14 \times 80 \times 80 = 3349.33 \text{ cm}^2$$

Area of the segment = Area of the sector $OACBO$ – Area of ΔAOB

$$= 3349.33 - 2271.28 = 1078.05 \text{ cm}^2$$

Surface Areas and Volumes

CHAPTER 12

Important Points

01 Solid Figures The objects which occupy space (*i.e.,* they have three dimensions) are called solids. The solid figures can be derived from the plane figures.

e.g., In Fig.(a), we have a paper cut in the form as shown. It is a plane figure but when we fold the paper along the dotted lines, a box can b[e] made as shown in Fig.(b).

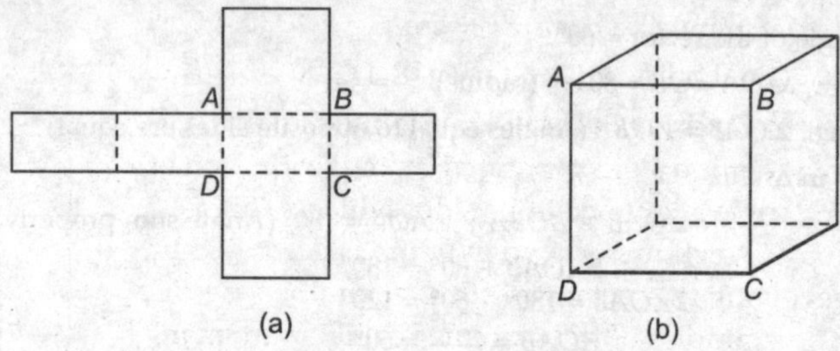

(a) (b)

02 Surface Area The sum of the areas of the plane figures making up the boundary of a solid figure is called its surface area *e.g.,* the area of paper in Fig.(a) is the surface area of box.

03 Volume The measure of part of space occupied by a solid is called its volume.

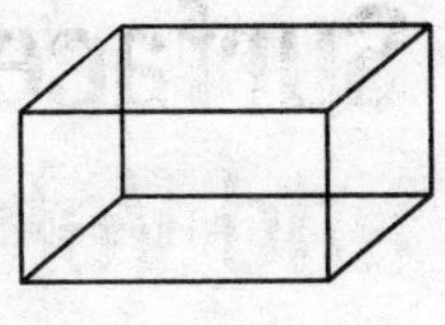

04 Parallelepiped (cuboid) A solid bounded by three pairs of parallel plane surfaces (or faces) is called a parallelepiped. A Parallelepiped whose faces are rectangles is called a rectangular parallelepiped or a rectangular solid or a cuboid.

(i) A cuboid has six rectangular plane surfaces called faces.

(ii) A cuboid has 8 corners called the vertices.

(iii) Volume of cuboid $= l \times b \times h$

where, l = length, b = breadth and h = height

(iv) Total surface area of cuboid $= 2\,(lb + bh + lh)$

(v) Area of the 4 walls $= 2\,(l + b) \cdot h$

05 Cube If the faces of a rectangular parallelepiped are squares, then it is called a cube.

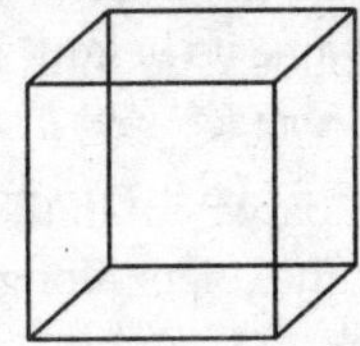

(i) Edge of a cube = Length = Breadth = Height

(ii) Volume of a cube $= (\text{Edge})^3$

(iii) Total Surface Area (TSA) of a cube $= 6 \times (\text{Edge})^2$

06 Right Circular Cylinder A right circular cylinder is a solid generated by the revolution of a rectangle about one of its sides which remains fixed. A cylinder shown in figure is described by revolving the rectangle $ABCD$ about the side BC. The examples of right circular cylinder are many such as water pipes, powder box, laboratory beakers etc.

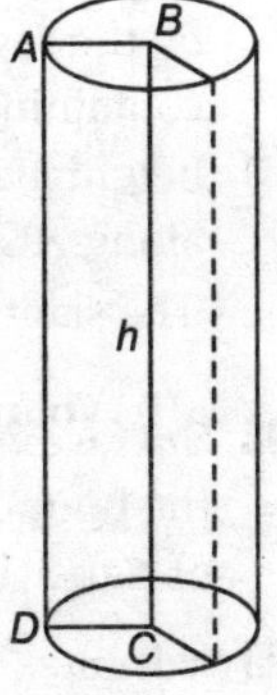

(i) Volume of the cylinder

$= (\text{Area of base}) \times \text{Height}$

$= \pi r^2 h$ cu units

where, r is the radius of the base and h is the height of the cylinder.

(ii) Curved surface area

$= \text{Circumference of the base} \times \text{Height}$

$= 2\pi rh$ sq units

(iii) Total surface area = Curved surface area + Area of two ends

$$= 2\,\pi r h + 2\pi\, r^2 = 2\pi\, r\,(h + r)$$

Also, note $\quad h = \dfrac{V}{\pi r^2} \Rightarrow r = \sqrt{\dfrac{V}{\pi\, h}}$

(iv) If we have two cylinder of same heights, then ratio of their volumes, $\dfrac{V_1}{V_2} = \left(\dfrac{r_1}{r_2}\right)^2$, where r_1 and r_2 are radii of respective cylinder.

07 Hollow Cylinder The volume of material in a hollow cylinder is the difference between the volume of a cylinder having the external dimensions and the volume of a cylinder having the internal dimensions.

Let R and r be the external and internal radii of the hollow cylinder and h be its height. Then,

(i) Volume of material $= \pi\,(R^2 - r^2)\,h$ sq. units

(ii) Total surface area $= 2\pi\,(R + r)(h + R - r)$ sq. units

(iii) Curved surface area

$$= 2\pi Rh + 2\pi\, rh = 2\pi\,(R + r)\,h \text{ sq. units}$$

(iv) Total outer surface area $= 2\pi\, rh + \pi R^2 + \pi\,(R^2 - r^2)$ sq. units

08 Right Circular Cone A right circular cone is a solid generated by the revolution of a right angled triangle about one of its sides containing the right angle as axis. In the adjoining figure a cone of height h and radius r is generated by revolving the right $\Delta\, AOB$ along AO.

The slant height of the cone $l = AC = \sqrt{r^2 + h^2}$

(i) Volume of cone $= \dfrac{1}{3}\pi\, r^2 h$ cu units

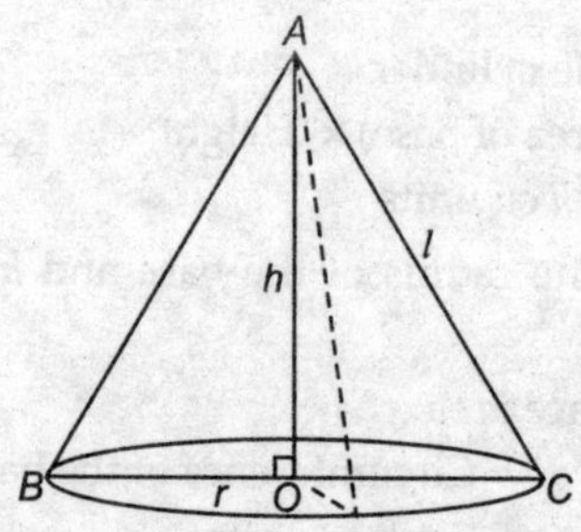

(ii) Curved surface area of cone = πrl sq units

(iii) Total surface area of a cone = $\pi r(l + r)$ sq units

(iv) If we have two cones of equal heights, then the ratio of their volumes, $\frac{V_1}{V_2} = \left(\frac{r_1}{r_2}\right)^2$, where, r_1 and r_2 are the radii of respective cones.

09 Sphere A sphere is a solid generated by the revolution of a semi-circle about its diameter.

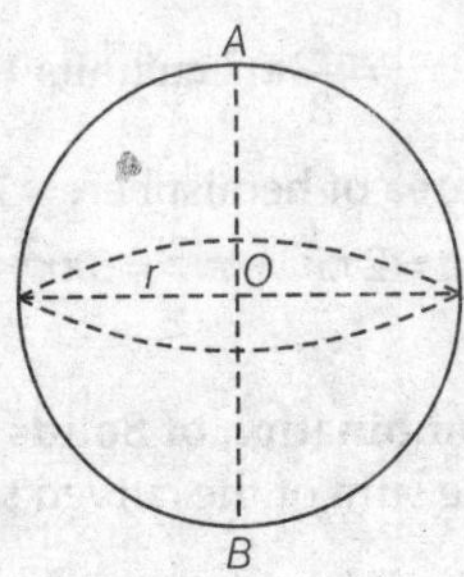

(i) A sphere is the locus of a point which moves in space such that its distance from a fixed point in space remains constant. The fixed point is called the centre of sphere and the constant distance is called the radius of sphere.

(ii) In the figure, O is centre and r is radius.

(iii) Volume of sphere = $\frac{4}{3}\pi r^3$ cu units

(iv) Surface area of sphere = $4\pi r^2$ sq units

(v) Volume of a hollow sphere = $\frac{4}{3}\pi(R^3 - r^3)$ cu units

where, r = inner radius and R = outer radius.

(vi) If we have two spheres of different radii, then ratio of their volumes $\frac{V_1}{V_2} = \left(\frac{r_1}{r_2}\right)^3$, where, r_1 and r_2 are the radii of respective spheres.

10 Hemisphere A plane passing through the centre cuts the spher in two equal parts each called a hemisphere.

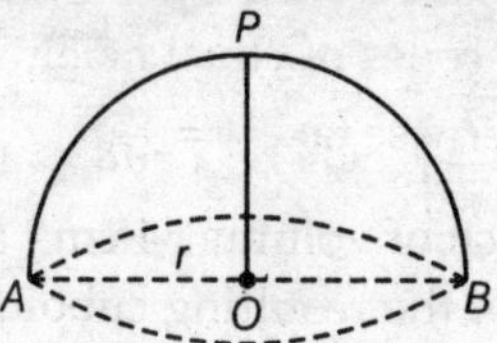

(i) Volume of hemisphere

$$= \frac{2}{3}\pi r^3 \text{ cu units}$$

(ii) Curved surface area of hemisphere $= 2\pi r^2$ sq units

(iii) Total surface area $= 2\pi r^2 + \pi r^2 = 3\pi r^2$ sq units

11 Surface Area of a Combination of Solids The total surface are of the new solid is the sum of the curved surface areas of each of the individual parts.

e.g.,

 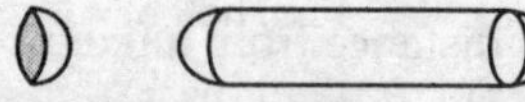

TSA of new solid = CSA of one hemisphere + CSA of cylinder + CSA of other hemisphere

where, TSA → Total Surface Area

and CSA → Curved Surface Area

Note The total surface area is not the sum of the total surface area of each of the individual parts.

Volume of a combination of solids The volume of the new solid is the sum of the volume of each of the individual parts.

e.g.,

Volume of the solid = Volume of cylinder + 2 × Volume of hemisphere

$$= \pi r^2 h + \frac{4}{3}\pi r^3$$

Exercise 12.1

Unless stated otherwise take $\pi = \frac{22}{7}$.

Question 1 2 cubes each of volume 64 cm^3 are joined end to end. Find the surface area of the resulting cuboid.

Sol. Given, the volume of a cube is 64 cm^3. Let side of the cube is a cm, then

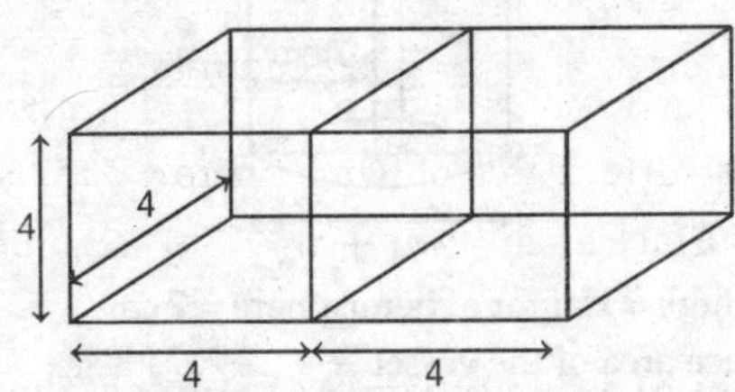

$$a^3 = 64 = 4^3 \Rightarrow a = 4 \text{ cm} \quad [\because \text{Volume of a cube} = (\text{side})^3]$$

When we join end to end of each cube, then length of the new cuboid become (4 + 4) = 8 cm, breadth = 4 cm, height = 4 cm.

$\therefore$ The surface area of the resulting cuboid $= 2(lb + bh + hl)$

$$= 2(8 \times 4 + 4 \times 4 + 4 \times 8)$$
$$= 2(32 + 16 + 32)$$
$$= 2(80) = 160 \text{ cm}^2$$

Question 2 A vessel is in the form of a hollow hemisphere mounted by a hollow cylinder. The diameter of the hemisphere is 14 cm and the total height of the vessel is 13 cm. Find the inner surface area of the vessel.

Sol. Given, vessel is a combination of hollow hemisphere and a hollow cylinder. Also, we have

$$AB = DC = 14 \text{ cm} \qquad \text{(Diameter)}$$

$\therefore$
$$OB = O'C = O'P$$
$$= \frac{AB}{2} = \frac{14}{2} = 7 \text{ cm} \qquad \text{(Radius)}$$

and
$$PO = 13 \text{ cm}$$

$\therefore$
$$OO' = PO - O'P$$
$$= 13 - 7 = 6 \text{ cm}$$

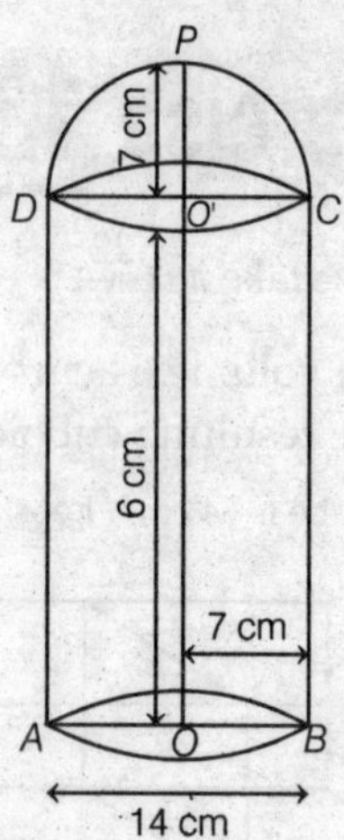

$\therefore$ Radius of hemisphere = Height of hemisphere = 7 cm

Now, the inner surface area of the vessel

$$= \text{Curved surface area of cylinder} + \text{Curved surface area of hemisphere}$$

$$= 2\pi rh + 2\pi r^2$$

$$= 2 \times \frac{22}{7} \times 7 \times 6 + 2 \times \frac{22}{7} \times (7)^2$$

$$= 2 \times 22 \times 6 + 2 \times 22 \times 7$$

$$= 44(6+7) = 44 \times 13$$

$$= 572 \text{ cm}^2$$

Question 3 A toy is in the form of a cone of radius 3.5 cm mounted on a hemisphere of same radius. The total height of the toy is 15.5 cm. Find the total surface area of the toy.

Sol. Given, toy is a combination of hemisphere and a cone.

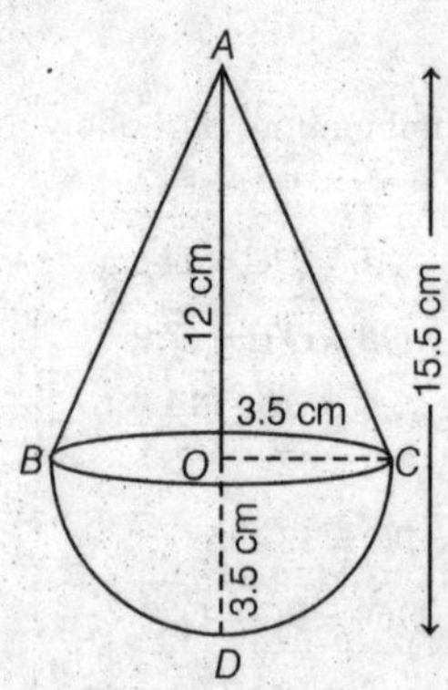

Also, we have $AD = 15.5$ cm

$OC = OD = OB = 3.5$ cm (Radius)

$OA = AD - OD$

$= 15.5 - 3.5 = 12$ cm

⇒ Height of the cone = 12 cm

and radius of the cone = 3.5 cm

∴ Total surface area of the toy = Curved surface area of cone + Curved surface area of hemisphere

$$= \pi r l + 2\pi r^2$$

$$= \pi r \sqrt{h^2 + r^2} + 2\pi r^2$$

$$= \frac{22}{7} \times 3.5 \times \sqrt{(12)^2 + (3.5)^2} + 2 \times \frac{22}{7} \times (3.5)^2$$

$$= 11\sqrt{144 + 12.25} + 22 \times 3.5$$

$$= 11\sqrt{156.25} + 11 \times 7$$

$$= 11(12.5) + 77 = 137.5 + 77$$

$$= 214.5 \text{ cm}^2$$

Question 4 A cubical block of side 7 cm is surmounted by a hemisphere. What is the greatest diameter the hemisphere can have? Find the surface area of the solid.

Sol. Given, a cubical block is surmounted by a hemisphere. Therefore, its diameter must be equal to the side of cube, *i.e.*, 7 cm.

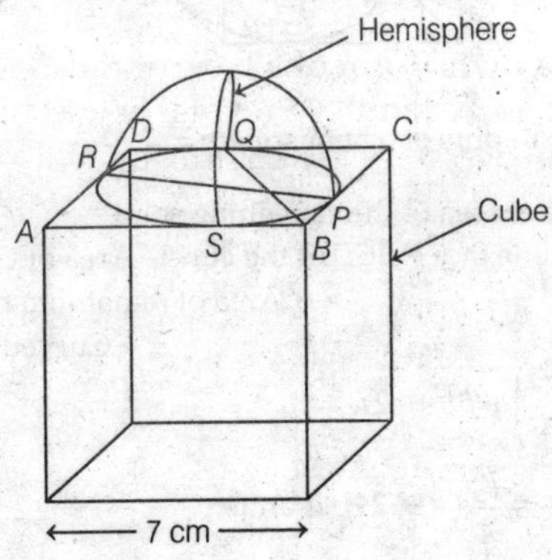

∴ Radius of hemisphere $(r) = \frac{7}{2}$ cm

Now, total curved surface area of solid

= Surface area of five faces of the cube

+ Surface area of hemisphere except circular face $PQRS$

+ {Area of face $ABCD$ – Area of circular space $PQRS$}

$$= 5\times(\text{side})^2 + 2\pi\,(\text{radius})^2 + \{(\text{side})^2 - \pi\,(\text{radius})^2\}$$

$$= 5\times(7)^2 + 2\times\frac{22}{7}\times\left(\frac{7}{2}\right)^2 + \left\{(7)^2 - \frac{22}{7}\times\left(\frac{7}{2}\right)^2\right\}$$

$$= 5\times 49 + 11\times 7 + \left(49 - \frac{77}{2}\right)$$

$$= 245 + 77 + 49 - \frac{77}{2}$$

$$= 294 + \frac{77}{2}$$

$$= \frac{665}{2} = 332.5\ \text{cm}^2$$

Question 5 A hemispherical depression is cut out from one face of a cubical wooden block such that the diameter l of the hemisphere is equal to the edge of the cube. Determine the surface area of the remaining solid.

Sol. Given, side of the cube = Diameter of the hemisphere = l

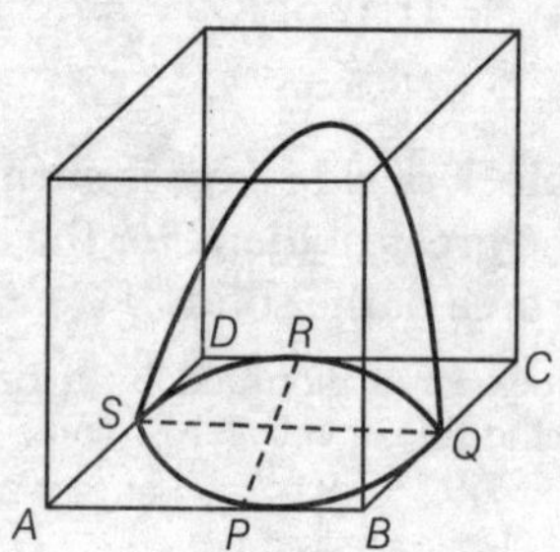

$\therefore$ Radius of a hemisphere $= \frac{l}{2}$

$\therefore$ Now, required surface area of the remaining solid

= {Area of one face *ABCD* of the cube – Area of circle *PQRS* + Area of remaining five faces of the cube + Curved area of hemisphere}

$$= \left(l^2 - \pi\frac{l^2}{4}\right) + 5l^2 + 2\pi\frac{l^2}{4}$$

$$= 6l^2 + \frac{\pi l^2}{4} = \frac{l^2}{4}(\pi + 24)\ \text{sq units}$$

estion 6 A medicine capsule is in the shape of a cylinder with ro hemispheres stuck to each of its ends (see figure). The length of e entire capsule is 14 mm and the diameter of the capsule is 5 mm. nd its surface area.

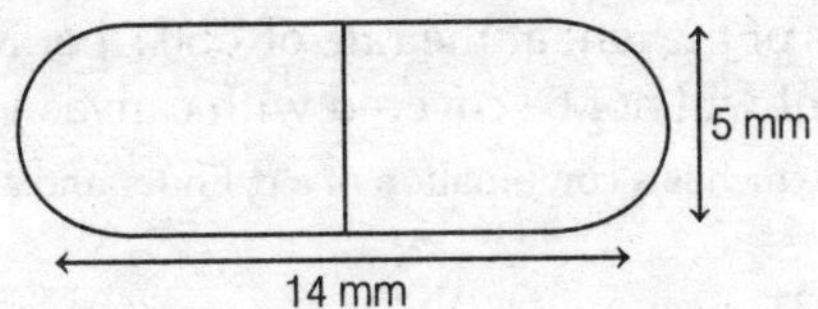

l. In the given medicine capsule, two hemisphere and one cylinder are cluded. Also, given the diameter of the capsule = 5 mm

$$\text{Radius} = \frac{5}{2} = 2.5 \text{ mm}$$

d length of the capsule = 14 mm

Length of the cylinder = 14 – (2.5 + 2.5) = 9 mm

ow, curved surface area of a hemisphere $= 2\pi r^2 = 2 \times \frac{22}{7} \times 2.5 \times 2.5$

$$= \frac{275}{7} \text{ mm}^2$$

so, curved surface area of the cylinder $= 2\pi r h = 2 \times \frac{22}{7} \times 2.5 \times 9$

$$= \frac{22}{7} \times 45 = \frac{990}{7} \text{ mm}^2$$

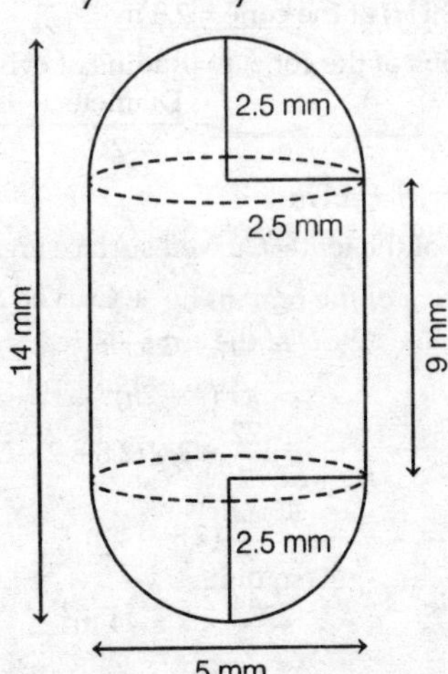

Required surface area of medicine capsule

= 2 × Curved surface area of the hemisphere + Curved surface area of the cylinder

$$= 2 \times \frac{275}{7} + \frac{990}{7} = \frac{550}{7} + \frac{990}{7} = \frac{1540}{7} = 220 \text{ mm}^2$$

Question 7 A tent is in the shape of a cylinder surmounted by a conical top. If the height and diameter of the cylindrical part are 2.1 m and 4 m respectively, and the slant height of the top is 2.8 m, find the area of the canvas used for making the tent. Also, find the cost of the canvas of the tent at the rate of ₹ 500 per m^2. (Note that the base of the tent will not be covered with canvas.)

Sol. Given, a tent which is a combination of a cylinder and a cone.

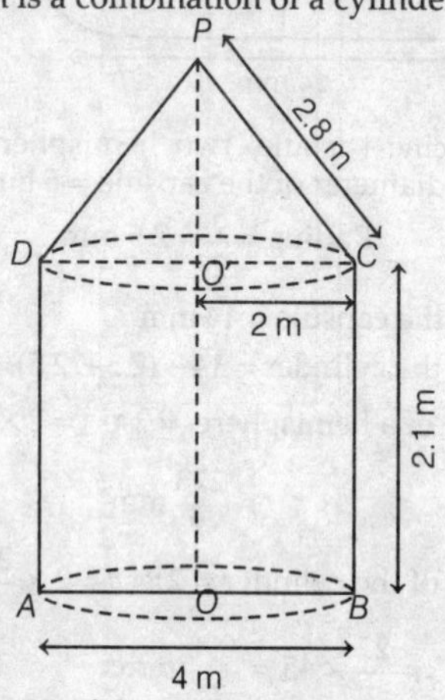

Also, we have slant height (l) of the cone = 2.8 m

$$\text{Radius of the cone, } r = \text{Radius of cylinder}$$

$$= \frac{\text{Diameter}}{2} = \frac{4}{2} = 2\,\text{m}$$

and height of the cylinder, h = 2.1 m

∴ Required surface area of the tent = Curved surface area of cone

+ Curved Surface area of cylind

$$= \pi r l + 2\pi r h$$

$$= \pi r (l + 2h)$$

$$= \frac{22}{7} \times 2 \times (2.8 + 2 \times 2.1)$$

$$= \frac{44}{7}(2.8 + 4.2)$$

$$= \frac{44}{7} \times 7 = 44\ \text{m}^2$$

Hence, the total cost of the canvas of the tent at the rate of ₹ 500 per m^2

= Curved surface area × Cost per m^2

= 44 × 500 = ₹ 22000

uestion 8 From a solid cylinder whose height is 2.4 cm and iameter 1.4 cm, a conical cavity of the same height and same iameter is hollowed out. Find the total surface area of the emaining solid to the nearest cm^2.

ol. Given, diameter of cylinder = Diameter of conical cavity = 1.4 cm

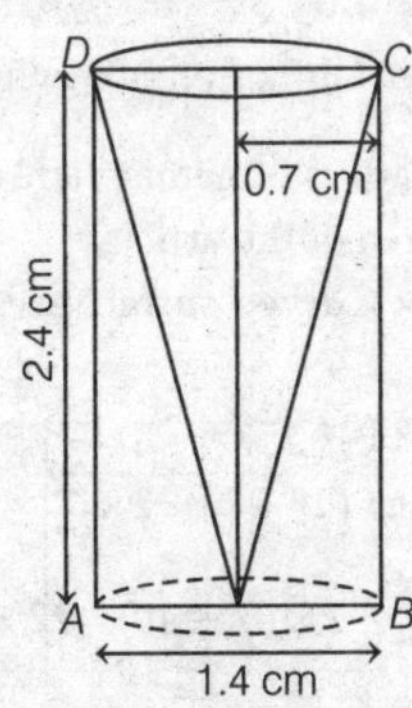

Radius of cylinder = Radius of conical cavity

$$= \frac{\text{Diameter}}{2}$$

$$= \frac{1.4}{2} = 0.7 \text{ cm}$$

nd height of the cylinder = Height of the conical cavity

$$= 2.4 \text{ cm}$$

Slant height of the conical cavity (l) $= \sqrt{h^2 + r^2}$

$$= \sqrt{(2.4)^2 + (0.7)^2}$$

$$= \sqrt{5.76 + 0.49} = \sqrt{6.25}$$

$$= 2.5 \text{ cm}$$

Hence, total surface area of remaining solid

= Curved surface area of conical cavity + Total surface area of cylinder without the top

$$= \pi r l + (2\pi r h + \pi r^2) = \pi r (l + 2h + r)$$

$$= \frac{22}{7} \times 0.7\,(2.5 + 4.8 + 0.7)$$

$$= 2.2 \times 8$$

$$= 17.6 \approx 18 \text{ cm}^2$$

Question 9 A wooden article was made by scooping out a hemisphere from each end of a solid cylinder, as shown in figure. If the height of the cylinder is 10 cm and its base is of radius 3.5 cm, find the total surface area of the article.

Sol Given,

Height of the cylinder, $h = 10$ cm

and radius of the cylinder = Radius of hemisphere $(r) = 3.5$ cm

Now, required total surface area of the article

$$= 2 \times \text{Curved surface area of hemisphere} + \text{Lateral surface area of cylinder}$$

$$= 2 \times (2\pi r^2) + 2\pi r h$$

$$= 2\pi r(2r + h) = 2 \times \frac{22}{7} \times 3.5 \times (2 \times 3.5 + 10)$$

$$= \frac{22}{7} \times 7 \times (7 + 10) = 22 \times 17 = 374 \text{ cm}^2$$

Exercise 12.2

Question 1 A solid is in the shape of a cone standing on a hemisphere with both their radii being equal to 1 cm and the height of the cone is equal to its radius. Find the volume of the solid in terms of π.

Sol Given, solid is a combination of a cone and a hemisphere.

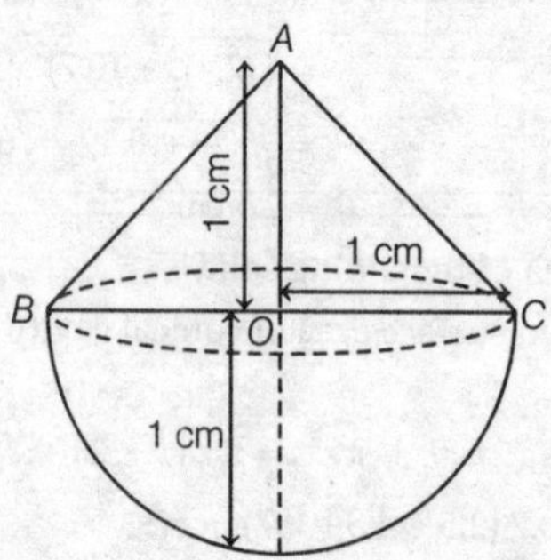

Also, we have radius of the cone (r) = Radius of the hemisphere = 1 cm

and height of the cone $(h) = 1$ cm

∴ Required volume of the solid = Volume of the cone + Volume of the hemisphere

$$= \frac{1}{3}\pi r^2 h + \frac{2}{3}\pi r^3$$
$$= \frac{1}{3}\pi (1)^2 (1) + \frac{2}{3}\pi (1)^3$$
$$= \frac{\pi}{3} + \frac{2}{3}\pi$$
$$= \frac{(\pi + 2\pi)}{3} = \frac{3\pi}{3} = \pi \text{ cm}^3$$

Question 2 Rachel, an engineering student, was asked to make a model shaped like a cylinder with two cones attached at its two ends by using a thin aluminium sheet. The diameter of the model is 3 cm and its length is 12 cm. If each cone has a height of 2 cm, find the volume of air contained in the model that Rachel made. (Assume the outer and inner dimensions of the model to be nearly the same.)

Sol. Given, model is a combination of a cylinder and two cones. Also, we have, diameter of the model, $BC = ED = 3$ cm.

∴ $$r = \frac{3}{2} = 1.5 \text{ cm}$$

Height of cone, $h_1 = 2$ cm and length of the model, $AF = 12$ cm

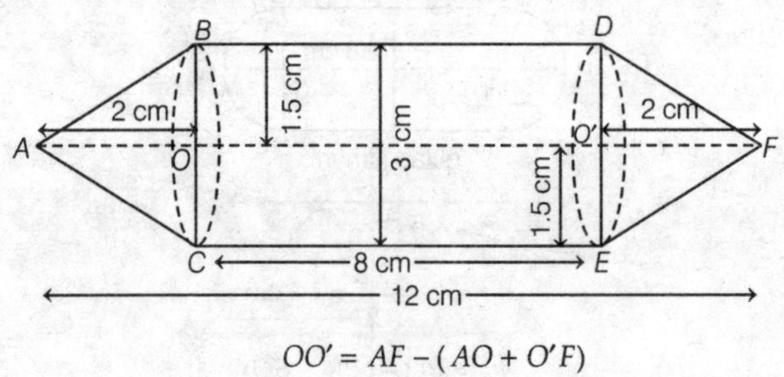

∴ $$OO' = AF - (AO + O'F)$$
$$= 12 - (2 + 2)$$
$$= 8 \text{ cm}$$

∴ Height of cylinder, $h_2 = 8$ cm

Now, volume of the air inside the model

$$= \text{Volume of air inside (cone + cylinder + cone)}$$
$$= \left(\frac{1}{3}\pi r^2 h_1 + \pi r^2 h_2 + \frac{1}{3}\pi r^2 h_1\right)$$
$$= \frac{1}{3}\pi r^2 (h_1 + 3h_2 + h_1)$$

$$= \frac{1}{3} \times \frac{22}{7} \times 1.5 \times 1.5\,(2 + 3 \times 8 + 2)$$
$$= \frac{22}{7} \times \frac{2.25}{3} \times (2 + 24 + 2)$$
$$= \frac{22}{7} \times 0.75 \times 28 = 22 \times 3 = 66 \text{ cm}^3$$

Question 3 A gulab jamun, contains sugar syrup upto about 30% of its volume. Find approximately how much syrup would be found in 45 gulab jamuns, each shaped like a cylinder with two hemispherical ends with length 5 cm and diameter 2.8 cm (see figure).

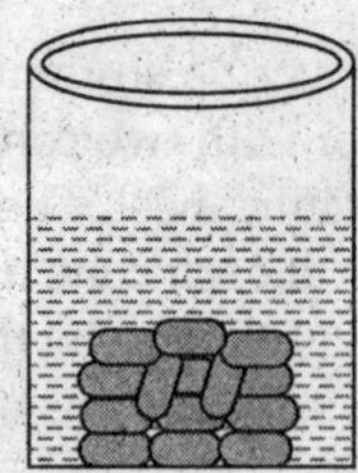

Sol. Let r be the radius of the hemisphere and cylinder both, h_1 be the height of the hemisphere which is equal to its radius and h_2 be the height of the cylinder. Given, length = 5 cm, diameter = 2.8 cm

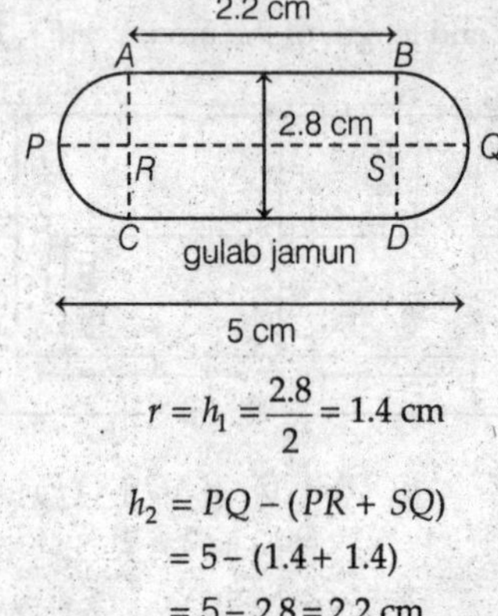

$\therefore \quad r = h_1 = \frac{2.8}{2} = 1.4$ cm

and
$$h_2 = PQ - (PR + SQ)$$
$$= 5 - (1.4 + 1.4)$$
$$= 5 - 2.8 = 2.2 \text{ cm}$$

$\therefore$ Volume of one gulab jamun = 2 × (Volume of hemisphere) + Volume of cylinder

$$= 2 \times \left\{\frac{2}{3}\pi r^3\right\} + \pi r^2 h_2$$
$$= \frac{4}{3}\pi r^3 + \pi r^2 h_2$$

$$= \pi r^2 \left\{\frac{4r}{3} + h_2\right\}$$

$$= \frac{22}{7} \times 1.4 \times 1.4 \left\{\frac{4}{3} \times 1.4 + 2.2\right\}$$

$$= \frac{22}{7} \times \frac{14}{10} \times \frac{14}{10} \left\{\frac{4}{3} \times \frac{14}{10} + \frac{22}{10}\right\}$$

$$= 22 \times \frac{1}{5} \times \frac{7}{5} \left\{\frac{28}{15} + \frac{11}{5}\right\}$$

$$= \frac{154}{25} \times \frac{61}{15} = \frac{9394}{375} \text{ cm}^3$$

∴ Volume of 45 gulab jamuns $= 45 \times \frac{9394}{375} = \frac{1}{75} \times 84546 = 1127.28 \text{ cm}^3$

∵ One gulab jamun, contains sugar syrup upto about 30% of its volume

i.e., $\left(\frac{9394}{375}\right) \times 30\%$

Hence, quantity of syrup found in 45 gulab jamuns

$$= 1127.28 \times \frac{30}{100}$$

$$= 1127.28 \times \frac{3}{10} = 338.184 \approx 338 \text{ cm}^3$$

Question 4 A pen stand made of wood is in the shape of a cuboid with four conical depressions to hold pens. The dimensions of the cuboid are 15 cm by 10 cm by 3.5 cm. The radius of each of the depressions is 0.5 cm and the depth is 1.4 cm. Find the volume of wood in the entire stand (see figure).

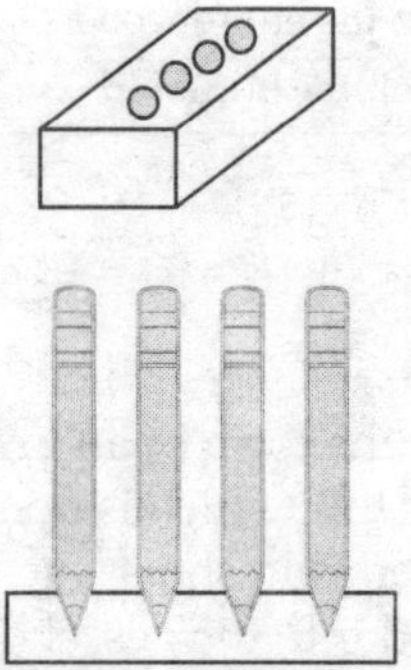

Sol. Given, length of cuboid $(l) = 15$ cm

Breadth of cuboid $(b) = 10$ cm

and Height of cuboid $(h) = 3.5$ cm

∴ Volume of cuboid $= l \times b \times h = 15 \times 10 \times 3.5 = 525 \text{ cm}^3$

Also, given that

Radius of conical depression $r = 0.5$ cm
and height of conical depression, $h = 1.4$

$\therefore$ Volume of a conical depression $= \frac{1}{3}\pi \times r^2 \times h$

$$= \frac{1}{3} \times \frac{22}{7} \times 0.5 \times 0.5 \times 1.4$$

$$= \frac{22}{3} \times \frac{1}{2} \times \frac{1}{2} \times \frac{2}{10} = \frac{11}{30} \text{ cm}^3$$

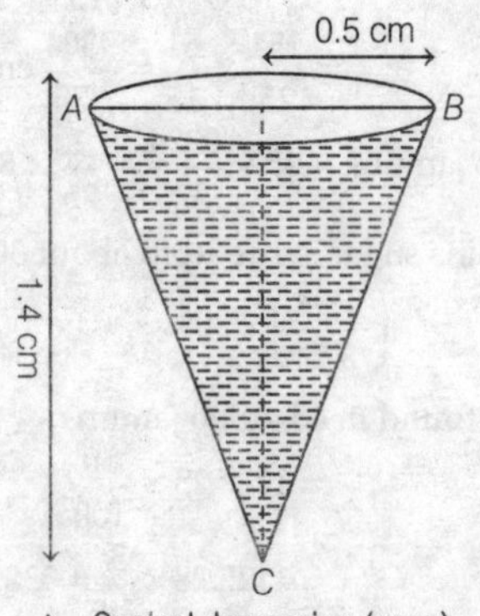

▲ Conical depression (cone)

$\therefore$ Volume of 4 conical depressions = 4 × Volume of a conical depression

$$= 4 \times \frac{11}{30}$$

$$= \frac{22}{15} \text{ cm}^3$$

Hence, the volume of wood in the entire wood

$$= \text{Volume of cuboid} - \text{Volume of 4 conical depressions}$$

$$= 525 - \frac{22}{15}$$

$$= 525 - 1.46$$

$$= 523.54 \text{ cm}^3$$

Question 5 A vessel is in the form of an inverted cone. Its height is 8 cm and the radius of its top, which is open, is 5 cm. It is filled with water upto the brim. When lead shots, each of which is a sphere of radius 0.5 cm are dropped into the vessel,one-fourth of the water flows out. Find the number of lead shots dropped in the vessel.

◎ ***Thinking Process*** Total number of lead shots $= \frac{\text{Volume of water}}{\text{Volume of one lead shot}}$

I. Given,

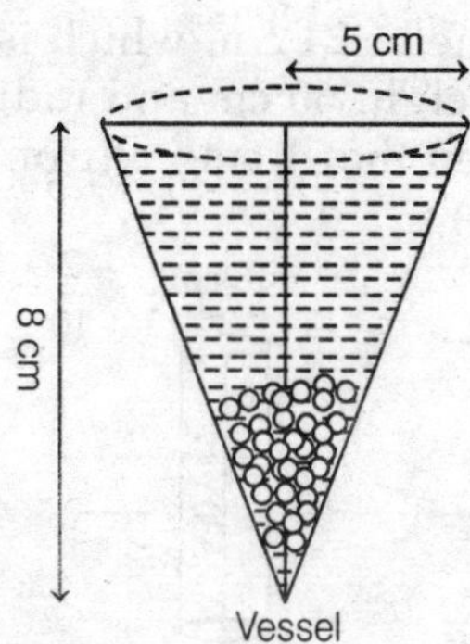

eight of the vessel $(h) = 8$ cm

d radius of the vessel $(r) = 5 \text{ cm} = \frac{1}{2}\text{cm}$

Volume of water filled in a vessel

$$= \frac{1}{3} \times \pi \times r \times r \times h$$
$$= \frac{1}{3} \times \frac{22}{7} \times 5 \times 5 \times 8$$
$$= \frac{4400}{21} \text{ cm}^3$$

so, given that,

e radius of a lead shots (sphere) = 0.5 cm

Volume of a lead shots (sphere) $= \frac{4}{3} \times \pi \times r \times r \times r$

$$= \frac{4}{3} \times \frac{22}{7} \times \frac{1}{2} \times \frac{1}{2} \times \frac{1}{2} = \frac{11}{21} \text{ cm}^3$$

t 'n' be the number of lead shots dropped in the vessel, then according to the ven condition.

< Volume of a lead shot (sphere)

$$= \frac{1}{4} \times \text{Volume of water filled in a vessel}$$

($\because$ Each lead shot flow out the water from the vessel equal to its volume)

$$n \times \frac{11}{21} = \frac{4400}{21} \times \frac{1}{4}$$
$$n \times 11 = 1100$$
$$n = 100$$

Required number of lead shots $(n) = 100$

Question 6 A solid iron pole consists of a cylinder of height 220 cm and base diameter 24 cm, which is surmounted by another cylinder of height 60 cm and radius 8 cm. Find the mass of the pole, given that 1 cm^3 of iron has approximately 8 g mass. (Use $\pi = 3.14$)

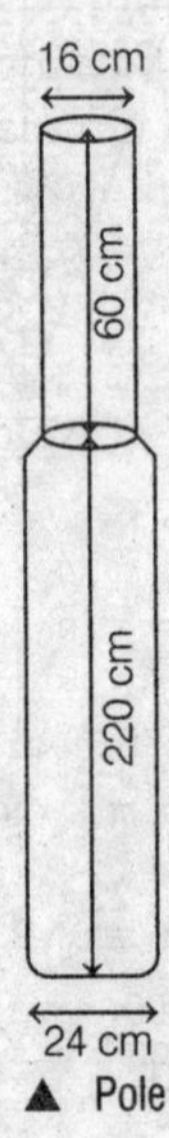

▲ Pole

Sol. Given,

Height of the first cylinder, $h_1 = 220$ cm

Radius of the first cylinder, $r_1 = \frac{24}{2} = 12$ cm

Height of the second cylinder, $h_2 = 60$ cm

and radius of the second cylinder, $r_2 = 8$ cm

$\therefore$ Volume of iron pole = Volume of first cylinder + Volume of second cylinder

$$= \pi r_1^2 h_1 + \pi r_2^2 h_2$$
$$= \pi (r_1^2 h_1 + r_2^2 h_2)$$
$$= 3.14 \{144 \times 220 + 64 \times 60\}$$
$$= 3.14 (31680 + 3840)$$
$$= 3.14 \times 35520 \text{ cm}^3$$

Also, given that,

1 cm^3 of iron has approximately mass $= 8 \text{ g} = \frac{8}{1000}$ kg

$\therefore$ (3.14×35520) cm^3 of iron has approximately mass

$$= 3.14 \times 35520 \times \frac{8}{1000}$$

$$= 3.14 \times 284.160 = 892.26 \text{ kg}$$

Question 7 A solid consisting of a right circular cone of height 120 cm and radius 60 cm standing on a hemisphere of radius 60 cm is placed upright in a right circular cylinder full of water such that it touches the bottom. Find the volume of water left in the cylinder, if the radius of the cylinder is 60 cm and its height is 180 cm.

Sol. Given,

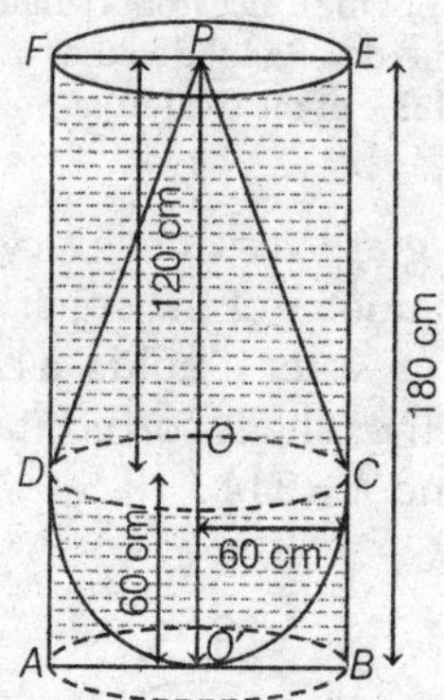

Height of the cylinder $(h) = 180$ cm $= 1.8$ m $\quad \left(\because 1 \text{ m} = 100 \text{ cm} \Rightarrow 1 \text{ cm} = \frac{1}{100} \text{ m}\right)$

and radius of the cylinder $(r) = 60$ cm $= 0.6$ m

$\therefore$ Volume of water filled in a right circular cylinder

$$= \pi r^2 h$$

$$= \frac{22}{7} \times 0.6 \times 0.6 \times 1.8$$

$$= \frac{14.256}{7} \text{ m}^3$$

Also, given solid is a combination of a cone and a hemisphere.

Height of the cone $(h_1) = 120$ cm $= 1.2$ m

Radius of the cone $(r_1) = 60$ cm $= 0.6$ m

and height/radius of the hemisphere $(r_2) = 60$ cm $= 0.6$ m

$\therefore$ Volume of the solid = Volume of the cone + Volume of the hemisphere

$$= \frac{1}{3} \times \pi r_1^2 h_1 + \frac{2}{3} \pi r_2^3$$

$$= \frac{1}{3} \times \frac{22}{7} \times (0.6)^2 \times (1.2) + \frac{2}{3} \times \frac{22}{7} \times (0.6)^3$$

$$= \frac{22}{21} \times (0.6)^2 \; \{1.2 + 2 \times 0.6\}$$

$$= \frac{22}{21} \times 0.36 \; (1.2 + 1.2)$$

$$= \frac{22}{21} \times 0.36 \times 2.4 = \frac{19.008}{21} = \frac{6.336}{7} \text{ m}^3$$

Hence, the volume of water left in the cylinder

= Volume of water filled in a right circular cylinder – Volume of the solid

$$= \frac{14.256}{7} - \frac{6.336}{7} = \frac{7.92}{7} = 1.131428 \text{ m}^3 \approx 1.131 \text{ m}^3$$

Note We know that, when a solid is placed in the right circular cylinder full with water, then it flow out the water from cylinder equal to its total volume. That means, if we need to find the volume of water left in the cylinder, then we subtract the volume of the solid from, volume the cylinder filled with water.

Question 8 A spherical glass vessel has a cylindrical neck 8 cm long, 2 cm in diameter; the diameter of the spherical part is 8.5 cm. By measuring the amount of water it holds, a child finds its volume to be 345 cm^3. Check whether she is correct, taking the above as the inside measurements and $\pi = 3.14$.

Sol. Not correct,

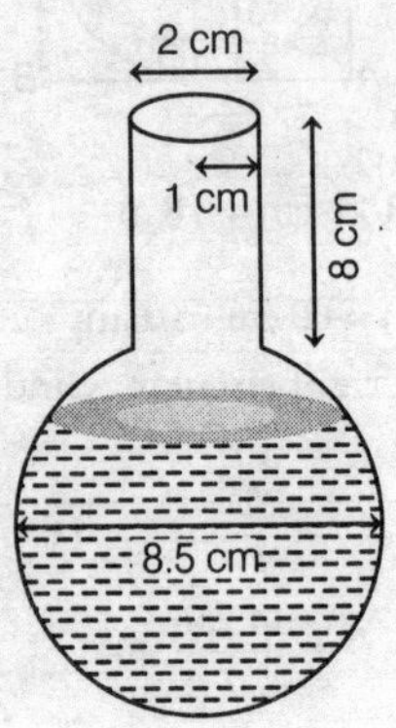

Given, spherical glass vessel is a combination of sphere as its base and a cylinder as its neck.

Also, we have height of the cylinder $(h_1) = 8$ cm

Radius of the cylinder $(r_1) = \frac{2}{2} = 1 \text{ cm}$

and radius of the sphere $(r_2) = \frac{8.5}{2}$ cm

∴ The volume of water filled in a spherical glass vessel

$$= \text{Volume of cylinder} + \text{Volume of sphere}$$

$$= \pi r_1^2 h_1 + \frac{4}{3}\pi r_2^3$$

$$= 3.14 \times 1 \times 1 \times 8 + \frac{4}{3} \times 3.14 \times \frac{8.5}{2} \times \frac{8.5}{2} \times \frac{8.5}{2}$$

$$= 25.12 + \frac{1928.3525}{6}$$

$$= 25.12 + 321.39 = 346.51$$

So, the correct answer is 346.51 cm^3.

DIKSHA APP Questions

Multiple Choice Questions

Q.1 A circular tent is cylindrical to a height of a 4 m and conical above it. If its diameter is 210 m and its slant height is 40 m. The total area of the canvas required in m^2 is

(a) 1560 (b) 15840

(c) 3960 (d) None of these

Sol. (b) Given, a tent which is a combination of a cylinder and a cone.

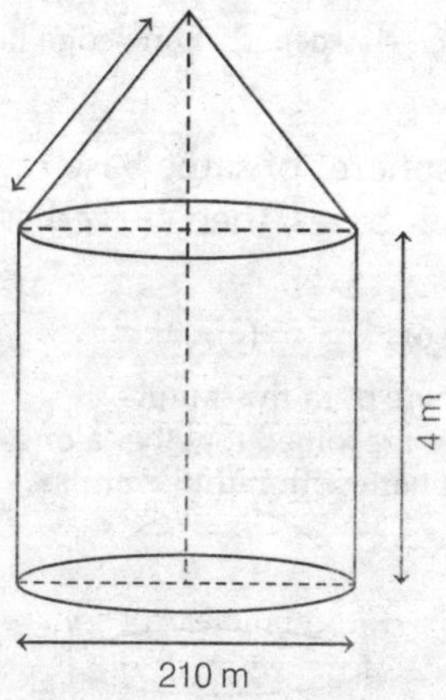

Also, we have slant height (l) of the cone = 40 m

Radius of the cone, r = Radius of cylinder

$$= \frac{\text{Diariameter}}{2}$$

$$= \frac{210}{2} = 105 \text{ m}$$

Height of the cylinder = 4 m

$\therefore$ Required surface area of the tent

$$= \text{CSA of cone} + \text{CSA of cylinder}$$
$$= \pi rl + 2\pi rh$$
$$= \pi r(l + 2h)$$
$$= \frac{22}{7} \times 105(40 + 2 \times 4)$$
$$= 22 \times 15(48) = 15840 \text{ m}^2$$

Q.2 A right circular cylinder of radius r cm and height h cm $(h \times 2r)$ just encloses a sphere of diameter

(a) r cm (b) $2r$ cm

(c) h cm (d) $2h$ cm

Sol. (b) As a right circular cylinder of radius r cm just encloses a sphere, both have the same radius. Hence, the sphere has a radius r cm.

So, the diameter of the sphere = 2 (radius) = $2r$ cm

Q.3 A cylindrical pencil sharpened at one edge is the combination of

(a) a cone and a cylinder (b) a cylinder and a sphere

(c) a hemisphere and a cylinder (d) two cylinders

Sol. (a) A cylindrical pencil sharpened at one edge has a conical shape on top of a cylinder.

Q.4 If two solid hemispheres of same base radius r are joined together along their bases, then curved surface area of this new solid is

(a) $8\pi r^2$ (b) $6\pi r^2$ (c) $3\pi r^2$ (d) $4\pi r^2$

Sol. (d) Given, a hemisphere of radius r units.

The two hemispheres are joined together along their bases. Then, the resultant solid is a sphere with radius r units.

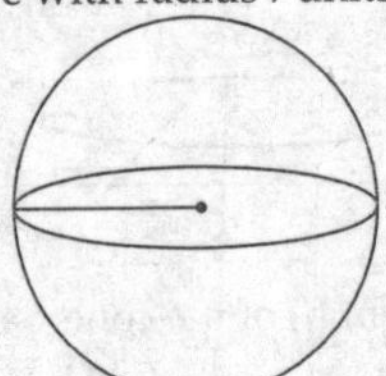

Hence, the surface area of the obtained solid = $4\pi r^2$

Q.5 If two solid cones of same radius r and slant height l are joined at their bases, then the curved surface area of the new solid is

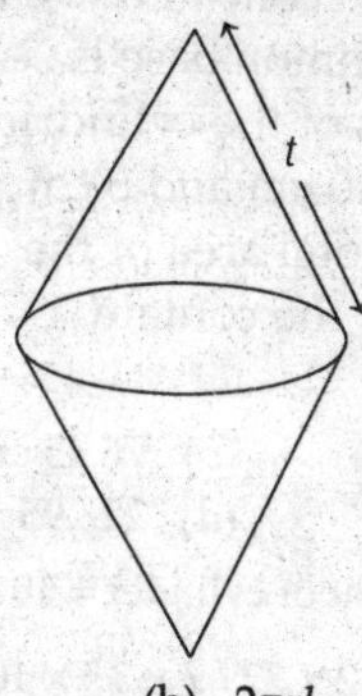

(a) $4\pi r^2$ (b) $2\pi rl$
(c) $2\pi rl$ (d) πrl

Sol. (b) Given, a cone with the radius r units and the slant height l units.

We know that CSA of a cone = πrl

When two cones are joined together then, the curved surface area of new solid = 2 × CSA of one cone = $2\pi rl$

Q.6 Four identical cubes of side 10 cm are joined to form a cuboid (with two cubes touching one another and the other two being placed on top of them). The total surface area of the resulting cuboid is

(a) 1200 cm^2 (b) 1600 cm^2
(c) 2400 cm^2 (d) 2000 cm^2

Sol. (b) When two cubes are placed touching each other and then two cubes are placed on top of them, a cuboid is formed. The cuboid has length = 20 cm, breadth = 10 cm, height = 20 cm

So, the total surface area = $2(lb + bh + lh)$

$$= 2(200 + 200 + 400) = 1600 \text{ cm}^2$$

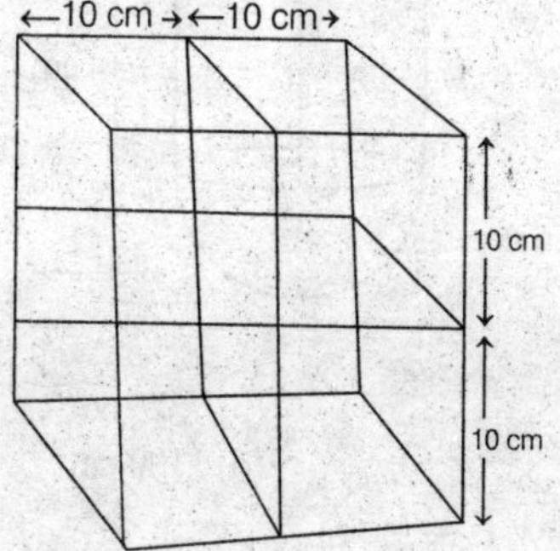

Q.7 A metal container is in the form of a right circular cylinder with a cone at one end. If the radius of the common base is 3.5 cm and the heights of the cylindrical and conical parts are 10 cm and 6 cm respectively, find the total area of the paper needed to cover the contain. (Take, $\pi = 22/7$)

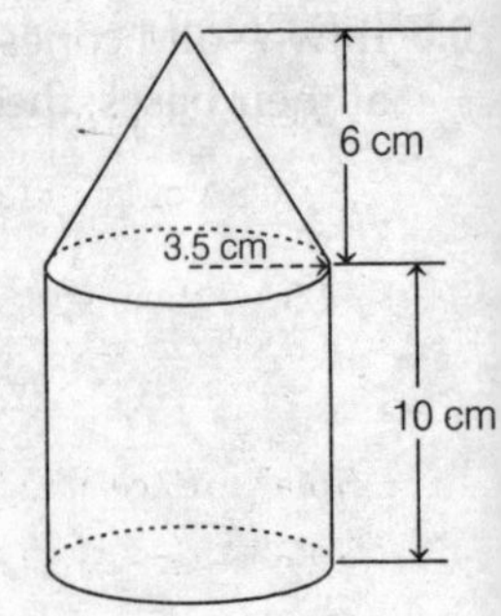

(a) 220 cm^2 (b) 76.45 cm^2
(c) 296.45 cm^2 (d) 226.95 cm^2

Sol. (c) Given, $r = 3.5$ cm, height of cylinder = 10 cm, height of cone of = 6 cm

CSA of cylinder = $2\pi rh = 2 \times 22/7 \times 3.5 \times 10 = 220$ cm^2

CSA of cone = πrl

$$l = \sqrt{(h^2 + r^2)} = \sqrt{(36 + 12.25)} = \sqrt{48.25} = 6.95 \text{ cm}$$

CSA of cone = $22/7 \times 3.5 \times 6.95 = 76.45$ cm^2

Total surface area of the solid = Area of paper needed to cover it

Total surface area of the solid = CSA of cylinder + CSA of cone

Total surface area of the solid = 220 + 76.45

$\therefore$ Area of paper needed to cover it = 296.45 cm^2

Q.8 A metal container made of tin sheets is in the form of a hollow cylinder mounted on a hollow hemisphere. If the diameter of the container is 8 cm and the total height of the container is 14 cm, find the total area of the tin sheets needed to make one such container. (Take, $\pi = 22/7$)

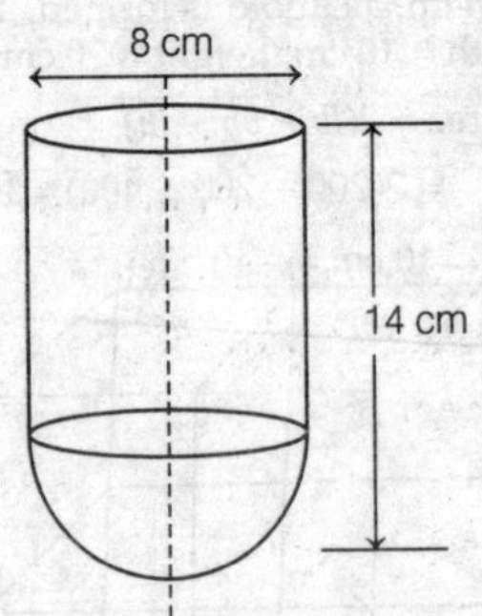

(a) 251 cm^2 (b) 325 cm^2
(c) 352 cm^2 (d) 100 cm^2

Sol. (c) Given, $r = 4$ cm, height of solid = 14 cm,

height of cylinder = 14 − 4 = 10 cm

$\therefore$ CSA of cylinder = $2\pi rh = 2 \times \frac{22}{7} \times 4 \times 10 \text{ cm}^2$

CSA of hemisphere = $2\pi r^2$

$$= 2 \times \frac{22}{7} \times 4 \times 4 \text{ cm}^2$$

Total surface area of the solid = Area of tin sheets needed to cover it.

Total surface area of the solid = CSA of cylinder + CSA of hemisphere

Total surface area of the solid = $2 \times \frac{22}{7}(40 + 16) = 352 \text{ cm}^2$

$\therefore$ Area of tin sheets needed = 352 cm^2

09 If the volume of a sphere is equal to its surface area numerically, then radius of the sphere is

(a) 2 units (b) 3 units (c) 4 units (d) 6 units

Sol. (b) Given, volume of sphere = surface area of sphere

Now, volume of sphere = $\frac{4}{3}\pi r^3$

and surface are of sphere = $4\pi r^2$

According to the condition

$$= \frac{4}{3}\pi r^3 = 4\pi r^2$$

$$\Rightarrow \quad \frac{1}{3}r^3 = r^2 \Rightarrow \frac{1}{3}r = 1$$

$$\Rightarrow \quad r = 3 \text{ units}$$

10 In a right angled triangle the sides including right angles are 3 cm and 4 cm. If the triangle is rotated about 4 cm, then the volume of the solid thus generated is

(a) $48\pi \text{ cm}^3$ (b) $12\pi \text{ cm}^3$

(c) $36\pi \text{ cm}^3$ (d) $16\pi \text{ cm}^3$

Sol. (b) Given, a right angle triangle have sides 3 cm and 4 cm.

After rotation about side AO we get a cone.

Radius of cone, $r = 3$ cm,

Height of cone, $h = 4$ cm

Hence, volume of cone = $\frac{1}{3}\pi r^2 h$

$$= \frac{1}{3} \times \pi \times 3 \times 3 \times 4$$

$$= 12\pi \text{ cm}^3$$

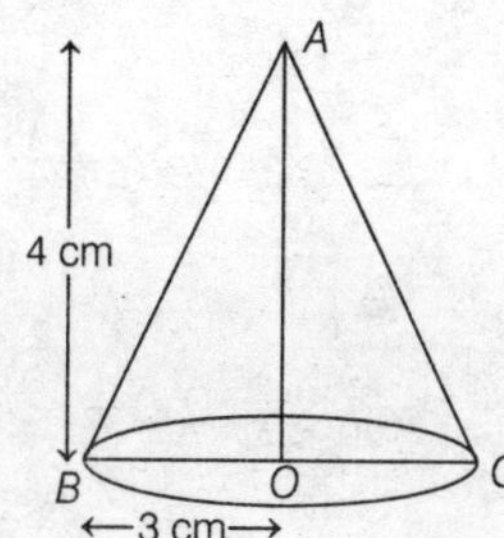

□ Subjective Type Questions

Q.1 A right circular cone of radius 3 cm, has a curved surface area of 47.1 cm^2. Find the volume of the cone. (usse $\pi = 3.14$)

Sol. Given, Radius of cone $(r) = 3$ cm

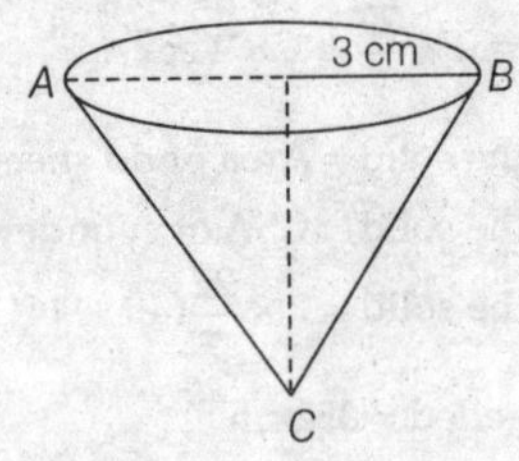

Curved surface area $= \pi rl = 47.1\,\text{cm}^2$, where $l =$ slant height of cone

$$\therefore l = \frac{47.1}{\pi r} = \frac{47.1}{3.14 \times 3} = 5\text{ cm}$$

We know that, $h = \sqrt{l^2 - r^2}$

$$\Rightarrow \quad = \sqrt{5^2 - 3^2} = \sqrt{25 - 9} = \sqrt{16} = 4\text{ cm}$$

Volume of cone $= \frac{1}{3} \times \pi r^2 h$

$$= \frac{1}{3} \times 3.14 \times 3 \times 3 \times 4 = 3.14 \times 3 \times 4 = 37.68\text{ cm}^2.$$

Hence, the volume of cone is 37.68 cm^2.

Q.2 The sum of the radius of base and height of a solid right circular cylinder is 37 cm. If the total surface area of the solid cylinder is 1628 sq. cm, find the volume of the cylinder. (use $\pi = 22/7$)

Sol. Given, $r + h = 37$ [where $r \rightarrow$ radius, $h \rightarrow$ height], and total surface area $= 1628\text{ cm}^2$

Total surface area of cylinder $= 2\pi r(h + r) = 2\pi rh + 2\pi r^2$

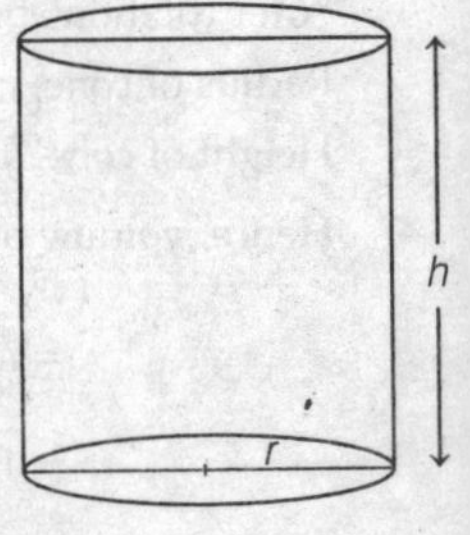

$$\Rightarrow \quad 2\pi r(h + r) = 1628$$

$$\Rightarrow \quad 2\pi r \times 37 = 1628$$

$$\Rightarrow \quad 2 \times \frac{22}{7} \times r \times 37 = 1628$$

$$\Rightarrow \quad r = \frac{1628 \times 7}{2 \times 22 \times 37} = 7\text{ cm}$$

Since, $r + h = 37$

$$\therefore \quad 7 + h = 37 \quad [\because r = 7\text{ cm}]$$

$$\Rightarrow \quad h = 37 - 7 = 30\text{ cm}$$

Hence, volume of cylinder = $\pi r^2 h$

$$= \frac{22}{7} \times 7 \times 7 \times 30 = 4620 \text{ cm}^3$$

Q.3 From a solid cylinder whose height is 12 cm and diameter 10 cm, a conical cavity with the same base and height is taken out. Find the total surface are of the remaining solid.

Sol. Given, diameter of the cylinder = Diameter of conical cavity = 10 cm

$\therefore$ Radius of cylinder = Radius of conical cavity

$$= \frac{10}{2} = 5 \text{ cm}$$

Height of the cylinder = Height of the conical cavity

$$= 12 \text{ cm}$$

$\therefore$ Slant height of the conical cavity, $l = \sqrt{h^2 + r^2}$

$\Rightarrow$ $l = \sqrt{12^2 + 5^2}$

$$= \sqrt{144 + 25}$$

$$= \sqrt{169} = 13 \text{ cm}$$

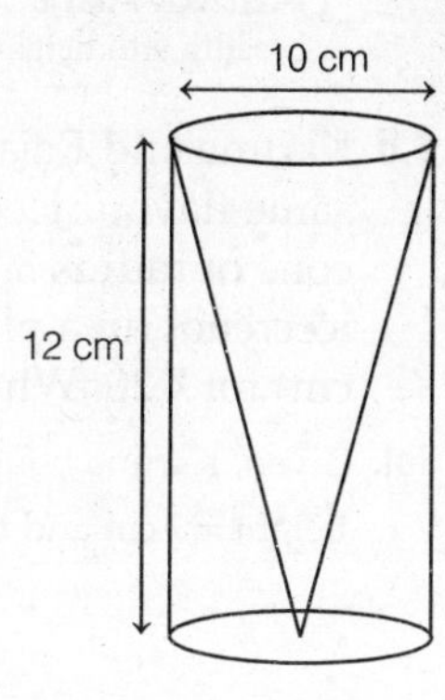

Hence, total surface area of remaining solid

= curved surface area of conical cavity + total surface area of cylinder without the top

$= \pi r l + (2\pi r h + \pi r^2)$

$$= \pi r[l + 2h + r]$$

$$= \frac{22}{7} \times 5\,[13 + 2 \times 12 + 5]$$

$$= \frac{22}{7} \times 5 \times 42$$

$$= 22 \times 5 \times 6$$

$$= 660 \text{ cm}^2$$

Q.4 Three identical cubes each of volume 343 cm^3 are joined end to end. Find the surface area of the resulting cuboid.

Sol. Given, volume of a cube = 343 cm^3

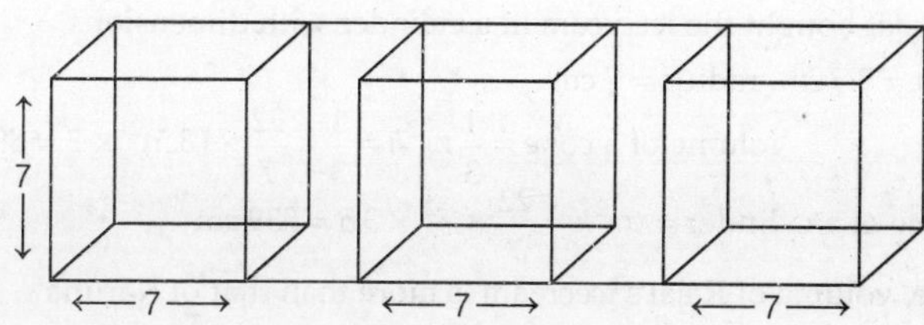

Also, volume of cube = s^3, where s is the side of cube.

$\Rightarrow \quad 343 = s^3$

$\Rightarrow \quad s = \sqrt[3]{343} = 7$ cm

Hence, side of the cube is 7 cm.

$\therefore$ Dimensions of the resulting cuboid

Length = 21 cm

Breadth = 7 cm

Height = 7 cm

Surface area of the resulting cuboid = $2(bh + lh + lb)$

$= 2(49 + 147 + 147)$

$= 2(343)$

$= 686 \text{ cm}^2$

Mistake Alert When two or more cubes are joined end to end, then the breadth and height at resulting cuboid will remain the same but not length.

Q.5 Karuna and Rajat went to an icecream parlour and purchased same flavour icecreams. Karuna bought icecream (in a plastic cone of radius 3.5 cm and height 7 cm) for ₹ 20. Rajat bought icecream (in a plastic cylinder for radius 7 cm and height 3.5 cm) for ₹ 20. Which is a better deal? Why ?

Sol. Given, Karuna bought the icecream in a cone with dimensions height = 7 cm and radius = 3.5 cm

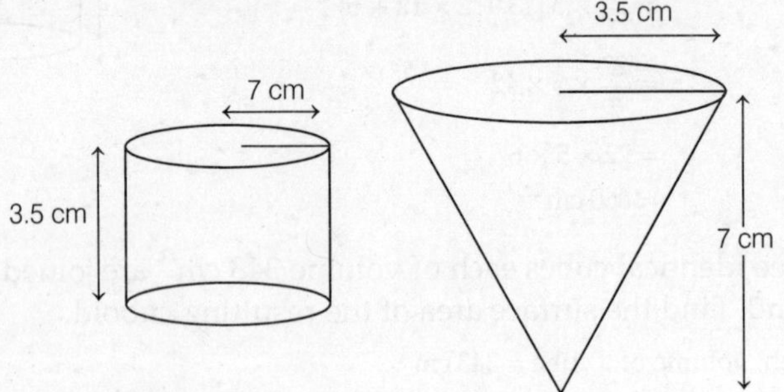

and Rajat bought the icecream in a cylinder with dimensions height = 3.5 cm, radius = 7 cm

$\therefore \quad$ Volume of a cone $= \frac{1}{3}\pi r^2 h = \frac{1}{3} \times \frac{22}{7} \times (3.5)^2 \times 7 = 89.83 \text{ cm}^3$

Volume of a cylinder $= \pi r^2 h = \frac{22}{7} \times 7^2 \times 3.5 = 539 \text{ cm}^3$

Hence, volume of Rajat's icecream is more than that of Karuna's.

Hence, Rajat got a better deal.

Q.6 Due to heavy floods in a state, thousands were rendered homeless. 50 schools collectively offered to the state government to provide place and the canvas for 1500 tents to be fixed by the government and decided to share the whole expenditure equally. The lower part of each tent is cylindrical of base radius 2.8 m and height 3.5 m, with conical upper part of same base radius but of height 2.1 m. If the canvas used to make the tents costs ₹ 120 per sq. m, find the amount shared by each school to set up the tents. What value is generated by above problem ?

Sol. We are given, radius of cylinderical part = 2.8 m

Height of cylinderical part = 3.5 m

Height at conical part = 2.1 m

Cost of canvas used to make tent = ₹ 120 per m^2

Therefore, slant height of conical part

$$l = \sqrt{r^2 + h^2} = \sqrt{(2.8)^2 + (2.1)^2} = \sqrt{7.84 + 4.41}$$

$$= \sqrt{12.25} = 3.5 \text{ cm}$$

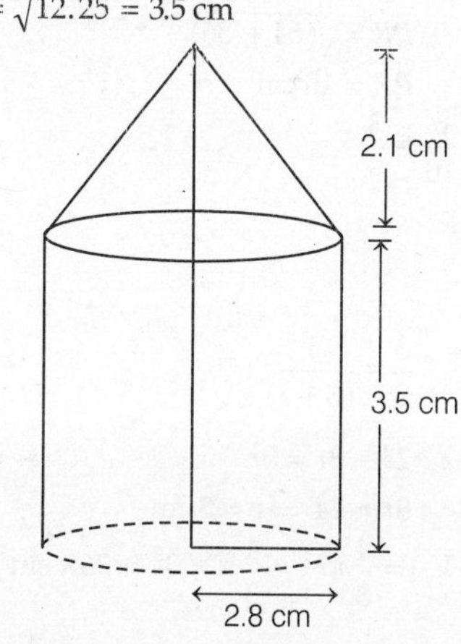

Area of tents = Curved surface area of cylindrical part + Curved surface area of conical part

$$= 2\pi rh + \pi rl$$

$$= 2 \times \frac{22}{7} \times 2.8 \times 3.5 + \frac{22}{7} \times 2.8 \times 3.5$$

$$= 61.6 + 30.8 = 92.4 \text{ m}^2$$

∴ Canvas required for 1500 tents = 1500 × 92.4 = 138600 m^2

Since, the cost of 1 sq. m canvas is ₹ 120.

$\therefore$ Cost of 1500 tents

$$= 138600 \times 120 = ₹\ 332640$$

School authorities are concerned about safety of children and their families.

Q.7 A conical vessel of radius 6 cm and height 8 cm is completely filled with water. A sphere is lowered into the water and its size is such that when it touches the sides, it is just immersed. What fraction of water overflows ?

Sol. Given, Radius of conical vessel $r = 6$ cm

Height of conical vessel $h = 8$ cm

Volume of conical vessel (V_c)

$$= \frac{1}{3}\pi r^2 h = \frac{1}{3}\pi \times 36 \times 8 = 96\pi$$

Let the radius of the sphere be r cm.

In right $\Delta PO'R$, by Pythagoras theorem

$$PR = \sqrt{(64 + 36)}$$

$$\Rightarrow \quad PR = 10 \text{ cm}$$

Hence, $\sin\theta = \frac{O'P}{PR} = \frac{6}{10} = \frac{3}{5}$ ...(i)

In right triangle OMR

$$\sin\theta = \frac{OM}{OR} = \frac{r}{OR}$$

$$\Rightarrow \quad \frac{3}{5} = \frac{r}{(8 - r)}$$ [Using Eq. (i)]

$$\Rightarrow \quad 24 - 3r = 5r$$

$$\Rightarrow \quad 8r = 24 \Rightarrow r = 3 \text{ cm}$$

$\therefore$ Volume of sphere $(V_s) = \frac{4}{3}\pi r^3 = \frac{4}{3}\pi \times 3^3 = 36\pi \text{ cm}^3$

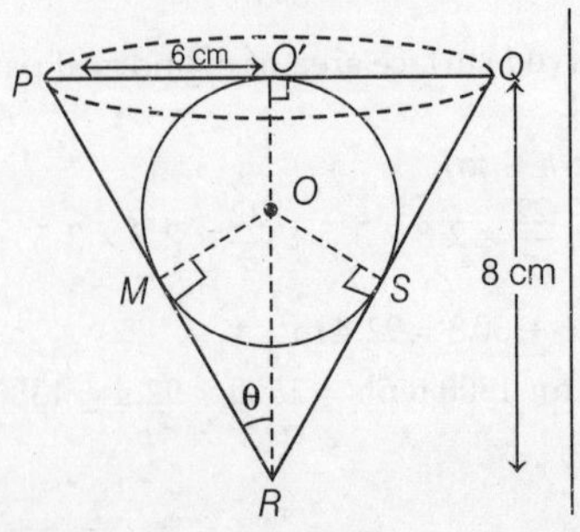

Now, Volume of the water = Volume of cone $(V_c) = 96\pi\ \text{cm}^3$

Clearly, volume of the water that flows out of cone is same as the volume of the sphere *i.e.*, V_s.

$\therefore$ Fraction of the water that flows out

$$V_s / V_c = \frac{36\pi}{96\pi} = \frac{3}{8}$$

Q.8 A solid toy is in the form of a right circular cylinder with a hemispherical shape at one end and a cone at the other end. Their common diameter is 4.2 cm and the height of the cylinder and conical portions are 12 cm and 7 cm respectively. Find the volume of the solid toy.

Sol. Given,

Height of conical portion = 7 cm

Height of cylindrical portion = 12 cm

Radius $= \frac{d}{2} = \frac{4.2}{2} = 2.1\ \text{cm}$

$\Rightarrow$ Volume of solid toy = Volume of conical portion + Volume of cylindrical portion + Volume of hemispherical portion

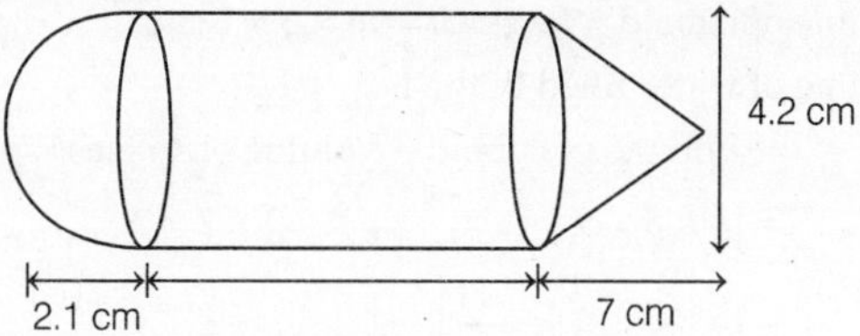

$$\Rightarrow \frac{1}{3}\pi r^2 h + \pi r^2 h + \frac{2}{3}\pi r^3$$

$$= \left(\frac{1}{3} + \frac{22}{7} \times 2.1 \times 2.1 \times 7\right) + \left(\frac{22}{7} \times 2.1 \times 2.1 \times 12\right) + \left(\frac{2}{3} \times \frac{22}{7} \times 2.1 \times 2.1 \times 2.1\right)$$

$$= \left(\frac{1}{3} \times 22 \times 0.3 \times 2.1 \times 7\right) + (22 \times 0.3 \times 2.1 \times 12) + \left(\frac{2}{3} \times 22 \times 0.3 \times 2.1 \times 2.1\right)$$

$$= (32.34) + (166.32) + (19.404) = 218.064\ \text{cm}^3$$

Q.9 16 glass spheres each of radius 2 cm are packed into a cuboidal box of internal dimensions 16 cm $\times$ 8 cm $\times$ 8 cm and then the box is filled with water. Find the volume of water filled in the box.

Sol. Given, radius of the sphere = 2 cm

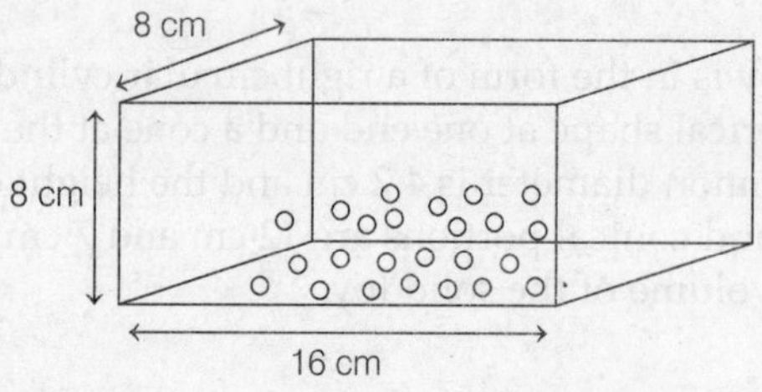

Volume of the one sphere $= \frac{4}{3}\pi r^3$

$$= \frac{4}{3} \times \frac{22}{7} \times 2 \times 2 \times 2 \text{ cm}^3$$

Therefore, Volume of 16 spheres $= 16 \times \frac{4}{3} \times \frac{22}{7} \times 2 \times 2 \times 2 \text{ cm}^3$

Now, volume of cuboid $= l \times b \times h = 16 \times 8 \times 8 \text{ cm}^3$

Now, volume of water filled in the box

$$= \text{Volume of cuboid} - \text{Volume of 16 glass spheres}$$

$$= 16 \times 8 \times 8 - 16 \times \frac{4}{3} \times \frac{22}{7} \times 2 \times 2 \times 2$$

$$= 16 \times 8 \times 8\left[1 - \frac{11}{21}\right]$$

$$= 16 \times 8 \times 8 \times \frac{10}{21}$$

$$= \frac{10240}{21}$$

$$= 487.6 \text{ cm}^3$$

Q.10 A well of diameter 4 m is dug 21 m deep. The earth taken out of it has been spread evenly all around it in the shape of circular ring of width 3 m to form an embankment find the height of the embament.

Sol. (b) Given, diameter of well = 4 cm

Then, radius, $r = \frac{\text{diameter}}{2} = \frac{4}{2} = 2$ cm

Deep of well = 21

Therefore, volume of earth taken out = $\pi r^2 h$

$= \pi \times 2 \times 2 \times 21$

$= 84\,\pi$ ...(i)

According to the given condition,

The embankment is in the shape of a circular ring with a width of 3 m.

Therefore, inner radius (*i.e.*, radius of the well) is 2 m.

So, the outer radius is 2 + 3 = 5 = cm

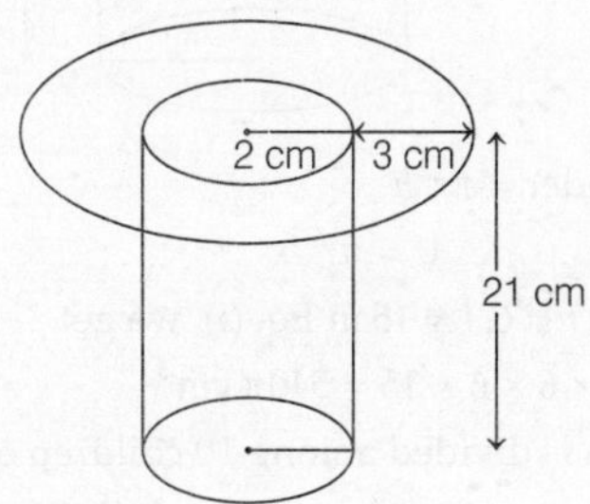

Since, volume of circular ring = $\pi(R^2 - r^2) \times h$

where, R = Outer radius, r = Inner radius.

i.e., volume of circular ring = $\pi \times (5^2 - 2^2) \times h$

$= \pi \times (25 - 4) \times h$

$= \pi \times 21 \times h$

$= 21\pi \times h$ ...(ii)

Since, volume of the earth taken out from the well is equal to volume of emboulement which is in the form of circular ring.

From Eq. (i) and Eq. (ii), we get

$84\,\pi = 21\,\pi \times h$

$\Rightarrow \quad h = 4$ cm

Hence, the height of embancement is 4 cm

Q.11 Cylindrical tub, whose diameter is 12 cm and height 15 cm is full of ice-cream. The whole ice-cream is to be divided into 10 chidren in equal ice-cream cones, with conical base surmounted by hemispherical top. If the height of conical portion is twice the diameter of base, find the diameter of conical part of ice-cream cone.

Sol. Given, Diameter of cylinder = 12 cm

Radius $r = \dfrac{\text{Diameter}}{2} = \dfrac{12}{2} = 6$ cm

Height = 15 cm

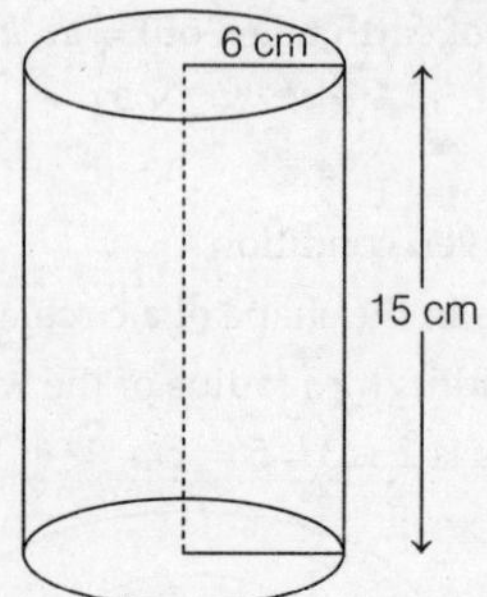

Volume of cylinder = $\pi r^2 h$

i.e., $V = \pi r^2 h$ ...(i)

On substituting $r = 6, l = 15$ in Eq. (i), we get

Volume, $V = \pi \times 6 \times 6 \times 15 = 540\pi \text{ cm}^3$

Since, ice-cream is divided among 10 children equally.

Therefore, amount of ice-cream for each child

$$= \frac{540}{10}\pi = 54\pi \quad \text{...(ii)}$$

Now, $OB = \frac{d}{2}$ = radius of hemispherical top.

Let diameter of the cone be d.

Then, radius of base of cone = $\frac{d}{2}$

The height of the coincal portion is twice the diameter of its base.

i.e., Height of cone = $2d$.

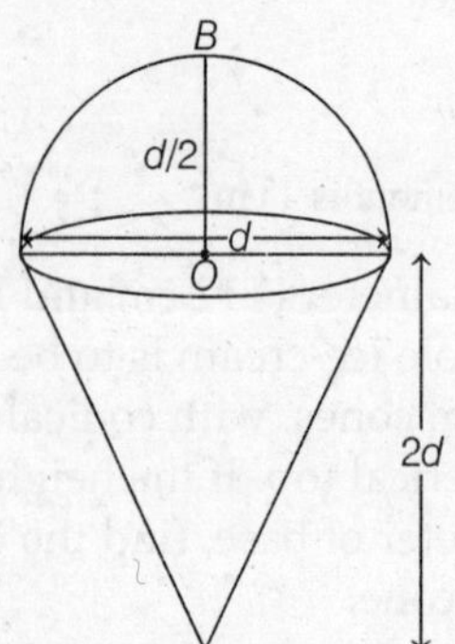

Volume V_c volume of cone = $\frac{1}{3}\pi r^2 h$

$$= \frac{1}{3}\pi \times \frac{d}{2} \times \frac{d}{2} \times 2d = \frac{1}{3} \times \frac{d^3}{2}$$

Radius of hemispherical top = Radius of cone

$$= \frac{d}{2}$$

Therefore, volume V_h of hemispherical top $= \frac{2}{3}\pi r^3$

$$= \frac{2}{3} \times \pi \times \frac{d}{2} \times \frac{d}{2} \times \frac{d}{2} = \frac{2}{3}\pi \times \frac{d^3}{8} = \frac{\pi}{3} \times \frac{d^3}{4}$$

The total volume V_{Total} for one conical ice-cream.

$$\Rightarrow \quad V_{\text{Total}} = V_c + V_h$$

$$= \frac{1}{3}\pi \times \frac{d^3}{2} + \frac{1}{3}\pi \times \frac{d^3}{4} = \frac{\pi d^3}{6} + \frac{\pi d^3}{12} = \frac{3\pi d^3}{12}$$

$$\Rightarrow \quad \frac{\pi d^3}{4} \quad \ldots\text{(iii)}$$

From Eq. (ii) and Eq. (iii), we get

$$\Rightarrow \quad 54\pi = \frac{\pi d^3}{4} \Rightarrow 216\pi = \pi d^3$$

$$\Rightarrow \quad d^3 = 216 \Rightarrow d = 6$$

Hence, the diameter of ice-cream cone is 6 cm.

Q.12 A 20 m deep well with diameter 7 m is dug and earth from digging is evenly spread out to form a platform 22 m by 14 m. Find the height of the platform.

Sol. Given, Depth of well = 20 m $\Rightarrow h = 20$ m

Diameter of well = 7 m

Then, radius of well $= \frac{7}{2}$ m

$$\Rightarrow \quad r = \frac{7}{2}$$

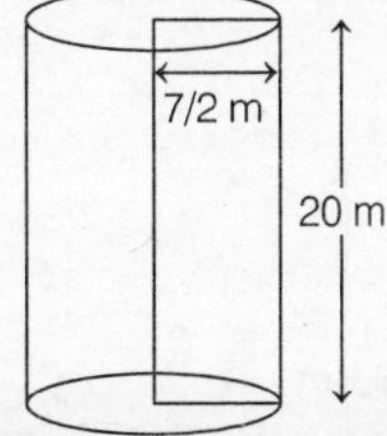

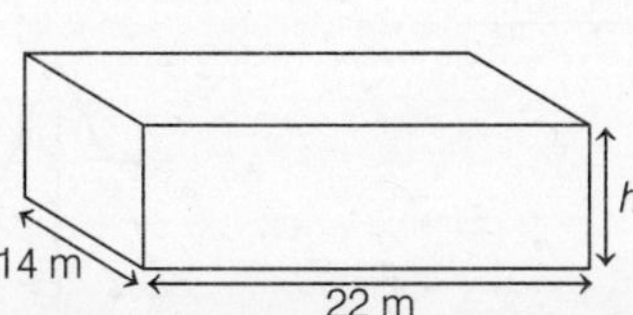

Earth dug out from the well is spread out to form a platform *i.e.,* in the cuboid form.

Length of platform = 22 m $\Rightarrow l = 22$ m

Breadth of platform = 14 m $\Rightarrow b = 14$ m

Let height of platform = h m.

Since, volume of earth dug out is equal to volume of earth spread out to a form of platform.

Therefore,

Volume of the well = Volume of the platform

Since, well is in the cylindrical form.

Therefore, volume of the well = $\pi r^2 h$

$$= \pi \times \left(\frac{7}{2}\right)^2 \times 20$$

$$= \pi \times \frac{7}{2} \times \frac{7}{2} \times 20 \quad \ldots(i)$$

Since, platform is in the form of cuboid.

Therefore, volume of the platform = $l \times b \times h$

$$= 22 \times 14 \times h \quad \ldots(ii)$$

According to the given condition,

Volume of well = Volume of platform

$$\Rightarrow \quad \pi \times \frac{7}{2} \times \frac{7}{2} \times 20 = 22 \times 14 \times h \quad \text{[Using Eq. (i) and (ii)]}$$

$$\Rightarrow \quad \frac{22}{7} \times \frac{7}{2} \times \frac{7}{2} \times 20 = 22 \times 14 \times h$$

$$\Rightarrow \quad h = \frac{20}{8} \Rightarrow h = 2.5 \text{ m.}$$

Hence, height of the plateform is 2.5 m.

Q.13 A heap of rice is in the form of a cone of diameter 9 m and height 3.5 m. Find the volume of the rice. How much canvas cloth is required to just cover the heap.

Sol. Given, diameter of conical heap = 9 m

Radius $r = \frac{\text{diameter}}{2} = \frac{9}{2}$ m

Height of conical heap, = 3.5 m

i.e., $h = 3.5$ m.

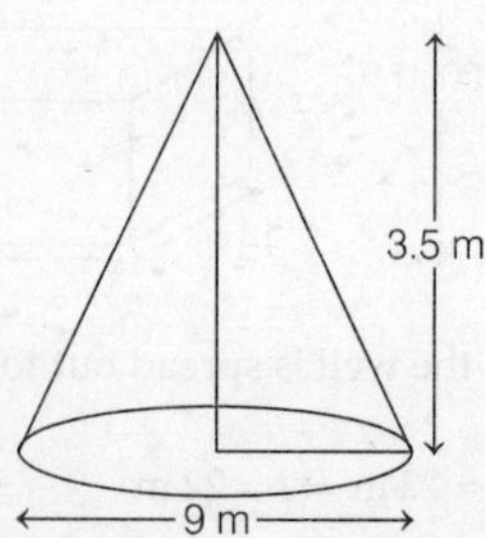

Volume of cone $= \frac{1}{3}\pi r^2 h$

$\Rightarrow$ Volume of heap of rice $= \frac{1}{3} \times \pi \times \frac{9}{2} \times \frac{9}{2} \times 3.5$

$= \frac{1}{3} \times \frac{22}{7} \times \frac{9}{2} \times \frac{9}{2} \times 3.5 = 74.25 \text{ m}^3$

Now, canvas cloth required to cover the heap = Curved surface area of the heap.

Curved surface area of cone $= \pi rl$

Slant height $l = \sqrt{h^2 + r^2}$

$= \sqrt{(3.5)^2 + \left(\frac{9}{2}\right)^2} = \sqrt{32.50} = 5.70$

Now, canvas cloth, required to cover the heap $= \pi rl$

$= \frac{22}{7} \times \left(\frac{9}{2}\right) \times 5.70 = 80.62 \text{ m}^2$

Hence, volume of the rice is 74.25 m^3 and required canvas cloth to cover the heap is 80.62 m^2.

Q.14 How many spherical lead shots each of diameter 4.2 cm can be obtained from a solid rectangular lead piece with dimensions 66 cm, 42 cm and 21 cm.

Sol. Given, a solid rectangular lead piece with dimensions 66 cm, 42 cm and 21 cm.

i.e., Length = 66 cm

Breadth = 42 cm

Height = 21 cm

and diameter of spherical lead shot = 4.2 cm

So, radius of shot, $r = \frac{\text{diameter}}{2} = \frac{4.2}{2} = 2.1 \text{ cm}$

Total number of lead shots $= \frac{\text{Volume of rectangular solid piece}}{\text{Volume of one spherical shot}}$

$\Rightarrow$ Total number of spherical lead shots $= \frac{l \times b \times h}{\frac{4}{3}\pi r^3}$

$= \frac{66 \times 42 \times 21}{\frac{4}{3} \times \frac{22}{7} \times 2.1 \times 2.1 \times 2.1}$

$= \frac{66 \times 42 \times 21 \times 3 \times 7}{4 \times 22 \times 2.1 \times 2.1 \times 2.1} = 1500$

Hence, total number of spherical lead shots = 1500

Statistics

CHAPTER 13

Important Points

01 As average represents the entire data, its value lies some where in between two extremes. For this reason, average is called measure of central tendency.

The measures of central tendency that in common use are

(i) Arithmetic mean or mean

(ii) Median

(iii) Mode

02 Mean of Raw Data The mean of n quantities $x_1, x_2, x_3, \ldots, x_n$ is

$$\text{Mean} = \frac{x_1 + x_2 + x_3 + \ldots + x_n}{n}$$

$$= \frac{\sum_{i=1}^{n} x_i}{n}$$

where, the Greek letter Σ (sigma) means "Summation".

03 Mean for a Frequency Distribution

(i) **Direct method**

Let x_i is the mid-point of the class marks and f_i is the corresponding frequencies, then

$$\text{Mean}(\overline{x}) = \frac{\sum_{i=1}^{n} f_i x_i}{\sum_{i=1}^{n} f_i} = \frac{\sum_{i=1}^{n} f_i x_i}{N}$$

where, $N = f_1 + f_2 + \ldots + f_n = \sum_{i=1}^{n} f_i$ = Total frequencies

(ii) **Mean by Shortcut Method or Assumed Mean Method** Firstly choose one among the x_i's as the 'assumed mean' and denote it by a and determine $d_i = x_i - a$ (where d_i's are called the deviations)

$$\therefore \quad \text{Mean } (\overline{x}) = a + \frac{\sum_{i=1}^{n} f_i d_i}{\sum_{i=1}^{n} f_i}$$

(iii) **Mean by Step Deviation Method**

In this method take $u_i = \dfrac{(x_i - a)}{h} = \dfrac{d_i}{h}$

$$\therefore \text{ Mean } (\overline{x}) = a + h \times \left(\frac{\sum_{i=1}^{n} f_i u_i}{\sum_{i=1}^{n} f_i} \right).$$

where, h is the width of the class.

Note The step deviation method will be convenient to apply, if all the d_i's have a common factor.

The mean obtained by all the three methods is the same.

The assumed mean method and step deviation method are just simplified forms of the direct method.

$$\text{Class Mark} = \frac{\text{Upper class limit} + \text{lower class limit}}{2}$$

04 Mode The item which occurs most frequently *i.e.,* most number of times is called mode.

e.g., Mode of the numbers 2, 3, 4, 4, 6, 6, 6, 6, 7, and 9 is 6 because it repeated most number of times *i.e.,* 4 times.

(i) **Mode of grouped data** In case of grouped data (discrete series), the mode is the observation with maximum frequency *i.e.,*

Marks obtained (out of 10)	1	2	3	4	6	7	9	10
Number of students	3	5	12	18	23	8	2	1

the mode of the distribution is 6 as it has the maximum frequency 23.

(ii) **Mode for continuous frequency distribution (grouped data)** In group data, mode is a value that lies in the model class and it is given by the formula,

$$\text{Mode} = l + \left(\frac{f_m - f_1}{2f_m - f_1 - f_2}\right) \times h$$

where, l = lower limit of the modal class

h = size of the class interval (assuming all class sizes to be equal)

f_m = frequency of the modal class

f_1 = frequency of the class preceding the modal class

f_2 = frequency of the class succeeding the modal class

Note If all the values in a data occur with equal frequency, then there is no mode. Modal class is the class with maximum frequency.

05 Median The median is a measure of central tendency which gives the value of the middle most observation in the data, when the observations are arranged either ascending or descending order of their magnitudes.

It divides the arranged series in two equal parts *i.e.*, 50% of the observations lie below the median and the remaining are above the median.

(i) **Median for individual series (ungrouped data)** Let n be the number of observations.

(a) If n is odd, then median = value of $\left(\frac{n+1}{2}\right)^{\text{th}}$ terms

(b) If n is even, then

$$\text{median} = \text{mean of the } \left(\frac{n}{2}\right)^{\text{th}} \text{ and } \left(\frac{n}{2}+1\right)^{\text{th}} \text{ terms}$$

$$= \frac{1}{2} \times \text{Value of} \left[\left(\frac{n}{2}\right)^{\text{th}} + \left(\frac{n}{2}+1\right)^{\text{th}}\right]$$

(ii) **Median of discrete series (grouped data)**

Firstly prepare a cumulative frequency table of the data.

(a) If n is odd, then median = Value of $\left(\frac{n+1}{2}\right)^{\text{th}}$ term

(b) If n is even, then median

$$= \frac{1}{2} \times \left[\text{Value of} \left\{\left(\frac{n}{2}\right)^{\text{th}} + \left(\frac{n}{2}+1\right)^{\text{th}}\right\} \text{term}\right]$$

(iii) **Median for continuous frequency distribution (grouped data)**

Use the following formula in addition to above steps

Then, $$\text{median} = l + \frac{\left(\frac{N}{2} - cf\right)}{f} \times h$$

Firstly find $\frac{N}{2}$ and determine the class interval in which they exist.

l = lower limit of median class

cf = cumulative frequency of class preceding the median class

f = frequency of the median class in which $\frac{N}{2}$ lies

h = class width (assuming class size to be equal)

N = number of observations

Note The cumulative frequency of a value is its frequency plus the frequencies of all smaller values.
Median class is the class interval whose cumulative frequency is greater than (and nearest to) $\frac{N}{2}$.

06 Relationship among Mean, Median and Mode There is an empirical relationship between the three measures of central tendency.

$$3 \text{ Median} = \text{Mode} + 2 \text{ Mean}$$

Exercise 13.1

Question 1 A survey was conducted by a group of students as a part of their environment awareness programme, in which they collected the following data regarding the number of plants in 20 houses in a locality. Find the mean number of plants per house.

Number of plants	0-2	2-4	4-6	6-8	8-10	10-12	12-14
Number of houses	1	2	1	5	6	2	3

Which method did you use for finding the mean and why?

Sol. Let us find mean of the data by direct method because the figures are small.

Class interval (Number of plants)	Frequency (f_i) (Number of houses)	Class mark (x_i)	$f_i \times x_i$
0-2	1	1	1
2-4	2	3	6
4-6	1	5	5
6-8	5	7	35
8-10	6	9	54
10-12	2	11	22
12-14	3	13	39
Total	$N = 20$		162

We have, $N = \sum_{i=1}^{7} f_i = 20$ and $\sum_{i=1}^{7} f_i x_i = 162$

Then, mean of the data is

$$\bar{x} = \frac{1}{N} \times \sum_{i=1}^{7} f_i x_i = \frac{1}{20} \times 162 = 8.1$$

Hence, the required mean number of plant per house is 8.1.

Mistake Alert Students may incorrectly calculate class marks by using the end point instead of the mid-point.

Question 2 Consider the following distribution of daily wages of 50 workers of a factory.

Daily wages (in ₹)	500-520	520-540	540-560	560-580	580-600
Number of workers	12	14	8	6	10

Find the mean daily wages of the workers of the factory by using an appropriate method.

Thinking Process Use the step deviation method to find the mean of the given distribution by the following formula, Mean $= a + \left(\frac{\sum f_i \times u_i}{N}\right)h$

Sol. Here, we use step deviation method for finding the mean of the data.

Daily wages (in ₹)	Number of workers (f_i)	Class mark (x_i)	$d_i = x_i - 550$	$u_i = \frac{d_i}{h} = \frac{x_i - 550}{20}$	$f_i \times u_i$
500-520	12	510	– 40	– 2	– 24
520-540	14	530	– 20	– 1	– 14
540-560	8	550 = a	0	0	0
560-580	6	570	20	1	6
580-600	10	590	40	2	20
Total	$N = 50$				– 12

We have, assumed mean $(a) = 550$, class width $(h) = 20$, $N = 50$ and $\sum_{i=1}^{5} f_i u_i = -12$

By step deviation method, we have

$$\text{Mean } = a + h \times \frac{1}{N} \times \sum_{i=1}^{5} f_i u_i$$

$$= ₹\left\{550 + 20 \times \frac{1}{50} \times (-12)\right\} = ₹\left\{150 - \frac{24}{5}\right\}$$

$$= ₹\{550 - 4.80\} = ₹\ 545.20$$

Hene, the mean daily wages of the workers of the factory is ₹ 545.20.

Question 3 The following distribution shows the daily pocket allowance of children of a locality. The mean pocket allowance is ₹ 18. Find the missing frequency f.

Daily pocket allowance (in ₹)	11-13	13-15	15-17	17-19	19-21	21-23	23-25
Number of children	7	6	9	13	f	5	4

Sol.

Daily pocket allowance (in ₹)	Number of children (f_i)	Class mark (x_i)	$d_i = x_i - 18$	$f_i \times d_i$
11-13	7	12	– 6	– 42
13-15	6	14	– 4	– 24
15-17	9	16	– 2	– 18
17-19	13	18 = a	0	0
19-21	f	20	2	$2f$
21-23	5	22	4	20
23-25	4	24	6	24
Total	$N = 44 + f$			$2f - 40$

It is given that mean = ₹ 18

From the table, we have

$$\text{Assumed mean } (a) = 18, N = 44 + f$$

and $$\sum_{i=1}^{7} f_i d_i = 2f - 40$$

Now, by assumed mean method, mean $= a + \dfrac{1}{N} \times \sum_{i=1}^{7} f_i d_i$

Then, substituting the value as given above, we have

$$18 = 18 + \frac{1}{(44+f)} \times (2f - 40)$$

$$\Rightarrow \quad 0 = \frac{2f - 40}{44 + f}$$

$$\Rightarrow \quad 2f = 40$$

$$\Rightarrow \quad f = 20 \qquad (\because f \neq -44)$$

Thus, the missing frequency is 20.

Question 4 Thirty women were examined in a hospital by a doctor and the number of heartbeats per minute were recorded and summarised as follows. Find the mean heartbeats per minute for these women, choosing a suitable method.

Number of heartbeats per minute	65-68	68-71	71-74	74-77	77-80	80-83	83-86
Number of women	2	4	3	8	7	4	2

Sol.

Number of heartbeats per minute	Number of women (f_i)	Class mark (x_i)	$u_i = \frac{x_i - a}{h} = \frac{x_i - 75.5}{3}$	$f_i \times u_i$
65-68	2	66.5	$u_1 = \frac{66.5 - 75.5}{3} = -3$	−6
68-71	4	69.5	$u_2 = \frac{69.5 - 75.5}{3} = -2$	−8
71-74	3	72.5	$u_3 = \frac{72.5 - 75.5}{3} = -1$	−3
74-77	8	75.5 = a	$u_4 = \frac{75.5 - 75.5}{3} = 0$	0
77-80	7	78.5	$u_5 = \frac{78.5 - 75.5}{3} = 1$	7
80-83	4	81.5	$u_6 = \frac{81.5 - 75.5}{3} = 2$	8
83-86	2	84.5	$u_7 = \frac{84.5 - 75.5}{3} = 3$	6
Total	$N = 30$			4

We have, assumed mean $(a) = 75.5$, class width $(h) = 3$,

Total observations $(N) = 30$ and $\sum_{i=1}^{7} f_i u_i = 4$

By step deviation method,

$$\text{Mean} = a + h \times \frac{1}{N} \times \sum_{i=1}^{7} f_i u_i$$

$$= 75.5 + 3 \times \frac{1}{30} \times 4$$

$$= 75.5 + 0.4$$

$$= 75.9 \text{ heartbeats}$$

Thus, the mean heartbeat per minute is 75.9

Question 5 In a retail market, fruit vendors were selling mangoes kept in packing boxes. These boxes contained varying number of mangoes. The following was the distribution of mangoes according to the number of boxes.

Number of mangoes	50-52	53-55	56-58	59-61	62-64
Number of boxes	15	110	135	115	25

Find the mean number of mangoes kept in a packing box. Which method of finding the mean did you choose?

Sol. Since, given data is not continuous, so, we subtract 0.5 from the lower limit of each class and add 0.5 to the upper limit of each class.

Number of mangoes	Number of boxes (f_i)	Class mark (x_i)	$u_i = \frac{x_i - a}{h} = \frac{x_i - 57}{3}$	$f_i \times u_i$
49.5-52.5	15	51	−2	−30
52.5-55.5	110	54	−1	−110
55.5-58.5	135	$a = 57$	0	0
58.5-61.5	115	60	1	115
61.5-64.5	25	63	2	50
Total	$N = 400$			25

We have, assumed mean $(a) = 57$, Class width $(h) = 3$, Total observations, $(N) = 400$ and $\sum_{i=1}^{5} f_i u_i = 25$

By step deviation method,

$$\text{Mean} = a + h \times \frac{1}{N} \times \sum_{i=1}^{5} f_i u_i$$

$$= 57 + 3 \times \frac{1}{400} \times 25$$

$$= 57 + \frac{75}{400}$$
$$= 57 + 0.19$$
$$= 57.19$$

Hence, the average number of mangoes to be kept the packing are 57.19.
The method chossen to find the mean is step deviation method.

Question 6 The table below shows the daily expenditure on food of 25 households in a locality.

Daily expenditure (in ₹)	100-150	150-200	200-250	250-300	300-350
Number of households	4	5	12	2	2

Find the mean daily expenditure on food by a suitable method.

Sol.

Daily expenditure (in ₹)	Number of households (f_i)	Class mark (x_i)	$u_i = \frac{x_i - a}{h} = \frac{x_i - 225}{50}$	$f_i \times u_i$
100-150	4	125	−2	−8
150-200	5	175	−1	−5
200-250	12	$a = 225$	0	0
250-300	2	275	1	2
300-350	2	325	2	4
Total	$N = 25$			−7

We have, assumed mean $(a) = 225$, class width, $(h) = 50$, Total observations $(N) = 25$ and $\sum_{i=1}^{5} f_i u_i = -7$

By step deviation method,

$$\text{Mean} = a + h \times \frac{1}{N} \times \sum_{i=1}^{5} f_i u_i$$
$$= 225 + 50 \times \frac{1}{25} \times (-7)$$
$$= 225 - 14$$
$$= ₹\ 211$$

Hence, the mean daily expenditure on food is ₹ 211.

Question 7 To find out the concentration of SO_2 in the air (in parts per million, *i.e.*, ppm), the data was collected for 30 localities in a certain city and is presented below.

Concentration of SO_2 (in ppm)	Frequency
0.00-0.04	4
0.04-0.08	9
0.08-0.12	9
0.12-0.16	2
0.16-0.20	4
0.20-0.24	2

Find the mean concentration of SO_2 in the air.

Sol.

Concentration of SO_2 (in ppm)	frequency f_i	Class mark (x_i)	$u_i = \frac{x_i - a}{h} = \frac{x_i - 0.10}{0.04}$	$f_i \times u_i$
0.00-0.04	4	0.02	−2	−8
0.04-0.08	9	0.06	−1	−9
0.08-0.12	9	0.10 = a	0	0
0.12-0.16	2	0.14	1	2
0.16-0.20	4	0.18	2	8
0.20-0.24	2	0.22	3	6
Total	$N = 30$			−1

We have, Assumed mean $(a) = 0.10$, class width $(h) = 0.04$,

Total observations $(N) = 30$ and $\sum_{i=1}^{6} f_i u_i = -1$

By step deviation method,

$$\text{Mean} = a + h \times \frac{1}{N} \times \sum_{i=1}^{6} f_i u_i$$

$$= 0.10 + 0.04 \times \frac{1}{30} \times (-1)$$

$$= 0.10 - \frac{0.04}{30}$$

$$= 0.10 - 0.001$$

$$= 0.099 \text{ ppm}$$

Hence, the mean concentration of SO_2 in the air is 0.099 ppm.

Question 8 A class teacher has the following absentee record of 40 students of a class for the whole term. Find the mean number of days a student was absent.

Number of days	0-6	6-10	10-14	14-20	20-28	28-38	38-40
Number of students	11	10	7	4	4	3	1

Sol.

Number of days	Number of students (f_i)	Class mark (x_i)	$d_i = x_i - a = x_i - 17$	$f_i \times d_i$
0-6	11	3	– 14	– 154
6-10	10	8	– 9	– 90
10-14	7	12	– 5	– 35
14-20	4	17 = a	0	0
20-28	4	24	7	28
28-38	3	33	16	48
38-40	1	39	22	22
Total	$N = 40$			– 181

We have, assumed mean (a) = 17, Total observations (N) = 40

and $\sum_{i=1}^{7} f_i d_i = -181$

By assumed mean method,

$$\text{Mean} = a + \frac{1}{N} \times \Sigma f_i d_i = 17 + \frac{1}{40} \times (-181) = 17 - 4.525 = 12.475 \approx 12.48 \text{ days.}$$

Hence, on an average a student was absent for 12.8 days.

Quick Solution

Number of days	Number of students (f_i)	Class mark (x_i)	$f_i \times x_i$
0-6	11	3	33
6-10	10	8	80
10-14	7	12	84
14-20	4	17	68
20-28	4	24	96
28-38	3	33	99
38-40	1	39	39
Total	$N = \Sigma f_i = 40$		$\Sigma f_i x_i = 499$

By direct method,

$$\text{Mean} = \frac{\Sigma f_i x_i}{\Sigma f_i} = \frac{499}{40} = 12.475 \approx 12.48$$

Question 9 The following table gives the literacy rate (in percentage) of 35 cities. Find the mean literacy rate.

Literacy rate (in %)	45-55	55-65	65-75	75-85	85-95
Number of cities	3	10	11	8	3

Solution

Literacy rate (in %)	Number of cities (f_i)	Class mark (x_i)	$u_i = \frac{x_i - a}{h} = \frac{x_i - 70}{10}$	$f_i \times u_i$
45-55	3	50	−2	−6
55-65	10	60	−1	−10
65-75	11	$a = 70$	0	0
75-85	8	80	1	8
85-95	3	90	2	6
Total	$N = 35$			−2

We have, Assumed mean $(a) = 70$, class width $(h) = 10$,

Total observations $(N) = 35$ and $\sum_{i=1}^{5} f_i u_i = -2$

By step deviation method,

$$\text{Mean} = a + h \times \frac{1}{N} \times \sum_{i=1}^{5} f_i u_i = 70 + 10 \times \frac{1}{35} \times (-2)$$

$$= 70 - \frac{4}{7} = 70 - 0.57 = 69.43\%$$

Hence, the average literary rate is 69.43%.

Quick Solution

Literacy rate (in %)	Number of cities (f_i)	Class mark (x_i)	$f_i \times x_i$
45-55	3	50	150
55-65	10	60	600
65-75	11	70	770
75-85	8	80	640
85-95	3	90	270
Total	$N\Sigma f_i = 35$		$\Sigma f_i x_i = 2430$

By direct method,

$$\text{Mean} = \frac{\Sigma f_i x_i}{\Sigma f_i} = \frac{2430}{35} = 69.43\%$$

Exercise 13.2

Question 1 The following table shows the ages of the patients admitted in a hospital during a year

Age (in years)	5-15	15-25	25-35	35-45	45-55	55-65
Number of patients	6	11	21	23	14	5

Find the mode and the mean of the data given above. Compare and interpret the two measures of central tendency.

Sol.

Age (in years)	Number of patients (f_i)	Class mark (x_i)	$u_i = \frac{x_i - a}{h} = \frac{x_i - 30}{10}$	$f_i \times u_i$
5-15	6	10	−2	−12
15-25	11	20	−1	−11
25-35	21	30 = a	0	0
35-45	23	40	1	23
45-55	14	50	2	28
55-65	5	60	3	15
Total	$N = 80$			43

We have, assumed mean $(a) = 30$, class width $(h) = 10$, Total observations, $(N) = 80$ and $\sum_{i=1}^{6} f_i u_i = 43$.

From the given data, we have the modal class 35-45.

($\because$ It has largest frequency among the given classes of the data)

So, lower limit of modal class $(l) = 35$, $f_m = 23$, $f_1 = 21$, $f_2 = 14$ and class width $(h) = 10$

$$\text{Mode} = l + \left\{\frac{f_m - f_1}{2f_m - f_1 - f_2}\right\} \times h$$

$$= 35 + \left\{\frac{23 - 21}{46 - 21 - 14}\right\} \times 10$$

$$= 35 + \frac{20}{11} = 35 + 1.8 = 36.8 \text{ years}$$

Now, let us find the mean of the data.

Now, by step deviation method,

$$\text{Mean} = a + h \times \frac{1}{N} \times \sum_{i=1}^{6} f_i u_i$$

$$= 30 + 10 \times \frac{1}{80} \times 43 = 30 + 5.37 = 35.37 \text{ years}$$

Thus, mode = 36.8 years and mean = 35.57 years So, we conclude that the maximum number of patients admitted in the hospital are of age 36.8 years (approx.), whereas on an average age of a patient admitted to the hospital is 35.37 years.

Mistake Alert Student may get confused between f_1, f_m and f_2 which may lead to incorrect results.

Question 2 The following data gives the information on the observed lifetimes (in hours) of 225 electrical components:

Lifetimes (in hours)	0-20	20-40	40-60	60-80	80-100	100-120
Frequency	10	35	52	61	38	29

Determine the modal lifetimes of the components.

Sol. Modal class of the given data is 60-80. Because it has highest frequency among the given classes of the data.

Here, lower limit of modal class (l) = 60, $f_m = 61$, $f_1 = 52$, $f_2 = 38$ and class width (h) = 20

$$\text{Mode} = l + \left\{\frac{f_m - f_1}{2f_m - f_1 - f_2}\right\} \times h$$

$$= 60 + \left\{\frac{61 - 52}{122 - 52 - 38}\right\} \times 20$$

$$= 60 + \frac{9 \times 20}{32} = 60 + \frac{45}{8}$$

$$= 60 + 5.625 = 65.625 \text{ hrs}$$

Hence, the model lifetimes of the components are 65.625 hrs.

Question 3 The following data gives the distribution of total monthly household expenditure of 200 families of a village. Find the modal monthly expenditure of the families. Also, find mean monthly expenditure

Expenditure (in ₹)	Number of families
1000-1500	24
1500-2000	40
2000-2500	33
2500-3000	28
3000-3500	30
3500-4000	22
4000-4500	16
4500-5000	7

Sol.

Expenditure (in ₹)	Number of families (f_i)	Class mark (x_i)	$u_i = \frac{x_i - a}{h} = \frac{x_i - 2750}{500}$	$f_i \times u_i$
1000-1500	24	1250	-3	-72
1500-2000	40	1750	-2	-80
2000-2500	33	2250	-1	-33
2500-3000	28	$2750 = a$	0	0
3000-3500	30	3250	1	30
3500-4000	22	3750	2	44
4000-4500	16	4250	3	48
4500-5000	7	4750	4	28
Total	$N = 200$			-35

Modal class of the data is 1500-2000, because it has highest frequency among the given classes of the data.

Lower modal class (l) = 1500, $f_m = 40$, $f_1 = 24$, $f_2 = 33$, class width (h) = 500

$$\text{Mode } = l + \left\{\frac{f_m - f_1}{2f_m - f_1 - f_2}\right\} \times h = 1500 + \left\{\frac{40 - 24}{80 - 24 - 33}\right\} \times 500$$

$$= 1500 + \frac{16 \times 500}{23} = 1500 + \frac{8000}{23}$$

$$= 1500 + 347.83 = ₹\ 1847.83$$

Now, from the table, we have, assumed mean (a) = 2750, class width (h) = 500,

Total observations (N) = 200 and $\sum_{i=1}^{8} f_i u_i = -35$

Now, by step deviation method,

$$\text{Mean} = a + h \times \frac{1}{N} \times \sum_{i=1}^{8} f_i u_i$$

$$= 2750 + 500 \times \frac{1}{200} \times (-35)$$

$$= 2750 - \frac{5 \times 35}{2}$$

$$= 2750 - 87.50 = ₹\ 2662.50$$

Thus, the modal monthly expenditure is ₹ 1847.83 and the mean monthly expenditure is ₹ 2662.50.

Question 4 The following distribution gives the state wise teacher-student ratio in higher secondary schools of India. Find the mode and mean of this data. Interpret, the two measures.

Number of students per teacher	Number of states/UT
15-20	3
20-25	8
25-30	9
30-35	10
35-40	3
40-45	0
45-50	0
50-55	2

Sol.

Number of students per teacher	Number of states /UT (f_i)	Class mark (x_i)	$u_i = \frac{x_i - a}{h} = \frac{x_i - 32.5}{5}$	$f_i \times u_i$
15-20	3	17.5	−3	−9
20-25	8	22.5	−2	−16
25-30	9	27.5	−1	−9
30-35	10	$32.5 = a$	0	0
35-40	3	37.5	1	3
40-45	0	42.5	2	0
45-50	0	47.5	3	0
50-55	2	52.5	4	8
Total	$N = 35$			−23

Since, highest frequency is 10, so its modal class is 30-35.
lower limit of modal class $(l) = 30$, $f_m = 10$, $f_1 = 9$, $f_2 = 3$ class width $(h) = 5$

$$\therefore \quad \text{Mode} = l + \left\{\frac{f_m - f_1}{2f_m - f_1 - f_2}\right\} \times h = 30 + \left\{\frac{10 - 9}{20 - 9 - 3}\right\} \times 5$$

$$= 30 + \frac{5}{8} = 30 + 0.625 = 30.625 \approx 30.6$$

Now, from the table, we have, assumed mean $(a) = 32.5$, Class width $(h) = 5$, Total observations $(N) = 35$ and $\sum_{i=1}^{8} f_i u_i = -23$

Now, by step deviation method,

$$\text{Mean} = a + h \times \frac{1}{N} \times \sum_{i=1}^{8} f_i u_i = 32.5 + 5 \times \frac{1}{35} \times (-23)$$

$$= 32.5 - \frac{23}{7} = 32.5 - 3.3 = 29.2$$

Hence, mode = 30.6 and mean = 29.2. We conclude that most states/ UT have a student teacher ratio of 30.6 and on an average ratio is 29.2.

Question 5 The given distribution shows the number of runs scored by some top batsmen of the world in one day international cricket matches

Runs scored	Number of batsmen
3000-4000	4
4000-5000	18
5000-6000	9
6000-7000	7
7000-8000	6
8000-9000	3
9000-10000	1
10000-11000	1

Find the mode of the data.

Thinking Process Use the formula, $\text{mod} = l + \left(\dfrac{f_m - f_1}{2f_m - f_1 - f_2}\right)h$ to get the required result.

Sol. Since, maximum frequency is 18, so its modal class is 4000-5000.

$\therefore$ limit of lower modal class $(l) = 4000$, $f_m = 18$, $f_1 = 4$, $f_2 = 9$, class width $(h) = 1000$

$$\therefore \quad \text{Mode} = l + \left\{\frac{f_m - f_1}{2f_m - f_1 - f_2}\right\} \times h = 4000 + \left\{\frac{18 - 4}{36 - 4 - 9}\right\} \times 1000$$

$$= 4000 + \frac{14000}{23} = 4000 + 608.7 = 4608.7 \text{ runs}$$

Hence, the required mode of the data is 4608.7 runs.

Question 6 A student noted the number of cars passing through a spot on a road for 100 period each of 3 minutes and summarized it in the given below. Find the mode of the data

Number of cars	0-10	10-20	20-30	30-40	40-50	50-60	60-70	70-80
Frequency	7	14	13	12	20	11	15	8

Sol. Since, maximum frequency is $f_m = 20$, so its modal class is (40-50)

$\therefore$ limit of lower modal class $(l) = 40$, $f_m = 20$, $f_1 = 12$, $f_2 = 11$, class width $(h) = 10$

$$\therefore \quad \text{Mode} = l + \left\{\frac{f_m - f_1}{2f_m - f_1 - f_2}\right\} \times h$$

$$= 40 + \left\{\frac{20 - 12}{40 - 12 - 11}\right\} \times 10$$

$$= 40 + \frac{80}{17} = 40 + 4.7 = 44.7 \text{ cars}$$

Hence, the required mode is 44.7 cars.

Exercise 13.3

Question 1 The following frequency distribution gives the monthly consumption of electricity of 68 consumers of a locality. Find the median, mean and mode of the data and compare them.

Monthly consumption (in units)	Number of consumers
65-85	4
85-105	5
105-125	13
125-145	20
145-165	14
165-185	8
185-205	4

Sol.

Monthly consumption (in units)	Number of consumers (f_i)	Cumulative frequency (cf)
65-85	4	4
85-105	5	9
105-125	13	22
125-145	20	42
145-165	14	56
165-185	8	64
185-205	4	68
Total	$N = 68$	

(i) Here, $N = 68 \Rightarrow \frac{N}{2} = 34$

So, we have the median class 125-145.

$\therefore$ Lower limit of median class $(l) = 125$, $N = 68$, $f = 20$, $cf = 22$, class width $(h) = 20$

$$\text{Median} = l + \left\{\frac{\frac{N}{2} - cf}{f}\right\} \times h$$

$$= 125 + \left\{\frac{34 - 22}{20}\right\} \times 20 = 125 + \frac{12}{20} \times 20$$

$$= 125 + 12 = 137 \text{ units}$$

(ii) Since, maximum frequency is 20, so its modal class is 125-145.

$\therefore$ $fm = 20, f_1 = 13, f_2 = 14$, limit of lower modal class $(l) = 125$ and class width $(h) = 20$

$$\text{Mode} = l + \left\{\frac{f_m - f_1}{2f_m - f_1 - f_2}\right\} \times h$$

$$= 125 + \left\{\frac{20 - 13}{40 - 13 - 14}\right\} \times 20$$

$$= 125 + \frac{7 \times 20}{13}$$

$$= 125 + \frac{140}{13}$$

$$= 125 + 10.77 = 135.77 \text{ units}$$

(iii)

Monthly consumption (in units)	Number of consumers (f_i)	Class mark (x_i)	$u_i = \frac{x_i - a}{h} = \frac{x_i - 135}{20}$	$f_i \times u_i$
65-85	4	75	-3	-12
85-105	5	95	-2	-10
105-125	13	115	-1	-13
125-145	20	$a = 135$	0	0
145-165	14	155	1	14
165-185	8	175	2	16
185-205	4	195	3	12
Total	$N = 68$			7

We have, total observations $(N) = 68$, assumed mean $(a) = 135$, class width $(h) = 20$ and $\sum_{i=1}^{7} f_i u_i = 7$

Now, by step deviation method

$$\text{Mean} = a + h \times \frac{1}{N} \times \sum_{i=1}^{7} f_i u_i$$

$$= 135 + 20 \times \frac{1}{68} \times 7$$

$$= 135 + \frac{35}{17}$$

$$= 135 + 2.05 = 137.05 \text{ units}$$

So, mean > median > mode

Question 2 If the median of the distribution given below is 28.5, find the values of x and y.

Class interval	Frequency
0-10	5
10-20	x
20-30	20
30-40	15
40-50	y
50-60	5
Total	60

Sol.

Class interval	Frequency (f)	Cumulative frequency
0-10	5	5
10-20	x	$5 + x = cf$
20-30	$20 = f$	$25 + x$
30-40	15	$40 + x$
40-50	y	$40 + x + y$
50-60	5	$45 + x + y$
Total	60	

Given, median = 28.5 lies in the class interval 20-30.
Then, median class is (20-30).
So, we have, lower limit of median class (l) = 20, $f = 20$, $cf = 5 + x$
class width (h) = 10, total observations (N) = 60

$$\text{Median } = l + \left\{\frac{\frac{N}{2} - cf}{f}\right\} \times h$$

$$\therefore \quad 28.5 = 20 + \frac{\left\{\frac{60}{2} - (5 + x)\right\}}{20} \times 10$$

$$\Rightarrow \quad 8.5 = \frac{25 - x}{2}$$

$$\Rightarrow \quad 17 = 25 - x$$

$$\Rightarrow \quad x = 8$$

From the given table, we have

i.e., $x + y + 45 = 60$

$\Rightarrow$ $x + y = 15$

$\Rightarrow$ $y = 15 - x = 15 - 8$

$\Rightarrow$ $y = 7$

Hence, the values of x and y are respectively 8 and 7.

Mistake Alert Students may mistakenly take the value of 'f' from the same median class instead of the value of 'f' before the median class.

Question 3 A life insurance agent found the following data for distribution of ages of 100 policy holders. Calculate the median age, if policies are only given to persons having age 18 years onwards but less than 60 years.

Age (in years)	Number of policy holders
Below 20	2
Below 25	6
Below 30	24
Below 35	45
Below 40	78
Below 45	89
Below 50	92
Below 55	98
Below 60	100

Sol.

Age (in years)	Number of policy holders	Cumulative frequency
Below 20	$2 = 2$	2
20-25	$6 - 2 = 4$	6
25-30	$24 - 6 = 18$	24
30-35	$45 - 24 = 21$	$45 = cf$
(Median class) 35-40	$78 - 45 = 33 = f$	78
40-45	$89 - 78 = 11$	89
45-50	$92 - 89 = 3$	92
50-55	$98 - 92 = 6$	98
55-60	$100 - 98 = 2$	100
Total	$N = 100$	

$$\because \quad \frac{N}{2} = \frac{100}{2} = 50$$

So, the median class in 35-40.

Here, lower limit of median class $(l) = 35$, $f = 33$, $cf = 45$, class width $(h) = 5$,

Total observations $(N) = 100$

$$\text{Median} = l + \left\{\frac{\frac{N}{2} - cf}{f}\right\} \times h$$

$$= 35 + \left\{\frac{50 - 45}{33}\right\} \times 5 = 35 + \frac{25}{33} = 35 + 0.76 = 35.76 \text{ years}$$

Hence, the median age is 35.76 years.

Question 4 The length of 40 leaves of a plant are measured correct to the nearest millimetre and the data obtained is represented in the following table :

Length (in mm)	Number of leaves
118-126	3
127-135	5
136-144	9
145-153	12
154-162	5
163-171	4
172-180	2

Find the median length of the leaves.

Thinking Process First, convert the given classes into continuous classes, then use the formula, median $= l + \left(\frac{\frac{N}{2} - cf}{f}\right) \times h$ of get the required result.

Sol. Since, given classes is not continuous, so it needs to be converted into continuous classes for finding the median, The classes, then change to 117.5-126.5, 126.5-135.5,...171.5-180.5.

Length (in mm)	Number of leaves f_i	Cumulative frequency
117.5-126.5	3	$3 = 3$
126.5-135.5	5	$3 + 5 = 8$
135.5-144.5	9	$8 + 9 = 17 = cf$
(Median class) 144.5-153.5	$12 = f$	$17 + 12 = 29$
153.5-162.5	5	$29 + 5 = 34$
162.5-171.5	4	$34 + 4 = 38$
171.5-180.5	2	$38 + 2 = 40$
Total	$N = 40$	

$\because \quad \frac{N}{2} = \frac{40}{2} = 20$

Since, cumulative frequency 20 lies in the interval 144.5-153.5.

So, median class is 144.5 – 153.5

Here, lower limit of median class (l) = 144.5, f = 12, cf = 17, class width (h) = 9, Total observations (N) = 40

$$\text{Median} = l + \left\{\frac{\frac{N}{2} - cf}{f}\right\} \times h$$

$$= 144.5 + \left\{\frac{20 - 17}{12}\right\} \times 9$$

$$= 144.5 + \frac{3 \times 3}{4} = 144.5 + \frac{9}{4} = 144.5 + 2.25$$

$$= 146.75 \text{ mm}$$

Hence, median length of the leaves is 146.75 mm.

Question 5 The following table gives the distribution of the life time of 400 neon lamps

Life time (in hours)	Number of lamps
1500-2000	14
2000-2500	56
2500-3000	60
3000-3500	86
3500-4000	74
4000-4500	62
4500-5000	48

Find the median life time of a lamp.

Sol.

Life time (in hours)	Number of lamps f_i	Cumulative frequency cf
1500-2000	14	14 = 14
2000-2500	56	14 + 56 = 70
2500-3000	60	70 + 60 = 130 = cf
(Median class) 3000-3500	86 = f	130 + 86 = 216
3500-4000	74	216 + 74 = 290
4000-4500	62	290 + 62 = 352
4500-5000	48	352 + 48 = 400
Total	$N = 400$	

$\because \qquad \frac{N}{2} = \frac{400}{2} = 200$

Since, cumulative frequency 200 lies in the interval 3000-3500.

So, median class is 3000 – 3500.

Here, lower limit of median class $(l) = 3000$, $f = 86$, $cf = 130$,

Class width $(h) = 500$, Total observations $(N) = 400$

$$\text{Median} = l + \left\{\frac{\frac{N}{2} - cf}{f}\right\} \times h$$

$$= 3000 + \frac{\{200 - 130\}}{86} \times 500$$

$$= 3000 + \frac{70 \times 500}{86}$$

$$= 3000 + \frac{35000}{86}$$

$$= 3000 + 406.98$$

$$= 3406.98 \text{ hours}$$

Hence, median life time of a lamp is 3406.98 hours.

Question 6 100 surnames were randomly picked up from a local telephone directory and the frequency distribution of the number of letters in the English alphabets in the surnames was obtained as follows :

Number of letters	1-4	4-7	7-10	10-13	13-16	16-19
Number of surnames	6	30	40	16	4	4

Determine the median number of letter in the surnames. Find the mean number of letters in the surnames? Also, find the modal size of the surnames.

Sol. (i)

Number of letters	Number of surnames	Cumulative frequency
1-4	6	6 = 6
4-7	30	6 + 30 = 36
7-10	40	36 + 40 = 76
10-13	16	76 + 16 = 92
13-16	4	92 + 4 = 96
16-19	4	96 + 4 = 100
Total	$N = 100$	

(i) $\because \qquad \frac{N}{2} = \frac{100}{2} = 50$

Since, cumulative frequency 50 lies in the interval 7-10.

So, median class is 7 – 10.

Here, lower limit of median class $(l) = 7$, $f = 40$, $cf = 36$, class width $(h) = 3$, Total observations $(N) = 100$

$$\text{Median} = l + \left\{\frac{\frac{N}{2} - cf}{f}\right\} \times h$$

$$= 7 + \left\{\frac{50 - 36}{40}\right\} \times 3$$

$$= 7 + \frac{14 \times 3}{40}$$

$$= 7 + \frac{21}{20} = 7 + 1.05 = 8.05$$

Hence, the median number of letters in the surnames is 8.05.

(ii) Modal class is 7-10, because it has maximum frequency *i.e.*, 40.

$\therefore$ Lower limit of modal class $(l) = 7$, $f_m = 40$, $f_1 = 30$, $f_2 = 16$, class width $(h) = 3$

$$\text{Mode} = l + \left\{\frac{f_m - f_1}{2f_m - f_1 - f_2}\right\} \times h = 7 + \left\{\frac{40 - 30}{80 - 30 - 16}\right\} \times 3$$

$$= 7 + \frac{30}{34} = 7 + 0.88 = 7.88$$

Hence, the modal size of the surnames is 7.88.

(iii)

Number of letters	f_i	Class mark x_i	$u_i = \frac{x_i - a}{h} = \frac{x_i - 8.5}{3}$	$f_i \times u_i$
1-4	6	2.5	– 2	– 12
4-7	30	5.5	– 1	– 30
7-10	40	$8.5 = a$	0	0
10-13	16	11.5	1	16
13-16	4	14.5	2	8
16-19	4	17.5	3	12
Total	$N = 100$			– 6

Here, total observations $(N) = 100$, assumed mean $(a) = 8.5$,

Class width $(h) = 3$ and $\sum_{i=1}^{6} f_i u_i = -6$

Now, by step deviation method,

$$\text{Mean} = a + h \times \frac{1}{N} \times \sum_{i=1}^{6} f_i u_i$$

$$= 8.5 + 3 \times \frac{1}{100} \times (-6)$$

$$= 8.5 - \frac{18}{100}$$

$$= 8.5 - 0.18$$

$$= 8.32$$

Hence, the mean number of letters in the surname is 8.32.

Question 7 The distribution below gives the weights of 30 students of a class. Find the median weight of the students.

Weight (in kg)	40-45	45-50	50-55	55-60	60-65	65-70	70-75
Number of students	2	3	8	6	6	3	2

Sol.

Weight (in kg)	Number of students (f_i)	Cumulative frequency
40-45	2	$2 = 2$
45-50	3	$2 + 3 = 5$
50-55	8	$5 + 8 = 13 = cf$
(median class) 55-60	$6 = f$	$13 + 6 = 19$
60-65	6	$19 + 6 = 25$
65-70	3	$25 + 3 = 28$
70-75	2	$28 + 2 = 30$
Total	$N = 30$	

$$\because \quad \frac{N}{2} = \frac{30}{2} = 15$$

Since, cumulative frequency 15 lies in the interval 55-60.

So, median class is 55-60.

Here, lower limit of median class $(l) = 55$, $f = 6$, $cf = 13$, class width $(h) = 5$,

Total observations $(N) = 30$

$$\text{Median} = l + \left\{ \frac{\frac{N}{2} - cf}{f} \right\} \times h$$

$$= 55 + \left\{ \frac{15 - 13}{6} \right\} \times 5$$

$$= 55 + \frac{5}{3}$$

$$= 55 + 1.67 = 56.67 \text{ kg}$$

Hence, the median weight of the students is 56.67 kg.

DIKSHA APP Questions

☐ Multiple Choice Questions

Q.1 While computing mean of grouped data, we assume that the frequencies are

(a) Evenly distributed over all the classes
(b) Centered at the class mark of the classes
(c) Centered at the upper limits of the classes
(d) Centered at the lower limits of the classes

Sol. (b) While computing the mean of grouped data, we assume that the frequencies are centered at the class mark of each class.

Q.2 The percentage of marks obtained by 100 students in an examinations are as fallows

Marks	130-135	135-140	140-145	145-150	159-155	155-160	150-165
Frequency	10	15	18	22	23	8	4

The comulative frequency of the class interval 150-155 is

(a) 90 (b) 80
(c) 100 (d) 88

Sol. (d)

Marks	Frequency	Cumulative frequency
130-135	10	10
135-140	15	25
140-145	18	43
145-150	22	65
150-155	23	88
155-160	8	96
160-165	4	100

The table shows that the cumulative frequency of the class interval 150-155 is 88.

Mistake Alert Student may mistakenly take the cumulative frequency of the class interval 150-155 to be 23 instead of 88.

Q.3 Consider the following frequency distribution of the heights of 60 students of a class

Height (in cm)	150-155	155-160	160-165	165-170	170-175	175-180
Number of students	15	13	10	8	9	5

The upper limit of the median class in the given data is

(a) 165 (b) 155
(c) 160 (d) 170

Sol. (a)

Height (in cm)	Number of students	Cumulative frequency
150-155	15	15
155-160	13	28
160-165	10	38
165-170	8	46
170-175	9	55
175-180	5	60
	$N = 60$	

Here, $N = 60$, gives $N/2 = 60/2 = 30$

So, the median class is 160-165. Hence, the upper limit of the median class is 165.

Q.4 The empirical relationship between the three measures of central tendency is

(a) 2 Mean = 3 Median − Mode
(b) 2 Mode = 3 Median − Mean
(c) Mode = 2 Mean − 3 Median
(d) 3 Median = 2 Mode + Median

Sol. (a) the empirical relationship between the three measures of central tendency is given by 3 Median = Mode + 2 Mean

$\Rightarrow$ 3 Median − Mode = 2 Mean

Q.5 If the mode of a data is 45 and mean is 27, then the median is

(a) 30 (b) 27
(c) 33 (d) None of these

◎ ***Thinking Process*** Use the formula 3 median = Node + 2 Mean to get the required result.

Sol. (c) Given, mode = 45 and mean = 27

We know that,

3 Median = Mode + 2 Mean

$\Rightarrow$ 3 Median = 45 + 2 × 27 = 45 + 54 = 99

$\Rightarrow$ Median = $\frac{99}{3}$ = 33

Q.6 If the mean of a frequency distribution is 60 and the median is 50, then find the mode using the empirical relationship

(a) 60 (b) 50 (c) 40 (d) 30

Sol. (d) Given, mean = 60, median = 50

We know that,

3 Median = Mode + 2 Mean

$\Rightarrow$ 3 × 50 = Mode + 2 × 60

$\Rightarrow$ 150 − 120 = Mode

$\Rightarrow$ Mode = 30

Q.7 The following frequency distribution gives the number of accidents that befell 150 workers working on a road project in a year. Find the mean of the following data.

Number of accidents	Number of workers (f_i)
0-5	60
5-10	52
10-15	34
15-20	4

(a) 6.9 (b) 9.6

(c) 10.35 (d) 9

Sol. (a)

Number of accidents	Number of workers (f_i)	x_i	$f_i \times x_i$
0-5	60	2.5	150
5-10	52	7.5	390
10-15	34	12.5	425
15-20	4	17.5	70
	$N = 150$		$\Sigma f_i x_i = 1035$

Here, $\Sigma f_i = 150$

and $\Sigma f_i x_i = 1035$

By direct method we have,

Mean = $\frac{\Sigma f_i x_i}{\Sigma f_i} = \frac{1035}{150} = 6.9$

Q.8 Find the the mean of the following frequency distribution by the assumed mean method.

Class Interval	Frequency (f_i)
63-65	4
65-67	3
67-69	7
69-71	8
71-73	8

(a) 68 (b) 68.886
(c) 67 (d) 69

Sol. (b)

Class Interval	Frequency (f_i)	Class Mark (x_i)	$d_i = x_i - a$ $= x_i - 68$	$f_i \times d_i$
63-65	4	64	–4	–16
65-67	3	66	–2	–6
67-69	7	68 = a	0	0
69-71	8	70	2	16
71-73	8	72	4	32
	$N = 30$			$\Sigma f_i d_i = 26$

Here, assumed mean, $a = 68$, $\Sigma f_i = 30$ and $\Sigma f_i d_i = 26$

$$\frac{\Sigma f_i d_i}{\Sigma f_i} = \frac{26}{30} = 0.866$$

Now, by the assumed mean method, we have

$$\text{Mean} = a + \frac{\Sigma f_i d_i}{\Sigma f_i} = 68 + 0.866 = 68.866$$

Q.9 During a Medical camp in school, the heights of Grade 7 boys were measured. The data is recorded in the following frequency distribution. Using the step deviation method, calculate the mean height of boys in Grade 7.

Height (cm)	Number of boys (f_i)
135-140	4
140-145	7
145-150	30
150-155	32
155-160	7

(a) 147.4375 cm (b) 149.5 cm
(c) 149.4375 cm (d) 147.5 cm

Sol. (c)

Height (cm)	Number of boys (f_i)	Class Mark (x_i)	$u_i = \frac{x_i - a}{h} = \frac{x_i - 147.5}{5}$	$f_i \times u_i$
135-140	4	137.5	–2	–8
140-145	7	142.5	–1	–7
145-150	30	147.5 = a	0	0
150-155	32	152.5	1	32
155-160	7	157.5	2	14
	$N = 80$			$\Sigma f_i u_i = 31$

We have, assumed mean, $(a) = 147.5$, class width $(h) = 5$, $\Sigma f_i = 80$, $\Sigma f_i u_i = 31$

Now, $$\frac{\Sigma f_i u_i}{\Sigma f_i} = \frac{31}{80} = 0.3875$$

$\therefore$ $$\text{Mean} = a + h\left[\frac{\Sigma f_i u_i}{\Sigma f_i}\right]$$

$$\text{Mean} = 147.5 + 5[0.3875] = 147.5 + 1.9375 = 149.4375$$

$\therefore$ Mean height of boys = 149.4375 cm

Q.10 Read the given data below and find the median class of the data.

Distance covered (Kms)	Number of cars
12-14	11
14-16	12
16-18	20
18-20	7

(a) 12-14 (b) 14-16 (c) 16-18 (d) 18-20

Sol. (c)

Distance covered (Kms)	Number of cars	Cumulative frequency
12-14	11	11
14-16	12	23
16-18	20	43
18-20	7	50
	$N = 50$	

Here, $N = 50 \Rightarrow \frac{n}{2} = 25$

Since, cumulative frequency 25 lies in class interval 16-18.

So, the median class is 16-18.

□ Subjective Type Questions

Q.1 Find the mean age of the following data

Age (in years)	10-30	30-50	50-70	70-90
Number of persons	15	12	18	5

Sol.

Age (in years)	Number of persons (f_i)	Class mark (x_i)	$d_i = x_i - a$	$f_i \times d_i$
10-30	15	20	–40	–600
30-50	12	40	–20	–240
50-70	18	$60 = a$	0	0
70-90	5	80	20	100
Total	$N = 50$			$\Sigma f_i d_i = -740$

We have, assumed mean, $a = 60$

Total observations, $N = 50$,

and $$\sum_{i=1}^{4} f_i d_i = -740$$

By assumed mean method,

$$\text{Mean} = a + \frac{1}{N} \times \Sigma f_i d_i$$

$$= 60 + \frac{1}{50} \times (-740) = 60 - 14.8 = 45.2$$

Hence, the mean for the given data is 45.2

Q.2 If the mode of given data is 24, find the missing frequencies for the following data

Class	0-10	10-20	20-30	30-40	40-50	50-60	Total
Frequency	7	8	x	4	5	y	50

Sol. Given, mode = 24

So, Modal class is 20-30

$$l = 20, f_m = x, f_2 = 4, f_1 = 8$$

$\therefore$ $$\text{Mode} = l + \left(\frac{f_m - f_1}{2f_m - f_1 - f_2}\right) \times h$$

$\Rightarrow$ $$24 = 20 + \left(\frac{x - 8}{2x - 8 - 4}\right) \times 10$$

$\Rightarrow$ $$24 - 20 = \frac{x - 8}{2x - 12} \times 10$$

$\Rightarrow \quad \dfrac{10x - 80}{2x - 12} = 4$

$\Rightarrow \quad 10x - 80 = 8x - 48$

$\Rightarrow \quad 2x = 32$

$\Rightarrow \quad x = 16$

Now, sum of all frequencies = 50 [given]

$\Rightarrow \quad 24 + x + y = 50$

$\Rightarrow \quad y + 40 = 50$

$\Rightarrow \quad y = 50 - 40$

$= 10$

Hence, $x = 16$ and $y = 10$

Q.3 The Median of the data is 28. Find the values of x and y if the total frequency is 50

Marks	0-10	10-20	20-30	30-40	40-50
Number of students	5	x	15	y	6

Sol.

Marks	Number of students (f_i)	Cumulative frequency
0-10	5	5
10-20	x	$5 + x$
20-30	15	$20 + x$
30-40	y	$20 + x + y$
40-50	6	$26 + x + y$
Total	$N = 26 + x + y$	

Given, median = 28

We have, sum of all frequencies = 50 = N

$\Rightarrow \quad 26 + x + y = 50$

$\Rightarrow \quad x + y = 24$ ...(i)

Since, median = 28 lies in the class interval 20-30.

So, we have, $l = 20, f = 15, cf = 5 + x, h + 10, N = 50$

$\therefore$ Median $= l + \dfrac{\left(\dfrac{N}{2} - cf\right)}{f} \times h$

$\Rightarrow \quad 28 = 20 + \dfrac{\left[\dfrac{50}{2} - (5 + x)\right]}{15} \times 10$

$$\Rightarrow \quad 28 = 20 + \frac{2}{3}(20 - x)$$

$$\Rightarrow \quad 8 = \frac{2}{3}(20 - x) \Rightarrow 12 = 20 - x \Rightarrow x = 8$$

On substituting $x = 8$ in Eq. (i), we get

$$8 + y = 24 \Rightarrow y = 16$$

Hence, $x = 8, y = 16$.

Q.4 The classification of children (according to age) playing in a playground was done. The data is represented in the form of the following frequency table

Age (years)	Number of Children
6-8	42
8-10	59
10-12	73
12-14	24

Find the mode for the frequency distribution.

Sol. Since highest frequency is 73.

$\therefore$ Modal class = 10-12

$l = 10, h = 2, f_m = 73, f_1 = 59, f_2 = 24$

$$\text{Mode} = l + \left(\frac{f_m - f_1}{2f_m - f_1 - f_2}\right) \times h$$

$$\text{Mode} = 10 + \left(\frac{73 - 59}{146 - 59 - 24}\right) \times 2 = 10 + \frac{14}{63} \times 2 = 10 + 0.44 = 10.44 \text{ years}$$

Q.5 If the mean of the following distribution is 54, find the missing frequency x

Class	0-20	20-40	40-60	60-80	80-100
Frequency	16	14	24	26	x

Sol.

Class interval	Class mark (x_i)	Frequency (f_i)	$f_i x_i$
0-20	10	16	160
20-40	30	14	420
40-60	50	24	1200
60-80	70	26	1820
80-100	90	x	$90x$
Total		$\Sigma f_i = 80 + x$	$\Sigma f_i x_i = 3600 + 90x$

$$\text{Mean} = \frac{\Sigma f_i x_i}{\Sigma f_i} \Rightarrow 54 = \frac{3600 + 90x}{80 + x}$$

$\Rightarrow$ $4320 + 54x = 3600 + 90x \Rightarrow 36x = 720 \Rightarrow x = 20$

Hence, the value of x is 20.

Q.6 The following table shows the distribution of weights of 100 candidates appearing for a competition. Determine the modal weight.

Weight (in kg)	50-55	55-60	60-65	65-70	70-75	75-80
Number of candidates	13	18	45	16	6	2

Sol.

Class Interval	f_i
50-55	13
55-60	18
60-65	45
65-70	16
70-75	6
75-80	2

Since, highest frequency is 45. So, the modal class is 60-65.

We have, $l = 60$, $f_m = 45$, $f_1 = 18$, $f_2 = 16$, $h = 5$

$$\text{Mode} = l + \left(\frac{f_m - f_1}{2f_m - f_1 - f_2}\right) \times h = 60 + \left(\frac{45 - 18}{2 \times 45 - 18 - 16}\right) \times 5 = 60 + \frac{135}{56}$$

$$= 60 + 2.41 = 62.41$$

Hence, modal weight is 62.41.

Q.7 Some students of class X donated for the welfare of old age persons. Their contributions are shown in the following frequency distribution

Amount in (₹)	0-20	20-40	40-60	60-80	80-100
Number of students	5	8	12	11	4

Find median and mode for their contribution.

Sol. Here, $N = 40$

Amount in (₹) (class interval)	Numbers of students (f_i)	cumulative frequency (cf)
0-20	5	5
20-40	8	13
40-60	12	25
60-80	11	36
80-100	4	40
Total	$N = \Sigma f_i = 40$	

$$\Rightarrow \quad \frac{N}{2} = 20$$

$\therefore$ Median class = 40 - 60

$$l = 40, f = 12, cf = 13, h = 60 - 40 = 20$$

$$\therefore \quad \text{Median} = l + \left(\frac{\frac{N}{2} - cf}{f}\right) \times h$$

$$= 40 + \left(\frac{20 - 13}{12}\right) \times 20 = 40 + \frac{7}{12} \times 20$$

$$= 40 + \frac{35}{3} = 40 + 11.66 = 51.66$$

For mode, modal class is 40 – 60 as highest frequency is 12.

$$l = 40, f_1 = 8, f_m = 12, f_2 = 11, h = 20$$

$$\text{Mode} = l + \left(\frac{f_m - f_1}{2f_m - f_1 - f_2}\right) \times h$$

$$= 40 + \left(\frac{12 - 8}{24 - 8 - 11}\right) \times 20 = 40 + \frac{80}{5} = 40 + 16 = 56$$

Q.8 The following data gives the information on the observed life times (in hours) of 150 electrical components.

Life time (in hours)	0-20	20-40	40-60	60-80	80-100
Frequency	15	10	35	50	40

Sol. Find the mode of the given data.

Life time (in hours)	Frequency
0-20	15
20-40	10
40-60	35
60-80	50
80-100	40

Since, highest frequency is 50.

So, modal class is 60 - 80

$\therefore \quad l = 60, f_1 = 35, f_m = 50, f_2 = 40, h = 20$

$$\text{Mode} = l + \left(\frac{f_m - f_1}{2f_m - f_1 - f_2}\right)h = 60 + \left[\frac{50 - 35}{(2 \times 50) - 35 - 40}\right] \times 20$$

$$= 60 + \left[\frac{15}{100 - 75}\right] \times 20 = 60 + \left[\frac{300}{25}\right] = 60 + 12 = 72$$

Q.9 Determine the missing frequency x, from the following data, when mode is 67.

Class	40-50	50-60	60-70	70-80	80-90
Frequency	5	x	15	12	7

Sol.

Class interval	Frequency
40-50	5
50-60	x
60-70	15
70-80	12
80-90	7

Mode = 67 [given]

$\therefore$ Modal class is 60-70

So, $l = 60, f_m = 15, f_1 = x, f_2 = 12, h = 10$

$$\therefore \text{Mode} = l + \left(\frac{f_m - f_1}{2f_m - f_1 - f_2}\right) \times h$$

$$\Rightarrow \quad 67 = 60 + \left(\frac{15 - x}{30 - x - 12}\right) \times 10$$

$$\Rightarrow \quad 67 = 60 + \left(\frac{15 - x}{18 - x}\right) \times 10$$

$$\Rightarrow \quad 67 = 60 + \frac{150 - 10x}{18 - x}$$

$$\Rightarrow \quad 7 = \frac{150 - 10x}{18 - x}$$

$$\Rightarrow \quad 126 - 7x = 150 - 10x$$

$$\Rightarrow \quad 10x - 7x = 150 - 126$$

$$\Rightarrow \quad 3x = 24$$

$$\Rightarrow \quad x = 8$$

Hence, the value of x is 8.

Q.10 Find the unknown values in the following table.

Class interval	Frequency	Cumulative frequency
0-10	5	5
10-20	7	x_1
20-30	x_2	18
30-40	5	x_3
40-50	x_4	30

Sol.

Class interval	Frequency	Cumulative frequency
0-10	5	5
10-20	7	x_1
20-30	x_2	18
30-40	5	x_3
40-50	x_4	30

From table, we get and $x_1 = 7 + 5 = 12,$

$$18 = x_1 + x_2 = 12 + x_2 \Rightarrow x_2 = 18 - 12 = 6,$$

$$x_3 = 18 + 5 = 23,$$

$$30 = x_3 + x_4 \Rightarrow x_4 = 30 - x_3 = 30 - 23 = 7$$

Hence, $x_1 = 12, x_2 = 6, x_3 = 23, x_4 = 7$

Q.11 The mode of a distribution is 55 and the modal class is 45-60 and the frequency preceding the modal class is 5 and the frequency after the modal class is 10. Find the frequency of the modal class.

Sol. Given, mode = 55

Modal class = 45 - 60

Frequency of class preceding modal class, $f_1 = 5$

Frequency of class succeeding modal class, $f_2 = 10$

Let frequency of the model class be f.

$$\text{Mode} = l + \left(\frac{f - f_1}{2f - f_1 - f_2}\right) \times h$$

$$\Rightarrow \quad 55 = 45 + \left(\frac{f - 5}{2f - 5 - 10}\right) \times 15$$

$$\Rightarrow \quad 10 = \frac{f - 5}{2f - 15} \times 15$$

$$\Rightarrow \quad \frac{10}{15} = \frac{f-5}{2f-15}$$

$$\Rightarrow \quad 20f - 150 = 15f - 75$$

$$\Rightarrow \quad 5f = 75 \Rightarrow f = 15$$

Hence, the required frequency of the modal class is 15.

Q.12 The lengths of 50 leaves of a plant are measured correct to the nearest millimetre and the data obtained is represented in the following table.

Length in (mm)	109-117	118-126	127-135	136-144	145-153	154-162	163-171
Number of Leaves	4	6	14	13	6	4	3

Find the mean length of the leaves.

Sol. Given frequency distribution is not continuous. So, first we have to make it continuous. To make data continuous, we subtract 0.5 from the lower limit of each class and add 0.5 to the the upper limit of each class.

Class Interval	x_i	f_i	$\mu_i = \frac{x_i - 140}{9}$	$f_i u_i$
108.5-117.5	113	4	–3	–12
117.5-126.5	122	6	–2	–12
126.5-135.5	131	14	–1	–14
135.5-144.5	$140 = a$	13	0	0
144.5-153.5	149	6	1	6
153.5-162.5	158	4	2	8
162.5-171.5	167	3	3	9
Total		$\Sigma f_i = 50$		$\Sigma f_i u_i = -15$

Here, assumed mean $(a) = 140$; class size $(b) = 9$

Now, mean $(\bar{x}) = a + \frac{\Sigma f_i u_i}{\Sigma f_i} \times h$

$$= 140 + 9\left(\frac{-15}{50}\right) = 140 - \frac{27}{10} = 140 - 2.7 = 137.30$$

Hence, mean length of the leaves = 137.30 mm.

Q.13 The mean of the following distribution is 18. Find the frequency f of the class 19-21.

Class	11-13	13-15	15-17	17-19	19-21	21-23	23-25
Frequency	3	6	9	13	f	5	4

Sol.

Class	x_i	f_i	$f_i x_i$
11-13	12	3	36
13-15	14	6	84
15-17	16	9	144
17-19	18	13	234
19-21	20	f	$20f$
21-23	22	5	110
23-25	24	4	96
Total		$40 + f$	$704 + 20f$

We have, $\Sigma f_i x_i = 704 + 20f$

$\Sigma f_i = 40 + f$

Mean = 18

$\Rightarrow \quad 18 = \dfrac{704 + 20f}{40 + f} \qquad \left[\because \text{Mean} = \dfrac{\Sigma f_i x_i}{\Sigma f_i}\right]$

$\Rightarrow \quad 720 + 18f = 704 + 20f \Rightarrow 2f = 16 \Rightarrow f = 8$

Hence, required value of f is 8.

Q.14 If the median of the following frequency distribution is 32.5. Find the values of f_1 and f_2

Class	0-10	10-20	20-30	30-40	40-50	50-60	60-70	Total
Frequency	f_1	5	9	12	f_2	3	2	40

Sol.

Class	Frequency	Cumulative Frequency
0-10	f_1	f_1
10-20	5	$5 + f_1$
20-30	9	$14 + f_1$
30-40	12	$26 + f_1$
40-50	f_2	$26 + f_1 + f_2$
50-60	3	$29 + f_1 + f_2$
60-70	2	$31 + f_1 + f_2$
Total	40	

Given, median = 32.5. Therefore, median class is 30-40.

So, we have, $l = 30, h = 10$

$f = 12, cf = (14 + f_1)$

$N = 20$ gives $\frac{N}{2} = 20$

Now, $32.5 = 30 + \frac{10}{12}(20 - 14 - f_1)$ $\left[\because \text{Median} = l + \frac{\left(\frac{N}{2} - cf\right)}{f} \times h\right]$

$\Rightarrow$ $2.5 = \frac{5}{6}(6 - f_1) \Rightarrow 15 = 30 - 5f_1 \Rightarrow f_1 = 15$

$\Rightarrow$ $f_i = 3$

Also, $31 + f_1 + f_2 = 40$

$\Rightarrow$ $31 + 3 + f_2 = 40$

$\Rightarrow$ $f_2 = 6$

Hence, the required values of f_1 and f_2 are 3 and 6 respectively.

Q.15 Mean of the following frequency distribution is 50. Find the value of p.

Classes	0-20	20-40	40-60	60-80	80-100
Frequency	17	p	32	24	19

Sol.

Classes	Frequency (f_i)	Mid value (x_i)	$f_i \times x_i$
0-20	17	10	170
20-40	p	30	$30p$
40-60	32	50	1600
60-80	24	70	1680
80-100	19	90	1710
Total	$N = 92 + p$		$5160 + 30p$

Arithmetic mean of the given distribution = 50

$\therefore$ Mean, $\overline{x} = \frac{\Sigma f_i x_i}{N}$

$\Rightarrow$ $50 = \frac{5160 + 30p}{92 + p}$

$\Rightarrow$ $4600 + 50p = 5160 + 30p$

$\Rightarrow$ $50p - 30p = 5160 - 4600$

$\Rightarrow$ $20p = 560$

$\therefore$ $p = 28$

Q.16 Compute the median marks for the following data

Marks	Number of Students
0 and above	50
10 and above	46
20 and above	40
30 and above	20
40 and above	10
50 and above	3
60 and above	0

Sol.

Marks	Number of Students	Cumulative frequency
0-10	$(50-46)=4$	4
10-20	$(46-40)=6$	10
20-30	$(40-20)=20$	30
30-40	$(20-10)=10$	40
40-50	$(10-3)=7$	47
50-60	$(3-0)+3$	50
60 above	0	50
Total	$N=50$	

Now, $\frac{N}{2}=\frac{50}{2}=25$

Hence, the median class is 20 - 30.

We have, $l=20,\ f=20, cf=10, h=10, N=50$

$$\text{Median } = l+\left(\frac{\frac{N}{2}-cf}{f}\right)\times h$$

$$=20+\frac{25-10}{20}\times 10$$

$$=20+\frac{15}{2}=20+7.5$$

$$=27.5$$

Hence, the median marks is 27.5

Probability

CHAPTER 14

Important Points

01 Outcomes and Sample Space A possible result of a random experiment is called its outcome.

e.g., In tossing a coin, the outcomes of this experiment are Head (H) and Tail (T) and the set of outcomes $\{H, T\}$ is called the sample space of the experiment.

Note By the phrase random experiment we mean that the experiment occurs without any bias or interference.

02 Elementary Event An event having only one outcome of the experiment is called an elementary event.

e.g., In tossing a coin, possible outcomes are Head (H) and Tail (T). Getting H or T are known as elementary events.

03 Occurrence of an Event An event A associated to a random experiment is said to occur, if any one of the elementary events associated to the event A is an outcome.

04 Impossible and Sure Event An event which is impossible to occur in called an impossible event and probability of impossible event is zero.

The empty set ϕ is called an impossible event.

e.g., Getting two heads in tossing a unbiased coin one time. Probability of sure event is 1. The event which is certain to occur is said to be sure event.

e.g., In tossing a die any number between 1 to 6, will come is a sure event.

06 Complementary Event The complementary event of A is the set of all sample points of the space other than the sample points of A and it is denoted by $\overline{A}$ or A'.
e.g., Let $S = \{1, 2, 3, 4, 5, 6\}$, if $A = \{1, 2, 4\}$, then $A' = \{3, 5, 6\}$

07 Probability Suppose there are n possible outcomes of an elementary events associated with a random experiment and m of them are favourable to an event A. Then the probability of happening or occurrence of event A is defined as the ratio $\frac{m}{n}$ and it is denoted by the symbol $P(A)$.

i.e., $P(A) = \frac{m}{n}$

or $$P(A) = \frac{\text{Number of favourable outcomes}}{\text{Number of possible outcomes of the event}}$$

Note (i) $0 \le P(A) \le 1$
(ii) If A is certain (sure) event, then $P(A) = 1$
(iii) If A is impossible event, then $P(A) = 0$.
(iv) $P(A) + P(\overline{A}) = 1$
(v) Probability of an event can never be negative.

- **Remember**
(i) In tossing of a coin, their is only head and tail.
(ii) In tossing of a die, numbers are 1, 2, 3, 4, 5 and 6.
(iii) In a deck of cards, their are 52 cards, which are divided into 4 suits, hearts (♥), diamonds (♦), clubs (♣) and spades (♠) of 13 cards each. Each of the suits have 3 face cards namely, King Queen and Jack and 10 number cards.

Exercise 14.1

Question 1 Complete the following statements
(i) Probability of an event E + Probability of the event 'not E' = ...
(ii) The probability of an event that cannot happen is .... Such an event is called ....
(iii) The probability of an event that is certain to happen is .... Such an event is called ....
(iv) The sum of the probabilities of all the elementary events of an experiment is ....
(v) The probability of an event is greater than or equal to .... and less than or equal to ....

Sol. (i) 1, Because the sum of probability of success and probability of failure is equal to one.

(ii) 0, Impossible event. (*e.g.*, suppose a die is tossed and determine the probability of getting 7. This type of events is called impossible events and probability of this event is 0.)

(iii) 1, Sure event. (*e.g.*, the event of getting number less than 7 in a single throw of a die is a sure event).

(iv) 1, [*e.g.*, suppose a die is tossed, then

$$P(1) + P(2) + P(3) + P(4) + P(5) + P(6) = 1]$$

(v) 0, 1, (since, the probability always lies between 0 and 1)

Question 2 Which of the following experiments have equally likely outcomes? Explain.

(i) A driver attempts to start a car. The car starts or does not start.

(ii) A player attempts to shoot a basketball. She/he shoots or misses the shot.

(iii) A trial is made to answer a true-false question. The answer is right or wrong.

(iv) A baby is born. It is a boy or a girl.

Sol. (i) Not equally likely, because the chance for a car to start depends on the condition of the car.

(ii) Not equally likely, because the shooting of a basketball depends upon ability of player.

(iii) Equally likely, because if a answer is true, then it cannot be false and if answer is false, then it cannot be true. So, both have equal possibility either true or false.

(iv) Equally likely, because when a baby is born, possibilities of a girl or a boy to be born are same.

Question 3 Why is tossing a coin considered to be a fair way of deciding which team should get the ball at the beginning of a football game?

Sol. When we toss a coin, we get either head or tail which are equally likely. Hence, the individual result of tossing a coin is completely unpredictable or unbiased.

Question 4 Which of the following cannot be the probability of an event?

(a) $\frac{2}{3}$ (b) -1.5 (c) 15% (d) 0.7

Sol. (b) The probability of an event cannot be negative in any case.

estion 5 If $P(E)=0.05$, what is the probability of 'not E'?

◎ *Thinking Process* Use the formula $P(E)+P(\bar{E})=1$ to determine the value of not 'E'.

l. Given, $P(E)=0.05$

know that, $P(E)+P(\bar{E})=1$

$$P(\bar{E})=1-0.05=0.95$$

estion 6 A bag contains lemon flavoured candies only. Malini kes out one candy without looking into the bag. What is the obability that she takes out

(i) an orange flavoured candy?

(ii) a lemon flavoured candy?

l. A bag contains only lemon flavoured candies so it does not contain an ange flavoured candy.

(i) Here, Number of orange flavoured candy is 0.

$\therefore$ P (an orange flavoured candy) = 0

(ii) P (a lemon flavoured candy) = 1

estion 7 It is given that in a group of 3 students, the probability 2 students not having the same birthday is 0.992. What is the obability that the 2 students have the same birthday?

l. Let $\bar{E}$ is the event of 2 students not having the same birthday.

$$P(\bar{E})=0.992$$

$$P(E)+P(\bar{E})=1$$

$$P(E)+0.0992=1$$

$$P(E)=1-0.992 \Rightarrow P(E)=0.008$$

, the probability of 2 students having the same birthday is 0.008.

uestion 8 A bag contains 3 red balls and 5 black balls. A ball is rawn at random from the bag. What is the probability that the ball rawn is (i) red? (ii) not red?

l. Total number of balls, $n(S)=3+5=8$

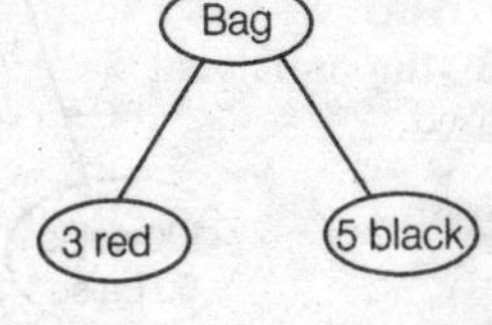

et, E be the event of drawing a red ball.

otal number favourable outcomes = $3n(E)$

(i) Probability of drawing a red ball = $\dfrac{n(E)}{n(S)}=\dfrac{3}{8}$

(ii) Probability of not drawing a red ball

$= 1 - P$ (Drawing a red ball)

$= 1-\dfrac{3}{8}=\dfrac{5}{8}$

Question 9 A box contains 5 red marbles, 8 white marbles and 4 green marbles. One marble is taken out of the box at random. What is the probability that the marble taken out will be (i) red? (ii) White? (iii) not green?

◎ ***Thinking Process*** To determine that the taken out marble is red or while use formula $P(A) = \dfrac{\text{Number of favourable outcomes}}{\text{Numebr of possible outcomes of the experiments}}$

Sol. Total number of marbles in a box, $n(S) = 5 + 8 + 4 = 17$

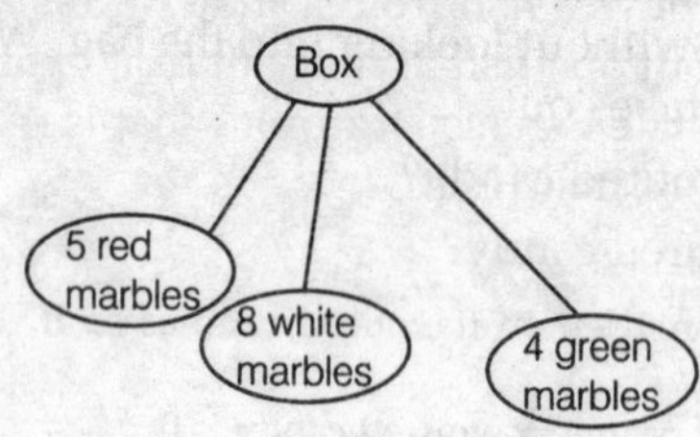

(i) Probability of taken out a red marble $= \dfrac{5}{17}$

(ii) Probability of taken out a white marble $= \dfrac{8}{17}$

(iii) Probability of taken out not a green marble

$$= \frac{\text{Either red or white marble}}{\text{Total number of marbles}} = \frac{5+8}{17} = \frac{13}{17}$$

Question 10 A piggy bank contains hundred 50 paise coins, fifty ₹ 1 coins, twenty ₹ 2 coins and ten ₹ 5 coins. If it is equally likely tha one of the coins will fall out when the bank is turned upside down, what is the probability that the coin (i) will be a 50 paise coin? (ii) will not be a ₹ 5 coin?

Sol. Given, number of 50 paise coins = 100

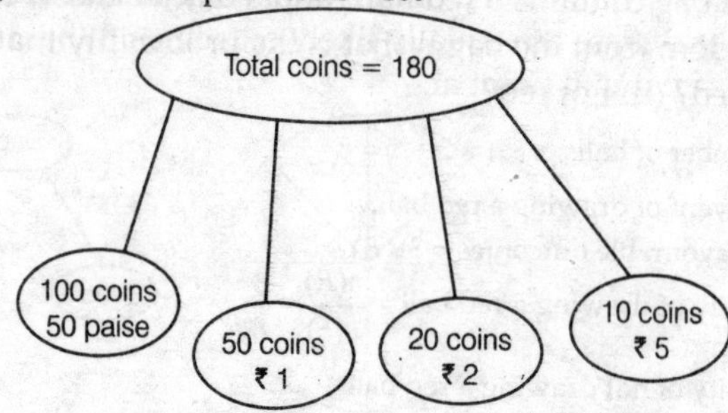

number of ₹ 1 coins = 50
number of ₹ 2 coins = 20
number of ₹ 5 coins = 10

$\therefore$ Total number of coins = 100 + 50 + 20 + 10 = 180

(i) P (50 paise coin) $= \frac{100}{180} = \frac{5}{9}$

(ii) P (will not be a ₹ 5 coin) $= \frac{180-10}{180} = \frac{170}{180} = \frac{17}{18}$

Question 11 Gopi buys a fish from a shop for his aquarium. The shopkeeper takes out one fish at random from a tank containing 5 male fish and 8 female fish (see figure). What is the probability that the fish taken out is a male fish?

Sol. Total number of fish in an aquarium = 5 male fish + 8 female fish = 13 fish

$\therefore$ Probability of taken out a male fish $= \frac{\text{Number of male fish}}{\text{Total number of fish}} = \frac{5}{13}$

Question 12 A game of chance consists of spinning at arrow which comes to rest pointing at one of the numbers 1, 2, 3, 4, 5, 6, 7 and 8 (see figure) and these are equally likely outcomes. What is the probability that it will point at

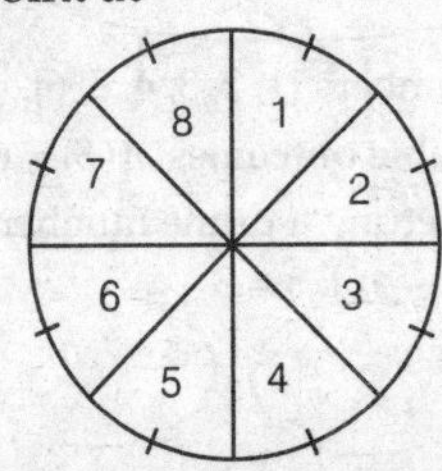

(i) 8? (ii) an odd number?
(iii) a number greater than 2? (iv) a number less than 9?

Sol. (i) Total number of points in a circle, $n(S) = 8$

Let E_1 be the event that arrow comes at number 8

$\therefore$ $n(E_1) = 1$

Probability that arrow comes at number 8 is

$$P(E_1) = \frac{n(E_1)}{n(S)} = \frac{1}{8}$$

(ii) Let E_2 be the event that arrow comes at an odd numbers

$= \{1, 3, 5, 7\}$

$\therefore$ $n(E_2) = 4$

$\therefore$ Probability that arrow comes at an odd number is

$$P(E_2) = \frac{n(E_2)}{n(S)} = \frac{4}{8} = \frac{1}{2}$$

(iii) Let E_3 be the event that arrow comes at a number greater than 2

$= \{3, 4, 5, 6, 7, 8\}$

$\therefore$ $n(E_3) = 6$

Probability that arrow comes at a number greater than 2 is

$$P(E_3) = \frac{n(E_3)}{n(S)} = \frac{6}{8} = \frac{3}{4}$$

(iv) Let E_4 be the event that arrow comes at a number less than 9 is

$= \{1, 2, 3, 4, 5, 6, 7, 8\}$

$\therefore$ $n(E_4) = 8$

Probability that arrow comes at a number less than 9 is

$$P(E_4) = \frac{n(E_4)}{n(S)} = \frac{8}{8} = 1$$

Question 13 A die is thrown once. Find the probability of getting

(i) a prime number

(ii) a number lying between 2 and 6

(iii) an odd number.

Thinking Process When a dice is thrown once, then outcomes are {1,2, 3, 4, 5, 6}.

Sol. In a die there are six numbers {1, 2, 3, 4, 5, 6}.

$\therefore$ Total number of possible outcomes, $n(S) = 6$

(i) Let E_1 be the event of getting a prime number = {2, 3, 5}

$\therefore$ $n(E_1) = 3$

Probability of getting a prime number $= \frac{n(E_1)}{n(S)} = \frac{3}{6} = \frac{1}{2}$

(ii) Let E_2 be the event of getting a number lying between 2 and 6
$= \{3, 4, 5\}$

$\therefore \quad n(E_2) = 3$

Probability of getting a number lying between 2 and 6

$$= \frac{n(E_2)}{n(S)} = \frac{3}{6} = \frac{1}{2}$$

Mistake Alert Between 2 and 6 does not include 2 and 6.

(iii) Let E_3 be the event of getting an odd number
$= \{1, 3, 5\}$

$\therefore \quad n(E_3) = 3$

Probability of getting on odd number

$$= \frac{n(E_3)}{n(S)} = \frac{3}{6} = \frac{1}{2}$$

Question 14 One card is drawn from a well-shuffled deck of 52 cards. Find the probability of getting

(i) a king of red colour
(ii) a face card
(iii) a red face card
(iv) the jack of hearts
(v) a spade
(vi) the queen of diamonds.

Sol. Total number of cards in one deck of cards, $n(S) = 52$

(i) Let E_1 be the event of getting a king of red colour

$\therefore \quad n(E_1) = 2$

[$\because$ In a deck of cards, 26 cards are red and 26 cards are black. There are four kings in a deck in which two are red and two are black]

Probability of getting a king of red colour

$$= \frac{n(E_1)}{n(S)} = \frac{2}{52} = \frac{1}{26}$$

(ii) Let E_2 be the event of getting a face card

$\therefore \quad n(E_2) = 12$

[$\because$ In a deck of cards, there are 12 face cards (4 king, 4 jack, 4 queen)]

Probability of getting a face card $= \frac{n(E_2)}{n(S)} = \frac{12}{52} = \frac{3}{13}$

(iii) Let E_3 be the event of getting a red face card

$\therefore$ $$n(E_3) = 6$$

[$\because$ In a deck of cards, there are 12 face cards (6 red, 6 black)]

Probability of getting a red face card $= \dfrac{n(E_3)}{n(S)} = \dfrac{6}{52} = \dfrac{3}{26}$

(iv) Let E_4 be the event of getting a jack of hearts

$\therefore$ $$n(E_4) = 1$$

[$\because$ There are four jack in a deck (1 heart, 1 club, 1 spade, 1 diamond]

Probability of getting a jack of heart $= \dfrac{n(E_4)}{n(S)} = \dfrac{1}{52}$

(v) Let E_5 be the event of getting a spade

$\therefore$ $$n(E_5) = 13$$

[$\because$ In a deck of cards, 13 spade, 13 club, 13 heart, 13 diamond]

Probability of getting a spade $= \dfrac{n(E_5)}{n(S)} = \dfrac{13}{52} = \dfrac{1}{4}$

(vi) Let E_6 be the event of getting a queen of diamond

$\therefore$ $$n(E_6) = 1$$

($\because$ In 13 diamond cards, three is only one queen)

Probability of getting a queen of diamond $= \dfrac{n(E_6)}{n(S)} = \dfrac{1}{52}$

Question 15 Five cards—the ten, jack, queen, king and ace of diamonds are well-shuffled with their face downwards. One card is then picked up at random.

(i) What is the probability that the card is the queen

(ii) If the queen is drawn and put a side, what is the probability that the

second card picked up is (a) an ace? (b) a queen?

Sol. (i) Total number of cards = 5

$\therefore$ P (picking a queen card) $= \dfrac{1}{5}$

(ii) Suppose, a queen is drawn and put a side. So, their are four cards left.

(a) P (the second card picked up an ace) $= \dfrac{1}{4}$

(b) P (the second card picked up an queen) $= \dfrac{0}{4} = 0$

($\because$ Queen is already drawn)

Question 16 12 defective pens are accidentally mixed with 132 good ones. It is not possible to just look at a pen and tell whether or not it is defective. One pen is taken out at random from this lot. Determine the probability that the pen taken out is a good one.

Sol. Total number of pens,

$$n(S) = 12 \text{ defective} + 132 \text{ good} = 144 \text{ pens}$$

Let E be the event of selecting a good pen

$$n(E) = 132$$

∴ Probability of selecting a good pen $= \dfrac{n(E)}{n(S)}$

$$= \frac{132}{144} = \frac{11}{12}$$

Question 17 (i) A lot of 20 bulbs contain 4 defective ones. One bulb is drawn at random from the lot. What is the probability that this bulb is defective?

(ii) Suppose, the bulb drawn in (i) is not defective and is not replaced. Now, one bulb is drawn at random from the rest. What is the probability that this bulb is not defective?

Sol. (i) Total number of bulbs, $n(S) = 20$

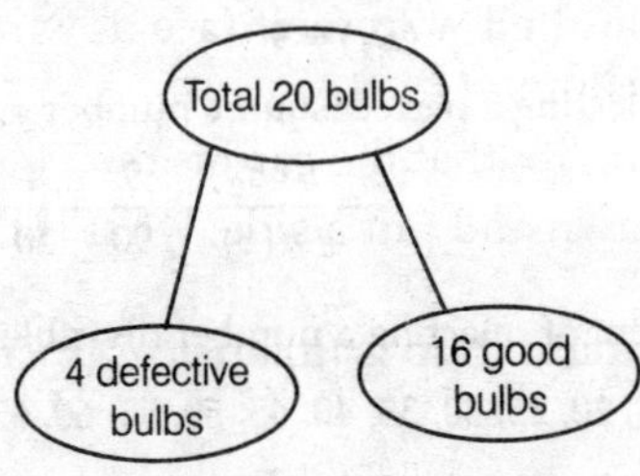

Let E_1 be the event of getting a defective bulb

$$\therefore \quad n(E_1) = 4$$

∴ Probability of selecting a defective bulb from the lot is

$$P(E_1) = \frac{n(E_1)}{n(S)} = \frac{4}{20} = \frac{1}{5}$$

(ii) Suppose, one good bulb is drawn and put outside.

Therefore, 15 good bulbs and 4 defective bulbs are remain in a lot.

Now, total number of bulbs $n(S_1) = 19$

Let E_2 be the event of selecting a good bulb,

$$n(E_2) = 15$$

$$\therefore \quad \text{Required probability} = \frac{n(E_2)}{n(S_1)} = \frac{15}{19}$$

Question 18 A box contains 90 discs which are numbered from 1 to 90. If one disc is drawn at random from the box, find the probability that it bears

(i) a two digit number
(ii) a perfect square number
(iii) a number divisible by 5

Sol. (i) Total number of disc in a box, $n(S) = 90$

Let E_1 be the event of selecting a two digit number

$$= \{10, 11, \ldots, 90\}$$

$$\therefore \quad n(E_1) = 81$$

Probability of getting a two digit number

$$= \frac{n(E)}{n(S)} = \frac{81}{90} = \frac{9}{10}$$

(ii) Let E_2 be the event of selecting a perfect square number

$$= \{1, 4, 9, 16, 25, 36, 49, 64, 81\}$$

$$\therefore \quad n(E_2) = 9$$

Probability of selecting a perfect square number

$$= \frac{n(E_2)}{n(S)} = \frac{9}{90} = \frac{1}{10}$$

(iii) Let E_3 be the event of selecting a number divisible by 5

$$= \{5, 10, 15, 20, 25, 30, 35, 40, 45, 50, 55, 60, 65, 70, 75, 80, 85, 90\}$$

$$\therefore \quad n(E_3) = 18$$

$$\therefore \quad \text{Required probability} = \frac{n(E_3)}{n(S)} = \frac{18}{90} = \frac{1}{5}$$

Question 19 A child has a die whose six faces show the letters as given below.

A	B	C	D	E	A

The die is thrown once. What is the probability of getting (i) A? (ii) D?

ol Total number of outcomes of a six face die, $n(S) = 6$

(i) Let E_1 be the event of getting a letter A

$$\therefore \quad n(E_1) = 2$$

Probability of getting a letter $A = \frac{n(E_1)}{n(S)} = \frac{2}{6} = \frac{1}{3}$

(ii) Let E_2 be the event of getting a letter D

$$\therefore \quad n(E_2) = 1$$

Probability of getting a letter $D = \frac{n(E_2)}{n(S)} = \frac{1}{6}$

Question 20 Suppose, you drop a die at random on the rectangular region shown in figure. What is the probability that it will land inside the circle with diameter 1 m?

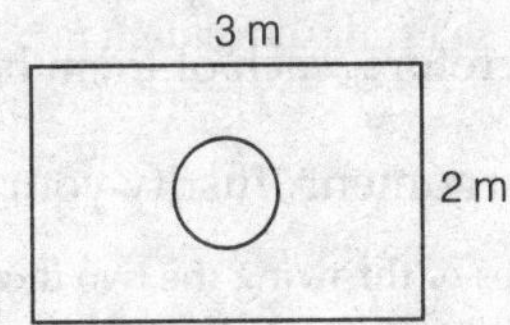

Sol. Area of rectangle $= 3 \times 2 = 6 \text{ m}^2$

and Area of circle $= \pi\left(\frac{1}{2}\right)^2 = \frac{\pi}{4} \text{ m}^2$ $\quad \left(\because \text{Diameter} = 1 \Rightarrow \text{radius} = \frac{1}{2}\right)$

$\therefore$ Probability that the die land inside the circle

$$= \frac{\text{Area of circle}}{\text{Area of rectangle}} = \frac{\pi/4}{6} = \frac{\pi}{24}$$

Question 21 A lot consists of 144 ball pens of which 20 are defective and the others are good. Nuri will buy a pen if it is good, but will not buy, if it is defective. The shopkeeper draws one pen at random and gives it to her. What is the probability that

(i) she will buy it?

(ii) she will not buy it?

Sol. Total number of ball pens, $n(S) = 144$

Let E be the event of getting a good ball pen

$$\therefore \quad n(E) = 144 - 20 = 124$$

(i) She will buy it only if it is a good pen.

$\therefore$ Required probability $= \frac{n(E)}{n(S)}$

$$= \frac{124}{144} = \frac{31}{36}$$

(ii) She will not buy if it is not a good pen.

$\therefore$ Required probability $= 1 - P(E)$

$$= 1 - \frac{31}{36} = \frac{5}{36} \qquad [\because P(E) + P(\bar{E}) = 1$$

Question 22 Two dice, one blue and one grey are thrown at the same time (i) complete the following table.

Event sum of 2 dice	2	3	4	5	6	7	8	9	10	11	12
Probability	$\frac{1}{36}$						$\frac{5}{36}$				$\frac{1}{36}$

(ii) A student argues that there are 11 possible outcomes 2, 3, 4,5, 6, 7, 8, 9, 10, 11 and 12. Therefore, each of them has a probability $\frac{1}{11}$.

Do you agree with this argument? Justify your answer.

Sol. Total possible outcomes of throwing the two dice, S

$$= \{(1, 1), (1, 2), (1, 3), (1, 4), (1, 5), (1, 6),$$
$$(2, 1), (2, 2), (2, 3), (2, 4), (2, 5), (2, 6),$$
$$(3, 1), (3, 2), (3, 3), (3, 4), (3, 5), (3, 6),$$
$$(4, 1), (4, 2), (4, 3), (4, 4), (4, 5), (4, 6),$$
$$(5, 1), (5, 2), (5, 3), (5, 4), (5, 5), (5, 6),$$
$$(6, 1), (6, 2), (6, 3), (6, 4), (6, 5), (6, 6)\}$$

$\therefore \quad n(S) = 36$

(a) Let E_1 be the sum of two dice is 3 = {(1, 2), (2, 1)}

$\therefore \quad n(E_1) = 2$

$\therefore \quad P(E_1) = \frac{n(E_1)}{n(S)} = \frac{2}{36} = \frac{1}{18}$

(b) Let E_2 be the sum of two dice is 4 = {(1, 3), (2, 2), (3, 1)}

$\therefore \quad n(E_2) = 3$

$\therefore \quad P(E_2) = \frac{n(E_2)}{n(S)} = \frac{3}{36} = \frac{1}{12}$

(c) Let E_3 be the sum of two dice is 5 = {(1, 4), (2, 3), (3, 2), (4, 1)}

$\therefore \quad n(E_3) = 4$

$\therefore \quad P(E_3) = \frac{n(E_3)}{n(S)} = \frac{4}{36} = \frac{1}{9}$

(d) Let E_4 be the sum of two dice is 6 = {(1, 5), (2, 4), (3, 3), (4, 2), (5, 1)}

$$\therefore \quad n(E_4) = 5$$

$$\therefore \quad P(E_4) = \frac{5}{36}$$

(e) Let E_5 be the sum of two dice is 7 = {(1, 6), (2, 5), (3, 4), (4, 3), (5, 2), (6, 1)}

$$\therefore \quad n(E_5) = 6$$

$$\therefore \quad P(E_5) = \frac{n(E_5)}{n(S)} = \frac{6}{36} = \frac{1}{6}$$

(f) Let E_7 be the sum of two dice is 9 = {(3, 6), (4, 5), (5, 4), (6, 3)}

$$\therefore \quad n(E_7) = 4$$

$$\therefore \quad P(E_7) = \frac{n(E_7)}{n(S)} = \frac{4}{36} = \frac{1}{9}$$

(g) Let E_8 be the sum of two dice is 10 = {(4, 6), (5, 5), (6, 4)}

$$\therefore \quad n(E_8) = 3$$

$$\therefore \quad P(E_8) = \frac{n(E_8)}{n(S)} = \frac{3}{36} = \frac{1}{12}$$

(h) Let E_9 be the sum of two dice is 11 = {(6, 5), (5, 6)}

$$\therefore \quad n(E_9) = 2$$

$$\therefore \quad P(E_9) = \frac{n(E_9)}{n(S)} = \frac{2}{36} = \frac{1}{18}$$

(ii) No, we do not agree with the argument because these events are not equally likely.

Question 23 A game consists of tossing a one rupee coin 3 times and noting its outcome each time. Hanif wins if all the tosses give the same result *i.e.,* three heads or three tails and losses otherwise. Calculate the probability that Hanif will lose the game.

Sol. The total possible outcomes on tossing a coin three times

= {(*HHH*), (*HHT*), (*HTH*), (*THH*), (*HTT*), (*THT*), (*TTH*), (*TTT*)}

Hanif will lose the game, if all the toses do not have same result.

i.e., {(*HHT*), (*HTH*), (*THH*), (*HTT*), (*THT*), (*TTH*)}

$$\therefore \quad \text{Required probability} = \frac{6}{8} = \frac{3}{4}$$

Question 24 A die is thrown twice. What is the probability that

(i) 5 will not come up either time?

(ii) 5 will come up atleast once?

[**Hint** Throwing a die twice and throwing two dice simultaneously are treated as the same experiment.]

◎ *Thinking Process* When a die is thrown twice the number of total outcomes or cases is $n(S) = 36$.

Sol. (i) Total number of outcomes.

$$n(S) = 6^2 = 36$$

Let $\bar{E}$ be the event that 5 will come up either time

$= \{(1, 5), (2, 5), (3, 5), (4, 5), (5,5), (6, 5), (5, 1), (5, 2), (5, 3), (5, 4), (5, 6)\}$

$\Rightarrow \quad n(\bar{E}) = 11$

and E be the event that 5 will not come up either time

$\therefore \quad n(E) = 36 - 11 = 25$

$\therefore$ Probability that 5 will not come up either time $= \dfrac{n(E)}{n(S)} = \dfrac{25}{36}$

(ii) Probability that, 5 will come up atleast once $= \dfrac{n(\bar{E})}{n(S)} = \dfrac{11}{36}$

Question 25 Which of the following arguments are correct and which are not correct? Give reasons for your answer. (i) If two coins are tossed simultaneously there are three possible outcomes—two heads, two tails or one of each. Therefore, for each of these outcomes, the probability is $\frac{1}{3}$. (ii) If a die is thrown, there are two possible outcomes—an odd number or an even number. Therefore, the probability of getting on odd number is $\frac{1}{2}$.

Sol. (i) Not correct.

The possible outcomes of tossing two coins

$$= \{(H, H), (H, T), (T, H), (T, T)\}$$

Then, $\quad P(H, H) = \frac{1}{4}, P(T, T) = \frac{1}{4}$

and $\quad P\{(H, T), (T, H)\} = \frac{2}{4} = \frac{1}{2}$

(ii) Correct. The total possible outcomes on a die = {1, 2, 3, 4, 5, 6}

Out of them odd numbers are {1, 3, 5} and even numbers are {2, 4, 6}.

$\therefore \quad P$ (getting odd numbers) $= \frac{3}{6} = \frac{1}{2}$

and P (getting even numbers) $= \frac{3}{6} = \frac{1}{2}$

Hence, both have same probability $\frac{1}{2}$.

DIKSHA APP Questions

Multiple Choice Questions

Q.1 A box contains 10 cards on which numbers from 1 to 10 are written. A card is taken out from the bag at random, the probability of that the number on the selected card is the multiple of 3.

(a) $\frac{1}{10}$

(b) $\frac{3}{10}$

(c) $\frac{7}{10}$

(d) $\frac{9}{10}$

Sol. (b) Total number of cards $n(s) = 10$

Let E be the event that the card selected is a multiple of 3.

Then, $n(E) = \{3, 6, 9\} = 3$

$$\therefore \quad P(E) = \frac{n(E)}{n(S)} = \frac{3}{10}$$

Q.2 Rekha is a tennis player. If the probability that Rekha winning the game is 0.62, then the probability that she losses the game is

(a) 0.08

(b) 0.5

(c) 1

(d) 0.38

Sol. (d) Let E be the event of Rekha winning the game.

$$\Rightarrow \quad P(E) = 0.62$$

$$\because \quad P(E) + P(\bar{E}) = 1$$

$$\Rightarrow \quad 0.62 + P(\bar{E}) = 1$$

$$\Rightarrow \quad P(\bar{E}) = 1 - 0.62 = 0.38$$

Q.3 A die is thrown once. The probability of getting perfect square number is

(a) $\frac{1}{6}$ (b) $\frac{2}{6}$

(c) $\frac{3}{6}$ (d) $\frac{5}{6}$

Sol. (b) Total number of outcomes $n(S) = 6$

Let E be the event of getting a perfect square number $\{1, 4\}$.

Then, $n(E) = 2$

$$\therefore \quad P(E) = \frac{n(E)}{n(S)} = \frac{2}{6} = \frac{1}{3}$$

Q.4 If the probability of an event (E) is 0.35, then the probability of 'not E' equals

(a) 0.65 (b) 0.35

(c) 1/0.35 (d) 1/0.65

Sol. (a) Given, $P(E) = 0.35$

We know, $P(E) + P(\bar{E}) = 1$

$$\Rightarrow \quad P(\bar{E}) = 1 - 0.35 = 0.65$$

Q.5 A letter of English alphabet is choosen at random. The probability that the letter is a consonant, is

(a) $\frac{3}{26}$ (b) $\frac{5}{26}$ (c) $\frac{1}{26}$ (d) $\frac{21}{26}$

Thinking Process Total number of consonant is = Total number of alphabets − Total number of vowels and number of vowels $= \{a, e, i, o, u\} = 5$, then number of consonents is $26 - 5 = 21$

Sol. (d) Total number of alphabets $n(S) = 26$

Let E be the event of alphabet being a consonant.

Then, $n(E) = 21$

$$\Rightarrow \quad P(E) = \frac{n(E)}{n(S)} = \frac{21}{26}$$

.6 A coin is tossed twice repeatedly. The probability of getting exactly one head is

(a) 1

(b) $\frac{1}{4}$

(c) $\frac{3}{4}$

(d) $\frac{1}{2}$

ol. (d) Possible outcomes = $\{TT, HH, HT, TH\}$

Total number of outcomes $n(S) = 4$
Let E be the event of getting exactly one head.

Then, $n(E) = 2 = \{HT, TH\}$

$$\therefore \qquad P(E) = \frac{n(E)}{n(S)} = \frac{2}{4} = \frac{1}{2}$$

.7 The probability of getting an even number when an unbiased die is thrown, is

(a) 1 (b) $\frac{1}{4}$

(c) $\frac{1}{3}$ (d) $\frac{1}{2}$

ol. (d) Total number of outcomes $n(S) = 6$

Let E be the event of getting an even number = $\{2, 4, 6\}$

Then, $n(E) = 3$

$$\therefore \qquad P(E) = \frac{n(E)}{n(S)} = \frac{3}{6} = \frac{1}{2}$$

.8 The probability that a vowel is chosen from the letters of the word 'UNIVERSITY' is

(a) $\frac{2}{5}$ (b) $\frac{3}{10}$

(c) $\frac{1}{5}$ (d) None of these

ol. (a) Total number of outcomes = 10

Let E be the event of getting a vowel = $\{U, I, E, I\}$
Then, $n(E) = 4$

$$\therefore \qquad P(E) = \frac{n(E)}{n(S)} = \frac{4}{10} = \frac{2}{5}$$

Q.9 A number is chosen at random from the numbers $-5, -4, -3, -2, -1, 0, 1, 2, 3, 4, 5$. Then, the probability that square of this number is less than or equal to 1 is

(a) $\frac{2}{1}$ (b) $\frac{6}{11}$

(c) $\frac{3}{11}$ (d) $\frac{1}{11}$

Sol. (c) Total number of outcomes $n(S) = 11$

Let E be the event that square of the chosen number is less than or equal to $1 = \{-1, 0, 1\}$

$\Rightarrow$ $n(E) = 3$

$\therefore$ $$P(E) = \frac{n(E)}{n(S)} = \frac{3}{11}$$

Q.10 The probability that a leap year will have 53 Fridays or 53 Saturdays is

(a) 0 (b) $\frac{2}{7}$

(c) $\frac{3}{7}$ (d) $\frac{1}{7}$

Sol. (c) There are 366 days in a leap year *i.e.,* there are 52 weeks and 2 days. Then, the possible combination of two consecutive days are :

Sunday- Monday,
Monday-Tuesday,
Tuesday-Wednesday,
Wednesday-Thursday,
Thursday-Friday,
Friday-Saturday,
And Saturday-Sunday

So, the total number of outcomes is $n(s) = 7$.

Let E be the event in which leap year has 53 Fridays or 53 Saturdays.

= {Thursday – Friday, Friday – Saturday, Saturday – Sunday}

Then, $n(E) = 3$

$\Rightarrow$ $$P(E) = \frac{n(E)}{n(S)} = \frac{3}{7}$$

Q.11 Probability that tomorrow will be holiday is 0.58. Probability that tomorrow will not be a holiday is

(a) 0.42 (b) 0.58 (c) 1 (d) 1.58

Sol. (a) Let E be the event that tomorrow will be a holiday.

$\Rightarrow$ $P(E) = 0.58$ (Giv

Now, we know, $P(E) + P(\overline{E}) = 1$

$\Rightarrow \quad 0.58 + P(\overline{E}) = 1$

$\Rightarrow \quad P(\overline{E}) = 1 - 0.58$

$\therefore \quad P(\overline{E}) = 0.42$

Q.12 Which of the following cannot be the probability of an event ?

(a) 0.7 (b) 0

(c) 1.2 (d) 18%

Sol. (c) We know that the probability of an event ranges between 0 and 1. Hence, the probability, in any case, cannot exceed 1.

Q.13 The probability of getting a rotten orange in a lot of 400 is 0.035. The number of rotten oranges in the lot is

(a) 7 (b) 14

(c) 21 (d) 28

Sol. (b) Total number of oranges $n(S) = 400$

Let E be the event of getting a rotten orange.

Then, $P(E) = 0.035$ (given)

Now, $P(E) = \dfrac{n(E)}{(S)}$

$\Rightarrow \quad 0.035 = \dfrac{n(E)}{400}$

$\Rightarrow \quad n(E) = 0.035 \times 400 = 14$

Hence, the number of rotten oranges is 14.

Q.14 A box of 400 cups contains 12 broken cups, one cup is taken out at random from this box, then the probability that is non-broken cup is

(a) 0.95

(b) 0.97

(c) 0.79

(d) 0.20

Sol. (b) Total number of cups $n(S) = 400$

Total number of Broken cups = 12

Let E be the event of takent out a broken cup.

Total number of non-broken cup $n(E) = 400 - 12 = 388$

$\therefore$ Probability of non-broken cup is $= \dfrac{n(E)}{n(S)} = \dfrac{388}{400} = 0.97$

Q.15 A jar contains 24 chocolates, some are brown and other are white in color . If a chocolate is drawn from the jar, the probability that it is brown is 2/3, then the number of white chocolates in the jar is

(a) 7 (b) 8

(c) 10 (d) 6

Sol. (b) Total number of chocolates in jar $n(S) = 24$

Let E be the event of drawing a brown chocolate.

Probability that the drawn chocolate is brown in colour is $P(E) = \frac{n(E)}{n(S)}$

$$\therefore \quad \frac{2}{3} = \frac{n(E)}{24} \quad \left[\because P(E) = \frac{2}{3}\right]$$

$$\Rightarrow \quad n(E) = \frac{48}{3}$$

$$\Rightarrow \quad n(E) = 16$$

Now, the number of white chocolates = Total number of chocolate – total number of brown chocolates

$= 24 - 16$

$= 8$

Hence, the number of white chocolates is 8.

□ Subjective Type Questions

Q.1 There are 100 cards in a bag on which numbers from 1 to 100 are written. A card is taken out from the bag at random. Find (i) the probability that the number on the selected card is divisible by 9 and is a perfect square (ii) and is a prime number greater than 80.

Sol. (i) Total possible cases = 100

Favourable cases when number is a perfect square and is divisible by 9 are 9, 36 and 81.

So, number of favourable cases = 3

$$\text{Required probability} = \frac{\text{Number of favourable cases}}{\text{Total possible cases}} = \frac{3}{100}$$

(ii) Favourable cases the prime numbers greater than 80 are 83, 89 and 97.

So, number of favourable cases = 3

$$\text{Required probability} = \frac{\text{Number of favourable cases}}{\text{Total possible cases}} = \frac{3}{100}$$

Q.2 From a pack of 52 playing cards, Jacks, Queens and Kings of red colour are removed. From the remaining, a card is drawn at random. Find the probability that drawn card is

(i) a black king.

(ii) a card of red colour.

(iii) a card of black colour.

Sol. Number of removed red colour cards = $3 \times 2 = 6$

Remaining cards = $52 - 6 = 46$

[$\because$ There are 2 queen, 2 Jacks and 2 Kings of red colour.]

(i) Number of black kings = 2

P(a black king) = $2 / 46 = 1 / 23$

(ii) Number of red colour cards = 26

Remaining red colour cards after removing Jaks, Queens and Kings of red colour = $26 - 6 = 20$

P (a card of red colour) = $20 / 46 = 10 / 23$

(iii) Number of black cards= 26

P (a black colour card) = $26 / 46 = 13 / 23$

Q.3 Three different coins are tossed together. Find the probability of getting.

(i) exactly two heads.

(ii) at least two heads.

(iii) at least two tails.

Sol. Possible outcomes when three coins are tossed {*HHH, HHT, HTT, TTT, THH, TTH, HTH, THT*}.

(i) Number of exactly two heads are *HHT, HTH* and *THH*.

P(exactly two heads) = $3 / 8$

(ii) In case of at least two heads, outcomes are *HHT, HTH, THH* and *HHH*.

P(at least two heads) = $4 / 8 = 1 / 2$

(iii) In case of least two tails, outcomes are *TTH, THT, HTT* and *TTT*.

P (at least two tails) = $4 / 8 = 1 / 2$

Q.4 A box consists of 100 shirts of which 88 are good, 8 have minor defects and 4 have major defects. Ramesh, a shopkeeper will buy only those shirts which are good but 'Kewal' another shopkeeper will not buy shirts with major defects. A shirt is taken out of the box at random. What is the probability that

(i) Ramesh will buy the selected shirt ?

(ii) 'Kewal' will buy the selected shirt ?

Sol. Number of total possible outcomes= 100

(i) Ramesh will purchase when shirt is good.

Favourable outcomes for Ramesh = number of good shirts = 88

$$P(\text{Ramesh buys a shirt}) = \frac{\text{Number of favourable outcomes}}{\text{Number of total possible outcomes}}$$

$$= \frac{88}{100} = \frac{22}{25}$$

(ii) Kewal will buy shirt if a shirt is not having major defect.

Number of favourable outcomes for Kewal = Number of shirts without major defect = 96

P (Kewal buys a shirt) = 96/100= 24 / 25

Q.5 Two different dice are thrown together. Find the probability of (i) getting a number greater than 3 on each dice and (ii) getting a total of 6 or 7 of the numbers on two dice.

Sol. Total number of outcomes, $n(S) = 36$

(i) Let E be the event that a number greater than 3 on each dice.

Then, $E = \{(4,4), (4, 5), (4, 6), (5, 4), (5, 5), (5, 6), (6, 4), (6, 5), (6, 6)\}$

$\Rightarrow \quad n(E) = 9$

Then, $P(E) = \frac{n(E)}{n(S)} = \frac{9}{36} = \frac{1}{4}$

(ii) Let F be the event that getting a total 6 or 7 of the numbers on the two dice.

Then, $F = (5, 1), (4, 2), (3, 3), (2, 4), (1, 5)(6, 1), (5, 2), (4, 3), (3, 4), (2, 5), (1, 6)$

$\Rightarrow \quad n(F) = 11$

Then, $P(E) = \frac{n(F)}{n(S)} = \frac{11}{36}$

Q.6 (i) In a single throw of a pair of different dice, what is the probability of (i) getting a prime number on each dice (ii) and a total of 9 or 11.

Sol. Total possible cases when two dice are thrown together = $6 \times 6 = 36$

(i) Favourable cases when both numbers are prime are (2, 2), (2, 3), (2, 5), (3, 2), (3, 3), (3, 5), (5, 2), (5, 3), (5, 5) *i.e.*, 9 outcomes.

$$P(\text{a prime number of each dice}) = \frac{\text{Favourable cases}}{\text{Total cases}} = \frac{9}{36} = \frac{1}{4}$$

(ii) Favourable cases when sum of numbers are 9 or 11 are (3, 6), (4, 5), (5, 4), (5, 6), (6, 3), (6, 5), *i.e.*, 6 outcomes.

$$P\text{(a total of 9 or 11)} = \frac{\text{Favourable outcomes}}{\text{Total possible outcomes}} = \frac{6}{36} = \frac{1}{6}$$

Q.7 A bag contains 5 red balls and some blue balls. If the probability of drawing a blue ball is double that of a red ball. Determine the number of blue balls in the bag.

Sol. Let the number of blue balls is the bag be x.

Then, total number of balls is the bag = $5 + x$

$\therefore$ Number of all possible outcomes = $5 + x$

Number of outcomes favourable to the event of drawing a blue ball = x

$\therefore$ Probability of drawing a blue ball = $\frac{x}{5+x}$

Similarly, probability of drawing a red ball $= \frac{5}{5+x}$

According to the condition, $\frac{x}{5+x} = 2\left(\frac{5}{5+x}\right)$

$x = 10$

Hence, the bag containg 10 blue balles.

Q.8 Find the probability of having 5 Mondays in the month of August.

Sol. Total number of days in the month of August are 31. *i.e.*, there are 4 weeks and 3 days.

Then, the 3 days can be

Sunday, Monday, Tuesday;
Monday, Tuesday, Wednesday;
Tuesday, Wednesday, Thursday;
Wednesday, Thursday, Friday;
Thursday, Friday, Saturday;
Friday, Saturday, Sunday;
and Saturday, Sunday, Monday

Let E be the event that one of the days is a Monday then $n(E) = 3$

$$\Rightarrow \quad P(E) = \frac{n(E)}{7} = \frac{3}{7}$$

Q.9 A dice is thrown twice. What is the probability that :

(a) 3 will not come up either time ?

(b) 3 will come up at least once ?

Sol. Total number of outcomes = 36

(a) Let E be the event that 3 come up either time or at least once

Then, $E = \{(3, 1), (3, 2), (3, 3), (3, 4), (3, 5), (3, 6), (1, 3), (2, 3), (4, 3), (5, 3), (6, 3)\}$

$\Rightarrow \quad n(E) = 11$

$\Rightarrow \quad P(E) = \dfrac{n(E)}{36} = \dfrac{11}{36}$

Now, the probability of 3 will not come up either time is

$$P(\overline{E}) = 1 - P(E)$$

$$= 1 - \frac{11}{36} = \frac{36-11}{36} = \frac{25}{36}$$

(b) $P(E) = \dfrac{11}{36}$ [$\because$ discussed already in (a) part]

Q.10 The quality control officer at a tire factory reported that 20 tires were defective out of a sample of 10,000 tires. A tire is selected, what are the chances that the tire selected is not defective ?

Sol. Total number of tires = 10000

Number of defective tires = 20

$$P\text{ (defective tires)} = \frac{20}{10000} = \frac{1}{500}$$

$$P\text{ (non defective tire)} = 1 - \frac{1}{500} = \frac{499}{500}$$

Q.11 Two different dice are thrown. Find the probability that the sum of the numbers appearing on the dice is 8.

Sol. Two dice are thrown, total number of outcomes : $n(S) = 36$

Let E be the event that the sum of numbers is equal to 8.

$$E = [(2, 6), (3, 5), (4, 4), (5, 3), (6, 2)] \Rightarrow n(E) = 5$$

$$P(E) = \frac{n(E)}{n(S)} \Rightarrow P(E) = \frac{5}{36}$$

Q.12 Find the probability that a non- leap year selected at random will contain 53 Sundays.

Sol. The non-leap years containing 52 weeks + one day.

Therefore, it contains 52 Sundays and the remaining day may be Sunday, Monday, Tuesday, Wednesday, Thursday, Friday and Saturday.

$\therefore \quad n(S) = 7$

Let A be the extra day is Sunday; $n(A) = 1$

$\because \quad P(A) = \dfrac{n(A)}{n(S)}$

$\Rightarrow \quad P(A) = \dfrac{1}{7}$

Q.13 A number is selected at random from first 50 natural numbers. Find the probability that it is a multiple of 3 and 4.

◎ *Thinking Process* Take the LCM of 3 and 4 which is 12 and find multiple of 12 less than 50.

Sol. $n(S) = 50$

Let A be the selected number is a multiple of 3 and 4.

$= [12, 24, 36, 48] \Rightarrow n(A) = 4$

$\because \quad P(A) = \dfrac{n(A)}{n(S)}$

$\Rightarrow \quad P(A) = \dfrac{4}{50} = \dfrac{2}{25}$

Q.14 From a group of 2 boys and 2 girls, two children are selected at random. Find the probability that one boy and one girl are selected.

Sol. Let two boys are B_1 and B_2 and 2 girls are G_1 and G_2.

Total number of teams $[B_1B_2, B_1G_1, B_1G_2, B_2G_1, B_2G_2, G_1G_2]$

$\therefore \quad n(S) = 6$

Let A be the event that one boy and one girl are selected $[B_1G_1, B_1G_2, B_2G_1, B_2G_2]$

$\because \quad n(A) = 4$

$\therefore \quad P(A) = \dfrac{n(A)}{n(S)} \Rightarrow P(A) = \dfrac{4}{6}$ or $\dfrac{2}{3}$

Q.15 A number x is selected at random from the numbers 1, 4, 9, 16 and another number is selected at random from the numbers 1, 2, 3, 4. Find the probability that the value of xy is more than 16.

Sol. Let x can be 1, 4, 9 or 16 and y can be 1, 2, 3 or 4.

Total number of cases of xy are {(1, 1), (1, 2)(1, 3)(1, 4), (4, 1)(4, 2)(4, 3) (4, 4), (9, 1)(9, 2), (9, 3)(9, 4), (16, 1), (16, 2),(16, 3)(16, 4)}

Number of cases when xy is more than 16 are (9×2), (9×3), (9×4), (16×2), (16×3), (16×4) *i.e.*, 6 cases.

P (value of xy more than 16) $= 6/16 = 3/8$

Q.16 A jar contains 54 marbles each of which is blue, green or white. The probability of selecting a blue marble at random from the jar is 1/3 and the probability of selecting a green marble at random is 4/9. How many white marbles does the jar contain ?

Sol. Total number of marbles = 54

Let B be the event of selecting a blue marble.

$$\Rightarrow \quad P(B) = \frac{1}{3} \quad \text{(given)}$$

Let G be the event of selecting a green marble.

$$\Rightarrow \quad P(G) = \frac{4}{9}$$

Let W be the event of selecting a white marble.

Since, total probability = 1

$$\Rightarrow \quad P(W) + P(G) + P(B) = 1$$

$$\Rightarrow \quad \frac{n(W)}{54} + \frac{4}{9} + \frac{1}{3} = 1$$

$$\left[\because P(W) = \frac{\text{Number of which marble}}{\text{Total numbers of marbles}}\right]$$

$$\Rightarrow \quad \frac{n(W)}{54} = 1 - \frac{4}{9} - \frac{1}{3}$$

$$= \frac{9-4-3}{9} = \frac{2}{9}$$

$$\Rightarrow \quad n(W) = \frac{2 \times 54}{9} = 12$$

Hence, Jar containing 12 white marbles.